Foreign Films

CineBooks Home Library Series
No. 3

Foreign Films

A guide to nearly 500 films on videocassette by foreign directors

CineBooks

CineBooks, Inc.
Evanston, Illinois, 1989

Editorial & Sales Offices
CINEBOOKS
990 Grove Street
Evanston, Illinois 60201

ISBN: 0-933997-22-1

CINEBOOKS, INC. is a McPherson's Publishing Company

Printed in the United States
First Edition

1 2 3 4 5 6 7 8 9 10

Table of Contents

Introduction

Until the advent of video, the opportunities to view most foreign films were extremely limited. Except for those few major foreign pictures from superstar "art film" directors (such as Federico Fellini's LA STRADA, Michelangelo Antonioni's BLOW-UP) which usually only played in large cities, the only place to view foreign movies were at college film societies. As the world film industry grew, more foreign films were shown in the US as art houses began to spring up throughout the country. The rise in popularity of such directors as Fellini or Ingmar Bergman, and the energy of the French New Wave directors—chiefly Jean-Luc Godard and Francois Truffaut—combined with the rise in college film study programs, contributed greatly to the growing interest. When Ingmar Bergman's WILD STRAWBERRIES and THE SEVENTH SEAL played to rave reviews in the US, distributors responded to the new market by releasing a number of earlier Bergman films. Just as film criticism of the 1960s revolved around the *politique des auteurs,* or the "auteur theory," so too did the distribution of foreign films as audiences made it clear they wanted more Bergman, more Fellini, more Truffaut, more Godard. Prize-winning films from international film festivals (Cannes and Venice, primarily) also were quick to come to US screens.

By the 1980s, the crowds for art films had grown, providing an actual marketplace, albeit a select one. Such sure-fire crowd-pleasers as Bergman's FANNY AND ALEXANDER, Wolfgang Petersen's THE BOAT, or Gabriel Axel's BABETTE'S FEAST became relatively major films, while less commercial pictures as Andrei Tarkovsky's THE SACRIFICE, Bertrand Tavernier's THE PASSION OF BEATRICE, or Marco Bellocchio's THE EYES, THE MOUTH soon disappeared without a trace—until they resurfaced on video. As a result of the video boom, films which had limited or no US release are finding a second life on video store shelves. Now it is just as easy for someone in Paris, Texas to see Wim Wenders' great KINGS OF THE ROAD, as it is for someone in New York, Chicago, or San Francisco. While it was almost impossible to see Luis Bunuel's long-banned 1930 surrealist classic L'AGE D'OR before the video age, one can now watch it at will. With the video boom, a large selection of Luis Bunuel's Mexican films are now surfacing, including the otherwise unseen 1951 film A WOMAN IN LOVE, a film so obscure it is absent from nearly all critical studies of the director. On video, one can now see the first feature film project of Ingmar Bergman—TORMENT, a 1946 Swedish picture directed by Alf Sjoberg and based on the young Bergman's script. As the audience and marketplace grow, so does the selection of foreign films on video. Sitting next to one another on the video shelves, as if no national borders exist, are such films as Tengiz Abuladze's REPENTANCE from the USSR, Roberto Rossellini's THE RISE TO POWER OF LOUIS XIV from France, Carl Theodor Dreyer's ORDET from

Denmark, Bernardo Bertolucci's 1900 from Italy, Carlos Saura's CRIA! from Spain, Hector Babenco's PIXOTE from Brazil, Fritz Lang's silent DESTINY from Germany, Zbynek Brynych's TRANSPORT FROM PARADISE from Czechoslovakia, and Dusan Makavejev's LOVE AFFAIR: OR THE CASE OF THE MISSING SWITCH-BOARD OPERATOR from Yugoslavia.

While most purists would rightfully argue that it is unacceptable to watch as beautiful a film as Max Ophuls' LOLA MONTES on videotape, it is equally unthinkable that many viewers may never see an Ophuls film. Watching a motion picture on videotape is, in many cases, a necessity. Fortunately some video distributors have taken the effort to resubtitle their films (many using yellow subtitles which stand-out against the "white tabletops" of many older prints) or, as in the case of LOLA MONTES, letterbox the picture so it may be viewed in its original widescreen format. Where possible, we have tried to note such changes in this book.

One added note on the selection process for this publication. Since time and space both have their limitations, and since video distributors both large and small continue to release new titles, it became necessary to deal with a cross-section of available titles. The emphasis was placed on directors, hence there is a larger selection of films by Luis Bunuel, Jean-Luc Godard, Francois Truffaut, Roberto Rossellini, Federico Fellini, Ingmar Bergman, Jean Renoir, and Wim Wenders than there are of such lesser-known directors as Philippe de Broca, Jacques Feyder, Ettore Scola, Jan Nemec or Moshe Mizrahi. Another factor in choosing the titles was availability. While Lev Kuleshov's 1927 exercise in creative editing, A KISS FOR MARY PICKFORD, is undoubtedly a more interesting film than Alberto Lattuada's sex romp THE CRICKET, the latter is on far more video shelves and therefore a review of the film is probably more valuable to the readers of these pages. We also elected not to restrict our selections to foreign-language films, instead trying to give equal time to the growing number of English-language foreign films (such as THE BIG BLUE or ROUND MIDNIGHT) or to those directors usually considered "foreign" who make forays into English-language filmmaking (Antonioni with BLOW-UP, ZABRISKIE POINT and THE PASSENGER; Makavejev with MONTENEGRO and THE COCA-COLA KID).

This volume includes reviews of some of the greatest achievements in the history of filmmaking, and our fondest hope is that FOREIGN FILMS will help some of these movies find new audiences among today's video renters and buyers.

—Daniel Curran

FILMS BY STAR RATINGS

All films included in this volume are listed below by star rating. The ratings indicate:
*****—masterpiece; ****—excellent; ***—good; **—fair; *—poor; zero—without merit

*****

A NOUS LA LIBERTE
AGUIRRE, THE WRATH OF GOD
ALEXANDER NEVSKY
BATTLE OF ALGIERS, THE
BATTLESHIP POTEMKIN
BEAUTY AND THE BEAST
BICYCLE THIEF, THE
BLUE ANGEL, THE
CABINET OF DR. CALIGARI, THE
CLAIRE'S KNEE
CONFORMIST, THE
CRIMINAL LIFE OF ARCHIBALDO DE LA CRUZ, THE
DAY FOR NIGHT
DIARY OF A LOST GIRL
DISCREET CHARM OF THE BOURGEOISIE, THE
EARTH
EXTERMINATING ANGEL, THE
FOUR HUNDRED BLOWS, THE
GRAND ILLUSION
JULES AND JIM
KINGS OF THE ROAD
LA DOLCE VITA
LA STRADA
L'AGE D'OR
LAST LAUGH, THE
LAST TANGO IN PARIS
LAST YEAR AT MARIENBAD
L'ATALANTE L'AVVENTURA
LE JOUR SE LEVE
LOLA MONTES
LOS OLVIDADOS
M
MASCULINE FEMININE
MR. HULOT'S HOLIDAY
MY LIFE TO LIVE
NAPOLEON
NOSFERATU
ORPHEUS
PASSION OF JOAN OF ARC, THE
PEPE LE MOKO
PLAYTIME
RAN
RASHOMON
REPULSION
RIFIFI
ROUND MIDNIGHT
RULES OF THE GAME, THE
SANSHO THE BAILIFF
SEVEN SAMURAI, THE
SHOESHINE
SHOOT THE PIANO PLAYER
TEN DAYS THAT SHOOK THE WORLD
TESTAMENT OF ORPHEUS, THE
UGETSU
UMBERTO D
VAMPYR
VIRIDIANA
WILD STRAWBERRIES
WINGS OF DESIRE
WOMAN IN THE DUNES

****

ALPHAVILLE
ASHES AND DIAMONDS
ASSAULT, THE
BAKER'S WIFE, THE
BALLAD OF A SOLDIER
BELLISSIMA
BERLIN ALEXANDERPLATZ
BETTY BLUE
BIZET'S CARMEN
BLACK ORPHEUS
BLOOD OF A POET, THE
BLOW-UP
BOAT, THE
BOB LE FLAMBEUR
BREATHLESS
CHLOE IN THE AFTERNOON
CLEAN SLATE (COUP DE TORCHON)
CLEO FROM 5 TO 7
CLOCKMAKER, THE
CONTEMPT
CRIA!
CRIES AND WHISPERS
CRIME OF MONSIEUR LANGE, THE
DAMNED, THE
DANTON
DAY OF WRATH
DEATH IN VENICE
DESTINY
DIABOLIQUE
DIARY OF A CHAMBERMAID
DIARY OF A COUNTRY PRIEST
DIRTY DISHES
DIVA
DR. MABUSE, THE GAMBLER, PART 1 & 2
DOUBLE SUICIDE
DRUNKEN ANGEL
EARRINGS OF MADAME DE . . ., THE
8 ½
EL BRUTO
EL NORTE
EVERY MAN FOR HIMSELF AND GOD AGAINST ALL
FAHRENHEIT 451
FANNY AND ALEXANDER
FAUST
FELLINI SATYRICON
FIRES ON THE PLAIN
FITZCARRALDO
FLOWERS OF ST. FRANCIS, THE
FRENCH CANCAN
FULL MOON IN PARIS
GARDEN OF THE FINZI-CONTINIS, THE
GATE OF HELL
GENERAL DELLA ROVERE
GERMANY, YEAR ZERO
GOLDEN COACH, THE
GOLEM, THE
GOSPEL ACCORDING TO ST. MATTHEW, THE
HAIL, MARY
HIDDEN FORTRESS, THE
HIGH AND LOW
HIMATSURI
HIROSHIMA, MON AMOUR
I VITELLONI
IREZUMI (SPIRIT OF TATTOO)
ITALIAN STRAW HAT, AN
IVAN THE TERRIBLE PART I AND II
JOUR DE FETE
JULIET OF THE SPIRITS
KAGEMUSHA
KAMERADSCHAFT
KANAL
KISS OF THE SPIDER WOMAN
KNIFE IN THE WATER
KRIEMHILD'S REVENGE
KWAIDAN
LA BETE HUMAINE
LA CAGE AUX FOLLES
LA RONDE
LA TERRA TREMA
LA TRAVIATA
LAST EMPEROR, THE
LE BEAU MARIAGE
LE DOULOS
LIFE OF OHARU
LOVE AFFAIR; OR THE CASE OF THE MISSING SWITCHBOARD OPERATOR
MAEDCHEN IN UNIFORM
MAN FACING SOUTHEAST
MARRIAGE OF MARIA BRAUN, THE

MARRIED WOMAN, THE
MAYERLING
MEPHISTO
MERRY CHRISTMAS, MR. LAWRENCE
METROPOLIS
MIRACLE IN MILAN
MR. KLEIN
MON ONCLE D'AMERIQUE
MOONLIGHTING
MURIEL
MY NIGHT AT MAUD'S
MY UNCLE
OPEN CITY
PAISAN
PARIS, TEXAS
PASSENGER, THE
PERSONA
PHANTOM OF LIBERTY, THE
PIXOTE
PROVIDENCE
REPENTANCE
SACRIFICE, THE
SEVENTH SEAL, THE
SHOP ON MAIN STREET, THE
SIEGFRIED
SISTERS OF THE GION
SMALL CHANGE
SPIES
STOLEN KISSES
STORY OF ADELE H., THE
SUNDAY IN THE COUNTRY, A
THAT OBSCURE OBJECT OF DESIRE
THERESE
THRONE OF BLOOD
TWENTY-FOUR EYES
TWO OF US, THE
TWO WOMEN
UMBRELLAS OF CHERBOURG, THE
UNDER THE ROOFS OF PARIS
VARIETY
WAGES OF FEAR, THE
WUTHERING HEIGHTS
Z

***1/2

ALICE IN THE CITIES
BAD GIRLS
BAD SLEEP WELL, THE
BAGDAD CAFE
BAND OF OUTSIDERS
BEAU PERE
BEYOND THE WALLS
BOUDU SAVED FROM DROWNING
BURMESE HARP, THE
CARMEN
CAT AND MOUSE
CESAR
CHOICE OF ARMS
CLOSELY WATCHED TRAINS
COCA-COLA KID, THE
CONFIDENTIALLY YOURS!
COUP DE GRACE
CRANES ARE FLYING, THE
DANGEROUS MOVES
DARK EYES
DEATHWATCH
DECLINE OF THE AMERICAN EMPIRE, THE
DIAMONDS OF THE NIGHT
DODES 'KA-DEN
DOWN AND DIRTY
EDITH AND MARCEL
ELENA AND HER MEN
ETERNAL RETURN, THE
FAMILY, THE
FANNY
FEAR
FIREMAN'S BALL, THE
FLOATING WEEDS
47 RONIN, THE (PARTS 1 & 2)
FUNNY, DIRTY LITTLE WAR, A
GET OUT YOUR HANDKERCHIEFS
GOALIE'S ANXIETY AT THE PENALTY KICK, THE
GOING PLACES
GREEN ROOM, THE
HAMMETT
HORROR CHAMBER OF DR. FAUSTUS, THE
INNOCENT, THE
JEAN DE FLORETTE
LA CIUDAD Y LOS PERROS
LA MARSEILLAISE
LAST METRO, THE
LE BEAU SERGE
LE PLAISIR
LES COMPERES
LOVE ON THE RUN
LOVES OF A BLONDE
MACBETH
MADAME ROSA
MAN AND A WOMAN, A
MAN IN LOVE, A
MANON OF THE SPRING
MARIUS
MEN
MEXICAN BUS RIDE
MILKY WAY, THE
MISHIMA
MOTHER
OFFICIAL STORY, THE
PADRE PADRONE
PANDORA'S BOX
PARDON MON AFFAIRE
PATHER PANCHALI
PAULINE AT THE BEACH
PEDESTRIAN, THE
QUESTION OF SILENCE
RED DESERT
RETURN OF MARTIN GUERRE, THE
REVOLT OF JOB, THE
SAMURAI TRILOGY, THE
SECRETS OF WOMEN
SEDUCTION OF MIMI, THE
SEVEN BEAUTIES
SOFT SKIN, THE
SOLDIER OF ORANGE
SPIRIT OF THE BEEHIVE, THE
STATE OF SIEGE
STATE OF THINGS, THE
STRAY DOG
SUGARBABY
SUMMER
SWEPT AWAY...BY AN UNUSUAL DESTINY IN THE BLUE SEA OF AUGUST
TALL BLOND MAN WITH ONE BLACK SHOE, THE
TAMPOPO
TAXING WOMAN, A
TCHAO PANTIN
TESTAMENT OF DR. MABUSE, THE
THREEPENNY OPERA, THE
TIN DRUM, THE
TONI
TORMENT
TWO ENGLISH GIRLS
VAGABOND
WALL, THE
WOMAN NEXT DOOR, THE
WOMAN WITHOUT LOVE
WORLD OF APU, THE
WRONG MOVE
YOJIMBO
YOL

***

AMARCORD
AMERICAN FRIEND, THE
AND NOW MY LOVE
AND THE SHIP SAILS ON
APARAJITO
ASSOCIATE, THE
BABETTE'S FEAST
BASILEUS QUARTET
BIG DEAL ON MADONNA STREET, THE
BLACK AND WHITE IN COLOR
BLIND TRUST
BYE-BYE BRAZIL
CARNIVAL IN FLANDERS
CESAR AND ROSALIE
COLONEL REDL
COUSIN, COUSINE
DAVID
DERSU UZALA
DESPAIR
DEVIL'S EYE, THE

DONA FLOR AND HER TWO HUSBANDS
DONKEY SKIN
DRIFTING
DUST
DYBBUK, THE
ECLIPSE
ECSTASY
EL AMOR BRUJO
ELUSIVE CORPORAL, THE
ENTRE NOUS
EYES, THE MOUTH, THE
FATHER
FRANTIC
FRENCH DETECTIVE, THE
FUNERAL, THE
GARDEN OF DELIGHTS, THE
GERTRUD
GERVAISE
GINGER & FRED
GO-MASTERS, THE
HARDER THEY COME, THE
HOLY INNOCENTS, THE
HOME AND THE WORLD, THE
HOUR OF THE STAR, THE
I SENT A LETTER TO MY LOVE
IKIRU
INVESTIGATION
KOLBERGLA CHEVRE
LA NUIT DE VARENNES
LA PASSANTE
LA TRUITE (THE TROUT)
L'ADDITION
LE DERNIER COMBAT
LE MILLION
LE SEX SHOP
LES ENFANTS TERRIBLES
LESSON IN LOVE, A
LOST HONOR OF KATHARINA BLUM, THE
LOVE AND ANARCHY
LOWER DEPTHS, THE (1936)
LOWER DEPTHS, THE (1957)
MACARTHUR'S CHILDREN
MAGICIAN, THE
MALICIOUS
MALOU
MAN AND A WOMAN: 20 YEARS LATER, A
MAN WHO LOVED WOMEN, THE
MONTENEGRO
MOON IN THE GUTTER, THE
MOSCOW DOES NOT BELIEVE IN TEARS
MY BEST FRIEND'S GIRL
MY LIFE AS A DOG
NEVER ON SUNDAY
NIGHT OF THE SHOOTING STARS, THE
NIGHTS OF CABIRIA, THE
1900
OSSESSIONE
PASSION OF DEATRICE
PICNIC ON THE GRASS
PLACE OF WEEPING
POIL DE CAROTTE
RED BEARD
RETURN OF THE TALL BLOND MAN WITH ONE BLACK SHOE, THE
RISE TO POWER OF LOUIS XIV, THE
SANJURO
SAWDUST AND TINSEL
SCENE OF THE CRIME
SCENES FROM A MARRIAGE
SHADOWS OF FORGOTTEN ANCESTORS
SILENCE, THE
SINCERELY CHARLOTTE
SKYLINE
SMILES OF A SUMMER NIGHT
SPETTERS
SUGAR CANE ALLEY
SUMMER INTERLUDE
SUNDAYS AND CYBELE
SWORD OF DOOM, THE
TENANT, THE
TESS
THREE BROTHERS
THROUGH A GLASS DARKLY
TRANSPORT FROM PARADISE
TWO DAUGHTERS
VIRGIN SPRING, THE
WANNSEE CONFERENCE, THE
WHERE THE GREEN ANTS DREAM
WOMAN IN FLAMES, A
YESTERDAY, TODAY, AND TOMORROW

****1/2**

A NOS AMOURS
ALSINO AND THE CONDOR
AU REVOIR LES ENFANTS
BATTLE OF AUSTERLITZ, THE
CAMILA
CHRIST STOPPED AT EBOLI
EL DIPUTADO
EMMANUELLE
ERENDIRA
FLIGHT OF THE EAGLE
FOUR BAGS FULL
FOURTH MAN, THE
FROM THE LIFE OF THE MARIONETTES
GOLDEN DEMON
GOOD MORNING BABYLON
HAPPY NEW YEAR
HENRY IV
IN THE NAME OF THE POPE KING
IPHIGENIA
JOKE OF DESTINY, A
JUPITER'S THIGH
KING OF HEARTS
LA BALANCE
LA BOUM
LAW OF DESIRE
LE BAL
LE CHAT
LE GRAND CHEMIN
LE MAGNIFIQUE
LES CARABINIERS
LOVE IN GERMANY, A
LUMIERE
MAKE ROOM FOR TOMORROW
MY NEW PARTNER
MYSTERY OF ALEXINA, THE
NEST, THE
NIGHT PORTER, THE
ORDET
PERIL
PORT OF CALL
SOTTO...SOTTO
SPRING SYMPHONY
SWANN IN LOVE
SYLVIA AND THE PHANTOM
TONIO KROGER
TWIST & SHOUT
WHERE'S PICONE?
WHITE SHEIK, THE
WIFEMISTRESS
WOLF AT THE DOOR, THE

******

AFTER THE REHEARSAL
AND GOD CREATED WOMAN
ARIAAUTUMN SONATA
BLOOD WEDDING
BLUE COUNTRY, THE
CRICKET, THE
DEVIL IN THE FLESH, THE
DIARY OF FORBIDDEN DREAMS
DIVINE NYMPH, THE
DREAMS
EL MUERTO
ELVIRA MADIGAN
FORBIDDEN GAMES
GABRIELA
GIFT, THE
GIRL ON A MOTORCYCLE, THE
HANNAH K.
HEAT OF DESIRE
HOUR OF THE WOLF, THE
INHERITANCE, THE
INHERITORS, THE
INVITATION AU VOYAGE
KAMIKAZE '89
LA CAGE AUX FOLLES II
LA CAGE AUX FOLLES 3: THE WEDDING
LADY CHATTERLEY'S LOVER

LE CAVALEUR (PRACTICE MAKES PERFECT)
MACARONI
MISS MARY
MY NAME IS IVAN
MY OTHER HUSBAND
ODD OBSESSION
ONE DEADLY SUMMER
QUERELLE
SEDUCED AND ABANDONED
SERPENT'S EGG, THE
STAY AS YOU ARE
STROMBOLI
SUBWAY
SWEET COUNTRY
THERESE AND ISABELLE
TILL MARRIAGE DO US PART
VERY CURIOUS GIRL, A
VERY PRIVATE AFFAIR, A
WINTER LIGHT, THE
ZABRISKIE POINT

***1/2**
BIG BLUE, THE
JACKO AND LISE
JULIA AND JULIA
LOVE SONGS
TENDRES COUSINES

*****
APHRODITE
CAMILLE 2000
COP AND THE GIRL, THE
FEMMES DE PARIS
HOLIDAY HOTELTHREE MEN AND A CRADLE

zero
L'ANNEE DES MEDUSES

FILMS BY COUNTRY

ALGERIA
LE BAL
Z

ARGENTINA
CAMILA
EL MUERTO
FUNNY, DIRTY LITTLE WAR, A
MAN FACING SOUTHEAST
MISS MARY
OFFICIAL STORY, THE

AUSTRALIA
COCA-COLA KID, THE

AUSTRIA
COLONEL REDL
COP AND THE GIRL, THE
GOALIE'S ANXIETY AT THE PENALTY KICK, THE
INHERITORS, THE
WANNSEE CONFERENCE, THE

BELGIUM
DUST
GET OUT YOUR HANDKERCHIEFS
JACKO AND LISE

BRAZIL
BLACK ORPHEUS
BYE BYE BRAZIL
DONA FLOR AND HER TWO HUSBANDS
GABRIELA
HOUR OF THE STAR, THE
KISS OF THE SPIDER WOMAN
PIXOTE

BRITAIN
ARIA
BLOW-UP
FAHRENHEIT 451
GIRL ON A MOTORCYCLE, THE
HAIL, MARY
MACBETH
MERRY CHRISTMAS, MR. LAWRENCE
MONTENEGRO
MOONLIGHTING
REPULSION
TESS

CANADA
BLIND TRUST
DECLINE OF THE AMERICAN EMPIRE, THE
LOVE SONGS

CHINA
GO-MASTERS, THE

COSTA RICA
ALSINO AND THE CONDOR

CUBA
ALSINO AND THE CONDOR

CZECHOSLOVAKIA
CLOSELY WATCHED TRAINS
DIAMONDS OF THE NIGHT
ECSTASY
FIREMAN'S BALL, THE
LOVES OF A BLONDE
SHOP ON MAIN STREET, THE
TRANSPORT FROM PARADISE

DENMARK
BABETTE'S FEAST
DAY OF WRATH
GERTRUD
ORDET
TWIST & SHOUT
WOLF AT THE DOOR, THE

EAST GERMANY
SPRING SYMPHONY

FRANCE
A NOS AMOURS
A NOUS LA LIBERTE
ALPHAVILLE
AMARCORD
AND GOD CREATED WOMAN
AND NOW MY LOVE
AND THE SHIP SAILS ON
APHRODITE
ASSOCIATE, THE
AU REVOIR LES ENFANTS
BAD GIRLS
BAKER'S WIFE, THE
BAND OF OUTSIDERS
BATTLE OF AUSTERLITZ, THE
BEAU PERE
BEAUTY AND THE BEAST
BETTY BLUE
BIG BLUE, THE
BIG DEAL ON MADONNA STREET, THE
BIZET'S CARMEN
BLACK AND WHITE IN COLOR
BLACK ORPHEUS
BLOOD OF A POET, THE
BLUE COUNTRY, THE
BOB LE FLAMBEUR
BOUDU SAVED FROM DROWNING
BREATHLESS
CARNIVAL IN FLANDERS
CAT AND MOUSE
CESAR
CESAR AND ROSALIE
CHLOE IN THE AFTERNOON
CHOICE OF ARMS
CHRIST STOPPED AT EBOLI
CLAIRE'S KNEE
CLEAN SLATE (COUP DE TORCHON)
CLEO FROM 5 TO 7
CLOCKMAKER, THE
CONFIDENTIALLY YOURS!
CONFORMIST, THE
CONTEMPT
COUP DE GRACE
COUSIN, COUSINE
CRIME OF MONSIEUR LANGE, THE
DANTON
DAY FOR NIGHT
DEATH IN VENICE
DEATHWATCH
DEVIL IN THE FLESH, THE
DIABOLIQUE
DIARY OF A CHAMBERMAID
DIARY OF A COUNTRY PRIEST
DIARY OF FORBIDDEN DREAMS
DIRTY DISHES
DISCREET CHARM OF THE BOURGEOISIE, THE
DIVA
DONKEY SKIN
DUST
EARRINGS OF MADAME DE . . ., THE
ECLIPSE
EDITH AND MARCEL
ELENA AND HER MEN
ELUSIVE CORPORAL, THE
EMMANUELLE
ENTRE NOUS
ERENDIRA
ETERNAL RETURN, THE
EYES, THE MOUTH, THE
FAMILY, THE
FANNY
FANNY AND ALEXANDER
FELLINI SATYRICON

FEMMES DE PARIS
FORBIDDEN GAMES
FOUR BAGS FULL
FOUR HUNDRED BLOWS, THE
FRANTIC
FRENCH CANCAN
FRENCH DETECTIVE, THE
FULL MOON IN PARIS
GENERAL DELLA ROVERE
GERMANY, YEAR ZERO
GERVAISE
GET OUT YOUR HANDKERCHIEFS
GIFT, THE
GINGER & FRED
GIRL ON A MOTORCYCLE, THE
GOING PLACES
GOLDEN COACH, THE
GOOD MORNING BABYLON
GOSPEL ACCORDING TO ST. MATTHEW, THE
GRAND ILLUSION
GREEN ROOM, THE
HAIL, MARY
HANNAH K.
HAPPY NEW YEAR
HEAT OF DESIRE
HIROSHIMA, MON AMOUR
HOLIDAY HOTEL
HORROR CHAMBER OF DR. FAUSTUS, THE
I SENT A LETTER TO MY LOVE
I VITELLONI
INNOCENT, THE
INVESTIGATION
INVITATION AU VOYAGE
ITALIAN STRAW HAT, AN
JACKO AND LISE
JEAN DE FLORETTE
JOUR DE FETE
JULES AND JIM
JULIET OF THE SPIRITS
JUPITER'S THIGH
KING OF HEARTS
LA BALANCE
LA BETE HUMAINE
LA BOUM
LA CAGE AUX FOLLES
LA CAGE AUX FOLLES II
LA CAGE AUX FOLLES 3: THE WEDDING
LA CHEVRE
LA DOLCE VITA
LA MARSEILLAISE
LA NUIT DE VARENNES
LA PASSANTE
LA RONDE
LA TRUITE (THE TROUT)
L'ADDITION
LADY CHATTERLEY'S LOVER
L'AGE D'OR
L'ANNEE DES MEDUSES
LAST METRO, THE
LAST TANGO IN PARIS
LAST YEAR AT MARIENBAD
L'ATALANTE
L'AVVENTURA
LE BAL
LE BEAU MARIAGE
LE BEAU SERGE
LE CAVALEUR (PRACTICE MAKES PERFECT)
LE CHAT
LE DERNIER COMBAT
LE DOULOS
LE GRAND CHEMIN
LE JOUR SE LEVE
LE MAGNIFIQUE
LE MILLION
LE PLAISIR
LE SEX SHOP
LES CARABINIERS
LES COMPERES
LES ENFANTS TERRIBLES
LOLA MONTES
LOVE IN GERMANY, A
LOVE ON THE RUN
LOVE SONGS
LOWER DEPTHS, THE (1936)
LUMIERE
MADAME ROSA
MAKE ROOM FOR TOMORROW
MAN AND A WOMAN, A
MAN AND A WOMAN: 20 YEARS LATER, A
MAN IN LOVE, A
MAN WHO LOVED WOMEN, THE
MANON OF THE SPRING
MARIUS
MARRIED WOMAN, THE
MASCULINE FEMININE
MAYERLING
MILKY WAY, THE
MR. HULOT'S HOLIDAY
MR. KLEIN
MON ONCLE D'AMERIQUE
MOON IN THE GUTTER, THE
MURIEL
MY BEST FRIEND'S GIRL
MY LIFE TO LIVE
MY NEW PARTNER
MY NIGHT AT MAUD'S
MY OTHER HUSBAND
MY UNCLE
MYSTERY OF ALEXINA, THE
NAPOLEON
NIGHTS OF CABIRIA, THE
ONE DEADLY SUMMER
ORPHEUS
PARDON MON AFFAIRE
PARIS, TEXAS
PASSION OF BEATRICE, THE
PASSION OF JOAN OF ARC, THE
PAULINE AT THE BEACH
PEPE LE MOKO
PERIL
PHANTOM OF LIBERTY, THE
PICNIC ON THE GRASS
PLAYTIME
POIL DE CAROTTE
PROVIDENCE
QUERELLE
RANRED DESERT
RETURN OF MARTIN GUERRE, THE
RETURN OF THE TALL BLOND MAN WITH ONE BLACK SHOE, THE
RIFIFI
RISE TO POWER OF LOUIS XIV, THE
ROUND MIDNIGHT
RULES OF THE GAME, THE
SACRIFICE, THE
SCENE OF THE CRIME
SEDUCED AND ABANDONED
SHOOT THE PIANO PLAYER
SINCERELY CHARLOTTE
SMALL CHANGE
SOFT SKIN, THE
STATE OF SIEGE
STOLEN KISSES
STORY OF ADELE H., THE
SUBWAY
SUGAR CANE ALLEY
SUMMER
SUNDAY IN THE COUNTRY, A
SUNDAYS AND CYBELE
SWANN IN LOVE
SYLVIA AND THE PHANTOM
TALL BLOND MAN WITH ONE BLACK SHOE, THE
TCHAO PANTIN
TENANT, THE
TENDRES COUSINES
TESS
TESTAMENT OF ORPHEUS, THE
THAT OBSCURE OBJECT OF DESIRE
THERESE
THREE MEN AND A CRADLE
TIN DRUM, THE
TONI
TONIO KROGER
TWO ENGLISH GIRLS
TWO OF US, THE
TWO WOMEN
UMBRELLAS OF CHERBOURG, THE
UNDER THE ROOFS OF PARIS
VAGABOND
VAMPYR
VERY CURIOUS GIRL, A
VERY PRIVATE AFFAIR, A

GERMANY

GREECE

HONG KONG

HUNGARY

INDIA

ISRAEL

ITALY

LA DOLCE VITA
LA NUIT DE VARENNES
LA STRADA
LA TERRA TREMA
LA TRAVIATA
LAST EMPEROR, THE
LAST TANGO IN PARIS
LAST YEAR AT MARIENBAD
L'AVVENTURA
LE BAL
LE MAGNIFIQUE
LE SEX SHOP
LES CARABINIERS
LOVE AND ANARCHY
MACARONI
MALICIOUS
MILKY WAY, THE
MIRACLE IN MILAN
MOON IN THE GUTTER, THE
MURIEL
NIGHT OF THE SHOOTING STARS, THE
NIGHT PORTER, THE
NIGHTS OF CABIRIA, THE
1900
OPEN CITY
OSSESSIONE
PADRE PADRONE
PAISAN
PASSENGER, THE
PASSION OF BEATRICE, THE
RED DESERT
SEDUCED AND ABANDONED
SEDUCTION OF MIMI, THE
SEVEN BEAUTIES
SOTTO...SOTTO
STATE OF SIEGE
STAY AS YOU ARE
STROMBOLI
SWEPT AWAY...BY AN UNUSUAL DESTINY IN THE BLUE SEA OF AUGUST
THREE BROTHERS
TILL MARRIAGE DO US PART
TWO WOMEN
UMBERTO D
VERY PRIVATE AFFAIR, A
WAGES OF FEAR, THE
WHERE'S PICONE?
WHITE SHEIK, THE
WIFEMISTRESS
YESTERDAY, TODAY, AND TOMORROW

IVORY COAST

BLACK AND WHITE IN COLOR

JAMAICA

HARDER THEY COME, THE

JAPAN

BAD SLEEP WELL, THE
BURMESE HARP, THE
DERSU UZALA
DODES 'KA-DEN
DOUBLE SUICIDE
DRUNKEN ANGEL
FIRES ON THE PLAIN
FLOATING WEEDS
47 RONIN, THE (PARTS 1 & 2)
FUNERAL, THE
GATE OF HELL
GO-MASTERS, THE
GOLDEN DEMON
HIDDEN FORTRESS, THE
HIGH AND LOW
HIMATSURI
HIROSHIMA, MON AMOUR
IKIRUIREZUMI (SPIRIT OF TATTOO)
KAGEMUSHA
KWAIDAN
LIFE OF OHARU
LOWER DEPTHS, THE (1957)
MACARTHUR'S CHILDREN
MERRY CHRISTMAS, MR. LAWRENCE
MOTHER
ODD OBSESSION
RAN
RASHOMON
RED BEARD
SAMURAI TRILOGY, THE
SANJURO
SANSHO THE BAILIFF
SEVEN SAMURAI, THE
SISTERS OF THE GION
STRAY DOG
SWORD OF DOOM, THE
TAMPOPO
TAXING WOMAN, A
THRONE OF BLOOD
TWENTY-FOUR EYES
UGETSU
WOMAN IN THE DUNES
YOJIMBO

MARTINIQUE

SUGAR CANE ALLEY

MEXICO

ALSINO AND THE CONDOR
CRIMINAL LIFE OF ARCHIBALDO DE LA CRUZ, THE
EL BRUTO
ERENDIRA
EXTERMINATING ANGEL, THE
LA CHEVRE
LOS OLVIDADOS
MEXICAN BUS RIDE
VIRIDIANA
WOMAN WITHOUT LOVE, A
WUTHERING HEIGHTS

THE NETHERLANDS

ASSAULT, THE
FOURTH MAN, THE
QUESTION OF SILENCE
SOLDIER OF ORANGE
SPETTERS

NEW ZEALAND

MERRY CHRISTMAS, MR. LAWRENCE

NICARAGUA

ALSINO AND THE CONDOR

NORWAY

FLIGHT OF THE EAGLE

PERU

LA CIUDAD Y LOS PERROS

POLAND

ASHES AND DIAMONDS
DANTON
DYBBUK, THE
KANAL
KNIFE IN THE WATER
TIN DRUM, THE

SOUTH AFRICA

PLACE OF WEEPING

SPAIN

BLOOD WEDDING
CAMILA
CARMEN
CRIA!
DISCREET CHARM OF THE BOURGEOISIE, THE
EL AMOR BRUJO
EL DIPUTADO
EL MUERTO
GARDEN OF DELIGHTS, THE
HEAT OF DESIRE
HOLY INNOCENTS, THE
LAW OF DESIRE
NEST, THE
SKYLINE
SPIRIT OF THE BEEHIVE, THE
STAY AS YOU ARE
THAT OBSCURE OBJECT OF DESIRE
VIRIDIANA

SWEDEN

AFTER THE REHEARSAL
AUTUMN SONATA
CRIES AND WHISPERS
DEVIL'S EYE, THE
DREAMS
ELVIRA MADIGAN
FANNY AND ALEXANDER
FLIGHT OF THE EAGLE
HOUR OF THE WOLF, THE

LESSON IN LOVE, A
MAGICIAN, THE
MASCULINE FEMININE
MONTENEGRO
MY LIFE AS A DOG
PERSONAPORT OF CALL
SACRIFICE, THE
SAWDUST AND TINSEL
SCENES FROM A MARRIAGE
SECRETS OF WOMEN
SEVENTH SEAL, THE
SILENCE, THE
SMILES OF A SUMMER NIGHT
SUMMER INTERLUDE
THROUGH A GLASS DARKLY
TORMENT
VIRGIN SPRING, THE
WILD STRAWBERRIES
WINTER LIGHT, THE

SWITZERLAND
DANGEROUS MOVES
HAIL, MARY
YOL

TAHITI
JACKO AND LISE

TURKEY
YOL

US
ARIA
CAMILLE 2000
EL NORTE
GOOD MORNING BABYLON
HAMMETT
KISS OF THE SPIDER WOMAN
LAST EMPEROR, THE
MISHIMA
NIGHT PORTER, THE
ROUND MIDNIGHT
SERPENT'S EGG, THE
STATE OF SIEGE
STATE OF THINGS, THE
SWEET COUNTRY
THERESE AND ISABELLE
THREEPENNY OPERA, THE
ZABRISKIE POINT

USSR
ALEXANDER NEVSKY
BALLAD OF A SOLDIER
BATTLESHIP POTEMKIN
CRANES ARE FLYING, THE
DERSU UZALA
EARTH
IVAN THE TERRIBLE PART I AND II
MOSCOW DOES NOT BELIEVE IN TEARS
MY NAME IS IVANREPENTANCE
SHADOWS OF FORGOTTEN ANCESTORS
TEN DAYS THAT SHOOK THE WORLD

WEST GERMANY
COP AND THE GIRL, THE
JULIET OF THE SPIRITS

YUGOSLAVIA
BATTLE OF AUSTERLITZ, THE
LOVE AFFAIR; OR THE CASE OF THE MISSING SWITCHBOARD OPERATOR
TIN DRUM, THE

FILMS BY GENRE

All films included in this volume are listed below by the genre best suited to the film. Those films which can be classified in more than one genre are listed under each of the genres in which they fit. For example, the Adventure/Biography AGUIRRE, THE WRATH OF GOD is listed under both of those genres.

ACTION
COP AND THE GIRL, THE
YOJIMBO

ADVENTURE
AGUIRRE, THE WRATH OF GOD
BIG BLUE, THE
DERSU UZALA
FLIGHT OF THE EAGLE
HIDDEN FORTRESS, THE
SAMURAI TRILOGY, THE
SANJURO
WAGES OF FEAR, THE

BIOGRAPHY
CHRIST STOPPED AT EBOLI
COLONEL REDL
DANTON
EDITH AND MARCEL
EVERY MAN FOR HIMSELF AND GOD AGAINST ALL
FLIGHT OF THE EAGLE
IVAN THE TERRIBLE PART I AND II
LAST EMPEROR, THE
MISHIMA
MYSTERY OF ALEXINA, THE
NAPOLEON
RISE TO POWER OF LOUIS XIV, THE
SPRING SYMPHONY
STORY OF ADELE H., THE
THERESE
WOLF AT THE DOOR, THE

COMEDY
A NOUS LA LIBERTE
AND NOW MY LOVE
AND THE SHIP SAILS ON
ASSOCIATE, THE
BAGDAD CAFE
BAKER'S WIFE, THE
BAND OF OUTSIDERS
BIG DEAL ON MADONNA STREET, THE
BLACK AND WHITE IN COLOR
BLUE COUNTRY, THE
BOUDU SAVED FROM DROWNING
BYE BYE BRAZIL
CAT AND MOUSE
CESAR AND ROSALIE
CLOSELY WATCHED TRAINS
COCA-COLA KID, THE
COUSIN, COUSINE
CRIME OF MONSIEUR LANGE, THE
CRIMINAL LIFE OF ARCHIBALDO DE LA CRUZ, THE
DARK EYES
DEVIL'S EYE, THE
DISCREET CHARM OF THE BOURGEOISIE, THE
DONA FLOR AND HER TWO HUSBANDS
DOWN AND DIRTY
EXTERMINATING ANGEL, THE
FAMILY, THE
FEMMES DE PARIS
FIREMAN'S BALL, THE
FOUR BAGS FULL
FUNERAL, THE
FUNNY, DIRTY LITTLE WAR, A
GET OUT YOUR HANDKERCHIEFS
GIFT, THE
GINGER & FRED
GOING PLACES
HOLIDAY HOTEL
ITALIAN STRAW HAT, AN
JOKE OF DESTINY, A
JOUR DE FETE
JUPITER'S THIGH
KING OF HEARTS
LA CAGE AUX FOLLES
LA CAGE AUX FOLLES II
LA CAGE AUX FOLLES 3: THE WEDDING
LA CHEVRE
LA NUIT DE VARENNES
LAW OF DESIRE
LE BEAU MARIAGE
LE CAVALEUR (PRACTICE MAKES PERFECT)
LE MAGNIFIQUE
LE MILLION
LE SEX SHOP
LES COMPERES
LESSON IN LOVE, A
LOVE AFFAIR; OR THE CASE OF THE MISSING SWITCHBOARD OPERATOR
LOVE ON THE RUN
LOVES OF A BLONDE
LOWER DEPTHS, THE (1936)
MACARONI
MALICIOUS
MAN WHO LOVED WOMEN, THE
MEN
MEXICAN BUS RIDE
MR. HULOT'S HOLIDAY
MOSCOW DOES NOT BELIEVE IN TEARS
MY BEST FRIEND'S GIRL
MY LIFE AS A DOG
MY NEW PARTNER
MY OTHER HUSBAND
MY UNCLE
NEVER ON SUNDAY
PARDON MON AFFAIRE
PAULINE AT THE BEACH
PLAYTIME
RETURN OF THE TALL BLOND MAN WITH ONE BLACK SHOE, THE
SECRETS OF WOMEN
SEVEN BEAUTIES
SINCERELY CHARLOTTE
SKYLINE
SMALL CHANGE
SMILES OF A SUMMER NIGHT
SOTTO...SOTTO
STAY AS YOU ARE
STOLEN KISSES
SUGARBABY
SWEPT AWAY...BY AN UNUSUAL DESTINY IN THE BLUE SEA OF AUGUST
SYLVIA AND THE PHANTOM
TALL BLOND MAN WITH ONE BLACK SHOE, THE
TAMPOPO
TAXING WOMAN, A
THREE MEN AND A CRADLE
TILL MARRIAGE DO US PART
TWO DAUGHTERS
TWO OF US, THE
WHERE'S PICONE?
WHITE SHEIK, THE
YESTERDAY, TODAY, AND TOMORROW

CRIME
ALPHAVILLE
BAND OF OUTSIDERS
BIG DEAL ON MADONNA STREET, THE
BOB LE FLAMBEUR
BREATHLESS
CHOICE OF ARMS
CLEAN SLATE (COUP DE TORCHON)
CONFIDENTIALLY YOURS!
COP AND THE GIRL, THE
DIVA
DR. MABUSE, THE GAMBLER, PART 1 & 2
FRENCH DETECTIVE, THE

GOALIE'S ANXIETY AT THE PENALTY KICK, THE
HAPPY NEW YEAR
HIGH AND LOW
INVESTIGATION
LA BALANCE
LE DOULOS
M
MY NEW PARTNER
PEPE LE MOKO
QUESTION OF SILENCE
RIFIFI
SHOOT THE PIANO PLAYER
STRAY DOG
SUBWAY
TCHAO PANTIN
TESTAMENT OF DR. MABUSE, THE

DANCE

BLOOD WEDDING
EL AMOR BRUJO

DRAMA

A NOS AMOURS
AFTER THE REHEARSAL
ALICE IN THE CITIES
ALSINO AND THE CONDOR
AMARCORD
AND GOD CREATED WOMAN
APARAJITO
APHRODITE
ASHES AND DIAMONDS
ASSAULT, THE
AU REVOIR LES ENFANTS
AUTUMN SONATA
BABETTE'S FEAST
BAD SLEEP WELL, THE
BAGDAD CAFE
BALLAD OF A SOLDIER
BASILEUS QUARTET
BELLISSIMA
BERLIN ALEXANDERPLATZ
BETTY BLUE
BEYOND THE WALLS
BICYCLE THIEF, THE
BLOW-UP
BLUE ANGEL, THE
BOUDU SAVED FROM DROWNING
BYE BYE BRAZIL
CAMILLE 2000
CARNIVAL IN FLANDERS
CESAR
CHLOE IN THE AFTERNOON
CLAIRE'S KNEE
CLEO FROM 5 TO 7
CLOCKMAKER, THE
CLOSELY WATCHED TRAINS
CONTEMPT
CRIA!
CRICKET, THE
CRIES AND WHISPERS
CRIME OF MONSIEUR LANGE, THE
CRIMINAL LIFE OF ARCHIBALDO DE LA CRUZ, THE
DAMNED, THE
DAVID
DAY FOR NIGHT
DAY OF WRATH
DEATH IN VENICE
DECLINE OF THE AMERICAN EMPIRE, THE
DESPAIR
DIAMONDS OF THE NIGHT
DIARY OF A CHAMBERMAID
DIARY OF A LOST GIRL
DIRTY DISHES
DISCREET CHARM OF THE BOURGEOISIE, THE
DIVINE NYMPH, THE
DODES 'KA-DEN
DOUBLE SUICIDE
DOWN AND DIRTY
DREAMS
DRIFTING
DRUNKEN ANGEL
DUST
EARRINGS OF MADAME DE . . ., THE
EARTH
ECLIPSE
ECSTASY
8 1/2
EL BRUTO
EL DIPUTADO
EL NORTE
ELENA AND HER MEN
ELUSIVE CORPORAL, THE
EMMANUELLE
ENTRE NOUS
EXTERMINATING ANGEL, THE
EYES, THE MOUTH, THE
FANNY
FANNY AND ALEXANDER
FATHER
FEAR
FITZCARRALDO
FLOATING WEEDS
FORBIDDEN GAMES
FOUR HUNDRED BLOWS, THE
FROM THE LIFE OF THE MARIONETTES
FULL MOON IN PARIS
GABRIELA
GARDEN OF DELIGHTS, THE
GARDEN OF THE FINZI-CONTINIS, THE
GENERAL DELLA ROVERE
GERMANY, YEAR ZERO
GERTRUD
GERVAISE
GINGER & FRED
GO-MASTERS, THE
GOALIE'S ANXIETY AT THE PENALTY KICK, THE
GOING PLACES
GOLDEN COACH, THE
GOLDEN DEMON
GREEN ROOM, THE
HANNAH K.
HARDER THEY COME, THE
HEAT OF DESIRE
HENRY IV
HIMATSURI
HIROSHIMA, MON AMOUR
HOLY INNOCENTS, THE
HOME AND THE WORLD, THE
HOUR OF THE STAR, THE
HOUR OF THE WOLF, THE
I SENT A LETTER TO MY LOVE
I VITELLONI
IKIRU
INHERITANCE, THE
INHERITORS, THE
INNOCENT, THE
INVESTIGATION
INVITATION AU VOYAGE
IPHIGENIA
IREZUMI (SPIRIT OF TATTOO)
JACKO AND LISE
JEAN DE FLORETTE
JULES AND JIM
JULIA AND JULIA
JULIET OF THE SPIRITS
KAGEMUSHA
KAMERADSCHAFT
KING OF HEARTS
KINGS OF THE ROAD
KNIFE IN THE WATER
LA BETE HUMAINE
LA BOUM
LA CIUDAD Y LOS PERROS
LA DOLCE VITA
LA PASSANTE
LA RONDE
LA STRADA
LA TERRA TREMA
LA TRUITE (THE TROUT)
LADY CHATTERLEY'S LOVER
L'AGE D'OR
L'ANNEE DES MEDUSES
LAST LAUGH, THE
LAST TANGO IN PARIS
LAST YEAR AT MARIENBAD
L'AVVENTURA
LE BEAU MARIAGE
LE BEAU SERGE
LE CHAT
LE GRAND CHEMIN
LE JOUR SE LEVE
LE PLAISIR

LE SEX SHOP
LES CARABINIERS
LES COMPERES
LES ENFANTS TERRIBLES
LIFE OF OHARU
LOLA MONTES
LOS OLVIDADOS
LOST HONOR OF KATHARINA BLUM, THE
LOVE AND ANARCHY
LOVE ON THE RUN
LOWER DEPTHS, THE (1936)
LOWER DEPTHS, THE (1957)
LUMIERE
MACARONI
MACARTHUR'S CHILDREN
MACBETH
MADAME ROSA
MAEDCHEN IN UNIFORM
MAGICIAN, THE
MAKE ROOM FOR TOMORROW
MALOU
MAN AND A WOMAN, A
MAN FACING SOUTHEAST
MAN WHO LOVED WOMEN, THE
MANON OF THE SPRING
MARIUS
MARRIAGE OF MARIA BRAUN, THE
MARRIED WOMAN, THE
MASCULINE FEMININE
MEPHISTOMEXICAN BUS RIDE
MISS MARY
MR. KLEIN
MON ONCLE D'AMERIQUE
MONTENEGRO
MOON IN THE GUTTER, THE
MOONLIGHTING
MOSCOW DOES NOT BELIEVE IN TEARS
MOTHER
MURIEL
MY LIFE AS A DOG
MY LIFE TO LIVE
MY NAME IS IVAN
MY NIGHT AT MAUD'S
MY OTHER HUSBAND
NEST, THE
NEVER ON SUNDAY
NIGHT OF THE SHOOTING STARS, THE
NIGHT PORTER, THE
NIGHTS OF CABIRIA, THE
1900
ODD OBSESSION
OFFICIAL STORY, THE
OPEN CITY
ORDET
OSSESSIONE
PADRE PADRONE
PANDORA'S BOX
PARIS, TEXAS
PASSENGER, THE
PASSION OF JOAN OF ARC, THE
PATHER PANCHALI
PAULINE AT THE BEACH
PEDESTRIAN, THE
PERSONA
PHANTOM OF LIBERTY, THE
PICNIC ON THE GRASS
PIXOTE
PLACE OF WEEPING
POIL DE CAROTTE
PORT OF CALL
PROVIDENCE
QUERELLE
RASHOMON
RED DESERT
REPENTANCE
REVOLT OF JOB, THE
ROUND MIDNIGHT
RULES OF THE GAME, THE
SACRIFICE, THE
SANSHO THE BAILIFF
SAWDUST AND TINSEL
SCENES FROM A MARRIAGE
SECRETS OF WOMEN
SEDUCED AND ABANDONED
SEDUCTION OF MIMI, THE
SERPENT'S EGG, THE
SEVEN BEAUTIES
SEVEN SAMURAI, THE
SEVENTH SEAL, THE
SHADOWS OF FORGOTTEN ANCESTORS
SHOP ON MAIN STREET, THE
SIEGFRIED
SILENCE, THE
SINCERELY CHARLOTTE
SISTERS OF THE GION
SMALL CHANGE
SOFT SKIN, THE
SOLDIER OF ORANGE
SOTTO...SOTTO
SPETTERS
SPIRIT OF THE BEEHIVE, THE
STATE OF THINGS, THE
STAY AS YOU ARE
STROMBOLI
SUGAR CANE ALLEY
SUGARBABY
SUMMER
SUMMER INTERLUDE
SUNDAY IN THE COUNTRY, A
SUNDAYS AND CYBELE
SWANN IN LOVE
SWEET COUNTRY
SWEPT AWAY...BY AN UNUSUAL DESTINY IN THE BLUE SEA OF AUGUST
SWORD OF DOOM, THE
SYLVIA AND THE PHANTOM
TAXING WOMAN, A
TCHAO PANTIN
TESS
TESTAMENT OF ORPHEUS, THE
THAT OBSCURE OBJECT OF DESIRE
THERESE AND ISABELLE
THREE BROTHERS
THRONE OF BLOOD
THROUGH A GLASS DARKLY
TIN DRUM, THE
TONI
TONIO KROGER
TORMENT
TRANSPORT FROM PARADISE
TWENTY-FOUR EYES
TWIST & SHOUT
TWO DAUGHTERS
TWO ENGLISH GIRLS
TWO OF US, THE
TWO WOMEN
UGETSU
UMBERTO D
UNDER THE ROOFS OF PARIS
VAGABOND
VARIETY
VERY CURIOUS GIRL, A
VERY PRIVATE AFFAIR, A
VIRGIN SPRING, THE
VIRIDIANA
WHERE THE GREEN ANTS DREAM
WIFEMISTRESS
WILD STRAWBERRIES
WINTER LIGHT, THE
WOMAN IN FLAMES, A
WOMAN IN THE DUNES
WOMAN NEXT DOOR, THE
WORLD OF APU, THE
WRONG MOVE
YESTERDAY, TODAY, AND TOMORROW
YOL
ZABRISKIE POINT

FANTASY

AMARCORD
BEAUTY AND THE BEAST
BLOOD OF A POET, THE
DIARY OF FORBIDDEN DREAMS
DONKEY SKIN
DYBBUK, THE
ERENDIRA
ETERNAL RETURN, THE
FAUST
KRIEMHILD'S REVENGE
METROPOLIS
MIRACLE IN MILAN
ORPHEUS
REPENTANCE

WINGS OF DESIRE

HISTORICAL
BATTLE OF AUSTERLITZ, THE
BATTLESHIP POTEMKIN
CAMILA
COLONEL REDL
COUP DE GRACE
DANTON
FELLINI SATYRICON
47 RONIN, THE (PARTS 1 & 2)
GATE OF HELL
GOOD MORNING BABYLON
IN THE NAME OF THE POPE KING
LA MARSEILLAISE
LA NUIT DE VARENNES
LAST EMPEROR, THE
MAYERLING
NAPOLEON
PASSION OF BEATRICE
RAN
RED BEARD
RETURN OF MARTIN GUERRE, THE
SAMURAI TRILOGY, THE
TEN DAYS THAT SHOOK THE WORLD
WANNSEE CONFERENCE, THE

HORROR
CABINET OF DR. CALIGARI, THE
DESTINY
GOLEM, THE
HORROR CHAMBER OF DR. FAUSTUS, THE
KWAIDAN
MNOSFERATU
REPULSION
TENANT, THE
VAMPYR

MUSICAL
FRENCH CANCAN
LA TRAVIATA
LE BAL
LOVE SONGS
SPRING SYMPHONY
THREEPENNY OPERA, THE
UMBRELLAS OF CHERBOURG, THE

MYSTERY
CAT AND MOUSE
HAMMETT

OPERA
ARIA
BIZET'S CARMEN
CARMEN

POLITICAL
CONFORMIST, THE
COUP DE GRACE
LOVE AND ANARCHY
REPENTANCE
STATE OF SIEGE
Z

PRISON
BEYOND THE WALLS
GRAND ILLUSION
KISS OF THE SPIDER WOMAN
L'ADDITION
MERRY CHRISTMAS, MR. LAWRENCE
SHOESHINE
WALL, THE

RELIGIOUS
DIARY OF A COUNTRY PRIEST
FLOWERS OF ST. FRANCIS, THE
GOSPEL ACCORDING TO ST. MATTHEW, THE
HAIL, MARY
MILKY WAY, THE

ROMANCE
AND NOW MY LOVE
BEAU PERE
BEAUTY AND THE BEAST
BLACK ORPHEUS
BLUE COUNTRY, THE
BREATHLESS
CAMILA
CESAR AND ROSALIE
CONFIDENTIALLY YOURS!
CRANES ARE FLYING, THE
DARK EYES
DEVIL IN THE FLESH, THE
DIVA
EDITH AND MARCEL
ELVIRA MADIGAN
ETERNAL RETURN, THE
GIRL ON A MOTORCYCLE, THE
HAPPY NEW YEAR
LAST METRO, THE
L'ATALANTE
LOVE IN GERMANY, A
MAN AND A WOMAN: 20 YEARS LATER, A
MAN IN LOVE, A
MAYERLING
PARDON MON AFFAIRE
PEPE LE MOKO
STOLEN KISSES
TENDRES COUSINES

SCIENCE FICTION
ALPHAVILLE
DEATHWATCH
FAHRENHEIT 451
KAMIKAZE '89
LE DERNIER COMBAT

SPY
RETURN OF THE TALL BLOND MAN WITH ONE BLACK SHOE, THE
SPIES
TALL BLOND MAN WITH ONE BLACK SHOE, THE

THRILLER
AMERICAN FRIEND, THE
BAD GIRLS
BLIND TRUST
DANGEROUS MOVES
DIABOLIQUE
FOURTH MAN, THE
FRANTIC
ONE DEADLY SUMMER
PERIL
SCENE OF THE CRIME
STATE OF SIEGE

WAR
ALEXANDER NEVSKY
ASHES AND DIAMONDS
ASSAULT, THE
BALLAD OF A SOLDIER
BATTLE OF ALGIERS, THE
BATTLE OF AUSTERLITZ, THE
BLACK AND WHITE IN COLOR
BOAT, THE
BURMESE HARP, THE
CRANES ARE FLYING, THE
ELUSIVE CORPORAL, THE
FIRES ON THE PLAIN
FORBIDDEN GAMES
FUNNY, DIRTY LITTLE WAR, A
GARDEN OF THE FINZI-CONTINIS, THE
GENERAL DELLA ROVERE
GRAND ILLUSION
KANAL
KOLBERG
LAST METRO, THE
LOVE IN GERMANY, A
MEPHISTO
MERRY CHRISTMAS, MR. LAWRENCE
NIGHT OF THE SHOOTING STARS, THE
OPEN CITY
PAISAN
SHOP ON MAIN STREET, THE
SOLDIER OF ORANGE
TRANSPORT FROM PARADISE
TWO WOMEN

WESTERN
EL MUERTO

Foreign Films

Film Reviews

A

A NOS AMOURS**½

(1983, Fr.) 102m Les Films du Livradois-Gaumont-FR3/ Triumph c (GB: TO OUR LOVES)

Sandrine Bonnaire *(Suzanne),* Dominique Besnehard *(Robert),* Maurice Pialat *(The Father),* Evelyne Ker *(The Mother),* Anne-Sophie Maille *(Anne),* Christophe Odent *(Michel),* Cyr Boitard *(Luc),* Maite Maille *(Martine),* Pierre-Loup Rajot *(Bernard),* Cyril Collard *(Jean-Pierre),* Nathalie Gureghian *(Nathalie),* Guenole Pascal *(Instructor),* Caroline Cibot *(Charline),* Jacques Fieschi *(Jacques),* Valerie Schlumberger *(Marie-France),* Tom Stevens *(American),* Tsilka Theodorou *(Fanny).*

A NOS AMOURS is the story of 15-year-old Suzanne (Sandrine Bonnaire, in her first role), who is in a hopeless situation—she can be loved but cannot feel love. Since she is only happy when she is with a guy, she sleeps with everyone who shows interest, except Luc (Cyr Boitard), the one boy who truly loves her. Her promiscuity not only makes her a popular item with the boys, but causes some jealousy among her girl friends. Her consistent late hours cause dissension in her family, especially in the case of her stern father (director Maurice Pialat), who slaps her, seemingly without remorse. When the father moves out, the family is thrown into severe turmoil as Bonnaire's inadequate brother assumes his father's role and her mother becomes a basket case. Bonnaire (who has since gone on to become one of France's top stars) makes quite an impression in the film—her character is a truly compelling romantic figure—but Pialat devotes much of his energy to the depiction of her home life (photographed in a style often compared to that of John Cassavetes). Although Suzanne's views on love and loving are the source of difficult emotional problems (allusions are made to psychiatric treatments), she appears completely sane in comparison to her wacked-out mother and brother, both of whom have slipped into a perverse relationship that would make Freud's day. One should see A NOS AMOURS solely for Bonnaire (Pialat has done better before and after this film), the greatest actress to come out of France since Isabelle Huppert appeared in THE LACEMAKER. In French with English subtitles.

p, Maurice Pialat; d, Maurice Pialat; w, Maurice Pialat, Arlette Langmann; ph, Jacques Loiseleux; ed, Yann Dedet, Sophie Coussein, Valerie Condroyer; m, Klaus Nomi, Henry Purcell.

Drama **(PR:O MPAA:R)**

A NOUS LA LIBERTE*****

(1931, Fr.) 97m Films Sonores Tobis bw (AKA: LIBERTY FOR US)

Henri Marchand *(Emile),* Raymond Cordy *(Louis),* Rolla France *(Jeanne),* Paul Olivier *(Uncle Paul Imaque),* Jacques Shelly *(Paul),* Andre Michaud *(Foreman),* Germaine Aussey *(Maud),* Alexander D'Arcy *(Gigolo),* William Burke *(Head Crook),* Vincent Hyspa *(Orator),* Leon Lorin *(Deaf Old Man).*

This classic satire on the dehumanization of industrial workers and man's desire for freedom is one of French director Rene Clair's greatest achievements, preceding Chaplin's indictment of the industrial revolution, MODERN TIMES, by five years. Clair's fast-paced and amusing experiment centers on the friendship between two prison inmates—Louis (Raymond Cordy), who escapes and becomes a phonograph company tycoon, and Emile (Henri Marchand), who upon his release is hired at his friend's factory. Filming without a script and thereby giving the actors freedom to improvise, Clair modeled his structure on that of the operetta. The film is filled with the music of Georges Auric, to which the movements of the assembly lines of actors are choreographed. Clair's message is an angry one—"a bitter pill," as he described it, which "would be more easily swallowed when coated with diverting music"—and later he would admit he was wrong in using the diverting operatic devices for his leftist attack on the factory owner's inhumane treatment of the proletariat. Whether or not Clair's execution was the best choice, A NOUS LA LIBERTE is a brilliantly crafted and wickedly funny satire, no less powerful today as it was in 1931. In French with English subtitles.

p, Rene Clair; d, Rene Clair; w, Rene Clair; ph, Georges Perinal; ed, Rene Le Hanaff; m, Georges Auric.

Comedy **(PR:A MPAA:NR)**

AFTER THE REHEARSAL**

(1984, Swed.) 72m Cinematograph-Personafilm/Triumph c (EFTER REPETITIONEN)

Erland Josephson *(Henrik Vogler),* Ingrid Thulin *(Rakel),* Lena Olin *(Anna Egerman),* Nadja Palmstjerna-Weiss *(Anna at age 12),* Bertil Guve *(Henrik at age 12).*

Filmed for Swedish television, AFTER THE REHEARSAL was announced as Ingmar Bergman's farewell to cinema (a claim that was also made upon FANNY AND ALEXANDER's release in 1983). Partly autobiographical, it concerns an aging theater director, Henrik Vogler (Erland Josephson), who looks back on the pain and suffering he has caused those around him, especially the actresses he has loved and left. After the rehearsal of his fifth production of August Strindberg's "Dream Play," the aging director rests his weary self on a couch that is part of the stage set. He is visited by Anna (Lena Olin), a young actress who has returned to the theater in search of a bracelet she supposedly left behind. There is a mutual attraction between actress and director as they discuss their lives and the theater—Henrik revealing to the young woman that he once had an affair with her mother. Then they imagine what their lives would be like if they were to have an affair. Though AFTER THE REHEARSAL is blessed with three superb performances (including that of Ingrid Thulin, as a has-been actress who attacks the director for having abandoned her), it is trapped in its staginess, leaving one to wonder why Bergman decided to bring it to the screen. Olin, Josephson, and cinematographer Sven Nykvist would meet again a few years later in THE UNBEARABLE LIGHTNESS OF BEING. In Swedish with English subtitles.

p, Jorn Donner; d, Ingmar Bergman; w, Ingmar Bergman; ph, Sven Nykvist; ed, Sylvia Ingemarsson.

Drama **(PR:C-O MPAA:R)**

AGUIRRE, THE WRATH OF GOD*****

(1972, Ger.) 93m Werner Herzog Prod./New Yorker c (AGUIRRE, DER ZORN GOTTES)

Klaus Kinski *(Don Lope de Aguirre),* Ruy Guerra *(Don Pedro de Ursua),* Del Negro *(Brother Gaspar de Carvajal, Narrator),* Helena Rojo *(Inez de Atienza),* Cecilia Rivera *(Flores),* Peter Berling *(Don Fernando de Guzman),* Danyel Edes *(Perucho),* Edward Roland *(Okello),* Armando Polanah *(Armando).*

In his most powerful fiction film, Werner Herzog shakes his fist at nature and the forces of destiny with this story of a 16th-century visionary/madman who is determined to conquer all the forces surrounding him. Klaus Kinski is Don Lope de Aguirre, one of a group of Spanish conquistadors traveling on foot over the Andes and exploring the jungles of Peru, claiming them as Spanish territories. Rather than send forward the entire group, many of whom are stricken with fever, the commanding officer sends a small scouting party ahead. When this party's leader also succumbs to the pressures of jungle exploration, the fiery Aguirre takes command, installing a puppet Emperor of Peru and assumes control of the party's men and property. His quest leads him down the raging Amazon in the direction of the mythical El Dorado, a land brimming with a wealth of gold. Under Aguirre's lead, the dispirited men are attacked by spear-wielding Indians or engulfed by whirlpools and rapids. By the film's end, Aguirre's men are dead, but nothing will stop the mad visionary. "Who is with me?" growls Aguirre, as his raft swirls out of control downriver, swarmed by countless tiny monkeys. It is in Aguirre that Herzog's link between Man and Nature is best drawn. Here is a character who is not of the same mold as other men—one who challenges the gods above with the words, "The Earth on which I tread hears me and trembles." In AGUIRRE, Herzog explores the violence that erupts when humankind tries to control forces greater than itself. With his next film, EVERY MAN FOR HIMSELF AND GOD AGAINST ALL, Herzog would suggest in the character of Kaspar Hauser the harmony that can exist between the same two forces. In German with English subtitles.

p, Werner Herzog; d, Werner Herzog; w, Werner Herzog; ph, Thomas Mauch (Eastmancolor); ed, Beate Mainka-Jellinghaus; m, Florian Fricke.

Adventure **(PR:O MPAA:NR)**

ALEXANDER NEVSKY*****

(1938, USSR) 107m Mosfilm/Artkino bw

Nikolai Cherkassov *(Prince Alexander Yaroslavich Nevsky),* Nikolai P. Okhlopkov *(Vassily Buslai),* A.L. Abrikossov *(Gavrilo Olexich),* Dimitri N. Orlov *(Ignat, Master Armourer),* V.K. Novikov *(Pavsha, Governor of Pskov),* N.N. Arski *(Domash, Nobleman of Novgorod),* V.O. Massalitinova *(Amefa Timofeyevna, Mother of Buslai),* Vera Ivasbeva *(Olga, a Novgorod Girl),* Anna Danilova *(Vassilissa),* V.L. Ersbov *(Master of the Teutonic Order),* S.K. Blinnikov *(Tverdillo, Traitorous Mayor of Pskov),* I.I. Lagutin *(Anani, a Monk),* L.A. Fenin *(The Bishop),* N.A. Rogozbin *(The Black-robed Monk).*

Sergei Eisenstein's classic tale of 13th-century Russia is as magnificent today as it must have been to its first viewers in 1938. One of the greatest achievements of Soviet (and world) cinema, this epic concerns a period in the mid-1200s, when the Teutonic Knights invaded Russia from one side while the Tartars closed in from the other. The motherland decays where invaders have plundered at will, destroying the earth and the morale of the populace. Finally, the moody and volatile Prince Nevsky (Nikolai Cherkassov) is summoned to lead his people in their struggle against the oppressors. A valiant and intelligent nobleman, Nevsky builds his army (a campaign that takes up half the film), then fights an incredible and decisive battle at the frozen Lake Peipus in 1242, where his strategy proves successful. The battle scenes are overwhelming—thousands and thousands of men (Eisenstein was given free use of the Russian army) fill the screen—the Teutonic Knights in their flowing crusaders' costumes, their heads topped with helmets fashioned in the forms of gargoyles, ogres, and fierce animals (purposely designed to frighten the enemy), and the Russian army of peasants and nobles all hacking with sword, mace, spear, pike, and axe, until the armor-burdened Germans fall victim to the lake's cracking ice. Eisenstein's attention to detail is meticulous down to every weapon and piece of equipment, every horse blanket and homemade shoe used in that long-ago era, and the mounting of his monument to Russia's ancient hero is no less than superb. Eisenstein, whose career was on the verge of dying, was rewarded for his work (a thinly veiled piece of Stalinist propaganda with the heroic Nevsky as Stalin and the savage Teutons as the Nazis) by being named head of Mosfilm Studios. In Russian with English subtitles.

p, Sergei Eisenstein; d, Sergei Eisenstein, Dmitri I. Vassiliev; w, Sergei Eisenstein, Pytor Pavlenko; ph, Eduard Tisse; ed, Sergei Eisenstein; m, Sergei Prokofiev.

War **(PR:C MPAA:NR)**

ALICE IN THE CITIES***½

(1974, Ger.) 110m Filmverlag der Autoren-WDR/Gray City bw (ALICE IN DEN STADTEN)

Rudiger Vogler *(Phillip Winter),* Yella Rottlander *(Alice van Damme),* Lisa Kreuzer *(Lisa, Alice's Mother),* Edda Kochl *(Angela, New York Girl Friend),* Didi Petrikat *(Woman at Beach),* Ernest Bohm *(Writer's Agent),* Sam Presti *(Used Car Salesman),* Lois Moran *(Ticket Agent),* Hans Hirschmuller *(Policeman),* Sybille Baier *(Woman),* Mirko *(Boy at Jukebox),* Wim Wenders *(Man at Jukebox).*

An ancestor of director Wim Wenders' 1984 film PARIS,

TEXAS, this low-budget West German picture made by Wenders a decade earlier documents the existence of Philip Winter (Rudiger Vogler), a German journalist who is traveling across the US' East Coast in search of a story. He finds that the only way he can capture America's landscapes, buildings, and signs is not by writing about them, but by taking Polaroid snapshots. While trying to return to Germany, Philip meets Lisa van Damme (Elisabeth Kreuzer) and her nine-year-old daughter, Alice (Yella Rottlander), who are also trying to arrange a flight home. When Lisa temporarily leaves Alice in Philip's care and it doesn't seem as if she will return, the unlikely pair drive through the streets of Wuppertal, West Germany, in search of Alice's grandmother's house. The beginning of a loosely connected Wenders road-movie trilogy (followed in 1975 by WRONG MOVE, and, one year later, KINGS OF THE ROAD—all three starring Vogler), ALICE IN THE CITIES is a relaxed, meditative film that favors the landscape and the road that stretches out ahead over the traditional film elements of story and dialog. Like Philip Winter, Wenders is a documentarian who fills his frame with images of American culture (a hot dog stand, a used car lot, Shea Stadium) and strains of American music ("Under the Boardwalk," Canned Heat, Chuck Berry) to tell his story, because he finds words insufficient. In English and German with English subtitles.

p, Jaochim von Mengershausen; d, Wim Wenders; w, Wim Wenders, Veith von Furstenberg; ph, Robby Muller, Martin Schafer; ed, Peter Przygodda, Barbara von Weitershausen; m, Can, Gustav Mahler.

Drama **(PR:A MPAA:NR)**

ALPHAVILLE****

(1965, Fr./It.) 98m Chaumiane-Filmstudio Athos/PATHE bw (AKA: ALPHAVILLE, A STRANGE CASE OF LEMMY CAUTION)

Eddie Constantine *(Lemmy Caution),* Anna Karina *(Natasha Von Braun),* Akim Tamiroff *(Henri Dickson),* Laszlo Szabo *(Engineer),* Howard Vernon *(Prof. Von Braun),* Michel Delahaye *(Von Braun's Assistant),* Jean-Andre Fieschi *(Prof. Heckel),* Jean-Louis Comolli *(Prof. Jeckell).*

Perhaps the most easily digestible of Jean-Luc Godard's films, ALPHAVILLE is often referred to as "science fiction," though the description is misleading and far from accurate. A hybrid of sci-fi and *film noir* styles, its real core is the surrealist poetry of the 1920s, specifically Paul Eluard's *Capital of Pain.* Pulp hero-intergalactic special agent Lemmy Caution (again essayed by Eddie Constantine) travels to the mysterious Alphaville (actually Paris) to investigate the disappearance of Henri Dickson (Akim Tamiroff), a member of Caution's agency, and to kill or capture Professor Von Braun (Howard Vernon), a scientist who invented the fascist Alpha-60 computer. En route he meets the professor's daughter Natasha (Anna Karina), who is incapable of loving and learns about the subject by studying Eluard's writings. Although Godard adheres to certain genre conventions in ALPHAVILLE (subtitled "The Strange Case of Lemmy Caution"), he is not a slave to them, continuing to discover the relationship between sound and image, and question the relationship between love and society. In French with English subtitles.

p, Andre Michelin; d, Jean-Luc Godard; w, Jean-Luc Godard; ph, Raoul Coutard; ed, Agnes Guillemot; m, Paul Misraki.

Crime/Science Fiction **(PR:A MPAA:NR)**

ALSINO AND THE CONDOR½**

(1982, Nicaragua/Costa Rica/Cuba/Mex.) 89m Cuban Institute of Cinematographic Art-Latin American Prod.-Costa Rican Cooperative/Libra Cinema 5 c (ALSINO Y EL CONDOR)

Dean Stockwell *(Frank),* Alan Esquivel *(Alsino),* Carmen Bunster *(Alsino's Grandmother),* Alejandro Parodi *(The Major),* Delia Casanova *(Rosario),* Marta Lorena Perez *(Lucia),* Reinaldo Miravalle *(Don Nazario, the Birdman),* Marcelo Gaete *(Lucia's Grandfather),* Jan Kees De Roy *(Dutch Adviser).*

ALSINO AND THE CONDOR presents a devastating view of Nicaragua torn to pieces by war, its people in poverty and starvation, all through the eyes of a wonderful little actor, Alan Esquivel, whose only desire is to escape the havoc and misery that surrounds him. Wishing he could fly, he spends his time daydreaming and imagining himself an exotic bird high above the jungles and rotting cities. He gets his first chance to fly when the friendly American helicopter pilot Frank (Dean Stockwell) takes the youngster up in his aircraft, which is painted with the symbol of a condor. But this is not enough for the boy. Flying in a helicopter is not the real thing, so he must continue to dream. Based on a popular children's novel, the film is an engrossing allegory of the situation in Latin America in which young Alsino is a representative of entire populations of oppressed people, his desire to fly a symbol of their quest for freedom. A low-budget multinational coproduction (the first film produced in Nicaragua after the Sandinista revolution), ALSINO AND THE CONDOR earned an Oscar nomination for Best Foreign Film. It was director Miguel Littin's second nomination; he had also received one in 1975 for LETTERS FROM MARUSIA. In Spanish with English subtitles.

p, Herman Littin; d, Miguel Littin; w, Miguel Littin, Isidora Aguirre, Tomas Perez Turrent (based on the book *Alsino* by Pedro Prado); ph, Jorge Herrera, Pablo Martinez; ed, Meriam Talavera; m, Leo Brower.

Drama **(PR:C MPAA:NR)**

AMARCORD***

(1973, Fr./It.) 127m F.C.-PECF/WB-NW c

Magali Noel *(Gradisca),* Bruno Zanin *(Titta),* Pupella Maggio *(Titta's Mother),* Armando Brancia *(Titta's Father),* Giuseppe Ianigro *(Titta's Grandfather),* Nando Orfei *(Pataca),* Ciccio Ingrassia *(Uncle Teo),* Luigi Rossi *(Lawyer),* Gennaro Ombra *(Bisein),* Josiane Tanzilli *(Volpina),* Antonietta Beluzzi *(Tobacconist),* Gianfilipo Carcano *(Don Baravelli),* Ferruccio Brembilla *(Fascist Lead-*

er), Dina Adorni *(Math Teacher),* Marcello di Falco *(The Prince),* Aristide Caporale *(Giudizio),* Fernando Vona *(Candela),* Donatella Gambini *(Aldina),* Franco Magno *(Zeus).*

A pictorial weaving of the bizarre fragments of Federico Fellini's imagination and memory, AMARCORD is set in a seaside village (very similar to Fellini's boyhood town of Rimini) in the 1930s. Incidents are viewed from the perspective of the impressionable young Titta (Bruno Zanin), and it is through his eyes that Fellini takes a penetrating look at family life, religion, education, and politics. Among the characters are Titta's constantly battling mother and father, and a priest who listens to confession only to spark his own deviant imagination. Though Italy is under the control of the Fascists, the regime's oppressiveness remains obscure to the naive villagers, who worship an immense, daunting banner of the face of *Il Duce.* Though there is hardly a character in AMARCORD left unscathed by Fellini's biting wit, the director still shows a great amount of love for these people. Unique personality traits, those things that reveal weaknesses, and thus humanness, are valued for the color and variety they add to the world. AMARCORD won the Academy Award for Best Foreign Film in 1974. As with a number of Fellini videocassettes, the film is unconvincingly dubbed.

p, Franco Cristaldi; d, Federico Fellini; w, Federico Fellini, Tonino Guerra; ph, Giuseppe Rotunno; ed, Ruggero Mastroianni; m, Nino Rota.

Drama/Fantasy (PR:O MPAA:R)

AMERICAN FRIEND, THE***

(1977, Ger.) 123m Road Movies-Les Films du Losange-WDR/New Yorker c

Bruno Ganz *(Jonathan Zimmermann),* Dennis Hopper *(Tom Ripley),* Lisa Kreuzer *(Marianne Zimmermann),* Gerard Blain *(Raoul Minot),* Nicholas Ray *(Derwatt/Pogash),* Samuel Fuller *(The American),* Peter Lilienthal *(Marcangelo),* Daniel Schmid *(Ingraham),* Jean Eustache *(Friendly Man),* Rudolf Schundler *(Gantner),* Sandy Whitelaw *(Doctor in Paris),* Lou Castel *(Rodolphe),* Andreas Dedecke *(Daniel),* David Blue *(Allan Winter),* Heinz Joachim Klein *(Dr. Gabriel),* Rosemarie Heinikel *(Mona),* Wim Wenders *(Bandaged Man in Ambulance).*

Heavily influenced by the American gangster film, this psychological thriller is the work of Germany's Wim Wenders. Based on a novel by Patricia Highsmith (whose STRANGERS ON A TRAIN was filmed by Alfred Hitchcock), it tells of two friends—Tom Ripley (Dennis Hopper), an eccentric and dangerous cowboy-criminal who deals in art forgeries, and Jonathan Zimmermann (Bruno Ganz), a humble family man from Hamburg who fears he is dying of leukemia. Like Robert Walker's deranged Bruno in STRANGERS ON A TRAIN, Ripley asks Jonathan (Farley Granger's Guy counterpart) to murder a perfect stranger. Ripley offers as payment a large sum of money from which Jonathan's family can benefit after his death. Jonathan agrees and as a result gets tugged deeper and deeper into a web of international crime. Wenders' debt to American gangster films is clear here, especially in the casting of two of the genre's kings—directors Sam Fuller and Nicholas Ray—as well as international directors Gerard Blain, Jean Eustache, Peter Lilienthal, Daniel Schmid, Sandy Whitelaw, and Wenders himself. Nonetheless, THE AMERICAN FRIEND is a profoundly original film that is as concerned with gangsters as with friendship, heroism, and dependence—common themes in all of Wenders' pictures. In German and English with English subtitles.

p, Michael Wiedemann, Pierre Cottrell; d, Wim Wenders; w, Wim Wenders (based on the novel *Ripley's Game* by Patricia Highsmith); ph, Robby Muller (Eastmancolor); ed, Peter Przygodda; m, Jurgen Knieper.

Thriller (PR:A-C MPAA:NR)

AND GOD CREATED WOMAN**

(1956, Fr.) 95m Iena-UCIL-Cocinor/Kingsley c (ET DIEU CREA LA FEMME; AKA: AND WOMAN. . .WAS CREATED)

Brigitte Bardot *(Juliette),* Curt Jurgens *(Eric),* Jean-Louis Trintignant *(Michel),* Christian Marquand *(Antoine),* Georges Poujouly *(Christian),* Jean Tissier *(M. Vigier-Lefranc),* Jeanne Marken *(Mme. Morin),* Marie Glory *(Mme.Tardieu),* Isabelle Corey *(Lucienne),* Jean Lefebvre *(Rene),* Philippe Grenier *(Perri),* Jacqueline Ventura *(Mme. Vigier-Lefrance),* Jany Mourney *(Bonne Femme),* Jacques Giron *(Roger).*

. . . but Roger Vadim created Brigitte Bardot. This is the film that made sex-kitten Bardot a household name, and that liberated French cinema by putting it in the hands of the young and the beautiful. And it managed to do these things without being a very good film. The story is a simple one—Juliette (BB) is a sexually dynamic orphan girl who marries Michel (Jean-Louis Trintignant), is pursued by the wealthy Eric (Curt Jurgens), and sleeps with Antoine (Christian Marquand), Michel's brother. Nonetheless, Michel fights for Juliette and manages to lure her back. Slight on story, AND GOD CREATED WOMAN is strong on energy—all of it coming from BB's brilliant screen presence. Her pouty lips, accentuated breasts, skimpy clothing, and wildly erotic mambo routine late in the film helped whip audiences into a BB feeding frenzy. They couldn't get enough of her in France, nor could they in America. While her effect on the American film scene was dubious (more and more soft-porn titillation was imported), her effect on the French film industry can be seen in the rise of the *Nouvelle Vague* directors, who were given greater opportunities in light of Vadim's commercial success. Vadim would continue along this same path, having increasingly less impact on the film world, and trying to create Woman again in an unsuccessful 1988 remake (in title only) starring Rebecca DeMornay. Bardot would have continued success without him, making one wonder if it was Bardot who created Vadim. (Dubbed in English.)

p, Raoul J. Levy; d, Roger Vadim; w, Roger Vadim, Raoul J. Levy; ph, Armand Thirard (CinemaScope, Eastmancolor); ed, Victoria Mercanton; m, Paul Misraki.

Drama (PR:O MPAA:NR)

AND NOW MY LOVE***

(1974, Fr.) 121m Rizzoli-Les Films 13/Joseph E. Levine-Avco Embassy c (TOUTE UNE VIE)

Marthe Keller *(Sarah/Her Mother, Rachel Stern/Her Grandmother),* Andre Dussollier *(Simon Duroc),* Charles Denner *(Sarah's Father, David Goldman/Sarah's Grandfather),* Carla Gravina *(Sarah's Italian Girl Friend),* Charles Gerard *(Charlie),* Gilbert Becaud *(Himself),* Alain Basnier *(Understudy),* Daniel Boulanger *(The General),* Elie Chouraqui *(Amorous Union Man),* Nathalie Courval *(Lawyer's Wife),* Andre Falcon *(Lawyer),* Angelo Infanti *(Stud),* Annie Kerani *(Simon's Lover),* Sam Letrone *(Restaurant Owner),* Gabriele Tinti *(Sarah's Six-day Husband),* Venantino Venantini *(Very Italian Man),* Harry Walter *(Sarah's Lover).*

This energetic, episodic view of three generations of Parisians is best described by one of it own characters, filmmaker Simon Duroc (Andre Dussolier) as he discusses his new film about the 20th century: "That film will begin in 1900 with the invention of movies and end when they invent happiness in the year 2000. It's going to be a mixture of subjects, a blend of styles. It will last almost three hours—for one single second of love. It will be the anatomy of love at first sight." This is AND NOW MY LOVE. The film begins as a silent film (complete with title cards), works its way to the present, and probes into the future. Along this historical route, we meet a collection of characters—a camera operator (Charles Denner) with his new model Lumiere who is subsequently killed in the trenches of WW I; the cameraman's son David Goldman (Denner again), a camp survivor who becomes a wealthy shoe manufacturer; Rachel Stern (Marthe Keller), his wife, who dies in childbirth; Goldman's daughter Sarah (Keller again), a spoiled rich brat who first loves a popular singer (Gilbert Becaud) and then loves Simon (Dussolier), an ex-con turned filmmaker who used to steal Becaud albums from record stores. Although the film starts off on a confusing foot (there are too many characters to follow), it fast becomes a virtual cornucopia of characters, stories, parallel romances, and filmmaking techniques. AND NOW MY LOVE is a semiautobiographical film for Claude Lelouch, who produced, directed, cowrote, and cophotographed. The two-hour running time is only for the US release (and, unfortunately, the videotape); the 150-minute French version carries the story into the future, with Sarah and Simon trying to raise a family in a heavily polluted New York City. (Dubbed into English.)

p, Claude Lelouch; d, Claude Lelouch; w, Claude Lelouch, Pierre Uytterhoeven; ph, Jean Collomb, Claude Lelouch (Technicolor); ed, George Klotz; m, Francis Lai, Gilbert Becaud.

Comedy/Romance **(PR:A-C MPAA:PG)**

AND THE SHIP SAILS ON***

(1983, It./Fr.) 132m RAI-Vides-Gaumont/Triumph c (E LA NAVE VA)

Freddie Jones *(Mr. Orlando),* Barbara Jefford *(Ildebranda Cuffari),* Victor Poletti *(Aureliano Fuciletto),* Peter Cellier *(Sir Reginald J. Dongby),* Elisa Marinardi *(Teresa Valegnani),* Norma West *(Lady Violet Dongby),* Paolo Paolini *(Maestro Albertino),* Sarah Jane Varley *(Dorothy),* Fiorenzo Serra *(Grand Duke of Harzock),* Pina Bausch *(Princess Lheremia),* Pasquale Zito *(Count of Bassano),* Linda Polan *(Ines Ruffo Saltini Ione),* Phillip Locke *(Prime Minister),* Jonathan Cecil *(Ricotin),* Maurice Barrier *(U.O. Ziloev),* Fred Williams *(Abatino Lepori),* Janet Suzman *(Edmea Tetua),* Elizabeth Norberg Schultz, Bernadette Lucarini *(Sopranos),* Bruno Baccaria *(Tenor),* Colin Higgins *(Police Chief),* Elizabeth Kaza *(Film Producer),* Umberto Zuanelli *(Maestro Rubetti 1),* Vittorio Zarfati *(Maestro Rubetti 2).*

This wacky and relatively unimportant Fellini film involves a shipload of eccentric passengers who set sail in 1914 for the small island of Cleo. The purpose of their voyage ("the voyage of life?" one character queries) is to scatter the ashes of their friend, a famous opera diva. While the first class cabins contain businessmen, opera colleagues, comedians, royalty, and various patrons of the arts, the steerage contains a whole slew of Serbo-Croatian freedom fighters on the run after assassinating Archduke Ferdinand—the catalysts of WW I. If that weren't enough variety, there is also a rhinoceros on board. Tensions rise when an Austro-Hungarian battleship arrives and demands that the revolutionaries be turned over to their custody. With a line of logic that is as scattered as the diva's ashes, AND THE SHIP SAILS ON is a difficult film to watch, mainly because it has no basis at all in the real world (it was photographed entirely on Cinecitta sets, which Fellini shows us). As a result, the frustrated audience is forced into just sitting back and watching. The film is worth seeing if only for the brilliant lengthy opening sequence, which begins as a scratchy, sepia-toned silent film and gradually but gloriously develops into a colorful sound picture. In Italian with English subtitles.

p, Franco Cristaldi; d, Federico Fellini; w, Federico Fellini, Tonino Guerra; ph, Giuseppe Rotunno; ed, Ruggero Mastroianni; m, Gianfranco Plenixio, Guiseppe Verdi, Pytor Ilich Tchaikovsky, Claude Debussy, Camille Saint-Saens, Johann Strauss, Franz Schubert.

Comedy **(PR:A MPAA:PG)**

APARAJITO***

(1959, India) 105m Epic/Aurora bw (GB: THE UNVANQUISHED)

Pinaki Sen Gupta *(Apu, as a boy),* Smaran Ghosal *(Apu, as an adolescent),* Karuna Banerji *(Mother),* Kanu Banerji *(Father),* Ramani Sen Gupta *(Old Uncle),* Charu Ghosh *(Nanda Babu),* Subodh Ganguly *(Headmaster),* Kali Charan Ray *(Press Proprietor),* Santi Gupta *(Landlord's Wife),* K.S. Pandey *(Pandey),* Sudipta Ray *(Nirupama),* Ajay Mitra *(Anil).*

The young Apu (Pinaki Sen Gupta) and his newly widowed mother (Karuna Banerji) struggle for existence in a small Indian town. Resisting a life in the priesthood, the boy persuades his mother to send him to school. Having done well in his studies over the years, Apu as a young adult (Smaran Ghosal) wins a scholarship to the university in Calcutta. Engulfed in city life and the demands of his school work, Apu gradually forgets about his mother. APARAJITO is the second chapter in THE APU TRILOGY (preceded by PATHER PANCHALI and followed by THE WORLD OF APU), perhaps the finest and certainly the most famous group of films to come out of India, in which director Satyajit Ray, a painter and commercial artist, devoted his time, money, and passion to a personal project that many considered impossible, the cinematic adaptation of the popular Bengali novel *Pather Panchali*. Although very slow moving and not as involving as the first and third episodes of Apu's fortunes, APARAJITO is a thoughtful, exotic, and poetic story of life in India. The beautiful black-and-white photography is accented by Ravi Shankar's traditional sitar score. The winner of the Golden Lion at the 1957 Venice Film Festival. In Bengali with English subtitles.

p, Satyajit Ray; d, Satyajit Ray; w, Satyajit Ray (based on the novel *Pather Panchali* by Bibhutibhusan Bandapaddhay); ph, Subroto Mitra; ed, Dulala Dutta; m, Ravi Shankar.

Drama **(PR:A MPAA:NR)**

APHRODITE*

(1982, Fr.) 90m Les Films de la Tour-Raoul Katz-Carlton-Almira/Atlantic Television c

Horst Bucholz, Valerie Kaprisky, Catherine Jourdan, Delia Boccardo, Capucine, Yves Massard, Paolo Baroni, Monica Nickel, Nicole Norden, Vanessa Weill, Lydia Dalbret, Daniel Beretta.

This silly, mildly erotic soft-core item stars Valerie Kaprisky, well-known in America as Richard Gere's costar in BREATHLESS, as a virginal French girl who is one of a number of aristocrats on a Mediterranean island in 1914. Horst Buchholz plays an arms dealer (the setting is just before the outbreak of WW I) who decides to stage a three-day reenactment of Pierre Louys' 1896 masterpiece of erotic literature, *Aphrodite*, with his guests as the stars and the entire island as their stage. The reluctant Kaprisky, of course, is a natural for the role of love goddess Aphrodite. The premise is an interesting one, but the filmmakers are concerned only with the eroticism, which becomes increasingly more decadent as the film rolls on. In the first few minutes alone one woman does an erotic dance in front of a one-way mirror, Kaprisky bathes herself, and there is a lesbian interlude between two guests, without any accompanying plot to speak of. APHRODITE may look like a French art film, but expect nothing more than an EMMANUELLE-type soft-core picture. Directed by Brit Robert Fuest, who brought us THE ABOMINABLE DR. PHIBES. Although some actors appear to be speaking English, the picture looks and sounds dubbed.

p, Adolphe Viezzi; d, Robert Fuest; w, Jean Melson, Jean Ardy (based on the novel by Pierre Louys); ph, Bernard Daillencourt; ed, Noelle Balenci; m, Jean-Pierre Stora, Anton Dvorak, Gustav Mahler, Cesar Frank, Nikolay Rimski-Korsakov.

Drama **(PR:O MPAA:NR)**

ARIA**

(1987, US/Brit.) 98m RVP-Virgin Vision/Miramax-WB bw

Theresa Russell *(King Zog),* Stephanie Lane *(Baroness),* Roy Hyatt, George Ellis Jones *(Chauffeurs),* Sevilla Delofski *(Maid),* Ruth Halliday *(Companion),* Arthur Cox *(Major),* Dennis Holmes *(Colonel),* Paul Collard *(Valet),* Danny Fitzgerald *(Mercedes Man),* Johnny Doyle *(Blind Balloon Man),* Derek Farmer *(Motorbike Man),* Michelle Read *(Nanny),* Maximillian Roeg *(Child),* Nicola Swain *(Marie),* Jackson Kyle *(Travis),* Marianne McLoughlin *(Kate),* Marion Peterson, Valerie Allain *(Young Girls),* Jacques Neuville, Jean Luc Corre, Bernard Gaudray, Dominique Mano, Patrice Tridian *(The Bodybuilders),* Buck Henry *(Preston),* Beverly D'Angelo *(Gilda),* Gary Kasper *(Jake),* Anita Morris *(Phoebe),* John Hostetter *(Elvis Impersonator),* Elizabeth Hurley *(Marietta),* Peter Birch *(Paul),* Louis-Marie Taillefer, Bridget Fonda, James Mathers *(The Lovers),* Angie Tetamontie, Esther Buchanan, Lorraine Cote, Renee Korn *(Las Vegas Ladies),* Bertha Weiss *(Lady with Glove),* Diane Thorne *(Bride),* Howie Maurer *(Groom),* Derick Coleman, Quentin Brown *(Indian Boys),* Linzi Drew *(Girl),* Amy Johnson *(Old Lady),* Tilda Swinton *(Young Girl),* Spencer Leigh *(Young Man),* John Hurt *(Actor),* Fernand Dumont *(Baritone Voice),* Voices of: Leontyne Price, Carlo Bergonzi, Robert Merrill, Anna Moffo, Enrico Caruso.

A grand idea with bland results, ARIA is an omnibus film that combines the talents of 10 directors and eight composers, but ends up with very little to show for it. It's more a showcase of brilliant packaging than of filmmaking, providing only a few segments of any real interest. In what is easily the most inventive episode, Jean-Luc Godard, excerpting Lully's "Armide," continues to experiment in modern sound construction and classical imagery. Without a conventional story line, the episode takes place in a gymnasium where a group of well-developed bodybuilders pump iron and a pair of barely-dressed young women do cleaning chores. Julian Temple, with cinematographer Oliver Stapleton, shows off some of the bravura camerwork delivered in ABSOLUTE BEGINNERS in a segment set to Verdi's "Rigoletto." His is the most entertaining and comical of the episodes, set in the gaudy Madonna Inn of San Luis Obispo, California, and follows two couples as they spend a sexually charged evening together. Franc Roddam set his tale to Wagner's "Tristan und Isolde," paralleling the passionate, perfect love of two innocent teenagers with the cheap, gunshot marriages of Las Vegas, and actually created a miniopera of perfect love that is strengthened by his choice of location—the loveless Las Vegas. Episodes by Ken Russell and Derek Jarman are visually delicious, but their connections to opera are pretty slim; Charles Sturridge offers a pleasant piece that is more of a moral tale than an operatic one. On the down side are the episodes by Nicolas Roeg, Bruce Beresford, Robert Altman, and Bill Bryden. Masterminded by producer Don Boyd, ARIA is a noble attempt to bring together the talents of some of today's more notable directors. Unfortunately, some of today's more notable directors aren't up to much more here than third-rate trash that would be jeered at any film school screening. The film has been called MTV for opera fans, but that does a disservice to the infinitely more daring rock video directors. One would think that giving free reign to a director would encourage him to take a few chances, but only Godard does so in his attempts to make a connection between sound and image, addressing the very root of opera—music and visuals—and doing so in a popular setting. Roddam, though his approach is a bit saccharine, has at least given us a story that is operatic; Temple also shows the visual and storytelling energy that one expects from opera. The remaining directors, however, failed to meet their cinematic challenge. What ARIA proves is that the top composers and stagers of opera today (Philip Glass and Robert Wilson, John Adams and Peter Sellars) are taking far greater steps in stretching the boundaries of their medium than this collection of supposedly top filmmakers are in stretching theirs. Instead of being a signal to other art forms that film, too, is an art, ARIA is a pitiful display of the lack of artistic imagination in filmmaking today.

p, Don Boyd; d, Nicolas Roeg, Charles Sturridge, Jean-Luc Godard, Julien Temple, Bruce Beresford, Robert Altman, Franc Roddam, Ken Russell, Derek Jarman, Bill Bryden; w, Nicolas Roeg, Charles Sturridge, Jean-Luc Godard, Julien Temple, Bruce Beresford, Robert Altman, Franc Roddam, Ken Russell, Derek Jarman, Bill Bryden, Don Boyd; ph, Harvey Harrison, Gale Tattersall, Carolyn Champetier, Oliver Stapleton, Dante Spinotti, Pierre Mignot, Frederick Elmes, Gabriel Beristain, Mike Southon, Christopher Hughes; ed, Marie Therese Boiche, Mike Cragg, Tony Lawson, Matthew Longfellow, Neil Abrahamson, Jennifer Auge, Rick Elgood, Michael Bradsell, Peter Cartwright, Angus Cook; m, Giuseppe Verdi, Jean Baptiste Lully, Erich Wolfgang Korngold, Jean Philippe Rameau, Richard Wagner, Giacomo Puccini, Gustave Charpentier, Ruggiero Leoncavallo.

Opera **(PR:O MPAA:R)**

ASHES AND DIAMONDS****

(1958, Pol.) 105m Film Polski/Janus bw (POPIOL Y DIAMENT)

Zbigniew Cybulski *(Maciek Chelmicki),* Eva Krzyzewska *(Krystyna),* Adam Pawlikowski *(Andrzej),* Waclaw Zastrzezynski *(Szczuka),* Bogumil Kobiela *(Drewnowski),* Jan Ciecierski *(Porter),* Stanislaw Milski *(Pienianzek),* Arthur Mlodnicki *(Kotowicz),* Halina Kwiatkoska *(Mrs. Staniewicz),* Ignancy Machowski *(Maj. Waga Staniewicz),* Zbigniew Skowronski *(Slomka),* Barbara Krafft *(Stefka),* Aleksander Sewruk *(Swiecki).*

A powerfully disturbing vision of war-torn Poland, ASHES AND DIAMONDS takes place on the 7th of May, 1945—the first day of peace since the outbreak of WW II. Although the non-Communists and Communists were allies in their battles against the Nazis, the differences between the factions have not lessened with the declaration of peace. The resistance force of "Armii krajowej" refuses to lay down arms and send two of their men—the young, rebellious Maciek (wonderfully acted by the bespectacled Zbigniew Cybulski) and the older, more professional-seeming Andrzej (Adam Pawlikowski)—on a mission to ambush Szczuka (Waclaw Zastrzezynski), the Communist Party District Secretary. The ambush fails, however, when the pair mistakenly machine gun two civilians returning home after being imprisoned in a German labor camp. During the next day and evening, Maciek battles with his conscience: he still has orders to kill Szczuka, but he begins to question the morality of Poles killing Poles. Director Andrzej Wajda displays his brilliance immediately in the film's opening minutes—the ambush, which takes place outside of an otherwise peaceful country church. He lays out the entire moral dilemma which faces Maciek: he is a Pole who brutally murders a fellow countryman, the dying man falling face first into the nearby chapel as the sorrowful Christ looks down from his cross. A film of great power, ASHES AND DIAMONDS (Wajda's third feature) is the third chapter of Wajda's "war trilogy," preceded in 1954 by A GENERATION and in 1957 by KANAL. Available in both dubbed and subtitled versions.

d, Andrzej Wajda; w, Andrzej Wajda, Jerzy Andrzejewski (based on the novel by Jerzy Andrzejewski); ph, Jerzy Wojcik; ed, Halina Nawrocka; m, Wroclaw Rhythm Quintet.

War/Drama **(PR:C MPAA:NR)**

ASSAULT, THE****

(1986, Neth.) 155m Cannon c

Derek de Lint *(Anton Steenwijk),* Marc van Uchelen *(Anton as a Boy),* Monique van de Ven *(Truus Coster/Saskia de Graaff),* John Kraaykamp *(Cor Takes),* Huub van der Lubbe *(Fake Ploeg/His Father),* Elly Weller *(Mrs. Beumer),* Ina van der Molen *(Karin Korteweg),* Frans Vorstman *(Father Steenwijk),* Edda Barends *(Mother Steenwijk),* Caspar De Boer *(Peter Steenwijk),* Wim de Haas *(Mr. Korteweg),* Hiske van der Linden *(Karin as a Young Girl),* Piet de Wijn *(Mr. Beumer),* Akkemay *(Sandra),* Kees Coolen *(Gerrit-Jan),* Eric van Heijst *(Mr. DeGraaff),* Mies de Heer *(Elisabeth),* Olliver Domnick *(SD Officer),* Amadeus August *(Haupsturmfuhrer),* Matthias Hell *(Sergeant),* Horst Reichel *(Officer),* Ludwig Haas *(General),* Mike Bendig *(Fake Ploeg as a Boy),* Michel van Rooij *(Cor Takes as a Young Man),* Guus Hermus *(Mr. van Lennep),* Manon Alving *(Mrs. de Graaff),* Tabe Bas *(Jaap),* Cas Baas *(Henk),* Okke Jager *(Vicar),* Eric van der Ronk *(Simon).*

A powerful motion picture that asks more questions than it answers, THE ASSAULT will haunt anyone who lived through WW II. The film takes place over a 40-year period, beginning in Holland as the war is waning and the Nazis realize they will be beaten. Anton (Marc van Uchelen) is a young lad living at home with his family. They are dining by candlelight one night during curfew when they see a local collaborator killed by a sniper. Fearing that they will be blamed for the death, the family watches in horror as their neighbors pull the dead body in front of their home. Soon Nazis are everywhere, the family is arrested and shot, the house is burned, and Anton is taken away to prison. He is eventually released, becomes a physician, marries, and has a family, but memory of that bleak night continues to hound him. THE ASSAULT, which won the Academy Award for Best Foreign Film, is a powerful indictment of the Nazi horror, though it seldom editorializes, seeming more like a documentary than a work of fiction. Although it begins as a picture about the war, it is much more than that—it is an exploration of the lives that were torn apart by Nazi occupation. Dubbed into English.

p, Fons Rademakers; d, Fons Rademakers; w, Gerard Soeteman (based on the novel by Harry Mulisch); ph, Theo van de Sande (Fujicolor); ed, Kees Linthorst; m, Jurriaan Andriessen.

Drama/War **(PR:C MPAA:PG)**

ASSOCIATE, THE***

(1982, Fr./Ger.) 94m EB-COL c (L'ASSOCIE)

Michel Serrault *(Julien Pardot),* Claudine Auger *(Agnes),* Catherine Alric *(Alice),* Judith Magre *(Mme. Brezol),* Mathieu Carriere *(Louis),* Bernard Haller *(Hellzer).*

This very funny comedy concerns a 50-year-old nebbish, Julien Pardot (Michel Serrault), who has never made it big in business because of his blah personality. To get around this problem, he invents a fictitious business partner from England named "Mr. Davis." With the help of Mr. Davis, Julien's financial counseling firm skyrockets to success. The elusive Englishman lends an air of mystery to the company that investors find appealing, but the more money he makes, the harder it is for Julien to keep up the charade. The fine cast is headed by Serrault, who was a big hit in LA CAGE AUX FOLLES, though much of the film's credit must go to the script, copenned by one of cinema's greatest writers, Jean-Claude Carriere. In French with English subtitles.

d, Rene Gainville; w, Rene Gainville, Jean-Claude Carriere (based on the novel *My Partner, Mr. Davis* by Jenaro Prieto); ph, Etienne Szabo (Fujicolor); ed, Raymonde Guyot; m, Mort Shuman.

Comedy **(PR:A MPAA:NR)**

AU REVOIR LES ENFANTS**½

(1987, Fr./Ger.) 104m Nouvelles-MK2-Stella-NEF/Orion c (Trans: Goodbye, Children)

Gaspard Manesse *(Julien Quentin),* Raphael Fejto *(Jean Bonnet),* Francine Racette *(Mme. Quentin),* Stanislas Carre de Malberg *(Francois Quentin),* Philippe Morier-Genoud *(Father Jean),* Francois Berleand *(Father Michel),* Francois Negret *(Joseph),* Peter Fitz *(Muller),* Pascal Rivet *(Boulanger),* Benoit Henriet *(Ciron),* Richard Leboeuf *(Sagard),* Xavier Legrand *(Babinot),* Arnaud Henriet *(Negus),* Jean-Sebastien Chauvin *(Laviron),* Luc Etienne *(Moreau),* Daniel Edinger *(Tinchaut),* Marcel Bellot *(Guibourg),* Ami Flammer *(Florent),* Irene Jacob *(Mlle. Davenne),* Jean-Paul Dubarry *(Father Hippolyte),* Jacqueline Staup *(Infirmary Nurse),* Jacqueline Paris *(Mme. Perrin).*

AU REVOIR LES ENFANTS is an honest and heartfelt, but curiously unemotional, quasi-autobiography from Louis Malle, set in January 1944 during the Nazi occupation of France. Twelve-year-old Julien (Gaspard Manesse) is sent to a provincial Catholic boarding school after spending the holidays with his mother. Julien is far more intelligent than all of his classmates, except one—Bonnet (Raphael Fejto), a new arrival who, like Julien, has a great love of books. Their friendship grows strong and eventually Julien learns Bonnet's secret—that he is one of three Jews being hidden from the Gestapo by the school's gutsy cleric, Father Jean (Morier-Genoud). Based on a traumatic incident of his own childhood, AU REVOIR LES ENFANTS is a deeply personal project that Malle has long wanted to essay. Unfortunately, the film never generates the emotional power one would expect from a story of personal tragedy centering around the horrors of the Holocaust. The film obviously hit home with a number of audiences, however, winning the Golden Lion at the 1987 Venice Film Festival and earning two Oscar nominations—Best Foreign Film and Best Screenplay. In French with English subtitles.

p, Louis Malle; d, Louis Malle; w, Louis Malle; ph, Renato Berta (Eastmancolor); ed, Emmanuelle Castro; m, Franz Schubert, Camille Saint-Saens.

Drama **(PR:A-C MPAA:PG)**

AUTUMN SONATA**

(1978, Swed.) 97m Personafilm/NEW WORLD c (HOSTSONATEN)

Ingrid Bergman *(Charlotte),* Liv Ullmann *(Eva),* Lena Nyman *(Helena),* Halvar Bjork *(Viktor),* Georg Lokkeberg *(Leonardo),* Knut Wigert *(Professor),* Eva Von Hanno *(Nurse),* Erland Josephson *(Josef),* Linn Ullmann *(Eva as a Child),* Arne Bang-Hansen *(Uncle Otto),* Gunnar Bjornstrand *(Paul),* Marianne Aminoff *(Charlotte's Secretary),* Mimi Pollak *(Piano Teacher).*

The meeting of the Bergmans—Ingmar and Ingrid—is reason alone to see AUTUMN SONATA. Ingrid's acting, as usual, is superb, and she is as beautiful here as she ever has been. Ingmar's directing, as usual, is superb, and he probes as deep into the psyche as he always has. The result, however accomplished and intelligent it may be, is a painful film that practically forces the audience to turn away. At its core is the psychological and emotional battle between a mother (Bergman) and her daughter Eva (Liv Ullmann). Despite her efforts to communicate with her mother, Eva cannot break through. Instead, the mother's favorite daughter has always been Helena (Lena Nyman), a woman dying of a mysterious disease who can communicate only in grunts and groans. Some have praised the direction and script for digging deeper into the feelings between mothers and daughters than any other film dares. Others, by contrast, have attacked the film for being incessantly talky, arcane, and boring. Ingmar devotees will most likely approve, while Ingrid fans will probably prefer CASABLANCA. The videocassette is unconvincingly dubbed.

p, Ingmar Bergman; d, Ingmar Bergman; w, Ingmar Bergman; ph, Sven Nykvist (Eastmancolor); ed, Sylvia Ingmarsdotter; m, Frederic Chopin, Johann Sebastian Bach, George Frideric Handel.

Drama **(PR:A-C MPAA:PG)**

B

BABETTE'S FEAST***

(1987, Den.) 102m Panorama-Nordisk-Danish Film Institute/Orion c (BABETTE'S GASTEBUD)

Ghita Norby *(Narrator),* Stephane Audran *(Babette Hersant),* Jean-Philippe Lafont *(Achille Papin),* Gudmar Wivesson *(Lorenz Lowenhielm as a Young Man),* Jarl Kulle *(Lorenz Lowenhielm as an Old Man),* Bibi Andersson *(Swedish Court Lady-in-Waiting),* Hanne Stensgaard *(Young Philippa),* Bodil Kjer *(Old Philippa),* Vibeke Hastrup *(Young Martina),* Birgitte Federspiel *(Old Martina),* Bendt Rothe *(Old Nielsen),* Ebbe Rode *(Christopher),* Lisbeth Movin *(The Widow),* Prebe Lerdorff Rye *(The Captain),* Pouel Kern *(The Vicar),* Axel Strobye *(Driver),* Ebba With *(Lorens' Aunt),* Else Petersen *(Solveig),* Therese Hojgaard Christensen *(Martha),* Asta Esper Andersen *(Anna),* Finn Nielsen *(Grocer).*

Winner of the Oscar for Best Foreign-Language Film of 1987, this quiet Danish film seemed an unlikely candidate for international success; instead of sex, violence, or nudity, it offers sermons and hymns, a dozen or so elderly Danes, and a feast to end all feasts. An expository flashback opens the film, delving into the frustrated love lives of Martina (Vibeke Hastrup) and Philippa (Hanne Stensgaard), the daughters of a prophetic minister in a small town on Denmark's rugged Jutland peninsula. The story then shifts to 1871, as Babette (Stephane Audran), whose husband and son were killed by the Paris Communards, arrives from France and enters the employ of the sisters, who are carrying on the work of their now-dead father's ministry. After 14 years of service with the sisters, Babette wins 10,000 Golden Francs in the French lottery, and uses it to prepare a sumptuous banquet in honor of the minister's 100th birthday. At first, the stoic townspeople are reluctant to participate fully in this "pagan" feast, but ultimately they joyously indulge in Babette's masterwork, and it is revealed that she was once the *chef de cuisine* at the famous Cafe Anglais in Paris. A gentle film that metaphorically examines the artist's relationship to her art, BABETTE'S FEAST is the sort of story that one cannot help but find uplifting. Yet, while director Gabriel Axel aims for the purity, grace, and austerity of the works of Carl Theodor Dreyer or Andrei Tarkovsky, his direction is often too saccharine to be spiritually affecting—there is much in BABETTE'S FEAST that is beautiful, but there is also much that is simply predictably charming. However, the performances, by such art-house favorites as Audran, Birgitte Federspiel (ORDET), Jean-Philippe Lafont (BIZET'S CARMEN), and Bergman veterans Jarl Kulle and Bibi Andersson, are uniformly wonderful. The story on which the film is based was the product of a bet between its author, Karen Blixen (aka Isak Dinesen, whom Meryl Streep portrayed in OUT OF AFRICA), and a friend who suggested that the best way to crack the American market was to write about food.

p, Just Betzer, Bo Christensen; d, Gabriel Axel; w, Gabriel Axel (based on the short story by Isak Dinesen); ph, Henning Kristiansen ; ed, Finn Henriksen; m, Per Norgard, Wolfgang Amadeus Mozart.

Drama **(PR:A MPAA:G)**

BAD GIRLS***½

(1968, Fr.) 104m Films la Boetie-Alexandra/Harris c (LES BICHES; AKA: THE HETEROSEXUALS; THE DOES; THE GIRLFRIENDS)

Stephane Audran *(Frederique),* Jaqueline Sassard *(Why),* Jean-Louis Trintignant *(Paul Thomas),* Nane Germon *(Violetta),* Serge Bento *(Bookseller),* Dominique Zardi *(Riais),* Henri Attal *(Robeque),* Claude Chabrol *(Filmmaker),* Henri Frances.

Although this videotape goes under the exploitative title of BAD GIRLS, it is really Claude Chabrol's LES BICHES, a suspenseful and erotic story of two lesbian lovers—Frederique (Stephane Audran), a wealthy and elegant woman, and Why (Jaqueline Sassard), a young bohemian who earns a living making charcoal drawings on the sidewalks of Paris. Frederique, who has already seduced Why and dragged her off to a lovely St. Tropez villa, upsets the balance when she next seduces architect Paul (Jean-Louis Trintignant). Why loves them both and cannot bear the thought of being left behind when Frederique and Paul run off to Paris together. One of the few Chabrol films available on videotape, LES BICHES features the director's favorite lead actress, Stephane Audran (then his wife), in yet another situation of suspense that, while Hitchcockian at its root, is pure Chabrol. The setup is a familiar one—a love triangle—but Chabrol's delicate treatment and highly controlled direction make this one of his finest efforts. (Dubbed into English.)

p, Andre Genoves; d, Claude Chabrol; w, Paul Gegauff, Claude Chabrol; ph, Jean Rabier (Eastmancolor); ed, Jacques Gaillard; m, Pierre Jansen, Jacques Baudry.

Thriller **(PR:O MPAA:R)**

BAD SLEEP WELL, THE***½

(1960, Jap.) 135m Tanaka-Kurosawa bw (WARUI YATSU HODO YOKU NEMURU; AKA: THE WORSE YOU ARE THE BETTER YOU SLEEP; THE ROSE IN THE MUD)

Toshiro Mifune *(Koichi Nishi),* Takeshi Kato *(Itakura),* Masayuki Mori *(Iwabuchi),* Takashi Shimura *(Moriyama),* Akira Nishimura *(Shirai),* Kamatari Fujiwara *(Wada),* Gen Shimizu *(Miura),* Kyoko Kagawa *(Kieko),* Tatsuya Mihashi *(Tatsuo),* Kyu Sazanka *(Kaneko),* Chishu Ryu *(Nonaka),* Seiji Miyaguchi *(Okakura),* Nobuo Nakamura *(Lawyer),* Susumu Fujita *(Commissioner),* Koji Mitsui *(Journalist).*

One of Akira Kurosawa's modern-day, or *gendai-geki*, films, THE BAD SLEEP WELL is a sociopolitical indictment of the feudalism that is prevalent even in the present-day Japanese hierarchy of business and politics. Nishi (Toshiro Mifune) is a fast-rising young executive about to further his acquisition of power through marriage to Keiko

(Kyoko Kagawa), the daughter of the firm's president, Iwabuchi (Masayuki Mori). Nishi, however, is something of a modern-day samurai—a heroic figure who has adopted a new identity in order to avenge the death of his father, a corporate vice-president whose death can be traced to Iwabuchi. Nishi's method of revenge is to become part of the family and, like a cancer, destroy Iwabuchi from the inside. But Nishi eventually discovers that there is no room for the noble hero in the ruthless world of high-powered executives and politicians. Although it is not one of Kurosawa's finest achievements, THE BAD SLEEP WELL becomes more interesting when viewed as a predecessor to HIGH AND LOW (1963), a more completely realized attack on Japanese society. In Japanese with English subtitles.

p, Tomoyuki Tanaka, Akira Kurosawa; d, Akira Kurosawa; w, Akira Kurosawa, Shinobu Hashimoto, Hideo Oguni, Ryuzo Kikushima, Eijiro Hisaita; ph, Yuzuru Aizawa; ed, Akira Kurosawa; m, Masaru Sato.

Drama **(PR:C MPAA:NR)**

BAGDAD CAFE*½**

(1987, Ger.) 91m Pelemele-BR-HR-Project/Island c (AKA: OUT OF ROSENHEIM)

Marianne Sagebrecht *(Jasmin Munchgstettner),* CCH Pounder *(Brenda),* Jack Palance *(Rudi Cox),* Christine Kaufmann *(Debbie),* Monica Calhoun *(Phyllis),* Darron Flagg *(Sal Junior),* George Aquilar *(Cahuenga),* G. Smokey Campbell *(Sal),* Hans Stadlbauer *(Munchgstettner),* Apesanahkwat *(Sheriff Arnie),* Alan S. Craig *(Eric),* Ronald Lee Jarvis *(Trucker Ron),* Mark Daneri *(Trucker Mark),* Ray Young *(Trucker Ray),* Gary Lee Davis *(Trucker Gary),* Baby Ashley.

Director Percy Adlon scored big on the art-house circuit with his 1985 film SUGARBABY, an eccentric love story starring the hefty Marianne Sagebrecht. For his followup, Adlon has again cast Sagebrecht and has set his first English-language film in the US, specifically at a run-down diner and motel in the middle of the Mojave Desert. Jasmin Munchgstettner (Sagebrecht), a German *hausfrau*, is abandoned in the desert after an argument with her husband. After wandering for some time under the scorching sun, Jasmin checks into a dusty motel run by Brenda (CCH Pounder), a tough-talking, no-nonsense black woman who treats her new boarder as if she's some sort of space alien. With time, however, the pair become the best of friends, turning the decrepit diner into the most exciting place west of Las Vegas, and Jasmin becomes one of the most popular women for miles around, especially catching the fancy of Rudy Cox (Jack Palance), a cosmic romantic who desperately wants to paint her portrait. BAGDAD CAFE is a visually exhilarating and consciously modern film, more concerned with projecting an atmosphere or spirit than with telling a story. Presented as a comedy-fable about the magic that develops at the meeting of two cultures, the film is difficult, perhaps impossible, not to like. (In English.)

p, Percy Adlon, Eleonore Adlon; d, Percy Adlon; w, Percy Adlon, Eleonore Adlon, Christopher Doherty (based on a story by Percy Adlon); ph, Bernd Heinl (Eastmancolor); ed, Norbert Herzner; m, Bob Telson, Johann Sebastian Bach.

Comedy/Drama **(PR:C MPAA:PG)**

BAKER'S WIFE, THE****

(1938, Fr.) 126m Les Films Marcel Pagnol bw (LA FEMME DU BOULANGER)

Raimu *(Aimable Castanier, the Baker),* Ginette Leclerc *(Aurelie Castanier),* Charles Moulin *(Dominique, the Shepherd),* Robert Vattier *(Priest),* Robert Bassac *(Schoolteacher),* Charpin *(Marquis de Venelles),* Charles Blavette *(Antonin),* Maupi *(Barnabe),* Alida Rouffe *(Celeste),* Odette Roger *(Miette),* Yvette Fournier *(Hermine),* Maximillienne Max *(Mme. Angele),* Charblay *(The Butcher),* Maffre *(Petugue),* Adrien Legros *(Barthelemy),* Jean Castan *(Esprit).*

Raimu, the star of Marcel Pagnol's trilogy MARIUS, FANNY, and CESAR, here teams again with Pagnol as the baker Aimable, a new addition to a French village that has lacked a quality baker for some time. The tasting of Aimable's first loaves of bread is an event eagerly awaited by all the locals, giving the villagers a chance to take time away from their daily complaints and neighborly disagreements. Aimable takes great pride in his bread—a pride equalled only by his affection for his coquettish wife Aurelie (Ginette Leclerc). The villagers agree that if their new baker's bread is as lovely as his wife, all will be content. Unfortunately for Aimable, however, the handsome shepherd Dominique (Charles Moulin) prefers Aurelie to a brioche, and she prefers his affection to slaving over a hot stove. When they run off together, Aimable is no longer able to continue his baking. Rather than risk losing another baker, the villagers band together in an effort to bring Aurelie back home. A touching film of comedy that borders on the tragic, THE BAKER'S WIFE is a brilliantly simple tale that seems effortlessly told by Pagnol and acted by the superb Raimu, and as a result became one of the most popular French films of all time in the US. Although the title refers to "the baker's wife," she is barely in the film. Instead, this is a film about the *effect* of the baker's wife—how her disappearance has near-disastrous results for the baker who loves her and for an entire village that depends, in turn, upon this baker. More than a light tragicomedy, THE BAKER'S WIFE has a socioeconomic importance, illustrating the equal weight borne by everyone in a society and how one person can, however unintentionally, disrupt an entire community simply by walking away from it. In French with English subtitles.

p, Marcel Pagnol; d, Marcel Pagnol; w, Marcel Pagnol (based in part on the novel *Jean Le Bleu* by Jean Giono); ph, George Benoit; ed, Suzanne de Troye; m, Vincent Scotto.

Comedy **(PR:A MPAA:NR)**

BALLAD OF A SOLDIER****

(1959, USSR) 89m Mosfilm/Kingsley bw (BALADA O SOLDATE)

Vladimir Ivashov *(Alyosha),* Shanna Prokhorenko *(Shura),* Antonina Maximova *(Alyosha's Mother),* Nikolai Kruchkov *(General),* Evgeni Urbanski *(Invalid).*

BALLAD OF A SOLDIER presents a moving, heart-rending profile of Alyosha (Vladimir Ivashov), a young soldier fighting on the front during WW II who performs the heroic act of disabling two German tanks and is rewarded with a six-day leave. As Alyosha makes the long journey home to see his mother (Antonina Maximova), he meets a variety of people—both friendly and antagonistic. More than a ballad of the soldier Alyosha, this startling, realistic picture is the ballad of all the Soviet people. An episodic and hauntingly visual film, BALLAD OF A SOLDIER is a fine example of the Soviet Realist tradition—a style of filmmaking paralleled by the more cinematically innovative techniques of such Soviet directors as Sergei Paradzhanov (SHADOWS OF FORGOTTEN ANCESTORS) and Andre Tarkovsky (MY NAME IS IVAN). Although the film is nationalistic, its appeal crossed all boundaries, and it took not only the Lenin Prize at the Moscow Film Festival, but a Gold Palm at the Cannes Film Festival and an Oscar nomination for Best Original Screenplay. In Russian with English subtitles.

d, Grigori Chukhrai; w, Valentin Yoshow, Grigori Chukhrai; ph, Vladimir Nikolayev, Yera Savelyeva; ed, M. Rooz; m, Mikhael Ziv.

Drama/War **(PR:A MPAA:NR)**

BAND OF OUTSIDERS*½**

(1964, Fr.) 95m Anouchka-Orsay/Royal bw (AKA: BANDE A PART; THE OUTSIDERS)

Anna Karina *(Odile),* Claude Brasseur *(Arthur),* Sami Frey *(Franz),* Louisa Colpeyn *(Mme. Victoria),* Daniele Girard *(English Teacher),* Ernest Menzer *(Arthur's Uncle),* Chantal Darget *(Arthur's Aunt),* Michele Seghers, Claude Makovski *(Pupils),* Georges Staquet *(Legionnaire),* Michel Delahaye *(Doorman at School),* Jean-Luc Godard *(Narrator).*

After the success of his debut feature, BREATHLESS, Jean-Luc Godard returned to the genre of the gangster film here, casting Anna Karina, Claude Brasseur, and Sami Frey as three young people who live as outsiders. As Godard has said about this trio: "They are more honest with themselves than with others. They are not among those who want to be cut off from the world, it is the world that is far from them." Meeting in an English language class, Odile (Karina), Arthur (Brasseur), and Franz (Frey) fast become friends. Odile has told Franz that she lives in a house where a large cache of loot has been hidden. Franz and his good friend Arthur decide, under the influence of the countless Hollywood films and pulp novels they've consumed, that they should burglarize the house. Odile, who shows an attraction to both men, makes up the third part of the criminal triangle. As anyone who has seen a Godard film might guess, there is very little concern for plot—the attraction of BAND OF OUTSIDERS lies not in its actual story so much as in Godard's telling of it. His voice-over narration is confrontational; his characters talk to the screen; there exists a strange, somewhat uneasy relationship between comedy and violence; and the frame is filled with various allusions to film, literature, and to Godard himself. This was Godard's seventh film in only five years and, as in Truffaut's SHOOT THE PIANO PLAYER, it is an attempt to find a new truth by retelling a familiar story in a new way. If this film seems to be nothing more than a playful attempt to re-create an old Hollywood genre, one must remember that Godard, in the height of self-awareness, playfully credits himself in this film as Jean-Luc Cinema Godard. In French with English subtitles.

p, Philippe Dussart; d, Jean-Luc Godard; w, Jean-Luc Godard (based on the novel *Fool's Gold* by Dolores Hitchens); ph, Raoul Coutard; ed, Agnes Guillemot, Francoise Collin; m, Michel Legrand.

Comedy/Crime **(PR:C MPAA:NR)**

BASILEUS QUARTET***

(1984, It.) 118m RAI-C.E.P./Libra-Cinema 5 c

Hector Alterio *(Alvaro),* Omero Antonutti *(Diego),* Pierre Malet *(Edo Morelli),* Francois Simon *(Oscar Guarneri),* Michel Vitold *(Guglielmo),* Alain Cuny *(Finkel),* Gabriele Ferzetti *(Mario Cantone),* Veronique Genest *(Sophia),* Lisa Kreuzer *(Lotte),* Euro Bulfoni, Francesco Carnelutti, Mimsy Farmer, Alessandro Haber.

This fascinating film explores the lives of three aging musicians, members of a world-famous string quartet who suddenly find themselves adrift when their lead violinist dies. They try to go their separate ways but are drawn back together by youthful prodigy Edo (Pierre Malet), who persuades them to re-form with him as lead violin. The others are amazed at his playing, and even more amazed at the life he leads off-stage—bedding groupies, smoking marijuana, and more. The others, who have denied themselves these pleasures for years, find their sacrifices made pointless; the nagging notion even creeps into their heads that Edo plays so brilliantly *because* he indulges in earthly delights. BASILEUS QUARTET raises a number of questions about aging, art, and self-expression, and does so with some beautiful performances (especially Omero Antonutti, of PADRE PADRONE), great music (Beethoven, Paganini, Debussy, *et al.*), and stunning locations (Paris, Vienna, Geneva, Venice). In Italian with English subtitles.

p, Arturo La Pegna; d, Fabio Carpi; w, Fabio Carpi; ph, Dante Spinotti; ed, Massimo Latini; m, Franz Schubert, Ludwig van Beethoven, Bedrich Smetana, Nicolo Paganini, Claude Debussy, Franz Joseph Haydn, Maurice Ravel, Richard Wagner, Richard Rodgers, Lorenz Hart, Vincenzo Bellini.

Drama **(PR:O MPAA:NR)**

BATTLE OF ALGIERS, THE***

(1966, It./Alger.) 120m Igor-Casbah/Rizzoli bw (LA BATTAGLIA DI ALGERI)

Yacef Saadi *(Saari Kader),* Jean Martin *(Colonel Mathieu),* Brahim Haggiag *(Ali La Pointe),* Tommaso Neri *(Captain Dubois),* Samia Kerbash *(One of the Girls),* Fawzia el Kader *(Halima),* Michele Kerbash *(Fathia),* Mohamed Ben Kassen *(Little Omar),* Ugo Paletti *(Captain).*

A frightening and powerful battle cry for Marxist revolutionaries, THE BATTLE OF ALGIERS tells the story of Algeria's struggle for independence from France. The film begins in Algiers in 1957, where a tortured Arab prisoner informs on Ali la Pointe (Brahim Haggiag), the last surviving member of the FLN (Algerian Liberation Front). As French soldiers surround Ali's apartment, Col. Mathieu (Jean Martin) issues a final warning to Ali and his family: surrender or be blown to pieces. With the form of the violent conflict clearly layed out—the revolutionary vs. the counterrevolutionary—the film shifts to 1954, as the Algerian conflict develops. Photographed in grainy black and white to suggest the style of documentaries and television news reports, THE BATTLE OF ALGIERS most closely resembles the neo-realism of Roberto Rossellini and the revolutionary technique of Sergei Eisenstein. Like Eisenstein, Gillo Pontecorvo has taken his camera to the actual locations of the revolution, re-created certain events, and cast local nonprofessionals. Only Martin is a professional actor, while Yacef Saadi, the film's coproducer, plays a revolutionary leader—a character based on his real-life role as the organizer of the resistance and the military commander of the FLN. What makes THE BATTLE OF ALGIERS acceptable (its content has been attacked for being morally too dangerous, and was reportedly used as a primer for terrorism in the late 1960s) is Pontecorvo's ability to present both sides as made up of multidimensional, nonheroic human beings, despite the fact that it is obvious where Pontecorvo's own sentiments lie. The film received the Golden Lion at Venice in 1966, and secured Oscar nominations for Best Foreign Film, Best Screenplay, and Best Director. Dubbed in English.

p, Antonio Musu, Yacef Saadi; d, Gillo Pontecorvo; w, Gillo Pontecorvo, Franco Solinas (based on a story by Pontecorvo, Solinas); ph, Marcello Gatti; ed, Mario Serandrei, Mario Morra; m, Gillo Pontecorvo, Ennio Morricone.

War **(PR:C MPAA:NR)**

BATTLE OF AUSTERLITZ, THE½**

(1960, Fr./It./Yugo.) 170m CFPI-Lyre-Galatea-Dubrava/LUX c (AKA: AUSTERLITZ)

Rossano Brazzi *(Lucien Bonaparte),* Claudia Cardinale *(Pauline Bonaparte),* Martine Carol *(Josephine),* Maria Ferrero *(Elise),* Ettore Manni *(Murat),* Jean Marais *(Carnot),* Georges Marchal *(Lannes),* Jack Palance *(Weirother),* Vittorio De Sica *(Pope Pius VII),* Michel Simon *(Grognard),* Orson Welles *(Robert Fulton),* Pierre Mondy *(Napoleon Bonaparte),* Elvire Popesco *(Laetizia Bonaparte),* Jean Mercure *(Tallyrand),* Leslie Caron *(Mme. de Vaudrey),* Polycarpe Pavlov *(Kutusov),* Nelly Kaplan *(Mme. Recamier),* J.L. Horbette *(Benjamin Constant),* Jacques Castelot, Jean-Louis Trintignant, Andre Certes, J.M. Bory, Lucien Raimbourg, Anna Moffo.

An ambitious effort from Abel Gance, the director of the brilliant silent epic NAPOLEON, THE BATTLE OF AUSTERLITZ again deals with the same period in French history. There is an undeniable grandeur to the film, even on videocassette, but it is still nearly impossible to judge Gance's original intent when the film is shown—shred to ribbons and in its reduced video format. The story concerns the titanic battle between Napoleon and the overwhelming armies of European allies, but the film never takes off. Even the battle scenes (which were so stunning in NAPOLEON) are disjointed and meaningless, as the 70-year-old Gance beats the drum too loudly for France's former days of glory. The $4 million price tag for this opus was staggering at the time, almost sending its producers into bankruptcy. Today one can pick up a public domain copy of the videocassette for as cheap as $5.99; unfortunately, these tapes are far inferior to the nicely packaged version from U.S.A. Home Video. If the name of Abel Gance doesn't seem enough reason to rent the film, then how about a cast that includes Orson Welles, Claudia Cardinale, Michel Simon, Vittorio De Sica, Jean Marais, Jack Palance, and Leslie Caron? The original script for the film was written in 1924 as part of a planned, but never completed, cycle of films about Napoleon's career.

p, Alexander Salkind, Michael Salkind; d, Abel Gance; w, Abel Gance; ph, Henri Alekan, R. Picon-Borel, Robert Foucard, Milan Babic (Dyaliscope, Eastmancolor); ed, Leonide Azar, Yvonne Martin; m, Jean Ledrut.

Historical/War **(PR:A MPAA:NR)**

BATTLESHIP POTEMKIN***

(1925, USSR) 67m Goskino bw (BRONENOSETS POTEMKIN; AKA: POTEMKIN)

Alexander Antonov *(Vakulinchuk),* Vladimir Barsky *(Comdr. Golikov),* Grigory Alexandrov *(Senior Officer Gilyarovsky),* Mikhail Gomorov *(Sailor Matyushenko),* Levchenko *(Boatswain),* Repnikova *(Woman on the Steps),* Marusov *(Officer),* I. Bobrov, A. Fait *(Recruits),* Sergei Eisenstein *(Priest),* Alexander Lyovshin *(Petty Officer),* Beatrice Vitoldi *(Mother with Baby Carriage),* Konstantin Feldman *(Student Feldman),* Protopopov *(Old Man),* Korobei *(Legless Veteran),* Yulia Eisenstein *(Lady Bringing Food to Mutineers),* Prokopenko *(Aba's Mother),* A. Glauberman *(Aba),* N. Poltautseva *(School Teacher),* Brodsky *(Intellectual),* Zerenin *(Student),* Sailors of the Red Navy, Citizens of Odessa, Members of the Proletcult Theatre.

Without a doubt one of the most important films in the development of cinema, this great historical epic from Sergei Eisenstein is perhaps the most written about and discussed film of all time, its "Odessa Steps" sequence probably the most analyzed of its film scenes. One simply cannot have a historical perspective on film without experiencing POTEMKIN. Set in Russia during the failed revolution of 1905, the film begins on board the Czarist battleship Potemkin, where the sailors whisper rumors of an uprising. Conditions are inhumane, the quarters cramped, and the meat is crawling with maggots. Tensions build, shots are fired, and a fallen comrade is lionized. When his body is placed on display for all the workers of Odessa to see, a revolutionary furor is sparked, and the citizens of the town unite with the ship's sailors in a move against the Czar. What is so brilliant about BATTLESHIP POTEMKIN is the convergence of Eisenstein's theme of revolution and his equally revolutionary technique of filmmaking, the likes of which had never before been seen and would forever influence the way the rest of the world made films. By experimenting with the rhythm of editing and juxtaposition of images, Eisenstein, in 65 minutes (at sound speed) and 1, 300 shots, was able to affect audiences in a purely filmic style that could not be duplicated in any other medium.

p, Jacob Bliokh; d, Sergei Eisenstein; w, Sergei Eisenstein, Nina Agadzhanova-Shutko, Nikolai Aseyev; ph, Eduard Tisse, V. Popov; ed, Sergei Eisenstein; m, Edmund Meisel.

Historical **(PR:C MPAA:NR)**

BEAU PERE***½

(1981, Fr.) 120m Sara-Antenne 2/New Line c (Trans: Step-father)

Patrick Dewaere *(Remi),* Ariel Besse *(Marion),* Maurice Ronet *(Charly),* Nicole Garcia *(Martine),* Nathalie Baye *(Charlotte),* Maurice Risch *(Nicolas),* Genevieve Mnich *(Simone),* Macha Meril *(Birthday Hostess),* Pierre Lerumeur *(Pediatrician),* Yves Gasc *(Landlord),* Rose Thierry *(Landlord's Wife),* Henri-Jacques Huet *(Restaurant Manager).*

BEAU PERE is a tender and sad love story about a jazz pianist Remy (Patrick Dewaere), whose life changes drastically when his live-in lover, Martine (Nicole Garcia), dies in a car accident, leaving him to care for her 14-year-old daughter, Marion (Ariel Besse). Without money or a future (his aspirations to fame have been overshadowed by his lack of talent), Remy feels an emptiness filled only by Marion's presence. On the precipice between adolescence and womanhood, Marion becomes attracted to 30-year-old Remy, eventually breaking down his resistance, not only to sleeping with a young girl, but to detaching himself from the memory of Martine. Their dependence on each other changes, however, when Marion rediscovers her love for her natural father (Maurice Ronet) and Remy falls for another woman (Nathalie Baye). BEAU PERE is a touching story (though not without spots of director Bertrand Blier's wicked humor) of that moment in a person's life when they most need someone beside them. Remy is caught for a moment without a lover, while Marion is simultaneously caught without a parent's love—and it is during this time of vulnerability that they have no choice but to fall in love. Besse, as the daughter, perfectly captures the innocence and sensuality that the role calls for, while Dewaere creates an entirely sympathetic character for whom one cannot help but feel pain. The cruel irony is that Dewaere, one of the most popular French actors of his time, committed suicide the following year. The videotape is dubbed in English, but be forewarned that the voices are atrocious, especially Marion's.

p, Alain Sarde; d, Bertrand Blier; w, Bertrand Blier (based on his novel); ph, Sacha Vierny; ed, Claudine Merlin; m, Philippe Sarde.

Romance **(PR:C-O MPAA:NR)**

BEAUTY AND THE BEAST*****

(1946, Fr.) 90m Discina/Lopert bw (LA BELLE ET LA BETE)

Jean Marais *(Avenant/The Beast/The Prince),* Josette Day *(Beauty),* Marcel Andre *(The Father),* Mila Parely *(Adelaide),* Nane Germon *(Felice),* Michel Auclair *(Ludovic),* Raoul Marco *(The Usurer),* Gilles Watteaux, Noel Blin.

Jean Cocteau has written that in order for a myth to live it must continually be told and retold, and this is just what Cocteau does in BEAUTY AND THE BEAST—bringing Mme. Marie Leprince de Beaumont's 1757 fairy tale to the screen. Beauty (Josette Day) and the Beast (Jean Marais) are given a new life in the cinema thanks to Cocteau's poetry, Henri Alekan's cinematography, Georges Auric's music, and Christian Berard's art direction. The legend is familiar: a merchant's beautiful daughter saves her father's life by agreeing to visit the diabolical Beast, a hideous-looking half-man, half-animal with magical powers. Beauty faints with horror upon their first meeting, but gradually grows to love the Beast, finding the soul that exists beneath his fangs and fur. While the narrative is basic and familiar, the film's visuals are not. A magical white horse blazes across the screen, the Beast's hands smoke after a kill, the hanging white laundry of Beauty's family billows in the breeze, the Beast's fantastical candelabras are human arms that extend from the walls and emerge from the dinner table. It is a credit to Cocteau's genius (and to that of his collaborators) that he has taken the unreal world of a fairy tale and made it as real as the world around us. In French with English subtitles.

p, Andre Paulve; d, Jean Cocteau; w, Jean Cocteau (based on the fairy tale by Mme. Marie Leprince de Beaumont); ph, Henri Alekan; ed, Claude Iberia; m, Georges Auric.

Fantasy/Romance **(PR:A MPAA:NR)**

BELLISSIMA****

(1951, It.) 116m Bellisima/I.F.E. bw

Anna Magnani *(Maddalena Cecconi),* Walter Chiari *(Alberto Annovazzi),* Tina Apicella *(Maria Cecconi),* Gastone Renzelli *(Spartaco Cecconi),* Arturo Bragaglia *(Photographer),* Alessandro Blasetti *(Himself),* Tecla Scarano *(Elocution Teacher),* Linda Sina *(Mimmetta),* Lola Braccini *(Photographer's Wife),* Vittorio Glori, Iris, Geo Taparelli, Mario Chiari, Filipo Mercati, Nora Ricci, Vittorina Benvenuti.

Somewhere between the neo-realism of LA TERRA TREMA and the baroque stylizations of THE LEOPARD and DEATH IN VENICE lay the stylized realism of BELLISSI-

MA. A transitional film for Luchino Visconti (as would be his follow-up to BELLISSIMA, SENSO), it is curious that BELLISSIMA has not received nearly as much attention in the US as have his other films. Thankfully, with its video release this remarkable film will now be available for those interested in Anna Magnani, Visconti, and/or the Italian neo-realist movement. The story is a simple one—Maddalena Cecconi (Magnani) is a working class mother who hears of a motion picture audition to find "the most beautiful *bambina* in Rome" and decides to enter her daughter Maria (Tina Apicella). Playing the pushy stage mother, Maddalena takes her child to CineCitta, the historic Italian film studio, for an audition, pitting Maria against hundreds of other little girls. Because Maria has no formal training, her natural talent stands apart from the other packaged and processed girls. Obsessed with the cinema, especially Montgomery Clift, Maddalena is convinced that the lives of actors and filmmakers are heavenly, but she receives a gradual and cruel awakening. Thanks to the superb performances of Magnani and little Apicella, BELLISSIMA effectively tells a tragicomic tale of how the cold reality of the world is imposed on common people, threatening to destroy what few hopes and dreams they have fought to retain. In addition to being a beautifully told story, BELLISSIMA is the first honest self-portrait of the cinema. In Italian with English subtitles.

p, Salvo D'Angelo; d, Luchino Visconti; w, Suso Cecchi D'Amico, Francesco Rosi (based on the story "La Bambina Piu Bella Del Mondo" by Cesare Zavattini); ph, Piero Portalupe; ed, Mario Serandrei; m, Franco Mannino.

Drama **(PR:A MPAA:NR)**

BERLIN ALEXANDERPLATZ****

(1979, Ger.) 930m Bavaria Atelier-RAI/Teleculture c

Gunter Lamprecht *(Franz Biberkopf),* Gottfried John *(Reinhold),* Barbara Sukowa *(Mieze),* Hanna Schygulla *(Eva),* Franz Buchrieser *(Meck),* Claus Holm *(Landlord),* Hark Bohm *(Mr. Luders),* Brigitte Mira *(Frau Bast),* Gunther Kaufmann *(Theo),* Margit Castensen *(An Angel),* Helmut Griem *(An Angel),* Elisabeth Trissenaar *(Lina),* Volker Spengler *(Bruno),* Udo Kier *(Man in Nightclub),* Karin Baal *(Minna),* Axel Bauer *(Dreske, the Communist),* Klaus Hohne *(Handicapped Rightwinger),* Jurgen Draeger *(Sausage Vendor),* Peter Kollek *(Nachum),* Mechthild Grossmann *(Paula),* Barbara Valentin *(Ida),* Hans Zander *(Eliser),* Roger Fritz *(Herbert Virchow),* Angela Schmidt *(Widow),* Fritz Scheiwy *(Willy),* Traute Hoess *(Emmi),* Annemarie Duringer *(Cilly),* Helen Vita *(Franze),* Ivan Desny *(Pums),* Vitus Zeplichal *(Rudi),* Gerhard Zwerenz *(Baumann),* Claus Wirt *(Max, the Barman),* Herbert Steinmetz *(Old Newspaper Vendor),* Christian Maybach, Sonja Neudorfer, Yaak Karsunke.

Over the short span of 17 years—from 1965, when he directed his first 10-minute film, up to his death on June 10, 1982—Rainer Werner Fassbinder directed some 90 hours of film and television. BERLIN ALEXANDERPLATZ, an adaptation of Alfred Doblin's massive novel made for German television, runs approximately 15 hours, and makes up one-seventh of Fassbinder's total output. Comprised of 13 episodes and an epilog, the film stars Gunter Lamprecht as the pimp Franz Biberkopf, released from prison after serving time for murdering a prostitute. Now that he has a certain freedom, he takes to the streets of Berlin in the late 1920s in search of his identity. He takes demeaning jobs (selling shoelaces and, later, sex manuals); works for the Nazi Party; builds a strange friendship with another man, Reinhold (Gottfried John); becomes involved with some gangsters; and even loses his arm. Simply recounting the plot, however, does no justice to Fassbinder or the film. What Doblin tried to do in his novel (written from 1927 to 1929) was to put into print the atmosphere of Berlin life. Acknowledging his debt to Doblin, Fassbinder has said, "I had quite simply, without realizing it, made Doblin's fantasy into my life." In that sense, BERLIN ALEXANDERPLATZ is not the story of Berlin, but the story of Fassbinder—and in these 15 hours the two are inseparable. Available in a handsome package of eight videotapes. Episode 1. Punishment Will Come; 2. How Can You Live If You Don't Want to Die?; 3. A Blow from a Hammer Can Hurt the Soul; 4. A Handful of People in the Depths of Silence; 5. A Reaper with the Power of God; 6. The Price of Love Is Always High; 7. Remember: An Oath Can Be Cut Off; 8. The Sun Still Warms and Sometimes Burns the Skin; 9. Of the Eternities Separating the Many from the Few; 10. Loneliness Causes Cracks in the Walls of Madness; 11. Knowledge Is Power, and the Early Bird Catches the Worm; 12. The Viper in the Soul of the Serpent; 13. The Outside and the Inside, and the Mystery of the Fear of Mystery; Epilog. Rainer Werner Fassbinder: My Dream of Franz Biberkopf's Dream. In German with English subtitles.

p, Peter Marthesheimer; d, Rainer Werner Fassbinder; w, Rainer Werner Fassbinder (based on the novel by Alfred Doblin); ph, Xaver Schwarzenberger; ed, Juliane Lorenz; m, Peer Raben.

Drama **(PR:O MPAA:NR)**

BETTY BLUE****

(1986, Fr.) 120m Constellation-Cargo/Alive c (37.2 LE MATIN)

Beatrice Dalle *(Betty),* Jean-Hugues Anglade *(Zorg),* Consuelo de Haviland *(Lisa),* Gerard Darmon *(Eddy),* Clementine Celarie *(Annie),* Jacques Mathou *(Bob),* Claude Confortes *(Owner),* Philippe Laudenbach *(Gyneco Publisher),* Vincent Lindon *(Policeman Richard),* Raoul Billeray *(Old Policeman),* Claude Aufaure *(Doctor),* Andre Julien *(Old Georges),* Nathalie Dalyan *(Maria),* Louis Bellanti *(Mario),* Bernard Robin *(Renter No. 2),* Nicolas Jalowyj *(Little Nicolas).*

By combining the energetic high-gloss finish of his debut feature, DIVA, with the raw poetic intensity of MOON IN THE GUTTER, Jean-Jacques Beineix has created in BETTY BLUE a brilliant, charming, and compelling tale of *amour fou*, or crazy, obsessive love. In a no-holds-barred opening, the camera zooms in on two naked lovers, Zorg (Jean-Hugues Anglade) and Betty (Beatrice Dalle), ecstatically making love, hiding nothing from the viewer—not their bodies, not their emotions, and not their love for each other. Soon Betty has discovered the one thing Zorg is hiding—an unpublished novel she is determined to get published, taking each rejection notice personally. If that's not tough enough on Betty, she starts hearing voices and is driven to poke out her own eye. With a passionate novel by Philippe Djian as source material, a delicate score by Gabriel Yared, and the warmth of the two leads, Beineix has created a romantic universe where nothing matters but love. Anglade, best known in the US as the "roller" in SUBWAY, is perfectly cast as Zorg, though the magical element in the film is the 21-year-old Dalle, a phenomenon who has subsequently taken Paris by storm, a fervor no less than that caused by Brigitte Bardot some 30 years earlier. Although Dalle has complained that "my skull is too flat, my ears stick out, my mouth is too big, my belly too round and my buttocks too heavy," the viewer's opinion is likely to differ. BETTY BLUE managed to receive eight Cesar nominations: Best Director/Best Picture, Best Actor, Best Actress, Best Supporting Actor (Gerard Darman), Best Supporting Actress (Clementine Celarie), Best Score, Best Editing, and Best Poster Design, winning only the latter. While not a box-office smash on this side of the Atlantic, BETTY BLUE did garner an Oscar nomination as Best Foreign Language Film. In French with English subtitles.

p, Claudie Ossard, Jean-Jacques Beineix; d, Jean-Jacques Beineix; w, Jean-Jacques Beineix (based on the novel *37.2 Le Matin* by Philippe Djian); ph, Jean-Francois Robin (Fujicolor); ed, Monique Prim; m, Gabriel Yared.

Drama **(PR:O MPAA:R)**

BEYOND THE WALLS***½

(1985, Israel) 103m April-Israel Fund/WB c (MEACHOREI HASORAGIM)

Arnon Zadok *(Uri),* Muhamad Bakri *(Issam),* Assi Dayan *(Assaf),* Rami Danon *(Fittusi),* Boaz Sharaabi *(The Nightingale),* Adib Jahashan *(Walid),* Roberto Polak *(Yechiel),* Haim Shinar *(Hoffman),* Naffi Salach *(Sanji),* Loueteof Noussir *(Fatchi).*

This Israeli-made prison film concerns rival gangs of Israeli and Arab convicts, led by Uri (Arnon Zadok) and Issam (Muhamad Bakri), in a maximum security prison. Tensions between the factions are high, but when a singing prisoner known as The Nightingale (Boaz Sharaabi) wins a talent contest and appears on national television, both groups cheer his victory and realize they have a common bond. Uri and Issam then begin to cooperate in a scheme to protest the harsh conditions in the prison. Nominated for an Academy Award as Best Foreign Language Film, BEYOND THE WALLS presents the Middle East crisis in microcosm. Although it must be praised as a political statement, it is less interesting as a film—the direction by Uri Barbash seems overwrought, punching up every little incident for its maximum symbolic and emotional impact. One of the most internationally renowned Israeli films, BEYOND THE WALLS earned the Critic's Prize at Venice, an Oscar nomination, and even received a brief US art-house release. More importantly, it paved the way for other Israeli filmmakers to attempt the same success. In Hebrew with English subtitles.

p, Rudy Cohen; d, Uri Barbash; w, Benny Barbash, Eran Pries, Uri Barbash; ph, Amnon Salomon; ed, Tova Asher; m, Ilan Virtzberg.

Drama/Prison **(PR:O MPAA:R)**

BICYCLE THIEF, THE*****

(1948, It.) 90m De Sica/Mayer-Burstyn bw (LADRI DI BICICLETTE; Trans: Bicycle Thieves)

Lamberto Maggiorani *(Antonio Ricci),* Lianella Carell *(Maria),* Enzo Staiola *(Bruno Ricci),* Elena Altieri *(Signora Santona),* Vittorio Antonucci *(The Thief),* Gino Saltamerenda *(Bajocco),* Fausto Guerzoni *(Amateur Actor),* Guilio Chiari, Michel Sakara, Carlo Jachino, Nando Bruno, Umberto Spadaro, Massimo Randisi.

THE BICYCLE THIEF is a landmark film on every level. It's honest, beautiful, and deceptively simple. Reviewers praised it unanimously upon its first release for its power, some even likening it to "King Lear." The film tells the story of ordinary, forgotten people, the kind of people who never have movies made about them. Antonio (Lamberto Maggiorani) is reasonably happily married and works hard to support his family, traveling back and forth to work on his bicycle. One day, his bike is stolen by a thief (Vittorio Antonucci). Since the bike is Antonio's very life—symbolizing his ability to earn a living and feed his family—his search for it becomes a sort of quest for the Grail. With his son Bruno (Enzo Staiola), Antonio searches throughout Rome, desperate to find the bike before he has to go to work on Monday morning. THE BICYCLE THIEF is a brilliant example of Vittorio De Sica's greatness and of the power of neo-realism. All roles were played by nonactors, the dialog is as spare as it can be in a talking picture, and the coarse black-and-white photography makes an audience feel as if they are watching a documentary. Cesare Zavattini received an Oscar nomination for his screenplay, and the film received a Special Academy Award as the "most outstanding" foreign film of the year, though the greatness of THE BICYCLE THIEF cannot be measured by awards or star ratings. In Italian with English subtitles.

p, Vittorio De Sica; d, Vittorio De Sica; w, Cesare Zavattini (based on the novel by Luigi Bartolini); ph, Carlo Montuori; ed, Eraldo Da Roma; m, Alessandro Cicognini.

Drama **(PR:A MPAA:NR)**

BIG BLUE, THE*½

(1988, Fr.) 120m Gaumont-Weintraub/COL c (LE GRAND BLEU)

Rosanna Arquette *(Joanna Cross),* Jean-Marc Barr *(Jacques Mayol),* Jean Reno *(Enzo Molinari),* Paul Shenar *(Dr. Laurence),* Sergio Castellitto *(Novelli),* Jean Bouise *(Uncle Louis),* Marc Duret, Griffin Dunne *(Duffy),* Andreas Voutsinas *(Priest),* Valentina Vargas *(Bonita),* Kimberley Beck *(Sally),* Patrick Fontana *(Alfredo),* Alessandra Vazzoler *(Mamma),* Geoffrey Carey *(Supervisor),* Bruce Guerre-Berthelot *(Young Jacques),* Gregory Forstner *(Young Enzo),* Claude Besson *(Jacques' Father),* Marika Gevaudan *(Angelica),* Jan Rouiller *(Noireuter),* Peter Semler

(Frank), Jacques Levy *(Doctor),* Eric Do *(Japanese Diver),* Andre Germe *(Filipino Diver),* Ronald Teuhi *(Tahitian Diver).*

Frenchman Luc Besson has been heralded as a *wunderkind* since his first film, LE DERNIER COMBAT, was released in 1983 by the then-24-year-old director. Although "BlueMania" has struck in France—where everything related to THE BIG BLUE is a smash, prompting its French rerelease at the beginning of 1989 with a longer, three-hour running time—the shock waves never made it to American shores. Costarring Rosanna Arquette, featuring a half-dozen exotic locations and much underwater photography, and bearing a hefty (for a French production) $12 million price tag, THE BIG BLUE is essentially a big-budget children's adventure about a boy and his dolphins. The plot concerns two brilliant deep-sea divers and former childhood friends—Enzo Molinari (Jean Reno), the world champion competition free-diver, and Jacques Mayol (Jean-Marc Barr), a meek, withdrawn young man who has no use for competition. Knowing his only true rival is Jacques, Enzo persuades his former friend to enter the upcoming world championship—a contest that grows increasingly dangerous as the two divers try to capture the depth record. In the meantime, Jacques falls in love with Johana (Arquette), a brainless, bumbling American who becomes an obstacle to his dream of ridding himself of all on-land connections and becoming one with the ocean and his beloved dolphins. While the plot is not without merit and the photography and locations are pleasing to the eye, the script and acting are about as bad as one can imagine. This is Besson's first film in English and his big bid for international recognition (it was the opening night presentation at the 1988 Cannes Film Festival), but the dialog, Barr's pathetically limp performance, and Arquette's daffy heroine make this adventure/romance far from exciting. In fairness to the taste of the French, it should be noted that THE BIG BLUE had a silly new ending and a wretched Bill Conti score tacked on for US release.

p, Patrice Ledoux; d, Luc Besson; w, Luc Besson, Robert Garland, Marilyn Goldin, Jacques Mayol, Marc Perrier (based on a story by Luc Besson); ph, Carlo Varini (CinemaScope); ed, Olivier Mauffroy; m, Eric Serra, Bill Conti.

Adventure (PR:A MPAA:PG)

BIG DEAL ON MADONNA STREET, THE***

(1958, It./Fr.) 91m Lux/United Motion Picture bw (IL SOLITI IGNOTI)

Vittorio Gassman *(Peppe),* Renato Salvatori *(Mario),* Rossana Rory *(Norma),* Carla Gravina *(Nicoletta),* Claudia Cardinale *(Carmelina),* Carlo Pisacane *(Campannelle),* Tiberio Murgia *(Ferribotte),* Memmo Carotenuto *(Cosimo),* Marcello Mastroianni *(Tiberio),* Toto *(Dante).*

This very funny spoof of RIFIFI stars Vittorio Gassman as Peppe, a bungling petty thief who leads a group of incompetent burglars in a plan to loot a jewelry store on Madonna Street. Peppe works out an elaborate route into the store via the adjoining apartment, but when he falls in love with the occupant, innumerable delays result. Tiberio (Marcello Mastroianni), another hard-pressed inept thief, cannot participate in the burglary as planned because his wife is working and he must perform baby-sitting chores. Capannelle (Carlo Pisacane) cannot concentrate on the plan because he is constantly eating, and the expert safecracker Dante (Toto), who explains in detail how to blow a safe, vanishes completely at the time of break-in. Not surprisingly, the burglary is a disaster. One of the greatest examples of Italian comedy to reach American shores, BIG DEAL ON MADONNA STREET satirizes all those procedural caper films that Hollywood turned out and the foreign homages that followed (such as RIFIFI and BOB LE FLAMBEUR). The entire burglarizing procedure, as directed by Mario Monicelli, is hilarious, thanks to the fine acting and the steady stream of sight gags that recall the classic comedies of silent days. CRACKERS, an unfunny remake from Louis Malle, appeared in 1984, and BIG DEAL ON MADONNA STREET—20 YEARS LATER surfaced in 1985. (In Italian; English subtitles.)

p, Franco Cristaldi; d, Mario Monicelli; w, Suso Cecchi D'Amico, Argo Scarpelli, Mario Monicelli; ph, Gianni Di Venanzo; ed, Adriana Novelli; m, Piero Umiliano.

Comedy/Crime (PR:A MPAA:NR)

BIZET'S CARMEN****

(1984, Fr./It.) 152m GAU-Marcel Dassault-Opera/ Triumph c (AKA: CARMEN)

Julia Migenes-Johnson *(Carmen),* Placido Domingo *(Don Jose),* Ruggero Raimondi *(Escamillo),* Faith Esham *(Micaela),* Jean-Philippe Lafont *(Dancairo),* Gerard Garino *(Remendado),* Susan Daniel *(Mercedes),* Lilian Watson *(Frasquita),* Jean Paul Bogart *(Zuniga),* Francois Le Roux *(Morales),* Julien Guiomar *(Lillas Pastia),* Accursio Di Leo *(Guide),* Maria Compano *(Manuelita),* Christina Hoyos, Juan Antonio Jimenez *(Court Dancers),* Enrique El Cojo *(Old Dancer/Innkeeper),* Santiago Lopez *(Escamillo's Double),* Antonio Gades Dance Company.

With any luck, this should be the last of the many adaptations of Merimee's story and Bizet's opera. Why the last? Because, so far, it's the best. Francesco Rosi's film was one of many versions of the tale to appear within a very short period, including Carlos Saura's flamenco rendering, CARMEN; Peter Brooks' minimal stage production, "La Tragedie de Carmen"; and Jean-Luc Godard's anti-adaptation, PRENOM: CARMEN, which is so far from an adaptation that it does not even include Bizet's score. Here Julia Migenes-Johnson is Carmen, a seductive cigarette factory worker who ruins the life of a Spanish officer, essayed by Placido Domingo. The film's chief plus is Rosi's direction, a return to the basics of the Merimee-Bizet tale that presents the setting as realistically as possible. Rosi and cinematographer Pasqualino De Santis have taken their actors and cameras into the Andalusian landscapes of Spain and given the warhorse of a story a different look. Choreographed by Antonio Gades, who performed the same task on the Carlos Saura version. Lorin Maazel served as the film's musical director. In French with English subtitles.

p, Patrice Ledoux; d, Francesco Rosi; w, Francesco Rosi, Tonino Guerra (based on the story by Prosper Merimee and the opera "Carmen" by Georges Bizet); ph, Pasqualino De Santis (Panavision, Eastmancolor); ed, Ruggero Mastroianni, Colette Semprun; m, Georges Bizet.

Opera **(PR:A-C MPAA:PG)**

BLACK AND WHITE IN COLOR***

(1976, Fr./Ivory Coast) 100m Reggane-Societe de Francaise-Smart-Societe Ivoirienne/AA c (LA VICTOIRE EN CHANTANT)

Jean Carmet *(Sgt. Bosselet),* Jacques Dufilho *(Paul Rechampot),* Catherine Rouvel *(Marinette),* Jacques Spiesser *(Hubert Fresnoy),* Dora Doll *(Maryvonne),* Maurice Barrier *(Caprice),* Claude Legros *(Jacques Rechampot),* Jacques Monnet *(Father Simon),* Peter Berling *(Father Jean De La Croix),* Marius Beugre Boignan *(Barthelemy),* Baye Macoumba Diop *(Lamartine),* Aboubakar Toure *(Fidel),* Dietor Schidor *(Lt. Kraft),* Marc Zuber *(English Major),* Helmut Eiker *(Haussman),* Mamadou Koulibaly *(Oscar),* Benjamin Memel Atchori *(Assomption),* Jean-Francoise Eyou N'Guessan *(Marius),* Inhabitants of Niofouin.

The winner of the 1976 Oscar for Best Foreign Film, this first feature from Jean-Jacques Annaud (THE NAME OF THE ROSE) is set in a French colonial outpost in 1915. When Hubert Fresnoy (Jacques Spiesser), a conscientious young geologist, writes home to Paris lamenting the "dangers" of Africa (chief among them boredom), he begs to be sent newspapers and books. Some time later the papers arrive, bringing the news—six months late—that France is at war with Germany. This poses a bit of a problem at the outpost for a number of reasons: the colonists are friendly with a group of neighboring Germans; their commander, Sgt. Bosselet (Jean Carmet), has never been to battle; and they have no trained army. Rather than go undefended, Bosselet orders the enlistment of all the healthy male natives that live in and around the outpost. Bosselet and his assistants teach the loin-clothed men to speak French, operate bayonets, wear shoes, and sing "La Marseillaise." The natives then receive the honor of being given a French name. BLACK AND WHITE IN COLOR is a biting satire on war, colonialism, and French patriotism, which juxtaposes scenes of gaiety and humor with the brutalities of racism and war. The result is something of a combination of Philippe de Broca's superb war satire, KING OF HEARTS, and Jamie Uys' THE GODS MUST BE CRAZY. Deserving special mention is the playful score by Pierre Bachelet. In French with English subtitles.

p, Arthur Cohn, Jacques Perrin, Giorgio Silvagni; d, Jean-Jacques Annaud; w, Jean-Jacques Annaud, George Conchon; ph, Claude Agostini, Nanamoudou Magasouba (Eastmancolor); ed, Francoise Bonnot, Michele Boehm; m, Pierre Bachelet.

Comedy/War **(PR:C-O MPAA:PG)**

BLACK ORPHEUS****

(1959, Fr./It./Braz.) 100m Dispatfilm-Gemma-Tupan/ Lopert c (ORFEU NEGRO)

Breno Mello *(Orfeo),* Marpessa Dawn *(Eurydice),* Lourdes de Oliveira *(Mira),* Lea Garcia *(Serafina),* Adhemar da Silva *(Death),* Alexandre Constantino *(Hermes),* Waldetar de Souza *(Chico),* Jorge dos Santos *(Benedito),* Aurino Cassiano *(Zeca),* Maria Alica.

The Orpheus myth is supplanted onto the soil of Rio de Janeiro during Carnaval—the one day of the year that calls for unrestrained celebration, music, dance, and costumes. Orfeo (Breno Mello) is a streetcar conductor and guitarist engaged to Mira (Lourdes de Oliveira), an exotic and vivacious woman who lives as if every day were Carnaval. However, anyone familiar with the legend of Orpheus (as the man in Rio's marriage office is) knows that he is destined to love Eurydice (Marpessa Dawn), personified here as a newcomer to Rio who arrives in town to visit her cousin Serafina (Lea Garcia). Eurydice has fled her hometown because she was being followed by a mysterious stranger—a stranger who has followed her to Rio and has disguised himself as Death for Carnaval. In order to save Eurydice from Death, Orfeo must travel into the Underworld and bring her back to the world of the living. From the opening shot, in which two Brazilian musicians literally burst through the frame, one can sense the explosiveness of BLACK ORPHEUS. Like Carnaval, the film frame dances, the soundtrack sings, and the costumes swirl in an explosion of color and light. Besides its exhilarating style, however, the film works as an effective translation of the classic Greek myth into a Brazilian romance. The second film from Marcel Camus, a Frenchman who traveled to Brazil to make this picture, BLACK ORPHEUS became an instant international success and was honored with the Golden Palm at Cannes and the Best Foreign Film Oscar at the Academy Awards. (In Portuguese; English subtitles.)

p, Sacha Gordine; d, Marcel Camus; w, Jacques Viot, Marcel Camus (based on the play "Orfeu da Conceicao" by Vinicius de Moraes); ph, Jean Bourgoin (CinemaScope, Eastmancolor); ed, Andree Feix; m, Antonio Carlos Jobim, Luis Bonfa.

Romance **(PR:A-C MPAA:NR)**

BLIND TRUST***

(1986, Can.) 87m Vision 4-L'Office du Film du Canada/ Vivafilm c (POUVOIR INTIME; AKA: INTIMATE POWER)

Marie Tifo *(Roxanne),* Pierre Curzi *(Ex-Con),* Jacques Godin *(Theo),* Eric Brisebois *(Robin),* Robert Gravel *(Martial),* Jacques Lussier *(Janvier),* Jean-Louis Millette *(Meurseault),* Yvan Ponton *(H.B.),* Richard Perron *(Thomas),* Yves Desgagnes *(Paul),* Bob Walsh *(Singer),* Pierrette Robitaille, Francine Ruel *(Tourists),* Rejean Gauvin, Pierre Brisset-Des Nos, Richard Blaimert, Jean-Raymond Chales, Michel Hinton, Andre Melancon, Bob Presner, Louis Maufette, Jean-Francois Leblanc, Lucien Francoeur, Regis Gautier, Rene Caron.

A dazzling and energetic twist on the gangster film, BLIND

TRUST keeps its audience tense for its duration and offers nearly nonstop splashes of color and sound. The film begins simply enough with a planned robbery of an armored car by Theo (Jacques Godin) and his amateur gang, including his son (Eric Brisebois), an ex-con (Pierre Curzi), and the ex-con's girl friend (Marie Tifo). A monkey wrench is thrown into the carefully laid plan, causing the son to panic and start firing at the guards, one of whom (unknown to the criminals) has taken refuge in the back of the armored car. The crooks drive to a secluded warehouse, where they intend to split up the loot, only to discover that the guard has locked himself in and is ready to fight. Their only choice is to force him out by any means necessary—methods that become increasingly desperate and sadistic. Directed with passion and verve by the 25-year-old Yves Simoneau, who has created a highly charged film of great style that explodes on the screen. (In French; English subtitles.)

p, Claude Bonin, Roger Frappier; d, Yves Simoneau; w, Yves Simoneau, Pierre Curzi; ph, Guy Dufaux; ed, Andre Corriveau; m, Richard Gregoire.

Thriller **(PR:C-O MPAA:NR)**

BLOOD OF A POET, THE*****

(1930, Fr.) 58m Vicomte de Noailles bw (LE SANG D'UN POETE)

Enrico Rivero *(The Poet),* Lee Miller *(Greek Statue),* Pauline Carton *(Child's Tutor),* Jean Desbordes *(The Friend),* Feral Benga *(The Black Angel),* Fernand Dichamps, Lucien Jager, Odette Talazac, Barbette, Jean Cocteau *(Narrator).*

Funded by the Vicomte de Noailles, who was also behind Luis Bunuel's L'AGE D'OR, this is Jean Cocteau's first step into filmmaking, just one of the many media in which the great poet worked. Divided into four episodes—"The Wounded Hand, or the Scars of the Poet," "Do Walls Have Ears?" "The Battle of the Snowballs," and "The Profanation of the Host"—THE BLOOD OF THE POET is a journey in which Cocteau attempts to "picture the poet's inner self." Taking great liberties with the notion of narrative film, it is a collection of all that is Cocteau—his dreams, his mirrors, his stars, his opium addiction, his deceptive images and sets, his mythology, and his obsession with dying. What is so remarkable about THE BLOOD OF THE POET is that Cocteau has created a lasting piece of art, a haunting poem, as exciting today as it was in 1930 and will be in 2030.

p, Vicomte de Noailles; d, Jean Cocteau; w, Jean Cocteau; ph, Georges Perinal; ed, Jean Cocteau; m, Georges Auric.

Fantasy **(PR:C MPAA:NR)**

BLOOD WEDDING**

(1981, Sp.) 72m Euro-Maghreb-Libra c (BODAS DE SANGRE)

Antonio Gades *(Leonardo),* Christina Hoyos *(Bride),* Juan Antonio Jimenez *(Groom),* Pilar Cardenas *(Mother),* Carmen Villena *(Wife),* El Guito, Elvira Andres, Marisa Nela, Lario Diaz, Azucena Flores, Antonio Quitana, Quico Franco *(Wedding Guests).*

This much-touted meeting of filmmaker Carlos Saura, choreographer Antonio Gades and playwright Federico Garcia Lorca has been praised to the heavens by aficionados of the dance film genre, though those who love the cinema or Garcia Lorca will hardly be as moved as they. BLOOD WEDDING opens backstage as the dancers pour in, open their makeup cases, fix their hair, and apply their greasepaint. Some time later, Gades and his troupe move out into their rehearsal space and begin practicing their flamenco version of Garcia Lorca's play. The film, which runs an economic 72 minutes, is a must for those interested in dance or devotees of the fine arts. (In Spanish; English subtitles.)

p, Emiliano Piedra; d, Carlos Saura; w, Antonio Areero, Alfredo Manas (based on the play by Federico Garcia Lorca); ph, Teo Escamilla (Eastmancolor); ed, Pablo del Amo; m, Emilio de Diego.

Dance **(PR:A MPAA:NR)**

BLOW-UP****

(1966, Brit./It.) 110m Bridge/Premier c

David Hemmings *(Thomas),* Vanessa Redgrave *(Jane),* Sarah Miles *(Patricia),* Jane Birkin, Gillian Hills *(Teenagers),* Peter Bowles *(Ron),* Harry Hutchinson *(Antiques Dealer),* John Castle *(Bill, the Painter),* Susan Broderick *(Antique Shop Owner),* Mary Khal *(Fashion Editor),* Ronan O'Casey *(Jane's Lover),* Tsai Chin *(Receptionist),* Jill Kennington, Peggy Moffitt, Rosaleen Murray, Ann Norman, Melanie Hampshire *(Models),* Julian Chagrin, Claude Chagrin *(Tennis Players),* The Yardbirds.

Michelangelo Antonioni's adaptation of Julio Cortazar's short story is an engrossing study of the image and one's perception of the image. Set against the backdrop of mod 1960s London, BLOW-UP follows a fashionable young photographer, Thomas (David Hemmings), as he snaps his surroundings. While wandering through a quiet park he begins taking photos of two lovers embracing. One of them, Jane (Vanessa Redgrave), chases after Thomas and demands that he return the negatives. Later, after developing the photos, Thomas thinks he sees something in the background—a man with a gun aimed at the back of Jane's partner. Returning that evening to the park, Thomas finds the man's corpse. But the following morning, when Thomas returns again, and corpse has vanished. Thomas blows the photo up larger and larger until it becomes an abstract and meaningless mass. One of the most successful art films ever made, BLOW-UP was Antonioni's leap into the commercial international film scene after much film festival attention for L'AVVENTURA; L'ECLISSE; LA NOTTE; and THE RED DESERT. Although much of BLOW-UP is brilliant, it looks increasingly silly with the passage of time. The mod scene succeeds today only as archival material, Hemmings is a difficult actor to care about, the dated Herbie Hancock score is nearly impossible to listen to, and the roving gang of mimes are downright irritating. What has curiously been ignored over the years is the fact that BLOW-UP is marvelously funny, though it's hard to gauge how much of this is intentional. Perhaps all along this film should have been viewed as an advancement of the great tradition of British comedies. Antonioni followed this one with an even funnier film—ZABRISKIE POINT. Jane Birkin is cast here in her first screen appearance, as one of the two giggling teenagers who playfully and erotically wrestle with Hemmings. (In English.)

p, Pierre Rouve, Carlo Ponti; d, Michelangelo Antonioni; w, Michelangelo Antonioni, Tonino Guerra, Edward Bond (based on the story "Las Babas Del Diablo" by Julio Cortazar); ph, Carlo di Palma (Metro Color); ed, Frank Clarke; m, Herbie Hancock, The Yardbirds, The Lovin' Spoonful.

Drama **(PR:O MPAA:NR)**

BLUE ANGEL, THE*****

(1930, Ger.) 99m UFA/PAR bw (DER BLAUE ENGEL)

Emil Jannings *(Professor Immanuel Rath),* Marlene Dietrich *(Lola-Lola Frohlich),* Kurt Gerron *(Kiepert, a Magician),* Rosa Valette *(Guste, his Wife),* Hans Albers *(Mazeppa),* Eduard von Winterstein *(Principal of the School),* Reinhold Bernt *(The Clown),* Hans Roth *(Beadle),* Rolf Muller *(Angst, a Student),* Robert Klein-Lork *(Goldstaub, a Student),* Karl Huszar-Puffy *(Publican),* Wilhelm Diegelmann *(Captain).*

The film that gave us the team of Josef von Sternberg and Marlene Dietrich, THE BLUE ANGEL is an unqualified masterpiece—a milestone in the careers of both the director and the actress, in the history of German film, and in the history of sound film. The story is that of a man's downfall because of his desire for a woman. The man, Prof. Immanuel Rath (Emil Jannings), is a pillar of the community who gives up everything in order to remain at the side of Lola-Lola (Dietrich), a leggy, sexually autonomous cabaret singer. A slave to Lola-Lola's love, Rath completely surrenders himself to this woman, and as a result lives in a state of humiliation and self-degradation. THE BLUE ANGEL's international success can be attributed to any number of elements in the film. The immortal Jannings, UFA's greatest actor and a victim of the transition from silents to sound, is astounding in an essentially silent performance. Dietrich is wholly captivating in her first role with Sternberg—a creative union from which arose the Dietrich persona that would become internationally recognizable. Unforgettable is her piercing rendition of "Falling in Love Again," which she sings directly to the obsessed Rath. It is, however, the genius of Sternberg to which THE BLUE ANGEL owes its greatness. His use of lighting, use of compositions, and use of silence as sound, his overall creation of a world that can seduce and destroy even its most upstanding citizen, attest to this filmmaker's greatness and to the stature of THE BLUE ANGEL. Filmed simultaneously in German and English, the film is available in two, slightly differing, videotape versions—in German with English subtitles, and in English.

p, Erich Pommer; d, Josef von Sternberg; w, Robert Liebmann, Karl Vollmoller, Carl Zuckmayer (based on the novel *Professor Unrat* by Heinrich Mann); ph, Gunther Rittau, Hans Schneeberger; ed, Walter Klee, Sam Winston; m, Friedrich Hollander.

Drama **(PR:A-C MPAA:NR)**

BLUE COUNTRY, THE**

(1977, Fr.) 102m GAU/Quartet c (LE PAYS BLEU; AKA: SINGLES COUNTRY)

Brigitte Fossey *(Louise),* Jacques Serres *(Mathias),* Ginette Garcin *(Zoe),* Armand Meffre *(Moise),* Ginette Mathieu *(Manon),* Roger Crouzet *(Fernand),* Albert Delpy *(Armand),* Pia Corcelle *(Armand's Wife),* Georges Lucas *(Fouchard),* Anne Roudier *(Mathias' Mother),* Theo Savon *(Felicien),* Pierre Maguelon *(Clovis),* Dora Doll *(Mathilde, Clovis' Wife),* Dominique Malmejat *(Joseph),* Micheline Bourday *(Vanessa),* Pierre Londiche *(Mercier),* Jean Lescot *(Theobald),* Serge Marzelle *(The Collector at P.T.T.),* Gill Moutier *(Mme. Malilorme),* Jean-Yves Gautier *(Nicky),* Noelle Leiris *(Sylvia),* Marie Cecora *(Suzy, the Butcher's Wife),* Patricia Kessler *(Peggy),* Gilbert Rivet *(Nora Santini),* Christine Azela *(Charlotte),* Jacky Kieki *(Agathe),* Alain Janey *(Jean-Marc),* Roger Souza *(The Hairdresser).*

Jean-Charles Tacchella's follow-up to the enormously successful COUSIN, COUSINE is a loosely structured collection of country vignettes with a large cast of eccentrics. Most of the folks in the quiet provincial town are content, or at least believe themselves to be so, but gradually these simple people find the urge growing inside them to discover what city life is all about. The differences between the urban and rural lifestyles are paralleled in the romance between ex-Parisian Louise (Brigitte Fossey) and country bumpkin Mathias (Jacques Serres). There are some very sweet, memorable moments in the film, and the ending is especially pleasant, but overall there isn't much here that hasn't been seen before. Were it not for the attention received by COUSIN, COUSINE, it's highly unlikely that THE BLUE COUNTRY would have ever made it to US shores. (In French; English subtitles.)

p, Jean-Charles Tacchella; d, Jean-Charles Tacchella; w, Jean-Charles Tacchella; ph, Edmond Sechan (Eastmancolor); ed, Agnes Guillemot; m, Gerard Anfosso.

Comedy/Romance **(PR:C MPAA:PG)**

BOAT, THE****

(1981, Ger.) 150m Bavaria Atelier/COL c (DAS BOOT)

Jurgen Prochnow *(The Captain),* Herbert Gronemeyer *(Lt. Werner/Correspondent),* Klaus Wennemann *(Chief Engineer),* Hubertus Bengsch *(1st Lt./Number One),* Martin Semmelrogge *(2nd Lieutenant),* Bernd Tauber *(Chief Quartermaster),* Erwin Leder *(Johann),* Martin May *(Ullmann),* Heinz Honig *(Hinrich),* U.A. Ochsen *(Chief Bosun),* Claude-Oliver Rudolph *(Ario),* Jan Fedder *(Pilgrim),* Ralph Richter *(Frenssen),* Joachim Bernhard *(Preacher),* Oliver Stritzel *(Schwalle),* Konrad Becker *(Bockstiegel),* Lutz Schnell *(Dufte),* Martin Hemme *(Bruckenwilli),* Roger Barth *(Thomas Boxhammer),* Christian Bendomir *(Gunther Franke),* Albert Kraml *(Norbert Fronwald),* Peter Pathenis

(Jean-Claude Hoffmann), Christian Seipolt *(Arno Kral),* Ferdinand Schaal *(Helmut Neumeier),* Rolf Weber *(Wilhelm Pietsch),* Lothar Zajicek *(Dirk Salomon),* Rita Cadillac *(Monique),* Otto Sander *(Thomsen),* Gunter Lamprecht *(Captain of the Weser),* Edwige Pierre *(Nadine),* Uwe Ochenknecht *(Boatman).*

A superbly filmed action movie, based on the actual experiences of WW II photographer Lothar-Guenther Buchheim, THE BOAT shows in detail the single cruise of a U-boat in 1941, replete with every known horror above and below the waves, as well as the mundane, boring hours spent at sea. Although most of the footage is devoted to the intense, noble captain (Jurgen Prochnow), the only fully developed character in the film is the boat itself, which undergoes numerous battles and attacks. The film is understandably and decidedly anti-Hitler and anti-Nazi, the submariners profiled as individual warriors upholding their own brand of honor and sneering in the direction of the Third Reich. The chief attraction of THE BOAT, however, is the incredible camerawork—the camera racing through the sub as it rises and submerges in and out of attack and moving through tiny openings. The result is a spectacular, lifelike re-creation of sea battle on the Atlantic. A technical marvel, THE BOAT is a breathtaking and powerful portrait of war and death. Originally released on videocassette as the subtitled DAS BOOT, though most copies now available are dubbed.

p, Gunter Rohrbach, Michael Bittins; d, Wolfgang Petersen; w, Wolfgang Petersen (based on the novel by Lothar-Guenther Buchheim); ph, Jost Vacano (Fujicolor); ed, Hannes Nikel; m, Klaus Doldinger.

War **(PR:C-O MPAA:R)**

BOB LE FLAMBEUR****

(1955, Fr.) 100m Studios Jenner-O.G.C.-Cyme-Play Art/ Triumph bw (Trans: Bob The Gambler)

Isabel Corey *(Anne),* Daniel Cauchy *(Paolo),* Robert Duchesne *(Bob Montagne),* Guy Decomble *(Inspector),* Andre Garet *(Roger),* Gerard Buhr *(Mark),* Claude Cerval *(Jean),* Colette Fleury *(Suzanne),* Simon Paris *(Yvonne),* Rene Havard, Howard Vernon, Germain Amiel, Yvette Amirante, Dominique Antoine, Yannick Arvel, Annick Bertrand, Duilio Carmine.

One of Jean-Pierre Melville's greatest efforts, unreleased in the US until 1982, this engaging black-and-white caper film stars Roger Duchesne as an aging gangster and compulsive gambler who is down on his luck. He has no other choice but to plan a heist of the Deauville Casino. Unfortunately for Bob, his two friends—Paulo (Daniel Cauchy), the young crook who idolizes him, and Anne (Isabelle Corey) his sensuous 16-year-old sex kitten—are proof that people today are not as loyal they were in Bob's youth. BOB LE FLAMBEUR, like Melville's later gangster film LE DOULOS, is an offering to the gods of Hollywood filmmaking and gangster mythmaking, an honest portrayal of that fictional character, the gangster hero. Melville films him lovingly—the upturned collar, the ever-present gun, and the hopeless philosophy that is as dark as the shadows of night. As American as Melville tries to be (he changed his name from Grumbach to Melville in honor of the author of *Moby Dick*), his films are entirely and unfailingly French. Coscripted by Auguste Le Breton, upon whose novel Jules Dassin based his classic gangster film RIFIFI, which Breton also coscripted. In French with English subtitles.

p, Jean-Pierre Melville; d, Jean-Pierre Melville; w, Jean-Pierre Melville, Auguste Le Breton; ph, Henri Decae; ed, Monique Bonnot; m, Eddie Barclay, Jo Boyer.

Crime **(PR:C MPAA:NR)**

BOUDU SAVED FROM DROWNING****

(1932, Fr.) 84m Societe Sirius/Pathe bw (AKA: BOUDU SAUVE DES EAUX)

Michel Simon *(Boudu),* Charles Granval *(Monsieur Lastingois),* Marcelle Hainia *(Madame Lastingois),* Severine Lerczynska *(Anne-Marie),* Jean Daste *(Student),* Max Dalban *(Godin),* Jean Gehret *(Vigour),* Jacques Becker *(Poet on Bench),* Jane Pierson *(Rose),* George Darnoux *(Marriage Guest).*

This wonderful early social comedy from Renoir (made in 1932 but lost, then finally released in 1967 in the US) is a satire on middle-class morality centering on Boudu (Michel Simon), an archetypal tramp about to commit suicide in grief, apparently, over the loss of his dog. He leaps into the Seine from the Pont des Arts, but is saved by bourgeois bookseller Lastingois (Charles Grahval), who takes Boudu home and tries to start him on the road to a productive, responsible life. Boudu, however, is a protohippie—a long-haired, bearded believer in freedom and anarchy. During his stay in Lastingois' very proper confines he turns the place into a shambles, seduces Lastingois' wife (Marcelle Hainia), and, when he strikes it rich in the lottery, marries the family's gold-digging maid (Severine Lerczynska). He is then faced with the choice of living as a socially responsible adult in a tuxedo or reasserting his own independence. The story is told in a realistic, humanistic manner as only Renoir can tell it, though much of the brilliance comes not from Renoir's technique but from Simon's extraordinary portrayal of Boudu. As Renoir has written: "Everything that an actor can be in a film, Michel Simon is in BOUDU. Everything!" Remade in 1986 as DOWN AND OUT IN BEVERLY HILLS, starring Nick Nolte. In French with English subtitles.

p, Michel Simon, Jean Gehret; d, Jean Renoir; w, Jean Renoir (based on a play by Rene Fauchois); ph, Jean-Paul Alphen; ed, Marguerite Renoir, Suzanne de Troye; m, Leo Daniderff, Raphael, Johann Strauss, Jean Boulze, Edouard Dumoulin.

Comedy/Drama **(PR:C MPAA:NR)**

BREATHLESS*****

(1959, Fr.) 89m Imperia-SNC bw (A BOUT DE SOUFFLE)

Jean-Paul Belmondo *(Michel Poiccard/Laszlo Kovacs),* Jean Seberg *(Patricia Franchini),* Daniel Boulanger *(Police Inspector),* Jean-Pierre Melville *(Parvulesco),* Liliane Robin *(Minouche),* Henri-Jacques Huet *(Antonio Berrutti),* Van Doude *(Journalist),* Claude Mansard *(Claudius Mansard),* Michel Fabre *(Plainclothesman),* Jean-Luc Godard *(Informer),* Jean Domarchi *(Drunk),* Richard Balducci *(Tolmatchoff),* Roger Hanin *(Carl Zombach),* Jean-Louis Richard *(Journalist),* Francois Moreuil *(Cameraman),* Philippe de Broca.

What Stravinsky's "La Sacre du Printemps" is to 20th-century music, what Joyce's *Ulysses* is to the 20th-century novel, what Picasso's "Demoiselles d'Avignon" is to 20th-century painting, that is what Jean-Luc Godard's first feature, BREATHLESS, is to film. BREATHLESS is a motion picture that stands apart from all that came before and that has revolutionized all that followed. Dedicated to the B-movies of Hollywood's Monogram Pictures, the film's structure is based on the conventions of the gangster film. Michel Poiccard, alias Laszlo Kovacs (Jean-Paul Belmondo), is a likeable but dangerously careless petty criminal who models himself after Bogart and becomes the subject of a police dragnet when he senselessly guns down a traffic cop. Without much money or a place to stay, Michel must depend on others' kindness. He tries every avenue possible to cash a check (signed "for deposit only") and hides out in the apartment of Patricia (Jean Seberg), a young American student he barely knows. While trying to avoid police detection, Michel finds himself falling dangerously in love with the confused Patricia. Rather than tell this story in a conventional mode, Godard pays little heed to the rules of the game. He is far more concerned with destroying previous film language and employing his own. He "jump cuts" with little concern for continuity, then by contrast dollies the camera for long, fluid takes. Some scenes have a documentary truth, while others are pulp fiction. As the title implies, Godard's technique and philosophy are designed to leave the viewer breathless—not to kill them, but to allow for Godard to breathe a new life into them. In French with English subtitles.

p, Georges de Beauregard; d, Jean-Luc Godard; w, Jean-Luc Godard (based on an idea by Francois Truffaut); ph, Raoul Coutard; ed, Cecile Decugis, Lila Herman; m, Martial Solal.

Crime/Romance (PR:A-C MPAA:NR)

BURMESE HARP, THE****

(1956, Jap.) 120m Nikkatsu/Brandon bw (BIRUMA NO TATEGOTO; AKA: HARP OF BURMA)

Shoji Yasui *(Private Mizushima),* Rentaro Mikuni *(Captain Inouye),* Taniye Kitabayashi *(Old Woman),* Tatsuya Mihashi *(Defense Commander),* Yunosuke Ito *(Village Head).*

THE BURMESE HARP is a lyrical antiwar film of great beauty that, along with FIRES ON THE PLAIN, is one of Kon Ichikawa's great films, and is the picture that brought this brilliant Japanese director international renown. Pvt. Mizushima (Shoji Yasui) has been commissioned to convince a Burmese unit of Japanese soldiers to surrender during the final days of WW II. He is unsuccessful, and, as a result, the unit is attacked. Only the injured Mizushima survives, and he is nursed back to health by a Buddhist monk. Mizushima, who is given a monk's robe to wear, then proceeds, in a great act of human dignity, to bury the dead as he transforms from soldier into monk. Also available on videotape as HARP OF BURMA, this film received another treatment in 1985 when Kon Ichikawa directed a remake in color. (In Japanese; English subtitles.)

p, Masayuki Takagi; d, Kon Ichikawa; w, Natto Wada (based on the novel by Michio Takeyama); ph, Minoru Yokoyama; ed, Masanori Tsujii; m, Akira Ifukube.

War (PR:C-O MPAA:NR)

BYE BYE BRAZIL***

(1980, Braz.) 110m Carnaval/Unifilm c (AKA: BYE-BYE BRASIL)

Jose Wilker *(Lord Cigano),* Betty Faria *(Salome),* Fabio Junior *(Cico),* Zaira Zambelli *(Dasdo),* Principe Nabor *(Swallow),* Jofre Soares *(Ze da Luz),* Marcos Vinicius *(Gent),* Jose Maria Lima *(Assistant),* Emanoel Cavalcanti *(Mayor),* Jose Marcio Passos *(Mayor's Assistant),* Rinaldo Gines *(Indian Chief),* Carlos Kroeber *(Driver),* Oscar Reis *(Smuggler),* Rodolfo Arena *(Peasant).*

Directed by Carlos Diegues (XICA DA SILVA), one of the principal members of the Brazilian "Cinema Novo" film movement, BYE BYE BRAZIL is a colorful, exotic collection of vignettes about modern Brazil. The film follows a carnival troupe as they travel throughout the country, wandering deep into the Amazonian jungles, in search of new places where they can put up their tents and put on a show. The eccentric troupe consists of Lord Cigano (Jose Wilker), a magician who organizes the troupe; Salome (Betty Faria), his mistress and the show's exotic dancer-prostitute; Cico (Fabio Junior), a young accordionist infatuated with Salome; Dasdo (Zaira Zambelli), his pregnant wife; and Swallow (Principe Nabor), a black, deaf-mute strongman. As time goes on, the troupe must face not only personal crises, but a financial crisis, which arises when the locals prefer to watch television instead of visit the carnival. An insightful and humorous look at two Brazils in conflict—the traditional Brazil versus the progressive Brazil, with its infusions of North American culture. In Portuguese with English subtitles.

p, Lucy Barreto; d, Carlos Diegues; w, Carlos Diegues; ph, Lauro Escorel; ed, Mair Tavares; m, Chico Buarque, Roberto Menescal, Dominguinhos, Bing Crosby, The Everly Brothers.

Comedy/Drama (PR:C-O MPAA:R)

C

CABINET OF DR. CALIGARI, THE*****

(1920, Ger.) 69m Decla-Bioscop/Goldwyn bw (DAS CABINETT DES DR. CALIGARI)

Werner Krauss *(Dr. Caligari),* Conrad Veidt *(Cesare),* Friedrich Feher *(Francis),* Lil Dagover *(Jane),* Hans Heinz von Twardowski *(Alan),* Rudolf Lettinger *(Dr. Olsen),* Rudolph Klein-Rogge *(A Criminal),* Ludwig Rex, Elsa Wagner, Henri Peters-Arnolds, Hans Lanser-Ludolff.

One of the landmarks in the history of cinema, THE CABINET OF DR. CALIGARI was one of the first self-conscious works of film "art," and has had a profound and lasting effect on the world's creative community. The film opens as two pale men sit on a park bench exchanging stories. The younger, Francis (Friedrich Feher), tells a fantastic tale of horror that transports the viewer to Holstenwall, a bizarre community with jagged roads, steeply pointed rooftops, and sloping walls. Into this town walks Dr. Caligari (Werner Krauss), a man of sinister appearance, who obtains a permit for his carnival. His chief attraction is the somnambulist Cesare (Conrad Veidt), but their arrival in Holstenwall mysteriously corresponds to a series of unexplained murders. THE CABINET OF DR. CALIGARI, with its disturbing and ambiguous framing story told by Francis, exploded onto the art world with shocking impact. The film's unique vision provided the spark needed to expand the Expressionist movement in Germany, and shortly thereafter throughout the world. German music, theater, painting, posters, literature, and architecture were all inspired by CALIGARI. Even more important than Robert Wiene's direction (the script was by the brilliant Carl Mayer and Czech poet Hans Janowitz; Fritz Lang was initially slated to direct, and the framing story was decided upon by producer Erich Pommer) is the stunningly original art direction by painters Hermann Warm and Walter Reimann and designer Walter Rohrig. They have created in their constructed village of Holstenwall a completely artificial universe—a stifling place without a sky, where sunlight and shadows are painted onto floors and walls, and where the angular contraptions called buildings defy all laws of architecture—a universe which could exist only in the mind of a madman. Budgeted at $18,000, the finished film was first screened in Berlin in February 1920, with a musical accompaniment that included selections from Schubert and Rossini. Some early prints were tinted with green, brown, and blue.

p, Erich Pommer; d, Robert Weine; w, Carl Meyer, Hans Janowitz; ph, Willy Hameister.

Horror **(PR:A MPAA:NR)**

CAMILA**½

(1984, Arg./Sp.) 105m GEA/European Classics c

Susu Pecoraro *(Camila O'Gorman),* Imanol Arias *(Fr. Ladislao Gutierrez),* Hector Alterio *(Adolfo O'Gorman),* Elena Tasisto *(Dona Joaquina O'Gorman),* Carlos Munoz *(Monsignor Elortondo),* Hector Pellegrini *(Commandant Soto),* Claudio Gallardou *(Br. Eduardo O'Gorman),* Boris Rubaja *(Ignacio),* Mona Maris *(La Perichona),* Lelio Incrocci, Armando Capo, Martin Coria, Olga Veyra, Cido Vianna, Juan Carlos Galbarsanini.

An Oscar nominee for Best Foreign Film, CAMILA takes as its subject the real-life Argentine legend of two doomed lovers—Camila O'Gorman (Susu Pecoraro) and Jesuit priest Ladislao Gutierrez (Imanol Arias)—who, in 1847, under the dictatorial Rosas government, were executed for the crime of sacrilege. Camila is the daughter of a Buenos Aires aristocrat (Hector Alterio) who governs his family with a hand as stern and ruthless as that of Rosas. She is considered strange by family and friends because, while her sisters marry into wealth and power, she has the romantic notion that one she should marry for love. Struggling with her blossoming sexual urges, she confesses an erotic dream to the parish priest, thinking him her usual confessor, but then finding out that he is the newly assigned Fr. Gutierrez. When she finally sets eyes on Gutierrez, Camila falls in love. The two initially resist their attraction to one another, but eventually leave the parish for a distant village, where they adopt new names and identities and run a small school. They are later arrested, imprisoned, and sentenced to death without benefit of trial. A powerful story of romance, CAMILA presents its lovers in a deliberately paced, soft-focus style, using very little dialog to bring forth their characters and emphasizing their gestures and expressions instead. Underneath the romance is an equally interesting look at the political climate in Argentina in the mid-1800s. CAMILA's tone remains, however, too emotionally guarded to capture the intensity of its protagonists' passionate love for one another, resulting in a film that seems as conventional and upper-class as the rigid mid-1800s aristocratic society it exposes. Available in both dubbed and subtitled (Spanish to English) versions.

p, Angel Baldo, Hector Gallardo, Edecio Imbert; d, Maria Luisa Bemberg; w, Luisa Bemberg, Beda Docampo Feijoo, Juan Bautista Stagnaro; ph, Fernando Arribas; ed, Luis Cesar D'Angiolillo; m, Luis Maria Serra.

Historical/Romance **(PR:O MPAA:NR)**

CAMILLE 2000*

(1969, US) 116m Audubon c

Daniele Gaubert *(Marguerite Gauthier),* Nino Castelnuovo *(Armand Duval),* Eleanora Rossi-Drago *(Prudence),* Philippe Forquet *(Duke De Varville),* Roberto Bisacco *(Gaston),* Massimo Serato *(Armand's Father),* Silvana Venturelli *(Olympe),* Zachary Adams *(Gody).*

Radley Metzger, who hit it big in the late 1960s with a series of "artsy" sex films, gives a futuristic treatment to Alexandre Dumas' (*fils*) novel *The Lady of the Camelias*, and adds a number of naked bodies to the proceedings, in CAMILLE 2000. While, technically, this is an American film (produced by a US company), it was shot in Rome with a European cast and crew and with typically lousy postdubbing. The buxom Daniele Gaubert plays Camille, a drug-addicted, incurably ill courtesan who sleeps her way into the heart of a local nobleman (Philippe Forquet), all the while longing for her true love, a lowly commoner (Nino Castelnuovo). Pretentious, overblown direction and generally awful performances detract from whatever eroticism could possibly develop from this mess. The best that can be said of the film is that the photography, art direction, and costumes (whether or not they are filled out) are not unpleasant to look at. In English.

p, Radley H. Metzger; d, Radley H. Metzger; w, Michael DeForrest (based on "The Lady of the Camellias" by Alexander Dumas fils); ph, Ennio Guarnieri (Panavision, Technicolor); ed, Humphrey Hinshelwood, Amedeo Safa; m, Piero Piccioni.

Drama **(PR:O MPAA:NR)**

CARMEN***½

(1983, Sp.) 102m Orion c

Antonio Gades *(Antonio),* Laura del Sol *(Carmen),* Paco de Lucia *(Paco),* Cristina Hoyos *(Cristina),* Juan Antonio Jimenez *(Juan),* Sebastian Moreno *(Escamillo),* Jose Yepes *(Pepe Giron),* Pepa Flores *(Pepa Flores).*

Another version of the Merimee/Bizet drama, this film uses rehearsals for the opera (not unlike director Carlos Saura's previous BLOOD WEDDING) as the setting for a story line similar to the performance piece itself. Laura del Sol (THE HIT) plays Carmen, here metamorphosed into a fiery actress-dancer who is slated to play her namesake in a flamenco dance version of the opera despite her lack of experience. Antonio Gades (the star of BLOOD WEDDING) is the choreographer who falls in love with his star. The dance sequences are excellent, as expected, with the added plus of del Sol's eroticism. In a major role is Paco de Lucia, the legendary flamenco guitarist. It should go without saying that Saura's dance films and Antonio Gades' choreography are must-sees for dance enthusiasts. Others may greet CARMEN with mixed emotions. In Spanish with English subtitles.

p, Emiliano Piedra; d, Carlos Saura; w, Carlos Saura, Antonio Gades; ph, Teo Escamilla (Eastmancolor); ed, Pedro Del Rey; m, Paco de Lucia, Georges Bizet.

Opera **(PR:C MPAA:R)**

CARNIVAL IN FLANDERS***

(1935, Fr.) 95m Film Sonoris Tobis/American Tobis bw (LA KERMESSE HEROIQUE)

Francoise Rosay *(Cornelia),* Jean Murat *(Duke d'Olivares),* Andre Alerme *(Burgomaster),* Louis Jouvet *(The Friar),* Lyne Clevers *(The Fishwife),* Micheline Cheirel *(Siska),* Maryse Wendling *(The Baker's Wife),* Ginette Gaubert *(The Innkeeper's Wife),* Marguerite Ducouret *(The Brewer's Wife),* Bernard Lancret *(Jan Brueghel),* Alfred Adam *(The Butcher),* Pierre Labry *(The Innkeeper),* Arthur Devere *(The Fishmonger),* Marcel Carpentier *(The Baker),* Alexander D'Arcy *(The Captain),* Claude Sainval *(2nd Spanish Lieutenant),* Delphin *(The Dwarf).*

This well-made French comedy, which was extremely popular upon its release but has dated poorly, details the temporary occupation of a small Flanders village by Spanish troops. Fearing the brutal treatment received by other towns at the hands of the invaders, the male citizens decide to "play dead." The town pretends to be in a state of mourning for their "late" mayor, who fakes his own death while the rest of the men remain hidden. Hoping that the Spanish army, led by the Duke (Jean Murat) and including a friar (Louis Jouvet), will soon proceed on their way, the women of the town treat them to an outpouring of hospitality that even leads to the bedroom. A pleasant enough farce, CARNIVAL IN FLANDERS is today best remembered for its superb acting, especially that of director Jacques Feyder's wife, Francoise Rosay. Set in 1616, the film does a fine job of re-creating the visual style of Flemish painters, particularly Jan Brueghel, whose character figures into the plot. Credit for the art direction goes to Alexandre Trauner, Lazare Meerson, and Georges Wakhevitch. In French with English subtitles.

d, Jacques Feyder; w, Charles Spaak, Jacques Feyder, Bernard Zimmer (based on a story by Charles Spaak); ph, Harry Stradling; ed, Jacques Brillouin; m, Louis Beydts.

Drama **(PR:A MPAA:NR)**

CAT AND MOUSE***½

(1975, Fr.) 107m Films 13-Robert A. McNeil/Quartet c (LE CHAT ET LA SOURIS)

Michele Morgan *(Mme. Richard),* Serge Reggiani *(Inspector Lechat),* Philippe Leotard *(Pierre, Lechat's Assistant),* Jean-Pierre Aumont *(Mon. Richard),* Valerie LeGrange *(Valerie),* Michel Peyrelon, Christine Laurent, Anne Libert, Jacques Francois, Judith Magre, Arlette Emmery, Jean Mermet, Philippe Labro, Sammy the Dog.

This thoroughly baffling murder mystery will fool even the most ardent and savvy viewer. Inspector Le*chat* (Serge Reggiani), the cat, is investigating the murder (or is it suicide?) of Mon. Richard (Jean-Pierre Aumont), an extremely wealthy businessman who dabbles in the production of soft-core sex films. He is found with a bullet hole in his head, his collection of priceless paintings stolen from the walls. His wife (Michele Morgan) stands to inherit everything and is naturally the chief suspect, but has a nearly airtight alibi. Richard's porn star lover is also suspected, and then there are his two underpaid servants. Together with his enthusiastic assistant (Philippe Leotard), Lechat tries his best to put the pieces together. Especially interesting is a lengthy sequence in which Lechat races against the clock through the Paris streets to test a suspect's alibi—all shot from a front-bumper point of view—first by car, then by motorcycle. Dubbed in English.

p, Claude Lelouch; d, Claude Lelouch; w, Claude Lelouch; ph, Jean Collomb; ed, Georges Klotz; m, Francis Lai.

Comedy/Mystery **(PR:A-C MPAA:PG)**

CESAR*½**

(1936, Fr.) 117m Pagnol/Siritzky bw

Raimu *(Cesar Olivier),* Pierre Fresnay *(Marius),* Orane Demazis *(Fanny),* Fernand Charpin *(Honore Panisse),* Andre Fouche *(Cesariot),* Alida Rouffe *(Honorine Cabinis),* Milly Mathis *(Aunt Claudine Foulon),* Robert Vattier *(M. Brun),* Paul Dullac *(Felix Escartefigue),* Maupi *(Chauffeur),* Edouard Delmont *(Dr. Felicien Venelle),* Doumel *(Fernand),* Thommeray *(The Priest Elzear),* Robert Bassac *(Pierre Dromard),* Charblay *(Bar Patron).*

The third part of Marcel Pagnol's "Marseilles Trilogy," CESAR completes the story begun in MARIUS and continued in FANNY. Cesariot (Andre Fouche) is the 18-year-old son of Marius (Pierre Fresnay) and Fanny (Orane Demazis), but his father disappeared before he was born and he believes the aging Panisse (Fernand Charpin), his stepfather, to be his biological parent. A priest begs Panisse to tell Cesariot about his real father, but he refuses. When Panisse dies, Fanny tells her son about his parentage and he is properly shocked to find that Cesar (Raimu), whom he had always thought to be his godfather, is actually his grandfather. The old man tells Cesariot about his father and where to find him. Magnificent performances, particularly from Raimu, highlight this fine film—the only one of the three directed by the trilogy's writer and producer, Pagnol. The receptive audiences that made the previous installments such a success did the same for this one, and the fact that the lovers of the first two—Marius and Fanny—were finally reunited after 20 years didn't hurt the box office, either. In French with English subtitles.

p, Marcel Pagnol; d, Marcel Pagnol; w, Marcel Pagnol; ph, Willy; ed, Suzanne de Troye, Jeanette Ginestet; m, Vincent Scotto.

Drama **(PR:A MPAA:NR)**

CESAR AND ROSALIE***

(1972, Fr./It./Ger.) 110m Fildebroc-UPF-Mega/PAR-Orion c (CESAR ET ROSALIE)

Yves Montand *(Cesar),* Romy Schneider *(Rosalie),* Sami Frey *(David),* Umberto Orsini *(Antoine),* Eva-Marie Meineke *(Lucie),* Bernard Le Coq *(Michel),* Gisella Hahn *(Carla),* Isabelle Huppert *(Marite),* Henri-Jacques Huet *(Marcel),* Pippo Merisi *(Albert),* Carlo Nell *(Julien),* Herve Sand *(Georges),* Betty Beckers, Jacques Dhery, Carole Lixon, Dimitri Petricenko, Celine Galland, Henri Coutet, Marcel Gassouk, David Tonelli, Martin Lartigue, Andre Cassan.

CESAR AND ROSALIE is an upper-class French romance in which Yves Montand, Romy Schneider, and Sami Frey are the three sides of a love triangle—an arrangement that seems tolerable to all three. Cesar (Montand), a likable scrap-metal dealer who lives life to the fullest, is in love with Rosalie (Schneider), who has a young daughter from a previous marriage. When family and friends gather for Rosalie's mother's wedding, an unexpected visitor arrives—David (Frey), Rosalie's former lover who disappeared from her life after breaking up her marriage. David's reappearance shakes Rosalie, who still loves him, especially after he admits to Montand that he is still in love with her. This intelligent and funny romance is directed with Claude Sautet's usual inoffensiveness, especially his all-too-complacent view of bourgeois life. What makes the film (at the time, one of France's top money-makers) worth watching is the interplay between Montand, Schneider, and Frey's characters, and the subtle attraction between Montand and Frey—two very different men bonded in their love for the same woman. In a supporting role is the 17-year-old Isabelle Huppert, in one of her very first film appearances. In French with English subtitles.

p, Michelle de Broca; d, Claude Sautet; w, Jean-Loup Dabadie, Claude Sautet, Claude Neron; ph, Jean Boffety (Eastmancolor); ed, Jacqueline Thiedot; m, Philippe Sarde.

Comedy/Romance **(PR:C MPAA:R)**

CHLOE IN THE AFTERNOON****

(1972, Fr.) 97m Les Films du Losange-Barbet Schroeder/COL c (L'AMOUR, L'APRES-MIDI)

Bernard Verley *(Frederic),* Zouzou *(Chloe),* Francoise Verley *(Helene),* Daniel Ceccaldi *(Gerard),* Malvina Penne *(Fabienne),* Babette Ferrier *(Martine),* Tina Michelino, Jean-Louis Livi, Pierre Nunzi, Irene Skobline, Frederique Hender, Claude-Jean Philippe, Silvia Badesco, Claude Bertrand, Sylvaine Charlet, Daniele Malat, Suze Randall, Francoise Fabian, Aurora Cornu, Marie-Christine Barrault, Haydee Politoff, Laurence de Monaghan.

This final installment of Eric Rohmer's "Six Moral Tales" focuses, for the first time in the series, on a married man, Frederic (Bernard Verley), a professional who spends very little time with his equally business-minded wife, Helene (Francoise Verley). The first part of the film is essentially a prolog, setting up Frederic's character. He is a man easily seduced—but only mentally. Frederic imagines what certain women (a series of cameos by previous Rohmer heroines) are like as they walk through the street; concocts romantic adventures with them; and, in one telling scene, purchases a shirt from a pretty salesgirl only because he cannot resist her charms. Having settled into marriage, he only dreams of love in the afternoon (as the title translates). Then, into his life walks Chloe (Zouzou), an attractive, sexy mystery woman who is determined to seduce Frederic. A fitting close to the series, which finally marries off one of Rohmer's romantic heroes, reunites all the previous Rohmer heroines, and addresses the basic theme of marital infidelity. In a greater degree than his previous films, Rohmer (to the surprise of those who find his work talky and boring) gives CHLOE IN THE AFTERNOON a great deal of suspense, not of the obvious sort, but of a quieter, emotional type, all the tension and conflict occurring within the character's head. In French with English subtitles.

p, Pierre Cottrell; d, Eric Rohmer; w, Eric Rohmer; ph, Nestor Almendros; ed, Cecile Decugis; m, Arie Dzierlatka.

Drama **(PR:O MPAA:R)**

CHOICE OF ARMS*½**

(1981, Fr.) 135m Sara-Antenne 2-Parafrance-Radio Monte Carlo c (LE CHOIX DES ARMES)

Yves Montand *(Noel Durieux),* Gerard Depardieu *(Mickey),* Catherine Deneuve *(Nicole Durieux),* Michel Galabru *(Bonnardot),* Gerard Lanvin *(Sarlat),* Jean-Claude Dauphin *(Ricky),* Richard Anconina *(Dany),* Jean Rougerie, Christian Marquand, Etienne Chicot, Pierre Forget.

A compelling and superbly directed *policier*, CHOICE OF ARMS pits the new, young breed of criminal—the crazed and disrespectful Mickey (Gerard Depardieu)—against an elder, retired underworld hood, the honorable Noel (Yves Montand). Mickey escapes from prison and takes temporary refuge at a ranch owned by Noel and his wife, Nicole (Catherine Deneuve). When Mickey refuses to play by Noel's rules, he takes off for Paris. Upon returning, he wrongly assumes that Noel informed on him and vows to kill both Noel and Nicole. A criminal of the old school—not unlike those who appear in the films of Jean-Pierre Melville—Noel leads a tranquil life, but is not beyond violent angry outbursts. He has fought long and hard to achieve his quiet lifestyle with his loving wife, and now must fight again. Although CHOICE OF ARMS does follow certain Hollywood genre expectations, Alain Corneau's direction stamps the film with a crisp, personal style of filmmaking that appears to pay more attention to a theoretical line (especially in his use of music and editing) than to a narrative or emotional one. Like his contemporary Bertrand Tavernier, Corneau achieves a balance between the theoretical and the emotional in his superb direction of actors. Depardieu turns in a forceful performance as the unpredictable Mickey, and Montand is an explosion waiting to happen as externally peaceful Noel. Unfortunately, the always beautiful Deneuve is cast here in another role in which she gets little chance to display much of her acting talent. In French with English subtitles.

p, Alain Sarde; d, Alain Corneau; w, Alain Corneau, Michel Grisolia; ph, Pierre-William Glenn (Panavision); ed, Thierry Derocles; m, Philippe Sarde.

Crime **(PR:C MPAA:NR)**

CHRIST STOPPED AT EBOLI½**

(1979, It./Fr.) 120m RAI-TV2-Vides Cinematografica-Action/Franklin Media c (CRISTO SI E FERMATO A EBOLI; AKA: EBOLI)

Gian Maria Volonte *(Carlo Levi),* Irene Papas *(Giulia),* Lea Massari *(Luisa Levi),* Paolo Bonacelli *(Don Luigi Magalone),* Alain Cuny *(Baron Rotundo),* Francois Simon *(Don Traiella).*

Francesco Rosi turns again to a historical figure (he has also filmed the lives of Salvatore Giuliano, Lucky Luciano, and Enrico Mattei) as the basis for this picture. This time Rosi's subject is the anti-Fascist writer-painter Carlo Levi, whose titular autobiographical novel has had worldwide success. The film follows a period in Levi's life of political exile in the tiny southern Italian village of Lucania, a place where Mussolini felt this northern intellectual could do no harm. Levi (Gian Maria Volonte) arrives in the mid-1930s via rail at Eboli station, a beautiful peasant town whose simple inhabitants have been kept at a comfortable distance from the Fascist happenings in the rest of the country. Through most of the film, Levi is a passive observer, resulting more in a dramatized ethnographic study than in a piece of narrative fiction. While CHRIST STOPPED AT EBOLI's episodic structure and slow pace tend to alienate even the most accepting viewer, Volonte's subtle and powerful performance is reason enough to see Rosi's film. In Italian with English subtitles.

p, Franco Cristaldi, Nicola Carraro; d, Francesco Rosi; w, Francesco Rosi, Tonino Guerra, Raffaele La Capria (based on the book *Christ Stopped At Eboli* by Carlo Levi); ph, Pasqualino De Santis; ed, Ruggero Mastroianni; m, Piero Piccioni.

Biography **(PR:A MPAA:NR)**

CLAIRE'S KNEE*****

(1970, Fr.) 103m Films du Losange/COL c (LE GENOU DE CLAIRE)

Jean-Claude Brialy *(Jerome),* Aurora Cornu *(Aurora),* Beatrice Romand *(Laura),* Laurence de Monaghan *(Claire),* Michele Montel *(Mme. Walter),* Gerard Falconetti *(Gilles),* Fabrice Luchini *(Vincent).*

A most truthful film about the inability to recognize one's own dishonesty and self-deception, CLAIRE'S KNEE, the fifth in Eric Rohmer's series of "Six Moral Tales," stars Jean-Claude Brialy as Jerome, a middle-aged intellectual who feels with his head and not his heart. A French diplomat who is about to be married to a woman he loves, but for whom he feels no passion, Jerome visits the provincial town where he was raised. Aurora (Romanian novelist Aurora Cornu, playing herself), hoping to spark some emotion in Jerome, informs him that a friend's 16-year-old daughter (Beatrice Romand) has a crush on him. Jerome's greater interest, however, is Claire (Laurence de Monaghan), a summery 17-year-old who is completely absorbed with her boy friend. Jerome channels his desire for her into a form of passion that, for him, is much more controllable—he wants only to touch her knee. One of Rohmer's greatest expressions of male-female relationships, CLAIRE'S KNEE is a quiet, simple picture (beautifully photographed by Nestor Almendros) that at first appears as light and airy as the summer days during which its action takes place. The portrait of Jerome, however, is of a man who, under his fairly charming and harmless demeanor, is eroding emotionally in keeping a frightening check on his passions, convincing even himself that he can control his desires. In order to do so, he must completely detach his actions from his heart and make a physical gesture (touching Claire's knee) completely devoid of romance or emotion. What makes this simple notion so poignant is that, by the film's end, it is only the audience, and not Jerome, who have understood this revelation. In French with English subtitles.

p, Pierre Cottrell; d, Eric Rohmer; w, Eric Rohmer; ph, Nestor Almendros; ed, Cecile Decugis.

Drama **(PR:C-O MPAA:GP)**

CLEAN SLATE (COUP DE TORCHON)****

(1981, Fr.) 128m Film de la Tour-Films A2-Little Bear/ Parafrance c (COUP DE TORCHON)

Philippe Noiret *(Lucien Cordier),* Isabelle Huppert *(Rose),* Jean-Pierre Marielle *(Le Peron/His Brother),* Stephane Audran *(Hughuette Cordier),* Eddy Mitchell *(Nono),* Guy Marchand *(Chavasson),* Irene Skobline *(Anne),* Michel Beaune *(Vanderbrouck),* Jean Champion *(Priest),* Victor Garrivier *(Mercaillou),* Gerard Hernandez *(Leonelli),* Abdoulaye Dico *(Fete Nat),* Daniel Langlet *(Paulo),* Francois Perrot *(Colonel).*

This violent and disturbing black comedy moves the action from the American South of Jim Thompson's pulp novel *Pop. 1280* to a French colonial town in 1938 Africa. There, Lucien Cordier (Philippe Noiret) is the police chief, a likable, bleary-eyed slob treated like dirt by most everyone he meets. Policing the town with anything but an iron fist, he prefers to turn a blind eye to vice and corruption. Then, having one day decided he's taken enough abuse, Lucien starts killing anyone who crosses him. Relying only slightly on a narrative drive, this two-hour-plus film concentrates instead on the creation of a character and his environment. Noiret is an excellent choice in the role, providing a perfect balance between the dangerous and the charming, the moral and the amoral, the killer and the victim. Isabelle Huppert, as his scruffy but alluring mistress, Rose, is an added bonus. Although his films vary radically from one to the next, director Bertrand Tavernier continues to walk the path of France's realist tradition. The influence is clear in his choice of production people—screenwriter Jean Aurenche (DEVIL IN THE FLESH; FORBIDDEN GAMES), production designer Alexandre Trauner (many of Marcel Carne's films, including CHILDREN OF PARADISE and LE JOUR SE LEVE), and production manager Louis Wipf (producer of Jean Renoir's FRENCH CANCAN and ELENA AND HER MEN). Available in both dubbed and subtitled (French into English) versions.

p, Adolphe Viezzi, Henri Lassa; d, Bertrand Tavernier; w, Bertrand Tavernier, Jean Aurenche (based on the novel *Pop. 1280* by Jim Thompson); ph, Pierre-William Glenn; ed, Armand Psenny; m, Philippe Sarde.

Crime **(PR:O MPAA:NR)**

CLEO FROM 5 TO 7****

(1961, Fr.) 90m Rome Paris Film bw (CLIO DE CINQ A SEPT)

Corinne Marchand *(Cleo),* Antoine Bourseiller *(Antoine),* Dorothee Blanck *(Dorothee),* Michel Legrand *(The Pianist),* Dominique Davray *(Angele),* Jose-Luis de Villalonga *(The Lover),* Jean-Claude Brialy, Anna Karina, Eddie Constantine, Sami Frey, Danielle Delorme, Jean-Luc Godard, Yves Robert, Alan Scott *(Actors in Comedy Film),* Robert Postec, Lucienne Marchand.

Agnes Varda's second feature opens with an overhead shot of a table, two pairs of women's hands, and a deck of tarot cards. The woman whose fortune is being read, Cleo (short for Cleopatra, played superbly by Corinne Marchand), is told she has cancer. Cleo, who is dreading the results of a recent medical test, believes her fortune. The rest of the film is a chronicle of the next 90 minutes in her life. A beautiful pop singer, Cleo wanders through the streets with a friend, buys herself a fur hat (in summer), takes a cab ride and hears a song of hers on the radio, meets with her two songwriters, and spends some time with a soldier preparing to leave for the war in Algeria. Photographed almost exclusively in the streets of Paris, CLEO FROM 5 TO 7 is a portrait of a woman whose view of life has previously never extended past her own vanity and singing success. Faced with the possibility of death, however, Cleo begins to perceive things differently—finding beauty and life in all things. Curiously, the only one of the film's scenes to fall completely flat is a silent comedy sketch that features Anna Karina, Jean-Luc Godard, Sami Frey, Jean-Claude Brialy, Eddie Constantine, and Yves Robert. One especially nice moment is a song, "Sans Toi" (by Michel Legrand and Varda), which Marchand delivers directly into the camera. In French with English subtitles.

p, Georges de Beauregard; d, Agnes Varda; w, Agnes Varda; ph, Jean Rabier; ed, Jeanne Verneau; m, Michel Legrand.

Drama **(PR:C MPAA:NR)**

CLOCKMAKER, THE****

(1974, Fr.) 105m Lira/Joseph Green c (L'HORLOGER DE SAINT-PAUL; AKA: THE WATCHMAKER OF LYON)

Philippe Noiret *(Michel Descombes),* Jean Rochefort *(Commissioner Guiboud),* Jacques Denis *(Antoine),* William Sabatier *(Lawyer),* Andree Tainsy *(Madeleine),* Sylvain Rougerie *(Bernard Descombes),* Christine Pascal *(Lilliane Terrini),* Cecile Vassort *(Martine),* Yves Afonso, Jacques Hilling, Clotilde Joano, Julien Bertheau, Johnny Wesseler, Tiffany Tavernier.

A first feature from former critic Bertrand Tavernier, THE CLOCKMAKER stars Philippe Noiret as Michel Descombes, a widowed Lyon watchmaker who leads a perfectly orderly life, plays by the rules, and has no intentions of ever stepping out of line. His life is thrown into disarray when police inspectors arrive at his shop to report that his only son, Bernard (Sylvain Rougerie), is suspected of murdering a hated factory foreman. Although Michel has what he considers a good relationship with his son, he comes to realize that he really doesn't know Bernard at all. Based on the novel by Georges Simenon, THE CLOCKMAKER is an introspective, intelligent, and sad (but ultimately positive) look, not at murderers and criminal investigations, but at a strong relationship between a father and son. Rather than resort to heavy-handed speechmaking or maudlin sentiment, Tavernier treats his material with the honesty and subtlety it deserves. This exceptional debut clearly marked Tavernier, one of the few realist directors in film, as a force with which to be reckoned. In French with English subtitles.

d, Bertrand Tavernier; w, Jean Aurenche, Pierre Bost (based on the novel *The Clockmaker of Everton* by Georges Simenon); ph, Pierre-William Glenn; ed, Armand

Psenny; m, Philippe Sarde.

Drama **(PR:O MPAA:NR)**

CLOSELY WATCHED TRAINS***½

(1966, Czech.) 89m Barrandov-Bohumil Smida-Ladislav Fikar/Sigma III bw (OSTRE SLEDOVANE VLAKY; AKA: CLOSELY OBSERVED TRAINS)

Vaclav Neckar *(Trainee Milos Hrma),* Jitka Bendova *(Conductor Masa),* Josef Somr *(Train Dispatcher Hubicka),* Vladimir Valenta *(Station Master Max),* Vlastimil Brodsky *(Counselor Zednicek),* Jiri Menzel *(Dr. Brabek),* Libuse Havelkova *(Max's Wife),* Alois Vachek *(Novak),* Jitka Zelenohorska *(Zdenka).*

The first feature from the 28-year-old Czech filmmaker Jiri Menzel is a comic, humanistic look at a teenage railway trainee, Milos (Vaclav Neckar), who is sent off to a desolate station in Bohemia during the German occupation of Czechoslovakia. Hidden away from much of the rest of the world, Milos and the very ordinary characters who pass through the station try to live as if they were not caught in the midst of WW II. With relative ease, Milos learns his trade, working under the experienced guidance of his mentor, Dispatcher Hubicka (Josef Somr), a bored womanizer who beds any female that happens by. Milos is less at ease, however, with the problems of manhood, which are all too quickly being thrust upon him. During the course of the film, Milos turns freedom fighter and experiences a variety of incidents, including sexual initiation, a botched suicide, and an act of heroism. The most commercially successful film of the Czech New Wave (which included such directors as Milos Forman, Ivan Passer, and Jan Nemec), CLOSELY WATCHED TRAINS went on to win an Oscar for Best Foreign Film. Comic, tragic, romantic, and realistic, it is a film of great warmth and honesty, photographed in wonderfully stark black and white and cast with an exceptional group of actors. Unfortunately, the subtitling is nearly impossible to read on the videocassette.

p, Zdenek Oves; d, Jiri Menzel; w, Jiri Menzel, Bohumil Hrabal (based on his novel); ph, Jaromir Sofr; ed, Jirina Lukesova; m, Jiri Sust.

Comedy/Drama **(PR:C MPAA:NR)**

COCA-COLA KID, THE***½

(1985, Aus.) 94m Smart Egg-Cinecom-Film Gallery c

Eric Roberts *(Becker),* Greta Scacchi *(Terri),* Bill Kerr *(T. George McDowell),* Chris Haywood *(Kim),* Kris McQuade *(Juliana),* Max Gilles *(Frank),* Tony Barry *(Bushman),* Paul Chubb *(Fred),* David Slingsby *(Waiter),* Tim Finn *(Philip),* Colleen Clifford *(Mrs. Haversham),* Esben Storm *(Country Hotel Manager),* Steve Dodd *(Mr. Joe),* David Argue *(Newspaper Vendor).*

When Coca-Cola's big bosses suspect that profits could be greater in Australia, they send in Becker (Eric Roberts), a quirky *wunderkind* troubleshooter who, as an ex-Marine, takes pride in the company and views Coca-Cola as a symbol of the United States. Arriving at the Australia office, he meets Terri (Greta Scacchi), a beautiful young secretary who wanders around the office in her stocking feet, lets her daughter photocopy her face on the office copier, and is nearly raped by her angry estranged husband. After studying a geographical representation of the areas where their product is being sold, Becker discovers a section of Australia that is completely void of the world's most popular beverage. This region prefers a local soft drink made by eccentric T. George McDowell (Bill Kerr), who years before fell in love with a girl from a Coca-Cola advertising poster. An embittered, trigger-happy old man, McDowell is now determined to keep Coca-Cola's imperialists off his land and continue his operations in a traditional, antiquated, steam-powered plant. In THE COCA-COLA KID, the Yugoslavian Dusan Makavejev has made a truly international picture that, like Coca-Cola, knows no borders, enlisting the contributions of an Australian writer, Frank Moorhouse; an American actor, Roberts; and a British actress, Scacchi. Scacchi, exuding a raw sexuality, makes a lasting impression, as does Roberts, who meets the challenge of playing a driven, obsessed character while also displaying a charming sense of humor. This is far from Makavejev's finest work (WR: MYSTERIES OF THE ORGANISM and SWEET MOVIE are much more challenging), but it is the film that has spread the director's political message to the widest audience, and therefore is, in a sense, more successful than all of his previous attempts combined.

p, David Roe, Sylvie Le Clezio; d, Dusan Makavejev; w, Frank Moorhouse (based on the short story collections, *The Americans, Baby, The Electrical Experience* by Frank Moorhouse); ph, Dean Semler (Panavision, Eastmancolor); ed, John Scott.

Comedy **(PR:O MPAA:R)**

COLONEL REDL***

(1985, Hung./Aust./Ger.) 144m Mafilm-Objectiv-Durniok-ORF-ZDF/Orion c (REDL EZREDES; OBERST REDL)

Klaus Maria Brandauer *(Alfred Redl),* Armin Mueller-Stahl *(Crown Prince Archduke Franz-Josef),* Gudrun Landgrebe *(Katalin Kubinyi),* Jan Niklas *(Kristof Kubinyi),* Hans-Christian Blech *(Col. von Roden),* Laszlo Mensaros *(Col. Ruzitska),* Andras Balint *(Dr. Gustav Sonnenschein),* Karoly Eperjes *(Lt. Jaromil Schorm),* Dorottya Udvaros *(Clarissa, Redl's Wife),* Laszlo Galffi *(Alfredo Velocchio),* Robert Ratonyi *(Baron Ullmann),* Gabor Svidrony *(Alfred Redl as a Child),* Eva Szabo *(Redl's Mother),* Gyorgy Racz *(Kristof Kubinyi as a Child),* Dora Lendvai *(Katalin Kubinyi as a Child),* Tamas Major *(Grandfather Kubinyi),* Maria Majlath *(Grandmother Kubinyi),* Flora Kadar *(Redl's Sister),* Agnes T. Katona *(Wilhelmina).*

Istvan Szabo's followup to MEPHISTO again stars Klaus Maria Brandauer, here as Col. Alfred Redl, who became head of the Austro-Hungarian military intelligence bureau in the early 1900s, despite being half-Jewish and from an impoverished family. His Gatsby-like strivings for aristocratic acceptance prove, however, to be his downfall when a czarist agent threatens to expose Redl's homosexual double life. Rather than sacrifice the status he has achieved, Redl reveals top secret information and eventually takes his own life. While not as richly textured or urgent as MEPHISTO, COLONEL REDL is an expertly made historical drama that, while fictionalizing some aspects, truthfully examines the desire for power and the catalysts of war. The film boasts yet another *tour de force* performance by Brandauer, as well as an equally strong portrayal by Armin Mueller-Stahl as the ruthless, power-hungry Archduke Redl serves. Winner of the Jury Prize at the Cannes Film Festival. In German with English subtitles.

p, Manfred Durniok, Joszef Marx; d, Istvan Szabo; w, Istvan Szabo, Peter Dobai (based on the play "A Patriot for Me" by John Osborne); ph, Lajos Koltai (Eastmancolor); ed, Zsuzsa Csekany; m, George Schumann, Johann Strauss, Frederic Chopin, Franz Liszt.

Biography/Historical (PR:O MPAA:R)

CONFIDENTIALLY YOURS!***½

(1983, Fr.) 111m Les Films du Carrosse-Films A2-Soprofilms/Spectrafilm bw (VIVEMENT DIMANCHE!; AKA: FINALLY, SUNDAY)

Fanny Ardant *(Barbara Becker)*, Jean-Louis Trintignant *(Julien Vercel)*, Philippe Laudenbach *(M. Clement)*, Caroline Sihol *(Marie-Christine Vercel)*, Philippe Morier-Genoud *(Supt. Santelli)*, Xavier Saint-Macary *(Bertrand Fabre)*, Jean-Pierre Kalfon *(Jacques Massoulier)*, Anik Belaubre *(Cashier)*, Jean-Louis Richard *(Louison)*, Yann Dedet *("Angel Face")*, Nicole Felix *(Scarred Woman)*, Georges Koulouris *(Det. Lablache)*, Roland Thenot *(Officer Jambrau)*, Pierre Gare *(Insp. Poivert)*, Jean-Pierre Kohut-Svelko *(Rowdy Slav)*, Pascale Pellegrin *(Secretarial Candidate)*, Jacques Vidal *(The King)*, Alain Gambin *(Theater Director)*, Pascal Deux *(Santelli's Sidekick)*, Frankie Diago *(Employee at Detective Agency)*, Isabelle Benet, Josiane Couedel *(M. Clement's Secretaries)*, Hilton McConnico *(Prostitute's Client)*, Marie-Aimee Debril, Christine Marmande *(Dog Groomers)*.

Discussing his film PARIS DOES STRANGE THINGS (ELENA ET LES HOMMES), Jean Renoir compared Ingrid Bergman to Venus and said that he "had been dying to make something gay with [her]; [he] wanted to see her smiling and laughing on the screen." One can imagine that Francois Truffaut had a similar thought when he cast Fanny Ardant in CONFIDENTIALLY YOURS. Worthy of comparison to Venus, Ardant is the reason this film exists. Based on the 1962 Charles Williams pulp novel *The Long, Saturday Night*, this final Truffaut film (he died in October 1984) is done in the style of the American *film noir* on which Truffaut was schooled. It's plot is an absurdly complex one, about businessman Julien Varcel (Jean-Louis Trintignant) who is charged with murder. In order to avoid detection, he remains holed up in his office, while Barbara (Ardant), the secretary he has just fired for her insolent behavior, tracks down clues to prove his innocence. The mystery of the film is not the killer's identity—this has never been a concern of Truffaut's—but the more important mystery of love. Barbara becomes an amateur sleuth, not because she cares about the murderer's identity, but because she loves Julien, though neither she nor Julien will initially admit to this. In order to prove her love to him, she must survive an Orphic descent into the seedy criminal underworld of gangsters, murderers, and prostitutes. Twisting the sequence of events that occurred in THE BRIDE WORE BLACK (in which a bride becomes a sleuth), CONFIDENTIALLY YOURS takes a more upbeat approach—the sleuth becomes a bride. CONFIDENTIALLY YOURS is Truffaut's testament of love for Ardant, the love of his later years and the mother of his youngest child. In this respect, Jean-Luc Godard's description of PARIS DOES STRANGE THINGS can certainly be applied to CONFIDENTIALLY YOURS: "It is the most intelligent film in the world." In French with English subtitles.

p, Armand Barbault; d, Francois Truffaut; w, Francois Truffaut, Suzanne Schiffman, Jean Aurel (based on the novel *The Long Saturday Night* by Charles Williams); ph, Nestor Almendros; ed, Martine Barraque; m, Georges Delerue.

Crime/Romance (PR:A-C MPAA:NR)

CONFORMIST, THE*****

(1970, It./Fr.) 110m Mars-Marianne-Maran/PAR c (IL CONFORMISTA)

Jean-Louis Trintignant *(Marcello Clerici)*, Stefania Sandrelli *(Giulia)*, Dominique Sanda *(Anna Quadri)*, Pierre Clementi *(Lino Seminara)*, Gastone Moschin *(Manganiello)*, Enzo Tarascio *(Prof. Quadri)*, Jose Quaglio *(Italo)*, Milly *(Marcello's Mother)*, Giuseppe Addobbati *(Marcello's Father)*, Yvonne Sanson *(Giulia's Mother)*, Fosco Giachetti *(Colonel)*, Benedetto Benedetti *(Minister)*, Gio Vagni Luca *(Secretary)*, Christian Alegny *(Raoul)*, Antonio Maestri *(Priest)*, Christian Belegue *(Gypsy)*, Pasquale Fortunato *(Marcello as a Child)*, Marta Lado *(Marcello's Daughter)*, Pierangelo Givera *(Male Nurse)*, Carlo Gaddi, Franco Pellerani, Claudio Cappelli, Umberto Silvestri *(Hired Killers)*.

Striving for normalcy, Marcello Clerici (Jean-Louis Trintignant) marries the dull, petty bourgeois Giulia (Stefania Sandrelli) and later joins the Italian Fascist movement, accepting an assignment to travel to Paris and assassinate Prof. Quadri (Enzo Tarascio), his former mentor. Before he can kill Quadri, Marcello becomes attracted to Anna (Dominique Sanda), the professor's seductive, lesbian wife, who is actually more interested in Giulia. His affiliation with the Fascists self-destructs, as does his own sexuality: plagued by the memory of a homosexual advance made to him as a child by his chauffeur, Marcello must battle his own desire for conformity. In THE CONFORMIST, Bernardo Bertolucci addresses the duality of man—the issue at the center of his entire body of work, whether it be a sexual conflict ("normalcy" vs. homosexuality/lesbianism/incest) or a political one (Marxism vs. fascism). Marcello Clerici is a man filled with contradictions and dualities, paralleled by those of the Italian government—both Clerici's and Mussolini's decline occurring simultaneously in 1943. Visually, THE CONFORMIST is one of the most stunning works of art ever created, its gliding camerawork, strange camera angles, and rich color (from the eye of Vittorio Storaro) becoming just as decadent and baroque as the bourgeois world into which Clerici is thrust. Bertolucci received an Oscar nomination for Best Adapted Screenplay. Dubbed into English.

p, Maurizio Lodi-Fe; d, Bernardo Bertolucci; w, Bernardo Bertolucci (based on the novel by Alberto Moravia); ph, Vittorio Storaro (Technicolor); ed, Franco Arcalli; m, Georges Delerue.

Political **(PR:C MPAA:R)**

CONTEMPT****

(1963, Fr./It.) 100m Concordia-C.C. Champion-Rome/EM c (LE MEPRIS; IL DISPREZZO)

Brigitte Bardot *(Camille Javal),* Michel Piccoli *(Paul Javal),* Jack Palance *(Jeremy Prokosh),* Fritz Lang *(Himself),* Giorgia Moll *(Francesca Vanini),* Jean-Luc Godard *(Lang's Assistant Director),* Linda Veras *(Siren).*

Paul Javal (Michel Piccoli) is a screenwriter who longs to write for the stage, but his extravagant wife, Camille (Brigitte Bardot), expects more financial rewards than the theater can offer. Paul is approached by crass American film producer Jeremy Prokosh (Jack Palance) to write a screenplay for his version of Homer's *Odyssey*, which is to be directed by the great German director Fritz Lang (playing himself). Paul accepts the job, but Camille is angry at his lack of conviction in the assignment, even though he accepted the job to benefit her. Camille turns to Prokosh, in what is apparently an affair. They take off together for a ride in Prokosh's sports car and meet a violent death under the wheels of a large truck. An adaptation of Alberto Moravia's novel *A Ghost At Noon*, CONTEMPT concerns itself with the art of adapting the novel for the screen. This idea is transferred to Prokosh and Lang's adaptation of the *Odyssey*, as Jean-Luc Godard specifically relates the characters in his film to those in Homer's and Moravia's work: Odysseus, Penelope, and Poseidon, respectively, are representative of Godard; his wife, Anna Karina; and distributor Joseph E. Levine. At the film's conception, Italian producer Carlo Ponti approached Godard about making a film. Godard suggested the Moravia novel with Kim Novak and Frank Sinatra in the leads. Not surprisingly, the pair refused. Ponti then suggested Sophia Loren and Marcello Mastroianni. Godard refused. Eventually Bardot was chosen, a decision welcomed enthusiastically by all involved because of the potential financial rewards the prospect of her flesh would bring. The only nudity, however, is in the film's relatively tame opening scene—Godard's one concession to this expectation. Godard cast himself as Lang's assistant director, clearly putting his philosophy in Lang's mouth and choosing the great German director because "he represents cinema, for which he is both the director and the voice of its conscience. From a more symbolic point of view, however, particularly since he is shooting a film on the *Odyssey*, he is also the voice of the gods, the man who looks at men." Dubbed in English.

p, Georges de Beauregard, Carlo Ponti, Joseph E. Levine; d, Jean-Luc Godard; w, Jean-Luc Godard (based on the novel *Il Disprezzo* by Alberto Moravia); ph, Raoul Coutard (CinemaScope); ed, Agnes Guillemot, Lila Lakshmanan; m, Georges Delerue.

Drama **(PR:C-O MPAA:NR)**

COP AND THE GIRL, THE*

(1985, Aust./W. Ger.) 92m Saskia-Trio-Neue-ZDF c (DER BULLE UND DAS MAEDCHEN)

Jurgen Prochnow *(The Cop),* Annette von Klier *(The Girl),* Franz Buchrieser *(Otto),* Stefan Meinke *(Rokker),* Krystyna Janda *(Gerlinde),* Daniel Olbrychski *(Fritz),* Ulrike Beimpold *(Prostitute),* Rolf Dahne *(Border Guard),* Haymon Maria Buttiger *(Schlager),* Eduard Erne, Klaus Goschl, Paul Wolff-Plotegg, Pavel Landowski.

The title tells the whole story. Jurgen Prochnow, best known for his role in THE BOAT (DAS BOOT), stars as The Cop, a cold, tough, quiet sort who has grown insensitive after years on the streets. During a routine bust of some teenage punks, The Cop meets The Girl (Annette von Klier), a pretty, feline 18-year-old who hangs out with a rough crowd, but, believe it or not, is a virgin. She owes some thug DM 150 and steals The Cop's gun in order to pay off the debt. Naturally, The Cop hunts down The Girl. The usual events follow, rather predictably: there are car chases, he saves her life, she tries to seduce him, he turns a cold shoulder, he starts feeling like a sensitive guy, and the next thing you know . . . The photography is slick (wet streets, blue and red neon signs—no different from your standard beer commercial), but otherwise this is no more than a third-rate action picture with German instead of American police cars. Dubbed into English.

p, Hanns Eckelkamp; d, Peter Keglevic; w, Pia Frolich, Peter Marthesheimer; ph, Edward Klosinski; ed, Susanne Schett, Karin Nowarra; m, Brynmor Jones, Alphaville, George Kranz.

Action/Crime **(PR:C-O MPAA:NR)**

COUP DE GRACE***½

(1976, Ger./Fr.) 96m Argos-Bioskop/Cinema V bw (DER FANGSCHUSS)

Margarethe von Trotta *(Sophie von Reval),* Matthias Habich *(Erich von Lhomond),* Rudiger Kirschstein *(Conrad von Reval),* Mathieu Carriere *(Volkmar von Plessen),* Valeska Gert *(Aunt Praskovia),* Marc Eyraud *(Dr. Paul Rugen),* Frederik Zichy *(Franz von Aland),* Bruno Thost *(Chopin),* Henry van Lyck *(Borschikoff),* Franz Morek.

Set in the Baltic states during the winter of 1919, just after the end of WW I, this historical fiction follows the lives of three aristocrats who, along with their servants and a haunting, heavily made-up old aunt (Valeska Gert), attempt to continue their day-to-day existence despite the bombings and fighting that disrupt their lives. Erich (Matthias Habich) is a Prussian officer who commands a garrison at the aristocratic estate of fellow soldier Konrad (Rudiger Kirchstein). Sophie (Margarethe von Trotta), Konrad's strong and independent sister, also lives there and is in love with the detached Erich, who does not reciprocate her affection, though he does seem to be attracted to Konrad. Despite her love for Erich, Sophie does not share the sympathies of the Prussian officer or of the Allied forces in their determination to crush the Bolshevik cause and execute its supporters. Shot in a cold, wintery black and white, this is an eerie, sometimes dreamlike picture that may be obscure (to most viewers) in its political and historical references, but not in its creation of atmosphere. This was the final professional collaboration for husband-and-wife filmmaking team Volker Schlondorff and von Trotta (who cowrote), both going on to direct films of their own. In German and French with English subtitles.

p, Eberhard Junkersdorf; d, Volker Schlondorff; w, Genevieve Dormann, Margarethe von Trotta, Jutta Bruckner (based on the novel by Marguerite Yourcenar); ph, Igor Luther, Peter Arnold; ed, Jane Sperr, Anette Dorn, Henri Colpi; m, Stanley Myers.

Historical/Political **(PR:C MPAA:NR)**

COUSIN, COUSINE***

(1976, Fr.) 95m Les Films Pomerau-Gaumont/Libra c

Marie-Christine Barrault *(Marthe),* Victor Lanoux *(Ludovic),* Marie-France Pisier *(Karine),* Guy Marchand *(Pascal),* Ginette Garcin *(Biju),* Sybil Maas *(Diane),* Jean Herbert *(Sacy),* Pierre Plessis *(Gobert),* Catherine Verlor *(Nelsa),* Hubert Gignoux *(Thomas),* Francoise Caillaud, Veronique Dancier, Catherine Day, Carine Delamare, Maite Delamare, Emmanuel Dessablet, Alain Douty, Pierre Forget, Anna Gaylor, Etoile Gomez, Marguerite Grimprel, Paul Handford, Marie-Paule Jourdan, Catherine Laborde, Sebastien Lebeaut.

A surprising popular success in the US, COUSIN, COUSINE is what is often described by dilettantes as "quintessentially French," perhaps because it has all those things that one associates with Gallicism (frank sexuality and matter-of-fact adultery, pretty countrysides and city cafes) and that uptight Americans fondly consider charming. Two families gather in celebration of their aging parents' marriage. During the festivities, Marthe (Marie-Christine Barrault) and Ludovic (Victor Lanoux), cousins by marriage, become friendly and agree to see each other more often. As both are sensible, intelligent, married people, they keep emotions in check and decide to have only a platonic relationship. Soon their spouses are assuming the worst, and inevitably the worst happens; by the end, however, all turns out for the best. COUSIN, COUSINE has some genuinely superb scenes, which range in emotion from the sad (the sudden death of one of the elderly newlyweds) to the romantic (a realistic, nonspectacular love scene between Marthe and Ludovic). Much of the film's success comes from the excellent rapport between Barrault and Lanoux in a thoroughly convincing portrayal of the hesitant lovers. Jean-Charles Tacchella, however, undermines his film by directing the scenes of bourgeois scandal as acceptably as possible, thereby creating a perfect wine-and-cheese "art film" guaranteed to offend no one. An Oscar nominee for Best Foreign Film (losing to BLACK AND WHITE IN COLOR), Best Actress, and Best Original Screenplay. The videocassette is dubbed into English.

p, Bertrand Javal; d, Jean-Charles Tacchella; w, Jean-Charles Tacchella, Daniele Thompson; ph, Georges Lendi (Eastmancolor); ed, Agnes Guillemot; m, Gerard Anfosso.

Comedy **(PR:O MPAA:R)**

CRANES ARE FLYING, THE***½

(1957, USSR) 97m Mosfilm/WB bw (LETYAT ZHURAVLI)

Tatyana Samoilova *(Veronica),* Alexei Batalov *(Boris),* Vasily Merkuryev *(Fyador Ivanovich),* Alexander Shvorin *(Mark),* Svetlana Kharitonova *(Irina),* Konstantine Niktin *(Volodya),* Valentine Zubkov *(Stepan),* Alla Bogdanova *(Grandmother).*

Free of much of the party-line propaganda one usually associates with Soviet films of its period, THE CRANES ARE FLYING is an antiwar love story, set during WW II, which centers on the romance between the pretty young Veronica (Tatyana Samoilova) and the sensitive factory worker Boris (Alexei Batalov). Boris, like hordes of other patriotic Soviet men, marches off to war, leaving behind the woman he loves. Veronica is eventually told of his death, but refuses to accept such horrible news. In the following years, she resigns herself to marrying Boris' draft-dodger brother, Fyodor (Vasily Merkuryev), for whom she feels no affection, partially because he raped her during an air raid but primarily because she still loves Boris. The film gained international attention and was one of the first postwar Soviet features to be seen in the West. A beautiful performance is given by the gorgeous Samoilova, the great niece of Stanislavsky and daughter of actor Yevgeni Samoilov. The Cannes Film Festival awarded Samoilova the Golden Palm for her electrifying performance, and named the film as Best Picture. The videocassette is subtitled.

p, Mikhail Kalatozov; d, Mikhail Kalatozov; w, Victor Rozov (based on his play); ph, Sergei Urussevsky; ed, M. Timofeyeva; m, Moisei Vaynberg.

Romance/War **(PR:A MPAA:NR)**

CRIA!****

(1975, Sp.) 110m Elias Querejeta/Jason Allyn c (AKA: THE SECRET OF ANNA)

Geraldine Chaplin *(Ana as an Adult/Her Mother Mariea),* Ana Torrent *(Ana as a Child),* Conchita Perez *(Irene),* Maite Sanchez *(Juana),* Monica Randall *(Paulina),* Florinda Chico *(Rosa),* Hector Alterio *(Anselmo),* German Cobos *(Nicolas Garontes),* Mirta Miller *(Amelia Garontes),* Josefina Diaz *(Abuela).*

A quietly haunting family album, CRIA! follows an upper-class Spanish family, specifically a young child, during the years following the Spanish Civil War. As the film opens, nine-year-old Ana (Ana Torrent) comes downstairs in her nightgown, awakened by the sounds of her father (Hector Alterio) making love. Behind his closed door, he gasps for breath and dies. Hurriedly leaving his room is Amelia (Mirta Miller), the wife of his best friend. This is the second death for Ana, her mother, Maria (Geraldine Chaplin), having died a few years earlier. Maria, however, has not left Ana's imagination and continues in this manner to return to her daughter's side, enabling the young girl to resist the attempts of her friendly but stern aunt Paulina (Monica Randall) to raise her and her sisters. A mesmerizing tale, CRIA! brilliantly weaves the tapestry of time—past and present—into a perfect blend of history. Rather than separate the past from the present, director Carlos Saura layers the two on top of one another. Characters who have died rejoin the living; others, like Ana, exist in any number of generations. Ana is seen not only as a young girl (the brilliant youngster Torrent) and as an adult (Chaplin), but also in the form of Maria (again Chaplin)—all of whom share the same time and space in the film. A remarkable achievement, which both examines the textures of a once-patriarchal family life and draws a parallel to the end of the Franco regime. In Spanish with English subtitles.

p, Carlos Saura; d, Carlos Saura; w, Carlos Saura; ph, Teo Escamilla; ed, Pablo G. del Amo; m, Federico Mompoll.

Drama **(PR:C MPAA:PG)**

CRICKET, THE**

(1979, It.) 90m Nir/Samuel Goldwyn c (LA CICALA)

Anthony Franciosa *(Hannibal Meneghetti),* Virna Lisi *(Wilma [Malinverni] Malen),* Renato Salvatori *(Carbide),* Clio Goldsmith *(Ninetta Leoni, "La Cicada"),* Barbara De Rossi *(Savaria),* Michael Coby, Mario Maranzana, Riccardo Garron, Imelde Marani, Corrado Olmi, Loris Bazoki, Ettore Mattia, Aristide Caporale, Natale Nazzareno.

Wilma (Virna Lisi), an aging showgirl-whore, becomes friends with a La Cicada (Clio Goldsmith, the "gift" of 1982's THE GIFT), a pretty, free-spirited young woman who would die before she would sleep with someone for money. They take to the road and eventually meet up with Hannibal (Anthony Franciosa), a former salesman whose nickname is Ulysses (he was a traveling salesman) and who has dreams of opening a truck stop/banquet hall/hotel/gas station. Wilma and La Cicada become his two catalysts for doing so. Hannibal marries Wilma and the three of them turn the club, named La Cicada, into a financial success. Although Hannibal is married to Wilma and doesn't seem to be interested in anyone else, she must prove his devotion. Wilma is satisfied that he does not desire La Cicada (as a favor to her friend, La Cicada parades around nude in front of Hannibal to test him), but begins to worry when her virginal 18-year-old daughter, Saveria (Barbara De Rossi) comes to stay with them. The mother-daughter relationship soon turns into a battle of whore vs. whore. Directed by the 75-year-old Alberto Lattuada, a one-time adherent of the Neo-Realist movement, THE CRICKET (entomologists may balk at the translation) is little more than titillating, voyeuristic, escapist fare. Despite Lattuada's fascination with the female anatomy (disembodied close-ups, breasts and bottoms bulging out of clothes, nude women frolicking under an Edenesque waterfall), there are enough interesting situations and character complexities to make up for at least part of the offensive chauvinism. The videocasette is dubbed in English.

p, Ibrahim Moussa; d, Alberto Lattuada; w, Alberto Lattuada, Franco Ferrini (based on the novel by Natale Prinetto, Marina D'Aunia); ph, Danilo Desideri, Sergio Montanari; m, Fred Buongusto.

Drama **(PR:O MPAA:NR)**

CRIES AND WHISPERS****

(1972, Swed.) 95m Cinematograph-Swedish Film Institute/NW c (VISKNINGAR OCH ROP)

Ingrid Thulin *(Karin),* Liv Ullmann *(Maria/Her Mother),* Harriet Andersson *(Agnes),* Kari Sylwan *(Anna),* Erland Josephson *(Doctor),* George Arlin *(Karin's Husband),* Henning Moritzen *(Maria's Husband),* Anders Ek *(Pastor),* Linn Ullmann *(Maria's Daughter),* Rosanna Mariano *(Agnes as a Child),* Lena Bergman *(Maria as a Child),* Monika Priede *(Karin as a Child).*

CRIES AND WHISPERS is a relentlessly depressing tale of a young woman who is dying of cancer and being comforted by her two sisters. Karin (Ingrid Thulin) and Maria (Liv Ullmann) return to the family home to be with sister Agnes (Harriet Andersson), who is under the care of Anna (Kari Sylwan), a longtime family retainer. Ingmar Bergman uses his four women metaphorically, as a representation of humanity, to see how they respond to anxiety, death, and what appears to be a wrathful rather than benevolent God. Karin is on the brink of suicide and, we learn, once mutilated her own genitalia rather than consummate her marriage; Maria is far earthier, and once had an affair that caused her husband to attempt suicide. Anna is the glue that holds these Chekhovian sisters together. She can accept God's will, and imparts her fatalism to Agnes. Anna lost a child early in life and understands what death is—neither hard nor bad, just a new voyage. Agnes, who is in terrible pain, cannot fully accept this; still, she is much closer to the housekeeper than she is to her sisters. There are many wordless moments in the film, and the silence is more eloquent than anything that might have been said. Bergman and cinematographer Sven Nykvist move the camera with remarkable fluidity, with the beauty of the photography in odd opposition to the almost unbearably stark subject matter. Nykvist's work took an Oscar, and Bergman was nominated as Best Writer and Best Director, with the movie also securing a nomination. Dubbed into English, as the video packaging assures us, by the actors and under the direction of the director.

p, Ingmar Bergman; d, Ingmar Bergman; w, Ingmar Bergman; ph, Sven Nykvist (Eastmancolor); ed, Siv Lundgren; m, Frederic Chopin, Johann Sebastian Bach.

Drama **(PR:C MPAA:R)**

CRIME OF MONSIEUR LANGE, THE****

(1936, Fr.) 90m Oberon-Brandon bw (LE CRIME DE M. LANGE)

Rene Lefevre *(Mon. Amedee Lange),* Florelle *(Valentine),* Henri Guisol *(Meunier),* Marcel Levesque *(Bessard),* Odette Talazac *(Mme. Bessard),* Maurice Baquet *(Charles Bessard),* Nadia Sibirskaia *(Estelle),* Jules Berry *(Batala),* Sylvia Bataille *(Edith),* Marcel Duhamel, Guy Decomble, Jean Daste, Paul Grimault *(Printers),* Jacques Brunius *(Baigneur),* Sylvain Itkine *(Retired Police Inspector),* Edmond Beauchamp *(Priest on Train),* Rene Genin *(Customer in Cafe).*

Mon. Amedee Lange (Rene Lefevre) is a meek author of French novels about the American West whose avaricious boss, Batala (Jules Berry) cheats him out of his earnings. Batala embezzles the company funds, flees, and is later reported dead in a train wreck. The employees of the publishing house are overjoyed and form a cooperative that achieves great success with Lange's "Arizona Jim" series. Lange falls in love with a woman from a neighboring laundry, but then Batala returns (he survived the wreck and took the clothes of a priest) and demands a share in the company's newfound prosperity. Lange decides to kill the villain. One of Jean Renoir's best films, THE CRIME OF MONSIEUR LANGE is also one of the most obvious examples of his Front Populaire (Popular Front) period of filmmaking—reflecting the social politics of its day and the belief that a collective could effectively overthrow a tyranny. This wonderfully entertaining and sharply scripted film is hampered by its poor sound quality, a result of Renoir's meager production budget. In French with English subtitles.

p, Andre Halley des Fontaines; d, Jean Renoir; w, Jean Castanier, Jean Renoir, Jacques Prevert (based on a story by Jean Castanier and Jean Renoir); ph, Jean Bachelet; ed, Marguerite Renoir; m, Jean Wiener.

Comedy/Drama **(PR:C-O MPAA:NR)**

CRIMINAL LIFE OF ARCHIBALDO DE LA CRUZ, THE*****

(1955, Mex.) 91m Alianza Cinematografica/Dan Talbot bw (ENSAYO DE UN CRIMEN; AKA: REHEARSAL FOR A CRIME)

Ernesto Alonso *(Archibaldo de la Cruz),* Miroslava Stern *(Lavinia),* Rita Macedo *(Patricia),* Ariadna Walter *(Carlota),* Rodolfo Landa *(Alejandro),* Andres Palma *(Cervantes),* Carlos Riquelme *(Chief of Police),* Jose Maria Linares Rivas *(Willy),* Leonor Llansas *(Governess),* Eva Calvo *(Mother),* Carlos Martinez Baena, Roberto Meyer.

This is one of Luis Bunuel's great achievements—a simple, graceful, and comic look at a man's tormented fantasy life. As a child, Archibaldo de la Cruz is emotionally scarred for life when his nanny is killed by a stray bullet after he has wished her death upon a music box he believes to be magical. As she dies, the guilt-stricken boy catches a glimpse of her exposed thigh. He goes through life believing that his murderous impulses and his sexual desires are interrelated. Every time he tries to kill a woman, however, she ends up dying (either accidentally or criminally) before he can take credit. The result is a perfectly realized story of passion, eroticism, violence, fantasy, guilt, and confession—the most important themes in Bunuel's career. Rarely has Bunuel's humor been as wicked and simultaneously touching as in this film. It also contains one of Bunuel's most memorable images: that of Archibaldo (Ernesto Alonso) burning a wax mannequin modeled after the woman he desires. When the frustrated Archibaldo misses his chance to kill the woman, he has no other choice but to burn her likeness in his pottery kiln—the wax image coming to a horrible melting life. In Spanish with English subtitles.

p, Alfonso Patino Gomez; d, Luis Bunuel; w, Luis Bunuel, Eduardo Ugarte Pages (based on a story by Rodolfo Usigli); ph, Augustin Jimenez; ed, Jorge Bustos; m, Jorge Perez.

Comedy/Drama **(PR:O MPAA:NR)**

D

DAMNED, THE****

(1969, It./Ger.) 155m Pegaso-Praesidens-Eichberg/WB-Seven Arts c (LA CADUTA DEGLI DEI; GOTTERDAMMERUNG)

Dirk Bogarde *(Friedrich Bruckmann),* Ingrid Thulin *(Baroness Sophie von Essenbeck),* Helmut Griem *(Aschenbach),* Helmut Berger *(Martin von Essenbeck),* Renaud Verley *(Gunther von Essenbeck),* Umberto Orsini, Rene Kolldehoff *(Baron Konstantin von Essenbeck),* Albrecht Schoenhals *(Baron Joachim von Essenbeck),* Charlotte Rampling *(Elisabeth Thallman),* Florinda Bolkan *(Olga),* Nora Ricci *(Governess),* Wolfgang Hillinger *(Yanek),* Bill Vanders *(Commissar),* Irina Vanka *(Lisa Keller),* Karin Mittendorf *(Thilde Thallman),* Howard Nelson Rubien *(Rector),* Warner Hasselmann *(Gestapo Officer),* Peter Dane *(Steel Worker),* Mark Salvage *(Police Inspector),* Karl Otto Alberty, John Frederick, Richard Beach *(Army Officers).*

Luchino Visconti's epic of decadence, set in Germany during the years 1933 and 1934, parallels a family of industrialists' decline with the rise of Nazism. The film opens with an extravagant dinner in celebration of the retirement of the family patriarch, Baron Joachim von Essenbeck (Albrecht Schoenhals), the magnate of a huge steel enterprise, and his appointment of an outsider, Friedrich Bruckmann (Dirk Bogarde) as temporary head. All seems very respectable and bourgeois, but the gathering turns strange when Joachim's grandson Martin (Helmut Berger) delivers his rendition of Marlene Dietrich's "Falling in Love Again" dressed in drag. Before the party is over, it is announced that the Reichstag has been burned, symbolizing the sabotage of German democracy. Later, as the highly organized SS plots to annihilate the SA (the populist fascist front), Martin, a bisexual, sadistic, pedophilic drug addict (who even rapes his own mother), engineers his plot to stop a takeover attempt by Friedrich and Sophie (Ingrid Thulin), Friedrich's lover and Martin's mother. THE DAMNED is Visconti at his most operatic (the German title is GOTTERDAMMERUNG, after Wagner), containing baroque sets and costumes, highly melodramatic acting, and orgiastic scenes of violence and sex. While it has been criticized on a number of levels (the equating of perverts and pedophiles with fascists has been done before, its English dialog is often poor, it indulges in its own distastefulness, it is too long, etc.), THE DAMNED is a spectacular, meticulously crafted film that cannot fail to elicit a response, whether disgust or appreciation, from an audience. In English.

p, Alfredo Levy, Ever Haggiag; d, Luchino Visconti; w, Luchino Visconti, Nicola Badalucco, Enrico Medioli; ph, Armando Nannuzzi, Pasquale De Santis; ed, Ruggero Mastroianni; m, Maurice Jarre.

Drama **(PR:O MPAA:X)**

DANGEROUS MOVES*½**

(1984, Switz.) 95m Arthur Cohn/Spectrafilm c (LA DIAGONALE DU FOU)

Michel Piccoli *(Akiva Liebskind),* Alexandre Arbatt *(Pavius Fromm),* Leslie Caron *(Henia Liebskind),* Liv Ullmann *(Marina),* Daniel Olbrychski *(Tac-Tac),* Michel Aumont *(Kerossian),* Serge Avedikian *(Fadenko),* Pierre Michael *(Yachvili),* Pierre Vial *(Anton Heller),* Wojtek Pszoniak *(Felton),* Jean-Hugues Anglade *(Miller),* Hubert Saint-Macary *(Foldes),* Bernhard Wicki *(Puhl),* Benoit Regent *(Barrabal),* Jacques Boudet *(Stuffli),* Jean-Paul Eydoux *(Carsen),* Albert Simono *(Dalcroze).*

This ingenious thriller takes place in the world of chess championships, using the politically neutral Geneva, Switzerland, as its backdrop. The reigning world chess champion, Akiva Liebskind (a bearded Michel Piccoli), is the pride of the Soviet Union, but his weak heart may mean the end of his reign. His competitor is Pavius Fromm (Alexandre Arbatt), a rebellious young Soviet exile. As the championship begins, Fromm attempts to disrupt the proceedings, and thereby Liebskind's concentration, by arriving late for his first move. His habitual tardiness and basic contempt for regulations force Liebskind to register a formal complaint with the jury. When Liebskind threatens to withdraw, Fromm buckles under and writes a formal apology rather than lose his chance to defeat the champion. As a result of their moves away from the chessboard, both men begin to deteriorate—Liebskind physically, Fromm mentally. The chess masters, however, are merely pawns in a larger political game involving the Soviet government and the West. Richard Dembo, in his debut feature, has managed to contrast skillfully the players' maneuvers with political power plays, yet avoids pretension. Rather than concentrating too much on the chess matches themselves (a knowledge of chess is helpful in viewing DANGEROUS MOVES, but by no means a requirement), Dembo brings to the screen an emotional battle between two powerful personalities—Liebskind, who refuses to be beaten, and Fromm, who refuses to lose. He also receives support from a solid who's who of European film, including actors Liv Ullmann, Leslie Caron, Bernhard Wicki, Daniel Olbrychski, Jean-Hugues Anglade; cameraman Raoul Coutard; and editor Agnes Guillemot. Named Best Foreign Film at the 1985 Academy Awards celebration. Available in a French-language version with English subtitles and in a dubbed version.

p, Arthur Cohn; d, Richard Dembo; w, Richard Dembo; ph, Raoul Coutard; ed, Agnes Guillemot; m, Gabriel Yared.

Thriller **(PR:C MPAA:NR)**

DANTON****

(1983, Fr./Pol.) 136m Gaumont-TF1-SFPC-Film Polski-Losange/Triumph c

Gerard Depardieu *(Georges Danton),* Wojciech Pszoniak *(Maximillian Robespierre),* Patrice Chereau *(Camille Desmoulins),* Angela Winkler *(Lucile Desmoulins),* Boguslaw Linda *(Saint Just),* Roland Blanche *(Lacroix),* Anne Alvaro *(Eleonore Duplay),* Roger Planchon *(Fouquier Tinville),* Serge Merlin *(Philippeaux),* Lucien Melki *(Fabre d'Eglantine),* Andrzej Seweryn *(Bourdon),* Franciszek Starowieyski *(David),* Emmanuelle Debever *(Louison Danton),* Jerzy Trela *(Billaud-Varenne),* Tadeusz Huk *(Couthon),* Jacques Villeret *(Westermann),* Krzysztof Globisz *(Amar),* Ronald Guttman *(Herman),* Gerard Hardy *(Tallien),* Stephane Jobert *(Panis),* Marian Kociniak *(Lindet),* Marek Kondrat *(Barere De Vieuzad),* Alain Mace *(Heron),* Bernard Maitre *(Legendre).*

This powerful drama of revolution is set in France 1794, during the second year of the *Republique*, and centers on the rivalry between the humanist Georges Danton (Gerard Depardieu) and "The Incorruptable" idealogue Maximillian de Robespierre (Wojciech Pszoniak). After temporarily retiring from politics and retreating to the countryside, Danton, the most popular of French revolutionaries, returns to Paris to stop the Reign of Terror led by Robespierre, his former compatriot in the Revolution whose efforts to keep the "pure patriots" in power have turned tyrannical. Although once a great freedom fighter and proponent of political, religious, and human rights, Robespierre and his Committee of Public Safety have become just as oppressive as the monarchs they overthrew. Despite the fact that Danton is a people's hero, Robespierre convinces himself that Danton, who hopes for an end to the bloodshed, must be executed in order to save the *Republique*. A stirring film of freedom made by Andrzej Wajda in his first directorial effort outside of Poland, DANTON is set in the eye of a hurricane. Although it has been criticized for being too static and theatrical, this is because the film takes care to show only the center of the Revolution—the battle between Danton and Robespierre, the unseen fight for freedom that takes place behind closed doors. Wajda avoids depicting the Revolution as it takes place in the streets and instead shows us the power that exists in the hands of government—those chosen few supposed to be the representatives of the people. In French with English subtitles.

p, Margaret Menegoz; d, Andrzej Wajda; w, Jean-Claude Carriere, Andrzej Wajda, Agnieszka Holland, Boleslaw Michalek, Jacek Gasiorowski (based on the play ""The Danton Affair" by Stanislawa Przybyszewska); ph, Igor Luther; ed, Halina Prugar-Ketling; m, Jean Prodromides.

Historical/Biography **(PR:O MPAA:PG)**

DARK EYES*½**

(1987, It.) 118m Excelsior-TV-RAI 1/Island c (OCI CIORNIE)

Marcello Mastroianni *(Romano),* Silvana Mangano *(Elisa),* Marthe Keller *(Tina),* Elena Sofonova *(Anna Sergeyevna),* Vsevolod Larionov *(Pavel),* Innokenti Smoktunovsky

(Governor of Sisoiev), Pina Cei *(Elisa's Mother),* Roberto Herlitzka *(Lawyer),* Dimitri Zolothukin *(Konstantin),* Paolo Baroni, Oleg Tabakov.

It is a special occurrence in film when an actor can capture an audience as Marcello Mastroianni does in DARK EYES, a film of such warmth, melancholy, tragedy, and beauty that one does not want it to end. Directed by Russian Nikita Mikhalkov (his first film outside the USSR), the film represents a union between a Soviet and Italian cast and crew, bringing a new, cross-cultural interpretation to the Chekhov stories upon which the film is based. Set at the turn of the century, the film stars Mastroianni as Romano, a paunchy, alcoholic waiter who works in the dining room of a cruise ship. While voyaging from Greece to Italy, he meets Pavel (Vsevolod Larionov), a jovial Russian on his honeymoon with his much younger Russian wife. Romano begins to reminisce to Pavel, and the film moves into flashback: as a young architecture student, Romano falls in love with Elisa (Silvana Mangano), a wealthy heiress, despite the objections of her high-society family. He eventually leaves her and retreats to a lavish health spa, where, as if he were a resident of heaven, Romano lives a relaxed life. He finds willing young ladies to sleep with, pulls an occasional practical joke, watches old women racing through the marble-columned grounds in their wheelchairs, wanders through the beautifully manicured lawns, and eats extravagant meals. At the spa he meets Anna Sergeyevna (Elena Sofonova), a timid, lovely, easily embarrassed young Russian woman with dark eyes and a lapdog. Mesmerized by her very presence and the magical sparkle of her hat pin, Romano becomes obsessed with Anna. As superb as Mastroianni is (he won the Best Actor prize at the Cannes Film Festival for his work here), it is not his performance alone that makes DARK EYES so enjoyable; there is also the discovery (for Western audiences) of the lovely Sofonova, a Soviet actress whose combination of fragility and strength is reminiscent of Audrey Hepburn. In Italian with English subtitles.

p, Silvia D'Amico Bendico, Carlo Cucchi; d, Nikita Mikhalkov; w, Alexander Adabachian, Nikita Mikhalkov, Suso Cecchi D'Amico (based on material from the Anton Chekhov stories "The Lady With the Little Dog," "The Name-Day Party," "Anna Around the Neck," "My Wife"); ph, Franco di Giacomo (Eastmancolor); ed, Enzo Meniconi; m, Francis Lai.

Romance/Comedy (PR:A-C MPAA:NR)

DAVID***

(1979, Ger.) 125m Pro-ject-FFAT-ZDF-Filmverlag-Dedra/Kino c

Walter Taub *(Rabbi Singer),* Irena Vrkljan *(Wife),* Eva Mattes *(Toni),* Mario Fischel *(David),* Dominique Horwitz *(Leo),* Torsten Henties *(David as Child),* Rudolph Sellner *(Krell).*

Coming on the heels of the American television mini-series "Holocaust," Peter Lilienthal's German-made entry focuses on the plight of David (Mario Fische), a teenage Jewish boy whose family is caught in the midst of the Nazi atrocities. His rabbi father (Czech actor Walter Taub) sees his synagogue burned down by the Nazis, who add the desecration of carving a swastika on the top of his bald head. After the family is forced to pay a shoemaker to hide their daughter (Eva Mattes) in his shop, David separates from them, hides out, makes money doing odd jobs, and eventually is able to escape to Israel. This powerful film from Lilienthal is of interest to American audiences chiefly because of its German origin. Lilienthal, a German Jew, is part of a generation of German filmmakers that, having been children during the war years, is not afraid to look back at the inhumanity of the previous generation. Although DAVID is relatively unknown in America, it received a measure of success in being named the best film of the 1979 Berlin Film Festival, beating out such better-known German pictures as Werner Herzog's NOSFERATU and Rainer Werner Fassbinder's THE MARRIAGE OF MARIA BRAUN. In German with English subtitles.

p, Joachim von Vietinghoff; d, Peter Lilienthal; w, Peter Lilienthal, Jurek Becker, Ulla Zieman (based on the novel by Joel Konig); ph, Al Ruban (Eastmancolor); ed, Siegrun Jager; m, Wojciech Kilar.

Drama (PR:C MPAA:NR)

DAY FOR NIGHT*****

(1973, Fr.) 115m PECF-PIC/WB c (LA NUIT AMERICAINE)

Francois Truffaut *(Ferrand),* Jacqueline Bissett *(Julie Baker-Nelson/Pamela),* Jean-Pierre Leaud *(Alphonse),* Valentina Cortese *(Severine),* Jean-Pierre Aumont *(Alexandre),* Dani *(Lilianna),* Alexandra Stewart *(Stacey),* Jean Champion *(Bertrand),* Nathalie Baye *(Joelle),* Bernard Menez *(Bernar),* Jean-Francois Stevenin *(1st Assistant Director),* Nike Arrighi *(Make-up Girl),* Gaston Joly *(Assistant Director),* David Markham *(Dr. Nelson),* Zenaide Rossi *(Assistant Director's Wife),* Maurice Seveno *(TV Reporter),* Zenaide Rossi *(Mme. Lajoie),* Christophe Vesque *(Boy with Cane in Dream),* Henry Graham [Graham Greene] *(English Insurance Broker),* Marcel Berbert *(French Insurance Broker).*

Quite simply, this is the best film ever made about the process of shooting a film—those few weeks in which technical personnel, cast members, lovers, and friends come together suddenly, then part just as suddenly. Francois Truffaut, the most reverent of filmmakers, plays the character he knows best—the film director. The first time we see Ferrand (Truffaut) he is in the midst of directing "I Want You to Meet Pamela," a French film shot in the La Victorine studios in the south of France. His cast includes a temperamental actor, Alphonse (Jean-Pierre Leaud), who wonders aloud, "Are women magic?"; Julie (Jacqueline Bisset), a famous actress recovering from a nervous breakdown; Alexandre (Jean-Pierre Aumont), a veteran actor, "continental lover," and closet homosexual; Severine (Valentina Cortese), a loud, alcoholic Italian actress who once was a great screen lover opposite Alexandre but who now cannot remember even the simplest dialog; and Stacey (Alexandra Stewart), a bit player whose pregnancy causes terrible scheduling problems. Given equal time is

Ferrand's crew—bumbling prop man Bernard (Bernard Menez); flaky makeup girl Odile (Nike Arrighi); script girl Lilianna (Dani), who cares nothing for film and gets the job only because she sleeps with Alphonse; unit manager Lajoie (Gaston Joly); producer Bertrand (Jean Champion); and the all-important production assistant, Joelle (Nathalie Baye). As one might expect, the characters themselves are more important than the thin plot—Ferrand trying to keep his production on track when his emotionally unstable leads, Alphonse and Julie, make the mistake of sleeping together for just one night. DAY FOR NIGHT provides all the needed proof that what goes on behind the screen is often of more interest than the film itself. It is a magical film, of awe-inspiring love and devotion, in which Truffaut reveals his world in a touching, comic, poetic manner. Paradoxically, however, it is one of Truffaut's least personal films, as he hides behind his alter ego Ferrand and interacts only on the most superficial levels with his cast and crew—by the film's end, it is Ferrand whom we know least. Dubbed into English.

p, Marcel Berbert; d, Francois Truffaut; w, Francois Truffaut, Suzanne Schiffman, Jean-Louis Richard; ph, Pierre-William Glenn (Eastmancolor, Panavision); ed, Yann Dedet, Martine Barraque; m, Georges Delerue.

Drama **(PR:A-C MPAA:PG)**

DAY OF WRATH****

(1943, Den.) 97m Palladium/Brandon bw (VREDENS DAG)

Thirkild Roose *(Absalon Pedersson),* Lisbeth Movin *(His Wife),* Sigrid Neiiendam *(His Mother),* Preben Lerdorff *(His Son by His First Marriage),* Albert Hoeberg *(The Bishop),* Olaf Ussing *(Laurentius),* Anna Svierkier *(Herlofs Marte).*

DAY OF WRATH was the first feature film directed by the great Danish director Carl Dreyer after his 1932 masterwork VAMPYR. In DAY OF WRATH, Dreyer returns to familiar territory—that of the witches, religion, and spiritualism that marked his earlier, silent masterpiece, THE PASSION OF JOAN OF ARC (1928). Set during the throes of a witch hunt in the 17th century, the film centers around a young woman, Anne (Lisbeth Movin), who is married to a much older, puritanical man she hates. She falls in love with his son, with whom she spends idyllic afternoons in the woods. Pressure begins to build, and she is heard to whisper aloud how she hungers for the death of her husband; soon afterwards, the husband dies, and she is accused of being a witch. The plot is deceptively simple and is barely representative of the film's power, for the film's brilliance lies not in its story but in Dreyer's direction. At a slow and deliberate pace, he allows the camera to linger, almost erotically, on images, waiting for the "right" look on a face or the correct movement of a hand. A study of good and evil, repression and oppression, sexuality and guilt, DAY OF WRATH is a truly spiritual film. In Danish with English subtitles.

p, Carl Theodor Dreyer; d, Carl Theodor Dreyer; w, Carl Theodor Dreyer, Poul Knudsen, Mogens Skot-Hansen (based on the novel by Wiers Jenssens); ph, Carl Anderson; ed, Edith Schlussel, Anne Marie Petersen; m, Poul Schierbeck.

Drama **(PR:C MPAA:NR)**

DEATH IN VENICE****

(1971, It./Fr.) 130m Alfa-Production Editions-Cinematographiques Francaises/WB c (MORTE A VENEZIA; MORT A VENISE)

Dirk Bogarde *(Gustav Von Aschenbach),* Bjorn Andresen *(Tadzio),* Silvana Mangano *(Tadzio's Mother),* Marisa Berenson *(Frau Von Aschenbach),* Mark Burns *(Alfred),* Romolo Valli *(Hotel Manager),* Nora Ricci *(Governess),* Carol Andre *(Esmeralda),* Masha Predit *(Singer),* Leslie French *(Travel Agent),* Franco Fabrizi *(Barber),* Sergio Garfagnoli *(Polish Youth),* Luigi Battaglia *(Scapegrace),* Ciro Cristofoletti *(Hotel Clerk),* Dominique Darel *(English Tourist).*

Luchino Visconti's powerful and controversial screen adaptation of Thomas Mann's novella stars Dirk Bogarde as Gustav von Aschenbach, an aging German composer (modeled after Gustav Mahler) who visits Venice while on the verge of a physical and mental breakdown. Plagued by fears that he can no longer feel emotion because he has been avoiding it for so long, he is unfazed by the boorish and obnoxious behavior of the bourgeois creatures around him. Then suddenly he sees a beautiful, blond boy named Tadzio (Bjorn Andresen), who is traveling with his mother and sisters. Gustav becomes obsessed with Tadzio and the ideal of classic beauty he represents. The boy is the most beautiful thing he has seen in his life, stirring feelings within him he thought he had lost. He seeks out the boy, but refrains from making contact with him; he just watches as the boy wanders through the dank, decaying city. Bogarde is superb as the dying composer who has one last rush of beauty and emotion in his life before he decays completely, like the cholera-infected Venice of 1911. The cinematography is beautiful, and, combined with Ferdinando Scarfiotti's art direction, yields a powerful remembrance of time and place past. Visconti also makes brilliant use of Mahler's Third and Fifth symphonies. The music haunts every frame of the film, as do the quiet whispers of sound that help create the film's almost unreal environment. The frailty of the soundtrack perfectly parallels Aschenbach's last days and his obsession with the face of the stunningly beautiful Tadzio. DEATH IN VENICE was met with almost universal disapproval and misunderstanding when it was first released, but despite its faults (the omissions from Mann's text, dependence on flashbacks, and overwrought arguments about art and music between Aschenbach and a colleague) it remains a film of great beauty. The videocassette is in English, with some characters dubbed.

p, Luchino Visconti; d, Luchino Visconti; w, Luchino Visconti, Nicola Badalucco (based on the novel by Thomas Mann); ph, Pasquale De Santis (Panavision, Technicolor); ed, Ruggero Mastroianni; m, Gustav Mahler, Ludwig van Beethoven, Modest Petrovich Mussorgsky.

Drama **(PR:C MPAA:GP)**

DEATHWATCH*½**

(1979, Fr./Ger.) 128m Selta-Little Bear-Sara-Gaumont-Antenne 2-SFP/Quartet c (LA MORT EN DIRECT)

Romy Schneider *(Katherine Mortenhoe),* Harvey Keitel *(Roddy),* Harry Dean Stanton *(Vincent Ferriman),* Therese Liotard *(Tracey),* Max von Sydow *(Gerald Mortenhoe),* Bernhard Wicki, Caroline Langrise, William Russell.

For followers of Bertrand Tavernier who know the director only through A SUNDAY IN THE COUNTRY or ROUND MIDNIGHT, the very realistic science-fiction film DEATH WATCH may come as a surprise. Set in Glasgow, the film takes place in a not-too-distant future when nearly all diseases have been conquered by medical science, leaving natural causes as society's prime killer. Katherine (Romy Schneider) is an independent, sensitive, and beautiful woman who has contracted a terminal disease; Vincent Ferriman (Harry Dean Stanton) is a crass television producer who finds her imminent demise perfect entertainment for a society that can't get enough of death; and Roddy (Harvey Keitel) is an employee who has had a video camera implanted in his head, sending everything he sees back to the TV station for editing and broadcast. As Roddy follows Katherine through the countryside, in effect shooting a narrative film, he finds himself becoming attracted to her. More than just a simple attack on electronic information in a modern technological society, DEATHWATCH (which could be read as Tavernier's PEEPING TOM) also addresses the issue of the objectification of women and depersonalization of death via the (implicitly male-oriented) media. The film is in English.

p, Gabriel Boustiani, Janine Rubeiz; d, Bertrand Tavernier; w, David Rayfiel, Bertrand Tavernier (based on the novel *The Continuous Katherine Mortenhoe* by David Compton); ph, Pierre-William Glenn (Panavision, Fujicolor); ed, Armand Psenny, Michael Ellis; m, Antoine Duhamel.

Science Fiction **(PR:O MPAA:R)**

DECLINE OF THE AMERICAN EMPIRE, THE*½**

(1986, Can.) 101m Malo-Natl. Film Board of Canada-Telefilm Canada-La Societe Generale Du Cinema Du Quebec/Cineplex Odeon c (LE DECLIN DE L'EMPIRE AMERICAIN)

Pierre Curzi *(Pierre),* Remy Girard *(Remy),* Yves Jacques *(Claude),* Daniel Briere *(Alain),* Dominique Michel *(Dominique),* Louise Portal *(Diane),* Dorothee Berryman *(Louise),* Genevieve Rioux *(Danielle),* Gabriel Arcand *(Mario).*

Four men swap stories of their sexual escapades while preparing an elaborate dinner; four women do the same while working out in a gym, and when the two groups come together, mutual betrayals come to light and shatter some illusions. On the surface, this is all that happens in this fine film, one of the most successful Canadian exports ever, but the sparkling wit of the dialog and the acutely observed jabs at the current preoccupation with sex distinguish THE DECLINE OF THE AMERICAN EMPIRE. The film's philosophy could best be summed up by a line uttered by one of the men: "Love—the kind that makes your heart race—lasts two years at best, then the compromises begin." Perhaps the most valid criticism of the film is that its questions are too easy, its answers too pat, and its characters too similar. On the other hand, the ensemble performance is impeccable, the technical credits flawless, and the whole thing quite enjoyable. Nominated for 13 Genies (Canada's equivalent of the Oscar), it won eight, including Best Picture, Best Director, Best Supporting Actor and Actress (Gabriel Arcand and Louise Portal). It was also nominated for an Academy Award for Best Foreign-Language Film. In French with English subtitles.

p, Rene Malo, Roger Frappier; d, Denys Arcand; w, Denys Arcand; ph, Guy Dufaux; ed, Monique Fortier; m, Francois Dompierre (from themes by George Frederick Handel).

Drama **(PR:O MPAA:R)**

DERSU UZALA***

(1975, Jap./USSR) 137m Toho-Mosfilm/Sovexport c (DERUSU USARA)

Maxim Munzuk *(Dersu Uzala),* Yuri Solomine *(Capt. Vladimir Arseniev),* Schemeikl Chokmorov *(Jan Bao),* Vladimir Klemena *(Turtwigin),* Svetlana Danielchanka *(Mrs. Arseniev).*

Capt. Arseniev (Yuri Solomine), leading a topographic expedition deep into the wilds of 19th-century Siberia, meets an old woodsman, Dersu Uzala (Maxim Munzuk), who shows him the ways of nature. The two men become close friends over a number of expeditions in which Dersu Uzala acts as guide. Each time, Arseniev tries to convince the hardy but aging Siberian to return to the city with him; each time, the latter refuses. Finally Dersu Uzala does go to the city, but finds he cannot readily adapt. Akira Kurosawa filmed in the USSR with an all-Soviet cast, the sole Japanese collaborator being cinematographer Asakadru Nakai, who photographed the film in 70mm. The first half of is wonderful, full of reverence for nature and the man who lives in it, but as the film goes on it becomes increasingly obvious, literal, and rather ponderous. What faults one may find, however, cannot detract from DERSU UZALA's magnificence. It is a picture, like so much of Kurosawa's work, of great humanism and respect. Best Foreign Film of the 1975 Academy Awards. In Russian with English subtitles.

p, Nikolai Sizov, Yoichi Matsue; d, Akira Kurosawa; w, Akira Kurosawa, Yuri Nagibin (based on the journals of Vladimir Arseniev); ph, Asakazu Nakai, Yuri Gantman, Fyodor Dobronavov; m, Isaac Schwalz.

Adventure **(PR:A MPAA:NR)**

DESPAIR***

(1977, Ger.) 119m Bavaria Atelier-SFP-Geria/Swan c

Dirk Bogarde *(Hermann Herman),* Andrea Ferreol *(Lydia Herman),* Volker Spengler *(Ardalion),* Klaus Lowitsch *(Felix Weber),* Alexander Allerson *(Mayer),* Bernhard Wicki *(Orlovius),* Peter Kern *(Muller),* Gottfried John *(Perebrodov),* Roger Fritz *(Inspector Braun),* Adrian Hoven *(Inspector Schelling),* Hark Bohm *(Doctor),* Voli Geiler

(Madam), Hans Zander *(Muller's Brother),* Y Sa Lo *(Elsie),* Liselotte Eder *(Secretary).*

Said the director of this film: "The reason I made DESPAIR comes from the awareness that in everyone's life there comes a point where not only the mind but the body, too, understands that it's over. I want to go on with my life, but there will be no new feelings or experiences for me. At this point people start to rearrange their lives." Set in Berlin in the 1930s, DESPAIR stars Dirk Bogarde as the Nabokovian Russian emigree Hermann Herman, an owner of a chocolate factory who is unhappy with the sameness of his life. Hoping to escape the trap of his dull existence and the advent of the Nazis, Hermann Herman flees from himself: one day, on a business trip, he meets a man who he is convinced is his double (though he looks nothing like him) and decides to exchange identities. Not only is DESPAIR Fassbinder's first English-language film, but it marks the first time he worked from another's screenplay—his collaboration with Tom Stoppard diminishing Fassbinder's usual aggressive style of filmmaking. Fassbinder has been criticized for his decision not to cast Bogarde in a dual role as Hermann Herman; instead, it is obvious from the start that the doppelganger exists only in Hermann's head, whereas Nabokov's novel obscures this fact until the end. Although Fassbinder's decision does cause confusion for the viewer, it is the move of a brave and intelligent director—forcing a distance between audience and story, and eliminating the otherwise inevitable shocker ending. While DESPAIR may not sound quite like a Fassbinder film, it is beautifully photographed by Michael Ballhaus in a frame filled with reflective glass and mirrors. The film is in English.

p, Peter Marthesheimer; d, Rainer Werner Fassbinder; w, Tom Stoppard (based on a novel by Vladimir Nabokov); ph, Michael Ballhaus (Eastmancolor); ed, Juliane Lorenz, Franz Walsch; m, Peer Raben.

Drama **(PR:O MPAA:NR)**

DESTINY****

(1921, Ger.) 114m Decla-Bioscop/Artclass bw (DER MUDE TOD: EIN DEUTSCHES VOLKSLIED IN 6 VERSEN; AKA: BETWEEN TWO WORLDS; BEYOND THE WALL; THE THREE LIGHTS; THE LIGHT WITHIN)

Lil Dagover *(Young Woman/Zobeida/Fiametta/Tiaotsien),* Bernhard Goetzke *(Death/El Mot/Archer),* Walter Janssen *(Young Man/Frank/Giovanfrancesco/Liang),* Rudolphe Klein-Rogge *(Dervish/Girolamo),* Georg John *(Beggar/Magician),* Eduard von Winterstein *(Caliph),* Max Adalbert *(Lawyer),* Paul Biensfeldt *(A Hi, Magician),* Karl Huszar *(Emperor),* Erika Unruh *(Aisha),* Lothar Muthel *(Confidant),* Hermann Picha *(Tailor),* Erik Pabst *(Teacher),* Hans Sternberg *(Mayor)*ACT Carl Ruckert *(Vicar),* Paul Rehkopf *(Sexton),* Edgar Klitzsch *(Doctor),* Marie Wismar *(Old Woman),* Aloisha Lehnert *(Mother),* Lewis Brody *(Moor).*

DESTINY is a dark and beautiful allegory of death and romance in which a young woman (Lil Dagover) tries to save her lover (Walter Janssen) from the hands of Death (Bernhard Goetzke). Weary of all his killing, Death agrees to spare the woman's lover if she can find someone to take his place. The visit to Death in his cathedral, which is decorated with a forest of thousands of flickering candles (each representing a lifespan), is intercut with the stories of three of these lights, or destinies. Set, respectively, in Baghdad during the time of the Arabian Nights, in 14th-century Venice, and in ancient China, the stories each feature the young woman trying to save a life from falling into the hands of death. When these three candles are extinguished, she gets one final chance to find someone to take her lover's place. A testament to Lang's genius and a thematic blueprint for many of his future films, DESTINY contains some of the most brilliant work of the German Expressionist period. Although the film loses some of its energy during the visits to Baghdad, Venice, and China, one cannot help but marvel at the beauty of Death's cathedral. In addition to the architecturally minded Lang, the film's style is a credit to art directors Hermann Warm, Walter Rohrig (both from 1920's CABINET OF DR. CALIGARI), and Robert Herlth, and lighting man Robert Hegerwald.

d, Fritz Lang; w, Fritz Lang, Thea von Harbou; ph, Erich Nitzschmann, Hermann Saalfrank, Fritz Arno Wagner; m, Peter Schirman.

Horror **(PR:A MPAA:NR)**

DEVIL IN THE FLESH, THE**

(1947, Fr.) 110m TRC/UNIV bw (LE DIABLE AU CORPS)

Micheline Presle *(Marthe Graingier),* Gerard Philipe *(Francois Jaubert),* Jean Debucourt *(Mons. Jaubert),* Denise Grey *(Mme. Grangier),* Pierre Palau *(Mons. Marin),* Jean Varas *(Jacques Lacombe),* Jeanne Perez *(Mme. Marin),* Germaine Ledoyen *(Mme. Jaubert),* Maurice Lagrenee *(Doctor),* Richard Francoeur *(Headwaiter),* Jacques Tati *(Soldier in Blue),* Charles Vissieres *(Anselme),* Andre Bervil *(Reporter),* Jean Relet, Michel Francois.

A scandalous picture in its day, DEVIL IN THE FLESH tells the tale of a 17-year-old, Francois (Gerard Philipe), in love with a married older woman (Micheline Presle) whose soldier husband has been assigned to the front. The story of the romance is told through the boy's eyes, in a flashback structure that points out the doomed nature of the affair. A number of people who saw the film were furious at the way the soldier—a man risking his life for his country—was deceived. Petitions were sent to the French government urging that the film be banned. Canada agreed to the ban, and New York state censors would show it only after certain cuts were made. The Legion of Decency condemned the picture for its "sordid and suggestive atmosphere." Notwithstanding the trouble it stirred up, THE DEVIL IN THE FLESH is a safe treatment by the French film industry of a subject that demands the passion of youth. While far from a terrible film, it is hardly the masterpiece it has been decreed. The story made it to the screen again in 1986's equally disappointing X-rated version directed by Marco Bellocchio. Starring Maruschka Detmers, that film received much unwarranted attention because of the inclusion of a brief fellatio scene. Both versions are based on the novel by Raymond Radiguet, who wrote his tale of romance at the age of 18, two years before his death. The videocassette is dubbed into English.

p, Paul Graetz; d, Claude Autant-Lara; w, Jean Aurenche, Pierre Bost (based on the novel by Raymond Radiguet); ph, Michel Kelber; ed, Madeleine Gug; m, Rene Cloerec.

Romance **(PR:C MPAA:NR)**

DEVIL'S EYE, THE***

(1960, Swed.) 90m ABSF bw (DJAVULENS OGA)

Jarl Kulle *(Don Juan),* Bibi Andersson *(Britt-Marie),* Axel Duberg *(Jonas),* Nils Poppe *(The Pastor),* Gertrud Fridh *(Renata),* Sture Lagerwall *(Pablo),* Stig Jarrel *(Satan),* Gunnar Bjornstrand *(The Actor),* Georg Funkquist *(Count Armand de Rochefoucauld),* Gunnar Sjoberg *(Marquis Giuseppe Maria de Maccopazza),* Allan Edwall *(The Ear Devil),* Torsten Winge *(Old Man),* Kristina Adolphsson.

This fanciful comedy by Ingmar Bergman details the efforts of the Devil to stop the swelling in his eye by sending Don Juan (Jarl Kulle) to seduce Britt-Marie (Bibi Andersson), the 20-year-old virgin daughter of a kindly country pastor—because, as an old Irish proverb states, "A virgin is a sty in the Devil's eye." Accompanied by his servant, Pablo (Sture Lagerwall), the great lover arrives to do the Devil's bidding, and while Don Juan is busy trying to corrupt the daughter, Pablo hopes to seduce the pastor's frustrated wife. Don Juan momentarily succeeds in causing a rift between Britt-Marie and her fiance, but then is challenged by the girl's indifference to him. Before Don Juan knows it, it is *he* who has fallen in love, an act that defies everything the devil represents. THE DEVIL'S EYE is a minor Bergman film, the broad comedy of which may surprise some of the director's followers. Fearing that viewers might misunderstand the film, Bergman wrote a program note, titled "Dear Frightened Audience," in which he assured them that it was indeed a comedy. Harkening back to his training in the theater, Bergman has divided the film into separate acts, each of which are introduced, self-reflexively, by a stage actor-narrator (Gunnar Bjornstrand). The videocassette is available in both dubbed and subtitled (Swedish into English) versions.

p, Allan Ekelund; d, Ingmar Bergman; w, Ingmar Bergman (based on the Danish radio play "Don Juan Vender tillbage" by Oluf Bang); ph, Gunnar Fischer; ed, Oscar Rosander; m, Domenico Scarlatti.

Comedy **(PR:C MPAA:NR)**

DIABOLIQUE****

(1955, Fr.) 107m Filmsonor/Vera bw (LES DIABOLIQUES; AKA: THE FIENDS)

Simone Signoret *(Nicole Horner),* Vera Clouzot *(Christina Delasalle),* Paul Meurisse *(Michel Delasalle),* Charles Vanel *(Inspector Fichet),* Jean Brochard *(Plantiveau),* Noel Roquevert *(Herboux),* Therese Dorny *(Mme. Herboux),* Pierre Larquey *(Drain),* Michel Serrault *(Raymond),* Yves-Marc Maurin *(Moinet),* Georges Poujouly *(Soudieu),* Jean Temerson *(Hotel Valet),* Georges Chamarat *(Dr. Loisy),* Jacques Varennes *(Prof. Bridoux).*

One of the most suspenseful films ever made, DIABOLIQUE revolves around a callous schoolmaster, Michel Delasalle (Paul Meurisse); his heiress wife, Christina (Vera Clouzot); and his mistress, Nicole (Simone Signoret). Nicole, a cold-blooded murderess, helps Christina poison and drown her husband. They dump the corpse in the pool of Michel's boarding school, but Christina grows increasingly fearful that Michel is still alive. An investigation of the schoolmaster's death proceeds, but when the pool is drained no body is found. Adding to the mystery is the testimony of schoolchildren who insist they've seen Michel. Director Henri-Georges Clouzot (who thrilled a decent number of folks with WAGES OF FEAR) keeps the viewer guessing to the final frames. The frightened wife of the "dead" man, Vera Clouzot, is the real-life Mrs. Clouzot. Authors Pierre Boileau and Thomas Narcejac, upon learning that Alfred Hitchcock was interested in acquiring the rights to *Celle Qui N'Etait Pas* (upon which DIABOLIQUE was based), set out to pen another novel that would surely interest Hitch—*D'Entre Les Mortes*, which would later become VERTIGO. DIABOLIQUE also includes one of the most effective "eyeball scenes" in filmmaking (second only to Bunuel and Dali's UN CHIEN ANDALOU) when the "dead" man rises from the bathtub. In French with English subtitles.

p, Henri-Georges Clouzot; d, Henri-Georges Clouzot; w, Henri-Georges Clouzot, Jerome Geronimi, Frederic Grendel, Rene Masson (based on the novel *The Woman Who Was No More* by Pierre Boileau, Thomas Narcejac); ph, Armand Thirard; ed, Madeleine Gug; m, Georges Van Parys.

Thriller **(PR:O MPAA:NR)**

DIAMONDS OF THE NIGHT***½

(1964, Czech.) 70m Ceskoslovensky-Impact bw (DEMANTY NOCI)

Ladislav Jansky *(1st Boy),* Antonin Kumbera *(2nd Boy),* Ilse Bischofova *(The Woman),* Jan Riha, Ivan Asic, August Bischof, Josef Koggel, Oskar Muller, Anton Schich, Rudolf Stolle, Josef Koblizek, Josef Kubat, Rudolf Lukasek.

DIAMONDS OF THE NIGHT is another outstanding example of Czech New Wave cinema, this time directed in 1964 by the 27-year-old Jan Nemec and based on the writings of a concentration camp survivor, Arnost Lustig. Running just over an hour, the film compresses four days in the lives of two Jewish boys (Ladislav Jansky and Antonin Kumbera) who, while being transferred to a Nazi concentration camp, jump from the transport and escape into the woods. Physically and mentally exhausted, hungry, lost, and desperate, they scrounge for food and shelter and are later chased and caught by a group of old men, only to be quickly released. As their fatigue grows, the boys begin to hallucinate, imagining that the trees are falling down upon them or that swarms of ants are crawling on their bodies. Perhaps even more impressive than the startling visual style—there is much hand-held camerawork, and a sense of realism (or, as Nemec would describe it, "dream realism")—is the sound, or lack thereof. The film is practically without dialog, and there are long stretches during which nothing is heard but the ticking of a clock or the sound of breathing. Available on videotape with Nemec's first short, 1959's LOAF OF BREAD, also based on an Arnost Lustig story. The videocassette is subtitled (Czechoslovakian into English).

d, Jan Nemec; w, Arnost Lustig, Jan Nemec; ph, Jaroslav Kucera; ed, Miroslav Hajek.

Drama **(PR:C MPAA:NR)**

DIARY OF A CHAMBERMAID****

(1964, Fr./It.) 97m Speva-Cine-Alliance-FS-Dear/Cocinor bw (LE JOURNAL D'UNE FEMME DE CHAMBRE; IL DIARIO DI UNA CAMERIERA)

Jeanne Moreau *(Celestine),* Georges Geret *(Joseph),* Michel Piccoli *(Mons. Monteil),* Francoise Lugagne *(Mme. Monteil),* Jean Ozenne *(Mons. Rabour),* Daniel Ivernel *(Capt. Mauger),* Jean-Claude Carriere *(Cure),* Gilberte Geniat *(Rose),* Bernard Musson *(Sacristan),* Muni *(Marianne),* Claude Jaeger *(Judge),* Dominique Sauvage *(Claire),* Madeleine Damien, Geymond Vital, Jean Franval, Marcel Rouze, Jeanne Perez.

A wonderfully vulgar film from the masterful Spanish director Luis Bunuel, DIARY OF A CHAMBERMAID is an adaptation in spirit of Octave Mirbeau's novel and Jean Renoir's 1946 film. Celestine (Jeanne Moreau) is a Parisian chambermaid who takes a new job in the country at the estate of a bourgeois womanizer, Mons. Monteil (Michel Piccoli), his frigid wife (Francoise Lugagne), and her likeable, foot-fetishist father (Jean Ozenne). Sexual vices are not limited to the bourgeoisie, however, as Joseph (Georges Geret), the filthy, fascist longtime servant, is found to be a sadistic rapist and murderer. Although Bunuel would regularly attack societal institutions, this film is one of his most overtly political. Set in the late 1920s, this chambermaid's diary sets up the social conditions of both political and sexual aggression that made the rise of fascism not only possible but—as Bunuel makes clear in the film's final shot of the stormy heavens—inevitable. His statement is a Surrealist one, presented in the most realistic of styles (which may surprise viewers who have only a peripheral familiarity with Bunuel's work). The director's wicked humor and unforgettable visual sense are perhaps best illustrated in his filming the rape and murder of an innocent young girl. Instead of narrating the attack in detail, Bunuel uses three shots—a wild boar running through the forest, a frightened rabbit, and the corpse's legs covered with the live snails she had been collecting. The videocassette has easy-to-read yellow subtitles (Spanish into English), but unfortunately does not letterbox the image and fails to do justice to the spectacular widescreen black-and-white photography.

p, Serge Silberman, Michel Safra; d, Luis Bunuel; w, Luis Bunuel, Jean-Claude Carriere (based on the novel *A Chambermaid's Diary* by Octave Mirbeau); ph, Roger Fellous (Franscope); ed, Louisette Hautecoeur.

Drama **(PR:O MPAA:NR)**

DIARY OF A COUNTRY PRIEST****

(1950, Fr.) 120m UGC bw (LE JOURNAL D'UN CURE DE CAMPAGNE)

Claude Laydu *(Priest of Ambricourt),* Jean Riveyre *(Count),* Andre Guibert *(Priest of Torcy),* Nicole Maurey *(Louise),* Nicole Ladmiral *(Chantal),* Marie-Monique Arkell *(Countess),* Martine Lemaire *(Seraphita),* Antoine Balpetre *(Dr. Delbende),* Jean Danet *(Olivier),* Gaston Severin *(Canon),* Jean Etievant *(Housekeeper),* Bernard Hubrenne *(Louis Dufrety).*

A frail, unnamed priest (Claude Laydu, an untrained actor) is assigned to his first parish—Ambricourt, a small and only somewhat religious town. He does as saintly priests are known to do—simply accepting the people around him as they are and attempting to strengthen their faith, while himself living a life of poverty, with bread and wine the only food he can eat without falling ill. His major achievement is bringing a withdrawn countess out of her hatred for God and into a state of peacefulness. Robert Bresson, returning to the screen after a five-year absence, succeeds in capturing the literary spirit of George Bernanos' book and retelling it in a cinematic language. It is a brilliant adaptation, remaining faithful to Bernanos without resorting to harmful omissions or additions, allowing its audience to enjoy the identical spiritual experience as the reader of the novel. DIARY OF A COUNTRY PRIEST shared the top prize at the Venice Film Fest with Kurosawa's RASHOMON. It is definitely not a film for everyone's tastes—Bresson's work is known for its slow, meditative pace—but a brilliant picture all the same. In French with English subtitles.

p, Leon Carre; d, Robert Bresson; w, Robert Bresson (based on the novel by George Bernanos); ph, Leonce-Henry Burel; ed, Paulette Robert; m, Jean-Jacques Grunenwald.

Religious **(PR:A MPAA:NR)**

DIARY OF A LOST GIRL*****

(1929, Ger.) 100m G.W. Pabst bw (DAS TAGEBUCH EINER VERLORENEN)

Louise Brooks *(Thymiane Henning),* Edith Meinhardt *(Erika),* Vera Pawlowa *(Aunt Frida),* Josef Rovensky *(Henning),* Fritz Rasp *(Meiner),* Andre Roanne *(Count Osdorff),* Arnold Korff *(Old Count Orsdorff),* Andrews Engelmann *(Director of the House of Correction),* Valeska Gert *(His Wife),* Franziska Kinz *(Meta),* Sybille Schmitz *(Elisabeth).*

While it is perhaps possible to define the influence that the great, though inconsistent, German director G.W. Pabst has had on film history, it is impossible to overrate the importance of Louise Brooks. Like such screen greats as Greta Garbo or Marlene Dietrich, Brooks (chiefly in this film and her previous Pabst production, PANDORA'S

BOX) had a mystique all her own—created as much by her on-screen persona as by her off-screen life. Having haunted film audiences' imaginations throughout the world with her erotic portrayal of Lulu in PANDORA'S BOX, Brooks returned again to Pabst's side to make the silent DIARY OF A LOST GIRL. A masterpiece of atmosphere (with art direction by the great Erno Metzner), the film is the story of a middle-class girl, Thymiane (Brooks), who is raped one night by her storekeeper father's assistant (Fritz Rasp). She becomes pregnant, and, in a series of downward turns, is sent to a boarding school run by a monstrously sadistic governess (Valeska Gert). Along with his brilliant naturalistic direction of Brooks, Pabst employs an equally brilliant style of rhythmic editing that keeps pushing scenes in a frenzied pace to their conclusion, only to have the whole process repeat again as Thymiane episodically falls further and further down.

p, G.W. Pabst; d, G.W. Pabst; w, Rudolf Leonhardt (based on the novel by Margarethe Boehme); ph, Sepp Allgeier.

Drama **(PR:C MPAA:NR)**

DIARY OF FORBIDDEN DREAMS**

(1972, It./Fr./Ger.) 112m CC Champion-Concordia-Dieter Geissler/Avco Enbassy c (AKA: CHE?; ROMAN POLANSKI'S DIARY OF FORBIDDEN DREAMS; WHAT?)

Marcello Mastroianni *(Alex),* Sydne Rome *(The Girl),* Romolo Valli *(Administrator),* Hugh Griffith *(Owner of Villa),* Guido Alberti *(Priest),* Gianfranco Piacentini *(Stud),* Carlo Delle Piane *(The Boy),* Roman Polanski *(Mosquito),* Roger Middleton *(Jimmy),* Henning Schlueter, Christiane Barry, Elisabeth Witte, Dieter Hallersorden, Mogen von Gadow, Cicely Brown, John Karlsen, Richard McNamara, Birgitta Nilsson.

This haphazard fantasy is of interest chiefly to devotees of Roman Polanski and, even more so, of Gerard Brach, his longtime screenwriting collaborator. An attempt at broad comedy, DIARY OF FORBIDDEN DREAMS is the story of The Girl, an American hippie (Sydne Rome) who wanders into the decadent environment of a seaside villa after nearly being raped while hitchhiking. She is given a room and, within moments, begins undressing under the peeping eye of Alex (Marcello Mastroianni), a former pimp, possible homosexual, and probable impotent pervert who defiantly insists he does not have any venereal diseases. Things are, at the very least, strange in the villa. One inhabitant constantly groans in his room; some mysterious character peeps into The Girl's room through a hole in the wall; two women wander through the terrace, both sporting fancy hats but only one wearing clothes; two young men play ping-pong, the sound of which drives Alex mad; and there is also a strange, Kafkaesque character, "Mosquito," played by Polanski himself. As if possessed by some sort of spirit of decadence, The Girl comes topless to the breakfast table. Some time later, her pants mysteriously disappear in the middle of the night. She even has a sexual rendezvous with Alex, who dons the skin of a tiger and demands to be "tamed" by the whip-cracking Girl. Throughout the entire adventure, The Girl carries a diary under her arm and writes curiously impersonal and unerotic entries. DAIRY OF FORBIDDEN DREAMS (its video title) is the least discussed of Polanski's films, but on some levels it may be his most revealing. It becomes most interesting when viewed as the second part of a Polanski-Brach trilogy that includes REPULSION and THE TENANT—in all three films, the central character is a psychological prisoner of perverse surroundings. Considering the subject of the film there is practically no sex, and the amount of nudity decreases as the story unfolds. Filmed in English, with some voices dubbed.

p, Carlo Ponti; d, Roman Polanski; w, Roman Polanski, Gerard Brach; ph, Marcello Gatti, Giuseppe Ruzzolini (Todd-AO 35, Technicolor); ed, Alastair McIntyre; m, Franz Schubert, Wolfgang Amadeus Mozart, Ludwig van Beethoven.

Fantasy **(PR:O MPAA:R)**

DIRTY DISHES****

(1978, Fr.) 99m Stephan/Quartet c (LA JUMENT VAPEUR)

Carole Laure *(Armelle Bertrand),* Pierre Santini *(Marc Bertrand),* Liliane Roveyre, Liza Braconnier, Daniel Sarki, Bernard Haller, Francoise Armel, Gilles Brissac, Luc Danet, Jean Degrave, Anne-Marie Descott, Jeanne Dory, Catherine Lachens, Pierre Lary, Jean-Claude Montalban, Jean-Jacques Moreau, Laurent Mozzinonacci, Roger Muni, Boris Najman, Agathe Nathanson, Louis Navarre, Odile Poisson.

One of the best cases of an unsung, and generally unseen, foreign film getting a chance to find an American audience on videotape is Joyce Bunuel's first feature, DIRTY DISHES, an excellent picture that has unfortunately gone unnoticed. This exciting and energetic film looks at the social and moral violence of housewifery. Armelle (Carole Laure) is a 30ish French housewife who, in the very first frame of the opening credit sequence, must wrestle with her vacuum cleaner and examine its dusty innards in order to complete her daily chores. The first scene provides a clue to the film's tone. Armelle and her husband, Marc (Pierre Santini), are picnicking in an idyllic, grassy setting. They dance wildly to some upbeat music while their two young children look on in amazement. This honeymoon soon ends, however, when a stranger drives up and verbally assaults them, then continues to terrorize the family, chasing them through the park and nearly crushing the head of one of the children under his front tire, until, just as suddenly as he arrived, he leaves. The story of a bored housewife has been told hundreds of times before, but rarely with so much insight, skill, or sense of impending danger. Bunuel (the American-born daughter-in-law of Luis Bunuel) directs the film at a feverish pace, and adroitly avoids stumbling over the usual cliches. Laure plays her role perfectly, turning in a wholly believable performance as the pretty ex-club dancer who gradually questions her decision to have a husband and family. The videotape is available in both dubbed and subtitled (French into English) versions.

p, Vera Belmont; d, Joyce Bunuel; w, Joyce Bunuel, Suzanne Baron; ph, Francois Protat; ed, Jean-Bernard Bonis;

m, Jean-Marie Senia.

Drama **(PR:O MPAA:NR)**

DISCREET CHARM OF THE BOURGEOISIE, THE*****

(1972, Fr./It./Sp.) 100m Greenwich-Jet-Dean/FOX c (LE CHARME DISCRET DE LA BOURGEOISIE)

Fernando Rey *(Ambassador Raphael Acosta),* Delphine Seyrig *(Mme. Simone Thevenot),* Stephane Audran *(Mme. Alice Senechal),* Bulle Ogier *(Florence),* Jean-Pierre Cassel *(Mon. Henri Senechal),* Paul Frankeur *(Mon. Francois Thevenot),* Julien Bertheau *(Bishop Dufour),* Claude Pieplu *(Colonel),* Michel Piccoli *(Home Secretary),* Muni *(Peasant Girl),* Milena Vukotic *(Ines the Maid),* Georges Douking *(Dying Gardener),* Bernard Musson *(Rochecachin),* Francois Maistre *(Delecluze),* Maria Gabriella Maione *(Guerrilla),* Pierre Maguelon, Ellen Bahl.

A carefully calculated and perfectly refined Surrealist attack on the rituals of the upper class, clergy, military, and the political sphere, THE DISCREET CHARM OF THE BOURGEOISIE is *so* couth that even many of Luis Bunuel's supporters mistakenly misread this brilliant joke as a sign that the then 72-year-old Spanish director had lost his bite. It is, however, every bit as wicked as the director's long-banned classic of 1930, L'AGE D'OR, only more . . . refined. The plot, which does no justice to a reading of the film, concerns the efforts of a group of middle-aged members of the bourgeoisie to sit down together for a dinner party. Sometimes they meet on the wrong evening, or they gather at a restaurant only to find the corpse of the recently deceased owner, or they are told that all beverages except water are out of stock, or they find that they are not at a dinner party at all, but on stage in front of an angry audience. These aborted meetings take place in "reality," though the film is interspersed with a number of "dreams" in which the characters imagine the worst possible events. Through all their attempts to cover up their truer, baser, and more venal nature (which encompasses drug smuggling, fascism, adultery, murder, and lustfulness), the members of this segment of society remain faithful to one another and continue to walk on together as if nothing can steer them from their path. Bunuel's wisdom and brilliance is clear when one realizes that, despite the film's dependence on dreams and absurdities, it presents a more truthful look at society than a thousand documentaries. Despite its content, and precisely because of its refinement, the film won the Oscar as Best Foreign Language Film—a perfect punch line to Bunuel's joke. In French with yellow English subtitles.

p, Serge Silberman; d, Luis Bunuel; w, Luis Bunuel, Jean-Claude Carriere; ph, Edmond Richard (Eastmancolor, Panavision); ed, Helene Plemiannikov; m, Galaxie Musique.

Comedy/Drama **(PR:C MPAA:PG)**

DIVA****

(1981, Fr.) 123m Galaxie-Greenwich/UA c

Frederic Andrei *(Jules),* Wilhelmenia Wiggins Fernandez *(Cynthia Hawkins),* Richard Bohringer *(Gorodish),* Thuy An Luu *(Alba),* Jacques Fabbri *(Saporta),* Chantal Deruaz *(Nadia),* Roland Bertin *(Weinstadt),* Gerard Darmon *(L'Antillais),* Dominique Pinon *(Le Cure),* Jean-Jacques Moreau *(Krantz),* Patrick Floersheim *(Zatopek),* Raymond Aquilon, Eugene Berthier, Gerard Chaillou, Andree Champeaux, Nathalie Dalian, Laurence Darpy, Michel Debrane, Etienne Draber, Laure Duthilleul, Nane Germon, Gebriel Gobin, Jim Adhi Limas, Louisette Malapert, Dimo Mally, Veneta Mally, Alain Marcel, Isabelle Mergault.

DIVA is a visually astonishing film with a complex plot concerning Jules (Frederic Andrei), a young Parisian mail carrier, and his love for Cynthia Hawkins (Wilhelmenia Wiggins Fernandez), a famous black American opera singer. Jules attends a performance by the diva, recording it secretly while a sinister Taiwanese man watches him. In a separate incident, a dazed girl walking through the Paris metro is murdered by two thugs—the greasy L'Antillais (Gerard Darmon) and the punkish, bald Le Cure (Dominique Pinon). As the girl dies, she slips an audiocassette into Jules' mailpouch on his moped. Jules now finds himself unwittingly caught in two plots: that of Taiwanese record pirates who want his recording of the diva, and that of a gang of pimps and drug runners who want the incriminating tape left in his mailpouch. In the process, Jules falls in love with Cynthia Hawkins, and meets a mysterious duo—Zen master Gorodish (Richard Bohringer) and his chic Vietnamese concubine, Alba (Thuy An Luu). The debut film from Jean-Jacques Beineix, DIVA is perhaps the most picturesque film to come out of France in years. Together with art director Hilton McConnico and cameraman Philippe Rousselot, Beineix creates awesome shot after awesome shot, so much so that many felt the film was too stylish. At times, the sensibility is very "new wave" (as in fashion and music, not the film movement); at other times, Beineix is intensely impressionistic. These qualities are even further enhanced by a perfect musical score, contributed by Vladimir Cosma, which makes use of Act I of Alfredo Catalani's opera "La Wally." The videocassette is subtitled (French into English); be wary of the atrociously dubbed cable television version.

p, Irene Silberman; d, Jean-Jacques Beineix; w, Jean-Jacques Beineix, Jean Van Hamme (based on a novel by Delacorta); ph, Philippe Rousselot (Eastmancolor); ed, Marie-Josephe Yoyotte, Monique Prim; m, Vladimir Cosma.

Crime/Romance **(PR:C MPAA:NR)**

DIVINE NYMPH, THE**

(1976, It.) 90m Filmarpa/Analysis c (DIVINA CREATURA)

Laura Antonelli *(Manoela Roderighi),* Terence Stamp *(Duke Daniele di Bagnasco),* Marcello Mastroianni *(Marquise Michele Barra),* Michele Placido *(Martino Ghiondelli),* Duilio Del Prete *(Armellini),* Ettore Manni *(Marco*

Pisani), Cecilia Polizzi *(Dany's Maid),* Marina Berti *(Manoela's Aunt),* Doris Duranti *(Signora Fones),* Ruth League *(Dany's Friend),* Piero Di Jorio *(Cameriere di Stefano),* Carlo Tamberlani *(Majordomo Pasqualino).*

This tame and rather uninteresting costume drama set among the Italian bourgeoisie of the 1920s stars the perenially nude Laura Antonelli as Manoela Roderighi, a pretty young woman who has a chance meeting with nobleman Daniele (Terence Stamp) while lunching with her fiance, Martino (Michele Placido). Daniele soon takes Manoela as his mistress and learns that she is full of secrets. Lying next to him in bed, she admits that she was raped when she was 15 by an older man who, unknown to Daniele, is Daniele's cousin Michele (Marcello Mastroianni). Later, as this triangle is fleshed out, Daniele delves deeper into Manoela's past and learns that she was forced into prostitution by Michele. It all looks quite luscious, with wonderfully baroque sets, gorgeous costumes, and the naked Antonelli, but there isn't much more here than an artsy Jackie Collins novel. Worthy of mention is Ennio Morricone's lively score—an interpretation of C.A. Bixio—and director Guiseppe Patroni Griffi's inventive and humorous use of quotes (Pushkin, Stendahl, etc.) to comment on the action. In English, with some characters dubbed.

p, Luigi Scattini, Mario Ferrari; d, Giuseppe Patroni Griffi; w, Giuseppe Patroni Griffi, A. Valdarnini (based on the novel *La Divina Fanciulla* by Luciano Zuccoli); ph, Giuseppe Rotunno; ed, Roberto Perpignani; m, Ennio Morricone, C.A. Bixio.

Drama (PR:O MPAA:NR)

DR. MABUSE, THE GAMBLER (PARTS I & II)****

(1922, Ger.) 120m & 93m Ullstein-Uco-Decla-Bioscop-Ufa bw (DR. MABUSE, DER SPIELER)

Rudolph Kelin-Rogge *(Mabuse),* Alfred Abel *(Count Told),* Aud Egede Nissen *(Cara Carozza),* Gertrude Welcker *(Countess Told),* Bernhard Goetzke *(Von Wenck),* Forster Larrinaga *(Sporri),* Paul Richter *(Edgar Hull),* Hans Adalbert von Schlettow *(Chauffeur),* Georg John *(Pesch),* Grete Berger *(Fine),* Julius Falkenstein *(Karsten),* Lydia Potechina *(Russian Woman),* Anita Berber *(Dancer),* Paul Biensfeldt *(Man with Gun),* Karl Platen *(Told's Servant),* Karl Huszar *(Hawasch),* Edgar Pauly *(Fat Man),* Julius Hermann *(Schramm),* Lil Dagover, Julie Brandt, Auguste Prasch-Grevenberg, Adele Sandrock, Max Adalbert, Gutav Botz, Heinrich Gotho, Leonhard Haskel, Erner Hubsch.

This two-part ("The Great Gambler" and "Inferno"), silent Fritz Lang entry follows the saga of master criminal Dr. Mabuse (Rudolph Klein-Rogge), a character Lang would return to in 1933's THE TESTAMENT OF DR. MABUSE and again in 1960's THE THOUSAND EYES OF DR. MABUSE. Mabuse, after winning a fortune during a stock market scam, meets the wealthy Edgar Hull (Paul Richter) and uses his power of hypnosis to bring Hull to financial ruin and seduce his mistress, the exotic dancer Cara Carozza (Aud Egede Nissen). Only police detective Von Wenck (Bernhard Goetzke) stands up to oppose the criminal. In Part II, Von Wenck resists Mabuse's attempts to destroy him and, with the help of the police, engineers a raid on the master criminal's headquarters. Made in 1922, the film foreshadows the madness that would bring the Nazi party to power in the form of the Mabuse character, a tyrannical monster whose influence on the public is so great that he controls their thoughts, actions, and desires—all in order for Mabuse to complete his great plan of world destruction and domination. An important document both politically and socially, DR. MABUSE, THE GAMBLER also displays Lang's technical genius, especially obvious in his magnificent art direction and the attention paid to architecture. The symmetry of the stock exchange, with its giant clock, and the Art Deco designs of the gambling room are but two examples of the achievements of art directors Stahl-Urach (who died during production) and Otto Hunte.

d, Fritz Lang; w, Fritz Lang, Thea von Harbou (based on the novel by Norbert Jacques); ph, Carl Hoffmann.

Crime (PR:A MPAA:NR)

DODES 'KA-DEN***½

(1970, Jap.) 139m Yonki no Kai/Toho c (DODESUKADAN; AKA: CLICKETYCLACK)

Yoshitaka Zushi *(Rokkuchan),* Kin Sugai *(Rokkuchan's Mother),* Junzaburo Ban *(Shima),* Kiyoko Tange *(Shima's Wife),* Michiko Hino, Tape Shimokawa, Keishi Furuyama *(Shima's Guests),* Hisashi Igawa *(Masuda),* Hideko Okiyama *(Masuda's Wife),* Kunie Tanaka *(Kawaguchi),* Jitsuko Yoshimura *(Kawaguchi's Wife),* Shinsuke Minami *(Ryo),* Yoko Kusunoki *(Ryo's Wife),* Toshiyuki Tonomura, Miika Oshida, Satoshi Hasegawa, Kumiko Ono, Tatsuhiko Yagishita *(Ryo's Children),* Tatsuo Matsumura *(Kyota),* Tsuji Imura *(Kyota's Wife),* Tomoko Yamazaki *(Kyota's Stepdaughter),* Masahiko Kametani *(Okabe),* Noboru Mitani *(Beggar),* Hiroyuki Kawase *(Beggar's Son),* Hiroshi Akutagawa *(Hei),* Tomoko Naraoka *(Ocho).*

Though DODESKA-DEN is void of a straight plot or structured narrative, director Akira Kurosawa was able to create in the film a highly emotional depiction of simple dreams, tragedies, and desires in an impoverished Tokyo slum. The title refers to the sound made by a slightly retarded boy as he impersonates a streetcar, a role he takes seriously as he struts down the streets of his own private universe. The boy is just one of many characters living in the shantytown whose hopes are best symbolized by a man who dreams of the palace he will build for himself and his son—a far cry from their actual home, a hollowed-out Volkswagen bug. This was, after three decades of filmmaking, Kurosawa's first film in color, and his eagerly awaited return to the screen after a five-year absence. Touching, sad, and humorous, it is a film of the imagination, in which a beautiful, colorful, palatial, and prosperous world exists only in the minds of its inhabitants. While not a box-office success, the film did earn an Oscar nomination for Best Foreign Film. In Japanese with English subtitles.

p, Yoichi Matsue; d, Akira Kurosawa; w, Akira Kurosawa, Hideo Oguni, Shinobu Hashimoto (based on the book by

Shugoro Yamamoto); ph, Takao Saito (Eastmancolor); m, Toru Takemitsu.

Drama **(PR:C MPAA:NR)**

DONA FLOR AND HER TWO HUSBANDS***

(1977, Braz.) 106m Gaumont-Coline/Carnival c (DONA FLOR E SEUS DOIS MARIDOS)

Sonia Braga *(Dona Flor),* Jose Wilker *(Vadhino),* Mauro Mendonca *(Teodoro),* Dinorah Brillanti *(Rozilda),* Nelson Xavier *(Mirandao),* Arthur Costa Filho *(Carlinhos),* Rui Rezende *(Cazuza),* Mario Gusmao.

This wonderfully sexy and funny comedy shattered Brazilian box-office records, chiefly because of the tremendously sensual presence of Sonia Braga. Dona Flor (Braga) is a beautiful woman whose gambling, whoring husband drops dead after an all-night carousal. She decides to marry again, choosing a middle-aged, devout, and boring pharmacist who rarely wants to make love. One night, as Dona Flor lies in bed next to her sleeping spouse, the ghost of her first husband appears, nude, in the room. She tries to get rid of him, but he refuses. Finally she succumbs to his blandishments and takes the ghost to bed with her, while the second husband continues to sleep. This entertaining and erotic picture, while perhaps not the most challenging film to come out of Brazil in the 1970s, is nevertheless enjoyable. Director Bruno Barreto and Braga teamed up again in 1983 in GABRIELA, with Marcello Mastroianni as the recipient of Braga's affections. Remade in 1982 as KISS ME GOODBYE with—are you ready for this?—Sally Field in the Dona Flor role. The videocassette is dubbed in English.

p, Luis Carlos Barreto, Newton Rique, Cia Serrador; d, Bruno Barreto; w, Bruno Barreto (based on a novel by Jorge Amado); ph, Maurilo Salles (Eastmancolor); ed, Raimundo Higino; m, Chico Buarque.

Comedy **(PR:O MPAA:R)**

DONKEY SKIN***

(1975, Fr.) 90m Parc-Marianne/Janus c (PEAU D'ANE)

Catherine Deneuve *(Peau d'Ane/Blue Queen),* Jacques Perrin *(Prince),* Jean Marais *(Blue King),* Delphine Seyrig *(Fairy Godmother),* Fernand Ledoux *(Red King),* Micheline Presle *(Red Queen),* Henri Cremieux, Sacha Pitoeff, Pierre Repp, Jean Servais, Georges Adet, Annick Berger, Romain Bouteille, Louise Chevalier, Sylvain Corthay, Michel Delahaye, Simone Guisin, Gabriel Jabbour, Bernard Musson, Patrick Prejean, Valerie Quincy.

DONKEY SKIN is an odd but charming combination of a number of fairy tales, blended with anachronistically modern touches and mixed up with adult themes disguised in the form of mythic euphemisms. Writer-director Jacques Demy, whose charming musical tale THE UMBRELLAS OF CHERBOURG (1964) won the Golden Palm at the Cannes Festival, has a knack—much like Jean Cocteau—for melding traditional fantasy with contemporary grown-up concerns. Viewers will recognize variations on "The Goose That Laid the Golden Egg," "Cinderella," and "Little Red Riding-Hood," among other classics, all rolled into a contiguous plot line. An incest theme is woven into the plot, but on a most ingenuous level. The Blue King (Jean Marais) governs a strange land that contains, among other assets, a national treasure, a donkey that excretes gems and valuable coins. The king's wife (Catherine Deneuve) and daughter (also Deneuve) are the rarest of beauties. On her deathbed, the Blue Queen makes the king promise to marry only someone more beautiful than she. The Blue King examines portraits of all the local princesses, but none will do—none, that is, save his daughter, who is thereupon selected to become her father's bride. Handled with style, grace, and good humor by Demy and a fine cast (namely Marais, Deneuve, and Delphine Seyrig, as a fairy godmother), the film is an enjoyable hour-and-a-half for adults that creates a wholly unique world of colorful sets, costumes and characters. As this is a Jacques Demy film, it of course has musical numbers written by Demy and Michel Legrand, in addition to excerpts of poems by Guillaume Apollinaire and Cocteau. In French with yellow English subtitles.

p, Mag Bodard; d, Jacques Demy; w, Jacques Demy (based on the fairy tale by Charles Perrault); ph, Ghislain Cloquet; ed, Anne-Marie Cotret; m, Michel Legrand.

Fantasy **(PR:C-O MPAA:NR)**

DOUBLE SUICIDE****

(1969, Jap.) 104m Hyogensha-Nippon/Toho bw (SHINJO TEN NO AMIJIMA; Trans: Double Suicide at Amijima)

Kichiemon Nakamura *(Jihei),* Shima Iwashita *(Koharu/Osan),* Hosei Kamatsu *(Tahei),* Yusuke Takita *(Magoemon),* Kamatari Fujiwara *(Yamatoya Owner),* Yoshi Kato *(Gosaemon),* Shizue Kawarazaki *(Osan's Mother),* Tokie Hidari *(Osugi).*

Although DOUBLE SUICIDE is set in 1690 and based on a puppet play from 1720 (by Monzaemon Chikamatsu), it is thoroughly modern cinema and one of the most inventive film adaptations you are likely to see. The picture opens with documentary-style shots of puppet masters preparing their dolls while a conversation between director Masahiro Shinoda and screenwriter Taeko Tomioka is heard on the soundtrack. Shinoda informs his collaborator that he has decided on the location (a cemetery) for the double suicide that will end his film. He then proceeds with the story, using real actors instead of puppets. This does not, however, prevent him from employing black-cloaked stage hands (*kuroko*) who are visible throughout the film and often interact with the lead actors. A film of social obligation (*giri*) and personal desire (*ninjo*), DOUBLE SUICIDE revolves around three characters: paper merchant Jihei (Kichiemon Nakamura); his devoted wife, Osan (Shima Iwashita); and the courtesan Koharu (Iwashita in a dual role), whom he loves and hopes to redeem. However, Jihei hasn't enough money to save Koharu, who is instead about to be claimed by the vile Tahei (Hosei Kamatsu), and Jihei and Koharu enter a suicide pact—their deaths being the only way to escape their societal obligations. In order to raise the needed money, Jihei is willing to ruin his wife's reputation, destroy his business, and orphan his two children. Photographed in exquisite black and white, DOUBLE SUICIDE is an emotionally powerful, thematically rich, and technically brilliant piece of art that stresses the violent opposition between desire and obligation. This is particularly exemplified in Shinoda's casting of Iwashita in the dual role of wife and courtesan: although wife and mistress are played by the same woman, Jihei's relationship to her as a wife is one of duty, while his relationship to her as a courtesan is one of intense erotic desire. The videotape, one of an excellent series from Sony Video, is in Japanese with easy-to-read English subtitles.

p, Masayuki Nakajima, Masahiro Shinoda; d, Masahiro Shinoda; w, Taeko Tomioka, Masahiro Shinoda, Toru Takemitsu (based on a puppet play by Monzaemon Chikamatsu); ph, Toichiro Narushima; m, Toru Takemitsu.

Drama **(PR:O MPAA:NR)**

DOWN AND DIRTY***½

(1976, It.) 115m C.C. Champion/New Line c (BRUTTI, SPORCHI E CATTIVI; Trans: Ugly, Dirty and Bad)

Nino Manfredi *(Giacinto),* Francisci Anniballi *(Domizio),* Maria Bosco *(Gaetana),* Giselda Castrini *(Lisetta),* Alfredo D'Ippolito *(Plinio),* Giancarlo Fanelli *(Paride),* Marian Fasoli *(Maria Lobera),* Ettore Garofolo *(Camilio),* Marco Marsili *(Vittoriano),* Franco Merli *(Fernando),* Linda Moretti *(Matilde),* Luciano Pagliuca *(Romolo),* Giuseppe Paravati *(Toto),* Silvana Priori *(Paride's Wife),* Giovanni Rovini *(Granny Antonecchia),* Adriana Russo *(Dore),* Maria Luisa Santella *(Iside),* Mario Santella *(Adolfo),* Ennio Antonelli *(Oste),* Marcella Battisti *(Marcella Celhoio),* Francesco Crescimone *(Commissario),* Beryl Cunningham *(Barracata Negra),* Silvia Ferluga *(Maga).*

A mean, nasty, vile, ugly, and wickedly funny look at the inhabitants of a squatters' slum outside of Rome, where the subproletariat lives a miserable existence, DOWN AND DIRTY focuses on Giacinto (Nino Manfredi), a brutal animal of a man who has won a million lira insurance settlement after losing an eye. Driven by greed and selfishness, Giacinto sleeps with a shotgun for fear that someone will steal his fortune. He refuses to spend even a small portion of his stash on his family—which consists of at least 20 people, all of whom live, eat, sleep, fight, and have sex in the same one-room shanty. He beats and stabs his wife, humiliates his children, drinks himself into a stupor, and gropes the local women. When he takes an obese, huge-chested whore (Maria Luisa Santella) as a mistress, lets her live under the same roof as his family, and then generously squanders his money on gifts for her, his relatives plot to murder him. An amazing picture from Ettore Scola, DOWN AND DIRTY presents an endless stream of human indignities (people living with rats, a drag queen seducing his sister-in-law, a proud mother displaying her daughter's nude centerfold, children spending the day locked in a cage that serves as a day-care center) with such a curious, crude sense of humor one cannot be sure whether to look away in horror or laugh. What is sure is that you cannot ignore these people, or their unfathomable living conditions—and this is Scola's intent. Shooting on location, with Manfredi as his only professional actor, Scola in DOWN AND DIRTY pays a heavy debt to the Neo-Realist tradition in Italy and produces a film worthy of Rossellini or De Sica. The videocassete, which is in Italian with English subtitles, is letterboxed.

d, Ettore Scola; w, Ettore Scola, Ruggero Maccari; ph, Dario Di Palma; ed, Raimondo Crociani; m, Armando Trovaioli.

Comedy/Drama **(PR:O MPAA:NR)**

DREAMS**

(1955, Swed.) 86m Sandrews/Janus bw
(KVINNODROM; AKA: JOURNEY INTO AUTUMN;
Trans: Women's Dreams)

Harriet Andersson *(Doris),* Eva Dahlbeck *(Susanne),* Gunnar Bjornstrand *(Consul Sonderby),* Ulf Palme *(Henrik Lobelius),* Inga Landgre *(Marta Lobelius),* Sven Lindberg *(Palle),* Naima Wifstrand *(Mrs. Aren),* Bengt-Ake Bengtsson *(Magnus),* Git Gay *(Model),* Ludde Gentzel *(Sundstrom),* Kerstin Hedeby *(Marianne),* Jessie Flaws *(Makeup Girl),* Marianne Nielson *(Fanny).*

Susanne (Eva Dahlbeck), the owner of a Stockholm modeling agency, and Doris (Harriet Andersson), a teenage model, travel together to Gothenburg on business. Once they arrive, the suicidal Susanne has a rendezvous with her married lover (Ulf Palme), though the romance sours when his wife appears. Meanwhile, the energetic Doris stirs the affections of a much older diplomat (Gunnar Bjornstrand) who cannot quite keep pace. Both women have their dreams—Susanne hopes to marry and begin a family; Doris hopes to gain a life of fame and luxury. This is not one of Ingmar Bergman's greats, but is a compelling film all the same. After DREAMS, he would direct, in swift succession, SMILES OF A SUMMER NIGHT; THE SEVENTH SEAL; and WILD STRAWBERRIES. In Swedish with English subtitles.

p, Ingmar Bergman; d, Ingmar Bergman; w, Ingmar Bergman; ph, Hilding Bladh; ed, Carl-Olav Skeppstedt.

Drama **(PR:C MPAA:NR)**

DRIFTING***

(1983, Israel) 80m Kislev/Nu-Image c (NAGOOA)

Jonathan Sagalle *(Robi),* Ami Traub *(Han),* Ben Levin *(Exri),* Dita Arel *(Rachel),* Boaz Torjemann *(Baba),* Mark Hassman *(Robi's Father).*

DRIFTING is an impressive and relatively successful debut feature, made on a shoestring budget of $100,000 and directed by one of Israel's most promising and controversial young directors, Amos Guttman. Robi (Jonathan Sagalle) is a young homosexual filmmaker who is trying to get a first feature made and who must work at his eccentric grandmother's grocery store to pay the bills. Since one of his lovers is married, Robi spends some evenings cruising for companionship. He is also visited by a former lover—a young woman who isn't aware of his homosexuality. Isolating himself in his room and spending most of his time in a gay milieu, Robi doesn't have to contend with society or politics, things which would only distract him from his greatest desire—to make films. The semiautobiographical DRIFTING has been described by some as "the best gay film ever made." Whether or not that is true, it did receive accolades at home despite its avoidance of broader topics, earning awards for Best Director, Best Actor, and Best Cinematography. In Hebrew with English subtitles.

d, Amos Guttman; w, Amos Guttman, Edna Mazia; ph, Yossi Wein; ed, Anna Finkelstein; m, Arik Rudich.

Drama **(PR:O MPAA:NR)**

DRUNKEN ANGEL****

(1948, Jap.) 102m Toho bw (YOIDORE TENSHI)

Toshiro Mifune *(Matsunaga),* Takashi Shimura *(Dr. Sanada),* Reisaburo Yamamoto *(Okada),* Michiyo Kogure *(Nanse),* Chieko Nakakita *(Miyo),* Noriko Sengoku *(Gin),* Eitaro Shindo *(Takahama),* Choko Iida *(Old Maid Servant).*

Akira Kurosawa's DRUNKEN ANGEL captures the mood of postwar Japan in the same way the Neo-Realist films of Italy did in that country. In a war-scarred town controlled by the Yakuza (Japanese gangsters), an alcoholic doctor runs a small clinic. A young gangster, Matsunaga (Toshiro Mifune), comes to have a bullet removed from his hand and is treated by Dr. Sanada (Takashi Shimura), who hates the Yakuza. Sanada discovers that Matsunaga has tuberculosis and, after arguments and fistfights, convinces Matsunaga to let him treat the illness, creating a love-hate relationship between the two. This was the first film on which Kurosawa had creative control and, although he had directed other pictures, it is the one in which his personal voice is first clearly heard. It was also the first starring role for Mifune, who, like his costar Shimura, turns in a mesmerizing performance. What makes the film so powerful is the characters' dependence on one another—Matsunaga's need for medical treatment and emotional support when faced with an incurable disease, and the humanist urge that compels Sanada to treat the gangster despite the fact that he hates everything the Yakuza represents. In Japanese with English subtitles.

p, Sojiro Motoki; d, Akira Kurosawa; w, Keinosuke Uegusa, Akira Kurosawa; ph, Takeo Ito; m, Fumio Hayasaka.

Drama **(PR:C MPAA:NR)**

DUST***

(1985, Fr./Bel.) 87m Man's-Daska-Flach-FR3-La Communaute Francaise de Belgique-De Ministerie van de Vlaamse Gemeenschap/Kino c

Jane Birkin *(Magda),* Trevor Howard *(The Father),* John Matshikiza *(Hendrik),* Nadine Uwampa *(Klein Anna),* Lourdes Christina Sayo *(Oud Anna),* Rene Diaz *(Jacob).*

Magda (Jane Birkin) is a matronly British woman living on a dusty, desolate farm in Cape Province, South Africa, with her indifferent father (Trevor Howard). Suffering from an emotional breakdown, Magda kills her father when she discovers that he has seduced the wife (Nadine Uwampa) of Hendrik (John Matshikiza), the farm foreman. She grows increasingly involved with the young black couple until Hendrik, disgusted by Birkin's self-induced deterioration, rapes her and then leaves the farm with his wife in tow. Carried by Birkin's wonderful performance and Howard's commanding portrayal of her father, the film evokes an atmosphere as erotic and raw as the land (shot in Spain, not South Africa) in which it is set. The winner of the Silver Lion at the 1985 Venice Film Festival, DUST is the second feature from Marion Hansel, one of Belgium's small core of women directors, which includes Chantal Ackerman and the heralded but relatively unknown Mary Jiminez. In English.

p, Michele Troncon; d, Marion Hansel; w, Marion Hansel (based on the novel *In the Heart of the Country* by Jean-Marie Coetzee); ph, Walther Vanden Ende (Fujicolor); ed, Susanna Rossberg; m, Martin St. Pierre.

Drama **(PR:O MPAA:NR)**

DYBBUK, THE***

(1938, Pol.) 122m Fencke/Foreign Cinema Arts bw

Abraham Morewski *(Rabbi Azrielke),* R. Samberg *(Messenger),* Moishe Libman *(Sender),* Lili Liliana *(Leah),* Dina Halpern *(Frade),* Gerszon Lamberger *(Nisson),* Leon Liebgold *(Channon),* Max Bozyk *(Nuta),* Samuel Landau *(Zalman),* S. Bronecki *(Nachman).*

This eerie filmization of a popular Yiddish play concerns two children promised to each other in marriage before they are born. Years pass and the young man, never having seen his bride-to-be, comes to her village to study cabalistic lore. He falls in love with her, but her father, Reb Sender (M. Libman) wants to renege on his promise and marry her to a wealthy man. In despair, the young man, Channon (L. Libgold), kills himself. His spirit leaves his body and possesses the body of his beloved, Leah (Lili Liliana), during her wedding. She is struck speechless and a wise old rabbi is brought in to perform the rites of exorcism. One of the few examples of prewar Polish cinema available on video, THE DYBBUK is a fascinating record not only of the height of Eastern European Yiddish theater's accomplishment before its annihilation, but of an almost utterly medieval Jewish way of life in which supernatural events were looked upon as common occurrences, a way of life likewise annihilated. The videotape is available only in its original Yiddish version.

p, Ludvig Previs; d, Machael Waszynski; w, S.A. Kacyzna, Marek Arenstein (based on a play by S. Ansky); ph, Albert Wywerka; ed, George Roland; m, Henryk Kon.

Fantasy **(PR:A MPAA:NR)**

E

EARRINGS OF MADAME DE . . ., THE****

(1953, Fr./It.) 105m Franco London-Indusfilms-Rizzoli/Arlan bw (MADAME DE. . .; AKA: THE DIAMOND EARRINGS)

Danielle Darrieux *(Countess Louise de. . .)*, Charles Boyer *(General Andre de. . .)*, Vittorio De Sica *(Baron Fabrizio Donati)*, Mireille Perrey *(Mme. de. . .'s Nurse)*, Jean Debucourt *(Mon. Remy, the Jeweler)*, Serge Lecointe *(Jerome, his Son)*, Lia di Leo *(Lola, the General's Mistress)*, Jean Galland *(M. de Bernac)*, Hubert Noel *(Henri de Maleville)*, Leon Walther *(Theater Manager)*, Madeleine Barbulee *(Mme. de. . .'s Friend)*, Guy Favieres *(Julien, the General's Valet)*, Paul Azais, Josselin.

One of the four great works—along with LA RONDE; LE PLAISIR; and LOLA MONTES—that closed Max Ophuls' career, THE EARRINGS OF MADAME DE . . . begins brilliantly as the Countess Louise de . . . (Danielle Darrieux, her character's last name deliberately obscured throughout the story and thereby more universal) searches through her belongings for something to sell. The camera moves along, focused on her hand, as she examines furs, a necklace, a cross, and finally a pair of diamond earrings that she received as a wedding present from her husband, Gen. Andre de . . . (Charles Boyer). This frivolous young woman apparently knows nothing about finances, which is why she must sell something, and clearly even less about romance, hence her choice to part with her wedding gift. When she pretends that the earrings have been stolen, the General begins a detailed search, gathering the servants and allowing the newspapers to print the story of their reported theft. Later the local jeweler (Jean Debucourt), discreetly returns the earrings, which he purchased from the Countess, to the General, to whom he sold them initially. The General then gives the earrings to his mistress, Lola (Lia di Leo), who is leaving for Constantinople. She loses them at a gambling table to Baron Fabrizio Donati (Vittorio De Sica), who, upon returning to Paris, meets and gradually falls in love with the Countess. Naturally, he must give the Countess a gift that will express his deepest affection. Masterfully told by Ophuls, both verbally and visually. As one comes to expect from the director, the camerawork is a marvel. We watch in awe as the camera dollies, tracks, and circles dizzyingly around the room to reveal selectively only those things Ophuls wants revealed. Perhaps the two best-known sequences are the economic opening, in which we learn nearly all we need to know about the Countess by watching her hands caress her finest material possessions; and the ballroom sequence, in which, though a series of camera moves and dissolves, we watch as the affectionate game-playing between the Countess and Baron Donati develops into a deep romance. In French with English subtitles.

p, H. Baum, Ralph Baum; d, Max Ophuls; w, Marcel Achard, Annette Wademant, Marcel Archard; ph, Christian Matras; ed, Borys Lewin; m, Oscar Strauss, Georges Van Parys.

Drama **(PR:A MPAA:NR)**

EARTH*****

(1930, USSR) 54m VUFKO/Artkino bw (ZEMLYA; AKA: SOIL)

Stepan Shkurat *(Opanas Trubenko)*, Semyon Savshenko *(Vasil, the Son)*, Pyotr Masokha *(Khoma)*, Mikola Nademski *(Grandfather Semen)*, V. Mikhailov *(Fr. Gerasim)*, Elena Maximova *(Natalka)*, Yulia Solntseva *(Vasil's Sister)*, P. Petrik *(Kravchina-Chuprina)*, I. Franko *(Arkhip Belokon, a Kulak)*.

One of film's great poetic masterpieces, EARTH is Alexander Dovzhenko's film about the land upon which he was raised—the Ukraine, where the USSR's first collective farm program began. Following a sketchy storyline involving the murder of a tractor-driving peasant by a landowner who opposes the new farm collective, Dovzhenko proceeded to create a film that is also a study of the land, the people, and the flow of nature. There are numerous moments of great beauty, such as the images of wheat fields blowing in the wind and the closeups of nature's abundance during harvesting, and then there are those faces—rough, weather-beaten, yet indomitable. There is the funeral sequence, when the hero's father stoically refuses a Christian service and conducts his own in the peasant tradition. To the old man this is part of nature's plan. Like the seasons and the crops, all things pass and return—in the Ukraine. EARTH, arguably the last great silent film, is a film of tremendous emotional power that must be seen to be appreciated. Silent, with English titles.

d, Alexander Dovzhenko; w, Alexander Dovzhenko; ph, Danilo Demutsky; ed, Alexander Dovzhenko; m, Leonid Revutsky.

Drama **(PR:A MPAA:NR)**

ECLIPSE***

(1962, Fr./It.) 123m Interopa-Cineriz-Paris/Times bw (L'ECLISSE)

Monica Vitti *(Vittoria)*, Alain Delon *(Piero)*, Francisco Rabal *(Riccardo)*, Lilla Brignone *(Vittoria's Mother)*, Louis Seigner *(Ercoli)*, Rossana Rory *(Anita)*, Mirella Ricciardi *(Marta)*, Cyrus Elias *(Drunk)*.

Vittoria (Monica Vitti) leaves Riccardo (Francisco Rabal), her companion of four years, and becomes involved with Piero (Alain Delon), a broker working for her mother. They fall in love, but realize they have little in common, so they bury their fears by making love and decide to continue the relationship as long as it will last. This was the third in a series of similarly styled films from Michelangelo Antonioni, the others being L'AVVENTURA (1960)—which first brought him international acclaim—and LA NOTTE (1961), all starring the enigmatic heroine Vitti as the capricious, love-weary blonde. It is not for the plot that one watches an Antonioni film; there is too little of it to be of much interest. Rather one watches—and, perhaps more importantly, hears—the modern world through his rendering of emotion, architecture, chaos, boredom, silence and incommunicability. In Italian with English subtitles.

p, Robert Hakim, Raymond Hakim; d, Michelangelo Antonioni; w, Michelangelo Antonioni, Tonino Guerra, Elio Bartolini, Ottiero Ottieri; ph, Gianni Di Venanzo; ed, Eraldo Da Roma; m, Giovanni Fusco.

Drama **(PR:C MPAA:NR)**

ECSTASY***

(1933, Czech.) 82m Elekta-Jewel bw (EXTASE; AKA: SYMPHONY OF LOVE)

Hedy Kiesler [Lamarr] *(Eva),* Zvonomir Rogoz *(Emile),* Aribert Mog *(Adam),* Leopold Kramer *(Eva's Father).*

Eva (Hedy Kiesler, who later became Hedy Lamarr) is a child bride whose husband ignores her on her wedding night. Later, in frustration, she has a sexual tryst in a hut with a roadway engineer. Taking a swim when her horse wanders away carrying her clothes, Eva chases the horse and bumps into the engineer, who hands over her clothes like a gentleman. She arranges to go away with him, but leaves him after her former husband commits suicide and subsequently appears with a baby, the offspring of this illicit affair, happy and fulfilled. The simple story is told with invention by director Gustav Machaty, who seems especially influenced by the editing techniques of Eisenstein. Nonetheless, the only reason ECSTASY is remembered today is because it contains the 15-year-old Hedy Lamarr's then-controversial nude bathing and, later, lovemaking scenes, in which she feigned the title emotion. Promoted in its day as "The most whispered about film in the world" and "The stark naked truth of a woman's desire for love." The videocasette is dubbed in English.

p, Frantisek Horky, Moriz Grunhut; d, Gustav Machaty; w, Gustav Machaty, Frantisek Horky, Vitezslav Nezval, Jacques A. Koerpel; ph, Jan Stallich, Hans Androschin; m, Giuseppe Becce.

Drama **(PR:O MPAA:NR)**

EDITH AND MARCEL*½**

(1983, Fr.) 140m Films 13-Parafrance/Miramax c (EDITH ET MARCEL)

Evelyne Bouix *(Edith Piaf/Margot de Villedieu),* Marcel Cerdan, Jr. *(Marcel Cerdan),* Charles Aznavour *(Himself),* Jacques Villeret *(Jacques Barbier),* Francis Huster *(Francis Roman),* Jean-Claude Brialy *(Loulou Barrier),* Jean Bouise *(Lucien Roupp),* Charles Gerard *(Charlot),* Charlotte de Turckheim *(Ginou),* Micky Sebastian *(Marinette),* Maurice Garrel *(Margot's Father),* Ginette Garcin *(Guite),* Philippe Khorsand *(Jo Longman),* Jany Gastaldi *(Momone),* Candice Patou *(Margot's Sister),* Tanya Lopert *(English Teacher),* Jean Rougerie *(Theater Director).*

This sad tale of romance devotes equal time to two love stories—that of singer Edith Piaf and boxer Marcel Cerdan, one of the most celebrated love affairs in France, and the romance between a chubby French POW and his schoolgirl pen pal, who correspond for four years and agree to marry without ever having met. Had these stories not existed, director Claude Lelouch would surely have invented them. The film begins in 1949, when Piaf (Evelyne Bouix) learns of the death of her lover, Marcel (played by Cerdan's son, Marcel, Jr.), who is killed in a plane crash over the Atlantic. The film then goes back to 1939: Edith and Marcel have not yet met, nor have POW Jacques (Jacques Villeret) and schoolgirl Margot (Bouix in a dual role). For the next hour, the film is about these lovers meeting. Piaf and Cerdan, who would eventually become the world middleweight champion and a hero to all of France, meet in a New York restaurant and become nearly inseparable, despite the presence of Marcel's wife and children in Casablanca; Jacques and Margot meet for the first time at a train station after the war, though Jacques is not quite the man Margot expected, especially since this Cyrano had his love letters penned by a far more eloquent army mate. For the remainder of the film, we watch the two romances ebb and flow, even crossing paths on one occasion, when Jacques and Margot attend a Piaf concert. Yes, EDITH AND MARCEL is terribly sentimental in the manner of a storybook fable, but no more so than so many of Piaf's great songs. The soundtrack is filled with her music (and that of one of her many collaborators, Charles Aznavour, who plays himself) and the result is a film that is not a biography, but an adaptation of the sad songs Piaf made famous. Bouix does an admirable job in her two roles and flawlessly lip-syncs Piaf's original recordings. Cerdan, Jr., is touching in a strangely powerful casting decision (as an actor, he must portray the love his father felt for a woman with whom his mother had to compete), which was made after the death of Patrick Dewaere, who was originally slated to star. In French with English subtitles.

p, Claude Lelouch; d, Claude Lelouch; w, Pierre Uytterhoeven, Gilles Durieux, Claude Lelouch; ph, Jean Boffety; ed, Hugues Darmois; m, Francis Lai, Edith Piaf.

Biography/Romance **(PR:A MPAA:NR)**

8 1/2****

(1963, It.) 140m Cineriz-Francinex/Embassy bw (OTTO E MEZZO; AKA: FEDERICO FELLINI'S 8 1/2)

Marcello Mastroianni *(Guido Anselmi),* Claudia Cardinale *(Claudia),* Anouk Aimee *(Luisa Anselmi),* Sandra Milo *(Carla),* Rossella Falk *(Rossella),* Barbara Steele *(Gloria Morin),* Mario Pisu *(Mezzabotta),* Guido Alberti *(The Producer),* Madeleine LeBeau *(French Actress),* Jean Rougeul *(Writer),* Caterina Boratto *(Fashionable Woman),* Annibale Ninchi *(Anselmi's Father),* Giuditta Rissone *(Anselmi's Mother),* Ian Dallas *(Mindreader),* Edra Gale *(La Saraghina),* Yvonne Casadei, Annie Gorassini *(Producer's Girl Friend),* Tito Masini *(The Cardinal),* Eugene Walter *(The Journalist),* Gilda Dahlberg *(Journalist's Wife),* Hedy Vessel *(Model),* Nadine Sanders *(Airline Hostess),* Georgia Simmons *(Anselmi's Grandmother),* Hazel Rogers *(Negro Dancer),* Riccardo Guglielmi *(Guido as a Farm Boy),* Marco Gemini *(Guido as a Schoolboy).*

After finishing six feature films, codirecting one film (THE WHITE SHEIK), and directing two short episodes of anthology films, Federico Fellini had made, according to his count, 7 1/2 films. Hence the title of his next—8 1/2. A brilliant film on filmmaking and the process of creating art, 8 1/2 comes about as close as anyone will be able to get to the inside of a human being's brain, specifically Fellini's. Marcello Mastroianni (playing a director not all that different from Fellini) is Guido Anselmi, a director coming off a big hit. He needs rest and goes to a spa to regain his strength. He cannot recuperate, however, being interrupted instead by his producer (Guido Alberti), his screenwriter (Jean Rougeul), his wife (Anouk Aimee), and his mistress (Sandra Milo)—all of whom want details from the director about his new sci-fi film. Hundreds of people are waiting in the wings, but Guido finds himself creatively blocked and fends off the inquiries of his actors, reporters, and especially his pain-in-the-neck screenwriter. Totally confused about what he wants to do next, Guido begins to fantasize. 8 1/2 is a beautifully photographed film, with superb performances, a haunting score from Nino Rota, and a confounding structure that often leaves the viewer guessing as to where the characters are—in the past? the present? the future? In the film or reality? It won an Oscar for Best Foreign-Language Film and Best Costume Design (black-and-white), and earned nominations for the director, screenwriters, and art director. Dubbed in English.

p, Angelo Rizzoli; d, Federico Fellini; w, Federico Fellini, Tullio Pinelli, Ennio Flaiano, Brunello Rondi (based on a story by Federico Fellini and Ennio Flaiano); ph, Gianni Di Venanzo; ed, Leo Catozzo; m, Nino Rota.

Drama **(PR:C MPAA:NR)**

EL AMOR BRUJO***

(1986, Sp.) 100m Piedra/Orion c (Trans: A Love Bewitched)

Antonio Gades *(Carmelo),* Cristina Hoyos *(Candela),* Laura del Sol *(Lucia),* Juan Antonio Jimenez *(Jose),* Emma Penella *(Aunt Rosario),* La Polaca *(Pastora),* Gomez de Jerez *(El Lobo),* Enrique Ortega *(Jose's Father),* Diego Pantoja *(Candela's Father),* Giovana *(Rocio),* Candy Roman *(Chulo),* Manolo Sevilla *(Singer).*

EL AMOR BRUJO is the third entry in Spanish director Carlos Saura's flamenco dance trilogy, preceded in 1981 by BLOOD WEDDING and in 1983 by CARMEN. This time Saura and his choreographer, Antonio Gades, have turned to the Manuel de Falla opera for their source of inspiration. Using much of the same cast from CARMEN—Laura del Sol has here been relegated to a supporting role, while Cristina Hoyos has been given the lead—Saura has set the film on an exotically colored and stylishly designed studio set of a Madrid shantytown. Jose (Juan Antonio Jimenez) and Candela (Hoyos) are two gypsies who have been betrothed since childhood, when their fathers, having drunk too much wine, decided on the arrangement. Early in the film a splendid wedding takes place, but we learn that each mate has another love interest. Carmelo (Gades) admires Candela from a distance, while Jose is having an affair with the gorgeous Lucia (del Sol). Following the critical and commercial success of CARMEN, which became one of Spain's highest-grossing pictures and received an Academy Award nomination as Best Foreign Film, EL AMOR BRUJO has been considerably less appreciated by critics and audiences alike, perhaps because the general audience is more familiar with Bizet's "Carmen" than with de Falla's "El Amor Brujo" (also known here as "Love, the Magician"). EL AMOR BRUJO is somewhat more stylized that its two predecessors, with some wonderfully fluid camera moves to highlight the cinematography. The dancing is equally astounding and, according to some enthusiasts, better with Hoyos having taken over the lead from del Sol. In Spanish with English subtitles.

p, Emiliano Piedra; d, Carlos Saura; w, Carlos Saura, Antonio Gades (based on the ballet by Manuel de Falla); ph, Teo Escamilla (Eastmancolor); ed, Pedro del Rey; m, Manuel de Falla.

Dance **(PR:A MPAA:PG)**

EL BRUTO****

(1952, Mex.) 80m Internacional Cinematografica/Plexus bw (AKA: THE BRUTE)

Pedro Armendariz *(Pedro, el Bruto),* Katy Jurado *(Paloma),* Andres Soler *(Don Andres Cabrea),* Rosita Arena *(Meche),* Roberto Meyer, Beatriz Ramos, Paco Martinez, Gloria Mestre, Paz Villegas, Jose Munoz, Diana Ochoa, Ignacio Villalbazo, Joaquin Roche, G. Bravo Sosa, Efrain Arauz, Lupe Carriles, Raquel Garcia.

This devastating, little-seen Mexican entry from Luis Bunuel was one of seven films he directed during 1951 and 1952 (only three of which he wrote). Pedro the Brute (Pedro Armendariz), a slaughterhouse worker who is all brawn and little brain, is indebted to Don Andres (Andres Soler), a callous landlord who is preparing to evict a number of families from their low-rent homes. When the tenants, who have nowhere to go, threaten to defy the court-issued eviction order, Don Andres hires Pedro to frighten them off. Unaware of his own awesome strength, Pedro hits the tenant organizer so hard he kills him. Meanwhile, Don Andres' sexually hungry mistress Paloma (Katy Jurado) makes amorous advances toward Pedro, with whom she openly discusses his stupidity. It is only later, as the frightened Pedro hides out from a band of murderous tenants, that his compassionate side is revealed. Injured in a fight, Pedro is treated by, and attracted to, the young, virginal Meche (Rosita Arenas), who is unaware that the man she nurses is her father's killer. Within the limits of a commercial, *film noir*-styled Mexican entertainment, the masterful Bunuel has created a moving and expertly crafted tale of brutality and compassion set in the context of class conflict. The Wellesian Pedro, in his self-discovery and his futile attempt to tame himself in the name of his love, is one of the most touching characters Bunuel has ever written. Thankfully, this film is now available on videotape, in Spanish with clearly legible English subtitles.

p, Oscar Dancigers; d, Luis Bunuel; w, Luis Alcoriza, Luis Bunuel; ph, Augustin Jimenez; ed, Jorge Bustos; m, Raul

Lavista.

Drama **(PR:A-C MPAA:NR)**

EL DIPUTADO**½

(1978, Sp.) 111m Figaro-Zeta-Ufesa/David Whitten c (Trans: The Deputy)

Jose Sacristan *(Roberto Orbea),* Maria Luisa San Jose *(Carmen Orbea),* Jose Luis Alonso *(Juanito),* Angel Pardo *(Nes),* Agustin Gonzalez *(Carres),* Enrique Vivo *(Moreno Pastrana),* Queta Claver *(Juanito's Mother),* Juan Antonio Bardem.

Spanish director Eloy de la Iglesia makes the connection between sexual and political preference in this post-Franco picture about an ex-homosexual lawyer, Roberto Orbea (Jose Sacristan) who is now married to a beautiful Marxist (Maria Luisa San Jose). Roberto has strong socialist leanings, but he keeps them hidden until he is arrested and thrown in prison. His time in jail reactivates his repressed homosexuality and he begins once again to pursue young boys. Meanwhile, Franco dies and all political prisoners are released. Roberto is now able to breathe freely, unafraid of repercussions resulting from his political beliefs. Unfortunately, hiding his renewed homosexuality presents a new problem: he develops a serious relationship with a young hustler (Jose Luis Alonso), but Roberto's Marxist preaching doesn't interest the boy. Originally released in Spain in 1978, EL DIPUTADO probably seemed more relevant and daring in post-Franco Spain than it does now to Americans. Despite the ingenious premise and depiction of homosexuality in an honest, realistic light, the film may turn off some viewers because of its stilted acting and militant speechmaking. The film's availability on videotape provides an excellent opportunity to see a commercial Spanish entry that made no impact on American shores. In Spanish with English subtitles.

d, Eloy de la Iglesia; w, Eloy de la Iglesia, Gonzalo Goicoachea; ph, Antonio Cuevas; ed, Julio Pena.

Drama **(PR:O MPAA:NR)**

EL MUERTO**

(1975, Arg./Sp.) 105m Aries-Impala c (Trans: The Dead Man)

Juan Jose Camero *(Benjamin Otalora),* Thelma Biral *(Azevedo's Mistress),* Francisco Rabal *(Azevedo Bandeira),* Raul Lavie *(Piru),* Jose Maria Gutierrez *(The Colonel),* Antonio Iranzo *(Ulpiano),* Jorge Vallalba *(Mocho),* Noemi Laserre *(Madam),* Ricardo Trigo, Fernando Iglesias *(Tacholas),* Rey Charol, Enrique Alonso, Juan Carlos Lamas, Max Berliner, Antonio Monaco, Miguel Zysman, Cristina Fernandez, Adolfo Estela.

A flat, uninteresting South American western from Hector Olivera, EL MUERTO stars Christopher Lambert lookalike Juan Jose Camero as Benjamin Otalora, a young man who flees Rio de Janeiro after knifing a man. He takes refuge in Montevideo and is befriended by Azevedo Bandeira (Francisco Rabal), a powerful and well-known smuggler who ships weapons and cattle across the Uruguayan border. Otalora proves his loyalty to Don Azevedo and is given an increasing amount of power in the smuggling operations. Soon, however, he begins working on his own, forming an alliance with Azevedo's right-hand man and even seducing his boss' mistress (Thelma Biral). Although it is based on a short story by Jorge Luis Borges, there is little (besides the subtitles) to distinguish this entry from your average horse opry. The story is screenwriting-by-numbers, the photography serviceable, the music curious and uncharacteristic, and the acting stilted. In Spanish with English subtitles.

p, Fernando Ayala; d, Hector Olivera; w, Fernando Ayala, Hector Olivera, Juan Carlos Onetti (based on the short story by Jorge Luis Borges); ph, Juan Carlos Desanzo; ed, Carlos Piaggo; m, Ariel Ramirez.

Western **(PR:C MPAA:NR)**

EL NORTE****

(1983, US) 139m Independent/Cinecom-Island Alive c

Zaide Silvia Gutierrez *(Rosa Xuncax),* David Villalpando *(Enrique Xuncax),* Ernesto Gomez Cruz *(Arturo Xuncax),* Alicia Del Lago *(Lupe Xuncax),* Eraclio Zepeda *(Pedro),* Stella Quan *(Josefita),* Emilio del Haro *(Truck Driver),* Rodolfo Alejandre *(Ramon),* Rodrigo Puebla *(Puma),* Trinidad Silva *(Monty),* Abel Franco *(Raimundo),* Mike Gomez *(Jaime),* Lupe Ontiveros *(Nacha),* John Martin *(Ed),* Ron Joseph *(Joel),* Larry Cedar *(Bruce),* Sheryl Bernstein *(Karen),* Gregory Enton *(Len),* Tony Plana *(Carlos),* Enrique Castillo *(Jorge),* Diane Civita *(Alice),* Jorge Moreno *(Man in Bus).*

A Spanish-language American film produced independently in association with the PBS TV series "American Playhouse," EL NORTE is an effective and moving drama about the strength of the human spirit and the will to survive. Enrique and Rosa Xuncax (David Villalpando and Zaide Silvia Gutierrez) are brother and sister, Guatemalan Indians, who are forced to flee their village when their politically active father is murdered and their mother is taken away by authorities. They decide to go to *el norte*, where—across the border in the US—the siblings feel their future lies. As difficult and demeaning as their illegal trek across the border is, it is not nearly as rough as their attempts to make a living in Los Angeles. The cinematic style alternates between straightforward, almost documentary storytelling and moments of surreal imagery that occur in the characters' dreams. Though there is certainly a political message maintained throughout the film, it is never made overt. Rather, situations are allowed to speak for themselves. Without big-name actors or a large budget, EL NORTE delivers a powerful and beautiful testament to the human spirit. (In Spanish; English subtitles.)

p, Anna Thomas; d, Gregory Nava; w, Anna Thomas, Gregory Nava; ph, James Glennon; ed, Betsy Blankett; m, Gustav Mahler, Samuel Barber, Giuseppe Verdi, The Folkloristas, Melecio Martinez, Emil Richards, Linda O'Brien.

Drama **(PR:O MPAA:R)**

ELENA AND HER MEN*½**

(1956, Fr./It.) 86m Franco-London-Gibe-Electra/WB c (ELENA ET LES HOMMES; AKA: PARIS DOES STRANGE THINGS)

Ingrid Bergman *(Princess Elena Sorokowska),* Jean Marais *(Gen. Francois Rollan),* Mel Ferrer *(Viscount Henri de Chevincourt),* Jean Claudio *(Lionel Villaret),* Jean Richard *(Hector, Rollan's Batman),* Magali Noel *(Lolotte, Elena's Maid),* Juliette Greco *(Miarka),* Pierre Bertin *(Martin-Michaud),* Jean Castanier *(Isnard),* Elina Labourdette *(Paulette),* Frederic Duvalles *(Gaudin),* Dora Doll *(Rosa la Rose),* Mirko Ellis *(Marbeau),* Jacques Hilling *(Lisbonne),* Jacques Jouanneau *(Eugene Godin),* Renaud Mary *(Fleury),* Gaston Modot *(The Leader of Gypsies),* Jacques Morel *(Duchene),* Michele Nadal *(Denise Godin),* Albert Remy *(Buchez),* Olga Valery *(Aunt Olga),* Leo Marjane *(The Street Singer),* Leon Larive *(Henri's Domestic),* Gregori Chmara *(Elena's Domestic),* Paul Demange *(A Spectator),* Jim Gerald *(Cafe Owner),* Robert Le Beal *(The Doctor),* Claire Gerard *(The Strolling Woman).*

Comparing the star of this picture with Venus, director Jean Renoir said that for a long time he "had been dying to make something gay with Ingrid Bergman, I wanted to see her laughing and smiling on the screen." She did that and much more in this critically assaulted tale of a beautiful Polish princess in Paris in the 1880s. As Princess Elena Sorokowska, she romances men in the hopes of bringing them great success and presents each with a marguerite, her favorite flower. She funnels her affections to Francois Rollan (Jean Marais), a general with plans to become a dictator after a coup d'etat. Because of her past successes in catapulting men to fame and good fortune, she believes she can do the same for him. It takes Henri di Chevincourt (Mel Ferrer), a young count and a friend, to convince her to change her feelings about immortalizing men. As with so many truly great movies, the public harshly attacked the film, which had been recut and dubbed by Warner Bros. "A mishmash," "a shock," and "a farrago" were just some of the critical stones hurled at Renoir, as was another suggestion that he throw the film in the Seine. On the plus side, however, Jean-Luc Godard has called it "the most intelligent film in the world." Though all the above descriptions are exaggerated, ELENA AND HER MEN is a fantastic film. It's filled with patented Renoirisms, from the utter sincerity of the emotions to the exceptional impressionistic composition. In French with English subtitles.

p, Louis Wipf; d, Jean Renoir; w, Jean Renoir, Jean Serge; ph, Claude Renoir (Technicolor); ed, Borys Lewin; m, Joseph Kosma.

Drama **(PR:A MPAA:NR)**

ELUSIVE CORPORAL, THE***

(1962, Fr.) 108m Cyclope/Pathe-Union bw (LE CAPORAL EPINGLE)

Jean-Pierre Cassel *(The Corporal),* Claude Brasseur *(Pater),* Claude Rich *(Ballochet),* Jean Carmet *(Emile),* Mario David *(Caruso),* Philippe Castelli *(Electrician),* Jacques Jouanneau *(Penche-a-Gauche),* Conny Froboess *(Erika),* Raymond Jourdan *(Dupieu),* O.E. Hasse *(Drunk on the Train),* Guy Bedos *(Stutterer),* Gerard Darrieu *(Cross-Eyed Man),* Sacha Briquet *(Escaping "Woman" Prisoner),* Lucien Raimbourg *(Station Guard).*

Where Jean Renoir's GRAND ILLUSION addressed life in POW camps during WW I, this effortlessly crafted (or so it appears) Renoir tale takes place during WW II, after the fall of France. The Corporal (Jean-Pierre Cassel) and two friends, Pater and Ballochet (Claude Brasseur and Claude Rich), try repeatedly to escape from prison, but each time their efforts are fruitless. They are separated, but, in time, reunited only to continue their attempts toward freedom. It is not long before they realize that there is no liberty, and that the prison walls are not the only ones confining them. Not by accident was this Renoir's first black-and-white film in over a decade. In this choice, Renoir drew a connection both to his past as a filmmaker and to Paris' past—emphasizing the senseless repetition of war and the timelessness and universality of the fight for liberty. In French with English subtitles.

p, Rene G. Vuattoux; d, Jean Renoir; w, Jean Renoir, Guy Lefranc (based on a novel by Jacques Perret); ph, Georges Leclerc; ed, Renee Lichtig; m, Joseph Kosma.

War/Drama **(PR:A MPAA:NR)**

ELVIRA MADIGAN**

(1967, Swed.) 90m Europa-Janco/Cinema V c

Pia Degermark *(Elvira),* Thommy Berggren *(Sixten Sparre),* Lennart Malmer *(Friend),* Nina Widerberg *(Little Girl),* Cleo Jensen *(Cook).*

A retelling of a famous love affair in 19th-century Sweden, this is the story of a tightrope performer (Pia Degermark) and an army lieutenant (Thommy Berggren) who both give up their previous lives—he leaving his wife and children, she deserting the circus troupe of which she is the top attraction—to find a new freedom for themselves. As the film begins, their romance appears perfect. As the story progresses, however, they realize that their idyllic state cannot continue, and vow to kill themselves rather than live apart. Universally praised as one of the most beautiful films of all time, "poetic" and "exquisite," ELVIRA MADIGAN is likewise one of the most *overrated* films of all time. Nothing on the screen even remotely suggests love or passion—unless, of course, one believes that romance exists only on those sunny days of Hallmark greeting cards in which lovers eat berries and cream and chase butterflies (in slow motion, what's more) through fields of long grass. Sixteen-year-old Degermark was named Best Actress at the Cannes Film Festival for her performance as the title character. The videotape is dubbed in English.

d, Bo Widerberg; w, Bo Widerberg; ph, Jorgen Persson; ed, Bo Widerberg (based on a ballad by Johan Lindstrom Saxon); m, Ulf Bjorlin, Wolfgang Amadeus Mozart, Antonio Vivaldi.

Romance **(PR:A-C MPAA:PG)**

EMMANUELLE½**

(1974, Fr.) 105m Trinacre-Orphee/COL c

Sylvia Kristel *(Emmanuelle),* Alain Cuny *(Marco),* Daniel Sarky *(Jean),* Jeanne Colletin *(Ariane),* Marika Green *(Bee),* Christine Boisson *(Marie-Ange).*

One of the classics of soft-core cinema, EMMANUELLE stars Sylvia Kristel as the title creature, the pretty wife of a French ambassador in Bangkok. It's not long before Emmanuelle discovers a burning sexual passion she has heretofore repressed. With the help of an attractive young teenager, Emmanuelle is exposed (literally) to the joys of eroticism. Although the film takes itself far too seriously and engages in much of the usual naughty Victoriana, it is a relatively well-made picture that became an international hit because of its appeal to both men and women. Many sequels followed, with Mia Nygren taking over the lead in 1984's EMMANUELLE 4. The Kristel-Nygren EMMANUELLE series (spelled with two "m"s) should not be confused with Laura Gemser's EMANUELLE (with one "m") films.

p, Yves Rousset-Rouard; d, Just Jaeckin; w, Jean-Louis Richard (based on the book by Emmanuelle Arsan); ph, Richard Suzuki; ed, Claudine Bouche.

Drama **(PR:O MPAA:X/R)**

ENTRE NOUS***

(1983, Fr.) 110m Partners-Alexandre-Hachette Premiere-Films A2-SFPC/UA c (COUP DE FOUDRE)

Miou-Miou *(Madeleine),* Isabelle Huppert *(Lena),* Jean-Pierre Bacri *(Costa),* Guy Marchand *(Michel),* Robin Renucci *(Raymond),* Patrick Bauchau *(Carlier),* Jacques Alric *(Monsieur Vernier),* Jacqueline Doyen *(Madame Vernier),* Patricia Champane *(Florence),* Saga Blanchard *(Sophie),* Guillaume LeGuellec *(Rene).*

This semi-autobiographical account from French director Diane Kurys exists, in some respects, as a prequel to her superb 1977 feature debut, PEPPERMINT SODA. The film opens during the German Occupation of France. Lena (Isabelle Huppert), a young Russian Jew, escapes from a prison camp by marrying a stranger, Michel (Guy Marchand). Meanwhile, in Paris, art student Madeleine (Miou-Miou) must start life anew when her husband is brutally gunned down before her. The scene then shifts to Lyons 1952 for a chance meeting between these two women. Lena is still wed to Michel and is the mother of two children, while Madeleine has remarried. They come to realize that they can only find support from each other and not from their boorish husbands. A resounding art-house success in the US and the recipient of an Oscar nomination for Best Foreign-Language Film, ENTRE NOUS (which, oddly, is the US release title) is an excellent examination of the bond of friendship. Like very few films before it, ENTRE NOUS focuses on a female friendship instead of the usual male "buddy" formula. Based in part on the experiences of the director's mother (the Lena character), this fictionalized account is one of great emotional truth, nothing if not honest. The relationship between Lena and Madeleine and between the women and their respective families is scripted, directed, and acted with a touch usually seen only in the French films of Renoir, Pagnol, or Truffaut. The picture's chief weakness is the curiously uninvolving episodic structure, beginning with the rocky 1940s prolog that opens the film. While ENTRE NOUS was universally praised, Kurys' superior 1987 follow-up, A MAN IN LOVE, was unduly condemned by nearly all who saw it. In French with English subtitles.

p, Ariel Zeitoun; d, Diane Kurys; w, Diane Kurys, Alain Le Henry (based on the book by Kurys, Olivier Cohen); ph, Bernard Lutic (CinemaScope); ed, Joele Van Effenterre; m, Luis Bacalov.

Drama **(PR:C MPAA:NR)**

ERENDIRA½**

(1983, Mex./Fr./Ger.) 103m Cine Qua Non-Triangle-Atlas Saskia/Miramax c

Irene Papas *(The Grandmother),* Claudia Ohana *(Erendira),* Michel Lonsdale *(The Senator),* Oliver Wehe *(Ulysses),* Ernesto Gomez Cruz *(The Grocer),* Pierre Vaneck *(Ulysses' Father),* Carlos Cardan *(The Smuggler),* Humberton Elizondo *(Blacaman),* Jorge Fegan *(The Commandant),* Francisco Mauri *(The Postman),* Sergio Calderon *(The Truck Driver),* Martin Palomares *(The Messenger),* Salvador Garcini *(The Juggler),* Felix Bussio Madrigal *(The Fiance),* Juan Antonio Ortiz Torres *(The Musician),* Delia Casanova *(The Narrator),* Rufus *(The Photographer).*

A hallucinatory picture that brings to the screen the images of famed Colombian writer Gabriel Garcia Marquez, ERENDIRA is the story of 14-year-old Erendira (Claudia Ohana), who lives in luxury with her witch of a grandmother (Irene Papas). One day, Erendira's carelessness in extinguishing a candelabra's flames leads to a fire that completely destroys everything her grandmother owns. The grandmother simply informs Erendira, "My poor darling, you will not be able to live long enough to pay me back," and sets off across the country with the young girl in tow. She sells off Erendira's virginity, then continues to prostitute the girl. The lengths of the lines stretching from Erendira's tent are astonishing, as is the girl's physical and mental stamina. Erendira then meets Ulysses (Oliver Wehe), an angelic customer who offers to take the girl away from her hell. This bizarre, labyrinthine picture should appeal to those familiar with Garcia Marquez and satisfy the desire to see his writings come to the screen in a faithful manner. The screenplay was based on a portion of his *One Hundred Years of Solitude*, which in turn inspired the novella *Innocent Erendira and Her Heartless Grandmother* and the short story "Death Beyond Constant Love." In Spanish with English subtitles.

p, Alain Queffelean; d, Ruy Guerra; w, Gabriel Garcia Marquez; ph, Denys Clerval; ed, Kenout Peltier; m, Maurice Lecoeur.

Fantasy **(PR:O MPAA:NR)**

ETERNAL RETURN, THE*½**

(1943, Fr.) 100m Discina bw (L'ETERNEL RETOUR; GB: LOVE ETERNAL)

Jean Marais *(Patrice)*, Madeleine Sologne *(Nathalie I)*, Jean Murat *(Marc)*, Yvonne de Bray *(Gertrude)*, Pierre Pieral *(Achille)*, Jean d'Yd *(Amedee)*, Junie Astor *(Nathalie II)*, Roland Toutain *(Lionel)*, Jeanne Marken *(Anne)*, Alexandre Rignault *(Morolt)*.

This modernized version of the Tristan and Isolde legend finds Patrice (Jean Marais) falling in love with two women named Nathalie (Madeleine Sologne and Junie Astor), one of whom (Sologne) has been betrothed to Patrice's wealthy uncle Marc (Jean Murat). Thinking that Nathalie I (Sologne) doesn't love him, Patrice proposes to Nathalie II. While the film is directed by Jean Delannoy, who is mediocre at best, the credit for its success belongs to scriptwriter Jean Cocteau. Although he had won praise 13 years earlier with THE BLOOD OF A POET, the painter-poet-playwright didn't gain real status in the cinema until this picture. Everything in it bears his mark, from the magical love potion to the idea of life continuing after death. It also marks the beginning of Cocteau's association with Marais, who would later appear in BEAUTY AND THE BEAST; THE EAGLE WITH TWO HEADS; LES PARENTS TERRIBLES; ORPHEUS; and THE TESTAMENT OF ORPHEUS. The wholly impersonal Delannoy, on the other hand, is best remembered today for his collaborations with others—Cocteau, Andre Gide (LA SYMPHONIE PASTORALE), and Jean-Paul Sartre (LES JEUX SONT FAITS). Pierre Pieral adds a demonic touch to the film with his portrayal of Achille, the hateful and monstrous dwarf. In French with English subtitles.

p, Andre Paulve; d, Jean Delannoy; w, Jean Cocteau; ph, Roger Hubert; ed, Suzanne Fauvel; m, Georges Auric.

Romance/Fantasy (PR:A MPAA:NR)

EVERY MAN FOR HIMSELF AND GOD AGAINST ALL****

(1975, Ger.) 110m ZDF-Herzog-Cine Intl./Cinema 5 c (JEDER FUR SICH UND GOTT GEGEN ALLE; AKA: THE MYSTERY OF KASPAR HAUSER)

Bruno S. *(Kaspar Hauser)*, Walter Ladengast *(Daumer)*, Brigitte Mira *(Kathe)*, Hans Musaus *(Unknown Man)*, Willy Semmelrogge *(Circus Director)*, Michael Kroecher *(Lord Stanhope)*, Henry van Lyck *(Calvary Captain)*, Enno Patalas *(Pastor Fuhrmann)*, Elis Pilgrim *(Pastor)*, Volker Prechtel *(Hiltel, the Prison Guard)*, Kidlat Tahmik *(Hombrecito)*, Gloria Doer *(Madame Hiltel)*, Helmut Doring *(Little King)*, Andi Gottwald *(Young Mozart)*, Herbert Achternbusch, Wolgang Bauer, Walter Steiner *(Farmboys)*, Florian Fricke *(Mons. Florian)*, Clemens Scheitz *(Registrar)*, Johannes Buzalski *(Police Officer)*, Dr. Willy Meyer-Furst *(Doctor)*, Wilhelm Bayer *(Calvary Captain)*, Franz Brumbach *(Bear Trainer)*, Alfred Edel *(Logic Professor)*, Herbert Fritsch *(Mayor)*.

The winner of the Grand Jury Award at the 1975 Cannes Film Festival, this haunting and uncharacteristically warm Werner Herzog film helped bring the visionary director an international reputation. The film is based on the documented story of a young man, Kaspar Hauser (Bruno S.), who, after living in a cellar for years with only a pet rocking horse, is abandoned by his protector and provider (a mysterious black-clad figure). Having been isolated from all humans except the godlike provider, Kaspar is suddenly thrust into civilization and, despite the fact that he can barely walk and cannot speak, is forced to adapt to society. His past remains a mystery to the townspeople, as does his purpose. Some attempt to teach him the mannerisms of the civilized, while others spy on his every move in an attempt to uncover some hidden identity. From the opening shot, of a wheat field blowing in the wind to the strains of Pachelbel's Canon, Herzog points to the connection between man and nature. It is Kaspar—discharged from the womb of nature (his dark, desolate cellar/prison) as a grown man different from all others, a pure soul uncorrupted by the demands of society—who is the embodiment of these two forces. To his fellow townspeople, Kaspar is an alien whose brain they must dissect after his mysterious death. After a careful examination, the scientists are thrilled with their discovery. They have solved this strange man's riddle—an enlarged liver and an abnormally shaped brain. This is the best, and only, answer they can find, who are unable to dissect their own brains. In German with English subtitles.

p, Werner Herzog; d, Werner Herzog; w, Werner Herzog; ph, Jorge Schmidt-Reitwein (Eastmancolor); ed, Beate Mainka-Jellinghaus; m, Johann Pachelbel, Tomaso Giovanni Albinoni, Orlando Di Lasso, Wolfgang Amadeus Mozart.

Biography (PR:A MPAA:NR)

EXTERMINATING ANGEL, THE*****

(1967, Mex.) 91m Uninci-SA Films 59-Altura bw (EL ANGEL EXTERMINADOR)

Silvia Pinal *(Letitia, the Valkyrie)*, Jacqueline Andere *(Senora Alicia Roc)*, Jose Baviera *(Leandro)*, Augusto Benedico *(Doctor)*, Luis Beristain *(Christian)*, Antonio Bravo *(Russell)*, Claudio Brook *(Majordomo)*, Cesar del Campo *(Colonel)*, Lucy Gallardo *(Lucia)*, Rosa Elena Durgel *(Silvia)*, Enrico Garcia Alvarez *(Senor Roc)*, Ofelia Guilmain *(Juana Avila)*, Nadia Haro Oliva *(Ana Maynar)*, Javier Loya *(Francisco Avila)*, Angel Merino *(Lucas)*, Javier Masse *(Eduardo)*, Ofelia Montesco *(Beatriz)*, Patricia Moran *(Rita)*, Patricia De Morelos *(Blanca)*, Bertha Moss *(Leonora)*, Enrique Rambal *(Nobile)*, Tito Junco *(Raul)*, Pancho Cordova.

A skillfully pointed blitzkrieg on the bourgeoisie from the master of iconoclastic assault, Luis Bunuel, THE EXTERMINATING ANGEL is an allegory about the savage interiors of a group of upper-class dinner guests who discover that they cannot leave the room in which they are gathered. Days and days pass, and their well-mannered facades are torn down by the animal natures that harbor within them. One guest (Antonio Bravo) dies and is irreverently stuffed into a cupboard; a pair of lovers (Javier Masse and Ofelia Montesco) commit suicide; a believer in witchcraft (Nadia Haro Oliva) hallucinates and brings forth demons; an incestuous brother and sister (Javier Loya and Ofelia Guilmain) steal morphine from a cancer-ridden guest. They even contemplate cannibalism—a fine way for the rich to act. The theme of entrapment in a hell of our own making, fashioned largely out of social conventions and traditions, is a familiar one in literature, but it has never been more successfully rendered in visual terms. Bunuel, like no other director, has continually exploded in the faces of the bourgeois the swiftest of blows, and in THE EXTERMINATING ANGEL he is in top form. His elegant kicks to the upper-crust crotch have not lost their potency from his first short, UN CHIEN ANDALOU (1928), to his final film, THAT OBSCURE OBJECT OF DESIRE (1977). In Spanish with English subtitles.

p, Gustavo Alatriste; d, Luis Bunuel; w, Luis Bunuel, Luis Alcoriza (based on the play "Los naufragos de la Calle de la Providentia" by Jose Bergamin); ph, Gabriel Figueroa; ed, Carlos Savage; m, Alessandro Scarlatti, Pietro Domenico Paradisi.

Comedy/Drama **(PR:O MPAA:NR)**

EYES, THE MOUTH, THE***

(1982, It./Fr.) 100m Odissya-Gaumont-RAI-TV/Triumph c (GLI OCCHI, LA BOCCA)

Lou Castel *(Giovanni Pallidissimi),* Angela Molina *(Vanda),* Emmanuelle Riva *(Mother),* Michel Piccoli *(Uncle Nigi),* Antonio Piovanelli *(Wanda's Father),* Giampaolo Saccarola *(Agostino),* Viviana Toniolo *(Adele),* Antonio Petrocelli *(Doctor),* Maria Romagnoli, Paolo Bacchi, Osanna Borsari, Daniele Mondini, Giada Mondini.

Giovanni Pallidissimi (Lou Castel), a washed-up actor who spends most of his time in Rome, returns to his bourgeois family's home to attend the funeral of his twin brother, Pippo, who committed suicide after being spurned by his fiancee, Vanda (Angela Molina). Giovanni's mother (Emmanuelle Riva) is a devout Catholic who is told that her son's death was an accident, since suicides reportedly go straight to hell. Pippo's uncle (Michel Piccoli) urges Vanda to pretend she was deeply in love with his nephew in order to quiet the mother's fears and to save face. She refuses to take part in their dishonesty and, by doing so, attracts the attention of Giovanni. Vanda and Giovanni give in to their desires and make love, but Giovanni must still face the ties that bind him to his mother and his dead brother's memory. Combining a high level of emotion with intellectual discourse, the film, which begins on New Year's Eve, confronts the necessity of detaching one's self from the past. While the main characters—Giovanni and Vanda—are attracted to each other for this reason, the theme is most brilliantly stated by director Marco Bellocchio with the inclusion of a scene from his highly acclaimed debut feature, FISTS IN THE POCKET, which starred a teenaged Castel in a similar role. Giovanni/Castel is no longer the same man who appeared in FISTS IN THE POCKET (he complains that he is old and fat and cannot find any more work), and the promised revolution of May 1968 never did come, but characters like Giovanni are still trapped in a search for freedom and love. In Italian with English subtitles.

p, Enzo Porcelli, Enea Ferrario; d, Marco Bellocchio; w, Marco Bellocchio, Vincenzo Cerami; ph, Giuseppe Lanci (Eastmancolor); ed, Sergio Nuti; m, Nicola Piovani.

Drama **(PR:O MPAA:R)**

F

FAHRENHEIT 451****

(1966, Brit.) 113m Anglo-Vineyard-Rank/UNIV c

Oskar Werner *(Montag),* Julie Christie *(Linda Montag/Clarisse),* Cyril Cusack *(Captain),* Anton Diffring *(Fabian),* Jeremy Spenser *(Man with Apple),* Bee Duffell *(Book Woman),* Gillian Lewis *(T.V. Announcer),* Ann Bell *(Doris),* Caroline Hunt *(Helen),* Anna Palk *(Jackie),* Roma Milne *(Neighbor),* Alex Scott *(The Life of Henry Brulard),* Dennis Gilmore *(The Martian Chronicles),* Fred Cox *(Pride),* Frank Cox *(Prejudice),* Michael Balfour *(Machiavelli's The Prince),* Judith Drynan *(Plato's Dialogues),* David Glover *(The Pickwick Papers),* Yvonne Blake *(The Jewish Question),* John Rae *(The Weir of Hermiston).*

Throughout nearly his entire career, Francois Truffaut was castigated for not making political films. He did, however, tackle political themes in two pictures—FAHRENHEIT 451, an adaptation of Ray Bradbury's sci-fi indictment of totalitarianism via book-burning, and THE LAST METRO, an original script that deals with the German occupation of France. In both cases the politics of the films address the suppression of two media of deep personal significance for Truffaut, namely books and the theater. His first film in English and first in color, FAHRENHEIT 451 (the title refers to the temperature at which paper burns) is set sometime in the future and follows Montag (Oskar Werner), a devoted and obedient "fireman" (he *sets* fires instead of extinguishing them) who burns books with a vengeance. Montag is superb at what he does and is able to ferret out books in the most obscure hiding places. One day he keeps a volume for himself, eager to learn why these tomes are so threatening that they must be destroyed, and is caught between his life as a civil servant—in which he follows orders and lives with a listless, TV-addicted wife, Linda (Julie Christie)—and his desire to live as a free man in a free society, inspired by schoolteacher Clarisse (Christie again). Severely underrated and misunderstood by critics who wanted Truffaut to continue making films like THE 400 BLOWS or JULES AND JIM, FAHRENHEIT 451 is a marvelously courageous personal statement that only becomes more fascinating with time. The finale, showing the "book people" who live secretly in the wilderness and "become" books by memorizing them, is one of the most memorable scenes of any Truffaut film. In English.

p, Lewis Allen; d, Francois Truffaut; w, Francois Truffaut, Jean-Louis Richard, David Rudkin, Helen Scott (based on the novel *Fahrenheit 451* by Ray Bradbury); ph, Nicolas Roeg (Technicolor); ed, Thom Noble; m, Bernard Herrmann.

Science Fiction **(PR:C MPAA:NR)**

FAMILY, THE***½

(1987, It./Fr.) 127m Maasfilm-Cinecitta-RAI TV Channel 1-Ariane/Vestron c (LA FAMIGLIA)

Vittorio Gassman *(Carlo),* Fanny Ardant *(Adriana),* Stefania Sandrelli *(Beatrice),* Andrea Occhipinti *(Young Carlo),* Jo Champa *(Young Adriana),* Alberto Gimignani, Massimo Dapporto, Carlo Dapporto, Cecilia Dazzi, Ottavia Piccolo, Athina Cenci, Alessandra Panelli, Monica Scattini, Ricky Tognazzi.

After venturing into pedestrian comedy in his previous film, MACARONI, director Ettore Scola returned to the single set limitations of his LE BAL for this pleasant drama, which covers 80 years in the life of one Italian family. The film opens in 1906 as the clan gathers in a large Rome apartment for a group photograph. A narrator, Carlo (Vittorio Gassman), points himself out in the picture—an infant who has just been baptized. Carlo narrates the entire film as time passes, Scola never showing the characters outside of their apartment. In addition to Carlo, the family includes his brother; his parents; the maid; his three matronly aunts; his wife, Beatrice (Stefania Sandrelli); and Beatrice's older and more worldly sister, Adriana (Fanny Ardant), whom Carlo really loves. Like so many of the films of Ingmar Bergman or Woody Allen, THE FAMILY goes to great lengths to re-create a family portrait album. Scola gives his audience a collection of characters, each with qualities and idiosyncracies that change and develop over the course of time. As a stylistic unifying thread, Scola uses a recurring dolly shot through the apartment's empty hall that symbolizes the passing of time. Filled with humor, sadness, and anger, the film also manages to encompass nearly all the major political and social events of 20th-century Italy. The videocassette is available in both dubbed and subtitled (Italian into English) versions.

p, Franco Committeri; d, Ettore Scola; w, Ruggero Maccari, Furio Scarpelli, Ettore Scola; ph, Ricardo Aronovich (Cinecitta color); ed, Ettore Scola; m, Armando Trovaioli.

Comedy **(PR:A MPAA:NR)**

FANNY***½

(1932, Fr.) 125m Pagnol-Siritzky bw

Raimu *(Cesar Olivier),* Orane Demazis *(Fanny),* Pierre Fresnay *(Marius),* Fernand Charpin *(Honore Panisse),* Alida Rouffe *(Honorine Cabanis),* Robert Vattier *(M. Brun),* Auguste Mouries, Milly Mathis, Maupi, Edouard Delmont.

The second installment of Marcel Pagnol's "Marseilles Trilogy" picks up just a short while after the end of MARIUS. After Marius (Pierre Fresnay) has gone to sea, it is learned that the girl he loves, Fanny (Orane Demazis), is pregnant. Because she has her reputation to think of, Fanny is persuaded by her family to marry the older, widowed sailmaker Panisse (Fernand Charpin), despite the fact that she is still deeply in love with Marius. After a year at sea, Marius returns and tries to convince the woman he loves to leave Marseilles with him. She, however, must consider the consequences and the feelings of Panisse, who has grown to love not only Fanny, but the child as well. Pagnol's warm, touching tale and has been a success wherever it has played, attesting to the story's total truthfulness that knows no nation's bounds. Written and produced by Pagnol and starring his troupe of actors, FANNY was filmed under the direction of Marc Allegret. In French with English subtitles.

p, Marcel Pagnol; d, Marc Allegret; w, Marcel Pagnol (based on the play by Marcel Pagnol); ph, Nicolas Toporkoff, Andre Dantan, Roger Hubert, Georges Benoit, Coutelain; ed, Raymond Lamy, Herman G. Weinberg; m, Vincent Scotto.

Drama **(PR:A-C MPAA:NR)**

FANNY AND ALEXANDER****

(1982, Swed./Fr./Ger.) 188m AB-Swedish Film Institute-Swedish TV 1-Gaumont-Personafilm-Tobis/Embassy c (FANNY OCH ALEXANDER)

Gunn Wallgren *(Widow/Grandmother Helena Ekdahl),* Boerje Ahlstedt *(Her Son, Prof. Carl Ekdahl),* Christina Schollin *(Lydia Ekdahl, His Wife),* Allan Edwall *(Helena's Son Oscar, Actor),* Ewa Froeling *(Oscar's Wife Emilie),* Pernilla Allwin *(Their Daughter Fanny, 8),* Bertil Guve *(Their Son, Alexander, 10),* Jarl Kulle *(Helena's Son Carl-Gustav),* Mona Malm *(His Wife, Alma),* Pernilla Wallgren *(His Mistress, Helena's Maid Maj),* Anna Bergman *(Hanna Schwarz),* Gunnar Bjornstrand *(Filip Landahl),* Jan Malmsjoe *(Bishop Edvard Vergerus),* Marianne Aminoff *(His Mother Blenda),* Kerstin Tidelius *(His Sister Henrietta),* Harriet Andersson *(Justina, Kitchen Maid),* Erland Josephson *(Isak Jacobi),* Stina Ekblad *(Ismael),* Mats Bergman *(Aron),* Kabi Laretei *(Aunt Anna),* Sonya Hedenbratt *(Aunt Emma),* Svea Holst *(Miss Ester),* Majlis Granlund *(Miss Vega),* Maria Granlund *(Petra),* Emilie Werko *(Jenny),* Christian Almgren *(Putte),* Kristina Adolphson *(Siri).*

Steering away from the heavy metaphysical questions his work previously posed, Ingmar Bergman created this film of magical proportions based on childhood memories of the turn of the century. FANNY AND ALEXANDER begins with the Ekdahl family's Christmas celebration, their large home serving as the meeting place for a merry celebration by both family members and servants, who dance about heedless of any form of social restraint. Late that night, 10-year-old Alexander (Bertil Guve) is tucked in by the buxom maid, who apologizes for being unable to spend the night with him because she has other obligations—namely bedding down with his Uncle Carl (Boerje Ahlstedt), a married man with children of his own, whose wife is completely aware of his pleasure-seeking adventures, but does nothing to stop them. The Christmas party's synthetic image of a happy, innocent life is quickly shattered when Alexander's acting father suffers a heart attack and dies, leaving the widow Ekdahl (Ewa Froeling) to be calmed by an understanding bishop (Jan Malmsjoe) whom she eventually marries, taking her two young children Fanny (Pernilla Allwin) and Alexander away from their warm family into the cold, strict world of the preacher. Not only does Bergman manage in FANNY AND ALEXANDER to capture the flavor and atmosphere of a 1907 Swedish town, he also expertly reveals events as seen through the eyes of a child, and, without any wordy dissertations on doctrines, makes powerful statements against oppressive religious zealots. The results are quite frightening, and far superior to the lengthy speeches and depressing anxiety that fill many earlier Bergman films. A magical film, FANNY AND ALEXANDER is likely to be the achievement for which Bergman will be most remembered. The videotape is available in both dubbed and subtitled (Swedish into English) versions.

d, Ingmar Bergman; w, Ingmar Bergman; ph, Sven Nykvist (Eastmancolor); ed, Sylvia Ingemarsson; m, Daniel Bell, Benjamin Britten, Frans Helmerson, Robert Schumson, Marianne Jacobs.

Drama **(PR:C-O MPAA:R)**

FATHER***

(1966, Hung.) 95m Mafilm/CD bw (APA)

Andras Balint *(Tako),* Miklos Gabor *(Father),* Klari Tolnay *(Mother),* Daniel Erdelyi *(Tako, as a Child),* Kati Solyom *(Anni),* Zsuzsa Rathonyi *(Mother, as a Young Woman),* Rita Bekes, Judit Halasz, Anna Nagy, Zsuzsa Balogh, Judit Zsolnai, Terez Nagy, Ila Loth, Geza Partos, Bela Asztalos, Geza Boszormenyi, Lajos Pozsar, Andras Kozak.

The much-heralded second feature from Istvan Szabo (MEPHISTO) and winner of the Grand Prize at the Moscow Film Festival, FATHER is actually about a son—Tako, a Hungarian boy who, after his father is killed at the end of WW II, conjures up a fantasy of what the parent must have been like. In the boy's imagination, he was a brave resistance fighter and a glorious hero. Tako's tales of this figure's courage naturally lead to his own assumption of leadership among his schoolmates; as he grows older, he finds that the stories of his father's heroism also attract women, who are enthralled by the tales of adventure. However, hungry for the truth about his heritage, he discovers that his father was an average man, never a great one. Told without sentiment, FATHER is a truly moving picture about a young man's attempt to find, not his father, but himself. Played superbly by three different actors in various stages of the character's life, Tako passes from youth to manhood, but cannot become a complete personality until he can come to terms with his obsession concerning the personality of his father. (In Hungarian; English subtitles.)

d, Istvan Szabo; w, Janos Hersko (based on a story by Szabo); ph, Sandor Sara; ed, Janos Rozsa; m, Janos Gonda.

Drama **(PR:A MPAA:NR)**

FAUST****

(1926, Ger.) 100m UFA bw

Emil Jannings *(The Devil),* Gosta Ekman *(Faust),* Camilla Horn, Yvette Guilbert, Wilhelm Dieterle *(Valentin),* Frida Richard *(Mother),* Eric Barclay *(Duke of Parma),* Hanna Ralph *(Duchess of Parma),* Werner Futterer *(Archangel).*

F.W. Murnau's visually stunning interpretation of the legend of Faust stars the great Emil Jannings as Faust's tempter, the Devil. In order to gain control of the world and spread his evil throughout all humanity, the Devil must secure the help of Faust (Gosta Ekman), an intelligent and highly respected member of his community. When the Devil sends a plague to Faust's village, Faust curses God and the heavens. Unable to stop the black death, he conjures up the Devil and enters into a pact with the evil force. Faust is soon swept away by the Devil's power and, after regaining his youth, falls in love with the Duchess of Parma. Instead of bringing her happiness, however, Faust can only bring death and misfortune into his love's life. Filled with awe-inspiring camerawork and superbly composed images highlighted by symbolically significant chiaroscuro lighting, Murnau's film also boasts the wonderful set design of Robert Herlth and Walter Rohrig and a powerful performance by Jannings. Silent with English titles.

d, F.W. Murnau; w, Hans Kyser; ph, Carl Hoffmann.

Fantasy **(PR:A MPAA:NR)**

FEAR***½

(1954, Ger./It.) 91m Aniene-Ariston/Astor bw (LA PAURA; DIE ANGST)

Ingrid Bergman *(Irene Wagner),* Mathias Wieman *(Professor Albert Wagner),* Renate Mannhardt *(Joanne Schultze),* Kurt Kreuger *(Heinrich Stoltz),* Elise Aulinger *(Marta, the Housekeeper),* Edith Schultze-Westrum, Steffie Struck, Annelore Wied.

A fascinating, psychologically based suspense film about marital infidelity and the guilt, fear, and need for confession which follow it, FEAR significantly marked the end of both the personal and professional relationships between Roberto Rossellini and Ingrid Bergman. The film opens with a nighttime rendezvous between Irene Wagner (Bergman) and her lover (Kurt Kreuger). As the two creep in and out of the shadows that almost completely obscure them, Irene confesses that she is unsure if she can continue the romance. Afterwards, as she returns home to her husband, Albert (Mathias Wieman), a scientist involved in a breakthrough experiment, Irene is met by the mysterious Joanna (Renate Mannhardt), a distraught woman who knows all about Irene's secret romance and blackmails her. What Irene does not know and what the audience learns some time later (but senses from the start), is that Albert has arranged for his wife to be blackmailed in the hope that she will confess her guilt. There are, however, variables in this experiment that he can't control, like Irene's threat to murder her blackmailer, then commit suicide. While neither Rossellini's nor Bergman's greatest work, the film is a mature, almost clinical look into the mind of a guilt-ridden individual. For those who know Rossellini only as a director of Neorealist dramas, FEAR—with its Hitchcockian elements (the suspense genre and Bergman as star) and German expressionist style (the psychological interplay of light and shadow and the source material, Stefan Zweig's novel *Angst*)—may come as something of a surprise. The videocassette is in English.

p, Roberto Rossellini; d, Roberto Rossellini; w, Roberto Rossellini, Sergio Amidei, Franz Treuberg (based on the novel *Der Angst* by Stefan Zweig); ph, Carlo Carlini, Heinz Schnackertz; ed, Jolanda Benvenuti, Walter Boos; m, Renzo Rossellini.

Drama **(PR:A MPAA:NR)**

FELLINI SATYRICON****

(1969, Fr./It.) 128m PEA-Artistes/UA c (AKA: SATYRICON)

Martin Potter *(Encolpius),* Hiram Keller *(Ascyltus),* Max Born *(Giton),* Capucine *(Tryphaena),* Salvo Randone *(Eumolpus),* Magali Noel *(Fortunata),* Alain Cuny *(Lichas),* Lucia Bose *(Suicide Wife),* Tanya Lopert *(Caesar),* Gordon Mitchell *(Robber),* Fanfulla *(Vernacchio),* Mario Romagnoli *(Trimalchio),* Donyale Luna *(Oenothea),* Giuseppe Sanvitale *(Habinnas),* Hylette Adolphe *(Oriental Slave Girl),* Joseph Wheeler *(Suicide Husband),* Genius *(Cinedo),* Danica La Loggia *(Scintilla),* Antonia Pietrosi *(Widow of Ephesus),* Wolfgang Hillinger *(Soldier at Tomb),* Elio Gigante *(Owner of Garden of Delights),* Pasquale Baldassare *(Hermaphrodite),* Sibilla Sedat *(Nymphomaniac).*

The bizarre characters and situations that had filled the films of Federico Fellini since his early VARIETY LIGHTS found their ultimate expression in this dreamy, hallucinatory depiction of ancient Rome. Based on the 1st century A.D. fragment by Gaius Petronius (with added inspiration from other writings of the period), this film strips away all the glamor and honor associated with the early Romans to expose a society in which morality has little or no significance. But Fellini's desire was not to criticize Rome, nor was it to set the history books straight; rather, he found the perfect setting with which to parallel the youth culture of the 1960s. Encolpius (Martin Potter) and Ascyltus (Hiram Keller) are two students whose adventures in a hotbed of decadence are the excuse for the threadbare plot that holds this extraordinary spectacle together. Their sole aim is the pursuit of hedonistic desires, and hedonism is just what Fellini gives his audience—there are orgies, concubines, nymphomaniacs, hermaphrodites, sadism, masochism, and no doubt a few more unidentifiable "isms" as well. It should go without saying that this may not be for all tastes. The videocassette is letter-boxed. In Italian with English subtitles.

p, Alberto Grimaldi; d, Federico Fellini; w, Federico Fellini, Bernardino Zapponi, Brunello Rondi (based on the play "Satyricon" by Gaius Petronius); ph, Giuseppe Rotunno (Panavision, DeLuxe Color); ed, Ruggero Mastroianni; m, Nino Rota, Ilhan Mimaroglu, Tod Dockstader, Andrew Rudin.

Historical **(PR:C-O MPAA:NR)**

FEMMES DE PARIS*

(1954, Fr.) 83m Optimax-CCF Lux/Fanfare c (AH! LES BELLES BACCHANTES; AKA: PEEK-A-BOO)

Robert Dhery *(Himself),* Colette Brosset *(Herself),* Louis de Funes *(Inspector Leboeuf),* Raymond Bussieres *(Plumber),* Rosine Luguet *(Plumber's Wife),* Jacqueline Maillan *(Theater Manager),* Sophie Mallet, Simone Claris, Liliane Autran, Caccia, Jacques Legras, Roger Saget, Gerard Calvi, Francis Blanche, Michel Serrault, Guy Pierrault, Jacques Jouanneau, Jacques Beauvais, Robert Destain.

With little more than a skeleton of a story, FEMMES DE PARIS is essentially a filmed record of Robert Dhery's stage revue, complete with dancing girls from the Lido. The minuscule plot revolves around the efforts of police inspector Lebeouf (Louis de Funes—his character name translated literally as MacBeef) as he attends the revue's rehearsal to make sure no decency laws are being broken. Also watching the show are a plumber (Raymond Bussieres) who would rather watch the rehearsals than work and his wife (Rosine Luguet), who performs a striptease to prove that she is just as appealing as the showgirls. There are a number of musical numbers performed, including "The Creation of the World" (scantily clad ladies dressed as the Moon, Water, Vegetation, etc.), "In the Rain" (a "Singing in the Rain"-type number with dancing girls in see-through raincoats), and the rather humorous comedy sketch "The Bathing Huts" (in which a male bather tries desperately to see the derriere of a pretty young femme). There's also an odd dance number set in a Chicago speakeasy in which a white thug beats up a black patron and strips the dress off his white dance partner—all without the recognition of a policeman on the beat. In French with English subtitles.

p, Edgar Bacquet; d, Jean Loubignac; w, Robert Dhery, Francis Blanche; ph, Rene Colas (Agfacolor); ed, Jacques Mavel; m, Gerard Calvi.

Comedy **(PR:O MPAA:NR)**

FIREMAN'S BALL, THE***½

(1967, Czech.) 73m Barrandov/Cinema V c (HORI MA PANENKO)

Vaclav Stockel *(Fire Brigade Commander),* Josef Svet *(Old Man),* Josef Kolb *(Josef),* Jan Vostrcil *(Committee Chairman),* Frantisek Debelka *(1st Committee Member),* Josef Sebanek *(2nd Committee Member),* Karel Valnoha *(3rd Committee Member),* Josef Rehorek *(4th Committee Member),* Marie Jezkova *(Josef's Wife),* Anina Lipoldva, Alena Kvetova, Mila Zelena *(Beauty Queen Candidates),* Vratislav Cermak, Vaclav Novotny, Frantisek Reinstein, Frantisek Paska.

This hilarious black comedy was made by Czech director Milos Forman and screenwriter Ivan Passer before both left Czechoslovakia for Hollywood, where their films would once again find critical acclaim. (Forman went on to direct ONE FLEW OVER THE CUCKOO'S NEST; HAIR; RAGTIME; and AMADEUS; Passer directed the vastly underappreciated CUTTER'S WAY.) THE FIREMAN'S BALL is a bizarre farce that uses a small, local event—in this case a retirement ball and beauty contest—to analyze larger social and political problems. Promised the presentation of a ceremonial hatchet at a ball given upon his retirement, a cancer-stricken, 86-year-old retired commander of a fire brigade sits helplessly as all hell breaks loose around him. A beauty contest organized as part of the evening's events fizzles when the contestants, barely a beauty among them, refuse to leave the bathroom, despite the firemen's best efforts to coax them out. The tension is broken when an alarm tears the fire company away from the festivities to fight a fire that is destroying another old man's home. Unfortunately, the fire truck sinks into the snow and is unable to function, forcing the firemen to watch helplessly as the house burns to the ground. To console the houseless old man, the firemen give him free raffle tickets to their ball, but the raffle prizes, and the tickets, are then stolen. Embarrassed, the master-of-ceremonies turns out the lights and encourages the thief to return the stolen items under cover of darkness, and when the lights go back on, it is the raffle's director who is caught returning one of the items. He suffers a heart attack and must be carried off by the firemen. The hall empties, leaving the guest of honor to discover that the case that holds his ceremonial fire hatchet is empty, his retirement gift having been purloined also. The *New York Times* reported that 40,000 Czech firemen resigned when the government released the film in their homeland—then Forman let it be known the film might be allegorical and they returned to their posts. Dubbed in English.

d, Milos Forman; w, Milos Forman, Ivan Passer, Jaroslav Papousek; ph, Miroslav Ondricek (Eastmancolor); ed, Miroslav Hajek; m, Karel Mares.

Comedy **(PR:C MPAA:NR)**

FIRES ON THE PLAIN****

(1959, Jap.) 105m Daiei/Harrison bw (NOBI)

Eiji Funakoshi *(Tamura),* Osamu Takizawa *(Yasuda),* Mickey Curtis *(Nagamatsu),* Mantaro Ushio *(Sergeant),* Kyu Sazanka *(Army Surgeon),* Yoshihiro Hamaguchi *(Officer),* Asao Sano, Masaya Tsukida, Hikaru Hoshi *(Soldiers).*

This grim, intense Japanese war drama concerns Tamura (Eiji Funakoshi), a tubercular soldier condemned to wander a battle-scarred landscape in the closing days of WW II. Separated from his unit and rejected by the hospital because he must have his own food in order to gain admittance, Tamura flees the advancing Americans and is forced to hide in the jungle, where he encounters all manners of death, disease, and horror. Stunningly composed in black and white on a widescreen DaieiScope canvas, FIRES ON THE PLAIN is beautiful to look at (its magnificent Philippine vistas swallowing the insignificant Tamura), though it is a philosophical horror to contemplate. The world director Kon Ichikawa has brought to the screen (based on the 1951 novel by Shohei Ooka) is difficult to bear—one of brutality, pain, death, destruction, and cannibalism, in short, the world of war—and in FIRES ON THE PLAIN Ichikawa has created one of cinema's greatest indictments of war and most painful, humanistic examinations of mankind. In Japanese with English subtitles, though the videocassette is unfortunately not letterboxed (except for the opening credit tease), thereby destroying the power and beauty of the visual composition.

p, Masaichi Nagata; d, Kon Ichikawa; w, Natto Wada (based on the novel by Shohei Ooka); ph, Setsuo Kobayashi (DaieiScope); ed, Hiroaki Fujii, Kon Ichikawa; m, Yasushi Akutagawa.

War **(PR:O MPAA:NR)**

FITZCARRALDO****

(1982, Ger.) 157m NW c

Klaus Kinski *(Brian Sweeney Fitzgerald/Fitzcarraldo),* Claudia Cardinale *(Molly),* Jose Lewgoy *(Don Aquilino),* Miguel Angel Fuentes *(Cholo),* Paul Hittscher *(Capt. Orinoco Paul),* Huerequeque Enrique Bohorquez *(The Cook),* Grande Othelo *(Station Master),* Peter Berling *(Opera Manager),* David Perez Espinosa *(Chief),* Milton Nascimento *(Black Man at Opera House),* Rui Polanah *(Rubber Baron),* Salvador Godinez *(Old Missionary),* Dieter Milz *(Young Missionary),* Bill Rose *(Notary),* Leoncio Bueno *(Prison Guard).*

A major filmmaking accomplishment that only Werner Herzog had the audacity to attempt, FITZCARRALDO stars Klaus Kinski as the title character, a dreamer who plans to bring opera and Enrico Caruso to the South American jungles. With limited funding, he must figure out how to finance the opera house, and ultimately decides to capitalize on South America's rubber industry. He discovers a hidden forest of rubber trees that is well protected by rapids, but the only way to get there is via a parallel river on the other side of a small group of mountains. Fitzcarraldo therefore hires local natives to pull his steamship over the mountain—320 tons up a 40-degree incline. The hauling of the boat is the poetic and symbolic heart of the movie, and no camera trickery is used in its filming. This is a real steamship being hauled over a real mountain—all at the command of Herzog (although, when one considers that Herzog previously stood at the lip of a live volcano for the filming of his short documentary LA SOUFFRIERE, this task must have seemed a picnic). The insurmountability of this labor of filmmaking parallels the character's determination to bring Caruso to the jungles, and herein lies the attraction of FITZCARRALDO—it is an artistic achievement that one watches for the drama of the film *and* of the filmmaking. Jason Robards was originally set to play the lead, but was forced to quit the film after catching a jungle illness. The resulting schedule delays also forced Mick Jagger, who was cast as Robards' sidekick, to drop out. Herzog was quoted as saying, "If I should abandon this film I should be a man without dreams . . . I live my life or end my life with this project." An excellent companion piece is Les Blank's BURDEN OF DREAMS, a documentary about the making of FITZCARRALDO. The videocassette is subtitled.

p, Werner Herzog, Lucki Stipetic; d, Werner Herzog; w, Werner Herzog; ph, Thomas Mauch; ed, Beate Mainka-Jellinghaus; m, Popol Vuh.

Drama **(PR:C MPAA:NR)**

FLIGHT OF THE EAGLE½**

(1982, Swed./Ger./Norway) 141m Bold-Svenska-Sveriges-Norsk-Polyphon/Summit c (INGENJOR ANDREES LUFTFARD; Trans: The Air Voyage of Engineer Andress)

Max von Sydow *(Salomon August Andree),* Goran Stangertz *(Nils Strindberg),* Sverre Anker Ousdal *(Knut Fraenkel),* Clement Harari *(Lachambre),* Eva von Hanno *(Guril Linder),* Lotta Larsson *(Anna Charlier),* Jon-Olof Strandberg *(Nils Ekholm),* Henric Holmberg *(GVE Svedenborg),* Mimi Pollak *(Mina Andree),* Cornelis Vreswijk *(Lundstrom),* Ulla Sjoblem *(Andree's Sister),* Ingvar Kjellson *(Alfred Nobel).*

Hauntingly beautiful photography of the Arctic region is the highlight of this film, based on the ill-fated Andree expedition of 1897. Max von Sydow plays the explorer S.A. Andree, who attempts to fly a balloon to the North Pole despite numerous warnings of the dangers involved. After only three days in the air, Andree and his two assistants, Nils Strindberg (Goran Stangertz), a descendent of August, and Knut Fraenkel (Sverre Anker Ousdal), a Norwegian athlete, crashed into the frozen tundra. Desperate and near death, they had little hope of making it back to civilization. With its picturesque photography, FLIGHT OF THE EAGLE definitely deserves to be seen on the big screen, though the latter half of the film, with the three men struggling across the icy wastes, tends to drag. What the film most lacks is that certain edge that separates expansive and lengthy films from truly great epic adventures. This lifelong project for director Jan Troell failed to find its hoped-for audience, although it was nominated for an Academy Award as Best Foreign-Language Film. A 180-minute version was shown on European television. In Swedish with English subtitles.

p, Goran Setterberg, Jorn Donner; d, Jan Troell; w, Georg Oddner, Ian Rakoff, Klaus Rifberg, Jan Troell (based on the novel by Per Olof Sundman); ph, Jan Troell, Mischa Gavruvsjov; ed, Jan Troell; m, Hans-Erik Philip, Carl-Axel Dominique.

Adventure/Biography (PR:A-C MPAA:NR)

FLOATING WEEDS*½**

(1959, Jap.) 119m Daiei-Altura c (UKIGUSA; AKA: THE DUCKWEED STORY; DRIFTING WEEDS)

Ganjiro Nakamura *(Komajuro),* Haruko Sugimura *(Oyoshi),* Hiroshi Kawaguchi *(Kiyoshi),* Machiko Kyo *(Sumiko),* Ayako Wakao *(Kayo),* Koji Mitsui *(Kichinosuke),* Mutsuko Sakura, Mantaro Ushio, Haruo Tanaka, Hitomi Nozoe, Chishu Ryu.

Although Yasujiro Ozu directed some 50 films, very few have been shown in the United States and even fewer are available on videotape. FLOATING WEEDS, released in the US 11 years after its first showing, is a remake of Ozu's 1934 silent version of the story. A variation on the theme of the family that pervades nearly all Ozu's pictures, the film concerns a familial group of theater performers. Komajuro (Ganjiro Nakamura) leads a traveling troupe to a seaside village, where he is reunited after a 12-year separation with his ex-mistress, Oyoshi (Haruko Sugimura), and his illegitimate son, Kiyoshi (Hiroshi Kawaguchi), who has been led to believe that Komajuro is his uncle. Instead of staying with his troupe, Komajuro lavishes attention on his son. Made jealous by this sudden shift of devotion, Sumiko (Machiko Kyo), Komajuro's current mistress, arranges to have one of the troupe's actresses, Kayo (Ayako Wakao), seduce the son, hoping that by hurting the son she can also hurt the father. This was the first color film by Ozu, who has been called the "most Japanese of Japanese directors," since his works have not been assimilated as easily into Western culture as have those of his compatriots, and, conversely, his filmmaking style seemingly shows no Western influences. Also available on videotape under the title DRIFTING WEEDS. (In Japanese; English subtitles.)

d, Yasujiro Ozu; w, Yasujiro Ozu, Kogo Noda (based on a story by Yasujiro Ozu and the film UKIGUSA MONOGATARI, screenplay by Tadeo Ikeda); ph, Kazuo Miyagawa (Daiei Color); m, Takanobu Saito.

Drama (PR:A MPAA:NR)

FLOWERS OF ST. FRANCIS, THE****

(1950, It.) 75m Cineriz-Rizzoli bw (FRANCESCO, GIULLARE DI DIO; AKA: THE ADVENTURES OF ST. FRANCIS OF ASSISI)

Aldo Fabrizi *(Nicolaio, the Tyrant),* Arabella Lemaitre *(Saint Clair),* Brother Nazario Gerardi *(Saint Francis).*

A film of great harmony and natural beauty, this short historical feature from Roberto Rossellini is a masterpiece of physical gestures. Acted, with the exception of Aldo Fabrizi, by nonprofessionals (all of whom are real-life Franciscans), the film captures the brothers' purity and their desire to live in harmony with nature. More important than the film's themes—man and nature, God and man, peace and defiance, love and hate, generosity and greed—is Rossellini's brilliance at capturing the monks' physical movements. Illustrating one character's line of dialog, "Souls are won over by examples, not words," Rossellini's direction gives us, not speeches or readings from scripture, but the hands and faces of these monks, their wonder, their peace, their simplicity. As these monks can say so much with their eyes, so too can Rossellini speak volumes with one frame of his film. In Italian with English subtitles.

p, Giuseppe Amato; d, Roberto Rossellini; w, Roberto Rossellini, Federico Fellini, Fr. Felix Morlion, Fr. Antonio Lisandrini (based on the life of Fioretti di San Francesco); ph, Otello Martelli; ed, Jolanda Benvenuti; m, Renzo Rossellini, Fr. Enrico Buondonno.

Religious (PR:A MPAA:NR)

FORBIDDEN GAMES**

(1953, Fr.) 90m Silver-Times bw (LES JEUX INTERDIT)

Brigitte Fossey *(Paulette),* Georges Poujouly *(Michel Dolle),* Lucien Hubert *(Dolle the Father),* Suzanne Courtal *(Mme. Dolle),* Jacques Marin *(Georges Dolle),* Laurence Badie *(Berthe Dolle),* Andre Wasley *(Gouard the Father),*

Amedee *(Francis Gouard),* Denise Perronne *(Jeanne Gouard),* Louis Sainteve *(Priest),* Pierre Merovee *(Raymond Dolle).*

For a time one of the most highly praised films ever about war and its effects, FORBIDDEN GAMES is a classic example of traditional, superficial filmmaking that today is little more than a museum piece. Disguising the artificiality of the Jean Aurenche-Pierre Bost script under the realism of Rene Clement's direction, FORBIDDEN GAMES begins with a harrowing sequence in which hundreds of refugees flee WW II Paris before the advance of the Germans. The parents and dog of little Paulette (Brigitte Fossey, in the role that launched her to stardom) are killed, leaving the orphan to be befriended by Michel (Georges Poujouly), an 11-year-old son of peasant parents (Lucien Hubert and Suzanne Courtal). The constant wartime reminder of death so greatly affects the children that they become obsessed with it, stealing crosses and constructing their own secret animal cemetery of moles, chickens, and insects—all of which are given elaborate memorial services by the pair. While Clement received resounding praise for his supposedly brilliant direction of children, the entire picture today seems forced, the young actors clearly "acting" instead of showing any real emotions or feelings. The film was a great critical success, and earned an honorary Oscar for Best Foreign Film released in 1952. Originally released at 102 minutes. In French with English subtitles.

p, Robert Dorfman; d, Rene Clement; w, Rene Clement, Jean Aurenche, Pierre Bost (based on the novel *Les Jeux Inconnus* by Francois Boyer); ph, Robert Juillard; ed, Roger Dwyre; m, Narcisco Yepes.

War/Drama **(PR:C MPAA:NR)**

47 RONIN, THE (PARTS I & II)***½

(1941, Jap.) 112m & 113m Shochiku bw (GENROKU CHUSHINGURA I-II; AKA: THE LOYAL 47 RONIN OF THE GENROKU ERA)

Chojuro Kawarazaki, Kanemon Nakamura, Kunitaro Kawarazaki, Yoshisaburo Arashi, Kikunojo Segawa, Kikunosuke Ichikawa, Tokusaburo Arashi, Ryotaro Kawanami, Joji Kaieda, Hiroshi Ouchi, Isamu Kosugi, Masao Shimizu, Utaemon Ichikawa, Sensho Ichikawa.

Extolling the strong will of the Japanese people, Kenji Mizoguchi's wartime, two-part historical epic about revenge and self-sacrifice is only one of dozens of versions of this popular tale, most of them based on a Kabuki play. The first part of the film concerns a group of samurai who become leaderless *ronin* when their master dies, focusing on the decision of 47 of them to take revenge on the man responsible. In the second part, after years of living apart, the loyal 47 carry out their deed and, to be reunited with their master, commit mass ritual suicide. Because Mizoguchi was forced to direct this ambitious film it is not generally considered as one of his finest works. But despite the director's reported lack of emotional and personal involvement in the project, THE 47 RONIN is, at the very least, a remarkable technical achievement. The sets (featuring life-size replicas) are astounding and beautifully detailed, and the camerawork, with its extensive use of tracking and crane shots, is simply breathtaking. The Sony videocassette, like all of those in the Japanese series, offers a crisp, English-subtitled print.

d, Kenji Mizoguchi; w, Kenichiro Hara, Yoshikata Yoda (based on a story by Seika Mayama); ph, Kohei Sugiyama; m, Shiro Fukai.

Historical **(PR:C MPAA:NR)**

FOUR BAGS FULL**½

(1956, Fr./It.) 82m Franco-London-Continentale/Trans-Lux bw (LA TRAVERSEE DE PARIS; Trans: The Trip Across Paris)

Jean Gabin *(Grandgil),* Bourvil *(Marcel Martin),* Jeanette Batti *(Mariette),* Louis de Funes *(Jambier),* Georgette Anys *(Waitress),* Robert Arnoux, Laurence Badie, Myno Burney, Germaine Delbat, Monette Dinay, Jean Dunot, Bernard Lajarrige.

Thrill-seeking artist Grandgil (Jean Gabin) joins meek cabbie Martin (Bourvil) to transport four suitcases of freshly butchered pork across Paris during the German occupation. What follows are a number of episodes—some comic, some tragic—in which the pair must avoid various inquiries, police confrontations, and even hungry dogs with keen noses. Bourvil gives one of the best performances of his career as the basically honest cabbie driven by circumstances to working in the black market, earning him the top prize at the Venice Film Festival. The direction, on the other hand, is less than compelling—the transitions between comic and dramatic episodes are weak, the characterizations are flabby, and the plot hobbles along to its rather predictable conclusion. In French with English subtitles.

d, Claude Autant-Lara; w, Jean Aurenche, Pierre Bost (based on a novel by Marcel Ayme); ph, Jacques Natteau; ed, Madeleine Gug; m, Rene Cloerec.

Comedy **(PR:A-C MPAA:NR)**

FOUR HUNDRED BLOWS, THE*****

(1959, Fr.) 93m Carrosse-SEDIF/Zenith bw (LES QUATRE CENTS COUPS)

Jean-Pierre Leaud *(Antoine Doinel),* Claire Maurier *(Mme. Doinel),* Albert Remy *(Antoine's Stepfather),* Guy Decomble *(Teacher),* Patrick Auffay *(Rene Bigey),* Georges Flamant *(Mon. Bigey),* Yvonne Claudie *(Mme. Bigey),* Robert Beauvais *(Director of the School),* Pierre Repp *(The English Teacher),* Claude Monsard *(Examining Magistrate),* Jacques Monod *(Commissioner),* Henri Virlojeux *(Night Watchman),* Richard Kanayan *(Abbou),* Jeanne Moreau *(Woman with Dog),* Jean-Claude Brialy *(Man in Street),* Jacques Demy *(Policeman),* Jean Douchet *(The Lover).*

This extraordinary film was the first feature film from Francois Truffaut, who was, until this film's release, best known as a hell-raising critic from *Cahiers du Cinema*. THE 400 BLOWS is not only one of the foremost films of the French New Wave, but also the first in a Truffaut series that included "Antoine and Colette" (an episode from LOVE AT TWENTY); STOLEN KISSES; BED AND BOARD; and LOVE ON THE RUN—all starring Jean-Pierre Leaud and spanning 20 years in his semiautobiographical character's life. Here Leaud plays Truffaut's 12-year-old alter ego, Antoine Doinel, a child more or less left to his own devices by his mother (Claire Maurier) and father (Albert Remy). He gets into trouble at school, runs away from home, and eventually ends up in an observation center for juvenile delinquents. THE 400 BLOWS—an idiomatic French expression for raising hell in protest—is a nonjudgmental film about injustice, pain, and the events in a young boy's life that make him the person he is. Neither good nor bad, Antoine is a child caught up in a maelstrom not of his making and is treated with warmth and compassion by Truffaut. The grace and perfection of THE 400 BLOWS has since caused it to become the standard against which all films on the subject of youth are judged, and Leaud's portrayal that to which all young performers' are compared. In addition to Truffaut's direction, Leaud's performance, and Henri Decae's poetic black-and-white photography, the film is remembered for its final freeze frame, perhaps the purest moment in all of cinema. In French with English subtitles.

p, Francois Truffaut; d, Francois Truffaut; w, Francois Truffaut, Marcel Moussy (based on a story by Truffaut); ph, Henri Decae (Dyaliscope); ed, Marie-Josephe Yoyotte; m, Jean Constantin.

Drama **(PR:A-C MPAA:NR)**

FOURTH MAN, THE½**

(1983, Neth.) 104m De Verenigde Nederlandsche-Spectrafilm c

Jeroen Krabbe *(Gerard Reve),* Renee Soutendijk *(Christine Halsslag),* Thom Hoffman *(Herman),* Dolf DeVries *(Dr. DeVries),* Geert De Jong *(Ria the Lady in Blue),* Hans Veerman *(Funeral Director),* Hero Muller *(Josefs),* Caroline De Beus *(Adrienne),* Reinout Bussemaker *(1st Husband),* Erik J. Meijer *(2nd Husband),* Ursul DeGeer *(3rd Husband),* Filip Bolluyt *(Surfer),* Hedda Lornie *(Sales Clerk in Bookstore),* Paul Nygaard *(Gerard's Boy Friend),* Guus van der Made *(Waiter on Train).*

A cryptic and intense thriller-black comedy from Dutch director Paul Verhoeven who, in 1987, delivered the blockbuster ROBOCOP, THE FOURTH MAN stars Jeroen Krabbe as Gerard Reve, a hard-drinking, fatalistic, bisexual writer who must supplement his paltry income by working the lecture circuit. During one speaking engagement he meets sensual, blonde spiderwoman Christine (Renee Soutendijk), whose three husbands have all died mysterious deaths. Reve's imagination begins to run wild—he has a nightmare that he is being castrated, has visions of the Virgin Mary, and "sees" Christine's dead lovers—as he becomes convinced that Christine loves her men and then devours them. Soon Reve becomes attracted to another lover of Christine's, Herman (Thom Hoffman), and the men wonder which of them will become the next victim. THE FOURTH MAN delivers a heavy dose of religious and sexual symbolism, a bit of gore, and a sharp-edged offering of perversity. While definitely not a film for everyone, those who like their films on the fringe will revel in this one's ideas. In Dutch with English subtitles.

p, Rob Houwer; d, Paul Verhoeven; w, Gerard Soeteman (based on the novel by Gerard Reve); ph, Jan De Bont; ed, Ine Schenkkan; m, Loek Dikker.

Thriller **(PR:O MPAA:NR)**

FRANTIC***

(1958, Fr.) 90m Nouvelles Editions/Times bw
(ASCENSEUR POUR L'ECHAFAUD)

Jeanne Moreau *(Florence Carala),* Maurice Ronet *(Julien Tavernier),* Georges Poujouly *(Louis),* Yori Bertin *(Veronique),* Jean Wall *(Simon Carala),* Ivan Petrovich *(Horst Bencker),* Lino Ventura *(Inspector Cherier),* Elga Andersen *(Madame Bencker),* Felix Marten *(Subervie),* Bandeira, Hubert Deschamps, Sylvianne Aisenstein.

This debut feature from the then-25-year-old Louis Malle quickly established the director as one of the most promising talents to come out of the French New Wave. Under the influence of American crime thrillers, Alfred Hitchcock, and Jean-Pierre Melville, Malle adapted a Noel Calef novel and turned it into an energetic and stylish tale starring Jeanne Moreau as Florence Carala, a woman in love with one of her husband's employees. She and her lover, Julien Tavernier (Maurice Ronet), engineer a plan to off her husband (Jean Wall). Having secretly attached a rope outside his boss' office window (one story above his own office), Julien climbs up the rope, shoots Florence's husband, and then returns to his own office. Later, after leaving the building, he glances upward, to see the rope—mute but deadly evidence of his involvement—dangling between the two offices. He reenters the building to retrieve the indicting hemp with which he may have fashioned a noose for himself, but a cost-conscious management has decreed that the building's electric power be shut off after working hours, and Julien finds himself trapped in an elevator between two floors. During his entrapment, two delinquent teenagers (Georges Poujouly and Yori Bertin) steal his car, discover a gun in the glove compartment, and murder a German couple—a crime that points to Julien. The enamored Florence turns detective on his behalf, determined to prove her lover's innocence. It is this film, as well as THE LOVERS and ZAZIE IN THE METRO, that shows Malle at his most exciting. Despite their numerous faults, these three films remind us that Malle was once something more than the safe, commercial director he has since become. (In French; English subtitles.)

p, Jean Thuillier; d, Louis Malle; w, Roger Nemier, Louis Malle (based on the play *Ascenseur Pour L'Echafaud* by Noel Calef); ph, Henri Decae; ed, Leonide Azar; m, Miles Davis.

Thriller **(PR:C MPAA:NR)**

FRENCH CANCAN****

(1955, Fr.) 93m Franco-London-Jolly/United c (AKA: ONLY THE FRENCH CAN)

Jean Gabin *(Danglard),* Maria Felix *(La Belle Abesse),* Francoise Arnoul *(Nini),* Jean-Roger Caussimon *(Baron Walter),* Gianni Esposito *(Prince Alexandre),* Philippe Clay *(Casimir),* Michel Piccoli *(Valorgueil),* Jean Paredes *(Coudrier),* Lydia Johnson *(Guibole),* Max Dalban *(Manager Of The Reine Blanche),* Jacques Jouanneau *(Bidon),* Jean-Marc Tennberg *(Savate),* Hubert Deschamps *(Isidore),* Franco Pastorino *(Paulo),* Valentine Tessier *(Mme. Olympe),* Albert Remy *(Barjolin),* Annik Morice *(Therese),* Dora Doll *(Le Genisse),* Anna Amendola *(Esther George),* Leo Campion *(The Commandant),* Mme. Paquerette *(Mimi Prunelle),* Sylvine Delannoy *(Titine),* Anne-Marie Mersen *(Paquita),* Michelle Nadal *(Bigoudi),* Gaston Gabaroche *(The Pianist),* Jaque Catelain *(The Minister),* Pierre Moncorbier *(The Bailiff),* Jean Mortier *(The Hotel Manager),* Numes Fils *(The Neighbor),* Robert Auboyneau *(The Elevator Attendant).*

After a 15-year hiatus from filmmaking in France, Jean Renoir returned with this high-spirited celebration of color and movement that brings to life the dawning days of the Moulin Rouge, complete with high-kicking, frilly, lacy chorus gals. Jean Gabin turns in one of his most memorable performances as Danglard, an aging theater impresario known for his ability to take common girls and transform them into dancehall sensations, as well as for successfully seducing them. Before long, he becomes captivated with a new girl and devotes his energies into making her a star, ignoring his previous love as Nini (Francoise Arnoul) becomes the next in his long line of targets when he spots her working as a laundry girl in 1880s Montmarte and decides to make her the star of his new "Moulin Rouge." A deceptively simple picture, FRENCH CANCAN transcends time and lets us relive an era previously vivid only in the posters and paintings of Toulouse-Lautrec and Jean's father, Auguste Renoir. Renoir, whose films have consistently served as training grounds for a number of prominent directors (Jacques Becker on LA CHIENNE, 1981; Yves Allegret and Luchino Visconti on the short A DAY IN THE COUNTRY, 1936; Robert Aldrich on THE SOUTHERNER, 1945), also gave a start to Jacques Rivette in this picture by letting him serve as a directorial trainee.

p, Louis Wipf; d, Jean Renoir; w, Jean Renoir (based on an idea by Andre-Paul Antoine); ph, Michel Kelber (Technicolor); ed, Borys Lewin; m, Georges Van Parys.

Musical **(PR:A MPAA:NR)**

FRENCH DETECTIVE, THE***

(1975, Fr.) 93m Les Films Ariane/Quartet c (ADIEU POULET)

Lino Ventura *(Commissioner Verjeat),* Patrick Dewaere *(Inspector Lefevre),* Victor Lanoux *(Pierre Lardatte),* Francoise Brion *(Marthe Rigaux),* Claude Rich *(Judge Delmesse),* Michel Peyrelon, Claude Brosset, Gerald Herold, Gerard Dessalles, Jacques Rispal, Patrick Feigelson, Henri Lambert, Chkristiane Tissot, Jean-Yves Gautier, Pierre Londiche, Jacques Serres, Eve Francis, Andre Malfuson.

Rouen police commissioner Verjeat (Lino Ventura) and his childish sidekick, Lefevre (Patrick Dewaere), try to find out who killed a fellow cop and trace the clues to bigshot politico Pierre Lardatte (Victor Lanoux). When the heat proves too much for Lardatte, he pressures the department to kick Verjeat upstairs. Verjeat and Lefevre turn the tables on their higher-ups, however, by concocting a bribery scheme that implicates them along with a crusading judge, keeping them under departmental investigation and thereby on the job. Ventura does a fine job as the decent, hardworking, veteran cop who is sick of playing politics with his department; Dewaere has less to do, and has shown more versatility and spontaneity in Bertrand Blier's films opposite Gerard Depardieu (GOING PLACES; GET OUT YOUR HANDKERCHIEFS). Pierre Granier-Deferre's direction is fairly run of the mill, but Francis Veber's intelligent and complex script saves the picture. The videocasette is available in both dubbed and subtitled (French into English) versions.

p, Georges Dancigers; d, Pierre Granier-Deferre; w, Francis Veber (based on the novel by Jean Laborde); ph, Jean Collomb; ed, Jean Ravel; m, Philippe Sarde.

Crime **(PR:C-O MPAA:NR)**

FROM THE LIFE OF THE MARIONETTES**½

(1980, Ger.) 104m Personafilm-ITC/Associated bw-c (AUS DEM LEBEN DES MARIONETTEN)

Robert Atzorn *(Peter Egerman),* Christine Buchegger *(Katarina Egerman),* Martin Benrath *(Mogens Jensen),* Rita Russek *(Katerina),* Lola Muethel *(Cordelia Egerman),* Walter Schmidinger *(Tim Mandelbaum),* Heinz Bennent *(Arthur Brenner),* Ruth Olafs *(Nurse),* Karl Heinz Pelser *(Interrogator).*

Just after rumors had been spread that Ingmar Bergman was to retire from the realm of feature film production to devote himself to his first love, the theater, he made yet another in-depth inquiry into the forces acting upon individual motivation with this film. Something of a follow-up to SCENES FROM A MARRIAGE, FROM THE LIFE OF THE MARIONETTES concentrates on the emotional and sexual repression that characterizes Peter Egerman's (Robert Atzorn) relationship to his wife (Christine Buchegger), the psychological antithesis of which is expressed in his bizarre sexual murder of a young prostitute. Bergman uses a mixture of black and white and color to relate the events that center around this event, with only the murder itself photographed in color and appearing at the beginning of the film. The rest, in black and white to lend an air of documentation, concentrates on the details that surround Egerman's alienating marriage, as well as a brief look at the police inquiry into the murder of the prostitute. Bergman's major theme appears to be that the philosophical traditions instigated by materialistic determinism have made man's emotional life a vast void; thus, the title signifies that the husband is just another puppet in the scheme of things, unable to properly respond to sensual and emotional arousal that varies from the routine structure.

p, Lew Grade, Martin Starger, Horst Wendtlandt, Ingmar Bergman; d, Ingmar Bergman; w, Ingmar Bergman; ph, Sven Nykvist; ed, Petra von Oelffen; m, Rolf Wilhelm.

Drama **(PR:O MPAA:NR)**

FULL MOON IN PARIS****

(1984, Fr.) 101m Losange-Ariane/Orion c (LES NUITS DE LA PLEINE LUNE)

Pascale Ogier *(Louise),* Fabrice Luchini *(Octave),* Tcheky Karyo *(Remi),* Christian Vadim *(Bastien),* Virginie Thevenet *(Camille),* Anne-Severine Liotard *(Marianne),* Laszlo Szabo *(Painter at Cafe),* Lisa Garneri *(Tina, the Babysitter),* Mathieu Schiffman *(Louise's Decorator Friend),* Herve Grandsart *(Remi's Friend Bertrand),* Noel Coffman *(Stanislas).*

This fourth entry in Eric Rohmer's "Comedies and Proverbs" series begins with the proverb, "He who has two women loses his soul. He who has two houses loses his mind." The remarkably effervescent Pascale Ogier stars as the quintessential Rohmer woman, loved and admired by the men around her but desperately confused as to the meaning of romance. A trainee at an interior design firm, Louise (Ogier) lives with her architect-tennis player lover, Remi (Tcheky Karyo), in a plastic suburb outside Paris. He wants to marry and settle down, but Louise is still young and enjoys dancing at parties until dawn. Remi's pressure proves too much for Louise and she takes an apartment in Paris in order "to experience loneliness." Ideally, she will spend her late party nights in Paris, sleep in her new apartment, and return to the suburbs the following afternoon. While in Paris she spends a great deal of time with Octave (Fabrice Luchini, in a role similar to the Octave of Jean Renoir's RULES OF THE GAME), a likable writer who is tortured by Louise's refusal to sleep with him. At one fateful party, Louise meets Bastien (Christian Vadim, son of Roger Vadim and Catherine Deneuve) and takes him back to her Paris apartment, only to realize her mistake and return to Remi in the suburbs with newfound affection. Remi, however, has fallen in love with someone else. What Rohmer has done in this film—and has done so successfully in the past—is to take a brief, intelligent, comic look at a young Frenchwoman and her ideas of love. Ogier (the 24-year-old daughter of actress Bulle Ogier) delivers her lines with an animated energy that is rarely captured on film, and knows how to dance on screen better than just about anyone. Her performance earned her a Best Actress award at the Venice Film Festival, but her career was tragically cut short by a fatal heart attack. In French with English subtitles.

p, Margaret Menegoz; d, Eric Rohmer; w, Eric Rohmer; ph, Renato Berta; ed, Cecile Decugis; m, Elli et Jacno.

Drama **(PR:O MPAA:R)**

FUNERAL, THE***

(1984, Jap.) 124m Itami-New Century/Electric Pictures c (OSOSHIKI; AKA: DEATH—JAPANESE STYLE)

Nobuko Miyamoto *(Chizuko Amamiya, the Eldest Daughter),* Tsutomu Yamazaki *(Wabisuke Inoue, the Son-in-Law),* Kin Sugai *(Kikue Amamiya, the Widow),* Chishu Ryu *(The Priest),* Shuji Otaki *(Shokichi Amamiya),* Ichiro Zaitsu *(Satomi),* Kiminobu Okumura *(Shinkichi Amamiya),* Haruna Takaso *(Yoshiko Saito).*

The first feature from Juzo Itami (TAMPOPO), one of Japan's fastest rising young talents, this is a black comedy about (what else?) a funeral. When a patriarch dies suddenly, his family—including his actress daughter (Nobuko Miyamato), her actor husband (Tsutomo Yamazaki), and their manager (Ichiro Zaitsu)—comes together for the three-day ceremony. Many of the scenes are familiar to anyone who has seen other similarly plotted films, but what makes THE FUNERAL so compelling is the fact that it takes place in Japan, a culture where burial rites are treated with the utmost respect. While THE FUNERAL is not as loopy as Itami's next picture, TAMPOPO, it is still one of the most energetic films to hit the international scene in some time. In Japanese with English subtitles.

p, Yasushi Tamaoki, Yutaka Okada; d, Juzo Itami; w, Juzo Itami; ph, Yonezo Maeda, Shinpai Asai (Fujicolor); ed, Akira Suzuki; m, Joji Yuasa.

Comedy **(PR:O MPAA:NR)**

FUNNY, DIRTY LITTLE WAR, A***½

(1983, Arg.) 80m Aries c (NO HABRA MAS PENAS NI OLVIDO)

Hector Bidonde *(Suprino),* Victor Laplace *(Reinaldo),* Federico Luppi *(Fuentes),* Miguel Angel Sola *(Juan),* Julio De Grazia *(Corp. Garcia),* Lautaro Murua *(Mayor Guglielmini),* Rodolfo Ranni *(Police chief),* Ulises Dumont *(Cervino),* Raul Rizzo *(Rossi),* Arturo Maly *(Toto),* Jose Maria Lopez *(Mateo Guastavino),* Maria Socas *(Girl),* Fernando Olmedo *(Ricardito),* Hector Canossa, Emilio Vidal *(Tacholas),* Augusto Larreta, Rodolfo Brindisi, Fernando Alvarez, Patrico Contreras, Norberto Diaz, Armando Capo, Carlos Usay, Salo Pasik.

This powerful black comedy takes place in 1974 in the rural Argentine town of Colonia Vela, where Peronist factions are split into two forces—the Marxist ultraleft and the Fascist ultraright. Although all shout "Viva Peron," they have different views on how he should govern—each group believing their impression of Juan Peron (who died in 1974) is the true one. When the town mayor (Lautaro Murua), the local union organizer (Victor Laplace), the Peronist boss (Hector Bidonde), and the local police chief (Rodolfo Ranni) conspire in a plot to oust the supposedly Marxist assistant (Jose Maria Lopez) to the town's deputy mayor, Ignacio Fuentes (Federico Luppi), Fuentes takes matters into his own hands. He barricades himself in City Hall along with some opportunistic supporters, one of whom (Julio De Grazia) is a likable but dopey patrolman who is instantly promoted to corporal and later sergeant. When Fuentes refuses to surrender, a battle breaks out and the little village of Colonia Vela becomes a microcosm of the country's political situation. The result is a shockingly potent film, paralleling violence and torture with some brilliant comedy. Scenes of cold and brutal violence are placed directly next to scenes of broad, slapstick humor—making the viewer more than a little ill at ease. Unfortunately, many of the political references will lose viewers who lack prior knowledge of Peronist politics. The film won the Silver Bear at the 1984 Berlin Film Festival, after which director Hector Olivera, curiously, followed up with three Roger Corman cheapies—BARBARIAN QUEEN; WIZARDS OF THE LOST KINGDOM; and COCAINE WARS. In Spanish with English subtitles.

p, Fernando Ayala, Luis Osvaldo Repetto; d, Hector Olivera; w, Hector Olivera, Roberto Cossa (based on the novel by Osvaldo Soriano); ph, Leonardo Rodriguez Solis; ed, Eduardo Lopez; m, Oscar Cardoza Ocampo.

Comedy/War **(PR:O MPAA:NR)**

G

GABRIELA**

(1983, Braz.) 102m Sultana/MGM-UA c

Sonia Braga *(Gabriela),* Marcello Mastroianni *(Nacib),* Antonio Cantafora *(Tonico Bastos),* Paulo Goulart *(Col. Joao Fulgencio),* Nelson Xavier *(Foreman),* Nuno Leal Maia *(Romulo),* Fernando Ramos *(Tuisca),* Nicole Puzzi *(Malvina),* Tania Boscoli *(Gloria),* Jofre Soares *(Col. Ramiro Bastos),* Paulo Pilla *(Prince),* Claudia Gimenez *(Dona Olga),* Ricardo Petraglia *(Prof. Josue),* Antonio Pedro *(Doctor),* Ivan Mesquita *(Col. Melk Tavares).*

This sexy, sultry, and erotic film is based on a 1925 novel by Jorge Amado, which was also adapted for a long-running Brazilian soap opera that likewise starred Sonia Braga. Nacib (a bloated, ancient-looking Marcello Mastroianni) is a bar owner who hires Gabriela (Braga) as his cook. It's 1925 in the Bahian village of Parati, where a great drought has come upon the land, and the filthy, downtrodden Gabriela and some of her thirsty compadres have emigrated to town from the country. The moment she meets Nacib, it's evident that she will be doing lots for the proprietor, in several departments. Once the mud is cleaned off her face, Gabriela begins to appear attractive to many of the other men in the village as well, and Nacib decides to put a stop to that by marrying her and insisting that she doff her old sexy clothing for more conservative togs. He also feels that it would be wrong for them to sleep with each other until they are married. Naturally, the pneumatic Gabriela pays little attention to this Henry Higgins' attempts to change her into a Latin version of Eliza Doolittle. A soft-core porn film that tries to hide its carnality under the cover of Amado's book, GABRIELA concerns itself chiefly with the story's sexual angle. The novel, however, was a comic look at life in the town of Ilheus, rich with interesting characters, satire, and politics. Worth seeing mainly for Braga, who displays—besides an ample amount of flesh—a freshness and energy that isn't often captured on film. The videocassette is available in both dubbed and subtitled (Portuguese into English) versions.

p, Harold Nebenzal, Ibrahim Moussa; d, Bruno Barreto; w, Leopaldo Serran, Flavio R. Tambellini, Bruno Barreto (based on the novel *Gabriela, Clove and Cinnamon* by Jorge Amado); ph, Carlo Di Palma (Technicolor); ed, Emmanuelle Castro; m, Antonio Carlos Jobim, Gal Costa.

Drama **(PR:O MPAA:R)**

GARDEN OF DELIGHTS, THE***

(1970, Sp.) 95m Elias Querejeta/Altura c (EL JARDIN DE LAS DELICIAS)

Jose Luis Lopez Vazquez *(Antonio),* Francisco Pierra *(Don Perdo),* Luchy Soto *(Luchy),* Lina Canalejas *(Aunt),* Julia Pena *(Julia),* Alberto Alonso *(Tony),* Charo Soriano *(Actress),* Esperanza Roy *(Nicole),* Mayrata O'Wisiedo *(Ana).*

With the release on videotape of THE GARDEN OF DELIGHTS, a little-seen Carlos Saura film from 1970 that played that year's New York Film Festival, one can see what must be ranked as one of film's most impressive acting performances—that of Jose Luiz Lopez Vazquez as Antonio, a wealthy industrialist who has lost his memory and all but the simplest physical skills in an automobile accident. At the start of the film, Antonio is confined to a wheelchair, barely able to move or speak. As he wheels down the hallway, his family—wife, father, aunt, son, and nurse—are getting ready, in the hope of jarring his memory, to play-act an event that occurred when Antonio was five. In this scene they lock him in a dark room with a large, grunting pig. Later they reenact his first communion, complete with a raid by angry, violent Republicans. In both cases, these re-creations of incidents in Antonio's youth do little to jar his memory. One-third of the way into the picture the audience learns why his impatient family is so determined to bring Antonio to his senses: he, and only he, knows the account number of a secret Swiss bank account. Without his Swiss millions, the industrial empire he created will be lost. Throughout nearly all of THE GARDEN OF DELIGHTS, Vazquez does little but sit motionless, yet it is nearly impossible to take one's eyes from his—in what looks like a blank stare, Vazquez is able to communicate volumes. Initially he does nothing more than try to write his signature or drink a milk shake. Gradually he regains some physical and verbal abilities, able to walk and mutter a few syllables. Somehow, we begin to realize that, although his body and memory cannot function, his brain is still hard at work, behind the mask that hides the unscrupulous industrialist. The videocassette is in Spanish with English subtitles.

p, Elias Querejeta; d, Carlos Saura; w, Rafael Azcona, Carlos Saura (based on a story by Saura); ph, Luis Cuadrado; ed, Pablo G. del Amo; m, Luis de Pablo.

Drama **(PR:C MPAA:NR)**

GARDEN OF THE FINZI-CONTINIS, THE****

(1971, It./Ger.) 103m Documento-CCC/Titanus c (IL GIARDINO DEL FINZI-CONTINI)

Dominique Sanda *(Micol),* Lino Capolicchio *(Giorgio),* Helmut Berger *(Alberto),* Fabio Testi *(Malnate),* Romolo Valli *(Giorgio's Father),* Raffaele Curi *(Ernesto),* Camillo Angelini-Rota *(Micol's Father),* Katina Viglietti *(Micol's Mother),* Inna Alexeiff *(Micol's Grandmother),* Barbara Pilavin, Gianpaolo Duregon, Katina Morisani, Cinzia Bruno, Marcella Gentile.

Vittorio De Sica, who made the great Neo-Realist films SHOESHINE; THE BICYCLE THIEF; and UMBERTO D, spent much of the latter half of his career acting in other director's work (Ophuls' THE EARRINGS OF MADAME DE . . ., Rossellini's GENERAL DELLA ROVERE). THE GARDEN OF THE FINZI-CONTINIS, however, is proof that the great director did not lose his touch. Set in Ferrara, Italy, during WW II, this story of love and culture unfurls effortlessly, albeit a trifle slowly. The Finzi-Continis are a wealthy Jewish-Italian family who cannot believe that the war will ever invade their hallowed garden walls. Rather than flee, they stay on in the false hope that they will not be betrayed. As they sit, posteriors barely touching their exquisite furniture, they realize that Fascism is not going to go away and that they must join the fight against it. Although this film bears very little resemblance to the director's early works (De Sica, like all other no longer state-funded filmmakers, had to become more concerned with his work's commercial appeal), THE GARDEN OF THE FINZI-CONTINIS is still directed with the same De Sica skill. Constructed with a heavy emphasis on flashbacks, the film is one of those few instances in which the flashbacks not only work, but are absolutely necessary, giving the viewer a historical perspective that its characters lack. De Sica's handling of the unknowns in the cast is exceptional, as is his direction of the wonderful Dominique Sanda. Because of its concern with Fascism; glossy, romantic photography; and use of Sanda, this picture directed by one of the veterans of Italian film serves as an interesting counterpart to THE CONFORMIST, directed by Bernardo Bertolucci, then one of the new voices in that country's cinema. Available on videocassette in a subtitled (Italian into English) version and a poorly dubbed version.

p, Arthur Cohn, Gianni Hecht Lucari; d, Vittorio De Sica; w, Cesare Zavattini, Vittorio Bonicelli, Ugo Pirro (based on the novel by Giorgio Bassani); ph, Ennio Guarnieri (Eastmancolor); ed, Adriana Novelli; m, Manuel De Sica.

War/Drama **(PR:C MPAA:R)**

GATE OF HELL****

(1953, Jap.) 89m Daiei c (JIGOKUMEN)

Machiko Kyo *(Lady Kesa),* Kazuo Hasegawa *(Moritoh),* Isao Yamagata *(Wataru),* Koreya Senda *(Kiyomori),* Yataro Kurokawa *(Shigemori),* Kikue Mohri *(Sawa),* Kotaro Bando *(Rokuroh),* Jun Tazaki *(Kogenta),* Tatsuya Ishiguro *(Yachuta),* Kenjiro Uemura *(Masanaka),* Gen Shimizu *(Saburosuke).*

A dazzlingly beautiful and simple Japanese tale set in the 12th century, GATE OF HELL concerns the heroic samurai Moritoh (matinee idol Kazuo Hasegawa), who is to be rewarded for his bravery by receiving, from his country's ruler, anything he desires. What Moritoh most desires is the beautiful Lady Kesa (Machiko Kyo), but she is already married. Attempts are made to persuade Kesa to leave her husband (Isao Yamagata), but her devotion to him is great, leaving Moritoh no other choice but to murder his rival. Less revered today than RASHOMON or UGETSU (both of which also starred the gorgeous Kyo), GATE OF HELL was the first Japanese color film to reach US shores and one of the pivotal Japanese releases of its day (premiering in the US in 1954)—helping to pave the way, along with Kurosawa and Mizoguchi's films, for a succession of Japanese releases in the US and building an international reputation for Japanese cinema. Although it was not widely appreciated in Japan, GATE OF HELL was much praised abroad, winning two Academy Awards and the Grand Prize at Cannes. In Japanese with English subtitles.

p, Masaichi Nagata; d, Teinosuke Kinugasa; w, Teinosuke Kinugasa (based on a play by Kan Kikuchi); ph, Kohei Sugiyama (Eastmancolor); m, Yasushi Akutagawa.

Historical **(PR:C-O MPAA:NR)**

GENERAL DELLA ROVERE****

(1959, It./Fr.) 160m Zebra-Gaumont/Continental bw (IL GENERALE DELLA ROVERE)

Vittorio De Sica *(Bardone/Grimaldi),* Hannes Messemer *(Col. Mueller),* Vittorio Caprioli *(Banchelli),* Guiseppe Rossetti *(Fabrizio/Pietro Valeri),* Sandra Milo *(Olga),* Giovanna Ralli *(Valeria),* Anne Vernon *(Chiara Fassio),* Baronessa Barzani *(Contessa della Rovere),* Kurt Polter *(German Officer),* Kurt Selge *(Schrantz),* Mary Greco *(The Madam),* Lucia Modugno *(The Prostitute),* Linda Veras *(German Attendant).*

GENERAL DELLA ROVERE was the film that returned Roberto Rossellini to international favor after he ended his filmmaking collaboration with Ingrid Bergman (FEAR, 1954, was their final work together) and embarked on the documentary course of INDIA. Although Rossellini (who took the project out of need) looks upon this film with shame, it is one of his great achievements, the story of a man who discovers his own morality by imitating the morals of another. Although its underlying themes are essentially Christian, the film is set during the German occupation of Genoa during the winter of 1943-44. After the leader of the Resistance, General della Rovere, is accidentally killed by Gestapo troops, the local Nazi commandant makes an offer to Bardone (Vittorio De Sica), an amoral low-life swindler, to impersonate the general. In that role, Bardone is sent to infiltrate a jail in Milan, where he is supposed to find and identify Fabrizio (Guiseppe Rossetti), the partisan leader della Rovere had planned to meet with before his death. Bardone, however, gradually begins to identify with his fellow prisoners and assumes the moral stance, if not the full personality, of della Rovere. Recalling Rossellini's great early achievements (OPEN CITY and PAISAN), GENERAL DELLA ROVERE is a powerful, beautifully acted picture, which—and this is the source of Rossellini's discontent with the work—retreads the ideas and forms of the director's past successes. But while it may represent a step backwards in the career of this great filmmaker, that does not diminish the film's undeniable autonomous strength. In Italian with English subtitles.

p, Morris Ergas; d, Roberto Rossellini; w, Sergio Amidei, Diego Fabbri, Indro Montanelli (based on a novel by Montanelli); ph, Carlo Carlini; ed, Anna Maria Montanari, Cesare Cavagna; m, Renzo Rossellini.

War/Drama **(PR:C MPAA:NR)**

GERMANY, YEAR ZERO****

(1947, It./Fr./Ger.) 75m Tevere-Salvo D'Angelo-Sadfilm/Superfilm bw (GERMANIA, ANNO ZERO)

Edmund Moeschke *(Edmund Koehler),* Franz Kruger *(Herr Koehler),* Barbara Hintz *(Eva Koehler),* Werner Pittschau *(Karlheinz Koehler),* Erich Guhne *(Prof. Enning),* Alexandra Manys, Baby Reckvell, Ingetraut Hintze, Hans Sange, Hedi Blankner.

It is perhaps appropriate that one of cinema's most frightening films concerns one of the most frightening periods in history. Directed by Roberto Rossellini on the streets of Berlin, GERMANY, YEAR ZERO takes place, as the title suggests, at a moment in time between two eras—between the awful violence of Hitler's fascism and the Holocaust and the German people's realization of the horrors of which their country was guilty. It is a film about that limbo between past and future—that interminable present—when history must start anew. The story follows Edmund (Edmund Moeschke), a 12-year-old boy who lives with nine adults in miserable conditions, surviving just barely on their meager ration cards, fearing each day that their heat or gas will be cut off. The boy's father is on his deathbed, and his brother, a former Nazi, must live in hiding (and therefore gets no ration card) to keep his past from catching up with him. It is therefore up to Edmund to take care of his family. He has no opportunity to live a child's life, or even attend school; too young to work, he spends his days trying to find food, barter on the black market, or do occasional jobs (such as selling records of Hitler's speeches to Allied soldiers). When he meets a former teacher (Erich Guhne), a homosexual fascist who procures young boys for a Nazi general, Edmund gets it into his head that the strong must have the courage to kill the weak. Since everything in his life revolves around the number of mouths he must feed, he decides to poison his father, reasoning that it is morally just to kill the sickly old man who has become just another mouth to feed. At this point young Edmund's Year Zero begins, but the moral weight of his actions proves too much to bear. The third part of Rossellini's "War Trilogy," preceded by OPEN CITY and PAISAN. The videocassette is in German with English subtitles, but is one of the least legible examples of subtitling you're likely to find.

p, Roberto Rossellini; d, Roberto Rossellini; w, Roberto Rossellini, Carlo Lizzani, Max Kolpet (based on a story by Rossellini); ph, Robert Juillard; ed, Eraldo Da Roma; m, Renzo Rossellini.

Drama **(PR:C MPAA:NR)**

GERTRUD***

(1964, Den.) 115m Palladium/Pathe bw

Nina Pens Rode *(Gertrud Kanning),* Bendt Rothe *(Gustav Kanning),* Ebbe Rode *(Gabriel Lidman),* Baard Owe *(Erland Jannson),* Axel Strobye *(Axel Nygren),* Anna Malberg *(Kanning's Mother),* Eduoard Mielche *(The Rector Magnificus),* Vera Gebuhr *(Kanning's Maid),* Karl Gustav Ahlefeldt, Lars Knutzon, William Knoblauch, Valso Holm, Ole Sarvig.

The unhappily married Gertrud (Nina Pens Rode) leaves her husband, accusing him of excessive devotion to his career. She has an affair with a young musician, but her hopes for romance are dashed when she learns that he has been bragging about their liaison. A poet from her past—their relationship having ended a long time ago when she learned that she hindered his creativity—reenters her life, after which she admits to her platonic friend Axel (Axel Strobye) that she is depressed because she falls in love only with men who cannot give her the full attention she desires. She goes to Paris, alone, and is reunited 30 years later with Strobye. In the finale, an aged Gertrud reads him a poem about love that she wrote when she was 16: "Look at me, am I beautiful? No, but I have loved." Carl Theodor Dreyer's fans had to wait 10 years for this, his final picture, and most were disappointed, although some praised the work as the director's greatest achievement since THE PASSION OF JOAN OF ARC. Composed of only 89 shots, GERTRUD is as filled with long (in duration *and* distance) shots as JOAN is with close-ups. Dreyer viewed the film as very much an experiment, calling it "a portrait of time from the beginning of the century." What presents the most difficulty is its talkiness (prompting one critic to call it a "two-hour study of sofas and pianos"), but it is in Dreyer's seemingly simple, noncinematic technique that one comes to realize the purity of his vision. In Danish with English subtitles.

p, Jorgen Nielsen; d, Carl Theodor Dreyer; w, Carl Theodor Dreyer (based on a play by Hjalmar Soderberg); ph, Henning Bendtsen, Arne Abrahamsen; ed, Edith Schlussel; m, Jorgen Jersild.

Drama **(PR:A MPAA:NR)**

GERVAISE***

(1956, Fr.) 120m Agnes Delahaie-Silver-CICC/Continental bw

Maria Schell *(Gervaise Macquart),* Francois Perier *(Henri Coupeau),* Suzy Delair *(Virginie),* Armand Mestral *(Lantier),* Jacques Harden *(Goujet),* Mathilde Casadesus *(Mme. Boche),* Jacques Hilling *(Mon. Boche),* Andre Wasley *(Pere Colombe),* Hubert de Lapparrent *(Mon. Lorilleaux),* Jany Holt *(Mme. Lorilleaux),* Lucien Hubert *(M. Poisson),* Chantal Gozzi *(Nana),* Florelle *(Maman Coupeau),* Pierre Duverger *(M. Gaudron),* Jacqueline Morane *(Mme. Gaudron),* Peignot *(M. Madinier),* Rachel Devirys *(Mme. Fau-*

connier), Max Elbeze *(Zidore),* Micheline Luccioni *(Clemence),* Helene Tossy *(Mme. Bijard),* Christian Denhez *(Etienne at 8),* Christian Ferez *(Etienne at 13),* Patrice Catineau *(Claude),* Marcelle Tery.

Based on a relatively obscure Zola novel about the evils of alcoholism, Rene Clement's film shifts the emphasis from a study of life in a gin-house to the downward spiral of one of its poverty-stricken characters, Gervaise (Maria Schell). The time is the 1850s, the location is the poorest section of Montmartre in Paris. Only 18 years old, Gervaise already has two children by her lover, Lantier (Armand Mestral), who leaves her. She goes to a local bathhouse and learns that he has fled with Virginie (Suzy Delair), the sister of a neighbor. Some time later, Gervaise marries the kind and gentle Coupeau (Francois Perier), with whom she has a daughter, and life finally seems to have a glimmer of hope. But while Gervaise is saving money so she can open her own laundry, Coupeau suffers an accident and is incapacitated for many months, which drains Gervaise's savings. A friendly blacksmith, Goujet (Jacques Harden), offers Gervaise the money to open her laundry, and it's not too hard to see that he is madly in love with her. As Gervaise finally opens her shop, Virginie reappears. This film, one of Clement's best, came at a time when the director was falling out of critical favor as a result of brutal attacks from the writers of *Cahiers du Cinema*. In spite of this, GERVAISE won numerous awards, including Best Actress (Schell) and Best Film at the Venice Film Festival and an Oscar nomination for Best Foreign Film. In French with English subtitles.

p, Annie Dorfmann; d, Rene Clement; w, Jean Aurenche, Pierre Bost (based on the novel *L'Assommoir* by Emile Zola); ph, Rene Juillard; ed, Henri Rust; m, Georges Auric.

Drama (PR:C MPAA:NR)

GET OUT YOUR HANDKERCHIEFS***½

(1977, Fr./Bel.) 108m Ariane-CAPAC-Belga-SODEP/ New Line c (PREPAREZ VOS MOUCHOIRS)

Gerard Depardieu *(Raoul),* Patrick Dewaere *(Stephane),* Carol Laure *(Solange),* Riton *(Christian Beloeil),* Michel Serrault *(Neighbor),* Eleonore Hirt *(Mrs. Beloeil),* Sylvie Joly *(Passerby),* Jean Rougerie *(Mr. Beloeil),* Liliane Rovere, Michel Beaune.

A more civilized, less offensive version of Bertrand Blier's earlier film GOING PLACES, GET OUT YOUR HANDKERCHIEFS again pairs Gerard Depardieu and Patrick Dewaere as a childlike duo who are completely emasculated by the mysterious woman in their lives. Solange (Carol Laure) is the unhappy wife of Raoul (Depardieu). Frustrated by his inability to make his wife happy, Raoul asks a complete stranger, Stephane (Dewaere), to give it a try. All Solange seems to do is knit sweaters with a completely expressionless face. Stephane is equally impotent, however, and succeeds only in becoming the best of friends with Raoul. It takes a third "man"—Christian (Riton), a 13-year-old genius the threesome meets at the boys' summer camp Stephane runs—to fulfill the unhappy woman. Solange, who has been unable to have a child with Raoul or Stephane, finally finds someone to love and care for, even if he is only 13. Besides Blier's sharp direction and screenplay, the film is memorable for the performances of Depardieu and Dewaere. These two superb actors seem so in tune with one another that one must judge their performance as a synthesized whole. Dubbed in English.

p, Paul Claudon; d, Bertrand Blier; w, Bertrand Blier; ph, Jean Penzer (Eastmancolor); ed, Claudine Merlin; m, Georges Delerue, Wolfgang Amadeus Mozart, Franz Schubert.

Comedy (PR:O MPAA:R)

GIFT, THE**

(1982, Fr./It.) 105m Goldwyn c

Pierre Mondy *(Gregoire),* Claudia Cardinale *(Antonella),* Clio Goldsmith *(Barbara),* Jacques Francois *(Loriol),* Cecile Magnet *(Charlotte),* Renzo Montagnani *(Emir Faycal),* Remi Laurent *(Laurent),* Leila Frechet *(Sandrine),* Henri Guybet *(Andre),* Yolande Gilot *(Jennifer),* Diulio Del Prete *(Umberto).*

A tame sex comedy that's neither sexy nor funny, THE GIFT concerns Gregoire (Pierre Mondy), a middle-aged banker getting ready to take an early retirement when in walks Barbara (Clio Goldsmith), a sultry young dream girl. Unknown to Gregoire, she is actually a prostitute who has been sent to the banker by his devilish coworkers. The pair runs off to Venice for a sexual adventure, with Gregoire hardly thinking of his wife (Claudia Cardinale). At best, THE GIFT is a mindless diversion, which at least features Cardinale. Otherwise, however, there is little here of interest. The videocassette is dubbed in English.

p, Gilbert de Goldschmidt; d, Michel Lang; w, Michel Lang (based on the play "Bankers Also Have Souls" by Valme and Terzolli); ph, Daniel Gaudry; m, Michel Legrand.

Comedy (PR:O MPAA:R)

GINGER & FRED***

(1986, It./Fr./Ger.) 126m PEA-Revcom-Stella-RAI 1/ MGM-UA c

Giulietta Masina *(Amelia Bonetti [Ginger]),* Marcello Mastroianni *(Pippo Botticella [Fred]),* Franco Fabrizi *(Show Host),* Frederick Von Ledenburg [Ledebur] *(Admiral Aulenti),* Martin Maria Blau *(Assistant Director),* Toto Mignone *(Toto),* Augusto Poderosi *(Transvestite),* Francesco Casale *(Mafioso),* Frederick Von Thun [Frederich Thun] *(Kidnaped Industrialist),* Jacques Henri Lartigue *(Brother Gerolamo),* Ezio Marano *(Writer),* Antoine Saint Jean *(Bandaged Man),* Antonio Iuorio *(Television Inspector),* Barbara Scoppa *(Pretty Journalist),* Elisabetta Flumeri *(Journalist),* Salvatore Billa *(Gable Double),* Ginestra Spinola *(Clairvoyant),* Stefania Marini *(CST Secretary),* Nando Pucci Negri *(On-Set Assistant),* Laurentina Guidotti *(Production Secretary),* Elena Cantarone *(Nurse),* Gianfranco Alpestre *(Kidnapped Lawyer),* Filippo Ascione *(Pianist),* Cosima Chiusoli *(Fiance of the Unfrocked Priest),* Claudio Ciocca *(Television Cameraman),* Sergio Ciulli

(Son of the Clairvoyant), Vittorio De Bisogno *(Television Director).*

GINGER & FRED tells a warm and very human story about two people who share a little bit of love, interwoven with director Federico Fellini's diatribe against the inanity of the modern television age. Amelia (Giuletta Masina) and Pippo (Marcello Mastroianni) are two aging hoofers who once made a name for themselves as the celebrity-impersonator dance team "Ginger and Fred." Although they bear no more resemblance to Rogers and Astaire than any one of a hundred impersonators does to Elvis, this team has had a few moments of glory that are now left to memory. After a long absence separation, the pair are reunited for a glitzy television variety show that also includes such acts as a troupe of midget Iberian dancers; celebrity lookalikes for Ronald Reagan, Telly Savalas, and Clark Gable; a lapsed priest who will marry onstage; and a man who has invented edible, vitamin-enriched panties. While their performance of "Cheek to Cheek" means very little to the 25 million viewers who plop themselves down in front of the television every night, it means the world to Amelia and Pippo. The well-guarded image of Fred and Ginger was clearly important to the real-life Ginger Rogers, who sued the filmmakers for $8 million, claiming that the movie damaged her reputation. Her claims were tossed out of court. In Italian with English subtitles.

p, Alberto Grimaldi; d, Federico Fellini; w, Federico Fellini, Tonino Guerra, Tullio Pinelli (based on a story by Federico Fellini and Tonino Guerra); ph, Tonino Delli Colli, Ennio Guarnieri; ed, Nino Baragli, Ugo De Rossi, Ruggero Mastroianni; m, Nicola Piovani.

Drama/Comedy **(PR:A-C MPAA:PG-13)**

GIRL ON A MOTORCYCLE, THE**

(1968, Fr./Brit.) 91m Mid-Atlantic-Ares/Claridge c (LA MOTOCYCLETTE; AKA: NAKED UNDER LEATHER)

Alain Delon *(Daniel),* Marianne Faithfull *(Rebecca),* Roger Mutton *(Raymond),* Marius Goring *(Rebecca's Father),* Catherine Jourdan *(Catherine),* Jean Leduc *(Jean),* Jacques Marin *(Pump Attendant),* Andre Maranne *(French Superintendent),* Marika Rivera *(German Waitress),* Richard Blake, Christopher Williams, Colin West, Kit Williams *(Students).*

One-time Rolling Stones groupie Marianne Faithfull is here clad in black leather as Rebecca, a bored housewife who hops on a motorcycle in Alsace and takes off for Heidelberg to meet her lover, Daniel (Alain Delon). During a long erotic ride through the countryside, she recalls various meetings with Daniel—some romantic, others sexual. As she nears his house, the bike seeming to increase in power, Rebecca is killed in a crash that sends her flying into the windshield of an oncoming car. This perversely morbid and erotic tale is blessed with Faithfull's aura, but damned by British director Jack Cardiff's pretensions. Originally released with an "X" rating but toned down to get its "R," it was filmed in both French and English versions, the latter of which is on videotape.

p, William Sassoon; d, Jack Cardiff; w, Ronald Duncan, Gillian Freeman (based on the novel *La Motocyclette* by Andre Pieyre de Mandiargues); ph, Jack Cardiff (Technicolor); ed, Peter Musgrave; m, Les Reed.

Romance **(PR:O MPAA:R)**

GO-MASTERS, THE***

(1982, Jap./Chi.) 133m Beijing-Toko Tokuma-Daiei/ Circle c (MIKAN NO TAIKYOKU; Trans: The Unfinished Game Of Go)

Sun Dao-lin *(Kuang Yi-shan),* Huang Zong-ying *(Kuang Yuan-Zhi),* Du Peng *(Guan Xiao-chuan),* Yu Shao-kang *(Dr. Zhang),* Liu Xin, Shen Guan-chu *(Kuang A-ming),* Mao Wei-hui, Shen Dan-ping *(Kuang A-hui),* Zhang Lei *(Xiao A-hui).*

The first Chinese-Japanese coproduction and the most widely seen Asian film on that continent, THE GO-MASTERS chronicles, in epic scale, 32 years in the lives of Kuang Yi-shan (Sun Dao-lin) of China and Rinsaku Matsunami (Rentaro Mikuni) of Japan. Both men are masters of Go, an ancient and extremely complex, chesslike game that involves military-style strategies and the conquering of territories. The film opens in 1946 at the close of WW II, revealing through flashbacks that Kuang sent his son to study Go in Japan under Rinsaku. The boy eventually became the national champion, wed his tutor's daughter, and with the start of WW II was pressured into declaring his allegiance to Japan. After going years without hearing from his child, Kuang travels to Japan only to learn of the son's death and to declare vengeance on Rinsaku. Reflecting its own underlying message of reconciliation, THE GO-MASTERS is itself a step towards peaceful relations between Asian nations. The film was not only coproduced by China and Japan, but also photographed in both countries, codirected by a Chinese and a Japanese, and made with technical crews from both countries. In Japanese and Mandarin with English subtitles.

p, Masahiro Sato, Wang Zhi-min; d, Duan Ji-shun, Junya Sato; w, Li Hong-zhou, Ge Kang-tong, Fumio Konami, Yasuko Ohno, Tetsuro Abe; ph, Luo De-an, Shohei Ando; m, Jiang Ding-xian, Hikaru Hayashi.

Drama **(PR:C MPAA:NR)**

GOALIE'S ANXIETY AT THE PENALTY KICK, THE***½

(1971, Ger./Aust.) 101m Filmverlag der Autoren-Osterreichischen Telefilm AG/Gray City c (DIE ANGST DES TORMANNS BEIM ELFMETER; AKA: THE ANXIETY OF THE GOALIE AT THE PENALTY KICK; THE GOALKEEPER'S FEAR OF THE PENALTY)

Arthur Brauss *(Joseph Bloch),* Kai Fischer *(Hertha Gabler),* Erika Pluhar *(Gloria),* Libgart Schwartz *(Anna, hotel maid),* Marie Bardeschewski *(Maria, Hertha's Waitress),* Michael Troost *(Salesman at Soccer Match),* Bert Fortell *(Customs Officer),* Edda Koechl *(Girl in Vienna),* Mario Kranz *(School Janitor),* Ernst Meister *(Tax Inspector),* Rosl Dorena *(Woman on Bus),* Rudi Schippel *(Cashier in Vienna),* Monika Poeschel, Sybile Danzer *(Hairdressers),*

Rudiger Vogler *(Village Idiot),* Karl Krittle *(Castle Gatekeeper),* Maria Engelstorfer *(Shopkeeper),* Otto Hoch-Fischer *(Innkeeper),* Wim Wenders *(Man in Bus Station),* Gerhard Toetschinger, Liane Golle, Ernst Koppens.

Wim Wenders' second feature film and his first collaboration with the Austrian novelist-poet-playwright Peter Handke is an adaptation of Handke's short novel about a soccer goalie driven to murder. From the start of Wenders' film, the personality of the goalie, Josef Bloch (Arthur Braus), is evident. While the game's action take place at one end of the field, Bloch waits at his net at the opposite end. As play nears, he takes little notice, walks in front of his net, and stands completely still as the ball is kicked past him. Bloch is a character who considers it pointless to try to evade or outwit the course of events. He leaves the team (whose popularity has taken them around the world) and begins to wander. He visits movie theaters, plays American songs on jukeboxes, drinks, encounters people, and observes life as it passes him by. After he meets a cinema cashier named Gloria (Erika Pluhar)—which, as she reminds him, is spelled G-L-O-R-I-A as in the rock'n'roll song by Them—Bloch returns with her to her apartment and, eventually, strangles her for no apparent reason. Although the film's plot is essentially that of a crime thriller, the director makes no concessions to genre expectations. Wenders, who has long professed his fascination with America, its films, and its music, cannot make an American-styled picture. Instead, he presents a meditative, fragmentary reconstruction of the killer's mind, his distorted perceptions, his personal (a)morality, and the otherwise unimportant events in his daily existence. While most directors insist of sensationalizing acts of violence and perpetuating the myth of the outlaw hero, Wenders, in this portrait of a killer, delivers one of film's most truthful depictions of the criminal. In German with English subtitles.

p, Peter Genee; d, Wim Wenders; w, Wim Wenders, Peter Handke (based on the novel by Handke); ph, Robby Muller; ed, Peter Przygodda; m, Jurgen Knieper.

Crime/Drama (PR:C MPAA:NR)

GOING PLACES***½

(1974, Fr.) 117m CAPAC-UPF-SN/Cinema 5 c (LES VALSEUSES)

Gerard Depardieu *(Jean-Claude),* Patrick Dewaere *(Pierrot),* Miou-Miou *(Marie-Ange),* Jeanne Moreau *(Jeanne Pirolle),* Jacques Chailleux *(Jacques Pirolle),* Michel Peyrelon *(Surgeon),* Brigitte Fossey *(Young Mother),* Isabelle Huppert *(Jacqueline),* Christiane Muller *(Jacqueline's Mother),* Christian Alers *(Jacqueline's Father),* Dominique Davray *(Ursula),* Jacques Rispal *(Beautician),* Marco Perrin *(Warden),* Gerard Boucaron *(Garage Owner),* Michel Pilorge *(Market Manager),* Eva Damien, Claude Vergnes.

This disagreeable but fascinating examination of youth is constructed as a buddy film/road movie and revolves around the friendship between Jean-Claude (Gerard Depardieu) and Pierrot (Patrick Dewaere), a couple of long-haired, disheveled petty thieves in their mid-20s. As the film begins, the duo is terrorizing a middle-aged woman—grabbing her ample behind, blowing kisses on her neck, and finally stealing her purse. So begins their spree, which, as crime sprees go, is relatively harmless. Along the way they steal cars, break into stores, insult people, seduce some semi-willing women, and even have sex with each other when no one else can be found, but do not seem to have a profound effect on anyone. After returning a stolen car, Pierrot is shot by the angry owner and superficially wounded in one testicle. His fear is that he'll never have a woman again. His anxiety proves unfounded, however, when the thieves meet Marie-Ange (Miou-Miou), a flighty young woman who doesn't mind disrobing for or having sex with them, but who doesn't seem to enjoy it either—infuriating these two macho men who are convinced they can make any woman melt in their arms. The first major film from Bertrand Blier (son of actor Bernard), GOING PLACES is an ugly and brutal, yet somehow charming, look at two young men who are wholly worthless as human beings. They have no future, and, despite the fact that they travel from one side of France to the other, they never get anywhere. They just go—fast and furious. The most significant moment in their lives (and in the film) is their meeting with Jeanne (Jeanne Moreau), an older woman just released from prison who laments that she is no longer young. She who has nothing is even worse off than Jean-Claude and Jacques, who at least have youth. The beautiful Moreau appears for only a short time in the film, but gives one of her most spectacular performances. The videocassette is dubbed in English.

p, Paul Claudon; d, Bertrand Blier; w, Bertrand Blier, Philippe Dumarcay (based on the novel by Bertand Blier); ph, Bruno Nuytten; ed, Kenout Peltier; m, Stephane Grappelli.

Comedy/Drama (PR:O MPAA:R)

GOLDEN COACH, THE****

(1952, Fr./It.) 105m Delphinus Hoche-Panaria/I.F.E. c (LE CARROSSE D'OR)

Anna Magnani *(Camilla),* Duncan Lamont *(Viceroy),* Paul Campbell *(Felipe),* Riccardo Rioli *(Ramon, the Bullfighter),* Odoardo Spadaro *(Don Antonio),* Nada Fiorelli *(Isabella),* Dante *(Harlequin),* George Higgins *(Martinez),* Ralph Truman *(Duke of Castro),* Gisella Mathews *(Marquise Altamirano),* Raf De La Torre *(Chief Justice),* Elena Altieri *(Duchess of Castro),* William Tubbs *(Innkeeper),* Jean Debucourt *(Bishop),* Lina Marengo *(The Old Actress),* Renato Chiantoni *(Captain Fracasse),* Giulio Tedeschi *(Baldassare),* Alfredo Kolner *(Florindo),* Alfredo Medini *(Polichinelle),* The Medini Brothers *(The Four Children).*

Marking Jean Renoir's return to France after his decade in Hollywood and his short period in India filming THE RIVER, THE GOLDEN COACH has often been seen as the key to the understanding of all of the director's work. Filmed in English at Rome's Cinecitta studios, the film stars Anna Magnani as Camilla, a commedia dell'arte performer who, with her ragtag troupe, arrives in a Latin American country to open a new theater. Already pursued by Felipe (Paul Campbell), Camilla captures the hearts of the vain bullfighter Ramon (Riccardo Rioli) and the Viceroy (Duncan Lamont). Swept away by Camilla's charms and attracted to the vulgar manner that is so alien to his aristocratic experience, the Viceroy presents her with his prized golden coach, a beautifully crafted vehicle that had been used solely for royal business. As the drama rolls on and Camilla struggles to differentiate between reality and the stage, all three of her suitors vie for her love—the Viceroy learning to feel "common" emotions; Ramon impressing her with his manliness; and Felipe inviting her to live with him in the wilderness among the "noble savages." Opening and closing with a stage curtain, THE GOLDEN COACH is Jean Renoir's invitation to sit back and enjoy the colorful, romantic, humorous spectacle of real life. While artists have often addressed the confusion of reality and fiction, few have done it with as much grace and love as Renoir. Much of the film's success, however, is due to the brilliant Magnani. THE GOLDEN COACH does not so much star Magnani, as it exists *because* of her. It is her film and everything in it thrives because of the life she breathes into it. In English.

p, Francesco Alliata; d, Jean Renoir; w, Jean Renoir, Renzo Avanzo, Jack Kirkland, Ginette Doynel, Giulio Macchi (based on the play "La Carrosse du Saint-Sacrement" by Prosper Merimee); ph, Claude Renoir (Technicolor), H. Ronald, Mario Serandrei; ed, David Hawkins, Mario Serandrei; m, Antonio Vivaldi.

Drama **(PR:A MPAA:NR)**

GOLDEN DEMON**½

(1954, Jap.) 95m Daiei/Edward Harrison c (KONJIKI YASHA)

Jun Negami *(Kan-ichi),* Fujiko Yamamoto *(Miya),* Kenji Sugawara *(Arao),* Mitsuko Mito *(Akagashi),* Kazuko Fushimi *(Aiko),* Eiji Funakoshi *(Tomiyama),* Shizue Natsukawa *(Mrs. Minowa),* Kumeko Urabe *(Tose),* Kinzo Shin *(Mrs. Shigisawa),* Shiko Saito *(Wanibuchi),* Teppei Endo *(Mr. Minowa),* Jun Miyazaki *(Kamata),* Yuki Hayakawa *(Kazahaya),* Yoshio Takee *(Yusa),* Sachiko Meguro *(Mrs. Yusa).*

A little-known film from the relatively obscure Japanese director Koji Shima, GOLDEN DEMON tells the tragic, late 19th-century tale of two star-crossed lovers forced to separate as a result of an arranged marriage. Kan-ichi (Jun Negami) is a young man in love with Miya (Fujiko Yamamoto), whom he has known since childhood and hopes to marry. However, when the wealthy Tomiyama (Eiji Funakoshi) asks the girl's parents for their daughter's hand, they agree over their daughter's objections. In order to avenge the loss of his beloved, whom he believes deserted him for money—that "golden demon"—Kan-ichi becomes a ruthless moneylender. While GOLDEN DEMON tends to pour on the sentiment in heavy doses, the superb color photography and the stylized acting lend much to this Romeo and Juliet story, which is based on a classic Japanese romance novel by Koyo Ozaki. The videocassette is available in both dubbed and subtitled (Japanese into English) versions.

p, Masaichi Nagata; d, Koji Shima; w, Koji Shima (based on the adaptation by Matsutaru Kawaguchi of the novel by Koyo Ozaki); ph, Michio Takahashi (Eastmancolor); m, Ichiro Saito.

Drama **(PR:C MPAA:NR)**

GOLEM, THE****

(1920, Ger.) 90m Ufa bw

Paul Wegener *(The Golem),* Albert Steinruck *(Rabbi Loew),* Lyda Salmonova *(Rabbi's Daughter),* Hans Strum *(Emperor Rudolf II of Hapsburg),* Ernest Deutsch *(Famulus),* Fritz Feld *(Jester),* Lathar Menthel *(Knight Florian),* Otto Gebuehr.

A pivotal work of German cinema and of the horror genre, THE GOLEM is a film of history, myth, and legend that nonetheless managed to play an important part in film's future. Upon receiving news that the tyrannical Hapsburg Emperor (Hans Strum) plans to drive the Jews from their Prague ghetto, Rabbi Loew (Albert Steinruck) conjures up a protector for his oppressed people—the Golem (Paul Wegener), a huge creature molded from clay and given life through a mystic ritual. The Rabbi, with the creature under his control, travels to the emperor's castle and, after letting the destructive Golem show his physical strength, persuades him to reverse his decree. When the Golem, who now desires more out of life than simply being the Rabbi's servant, falls in love with the Loew's daughter (Lyda Salmonova), he must fight against his creator for the right to exist. This was the third time (previous versions were in 1914 and 1917) that Wegener brought the Golem legend to the screen, each time casting himself in the lead, and his superb performance (a model for Karloff's Frankenstein), the photography of the legendary Karl Freund, and the masterful set design of Hans Poelzig (who reconstructed a portion of old Prague in the UFA studios) make this seminal horror film extremely powerful today. The videotape version is listed under a variety of running times, ranging anywhere from 70 to 118 minutes. The complete version, however, runs approximately 90 minutes.

d, Paul Wegener, Carl Boese; w, Paul Wegener, Henrik Galeen; ph, Karl Freund.

Horror **(PR:A-C MPAA:NR)**

GOOD MORNING BABYLON**½

(1987, It./Fr./US) 116m Filmitre-MK2-Pressman-RA-Films A2/Vestron c (GOOD MORNING BABILONIA)

Vincent Spano *(Nicola Bonnano),* Joaquim de Almeida *(Andrea Bonnano),* Greta Scacchi *(Edna),* Desiree Becker *(Mabel),* Omero Antonutti *(Bonnano, Nicola & Andrea's Father),* Charles Dance *(D.W. Griffith),* Berangere Bonvoisin *(Mrs. Moglie Griffith),* David Brandon *(Grass),* Brian Freilino *(Thompson),* Margarita Lozano *(The Venetian),* Massimo Venturiello *(Duccio),* Andrea Prodan *(Irish Cameraman),* Dorotea Ausenda, Ugo Bencini, Daniel Bosch, Renzo Cantini, Marco Cavicchioli, Fiorenza d'Alessandro, Lionello Pio Di Savoia, Maurizio Fardo, Domenico Fiore, Mirio Guidelli.

The dawn of Hollywood is brought to the screen in this fable about two Italian brothers—Nicola and Andrea Bonnano (Vincent Spano and Joaquim de Almeida)—whose craftsmanship augments D.W. Griffith's 1916 masterpiece INTOLERANCE. The film begins in Tuscany, 1913, as a master restorer of facades (Omero Antonutti) and his sons put the finishing touches on an exquisite old basilica. Afterwards, the patriarch announces that he is selling his unprofitable company. His two favorite sons, Nicola and Andrea, who inherited his "hands of gold," vow to make a fortune in America and then return to buy back the family business. After a transatlantic voyage that purposely recalls the Charles Chaplin short THE IMMIGRANT, the brothers arrive in New York with wide-eyed awe. Their dreams of being discovered as great artisans are far from realized, however, when they earn their first wages as pig caretakers. Eventually they arrive in Hollywood, but instead of finding powerful positions they are taken on as laborers. The fact that they are "the sons of the sons of the sons of Michelangelo and Leonardo" impresses no one—except two pretty extras (Greta Scacchi and Desiree Becker) with whom they fall in love. Finally, however, their design for the gigantic elephants of INTOLERANCE's "Babylon" sequence is spotted by Griffith (Charles Dance), and fortune follows. Brothers Paolo and Vittorio Taviani have made clear their attempt to create a fable, but, unfortunately, GOOD MORNING BABYLON succeeds on that level only, ignoring logic, history, and solid characterization. One of the most disappointing major releases in recent years, GOOD MORNING BABYLON promised to capture the dawn of cinema, and of Hollywood as the birthplace of a new, collaborative community of artisans not unlike the great craftsmen who spent years creating Italian cathedrals, but the result shows as much dimension as a movie set facade. In English and Italian with English subtitles.

p, Giuliani G. De Negri; d, Paolo Taviani, Vittorio Taviani; w, Paolo Taviani, Vittorio Taviani, Tonino Guerra (based on an idea by Lloyd Fonvielle); ph, Giuseppe Lanci (Eastmancolor); ed, Roberto Perpignani; m, Nicola Piovani.

Historical **(PR:C-O MPAA:PG-13)**

GOSPEL ACCORDING TO ST. MATTHEW, THE****

(1964, Fr./It.) 136m L'Arco-CCF/CD bw (IL VANGELO SECONDO MATTEO; L'EVANGILE SELON SAINT-MATTHIEU)

Enrique Irazoqui *(Jesus Christ),* Margherita Caruso *(Mary, as a Girl),* Susanna Pasolini *(Mary, as a Woman),* Marcello Morante *(Joseph),* Mario Socrate *(John the Baptist),* Settimo Di Porto *(Peter),* Otello Sestili *(Judas),* Ferruccio Nuzzo *(Matthew),* Giacomo Morante *(John),* Alfonso Gatto *(Andrew),* Enzo Siciliano *(Simon),* Giorgio Agamben *(Philip),* Guido Cerretani *(Bartholomew),* Luigi Barbini *(James, Son of Alpheus),* Marcello Galdini *(James, Son of Zebedee),* Elio Spaziani *(Thaddeus),* Rosario Migale *(Thomas),* Rodolfo Wilcock *(Caiaphas),* Alessandro Tasca *(Pontius Pilate),* Amerigo Bevilacqua *(Herod the Great),* Francesco Leonetti *(Herod Antipas),* Franca Cupane *(Herodias),* Paola Tedesco *(Salome),* Rossana Di Rocco *(Angel),* Eliseo Boschi *(Joseph of Arimathea),* Natalia Ginzburg *(Mary of Bethany),* Renato Terra *(A Pharisee),* Enrico Maria Salerno *(Voice of Jesus).*

Pier Paolo Pasolini's epic film tells the life story of Jesus in a semidocumentary filmmaking style enacted by nonprofessional actors, including the director's mother as the Virgin Mary. Hailed by many as the greatest adaptation of the life of Christ (though the praise heaped upon THE LAST TEMPTATION OF CHRIST may now change that), this picture was dedicated to Pope John XXIII, who brought the Catholic Church into the 20th century. It may come as a surprise to those who see this honest and moving film that Pasolini was not only an atheist, but a homosexual and Marxist as well. The film won a special jury prize at the Venice Film Festival and received three Oscar nominations—Luis Enriquez Bacalov for his score (arrangements of Bach, Mozart, Webern, and Prokofiev), Luigi Scaccianoce for black-and-white art direction, and Danilo Donati for black-and-white costume design. As if to underline the unorthodox nature of the film, Pasolini has included on his soundtrack the American spiritual "Sometimes I Feel Like a Motherless Child," sung by Odetta. The videotape is available in both dubbed and subtitled (Italian into English) versions.

p, Alfredo Bini; d, Pier Paolo Pasolini; w, Pier Paolo Pasolini (based on the gospel according to St. Matthew); ph, Tonino Delli Colli; ed, Nino Baragli; m, Luis Bacalov, Johann Sebastian Bach, Wolfgang Amadeus Mozart, Sergei Prokofiev, Anton Webern.

Religious **(PR:A MPAA:NR)**

GRAND ILLUSION*****

(1937, Fr.) 95m RAC/World bw (LA GRANDE ILLUSION)

Jean Gabin *(Marechal),* Pierre Fresnay *(Capt. de Boeildieu),* Erich von Stroheim *(Von Rauffenstein),* Marcel Dalio *(Rosenthal),* Dita Parlo *(Elsa, the farm woman),* Julien Carette *(Cartier),* Gaston Modot *(A Surveyor),* Georges Peclet *(A Soldier),* Edouard Daste *(A Teacher),* Sylvain Itkine *(Demolder),* Jacques Becker *(The English Officer),* Werner Florian *(Arthur Krantz),* Claude Sainval, Michel Salina.

One of the undeniably great films in the history of cinema, Jean Renoir's GRAND ILLUSION is a comment on the borders that divide people, classes, armies, and countries. The film opens during WW I, as Marechal (Jean Gabin) and Boeildieu (Pierre Fresnay) are shot down by German ace Von Rauffenstein (Erich von Stroheim). Marechal and Boeildieu survive the crash and are invited to lunch by Von Rauffenstein before ground troops arrive to cart the French officers off to a POW camp. Although Marechal and Boeildieu are compatriots, Boeildieu has more in common with Von Rauffenstein, as both of them are members of the white-gloved aristocracy. After lunch, the Frenchmen are placed in a barracks where French officer Rosenthal (Marcel Dalio), a Jew, befriends them, along with several British officers who have also been taken prisoner. The newcomers join the others in working on an escape tunnel beneath the barracks, but a French victory on the Western Front is a sign that the war is turning in the favor of the French. Marechal, Boeildieu, and the rest of the French prisoners are transferred to another prison, where they again meet Von Rauffenstein. Now confined to a neck brace after sustaining an injury in combat, the Commandant warmly welcomes the Frenchmen, pointing out that his prison, Wintersborn, is escape proof. He treats his prisoners with great deference, having them to dinner and extending what meager courtesies he can, talking with Boeildieu about how this war will bring to an end the gentlemanly class of officers, dispensing with the honor and dignity of their rank and bloodlines. Caught somewhere between his loyalty to a member of his class (Von Rauffenstein) and to his country, Boeildieu once again agrees to assist his fellow prisoners in their escape attempts. Directed with patience and care by Renoir, the film was banned in Germany by Nazi Propaganda Minister Josef Goebbels, who labeled it "Cinematographic Enemy Number 1" and compelled his Italian counterpart to have the film banned in that country, although the 1937 Venice Film Festival gave the film a Best Artistic Ensemble award. It was thought that all European prints of GRAND ILLUSION were destroyed by the Nazis, but American troops uncovered a negative in Munich in 1945 (preserved, strangely, by the Germans themselves), leading to the edited film's reconstruction. Gabin, Fresnay, Dalio, and von Stroheim all give impressive performances in this beautifully directed and written film. In French with English subtitles.

p, Raymond Blondy; d, Jean Renoir; w, Jean Renoir, Charles Spaak; ph, Christian Matras; ed, Marguerite Renoir; m, Joseph Kosma.

War/Prison **(PR:A MPAA:NR)**

GREEN ROOM, THE*½**

(1978, Fr.) 94m Carrosse-Artistes/NW c (LA CHAMBRE VERTE)

Francois Truffaut *(Julien Davenne),* Nathalie Baye *(Cecilia Mandel),* Jean Daste *(Bernard Humbert),* Jean-Pierre Moulin *(Gerard Mazet),* Antoine Vitez *(Bishop's secretary),* Jane Lobre *(Mme. Rambaud),* Monique Dury *(Monique),* Laurence Ragon *(Julie Davenne),* Marcel Berbert *(Dr. Jardine),* Christian Lentretien *(Orator in Cemetery),* Patrick Maleon *(Georges as a Boy),* Annie Miller *(Genevieve Mazet),* Marie Jadoul *(Yvonne Mazet),* Jean-Pierre Ducos *(Priest in Mortuary),* Guy d'Ablon *(Wax-Dummy Maker),* Alphonse Simon *(One-legged Man at The Globe),* Henri Bienvenu *(The Auctioneer),* Thi Loan N'Guyen *(Apprentice Artisan),* Nathan Miller *(Genevieve Mazet's Son),* Anna Paniez *(Girl at Piano).*

Francois Truffaut's testimony of obsession is perhaps the most unheralded film of his career, and surely one of his most personal. Truffaut himself plays Julien Davenne, a secretive man who excels at writing obituaries for a failing journal. He is stubbornly obsessed with death, believing that the dead are not given the love and attention they deserve. The reason for his reverence is two-fold: he has suffered both the guilt of returning from WW I unharmed while everyone he knew was killed or injured, and the sudden death of his newlywed wife. In her memory he constructs a shrine, complete with a frightening, lifesize wax figurine. He meets former acquaintance Cecilia (Nathalie Baye) and begins running into her on a steady basis at the cemetery. While wandering through the grounds there, Julien discovers an old chapel in need of restoration, which he remodels as elaborate temple for the dead. On the surface, THE GREEN ROOM is an excessively depressing and strange portrait of a man who values death over life, but underneath this lies its study of a man driven by his obsessions, overflowing with exalted energy. Just as Julien Davenne is obsessed with the dead, or as Antoine Doinel is obsessed with woman, so Truffaut was obsessed with the cinema. For fans of Truffaut, who died in 1984, THE GREEN ROOM is an especially chilling experience. There's also the odd coincidence of Oskar Werner's picture being included in the shrine—Werner died just days after Truffaut. In French with English subtitles.

d, Francois Truffaut; w, Francois Truffaut, Jean Gruault (based on themes in the writings of Henry James); ph, Nestor Almendros (Eastmancolor); ed, Martine Barraque; m, Maurice Jaubert.

Drama **(PR:C-O MPAA:PG)**

H

HAIL, MARY****

(1985, Fr./Switz./Brit.) 86m Pegase-JLG-Sara-SSR-Channel 4/Gaumont-New Yorker c (JE VOUS SALUE MARIE)

Myriem Roussel *(Mary),* Thierry Rode *(Joseph),* Philippe Lacoste *(The Angel),* Juliette Binoche *(Juliette),* Manon Anderson *(Girl),* Malachi Jara Kohan *(Jesus),* Dick *(Arthur),* Johann Leysen *(Professor),* Anne Gauthier *(Eva).*

Ever since his first film, BREATHLESS (1959), Jean-Luc Godard has managed to destroy the conventions of cinema and cause critical outrage in the process. Remaining true to form, Godard, some 25 years later, again whipped his critics into a frenzy with HAIL MARY—not long after the New Wave had been pronounced dead by many. By updating the story of the Virgin Mary, Godard produced, as the critics billed it, "the most controversial film of our time," and for once the advertisements weren't lying. Myriem Roussel is Mary, a young woman who pumps gas, plays basketball, and has a taxi driver boy friend named Joseph (Thierry Rode). Although another woman is anxious to sleep with Joseph, he chooses instead to chase the chaste Mary. One day, Mary learns that she is to give birth to the Son of God; Joseph, however, cannot believe that Mary is pregnant *and* a virgin. But after they are wed, Mary teaches Joseph to love her from a distance, revering her without touching her—Godard's personal definition of faith. Sight unseen, HAIL MARY was protested in many cities throughout the world, and banned in others, including Rome, where Pope John Paul II officially condemned the film. Curiously, Godard had originally intended to make a film about incest—planning to concentrate on a man's impossible love for his unattainable daughter—but as the film evolved, it became the story of Joseph's love for his unattainable Mary. Since BREATHLESS Godard has been fascinated with the idea of a man becoming obsessed with a woman he cannot attain or possess, and HAIL, MARY takes this preoccupation to the extreme. Included on the videocassette is the short THE BOOK OF MARY (LE LIVRE DE MARIE), directed by longtime Godard associate Anne-Marie Mieville. In French with English subtitles.

d, Jean-Luc Godard; w, Jean-Luc Godard; ph, Jean-Bernard Menoud, Jacques Frimann; m, Johann Sebastian Bach, Anton Dvorak, John Coltrane.

Religious **(PR:O MPAA:NR)**

HAMMETT***½

(1982, US) 94m Orion-Zoetrope/WB c

Frederic Forrest *(Hammett),* Peter Boyle *(Jimmy Ryan),* Marilu Henner *(Kit Conger/Sue Alabama),* Roy Kinnear *(English Eddie Hagedorn),* Elisha Cook *(Eli, the Taxi Driver),* Lydia Lei *(Crystal Ling),* R.G. Armstrong *(Lt. Pat O'Mara),* Richard Bradford *(Detective Tom Bradford),* Michael Chow *(Fon Wei Tau),* David Patrick Kelly *(Punk),* Sylvia Sidney *(Donaldina Cameron),* Jack Nance *(Gary Salt),* Elmer L. Kline *(Doc Fallon),* Royal Dano *(Pops),* Samuel Fuller *(Old Billiard Player),* Lloyd Kino *(Barber),* Fox Harris *(Frank),* Rose Wong *(Laundress),* Liz Roberson *(Lady in Library),* Jean Francois Ferreol *(French Sailor),* Alison Hong *(Young Girl),* Patricia Kong *(Girl at Fong's),* Lisa Lu *(Donaldina's Assistant),* Andrew Winner *(Bank Guard),* Kenji Shibuya *(Chinese Bouncer),* James Quinn *(Fong's Bodyguard).*

Impressed by Wim Wenders' obvious talent, Francis Coppola invited the German director to come to America (a dream come true for any of Wenders' wandering characters) and make a Hollywood film. The project chosen was a highly fictionalized account of the exploits of famed detective novelist Dashiell Hammett. Set in 1920s San Francisco, the film follows Hammett (Frederic Forrest) as he leaves the Pinkerton Detective Agency to devote himself to writing, and is recruited by his former boss, Jimmy Ryan (Peter Boyle), to help crack a particularly tough case involving a Chinese prostitute. Like THE AMERICAN FRIEND, Wenders' previous picture, HAMMETT is less concerned with its story line (though more so than Wenders' previous films) than it is with focusing on an American myth. Unfortunately, Hollywood filmmaking was not what Wenders expected, as he and Coppola clashed over the film's direction. Wenders, who had already made seven features and was an internationally renowned director, was handcuffed by Coppola, who not only hired the director, but also used much of the cast and crew of his own Zoetrope studio. In between HAMMETT's production delays, Wenders made the low-budget black-and-white THE STATE OF THINGS, a film about the difficulties of filmmaking and the elusiveness of an American film producer. In English.

p, Fred Roos, Ronald Colby, Don Guest; d, Wim Wenders; w, Ross Thomas, Dennis O'Flaherty, Thomas Pope (based on the novel *Hammett* by Joe Gores); ph, Philip Lathrop, Joseph Biroc (Technicolor); ed, Barry Malkin, Marc Laub, Robert Q. Lovett, Wendy Roberts; m, John Barry.

Mystery **(PR:C MPAA:PG)**

HANNAH K.**

(1983, Fr.) 108m KG-Gaumont/UNIV c

Jill Clayburgh *(Hannah Kaufman),* Jean Yanne *(Victor Bonnet),* Gabriel Byrne *(Josue Herzog),* Muhamad Bakri *(Selim Bakri),* David Clennon *(Amnon),* Shimon Finkel *(Prof. Leventhal),* Oded Kotler *(The Stranger),* Michael Bat-Adam *(Russian Woman),* Dafna Levy *(Dafna),* Dan Muggia *(Capt. Allenby Bridge),* Robert Sommer *(Court President),* Ronald Guttman *(Judge),* Bruno Corazzari *(Court President),* Amnon Kapeliouk *(Judge),* Dalik Wolinitz *(Sergeant),* Luca Barbareschi *(Young Lawyer),* Gideon Amir *(Court Lawyer),* William Berger *(German Journalist),* Murray Gronwall *(Jail Interpreter),* Cyrus Elias *(Guard in Jail Parlor),* Izviad Arad *(Tourist Guide),* Jacques Cohen *(Ex-Soldier at Airport),* Uri Gavriel *(Barman at Airport),* Manuel Cauchi *(Barman at Beach),* Sinay Peter *(Airport Control).*

This frustrating film from Constantin Costa-Gavras stars Jill Clayburgh as Hannah Kaufman, an American Jewish lawyer who defends a young Palestinian, Selim Bakri (Mohamed Bakri), who sues Israel for the right to live on his ancestral land on the Left Bank. Josue Herzog (Gabriel Byrne), the arrogant young Israeli who represents the government in the case, is also the man whose child Hannah is bearing. When she and Selim also become lovers, politics and romance become painfully and inextricably linked for the idealistic American. Surprisingly, for a Costra-Gavras film, HANNAH K.'s potential for political provocation is clouded by the script's contrived romantic flip-flops. Clayburgh's character is weak, and hence unsympathetic, while Byrne's Israeli is so obnoxious one can't help but root for Bakri's noble Arab. It may be too much to expect an "objective" examination of such an explosive issue in any film, let alone one by such a champion of the oppressed as Costa-Gavras, but those expecting the gripping dramatic tension of the director's Z; STATE OF SIEGE; or MISSING are likely to be disappointed by HANNAK K. In English.

p, Michele Ray-Gavras; d, Constantin Costa-Gavras; w, Constantin Costa-Gavras, Franco Solinas; ph, Ricardo Aronovich (Panavision, Fujicolor); ed, Francoise Bonnot; m, Gabriel Yared.

Drama **(PR:C MPAA:R)**

HAPPY NEW YEAR**½

(1973, Fr./It.) 114m Les Films 13-Rizzoli/Joseph E. Levine-Avco Embassy bw (LA BONNE ANNEE)

Lino Ventura *(Simon),* Francoise Fabian *(Francoise),* Charles Gerard *(Charlot),* Andre Falcon *(Jeweler),* Claude Mann *(Intellectual),* Frederic de Pasquale *(Lover),* Bettina Rheims *(Salesgirl),* Mireille Mathieu, Lilo, Gerard Sire,

Silvano Tranquilli, Andre Barello, Norman de la Chesnaye, Michel Bertay, Pierre Edeline, Pierre Pontiche, Michou, Joseph Rythmann, Georges Staquet, Harry Walter, Jacques Villedieu, Robert Atelian, Alain Basnier, Gaya Becaud, Eugene Bellin, Denise Cassotti, Sabine Cocheteux, Andre Davalan, Catherine Desage.

An entertaining but vacuous effort from Claude Lelouch, HAPPY NEW YEAR combines the tenderness of a love story, the suspense of a caper film, and the hard-edged sensitivity of a male buddy picture. Simon (Lino Ventura), a con man just released from prison, teams with another former inmate, Charlot (Charles Gerard), and plots an elaborate heist of a jewelry store. While casing the store, Simon notices Francoise (Francoise Fabian), a pretty antique dealer whose shop is located next to his target, and, in short order, concocts a scheme to win her over. The result is a pleasant tale that uses a slightly tricky structural device (most of the film, photographed in color, is a flashback from the far superior black-and-white opening and closing scenes) as a crutch for the otherwise standard script. Most of the fun comes from the caper setup, as Simon masquerades as a frail octogenarian who visits the store to purchase expensive jewelery for his dying sister. There are also numerous references to other films (notably Lelouch's own A MAN AND A WOMAN) and filmmakers, including Bertolucci, Bellocchio, Lean, Chaplin, Minnelli. Remade in 1985 (though released in 1987) by John G. Avildsen with Peter Falk in the Lino Ventura role. The videocassette is available in both subtitled and dubbed (French into English) versions.

p, Claude Lelouch; d, Claude Lelouch; w, Claude Lelouch, Pierre Uytterhoeven; ph, Claude Lelouch, Jean Collomb; ed, Georges Klotz; m, Francis Lai.

Crime/Romance (PR:C MPAA:NR)

HARDER THEY COME, THE***

(1973, Jamaica) 98m Intl. Films/NW c

Jimmy Cliff *(Ivan),* Carl Bradshaw *(Jose),* Janet Bartley *(Elsa),* Ras Daniel Hartman *(Pedro),* Basil Keane *(Preacher),* Bobby Charlton *(Hilton),* Winston Stona *(Detective).*

This outstanding Jamaican feature became a major cult favorite in the US and did much to popularize reggae with its fabulous musical score. Reggae star Jimmy Cliff plays Ivan, a young Jamaican singer from the country who arrives in Kingston with the hope of becoming a star. Work is hard to come by, though, and after a rude awakening on the city streets, Ivan becomes a handyman for a local preacher, running into trouble when he begins an affair with the clergyman's ward Elsa (Janet Bartley). When an argument over a bicycle turns into a knife fight, Ivan is sent to jail. After his release he moves in with Elsa and pursues the island's biggest record producer, Hilton (Bobby Charlton), who allows him to record "The Harder They Come." However, Hilton offers him a paltry $20 for the song, and when Ivan balks, releases it without any promotion. Penniless, Ivan has no choice but to get involved in the ganja (marijuana) trade. THE HARDER THEY COME is a gritty, realistic view of urban Jamaica that concentrates on the squalor of shantytowns tourists never see. Cliff is superb as the determined young man who rises to cult status, mirroring his own real-life ascendence to worldwide fame as a reggae artist. The film is, for the most part, in English, though the Jamaican patois requires subtitling in some sections.

p, Perry Henzell; d, Perry Henzell; w, Perry Henzell, Trevor D. Rhone; ph, Peter Jassop, David McDonald (Metrocolor); ed, John Victor Smith, Seicland Anderson, Richard White; m, Jimmy Cliff, Desmond Dekker, The Slickers.

Drama (PR:C MPAA:R)

HEAT OF DESIRE**

(1981, Fr./Sp.) 89m Cineproduction-Gaumont-Dara/Triumph c (PLEIN SUD)

Patrick Dewaere *(Serge Laine),* Clio Goldsmith *(Carol),* Jeanne Moreau *(Helene),* Guy Marchand *(Max),* Pierre Dux *(Rognon),* Jose Luis Lopez Vazquez *(Martinez),* Nicole Jamet *(Serge's Wife),* Roland Amstutz *(Jeannot),* Beatrice Camurat *(Pepita),* Luis Andres *(Hotel Director),* Alejo Del Peral *(Hotel Receptionist),* Nicole Jamet *(Nicole Laine),* Carlos Luchetti, Robert Rimbaud, Juan Vinallonga, Jean Antonilos, Jaume Comas, Gerard Cuvier, Jordy Bifill, Jacqueline Dufranne.

A feeble attempt at bringing passion to the screen, HEAT OF DESIRE stars Patrick Dewaere as Serge Laine, a foolish lecturer who is about to take his wife with him to Barcelona for a speaking engagement. Fate intervenes, however, and he becomes the object of another woman's desires. The bored mistress of a politician, Carol (Clio Goldsmith), decides to have a steamy affair with the first man who walks by her window—Serge. They run off to Barcelona together, leaving behind Serge's wife, and there he devotes all his time and money to Carol, who enjoys nothing more than playing sex games in posh hotel rooms. Of course, she is also mysterious, unpredictable, exotic, and exciting, and Serge steadily deteriorates, embarrasses himself during his lecture, and finds himself penniless, having to steal to satisfy his desire to see Carol. Once again a filmmaker falls flat trying to repeat the success of LAST TANGO IN PARIS—an intelligent, artistic film revolving around sexual desire. HEAT OF DESIRE is a meaningless morality tale about passion and its consequences that predictably shows Carol's psychological domination, Ivan's downfall, and a great deal of flesh. The film is perhaps worth watching, however, just for the sensational Dewaere, who plays a role that is far more low-key than those he has done for Bertrand Blier. When one considers that Dewaere committed suicide not long after the completion of this film, his character's downfall becomes frightfully real. In French with English subtitles.

p, Lise Fayolle, Giorgio Silvagni; d, Luc Beraud; w, Luc Beraud, Claude Miller, Jean-Louis Comolli, Jean-Andre Fieschi; ph, Bernard Lutic; ed, Joele Van Effenterre; m, Eric Demarsan.

Drama (PR:O MPAA:R)

HENRY IV***

(1984, It.) 95m Odyssa/Orion c (ENRICO IV)

Marcello Mastroianni *(Henry IV),* Claudia Cardinale *(Matilda),* Leopoldo Trieste *(Psychiatrist),* Paolo Bonacelli *(Belcredi),* Gianfelice Imparato *(Di Nolli),* Claudio Spadaro *(Lolo),* Giuseppe Cederna *(Fino Pagliuca),* Giacomo Bertozzi *(Giacomo),* Fabrizio Macciantelli *(Fabrizio),* Luciano Bartoli *(Young Henry IV),* Latou Chardons *(Frida),* Gianluigi Sedda, Maria Loos, Luciano Branchi.

An adaptation of Luigi Pirandello's noted play, Marco Bellocchio's surprising follow-up to THE EYES, THE MOUTH stars Marcello Mastroianni as a wealthy gentleman who, following a fall from a horse some 20 years earlier, has seemingly become convinced that he is none other than 11th-century Holy Roman Emperor Henry IV. Having spent the last two decades living in a castle, wearing a crown and decorative robes, this Henry IV romps merrily in his own delusions. When a group of family and friends visits, hoping to bring him back to reality, they play along with his game, wearing the appropriate robes and dresses and taking historical names. In time, however, they begin to realize that, perhaps, their Henry IV isn't crazy after all. Like previous Bellocchio characters—those played by Lou Castel in FISTS IN THE POCKET and THE EYES, THE MOUTH, and the role essayed by Maruschka Detmers in the X-rated remake of THE DEVIL IN THE FLESH—Mastroianni's Henry IV rebels against the privileged class he despises. He knows the rules of his class, but rather than oppose them openly, he circumvents them by pretending to be a madman. The film is admittedly "freely adapted" from Pirandello, which should warn the playwright's devotees that Bellocchio has not remained entirely faithful to the play. In Italian with English subtitles.

p, Enzo Porcelli; d, Marco Bellocchio; w, Marco Bellocchio, Tonino Guerra (based on the play by Luigi Pirandello); ph, Giuseppe Lanci; ed, Mirco Garrone; m, Astor Piazzola.

Drama **(PR:C MPAA:PG-13)**

HIDDEN FORTRESS, THE****

(1958, Jap.) 137m Toho-Albex bw (KAKUSHI TORIDE NO SAN AKUNIN; AKA: THREE RASCALS IN THE HIDDEN FORTRESS; THREE BAD MEN IN THE HIDDEN FORTRESS)

Toshiro Mifune *(Rokurota),* Misa Uehara *(Lady Yukihime),* Minoru Chiaki *(Tahei),* Kamatari Fujiwara *(Matashichi),* Susumu Fujita *(The Grateful Soldier),* Takashi Shimura *(The Old General),* Eiko Miyoshi *(The Old Woman),* Toshiko Higuchi *(The Farmer's Daughter),* Kichijiro Ueda *(Girl-Dealer).*

Two unlikely looking soldiers, Tahei (Minoru Chiaki) and Matashichi (Kamatari Fujiwara), flee following the defeat of their army. They stumble across a gold bar hidden in some firewood, but before they can take it, Rokurota (Toshiro Mifune), a general, appears. He enlists the two to help him take a wagon load of gold—plus deposed princess Lady Yukihime (Misa Uehara)—to safety in the next province. One of Akira Kurosawa's best works—with an odd mix of periods, from Medieval to modern—HIDDEN FORTRESS is filled with humor and excitement, owing more to Hollywood adventure films than to the Japanese tradition. George Lucas claimed that this film was the chief inspiration for STAR WARS, and it is easy to see the resemblance, especially in Chiaki and Fujiwara, who were copied in metal to make R2-D2 and C-3PO. Originally released in the US in a truncated 90-minute print, THE HIDDEN FORTRESS quickly disappeared and was not released in a full-length version until 1983. The video release is both subtitled (Japanese into English) and letterboxed.

d, Akira Kurosawa; w, Ryuzo Kikushima, Hideo Oguni, Shinobu Hashimoto, Akira Kurosawa; ph, Kazuo Yamazaki; m, Masaru Sato.

Adventure **(PR:C MPAA:NR)**

HIGH AND LOW****

(1963, Jap.) 142m Toho-Continental bw-c (TENGOKU TO JIGOKU)

Toshiro Mifune *(Kingo Gondo),* Tatsuya Nakadai *(Inspector Tokura),* Kyoko Kagawa *(Reiko, Gondo's Wife),* Tatsuya Mihashi *(Kawanishi),* Yutaka Sada *(Aoki),* Kenjiro Ishiyama *(Detective Taguchi),* Tsutomu Yamazaki *(The Kidnaper),* Takashi Shimura *(Director),* Susumu Fujita *(Commissioner),* Ko Kimura *(Detective Arai),* Takeshi Kato *(Detective Nakao),* Yoshio Tsuchiya *(Detective Murata),* Hiroshi Unayama *(Detective Shimada),* Koji Mitsui *(Newspaperman).*

Based on a crime novel by Ed McBain, this brilliant Kurosawa film stars Toshiro Mifune as Kingo Gondo, a rich industrialist who receives word that his son has been kidnaped by a madman demanding an outrageous ransom that will ruin Gondo financially if he pays it. Before Gondo can make a decision, his son enters the house, and we learn that it is his playmate, the chauffeur's son, who has been kidnaped. Gondo is then faced with a tough moral decision: is his chauffeur's son worth as much as his own? When the kidnaper calls and admits his mistake, but demands payment anyway, Gondo initially refuses, but is conscience stricken. In HIGH AND LOW Kurosawa succeeds in developing a highly visual structural style within the wide-screen format. The first half of the film takes place in the living room of Gondo's hilltop house and is characterized by static shots that hold for several minutes on a single composition. Time transitions are handled by wipes, creating a charged atmosphere. This steadiness is broken suddenly for the second half of the film (which involves the criminal manhunt), shot with a normal amount of motion and cutting—its pace frenetic in comparison with the first half of the film. The videocassette is both subtitled (Japanese into English) and letterboxed.

p, Tomoyuki Tanaka, Ryuzo Kikushima; d, Akira Kurosawa; w, Akira Kurosawa, Hideo Oguni, Ryuzo Kikushima, Eijiro Hisaita (based on the novel *King's Ransom* by Ed McBain [Evan Hunter]); ph, Choichi Nakai, Takao Saito (Tohoscope); m, Masaru Sato.

Crime **(PR:C-O MPAA:NR)**

HIMATSURI****

(1985, Jap.) 120m Gunro-Seibu-Cine Saison/Kino c (AKA: FIRE FESTIVAL)

Kinya Kitaoji *(Tatsuo),* Kiowako Taichi *(Kimiko),* Ryota Nakamoto *(Ryota),* Norihei Miki *(Yamakawa),* Rikiya Yasuoka *(Toshio),* Junko Miyashita *(Sachiko),* Kin Sugai *(Tatsuo's Mother),* Sachiko Matsushita, Masako Yagi *(Tatsuo's Sisters),* Jukei Fujioka, Kenji Kobayashi, Ippei Sooda *(Lumbermen),* Aoi Nakajima *(Sister),* Kenzo Kaneko *(Husband),* Ban Kojika *(Smith),* Masato Ibu *(Baker),* Kosanji Yanagiya *(Boatman).*

In 1980, a man living in a remote Japanese village brutally murdered several members of his family before committing suicide. In HIMATSURI, director Mitsuo Yanagimachi uses this incident to create a unique and highly intense story of one man's fight against the encroaching specter of Western modernism in rural Japan. Tatsuo (Kinya Kitaoji), a man of contradictory and often violent passions, engages in numerous affairs with no regard for his family's feelings and takes great pride in his skills as a survivalist. Living in an area where the ancient Shinto religion is firmly entrenched, Tatsuo boldly flaunts his arrogant attitudes by exposing himself before swimming in a sacred lake. Yet Tatsuo is not without some principles; although he openly mocks the sacred codes reverently observed by the locals, he harbors deep respect for the natural beauty of the land. HIMATSURI, much like Paul Schrader's MISHIMA, deals with the conflict between modernism and Japanese traditions. Tatsuo, overbearing and little concerned for others, does, however, maintain a germ of interest in tradition, and it spreads steadily through his consciousness. Yanagimachi's direction emphasizes the relationship between man and nature, a harmony that grows more profound as the story unfolds. In Japanese with English subtitles.

d, Mitsuo Yanagimachi; w, Kenji Nakagami; ph, Masaki Tamura (Eastmancolor); ed, Sachiko Yamaji; m, Toru Takemitsu.

Drama **(PR:O MPAA:NR)**

HIROSHIMA, MON AMOUR*****

(1959, Fr./Jap.) 88m Argos-Daiei-Como-Pathe/Zenith bw

Emmanuelle Riva *(Elle),* Eiji Okada *(Lui),* Stella Dassas *(Mother),* Pierre Barbaud *(Father),* Bernard Fresson *(German Lover).*

It has been often, and accurately, stated that HIROSHIMA MON AMOUR is as important to the development of film art as CITIZEN KANE is. The first feature film from Alain Resnais, previously known for his incredibly moving documentaries, it was adapted from a script by Frenchwoman Marguerite Duras, one of the 20th century's greatest authors. The combination of Duras' text and Resnais' blend of sound and image results in a film that is completely modern. The story, which manages to be both complex (in its manipulation of past and present) and simple (the brevity of its love affair), is about a married Japanese architect (Eiji Okada) and a married French actress (Emmanuelle Riva) who have a two-day affair in Hiroshima. The pain "She" (their names are never used) feels for the dead of Hiroshima reminds her of the pain she felt when the young German soldier she loved in Nevers was killed on the day that town was liberated. Castigated by her family, She was imprisoned in a dark cellar, viewed as a disgrace for having loved the enemy. She projects the entire experience of the Japanese city—the bomb, the death, the suffering, the physical mutilation—onto her lover, whom she calls "Hiroshima," but she knows that someday she will forget him. Interweaving sound and image, brutal documentary footage and tender lovemaking, the past and the present, the past and the remembered past, the city and the individual, and passion and despair, Resnais has created a breathtaking picture that, like so many great works of art, can never be fully appreciated or understood. It is a film that must be felt—a film that combines the soft, loving caresses of two intertwined bodies with the burnt, blistering flesh of a dying victim of atomic warfare—yet the feelings it evokes defy understanding or explanation. In French with English subtitles.

p, Samy Halfon; d, Alain Resnais; w, Marguerite Duras; ph, Sacha Vierny, Michio Takahashi; ed, Henri Colpi, Jasmine Chasney, Anne Sarraute; m, Georges Delerue, Giovanni Fusco.

Drama **(PR:C-O MPAA:NR)**

HOLIDAY HOTEL*

(1978, Fr.) 115m Production 2000/Quartet c (L'HOTEL DE LA PLAGE; Trans: The Beach Hotel)

Sophie Barjac, Myriem Boyer, Daniel Ceccaldi, Michele Grellier, Bruno Gullain, Francis Lemaire, Robert Lombard, Bruno Du Louvat, Guy Marchand, Jean-Paul Muel, Anne Parillaud, Michel Robin, Martine Sarcey, Bernard Soufflet, Rosine Cardoret.

One of the dumbest French comedies to make it to video (and there are more than a few), HOLIDAY HOTEL is essentially a regional comedy about vacationers at a seaside resort in Brittany. The story is overflowing with characters who have one thing on their mind—sex. Male or female, young, old, or middle-age, everyone pursues it, with comic adventures the result. Most of the humor is crude and mean-spirited, though it is given a pleasant coating of French pop music. Available in both dubbed and subtitled (French into English) versions.

d, Michel Lang; w, Michel Lang; ph, Daniel Gaudry; ed, Helene Plemiannikov; m, Mort Shuman.

Comedy **(PR:C-O MPAA:NR)**

HOLY INNOCENTS, THE***

(1984, Sp.) 108m Ganesh-Samuel Goldwyn c (LOS SANTOS INOCENTES)

Alfredo Landa *(Paco),* Francisco Rabal *(Azarias),* Terele Pavez *(Regula),* Belen Ballesteros *(Nieves),* Juan Sanchez *(Quirce),* Juan Diego *(Master Ivan),* Agustin Gonzalez *(Don Pedro),* Susana Sanchez *(Little One),* Agata Lys *(Dona Purita),* Mary Carillo *(Marchioness),* Maribel Martin

(Miriam), Jose Guardiola *(Senorito de la Jara),* Manuel Zarzo *(Physician).*

Grounded in realism, THE HOLY INNOCENTS is a socially relevant tale of class struggle in Franco-era Spain. Paco (Alfredo Landa) is a devoted laborer who, with his wife (Terele Pavez) and his mute, crippled daughter (Susana Sanchez), works the land and displays a special talent for tracking birds. Master Ivan (Juan Diego), a vile, upper-class sportsman, enlists Paco's help on a bird hunt, but is less than compassionate when his guide breaks his foot, forcing Paco to continue. It is the relationship between the ruling class and the peasants revealed in this situation that is most indicative of the film's sentiments. The peasants are degraded by the rich despite their dependence on the peasants' knowledge of nature and their working of the land. According to director Mario Camus, the film's title refers not only to the peasant class but to all classes. "It also offers something very welcome," Camus has said, "and that is that the poor people are happy people because they are vital human beings, and manifest themselves in more spontaneous ways. They have nothing more than that world, and it fills them." The 1984 Cannes Film Festival honored Landa and veteran actor Francisco Rabal, who plays Paco's eccentric older brother, with a shared Best Actor Award. In Spanish with English subtitles.

p, Julian Mateos; d, Mario Camus; w, Mario Camus, Antonio Larreta, Manuel Matji (based on the novel by Miguel Delibes); ph, Hans Burmann (Eastmancolor); ed, Jose Maria Biurrun; m, Anton Garcia Abril.

Drama **(PR:O MPAA:PG)**

HOME AND THE WORLD, THE***

(1984, India) 140m Natl. Film Development Corp. of India/European Classics c (GHARE BAIRE)

Soumitra Chatterjee *(Sandip Mukherjee),* Victor Bannerjee *(Nikhilesh Choudhury),* Swatilekha Chatterjee *(Bimala Choudhury),* Gopa Aich *(Sister-in-Law),* Jennifer Kapoor *(Miss Gilby),* Manoj Mitra *(Headmaster),* Indrapramit Roy *(Amulya),* Bimala Chatterjee *(Kulada).*

This graceful film by Satyajit Ray is as much a tragic love story as it is an examination of political turmoil in India in 1908. Victor Bannerjee stars as Nikhilesh Choudhury, a highly educated Hindu who lives with his wife, Bimala (Swatilekha Chatterjee), in colonial East Bengal. Political tension grows when Lord Curzon, the British governor-general of India, enacts a plan to "divide and rule" the Hindus and Muslims. Because of the resulting unrest, Sandip Mukherjee (Soumitra Chatterjee), a fiery rebel and friend of Nikhilesh's, pays a visit to the town. Unconvinced that his wife truly loves him, Nikhelesh encourages Bimala to come out of *purdah* (orthodox seclusion) to meet other men, namely his rebellious friend. If she remains faithful after having met others, then Nikhelesh feels he can be certain of her love. His plan backfires, however, and Bimala falls in love with the rebel. What's more, political differences arise between the two men. Based on a novel by Nobel Prize-winning author Rabindranath Tagore, THE HOME AND THE WORLD was to have come to the screen 30 years earlier as Ray's first film. Tagore, a friend of Ray's family, had published his book in 1919 to much acclaim, and Ray, who had only a passing interest in film at the time, read the book and wrote a screenplay based on it. It wasn't until 1980, however, that the great Indian filmmaker returned to the project. In Bengali and English with English subtitles.

d, Satyajit Ray; w, Satyajit Ray (based on the novel by Rabindranath Tagore); ph, Soumandu Roy (Eastmancolor); ed, Dulal Dutta; m, Satyajit Ray.

Drama **(PR:C MPAA:NR)**

HORROR CHAMBER OF DR. FAUSTUS, THE*½**

(1959, Fr./It.) 84m Champs-Elysees-Lux/Lopert bw (LES YEUX SANS VISAGE; OCCHI SENZA VOLTO; AKA: EYES WITHOUT A FACE)

Pierre Brasseur *(Prof. Genessier),* Alida Valli *(Louise),* Edith Scob *(Christiane),* Francois Guerin *(Jacques),* Juliette Mayniel *(Edna Gruber),* Beatrice Altariba *(Paulette),* Alexandre Rignault *(Inspector Parot),* Rene Genin *(Bereaved Father),* Claude Brasseur, Michel Etcheverry, Yvette Etievant, Lucien Hubert, Marcel Peres.

At the center of this eerie, poetic horror thriller is famed plastic surgeon Dr. Genessier (Pierre Brasseur), who, obsessed with reconstructing the disfigured face of his daughter Christiane (Edith Scob), sends his loyal female assistant (Alida Valli) to the Sorbonne to lure young women to his laboratory. Dr. Genessier then proceeds to remove their faces in an attempt to graft the flesh onto Christiane's accident-scarred visage—hidden behind a mask that reveals only her melancholy eyes. Adapted by Pierre Boileau and Thomas Narcejac (who collaborated on DIABOLIQUE and VERTIGO) from a novel written by Jean Redon, THE HORROR CHAMBER OF DOCTOR FAUSTUS is a blood-curdling picture directed by Georges Franju at an even, distant pace that builds tension to an almost unbearable level. Having found fame first as documentarian, Franju presents this thriller in the same manner as the gruesome, but brilliant, LES SANG DES BETES (Blood of the Beasts), his unflinching, unrelenting, poetic documentary about a slaughterhouse. The sickening scene in which the scalpel-wielding Dr. Genessier removes his victim's face in one flap of grotesque flesh is photographed without even the slightest hint of sensationalism. Instead, it is as if Franju *and* Dr. Genessier have seen this happen a thousand times before. In French with English subtitles.

p, Jules Borkon; d, Georges Franju; w, Georges Franju, Jean Redon, Claude Sautet, Pierre Boileau, Thomas Narcejac (based on the novel *Les yeux sans visage* by Jean Redon); ph, Eugene Shuftan; ed, Gilbert Natot; m, Maurice Jarre.

Horror **(PR:O MPAA:NR)**

HOUR OF THE STAR, THE***

(1986, Braz.) 96m Embrafilme/Kino c (A HORA DA ESTRELA)

Marcelia Cartaxo *(Macabea),* Jose Dumont *(Olimpico),*

Tamara Taxman *(Gloria),* Fernanda Montenegro *(Mme. Carlotta),* Umberto Magnani, Denoy de Oliveira, Claudia Rezende.

Macabea (Marcelia Cartaxo), a frumpy 19-year-old orphan from northern Brazil, reveals herself in beautifully simple terms: "I am a typist, I am a virgin, and I like Coca-Cola." Uneducated, unwashed, and unnoticed by most of the people around her, Macabea has no confidence and no desire to be anything but someone's wife. Sharing a broken-down one-room apartment with three other young women, she is unable to adjust to their ways. She doesn't have a lover, knows nothing about hygiene or cosmetics, and is even too bashful to undress in front of the others. On weekends, while her friends meet with their lovers, Macabea indulges in her favorite pastime—riding the subway. Then she meets the swarthy Olimpico (Jose Dumont). They chat, he asks her to take a walk with him, and they become friends. He tells her of his great plan to become a congressman, though he is too uneducated to explain what one does. Macabea, believing that she's found a man who can look after her, now has a reason to improve her life. THE HOUR OF THE STAR is an impressive effort from first-time director Suzana Amaral, who, at age 52, after raising nine children and graduating from the NYU Film School, returned to her native Sao Paulo, Brazil, to make the film. Based on a 1977 novella, it approaches the style of Neo-Realism in both its photography and the plight of its poor heroine, depending heavily on the excellent debut performance of 23-year-old stage actress Cartaxo. In Portuguese with English subtitles.

d, Suzana Amaral; w, Suzana Amaral, Alfredo Oroz (based on the novel by Clarice Lispector); ph, Edgar Moura; ed, Ide Lacreta; m, Marcus Vinicius.

Drama **(PR:O MPAA:NR)**

HOUR OF THE WOLF, THE**

(1968, Swed.) 88m Svensk-Lopert bw (VARGTIMMEN)

Liv Ullmann *(Alma Borg),* Max von Sydow *(Johan Borg),* Erland Josephson *(Baron von Merkens),* Gertrud Fridh *(Corinne von Merkens),* Gudrun Brost *(Gamla Fru von Merkens),* Bertil Anderberg *(Ernst von Merkens),* Georg Rydeberg *(Arkivarie Lindhorst),* Ulf Johanson *(Kurator Heerbrand),* Naima Wifstrand *(Old Lady With Hat),* Ingrid Thulin *(Veronica Vogler),* Lenn Hjortzberg *(Kapellmastare Kreisler),* Agda Helin *(Maidservant),* Mikael Rundqvist *(Young Boy),* Mona Seilitz *(Woman in Mortuary),* Folke Sundquist *(Tamino I. Trollflojten).*

This Bergman discourse on the nature of art, and the artist's relation to society, is shrouded in the trappings of gothic horror and stars Max von Sydow as Johan Borg, a painter haunted by bad dreams and apparitions while secluded on an island with his pregnant wife Alma (Liv Ullmann). Both of them experience a series of haunting visions: Johan sees a beautiful boy, a ghost able to walk on walls, and an ancient woman who tears off her face; Alma is approached by a woman (who may or may not be an apparition) who instructs her to read her husband's diary. There she learns of Johan's love affair. Generally considered one of Bergman's lesser pictures (though it does have its supporters), THE HOUR OF THE WOLF was originally to be shot before PERSONA, in 1965, as "The Cannibals." In Swedish with English subtitles.

d, Ingmar Bergman; w, Ingmar Bergman; ph, Sven Nykvist; ed, Ulla Ryghe; m, Lars Johan Werle.

Drama **(PR:O MPAA:NR)**

I

I SENT A LETTER TO MY LOVE***

(1980, Fr.) 112m Cine Production-FR3/Atlantic c (CHERE INCONNUE)

Simone Signoret *(Louise),* Jean Rochefort *(Gilles),* Delphine Seyrig *(Yvette),* Genevieve Fontanel *(Beatrice),* Dominique Labourier *(Catherine),* Gillette Barbie, Marion Loran, Jean Obe, Madeleine Ozeray, Danielle Altenburger, Claudine Delvaux, Pierre Gallon, Florence Haziot.

Simone Signoret gives a touching performance here as Louise, an aging woman whose devotion to her paralyzed, wheelchair-bound brother, Gilles (Jean Rochefort), has not allowed her to taste some of the sweeter things in life. Neither sibling has much contact with the outside world—Gilles gazes at the Atlantic through his telescope, Louise dreams of taking a vacation to America—except through their close friend Yvette (Delphine Seyrig), an aging local baker who has a fondness for Gilles. Hoping to find a mate, Louise places an ad in the local newspaper to that effect and receives only one response—from Gilles. Rather than reveal herself to him, the needy Louise continues to correspond under the *nom de plume* "Beatrice Deschamps," eagerly awaiting his increasingly amorous and erotic letters, until the time comes for "Beatrice" to meet Gilles. This slow-moving story, which reteams director Moshe Mizrahi and Signoret after their Oscar-winning MADAME ROSA, relies chiefly on its three poignant and sensitive performances. Signoret, Rochefort and Seyrig never look like glamourous movie stars, instead completely capturing the mannerisms of aging adults frustrated by the monotony of their day-to-day existence. Despite some complex ideas in Gerard Brach's script, Mizrahi's direction is less than inspired. The videocassette is inoffensively dubbed in English.

p, Lise Fayolle, Giorgio Silvagni; d, Moshe Mizrahi; w, Moshe Mizrahi, Gerard Brach (based on the novel by Bernice Rubens); ph, Ghislain Cloquet; ed, Francoise Bonnot; m, Philippe Sarde.

Drama **(PR:A MPAA:PG)**

I VITELLONI****

(1953, It./Fr.) 104m Peg-Cite/AFI-Janus bw (AKA: THE YOUNG AND THE PASSIONATE; VITELLONI; THE WASTRELS)

Franco Interlenghi *(Moraldo),* Franco Fabrizi *(Fausto),* Alberto Sordi *(Alberto),* Leopoldo Trieste *(Leopoldo),* Riccardo Fellini *(Riccardo),* Elenora Ruffo *(Sandra),* Lida Baarova *(Guilia, Michele's wife),* Arlette Sauvage *(Woman in the Cinema),* Maja Nipora *(Actress),* Jean Brochard *(Fausto's Father),* Claude Farere *(Alberto's Sister),* Carlo Romano *(Michele),* Silvio Bagolini *(Giudizio),* Vira Silenti *(Leopoldo's "Chinese" Date).*

This semiautobiographical work by Federico Fellini was the first film to bring him a measure of world attention, succeeding at the box office where his previous THE WHITE SHEIK had failed. As in AMARCORD (his film of nearly two decades later), the setting is the seaside town of Rimini, Fellini's birthplace and the wellspring of the experiences that were to color this and other films. The plot follows the adventures of five youths who refuse to grow up and accept responsibility. Only one of the gang, Moraldo (Franco Interlenghi, the young boy from SHOESHINE) comes to understand that life in the small town is a relatively empty existence, while his friends are content to play meaningless games that lend momentary security but ultimately make them puppets to forces beyond their control. Of the gang, Fausto's (Franco Fabrizi) plight is given the most attention. As the group's Don Juan, he is looked up to by the others, but he eventually gets one woman pregnant and is forced into a marriage that will undoubtedly prove tragic. Alberto (Alberto Sordi), the effeminate one, is basically a lazy oaf, dependent upon his sister for support. In a fascinatingly filmed festival scene, Alberto's plight is revealed as he dances, in a drunken stupor, dressed like a woman. I VITELLONI is filled with the cinematic excesses that were to clutter Fellini's later films, though here they seem much more insightful in describing the tribulations of adolescent rites of passage. The videocassette is in Italian with English subtitles.

p, Lorenzo Pegoraro; d, Federico Fellini; w, Federico Fellini, Tullio Pinelli, Ennio Flaiano (based on the story by Fellini, Flaiano, Pinelli); ph, Otello Martelli, Luciano Trasatti, Carlo Carlini; ed, Rolando Benedetti; m, Nino Rota.

Drama **(PR:C MPAA:NR)**

IKIRU***

(1952, Jap.) 140m Toho/Brando bw (AKA: DOOMED, LIVING)

Takashi Shimura *(Kanji Watanabe),* Nobuo Kaneko *(Mitsuo Watanabe),* Kyoko Seki *(Kazue Watanabe),* Miki Odagiri *(Toyo),* Kamatari Fujiwara *(Ono),* Makoto Koburi *(Klichi Watanabe),* Kumeko Urabe *(Tatsu Watanabe),* Yoshie Minami *(Hayoshi, the Maid),* Nobuo Nakamura *(Deputy Mayor),* Minosuke Yamada *(Saito),* Haruo Tanak *(Sakai),* Bokuzen Hidari *(Ohara),* Minoru Chiaki *(Noguchi),* Shinichi Himori *(Kimura),* Kazao Abe *(City Assemblyman),* Masao Shimizu *(Doctor),* Yunosuke Ito *(Novelist),* Ko Kimura *(Intern),* Atsushi Watanabe *(Patient),* Yatsuko Tanami *(Hostess).*

In IKIRU, Akira Kurosawa has created a subtle and moving account of a man who searches for meaning in the final days of his shallow existence. Kanji Watanabe (Takashi Shimura) is a clerk in a government office who discovers that he has cancer and, at most, only a year to live. Up to this point he has lived strictly according to the book, never allowing for any fluctuations from routine. Now, realizing that he is about to die, with two children who offer him no comfort, Kanji must find something to make him feel that his life has not been a total waste. The movement of IKIRU is extremely low-key, and the overall emotional impact is quite powerful, with the character of Kanji serving as a metaphor for human individuality in postwar Japan. Though Japanese culture is Kurosawa's main target, this theme easily becomes a universal one. In Japanese with English subtitles.

d, Akira Kurosawa; w, Akira Kurosawa, Hideo Oguni, Shinobu Hashimoto; ph, Asakazu Nakai; m, Fumio Hayasaka.

Drama **(PR:A MPAA:NR)**

IN THE NAME OF THE POPE KING½**

(1978, It.) 107m Juppiter Generale Cinematografica/ Rizzoli c (IN NOME DEL PAPA RE)

Nino Manfredi *(Don Colombo),* Danilo Mattei *(Cesare Costa),* Carmen Scarpitta *(Contessa Flaminia),* Giovanella Grifeo *(Teresa),* Carlo Bagno *(Perpetuo),* Salvo Randone *(Papa Nero),* Gabriella Giacobe, Luigi Basagaluppi.

Director Luigi Magni has given history a popular, youthful slant in this story, set in 1867 as troops are about to enter Rome in the name of separating the powers of the State from those of the Pope. Nino Manfredi is Don Colombo, a Papal magistrate whose troubled conscience and hope for a less authoritarian government has driven him to submit his resignation. Before he can do so, however, a band of young terrorists bomb a garrison at Zouave, and more pressure is placed on the already torn Don Colombo when he learns that one of the terrorists is the son he fathered illegitimately some 20 years ago. While it is a bit slow and talky for those unfamiliar with the government of the Papal States, IN THE NAME OF THE POPE KING is a relatively accessible film with a fine performance from Manfredi that falls somewhere between the comic and the tragic. The videocassette is in Italian with English subtitles.

p, Franco Committeri; d, Luigi Magni; w, Luigi Magni; ph, Danilo Desideri (Eastmancolor); ed, Ruggero Mastroianni; m, Armando Trovaioli.

Historical **(PR:O MPAA:NR)**

INHERITANCE, THE**

(1976, It.) 105m FLAG/SJ Intl. c (L'EREDITA' FERRAMONTI)

Anthony Quinn *(Gregorio Ferramonti),* Fabio Testi *(Mario Ferramonti),* Dominique Sanda *(Irene),* Luigi Proietti *(Pippo Ferramonti),* Adriana Asti *(Teta Ferramonti),* Paolo Bonacelli *(Paolo Furlin),* Harald Bromley.

Gregorio Ferramonti (Anthony Quinn) is a despicable southern Italian baker who retires and sells his shop, dividing the profits and doling them out to his three grown children as their inheritance. However, one son, Mario (Fabio Testi), is a gambling playboy whose debts have been paid off by Gregorio—therefore no inheritance. Gregorio's only daughter, Teta (Adriana Asta), married a man her father despises, and is denied her portion. Only Pippo (Luigi Proietti), Gregorio's boot-licking, idiot son, is given his share of the legacy. After 20 years of slaving and sweating in his father's bakery, he is determined to open a hardware store, despite the fact that he knows nothing about the business. He's aided by Irena (Dominique Sanda), a manipulative and intelligent working who woman helps Pippo secure government construction contracts. In the process, she reunites the siblings (who previously weren't on speaking terms), makes eyes at the suave Mario, and puts a move on the hated patriarch. THE INHERITANCE has plenty of what makes soap opera the wonderfully trashy art form it is: magnificent settings, powerful and unscrupulous characters, and plenty of sexual encounters. The ludicrous dialog is dubbed in English.

p, Gianni Hecht Lucari; d, Mauro Bolognini; w, Ugo Pirro, Sergio Bazzini (based on a novel by Gaetano Carlo); ph, Ennio Guarnieri (Eastmancolor); ed, Fima Noveck; m, Ennio Morricone.

Drama **(PR:O MPAA:R)**

INHERITORS, THE**

(1982, Aust.) 89m Monarex-Island Alive-Bannert c (DIE ERBEN)

Nikolas Vogel *(Thomas Feigl),* Roger Schauer *(Charly),* Anneliese Stoeckl-Eberhard *(Thomas' Mother),* Jaromir Borek *(Thomas' Father),* Klaus Novak *(Ernst, Thomas' Brother),* Johanna Tomek *(Charly's Mother),* Frank Dietrich *(Charly's Father),* Edd Stavjanik *(Schweiger),* Gabriele Bolen *(Charly's Girl Friend),* Titanila Kraus *(Anna),* Michael Janisch *(Gunther),* Wolfgang Gasser *(Norbert Furst),* Helmut Kahn *(Speaker at Nazi Rally),* Ottwald John *(Nazi Camp Trainer),* Rudi Schippel, Gerald Distl, Sascha Stein, Evelyn Faber, Guenter Treptow.

This well-intentioned film is unfortunately marred by simplistic psychology and inept execution. Thomas Feigl (Nikolas Vogel) is a 16-year-old German youth who comes from an unhappy home and, after meeting another youth his age, finds an escape as a member of the neo-Nazi Unity Party. Along with his neo-Nazi friends, Thomas attends Nazi rallies and witnesses brutal violence. Later they meet a veteran of WW II who proudly displays a lampshade made of human skin—a macabre "souvenir" of Auschwitz. As Thomas' involvement with the group grows deeper, so too does his alienation from both family and school. Writer-director Walter Bannert supplies too many perfunctory motives for Thomas' story to be effective, selling short both the importance of his subject and the profundity of his theme. Thomas' home life is a collection of cliches, while the recollections of old-time Nazis are presented with little insight. Instead of exploring such moments, Bannert seems more concerned to exploit them. A brutal and difficult film about an admittedly brutal situation, THE INHERITORS plays more like a horror film than an insightful drama. In German with English subtitles.

p, Walter Bannert; d, Walter Bannert; w, Walter Bannert, Erich A. Richter; ph, Hanus Polak; ed, Walter Bannert; m, Gustav Mahler.

Drama **(PR:O MPAA:NR)**

INNOCENT, THE***½

(1976, Fr./It.) 112m Rizzoli-Les Films Jacques Leitienne-Franco Riz c (L'INNOCENTE)

Giancarlo Giannini *(Tullio Hermil),* Laura Antonelli *(Guiliana Hermil),* Jennifer O'Neill *(Teresa Raffo),* Rina Morelli *(Tullio's Mother),* Massimo Girotti *(Count Stefano Egano),* Didier Haudepin *(Federico Hermil),* Marie Dubois *(Princess di Fundi),* Roberta Paladini *(Mrs. Elviretta),* Claude Mann *(The Prince),* Marc Porel *(Filippo d'Arborio),* Philippe Hersent, Elvira Cortese, Siria Betti, Enzo Musumeci Greco, Alessandra Vazzoler, Marina Pierro.

Luchino Visconti's final film, released just two months after his death, is an adaptation of Gabriele D'Annunzio's 1892 novel about the decadence of the aristocracy of late 19th-century Italy, where hedonistic pursuits are veiled under a decor of social respectability. Tullio Hermil (Giancarlo Giannini) is an atheistic aristocrat married to Guiliana (Laura Antonelli) and carrying on a fairly open affair with the manipulative Teresa (Jennifer O'Neill). Despite his history of dalliances, Tullio not only expects his wife to understand his position, but begs and demands that she listen to his romantic woes and, if at all possible, think of a way to prevent him from seeing his mistress. Tullio views his wife as a wife and friend, but never a mistress—until he learns that she is having a passionate affair with a successful young novelist, Filipo d'Arborio (Marc Porel). Visconti takes great care to represent details of bourgeois extravagance with his lush visuals and elaborate ornamentation, displaying that remarkable command of the screen that one had come to expect from this great veteran filmmaker. Although Giannini, who is primarily considered as a comic performer, is compelling as the evil but somehow sympathetic antihero Tullio, he gets little help from either Antonelli or O'Neill, both of whom are extremely beautiful but do little to ignite the spark essential to their roles. Much of Visconti's effort goes to waste on the videocassette version, which pays no attention to the film's original ratio or the framing of the characters, who are often barely visible at the edges of the frame. The videocassette is available only in the original English-dubbed version.

p, Giovanni Bertolucci; d, Luchino Visconti; w, Suso Cecchi D'Amico, Enrico Medioli, Luchino Visconti (based on the novel *L'Innocente* by Gabriele D'Annunzio); ph, Pasqualino De Santis (Technovision, Technicolor); ed, Ruggero Mastroianni; m, Franco Mannino, Frederic Chopin, Wolfgang Amadeus Mozart, Franz Liszt, Christoph Gluck.

Drama **(PR:O MPAA:R)**

INVESTIGATION***

(1979, Fr.) 116m Planfilm-Films de la Tour-Jacques Roitfeld-Drouette/Quartet c (UN SI JOLI VILLAGE; Trans: Such A Lovely Village)

Victor Lanoux *(Stephan Bertin),* Jean Carmet *(Judge Noblet),* Valerie Mairesse *(Muriel Olivier),* Michel Robin *(Gaspard),* Jacques Richard *(Maurois),* Gerard Jugnot *(Freval),* Francis Lemaire *(Demaison),* Anne Bellac, Alain Doutey, Jean Vigny, Gerard Caillaud, Roland Amstutz, Christian de Tiliere, Jacques Canselier.

A compelling psychological thriller, INVESTIGATION concerns the powerful, well-liked owner of a small town tanning factory, Stephan Bertin (Victor Lanoux), who kills his wife when she refuses to grant him a divorce. When her disappearance is investigated by Judge Noblet (Jean Carmet), a soft-spoken city bureaucrat, the callous Bertin simply and matter-of-factly pretends that his wife has left him—something most locals believe, since it's well-known that Bertin and the village's now-pregnant schoolteacher, Muriel (Valerie Mairesse), have been having an affair. Acting only on a gut instinct, Noblet tries to build a case against Bertin. Bertin counters with a threat to shutter his tannery—an action that unites the workers and engages wide sympathy for the little village. Despite the mounting odds against him, Noblet continues his fight. A low-key suspenser with excellent performances from the brutish Lanoux and the civilized Carmet, both of whom are engaged in a fight to the finish, the film is on one level about their personal battle and the on-going investigation. Its most interesting aspect, however (hence the original title), is the complicity of the locals, who care more for prosperity than they do about bringing a murderer to justice. In French with English subtitles.

d, Etienne Perier; w, Etienne Perier, Andre G. Brunelin (based on the novel *Le Moindre Mal* by Jean Laborde); ph, Jean Charvein; ed, Renee Lichtig; m, Paul Misraki.

Crime/Drama **(PR:O MPAA:NR)**

INVITATION AU VOYAGE**

(1982, Fr.) 93m NEF/Triumph c (Trans: Invitation To A Journey)

Laurent Malet *(Lucien),* Nina Scott *(Jeanne),* Aurore Clement *(Women on the Turnpike),* Mario Adorf *(Timour),* Raymond Bussieres *(Old Man).*

A kind of hybrid, with the hip tone of Jean-Jacques Beineix's DIVA, the incest of Jean Cocteau and Jean-Pierre Melville's LES ENFANTS TERRIBLES, and the cross-dressing of Roman Polanski's THE TENANT, INVITATION AU VOYAGE is a psychological road movie about the 20ish Lucien (Laurent Malet) and his twin sister, Jeanne (Nina Scott). Everything they do they do together, until they receive a sign from above—literally—when a hanging lamp falls into Jeanne's bathtub, electrocuting her. A distraught Lucien pulls naked sis from the tub, stuffs her into a cello case, straps the case to the roof of his car, and begins his odyssey across Paris. Although there are some nice moments, it's all a bit too hip and obscure to care about. California-born Italian director Peter Del Monte further explored the idea of dual identities in his 1988 picture JULIA AND JULIA. In French with English subtitles.

p, Claude Nedjar; d, Peter Del Monte; w, Peter Del Monte, Franco Ferrini (based on the novel *Moi, Ma Soeur* by Jean Bany); ph, Bruno Nuytten; ed, Agnes Guillemot; m, Gabriel Yared.

Drama **(PR:O MPAA:R)**

IPHIGENIA**½

(1977, Gr.) 130m Greek Film Center/Cinema 5 c

Irene Papas *(Clytemnestra),* Costa Kazakos *(Agamemnon),* Costa Carras *(Menelaus),* Tatiana Papamoskou *(Iphigenia),* Christos Tsangas *(Ulysses),* Panos Michalopoulos *(Achilles),* Angelos Yannoulis *(Servant),* Dimitri Aronis *(Calchas),* Georges Vourvahakis *(Orestes),* Irene Koumarianou *(Nurse),* Georges Economou *(Messenger).*

This Greek tragedy based on Euripides' play of 407 B.C. tells the story of King Agamemnon (Costa Kazakos), the leader of the Greek army, as he prepares to launch a thousand ships in order to retrieve the kidnapped Helen, wife of his elder brother, Menelaus (Costa Carras). As his fleet lies becalmed, Agamemnon and Menelaus appeal to the gods and are told through their oracles that Agamemnon must sacrifice his 12-year-old daughter, Iphigenia (Tatiana Papamoskou). Clytemnestra (Irene Papas) is the tragic heroine who begs Agamemnon to reconsider and spare their daughter. This marked director Michael Cacoyannis' third adaptation of a Greek tragedy, following 1961's ELECTRA, which brought him international renown, and 1971's THE TROJAN WOMEN. While Papas' performance is superb, albeit familiar, and the photography beautiful, the well-crafted IPHIGENIA is still not a film for all audiences. Cacoyannis is better suited than most to adapt Greek tragedies, but the resulting film inspires less awe than one would hope. In Greek with English subtitles.

d, Michael Cacoyannis; w, Michael Cacoyannis (based on the play "Iphigenia In Aulis" by Euripides); ph, Georges Arvantis; ed, Michael Cacoyannis, Takis Yannopoulos; m, Mikis Theodorakis.

Drama **(PR:A MPAA:NR)**

IREZUMI (SPIRIT OF TATTOO)****

(1982, Jap.) 88m Daiei/Almi Classics c (SEKKA TOMURAI ZASHI; Trans: The Final Incision Of The Snowflake)

Tomisaburo Wakayama *(Kyogoro),* Tasayo Utsunomiya *(Akane),* Yusuke Takita *(Fujieda),* Masaki Kyomoto *(Harutsune),* Harue Kyo *(Katsuko),* Naomi Shiraishi *(Haruna),* Taiji Tonoyama *(Horiatsu).*

IREZUMI is a strikingly visual film about the beautiful young Akane (Tasayo Utsonomiya), who performs for her lover the sacrifice of having her back tattooed. Her greatest fear is that she will lose this man, a file clerk with a fetish for beautiful skin and tattoos, and for two years she commutes from Tokyo to Kyoto, where Kyogoro (Tamisaburo Wakayama), a renowned tattoo artist who has come out of retirement for Akane, devotes the remainder of his life to completing this final tattoo. His method, of which he is deeply ashamed, is unique: Akane lies atop Kyogoro's nude, heavily tattooed young apprentice, moaning from the pain of the pricking tattoo needle and tightly gripping the man beneath her. Kyogoro believes that this brings the tattoo to life, giving it a soul and spirit all its own. As mysterious and foreign as it is kinky and erotic, IREZUMI explores the yin-yang principle of complete existence emerging from two opposites. While she is tattooed, Akane experiences intense extremes of both pleasure and pain, which breathes life into Kyogoro's art. Later, Kyogoro's apprentice creates his first tattoo—a tiny snowflake—which burns Akane's tender flesh like fire. Director Yoichi Takabayashi, whose first film, 1973's GAKI ZOSHI (The Water Was So Clear) also dealt with spirituality and eroticism, directs with a delicate sense of beauty, his visuals carefully capturing the movements and colors of the tattoo master at work and the living piece of art Akane becomes. The videocassette offers a vibrant print in Japanese with English subtitles.

p, Yasuyoshi Tokuma, Masumi Kanamaru; d, Yoichi Takabayashi; w, Chiho Katsura (based on the novel by Baku Akae); ph, Hideo Fujii; m, Masaru Sato.

Drama **(PR:O MPAA:NR)**

ITALIAN STRAW HAT, AN****

(1927, Fr.) 72m Albatros-Sequana/Kamenka bw (UN CHAPEAU DE PAILLE D'ITALIE)

Albert Prejean *(Fadinard, the Bridegroom),* Olga Tschechowa *(Mme. Anais de Beauperthuis),* Marise Maia *(Helene),* Alice Tissot *(Cousin Alice),* Yvonneck *(Nonancourt),* Paul Olivier *(Uncle Vezinet),* Jim Gerald *(Beauperthuis),* Vital Geymond *(Lt. Tavernier),* Alex Bondi *(Cousin Alex),* Jane Pierson *(Aunt Jane),* Alex Allin *(Felix, a Servant),* Volbert *(Mayor),* Valentine Tessier *(Customer in Store).*

One of the classics of French silent cinema and the first great film from then-30-year-old director Rene Clair, AN ITALIAN STRAW HAT is a superb visual comedy about Fadinard (Albert Prejean) who is on his way to his wedding. En route, however, his hungry horse makes a meal of a hat worn by a married woman, Anais (Olga Tschekowa), who is dallying in the park with her lover, a threatening army officer. The two lovers fear that Anais' husband will become suspicious if she returns home without her straw hat, and the army officer vows to destroy every piece of furniture in Fadinard's new apartment if the groom-to-be doesn't run right out and find a replacement. Naturally, this is easier said than done, and Fadinard sets off on a comic chase to purchase the hat before the appointed time of his wedding. Clair, whose associations with the French Dadaists and Surrealists has made him something of a favorite among Parisian intellectuals, managed in AN ITALIAN STRAW HAT to take a swipe at bourgeois social conventions while putting into practice his belief that film should be a purely visual art form. Using very few intertitles, Clair relied on his visuals to create character and to propel the narrative, and, as a result, proved himself very much the equal of Chaplin and Keaton as a comic filmmaker.

p, Alexander Kamenka; d, Rene Clair; w, Rene Clair (based on the play *Un Chapeau de Paille d'Italie* by Eugene Labiche, Marc Michel); ph, Maurice Desfassiaux, Nicolas Roudakoff; ed, Rene Clair.

Comedy **(PR:A MPAA:NR)**

IVAN THE TERRIBLE PART I AND II****

(1945, USSR) 99m & 90m Alma-Ata-Mosfilm/Sovexportfilm-Artkino-Janus bw (IVAN GROZNY)

Nikolai Cherkassov *(Czar Ivan IV),* Ludmila Tselikovskaya *(Anastasia Romanovna),* Serafima Birman *(The Boyarina Efrosinia Staritskaya, Czar's Aunt),* Pavel Kadochnikov *(Vladimir Andreyevich Staritsky),* Nikolai Nazvanov *(Prince Andrei Kurbsky),* Andrei Abrikosov *(Boyar Fyodor Kolychev),* Alexander Mgebrov *(Archbishop Pimen),* Vladimir Balashov *(Pyotyr Volynets),* Mikhail Zharov *(Malyuta Skuratov),* Mikhail Kuznetsov *(Fyodor Basmanov),* Eric Pyriev *(Young Ivan),* Alexei Buchma *(Alexei Basmanov),* Pavel Massalsky *(King Sigismund Augustus),* Vsevolod Pudovkin *(Nikola),* Maxim Mikhailov *(Archdeacon),* Erik Pyriev *(Czar Ivan as a Child),* Ada Voitsik *(Yelena Glinskaya).*

The first two parts of Sergei Eisenstein's intended trilogy about the 16th-century Russian hero Czar Ivan IV. Part I, completed in 1945, chronicles the ruler's coronation, marriage, illness and unexplained sudden recovery, the poisoning of his wife, and his battles against conspirators. By the end of Part I, Ivan declares his intention to return from Alexandrov to Moscow at the will of his people. Part II (subtitled "The Boyer's Plot"), which was filmed shortly after Part I but not released until 1958, follows Czar Ivan on his return, his confrontations with his enemies, the poisoning of his mother, and his discovery of an assassination plot. The black-and-white film ends with a brilliantly colored banquet scene. Although the scenario for Part III (subtitled "The Battles of Ivan") was approved by Stalin (oddly enough, since it is Stalin who censored Part II because of its negative portrayal of Ivan's secret police), Eisenstein, who died in 1948, never completed the project. For those viewers familiar only with Eisenstein's BATTLESHIP POTEMKIN, the shift from that film's revolutionary editing style to IVAN's emphasis on composition and lighting will be quite a surprise. IVAN THE TERRIBLE is a vast, important, and occasionally difficult historical effort that closes Eisenstein's legendary career. Sergei Prokofiev was commissioned to provide the film's remarkable score. Both videocassettes are in Russian with English subtitles.

d, Sergei Eisenstein; w, Sergei Eisenstein; ph, Eduard Tisse, Andrei Moskvin; ed, Sergei Eisenstein; m, Sergei Prokofiev.

Biography **(PR:A MPAA:NR)**

J

JACKO AND LISE*½

(1979, Fr./Bel./Tahiti) 92m Belstar-AMS-Cathala-la Tour-Pacific-SODEP-BELGA/Quartet c (BOBO JACCO)

Laurent Malet *(Jacco),* Annie Girardot *(Magda),* Michel Montanary *(Freddie),* Evelyn Bouix *(Lise),* Jean-Claude Brialy *(Guillaume),* Francisca Barsin *(Freddie's Mother),* Michel Berto *(Department Head),* Arlette Biernau *(Lise's Grandmother),* Robert Corhay *(Bedeau),* Angela de Bona *(Vera),* Andre Deflandre *(Tramway Driver),* Jean-Andre Dumont *(Jacco's Father),* Daniel Dury *(Office Caretaker),* Simone Ettekoven *(Josephine),* Carine Francois *(Woman Cinephile),* Arnold Gelderman *(First Poker Player),* Philippe Geluck *(Cinephile),* Luc Van Grunderbeeck *(Drageur),* Alain Lahaye *(Alexandre),* Jacques Lippe *(Old Cop),* Gaetan Marynissen *(Freddie's Brother),* Jules Nijs *(Peasant),* Jean Pascal *(Old Man),* Denyse Periez *(Jacco's Mother).*

Jacco (Laurent Malet) is a young, curly-haired delinquent who is best pals with Freddie (Michel Montanary). The two of them raise hell wherever they go—getting drunk in church and falling off the pews, singing loudly while wandering the streets in the middle of the night, and sleeping with any women they can find. Freddie is the playboy, while Jacco (short for Jacques, and changed to Jacko for the US release title) seems content in his romance with Magda (Annie Girardot), a bar owner nearly twice his age. It's about an hour into the film when Jacco meets Lise (Evelyne Bouix), a pretty, short-haired young woman engaged to marry Guillaume (Jean-Claude Brialy), a wealthy businessman. The slight attraction between Jacco and Lise grows into a deep love, as both of them shut out the wider world for as long as possible. Eventually, however, the pressures on the relationship prove too great. First-time director Walter Bal tries to combines elements of Truffaut's JULES AND JIM (the bond of friendship tested when one friend falls in love) and Bertrand Blier's GOING PLACES (the vulgar carousing and homoeroticism), but succeeds only in creating two one-dimensional yahoos who are far more obnoxious than they are rebellious. The film only comes alive in the final half-hour with the appearance of Bouix, who in 1984 would play Edith Piaf in Claude Lelouch's EDITH AND MARCEL. Otherwise, the film is a tedious ninety minutes with a third-rate pop rock score. In French with English subtitles.

p, Jacques Dorfman, Laurent Meyniel, Norbert Saada; d, Walter Bal; w, Walter Bal; ph, Pascal Gennesseaux; ed, Michel Lewin; m, Jacques Revaux.

Drama **(PR:C MPAA:NR)**

JEAN DE FLORETTE***½

(1986, Fr.) 122m Renn-Films A2-RAI 2-DD/Orion c

Yves Montand *(Cesar Soubeyran/"Le Papet"),* Gerard Depardieu *(Jean de Florette [Cadoret]),* Daniel Auteuil *(Ugolin Soubeyran/"Galignette"),* Elisabeth Depardieu *(Aimee Cadoret),* Ernestine Mazurowna *(Manon Cadoret),* Marcel Champel *(Pique- Bouffigue),* Armand Meffre *(Philoxene),* Andre Dupon *(Pamphile),* Pierre Nougaro *(Casimir),* Marc Betton *(Martial),* Jean Maurel *(Anglade),* Roger Souza *(Ange),* Bertino Benedetto *(Giuseppe),* Margarita Lozano *(Baptistine),* Pierre Jean Rippert *(Pascal),* Didier Pain *(Eliacin),* Fransined *(Florist),* Christian Tamisier *(Doctor),* Marcel Berbert *(Notary),* Jo Doumerg *(Muledriver),* Chantal Liennel *(Amandine, Papet's Servant).*

The most talked-about French production in many years, this picture and its sequel, MANON OF THE SPRING (MANON DES SOURCES), were completed at a combined record-breaking budget of $17 million (about eight times the cost of the average French picture). Shot back to back with its successor, JEAN DE FLORETTE is set in a French farming village tucked into a rocky but picturesque hillside. As the film begins, Le Papet (Yves Montand), a coarse local reputed to be a swindler, welcomes the return to the village of his nephew, Ugolin (Daniel Auteuil). A grimy, idiotic misfit, Ugolin has dreams of growing carnations for sale at the local marketplace. Carnations, however, need a great deal of water—a sparse commodity in the village. When Le Papet realizes that Ugolin's idea is potentially profitable, he sets his sights on a neighboring farm that, he knows, contains an untapped natural spring. It is owned by Jean Cadoret (Gerard Depardieu), a hunchbacked tax collector who has bid farewell to city life in favor of a return to nature. Refusing to let the farm slip through their fingers, Le Papet and Ugolin dig up the spring and cover the opening with cement, letting Jean work himself to death in the hope that they will eventually take over his farm. Directed by Claude Berri, JEAN DE FLORETTE is a throwback to the pre-Nouvelle Vague days of French cinema, when the Tradition of Quality was the norm. Based on Marcel Pagnol's two-part novel *L'Eau des Collines* (The Water of the Hills), which, in turn, was based on an unsuccessful 1952 film Pagnol directed, the film offers the same sort of complex characterizations, careful scripting, beautiful country images, and heightened realism that marked such films as Pagnol's early "Marseilles Trilogy"—MARIUS (1931), FANNY (1932), and CESAR (1934). Berri sets up a number of forces, all pitted against each other—Jean's will against nature's persistence, Jean's knowledge against nature's unpredictability, Jean's vision against Le Papet's greed, and Ugolin's aspirations against his own conscience—and the result is a grand but somehow unfulfilling picture. (SEE: MANON OF THE SPRING). In French with easy-to-read yellow English subtitles.

p, Pierre Grunstein; d, Claude Berri; w, Claude Berri, Gerard Brach (based on the novel by Marcel Pagnol); ph, Bruno Nuytten (Technovision, Eastmancolor); ed, Arlette Langmann, Herve de Luze, Noelle Boisson; m, Jean-Claude Petit.

Drama **(PR:C MPAA:PG)**

JOKE OF DESTINY, A**½

(1983, It.) 105m Radiovideo/Samuel Goldwyn c (SCHERZO DEL DESTINO IN AGGUATO DIETRO L'ANGLO COME UN BRIGANTE DI STRADA; AKA: A JOKE OF DESTINY LYING IN WAIT AROUND THE CORNER LIKE A STREET BANDIT)

Ugo Tognazzi *(Vincenzo De Andreiis),* Piera Degli Esposti *(Maria Teresa De Andreiis),* Gastone Moschin *(Minister of the Interior),* Roberto Herlitzka *(Minister's Assistant),* Renzo Montagnani *(Pautasso),* Enzo Jannacci *(Gigi Pedrinelli),* Valeria Golino *(Adalgisa),* Massimo Wertmuller *(Beniamino),* Livia Cerini *(Pot-Smoking Grandmother),* Antonella D'Agostino *(Wife of Minister),* Pina Cei *(Maria's Sister),* Pierluigi Misasi *(Driver).*

The full title is A JOKE OF DESTINY LYING IN WAIT AROUND THE CORNER LIKE A STREET BANDIT and, as might be suspected of any title that long, it comes from the mind of Lina Wertmuller. A satire on the dangers of technology, the film takes a small incident—the imprisonment of the Italian Minister of the Interior (Gastone Moschin) in his specially designed, super high-tech, antiterrorist limousine—and turns it into an intelligent, though not terribly funny, comedy. Vincenzo De Andreiis (Ugo Tognazzi), a boot-licking member of the Italian parliament whose undersecretaryship was vetoed by the minister, is out for a stroll when he finds the stalled limousine and has it pushed into the garage on his estate. After this, a variety of peculiar situations occur—situations which, judging from the title, were destined to happen as a result of technological advances. A pair of technical experts, whose names translate as "Godhelpus" and "Praytogod," do their best to free the minister. Telephone calls for help are repeatedly connected to a local pizza parlor. Vincenzo's wife, Maria Teresa (Piera Degli Esposti) has an affair with a Red Brigade terrorist (Enzo Jannacci). Vincenzo's daughter, Adalgisa (Valeria Golino), takes a pair of handcuffs and shackles herself to an unwitting policeman, pleading for the man to "deflower" her. Curiously, Wertmuller's comedy falls flat, but if one believes her intent is not to make audiences laugh but to make them think about the absurdity of technological dependence, then the film can be viewed as a success. Fans of Golino, who made a big splash in 1988 with RAIN MAN and BIG TOP PEE-WEE, will delight in seeing the peppy 16-year-old in her first film role. The letter-boxed videocassette is in Italian with English subtitles.

p, Giuseppe Giovannini; d, Lina Wertmuller; w, Lina Wertmuller, Age (based on a story by Wertmuller, Silvia D'Amico Bendico); ph, Camillio Bazzoni; ed, Franco Fraticelli; m, Paolo Conte.

Comedy **(PR:A-C MPAA:PG)**

JOUR DE FETE****

(1949, Fr.) 90m Cady/Meyer-Kingsley bw (AKA: HOLIDAY; THE BIG DAY; THE BIG NIGHT; THE VILLAGE FAIR)

Jacques Tati *(Francois, the Postman),* Guy Decomble *(Roger, the Circus Owner),* Paul Frankeur *(Marcel, Roger's Circus Partner),* Santa Relli *(Roger's Wife),* Maine Vallee *(Jeanette, the Young Girl),* Roger Rafal *(Barber),* Beauvais *(Cafe Proprietor),* Delcassan *(Old Cinema Operator),* Inhabitants of Sainte-Severe-sur-Indre.

This first feature from Jacques Tati is actually a lengthened version of his 1947 short L'ECOLE DES FACTEURS, and helped give Tati somewhat of an international reputation as one of the best, if not the very best, film comics to come out of France. Tati stars as Francois, the postman of a small sleepy village. He becomes obsessed with applying to his job the methods of the American postal system, as seen in a short educational film. This simple premise provides an abundance of opportunities for the gangly and buffoonish Tati to engage in some spectacular jokes. The emphasis of Tati's work is visual, with music and dialog used only commentatively. As a result, Tati's style, like the styles of the great silent comedians, crossed language barriers and found Tati an international following. In French with English subtitles.

p, Fred Orain; d, Jacques Tati; w, Jacques Tati, Rene Wheeler, Henri Marquet; ph, Jean Mercanton, Marcel Franchi; ed, Marcel Moreau; m, Jean Yatove.

Comedy **(PR:A MPAA:NR)**

JULES AND JIM*****

(1962, Fr.) 104m Carrosse-SEDIF/Janus bw (JULES ET JIM)

Jeanne Moreau *(Catherine),* Oskar Werner *(Jules),* Henri Serre *(Jim),* Marie Dubois *(Therese),* Vanna Urbino *(Gilberte),* Sabine Haudepin *(Sabine),* Boris Bassiak *(Albert),* Kate Noelle *(Birgitta),* Anny Nelsen *(Lucie),* Christiane Wagner *(Helga),* Jean-Louis Richard, Michel Varesano *(Customers in Cafe),* Pierre Fabre *(Drunkard in Cafe),* Danielle Bassiak *(Albert's Friend).*

Arguably Francois Truffaut's greatest achievement, JULES AND JIM stands as a shrine to those lovers who have known obsession and been destroyed by it. The film begins in Paris in 1912 when two writers—Jules (Oskar Werner), a shy German, and Jim (Henri Serre), a dark-haired Parisian—become obsessed with an ancient stone carving of a woman. Their life changes when they meet Catherine (Jeanne Moreau), the personification of the stone goddess, whose smile enchants both men. Jules begins to court her, but only with Jim's blessing. The three become great friends, though Catherine's unpredictability flares whenever she feels she is being ignored (at one point, she jumps into the Seine when Jules and Jim's heated discussion of a Strindberg play does not include her).

Although Catherine gives Jules a child, Sabine (the adorable, bespectacled Sabine Haudepin), her ever-changing moods are not those of a mother or a wife, and she begins an affair with Jim. Jules, however, refuses to leave her, or even to get angry—he only wants to be near her and his friend. The film is a celebration both of love and cinema, as Truffaut directs with equal concern for his characters and for film technique—one never overshadowing the other. Scripted from Henri-Pierre Roche's novel, the screenplay has not a wasted word or gesture, every element working together perfectly to create three unique and interdependent characters. As in love with Catherine as Jules and Jim are, Truffaut photographs her with the greatest love and admiration. Just as Jules and Jim respond lovingly to Catherine's every move and just as the camera swirls and dollies around the ancient stone carving of the film's early scenes, so too does Truffaut's filmmaking revolve around the great Moreau, who gives the performance of her career and one of the most memorable performances in cinema history. The videocassette is in French with English subtitles, but the powerful widescreen ratio of Raoul Coutard's black-and-white photography is unfortunately lost on the small screen.

p, Marcel Berbert; d, Francois Truffaut; w, Francois Truffaut, Jean Gruault (based on the novel *Jules et Jim* by Henri-Pierre Roche); ph, Raoul Coutard (Franscope); ed, Claudine Bouche; m, Georges Delerue.

Drama **(PR:C-O MPAA:NR)**

JULIA AND JULIA*½

(1988, It.) 97m RAI-TV/Cinecom c (GUILIA E GUILIA)

Kathleen Turner *(Julia),* Sting *(Daniel Osler),* Gabriel Byrne *(Paolo),* Gabriele Ferzetti *(Paolo's Father),* Angela Goodwin *(Paolo's Mother),* Lidia Broccolino *(Carla),* Alexander Van Wyk *(Marco),* Renato Scarpa *(Commissioner).*

With JULIA AND JULIA, the American-born Italian director Peter Del Monte makes his first English-language picture, and, perhaps more importantly, the first feature-length film shot in HDVS, a high-definition video system that is transferred to 35mm film for distribution. While the technology may be revolutionary, the film is far less noteworthy. Kathleen Turner stars as the title Julias. As the film gets under way, we realize that today is Julia's wedding day. As she and her new husband, Paolo (Gabriel Byrne), are driving in Italy, they are run off the road and Paolo is killed. Unable to get over her loss, Julia subsequently lives a seemingly empty life in Trieste. One evening, however, after driving through an inexplicable fog, Julia arrives at her apartment only to find someone else living there—someone who claims to have been there for years. Julia is eventually reunited with Paolo (now alive?) and, to her surprise, a son to whom she doesn't remember giving birth. This apparently happy outcome is again turned topsy-turvy when she arrives at work, but no one recognizes her. In her pocket she finds a hotel room key and, going there after some hesitation, she finds herself is reunited with her lover, Daniel (Sting), whom she doesn't remember any better than she remembers her baby. This pattern goes on for some time, then the film ends. There are certain debates in the history of civilization that just aren't worth pondering for long, like "If a tree falls in the forest and no one is around for miles to hear it, does it make a sound?" or "What are Razzles—a candy or a gum?" With the release of JULIA AND JULIA, we can now add, "What is JULIA AND JULIA about, really?" Turner seems to try with her material but it's basically a one-note performance of perplexity. Sting and Byrne are in the film, but there's little more that one can say about their performances—they're just pawns in Del Monte's "Twilight Zone"-style mind game. In English.

d, Peter Del Monte; w, Silvia Napolitano, Peter Del Monte, Sandro Petraglia (based on a story by Peter Del Monte, Silvia Napolitano); ph, Giuseppe Rotunno (Technicolor); ed, Michael Chandler; m, Maurice Jarre.

Drama **(PR:C-O MPAA:NR)**

JULIET OF THE SPIRITS****

(1965, Fr./It./W. Ger.) 148m Federiz-Francoriz-Rizzoli-Eichberg/Rizzoli c (GIULIETTA DEGLI SPIRITI; JULIETTE DES ESPRITS; JULIA UND DIE GEISTER)

Giulietta Masina *(Juliet),* Alba Cancellieri *(Juliet as a Child),* Mario Pisu *(Giorgio),* Caterina Boratto *(Juliet's Mother),* Luisa Della Noce *(Adele),* Sylva Koscina *(Sylva),* Sabrina Gigli, Rosella di Sepio *(Granddaughters),* Lou Gilbert *(Grandfather),* Valentina Cortese *(Valentina),* Silvana Jachino *(Dolores),* Elena Fondra *(Elena),* Jose-Luis de Vilallonga, Cesarino Miceli Picardi *(Friends of Giorgio),* Milena Vucotich, Elisabetta Gray *(Juliet's Maids),* Sandra Milo *(Susy/Iris/Fanny),* Irina Alexeieva *(Susy's Grandmother),* Alessandra Mannoukine *(Susy's Mother),* Gilberto Galvan *(Susy's Chauffeur).*

Juliet (Giulietta Masina) is a married woman in her mid-30s, more or less resigned to a dull life with her dull husband, Giorgio (Mario Pisu), who pays her little attention. At first she thinks it's just the pressures of business that cause him to be so diffident, but soon she begins to wonder if he may have someone else. One night, Giorgio and some friends hold a seance and Juliet discovers that she can conjure up various spirits. These wraiths tell her that she deserves some enjoyment in life and should give herself a treat. Checking to see if her suspicions about Giorgio are correct, Juliet hires a sleuth who corroborates her worst fears about his extramarital life—news that forces the distraught wife to change her lifestyle and move out from under the shadow of her unloving husband. A feminized version of 8 1/2—both Masina's and Pisu's characters drifting in and out of fantasy in order to come to grips with reality—JULIET OF THE SPIRITS will likely appeal to fans of that previous Fellini picture. This was Fellini's first color feature, and one can tell—the results as spectacular and festive as one would imagine Fellini's first use of color would be. Dubbed in English.

p, Angelo Rizzoli; d, Federico Fellini; w, Federico Fellini, Tullio Pinelli, Ennio Flaiano, Brunello Rondi (based on a story by Federico Fellini, Tullio Pinelli); ph, Gianni De Venanzo (Technicolor); ed, Ruggero Mastroianni; m, Nino Rota.

Drama **(PR:A-C MPAA:NR)**

JUPITER'S THIGH½**

(1980, Fr.) 102m Ariane-Mondex-FR3/Quartet c (ON A VOLE LA CUISSE DE JUPITER)

Annie Girardot *(Lise Tanquerelle),* Philippe Noiret *(Antoine Lemercier),* Francis Perrin *(Charles-Hubert Pochet),* Catherine Alric *(Agnes Pochet),* Marc Dudicourt *(Spiratos),* Alexandre Mnouchkine *(Von Blankenberg).*

This is a silly but entertaining comic adventure from Philippe de Broca about a pair of middle-aged newlyweds—Prof. Antoine Lemercier (Philippe Noiret), an expert in Greek history, and Police Commissioner Lise Tanquerelle (Annie Girardot), a master criminal investigator—who honeymoon in Greece. Upon their arrival, they meet Charles-Hubert Pochet (Francis Perrin), a young archaeologist who has just unearthed a chunk of statue—the buttocks of Venus Heroclitus (why the film is called JUPITER'S THIGH is anyone's guess). The discovery is of great importance and will bring Charles-Hubert international renown, but by nightfall it is stolen, thanks to his greedy wife, Agnes (Catherine Alric). Agnes has arranged for the fragment to be sold so she can buy a new car. Unfortunately for all involved, the man who wants the buttocks is a ruthless killer, and before long Lemercier and Charles-Hubert are murder suspects. Of course, it's left up to Inspector Tanquerelle to prove their innocence. While the film doesn't match de Broca's better efforts—THAT MAN FROM RIO; KING OF HEARTS; or even 1977's DEAR INSPECTOR, which introduced us to Prof. Lemercier and Inspector Tanquerelle—JUPITER'S THIGH is a pleasant enough way to spend an evening. If the silliness of the proceedings or Noiret's performance don't win you over, maybe the Greek settings and score will. The videocassette is in French and Greek with English subtitles.

p, Alexandre Mnouchkine, Georges Dancigers, Robert Amon; d, Philippe de Broca; w, Philippe de Broca, Michel Audiard (based on the character created by Jean-Paul Rouland, Claude Olivier); ph, Jean-Paul Schwartz (Eastmancolor); ed, Henri Lanoe; m, George Hatzinassios.

Comedy **(PR:C MPAA:NR)**

K

KAGEMUSHA****

(1980, Jap.) 179m Toho-Kurosawa/FOX c (AKA: THE DOUBLE; THE SHADOW WARRIOR)

Tatsuya Nakadai *(Shingen Takeda/Kagemusha),* Tsutomo Yamazaki *(Nobukado Takeda),* Kenichi Hagiwara *(Katsuyori Takeda),* Kota Yui *(Takemaru Takeda),* Shuji Otaki *(Masakage Yamagata),* Hideo Murata *(Baba),* Daisuke Ryu *(Nobunaga Oda),* Kaori Momoi *(Otsuyanokata),* Masayuki Yui *(Ieyasu Tokugawa).*

After a long period of inactivity, Akira Kurosawa returned to the genre of which he is the undisputed master, the samurai film, with KAGEMUSHA. Tatsuya Nakadai plays a 16th-century warlord, Shingen Takeda, who uses doubles for himself on the battlefield, thereby instilling confidence and fear through his constant presence while his clan fights to establish dominance in Japan. When he is killed, his current "shadow warrior," or kagemusha—in actuality a petty thief (again played by Tatsuya Nakadai)—must take over so that the army's morale will not die. Trained in secret by Shingen's assistants, the man genuinely begins to acquire some of his master's attributes, but is eventually exposed as a fake and banished from court. In the climactic battle, however, the deposed kagemusha is unable to restrain himself and grabs the clan's standard, rushing into the thick of the fray. Kurosawa's epic is alive with color, the spectacular visuals overlying a somber exploration of traditionalism, loyalty, and identity set against a background of political intrigue and the 16th-century clan warfare ended by the Tokugawa shogunate. The massive battle scenes rank with the director's best, employing brilliant color and contrasts of light amidst the enormous cast with great style. Made and distributed with the financial aid and clout of George Lucas and Francis Ford Coppola, KAGEMUSHA was cowinner (with Bob Fosse's ALL THAT JAZZ) of the Golden Palm at the Cannes Film Festival. Its worldwide success prefigured and paved the way for the great RAN (1985), Kurosawa's epic adaptation of "King Lear." In Japanese with English subtitles.

p, Akira Kurosawa, Tomoyuki Tanaka; d, Akira Kurosawa; w, Akira Kurosawa, Masato Ide; ph, Takao Saito, Shoji Ueda, Kazuo Miyagawa, Asaichi Nakai (Panavision, Eastmancolor); ed, Keisuke Iwatani; m, Shinichiro Ikebe.

Drama **(PR:C MPAA:PG)**

KAMERADSCHAFT****

(1931, Ger.) 93m Nero-Gaumont-Franco-Film-Aubert bw (AKA: COMRADESHIP)

Fritz Kampers *(Wilderer),* Gustav Puttjer *(Kaplan),* Alexander Granach *(Kaspers),* Andree Ducret *(Francoise),* Georges Charlia *(Jean),* Ernst Busch *(Wittkopp),* Daniel Mandaille *(Emile),* Pierre Louis *(Georges),* Alex Bernard *(Grandfather).*

A heartfelt plea for peace and internationalism, KAMERADSCHAFT is set in the Lorraine mining region on the French-German border in the aftermath of WW I, though it is based on a actual 1906 mining disaster that claimed 1200 lives. Combining Expressionism and realism (predating the Italian Neo-Realists), G.W. Pabst introduces the viewer to the German and French miners. Separated by mine walls and metal bars below, and by armed border patrols above, they have little contact with one another, but when a series of explosions causes a cave-in on the French side, German hearts bleed. Wittkopp (Ernst Busch) appeals to his bosses to send a rescue team, while underground a trio of German miners breaks through a set of steel bars that mark the 1919 border. Meanwhile, on the French side, an old, retired miner (Alex Bernard) sneaks into the shaft hoping to rescue his young grandson (Pierre Louis). Although occasionally over-sentimental, Pabst's plea for a peaceful future is both noble and honest, his direction of the heartbreak and devastation enhanced by the brilliant photography by Fritz Arno Wagner and Robert Baberske, and the frighteningly real set design by Erno Metzner and Karl Vollbrecht. The videocassette is in German and French with easy-to-read yellow English subtitles.

p, Seymour Nebenzahl; d, G.W. Pabst; w, Karl Otten, Peter Martin Lampel, Ladislaus Vajda; ph, Fritz Arno Wagner, Robert Baberske; ed, Hans Oser.

Drama **(PR:A-C MPAA:NR)**

KAMIKAZE '89**

(1982, Ger.) 106m Trio-Oase c

Rainer Werner Fassbinder *(Police Lieutenant Jansen),* Gunther Kaufmann *(Anton),* Boy Gobert *(Blue Panther),* Arnold Marquis *(Police Chief),* Richy Muller *(Nephew),* Nicole Heesters *(Barbara),* Brigitte Mira *(Personnel Director),* Jorg Holm *(Vice President),* Hans Wyprachtiger *(Zerling),* Petra Jokisch *(Elena Farr),* Ute Fitz-Koska *(Police Doctor),* Frank Ripploh *(Gangster),* Hans- Eckardt Eckardt *(Policeman),* Christoph Baumann *(Plainclothesman),* Juliane Lorenz *(Nurse),* Christel Harthaus *(Policewoman),* Franco Nero *(Weiss).*

This peculiar, high-camp film stars the bigger-than-life German director Rainer Werner Fassbinder as Jansen, a futuristic police lieutenant who must locate a bomb that has apparently been planted in a 30-story office building. The result, an amalgam of West Berlin punk sensibilities and *film noir*/comic book archetypes, is as odd and exciting as it is unwatchable and confusing. For those rabid Rainer-maniacs who can't get enough of the late, great director, KAMIKAZE '89 is a must—if only to see Fassbinder in his leopard-skin suit. Others will probably find the goings-on rather trying. In German with English subtitles.

p, Regina Ziegler; d, Wolf Gremm; w, Robert Katz, Wolf Gremm (based on the novel *Murder on the 31st Floor* by Per Wahloo and Maj Sowall); ph, Xaver Schwarzenberger; ed, Thorsten Nater; m, Edgar Froese.

Science Fiction **(PR:O MPAA:NR)**

KANAL****

(1957, Pol.) 96m Polski/MJP-Kingsley bw (AKA: THEY LOVED LIFE)

Teresa Izewska *(Daisy Stokrotka),* Tadeusz Janczar *(Cpl. Korab),* Wienczyslaw Glinski *(Lt. Zadra),* Tadeusz Gwiazdowski *(Sgt. Kula),* Stanislaw Mikulski *(The Slim [Smukly]),* Wladyslaw Sheybal *(Composer),* Emil Karewiez *(The Wise [Madry]),* Teresa Berezowska *(Halinka),* Adam Pawlikowski *(German Officer),* Zofia Lindorf, Students of the Lodz Film School.

This second feature from Andrzej Wajda takes place during the final days of the Warsaw Uprising in 1944 as three groups of Poles, no longer able to hold off the enemy, retreat to the *kanaly*, the city's sewer system. The viewer is told from the very start to "watch them closely, these are the last hours of their lives," and with this dark foreknowledge we watch as they live an underground existence free from the oppression and lost ideals of their lives above ground, even as they try to escape. Although we know that death awaits them, we also know that escape from the sewers is only a relative freedom. Wajda spares his audience nothing, showing death, betrayal, suffering, suicide, capture, and despair, yet his characters fight on, hoping to see sunlight pouring into the sewer, even if it is filtered through the barrier of a metal grate. The videocassette is available in both dubbed and subtitled (Polish into English) versions.

p, Stanislaw Adler; d, Andrzej Wajda; w, Jerzy Stefan Stawinski (based on a short story by Jerzy Stefan Stawinski); ph, Jerzy Lipman; ed, Halina Nawrocka; m, Jan Krenz.

War **(PR:C MPAA:NR)**

KING OF HEARTS***½

(1967, Fr./It.) 100m Artistes-Montoro-Fildebroc/Lopert-UA c (LE ROI DE COEUR; TUTTI PAZZIO MENO LO)

Alan Bates *(Pvt. Charles Plumpick),* Pierre Brasseur *(Gen. Geranium),* Jean-Claude Brialy *(The Duke),* Genevieve Bujold *(Coquelicot),* Adolfo Celi *(Col. Alexander MacBibenbrook),* Micheline Presle *(Mme. Eglantine),* Francoise Christophe *(The Duchess),* Julien Guiomar *(Bishop Daisy),* Michel Serrault *(The Crazy Barber),* Marc Dudicourt *(Lt. Hamburger),* Daniel Boulanger *(Col. Helmut von Krack),* Jacques Balutin *(Mac Fish),* Pierre Palau *(Alberic),* Madeleine Clervanne *(Brunehaut).*

Breathing new life into old themes, Philippe de Broca's charming antiwar "dramedy" KING OF HEARTS has been a perennial favorite on college campuses since it first reached the screen in 1967, at the height of the Vietnam War. Set during WW I, the film begins as the occupying Germans retreat from the town of Marville, France, but not before leaving behind a time bomb. The fleeing townspeople tell the approaching British forces about the hidden explosive, and Pvt. Charles Plumpick (Alan Bates), a poetry-loving Scotsman, is dispatched to locate the bomb. To avoid the German rear guard, Plumpick ducks into Marville's insane asylum, where the inmates hail him as the "King of Hearts" before retaking the town and resuming their former lives, albeit in a decidedly loony fashion. In the process of trying to find and defuse the bomb Plumpick comes to love the crazy but gentle citizens, especially Coquelicot (Genevieve Bujold). In time, the Germans and British clash in Marville, littering the town with bodies, and when the "real" villagers return, Plumpick is left with a choice: to go back to soldiering or join the "crazy" folks in the asylum. In addition to its strong antiwar message, KING OF HEARTS ponders the old question, Who's crazier, the people who accept life's brutality or those who reject it? Some have said that de Broca states his case with a heavy hand—and he does—but for those willing to open themselves to a humorous treatment of this all-too-serious subject, KING OF HEARTS will be both touching and life-affirming. The videocassette is dubbed in English.

p, Philippe de Broca; d, Philippe de Broca; w, Daniel Boulanger (based on an idea by Maurice Bessy); ph, Pierre L'Homme (Techniscope, DeLuxe Color); ed, Francoise Javet; m, Georges Delerue.

Comedy/Drama **(PR:C MPAA:NR)**

KINGS OF THE ROAD*****

(1976, Ger.) 176m Wim Wenders bw (IM LAUF DER ZEIT)

Rudiger Vogler *(Bruno Winter),* Hanns Zischler *(Robert "Kamikaze" Lander),* Lisa Kreuzer *(Pauline),* Rudolf Schuendler *(Robert's Father),* Marquard Bohm *(Man Whose Wife Commits Suicide),* Dieter Traier *(Paul, Robert's Friend),* Franziska Stommer *(Female Theater Owner),* Peter Kaiser *(Projectionist),* Patrick Kreuzer *(Boy at Train Station),* Wim Wenders *(Theater Patron).*

One of the seminal films of the New German Cinema, KINGS OF THE ROAD is, along with the recent WINGS OF DESIRE, one of Wim Wenders' greatest achievements. The ultimate road movie, this three-hour picture traces the small adventures of two men as they wander along the back roads of Germany, moving from one small town to the next. One morning Bruno (Rudiger Vogler), a motion picture projector repairman who lives in his van, sees a Volkswagen plunge off a dock and into the Elbe River, a natural border between East and West Germany. Out of the water comes Robert (Hanns Zischler), a linguist who has just made a half-hearted suicide attempt. Robert accepts a ride from Bruno and, as they travel cross-country on Bruno's repair route, their friendship grows strong. They drink, meet people, wander the streets, and sing along to American songs, especially Roger Miller's "King of the Road." The story is simple and told in the main without dialog (Wenders and crew set out with an itinerary, but no script), and the film's core is not narrative—instead, as the translated title tells us, it is "the course of time" that holds Wenders' interest. The changes that occur throughout history (symbolized by crumbling small-town movie houses) are the film's central concern, hence its length. Scenes are filmed in real time, as we watch the characters shave, wash, think, talk, and even defecate. KINGS OF THE ROAD becomes an even more revealing entry in Wenders' canon when one views it in light of WINGS OF DESIRE: Both films examining the borders or walls that exist between people, between past and present, and between the two Germanys. No mention of this film can go without citing the power of the naturally lit, black-and-white images captured by Robby Muller. In German with English subtitles.

p, Michael Wiedemann; d, Wim Wenders; w, Wim Wenders; ph, Robby Muller; ed, Peter Przygodda; m, Axel Linstadt, Roger Miller, Chris Montez, Christian St. Peters.

Drama **(PR:C MPAA:NR)**

KISS OF THE SPIDER WOMAN****

(1985, US/Braz.) 119m HB/Island Alive bw-c

William Hurt *(Luis Molina),* Raul Julia *(Valentin Arregui),* Sonia Braga *(Leni Lamaison/Marta/Spider Woman),* Jose Lewgoy *(Warden),* Milton Goncalves *(Pedro),* Miriam Pires *(Mother),* Nuno Leal Maia *(Gabriel),* Fernando Torres *(Americo),* Patricio Bisso *(Greta),* Herson Capri *(Werner),* Denise Dummont *(Michele),* Nildo Parente *(Leader of Resistance),* Antonio Petrin *(Clubfoot),* Wilson Grey *(Flunky),* Miguel Falabella *(Lieutenant),* Walter Breda, Luis Guilherme, Walmir Barros *(Agents),* Luis Serra *(Prison Doctor),* Ana Maria Braga *(Lidia),* Benjamin Cattan, Oswaldo Barreto, Sergio Bright, Claudio Curi *(Molina's Friends),* Lineu Dias *(Bank Cashier),* Joe Kantor *(Judge),* Luis Roberto Galizia *(Nurse),* Pericles Campos, Edmilson Santos, Walter Vicca, Kenichi Kaneko *(Prison Guards),* Georges Schlesinger, Carlos Fariello, Frederico Botelho *(Jewish Smugglers),* Sylvio Band, Paulo Ludmer *(Rabbis),* Elvira Bisso *(Maid).*

Based on Manuel Puig's novel of the same name, KISS OF THE SPIDER WOMAN treats its unusual premise with an often lyrical grace. In a South American country, Molina (William Hurt), a flamboyant homosexual jailed for taking liberties with a minor, shares a cell with Arregui (Raul Julia), a political prisoner. Although the macho revolutionary initially dislikes Molina, he is eventually drawn in by the latter's reenactment of films, including a Nazi propaganda piece about a cabaret singer and a B picture featuring the "Spider Woman" (both "starring" Sonia Braga). Arregui also dreams of his lover outside (Braga again), memories that help him withstand torture. The two men slowly grow closer in a relationship that culminates with Molina's release. Hurt (named Best Actor on Oscar night and at Cannes) and Julia each create a distinct persona while developing a wholly believable, interdependent relationship, and Braga does a wonderful job of differentiating among her roles and their varying levels of fantasy. Hector Babenco's direction is a masterwork of detailed camera choreography, and the film-within-a-film episodes beautifully complement the prisoners' relationship. The film also received Oscar nominations for Best Picture and Best Director. In English.

p, David Weisman; d, Hector Babenco; w, Leonard Schrader (based on the novel by Manuel Puig); ph, Rodolfo Sanchez (MGM Color); ed, Mauro Alice, Lee Percy; m, John Neschling, Wally Badarou.

Prison **(PR:O MPAA:R)**

KNIFE IN THE WATER****

(1962, Pol.) 94m Film Polski-Kanawha bw (NOZ W WODZIE)

Leon Niemczyk *(Andrzej),* Jolanta Umecka *(Christine),* Zygmunt Malanowicz *(The Young Man).*

Roman Polanski's first feature immediately established him as a filmmaker to be reckoned with, winning top honors at the Venice Film Festival, a Best Foreign Film Oscar nomination, and a place on the cover of *Time* in conjunction with the first New York Film Festival. Polanski's career-long fascination with human cruelty and violence is already evident, as is his intense interest in exploring the complex tensions involved in close relations. When Andrzej (Leon Niemczyk), a successful sportswriter on holiday with his wife, Christine (Jolanta Umecka), picks up a hitchhiker (Zygmunt Malanowicz), the couple asks the young man (nameless throughout) to join them on a short boating excursion. Jealous of the blonde boy's youth and looks, Andrzej boasts of his physical prowess, faulting his guest's inexperience at sea. Tension between the men intensifies, with the pocket knife that represents the hitchhiker's particular skill lending a continual suggestion of violence, and eventually leading to a skirmish between him and Andrzej. Filmed in black and white, Polanski's debut feature is extremely assured, concise, and telling in its characterizations. KNIFE IN THE WATER is also notable in the career of another Polish filmmaker, coscenarist Jerzy Skolimowski, who had already begun to direct but emerged internationally in 1982 with MOONLIGHTING. In Polish with English subtitles.

p, Stanislaw Zylewicz; d, Roman Polanski; w, Roman Polanski, Jerzy Skolimowski, Jakub Goldberg; ph, Jerzy Lipman; ed, Halina Prugar-Ketling; m, Krzysztof Komeda.

Drama **(PR:O MPAA:NR)**

KOLBERG***

(1945, Ger.) 99m UFA-Farbfilm c (AKA: BURNING HEARTS)

Kristina Soderbaum *(Maria),* Heinrich George *(Nettelbeck),* Horst Caspar *(Gen. Gneisenau),* Paul Wegener *(Col. von Loucadou),* Gustav Diessl *(Maj. Schill),* Otto Wernicke *(Werner, a Farmer),* Irene von Meyendorff *(Queen),* Kurt Meisel *(Claus),* Jaspar von Oertzen *(Prince Louis Ferdinand),* Hans Herrmann Schlaufuss *(Zaufke),* Paul Bildt *(Rektor),* Franz Schafheitlin *(Franselow),* Charles Schauten *(Napoleon),* Heinz Lausch *(Friedrich),* Josef Dahmen *(Franz),* Franz Herterich *(Kaiser Franz II),* Frau Schroder-Wegener *(Frau von Voss),* Fritz Hoopts *(Timm),* Werner Scharf *(Gen. Teulie),* Theo Schall *(Gen. Loison).*

KOLBERG is Joseph Goebbels' attempt to outdo GONE WITH THE WIND and reportedly the most expensive German film ever, with over 90 hours of footage and film stock designed by Nazi chemists specifically for this picture. This propaganda story concerns the heroic attempts of a Prussian town, Kolberg, to ward off advancing French troops during the Napoleonic wars. Nettelbeck (Heinrich George, who was to die in a Russian prison camp in 1946) is the town mayor who organizes civilians to fight the French; Maria (Kristina Soderbaum, the director's wife) is a farmer's daughter who convinces her brothers and lover to die for the glory of Prussia. After a year in production, the film premiered during WW II at La Rochelle, with the advancing Allies just miles away. Future showings were extremely limited by the war. Although not credited, Goebbels was a major contributor to the script. A total of 187, 000 Wehrmacht extras were reassigned from various besieged fronts to lend authenticity to the movie, a testament to the fact that both Goebbels and Hitler believed the picture to be at least as important to morale at that time as a military victory. Although, as a product of Naziism, directed by a devout party man and anti-Semite, its worth can be debated, the film is not without some astounding production values and a certain historical importance. In German with English subtitles.

d, Veit Harlan; w, Veit Harlan, Alfred Braun; ph, Bruno Mondi; m, Norbert Schultze.

War **(PR:O MPAA:NR)**

KRIEMHILD'S REVENGE****

(1924, Ger.) 95m UFA bw (KRIEMHILDS RACHE)

Margarethe Schon *(Kriemhild),* Theodor Loos *(King Gunther),* Hanna Ralph *(Brunhild),* Georg John *(Blaodel),* Hans Carl Muller *(Gerenot),* Bernhard Goetzke *(Volker von Alzey),* Hans Adalbert von Schlettow *(Hagen Tronje),* Rudolf Rittner *(Markgraf Rudiger von Bechlarn),* Fritz Alberti *(Dietrich von Bern),* Georg August Koch *(Hildebrand),* Rudolph Klein-Rogge *(King Etzel),* Hubert Heinrich *(Werbel),* Grete Berger *(A Hun),* Rose Lichtenstein.

Part two of Fritz Lang's epic saga DIE NIBELUNGEN (the first of the two-part series is SIEGFRIED, released the same year), KRIEMHILD'S REVENGE was filmed as a single entity over a nine-month period and picks up after the death of Siegfried. The final events of SIEGFRIED are reprised as the slain hero's widow, Kriemhild (Margarethe Schon), standing at her late husband's bier, bitterly accuses Hagen Tronje (Hans Adalbert von Schlettow), her sinister half-brother, of his murder. She urges her brother the king (Theodor Loos) to visit justice on the villain. On the advice of young courtier Gerenot (Hans Carl Muller), the weakling king elects to do nothing to avenge Siegfried, averring that the family must stick together. Now realizing the king's complicity in the killing, Kriemhild plots vengeance against her own clan. Having handled this historical legend brilliantly for the German film studio UFA and for producer Erich Pommer, Lang would now turn his attention to his coming futuristic masterpiece, METROPOLIS. (SEE: SIEGFRIED).

p, Erich Pommer; d, Fritz Lang; w, Thea von Harbou (based on the anonymous poem "Das Nibelungenlied" and various Nordic legends); ph, Carl Hoffmann, Gunther Rittau.

Fantasy **(PR:C MPAA:NR)**

KWAIDAN****

(1964, Jap.) 164m Bungei-Ninjin-Toho/Continental c (KAIDAN)

"Black Hair": Rentaro Mikuni *(Samurai),* Michiyo Aratama *(1st Wife),* Misako Watanabe *(2nd Wife),* "The Woman of the Snow": Keiko Kishi *(Yuki/Snow Woman),* Tatsuya Nakadai *(Minokichi),* Mariko Okada *(Minokichi's Mother),* "Hoichi, the Earless": Katsuo Nakamura *(Hoichi),* Rentaro Mikuni *(Samurai Spirit),* Ganjiro Nakamura *(Head Priest),* Takashi Shimura *(Priest),* Tetsuro Tamba *(Yoshitsune),* Joichi Hayashi *(Attendant),* "In a Cup of Tea": Ganemon Nakamura *(Kannai),* Noboru Nakaya *(Heinai).*

Four short supernatural stories based on the tales of Lafcadio Hearn, an American who settled in Japan in 1890 and eventually became a citizen of that country, comprise KWAIDAN. Directed with an eerie visual sense by Masaki Kobayashi and containing some spectacular art direction by Shigemasa Toda, the stories each involve an encounter with a ghost—in Hearn's tales a supernatural being who appears to be corporeal but is actually one of the dear departed left to wander aimlessly through the real world. Included are "Black Hair," the tale of a samurai (Rentaro Mikuni) who returns to the wife he deserted years before and, after sleeping with her, discovers her skeletal remains and long black tresses in his bed; "The Woman of the Snow," a story cut from the US theatrical release about a young woodcutter (Tatsuya Nakadai) saved from death by a mysterious snow maiden who swears to kill him should he ever reveal what has occurred; "Hoichi, the Earless," the tale of a blind musician (Katsuo Nakamura) whose ears are cut off, as he sings, at the request of a samurai ghost for a dead infant lord; and finally "In a Cup of Tea," a story about a guard (Ganemon Nakamura) who sees a samurai's face in his teacup and absorbs the ghost's soul into his body after drinking. A celebration of the marvelous from director Kobayashi, KWAIDAN's haunting poetry is conveyed not only in its beautiful color images, but also through the chilling soundtrack. Winner of the Special Jury Prize at the 1965 Cannes Film festival. The videocassette is in Japanese with English subtitles, though the widescreen Tohoscope compositions are lost on tape.

p, Shigeru Watasuki; d, Masaki Kobayashi; w, Yoko Mizuki (based on the stories of Lafcadio Hearn); ph, Yoshio Miyajima (Tohoscope, Eastmancolor); ed, Hisashi Sagara; m, Toru Takemitsu.

Horror **(PR:O MPAA:NR)**

L

LA BALANCE**½

(1982, Fr.) 102m Ariane-Films A2-Spectrafilm/Gala c (AKA: THE NARK)

Nathalie Baye *(Nicole),* Philippe Leotard *(Dede),* Richard Berry *(Palouzi),* Christophe Malavoy *(Tintin),* Jean-Paul Connart *(Le Belge),* Bernard Freyd *(Le Capitaine),* Albert Dray *(Carlini),* Florent Pagny *(Simoni),* Jean-Daniel Laval *(Arnaud),* Luc-Antoine Diquero *(Picard),* Maurice Ronet *(Massina),* Tcheky Karyo *(Petrovic),* Anne-Claude Salimo *(Sabrina),* Michel Anphoux *(Guy),* Raouf Ben Yaghlane *(Djerbi),* Robert Atlan *(Ayouche),* Guy Dhers *(Calemard),* Francois Berleand *(Inspector Mondaine),* Sam Karmann *(Paulo),* Galia Dujardin, Andrey Laxinni.

American expatriate director Bob Swaim took the standard Hollywood gangster expectations, added a decidedly Parisian spin and some authentic local grit, and wound up giving the European audience just what it wanted. One-time mobster Dede (Philippe Leotard) and prostitute Nicole (Nathalie Baye) play a power game with the sleazy cops trying to pressure them into informing. Dede and Nicole are trying to live a quiet existence on the money she earns from her tricks; however, cop Palouzi (Berry) is less concerned with their struggles than he is with busting a crime ring headed by a former associate of Dede's. If Dede cooperates, the police will leave them alone. Unfortunately for Dede, he doesn't like the idea of being a stoolie or winding up dead. There are some nice moments here—the colorful opening sequence and an unlikely traffic jam shootout that results in a cop's Walkman stopping a bullet—but it all just adds up to some gritty Saturday night entertainment without much thought involved. Loved by the French, LA BALANCE garnered a number of Cesars, including one for Best Picture. The videocassette is dubbed in English.

p, Georges Dancigers, Alexandre Mnouchkine; d, Bob Swaim; w, Bob Swaim, M. Fabiani; ph, Bernard Zitzermann (Eastmancolor); ed, Francoise Javet; m, Roland Bocquet.

Crime **(PR:O MPAA:R)**

LA BETE HUMAINE****

(1938, Fr.) 105m Paris/Juno bw (AKA: THE HUMAN BEAST)

Jean Gabin *(Jacques Lantier),* Simone Simon *(Severine),* Fernand Ledoux *(Roubaud),* Julien Carette *(Pecqueux),* Blanchette Brunoy *(Flore),* Jean Renoir *(Cabuche),* Gerard Landry *(Dauvergne's Son),* Jenny Helia *(Philomene),* Colette Regis *(Victoire),* Jacques Berlioz *(Grand-Morin),* Leon Larive *(Grand-Morin's servant),* Georges Spanelly *(Camy-Lamothe),* Emile Genevois, Jacques Brunius *(Farmhands),* Marcel Perez *(Lampmaker),* Claire Gerard *(Traveler),* Tony Corteggiani *(Supervisor),* Guy Decomble *(Gate Keeper).*

Locomotive engineer Jacques Lantier (Jean Gabin) is infatuated with Severin (Simone Simon), the beautiful but dangerous young wife of assistant stationmaster Roubaud (Fernand Ledoux). When Roubaud learns that Severin secured his job by sleeping with his superior, he goes mad with jealousy. With the aid of Severin, he kills his superior, an act blamed on an innocent poacher but witnessed by Lantier. Roubaud then sends his wife to Lantier as a means of ensuring the engineer's silence. Again Severin's bedroom prowess secures a lover's loyalty, resulting in a romance between the pair, whereupon Severin tries to persuade Lantier to kill Roubaud. Based on the novel by Emile Zola (whose *Nana* was also adapted by Jean Renoir in 1926), LA BETE HUMAINE features one of Jean Gabin's greatest performances—one with even more force than the locomotive he powers. The catlike Simon is perfect as the persuasive beauty who drives both of the men in her life to their destructive deeds, her unattainable love their tragic downfall. This picture was remade by Fritz Lang as HUMAN DESIRE, Lang's second remake of a Renoir film. The first was SCARLET STREET, a remake of LA CHIENNE. In French with English subtitles.

p, Robert Hakim, Raymond Hakim; d, Jean Renoir; w, Jean Renoir (based on the novel by Emile Zola); ph, Curt Courant; ed, Marguerite Renoir, Suzanne de Troeye; m, Joseph Kosma.

Drama **(PR:A MPAA:NR)**

LA BOUM**½

(1981, Fr.) 108m Triumph c

Claude Brasseur *(Francois),* Brigitte Fossey *(Francoise),* Sophie Marceau *(Vic),* Denise Grey *(Poupette),* Dominque Lavanant *(Vanessa),* Bernard Giraudeau *(Eric).*

Vic (Sophie Marceau) is a spunky 13-year-old French girl who is trying to make it through adolescence despite the shaky relationship of her likable parents (Claude Brasseur and Brigitte Fossey). Blossoming into a young woman, she discovers the Parisian social scene and all its vices—boys, dancing, drinking—through a series of *boums*, teen parties. The situations are just what you'd expect from such a film—cute, charming, funny, awkward, and nostalgic. What separates this film from scores of others just like it is the bubbly Marceau. A huge box-office hit in France, LA BOUM spawned an unimaginatively titled sequel, LA BOUM II, in 1983. In French with English subtitles.

p, Alain Poire; d, Claude Pinoteau; w, Daniele Thompson, Claude Pinoteau; ph, Edmond Sechan; ed, Marie-Josephe Yoyotte; m, Vladimir Cosma.

Drama **(PR:A MPAA:PG)**

LA CAGE AUX FOLLES****

(1979, Fr./It.) 103m Artistes-DaMa/UA c (AKA: THE MAD CAGE; BIRDS OF A FEATHER)

Ugo Tognazzi *(Renato),* Michel Serrault *(Albin/"Zaza"),* Michel Galabru *(Charrier),* Claire Maurier *(Simone),* Remy Laurent *(Laurent),* Benny Luke *(Jacob),* Carmen Scarpitta *(Madame Charrier),* Luisa Maneri *(Andrea).*

In less sure hands, this could have wound up as a disaster, but director Edouard Molinaro was able to skillfully lens the long-running play (more than seven years) and wring every drop of humor from it. Renato (Ugo Tognazzi) and Albin (Michel Serrault) have been lovers for more than 20 years. Albin is the lead "drag queen" of La Cage Aux Folles, a Saint Tropez nightclub, and Renato, the more masculine of the two, runs the day-to-day operations of the boite. Many years before, Renato stepped out of his gay lifestyle long enough to father Laurent (Remy Laurent) in a one-night stand, and since then both men have raised the boy. Now, Laurent comes home from college with the news that he is engaged to Andrea (Luisa Maneri), whose father, Charrier (Michel Galabru), is the secretary of the blue-nosed Union of Moral Order. As a result, Laurent has lied about his parentage and told his future father-in-law that his father is a cultural attache. From this set-up alone, one can guess that the situations that follow—revolving around Charrier's meeting with Renato—lead to some riotous results. LA CAGE AUX FOLLES earned more than $40 million, and spawned a pair of dreadful sequels and a fabulously successful stage musical. Serrault won a Cesar as Best Actor and the film was nominated for Best Direction, Screenplay, and Costume Design Oscars. Despite the apparent risk of making a movie with two gay leads, it was basically an old-fashioned bedroom farce, and tamer than most, at that. French dubbed into English.

p, Marcello Danon; d, Edouard Molinaro; w, Marcello Danon, Edouard Molinaro, Francis Veber, Jean Poiret (based on the play by Jean Poiret); ph, Armando Mannuzzi (Eastmancolor); ed, Robert Isnardon, Monique Isnardon; m, Ennio Morricone.

Comedy **(PR:O MPAA:R)**

LA CAGE AUX FOLLES II**

(1980, It./Fr.) 100m Da Ma/UA c

Ugo Tognazzi *(Renato Baldi),* Michel Serrault *(Albin Mougeotte/Zaza Napoli),* Gianni Frisoni *(Barman at Cabaret),* Mark Bodin *(Caramel),* Benny Luke *(Jacob),* Gianrico Tondinelli *(Walter),* Philippe Cronenberver *(Waiter/Negresco),* Francis Missana *(Handsome Young Man),* Marie-Claude Douquet *(Pretty Girl),* Ricardo Berlingeri *(Desk Clerk-Hotel de Lys),* Piero Morgia *(Killer in Hotel),* Marcel Bozzuffi *(Broca),* Michel Galabru *(Simon Charrier),* Giovanni Vettorazzo *(Milan),* Pierre Desmet *(Proprietor Le Roi du Bleu),* Tom Felleghy *(Andrew Manderstam),* Danilo Recanatesi *(Dr. Boquillon),* Nello Pazzafini *(Mangin),* Renato Basso *(Rouget),* Antonio Francioni *(Michaux),* Nazareno Natale *(Demis),* Stelio Candelli *(Hans).*

Spurred by the huge success of LA CAGE AUX FOLLES, the producers rushed this sequel into the works and came up short in every way. Whereas the first film had lots of heart, this is just another spy picture with the added twist that the two heroes are heroines with baritone voices. Albin (Michel Serrault) thinks that Renato (Ugo Tognazzi) no longer finds him attractive so he seeks to make him jealous, dresses up in drag, and is picked up in a cafe by a spy who is escaping enemy agents. The spy uses Albin as his getaway cover but, in no time, Albin has the precious microfilm in his possession. Benny Luke reprises his role as the maid, as does Michel Galabru as Albin and Renato's son's father-in-law (see LA CAGE AU FOLLES, above). Whatever comedy is in the picture is provided by Serrault as he sings, tries to be macho (as he did in the first film), faces down the villains, etc. Tognazzi, on the other hand, doesn't have much to do and the picture just sort of lies there. The producers had planned to make a few more CAGE sequels but this was such a dud that only one more shot was fired in 1985, thankfully. Italian dubbed into English.

p, Marcello Danon; d, Edouard Molinaro; w, Francis Veber (based on a story by Marcello Danon, Jean Poiret Francis Veber); ph, Armando Nannuzzi (Technicolor); ed, Robert Isnardon; m, Ennio Morricone.

Comedy **(PR:A-C MPAA:R)**

LA CAGE AUX FOLLES 3: THE WEDDING**

(1985, Fr./It.) 87m DaMa-COL/WB-COL-Tri-Star c

Michel Serrault *(Albin Mougeotte),* Ugo Tognazzi *(Renato Baldi),* Benny Luke *(Jacob),* Stephane Audran *(Matrimonia),* Antonella Interlenghi *(Cindy),* Saverio Vallone *(Mortimer),* Gianluca Favilla *(Dulac),* Umberto Ramo *(Kennedy).*

The third time was not a charm as the same actors came

back for yet another go-around at drag comedy. It took no less than seven writers to conjure up this story, which is, at best, serviceable. Albin (Michel Serrault), the flashy member of the French cinema's best-loved gay couple, is still living with Renato (Ugo Tognazzi), the straighter of the duo. Their nightclub in St Tropez has fallen upon hard times, and Albin is preparing to star in a new revue they hope will bring the customers flocking back. If they can raise enough money to pay for new costumes, he will be the "Queen of Bees," and when Albin's uncle dies in Scotland and leaves his nephew a hefty inheritance, Renato is thrilled. There is a catch, however; to collect Albin will have to marry and sire a child within 18 months. Benny Luke and Michel Galabru again reprise their roles, but this time director Edouard Molinaro hands over the duties to Georges Lautner. Although this is a pleasant enough picture and Serrault's hysterical characterization offers plenty of laughs, both this entry and LA CAGE AUX FOLLES II pale in comparison with the original. Italian dubbed into English.

p, Marcello Danon; d, Georges Lautner; w, Philippe Nicaud, Christine Carere, Marcello Danon, Jacques Audiard, Michel Audiard, Georges Lautner, Gerard Lamballe (based on the characters in Jean Poiret's play); ph, Luciano Tovoli (Eastmancolor); ed, Michelle David; m, Ennio Morricone.

Comedy **(PR:C MPAA:NR)**

LA CHEVRE***

(1981, Fr./Mex.) 91m GAU-Fideline-Conacine/European Classics c

Pierre Richard *(Francois Perrin),* Gerard Depardieu *(Campana),* Corynne Charbit *(Marie Bens),* Michel Robin *(Mr. Bens),* Andre Valardy *(Meyer),* Pedro Armendariz, Jr. *(Custao),* Maritza Olivares, Jorge Luke, Sergio Calderon, Robert Balban, Michel Fortin, Jean-Louis Fortuit, Jacqueline Noelle, Marjorie Godin, Pulchier Castan.

The French box-office champ in 1981, LA CHEVRE, a lightweight comedy from the predictable Francis Veber, managed to send audiences home laughing in its native country, though it wasn't released in the US until 1985. Veber, cowriter of THE TALL BLOND MAN WITH ONE BLACK SHOE and its sequel, THE RETURN OF THE TALL BLOND MAN WITH ONE BLACK SHOE, continues the exploits of klutzy amateur detective Francois Perrin (Pierre Richard), who is here paired with logic-obsessed investigator Campana (Gerard Depardieu). When accident-prone heiress Marie Bens (Corynne Charbit) disappears in Rio, her father sends Perrin and Campana to track her. Perrin, who is equally as clumsy as Bens, retraces her steps exactly, falling into the same traps and stumbling over the same clues. Not surprisingly, Campana is amazed that Perrin's methods prove more effective than logic and deduction. Of course, it all works out neatly in the end. A highly entertaining, funny, well-crafted film that boasts a wonderful chemistry between its stars. Depardieu, Richard, and Veber would team up again in 1983 in the superior LES COMPERES. In French with English subtitles.

p, Alain Poire; d, Francis Veber; w, Francis Veber; ph, Alex Phillips; ed, Albert Jurgenson; m, Vladimir Cosma.

Comedy **(PR:A MPAA:NR)**

LA CIUDAD Y LOS PERROS***½

(1985, Peru) 144m Cinevista c (AKA: THE CITY AND THE DOGS)

Pablo Serra *(Poet),* Gustavo Bueno *(Lt. Gamboa),* Juan Manuel Ochoa *(Jaguar),* Luis Alvarez *(Colonel),* Eduardo Adrianzen *(Slave),* Liliana Navarro *(Teresa),* Miguel Iza *(Arrospide).*

Based on a novel by Mario Vargas Llosa, this often engrossing tale of shifting loyalties and revenge is set in the volatile, hierarchical, rigidly codified world of a boys' military academy. The unofficial leaders among the students are called "The Circle," a powerful unit that trades in contraband. Another boy (Pablo Serra), known as "The Poet," has found his niche by writing love letters and erotic stories for his classmates, and is the only confidante—although an untrustworthy one—of "The Slave" (Eduardo Adrianzen), a cowardly scapegoat. When The Slave is killed under mysterious circumstances, the stage is set for a confrontation between The Poet and The Circle's leader (Juan Manuel Ochoa), with critical results for the brutal army official who oversees the boys' activities (Gustavo Bueno). Producer-director Francisco J. Lombardi's portrayal of the boys' daily discipline is as unflinching as any of the boot camp scenes in FULL METAL JACKET; in the opening scenes, particularly, we are presented with a surrealistic glimpse of the inferno. The film is especially compelling in its study of the multifaceted nature of honor, with the various cadres and relationships marked by strict codes of behavior that prohibit even the smallest deviation. Aided by his first-rate ensemble cast, Lombardi succeeds in giving a strong sense of underlying tension to the emotionally charged events.

p, Francisco J. Lombardi; d, Francisco J. Lombardi; w, Jose Watanabe (based on the novel by Mario Vargas Llosa); ph, Pili Flores Guerra.

Drama **(PR:O MPAA:NR)**

LA DOLCE VITA*****

(1960, It./Fr.) 180m Riama-Pathe-Gray-Astor/AIP bw

Marcello Mastroianni *(Marcello Rubini),* Anita Ekberg *(Sylvia),* Anouk Aimee *(Maddalena),* Yvonne Furneaux *(Emma),* Magali Noel *(Fanny),* Alain Cuny *(Steiner),* Nadia Gray *(Nadia),* Lex Barker *(Robert),* Annibale Ninchi *(Marcello's Father),* Walter Santesso *(Paparazzo),* Jacques Sernas *(Matinee Idol),* Valeria Ciangottini *(Paola),* Alan Dijon *(Frankie Stout),* Renee Longarini *(Signora Steiner),* Polidor *(Clown),* Giulio Questi *(Don Giulio),* Leonardo Botta *(Doctor),* Harriet White *(Sylvia's Secretary),* Gio Staiano *(Effeminate Male),* Carlo Di Maggio *(Producer),* Adriano Celentano *(Rock-n-Roll Singer),* Alfredo Rizzo *(Television Director),* Marianna Leibl *(Yvonne's Companion),* Iris Tree *(Poetess),* Lilly Granado *(Lucy),* Gloria Jones *(Gloria),* Nico Otzak *(Sophisticated Prostitute).*

This beautifully photographed and confounding picture begins as a large statue of Christ is flown over the city by a helicopter, hanging from a cable with its arms outstretched and casting a shadow over the buildings below. Following in a second chopper is Marcello Rubini (Marcello Mastroianni), a gossip writer for the local scandal sheet, whose mouth waters at the female sunbathers on the rooftops below. What follows is Marcello's hedonistic journey through Rome, where he witnesses the decadence and shallowness of "the sweet life" around him, yet refuses to take a stance or gather an opinion on the world around him. The central event in the film is his meeting with movie starlet Sylvia (Anita Ekberg). He is soon infatuated with the buxom blonde and takes her on a whirlwind tour of Rome, including all the usual spots—the Trevi Fountain, St. Peter's Basilica, the Caracalla Baths—and one less usual spot, a dingy nightclub nestled in an ancient Roman ruin. After receiving a beating from Sylvia's fiance Robert (Lex Barker), Marcello covers a story about two small children who have had a vision of the Blessed Virgin—a "miracle" which turns out to be a hoax. While its meanings are as varied as its viewers, LA DOLCE VITA contains humor, darkness, nobility, and tawdriness and a breadth of vision that blend together to become a total cinematic experience. While the viewer is not always sure where Fellini is taking us (even Fellini has seemed unsure when confronted with revealing the film's meaning), the journey is still a pleasure. In and of itself, LA DOLCE VITA may be an impenetrable moral tale, but when compared to his earlier picture I VITELLONI, with Mastroianni's character (initially named Moraldo) seen as an extension of the young Moraldo, Fellini's intentions become clearer. One other clue may be Fellini's early title for the film, "Babylon—2,000 Years After Christ." Winner of the Grand Prize at the Cannes Film Festival. In Italian with English subtitles.

p, Giuseppe Amato, Angelo Rizzoli; d, Federico Fellini; w, Federico Fellini, Ennio Flaiano, Tullio Pinelli, Brunello Rondi (based on a story by Fellini, Flaiano, Pinelli); ph, Otello Martelli (Totalscope); ed, Leo Catozzo; m, Nino Rota.

Drama **(PR:C MPAA:NR)**

LA MARSEILLAISE***½

(1938, Fr.) 130m La Marseillaise Society/World bw

Pierre Renoir *(Louis XVI),* Lise Delamare *(Marie Antoinette),* Leon Larive *(Picard),* William Haguet *(La Rochefoucald-Liancourt),* Louis Jouvet *(Roederer),* Aime Clairond *(M. de Saint-Laurent),* Maurice Escande *(Le Seigneur du Village),* Andre Zibral *(M. de Saint Merri),* Andrex *(Arnaud),* Ardisson *(Bomier),* Paul Dullac *(Javel),* Fernand Flamant *(Ardisson),* Jean-Louis Allibert *(Moissan),* Nadia Siberskaia *(Louison),* Jeanna Hella *(The Interpellant),* G. Lefebure *(Mme. Elizabeth),* Pamela Stirling, Genia Vaury *(Servants),* Jean Aquistapace *(The Mayor),* Georges Spanelly *(La Chesnaye),* Pierre Nay *(Dubouchage),* Jaque Catelain *(Capt. Langlade),* Edmond Castle *(Leroux),* Jean Ayme *(M. de Fougerolles),* Irene Joachim *(Mme. de Saint-Laurent),* Alex Truchy *(Cuculiere).*

The story is of the march on Paris by a battalion of 500 volunteers that arrives in time to capture the Tuilleries, leading to the publication of the Brunswick Manifesto and the overthrow of the monarchy of Louis XVI. Essentially the film contrasts the lives of commoners and aristocracy as the grand march proceeds from Marseilles to Paris, to the accompaniment of the most patriotic French song, "La Marseillaise," which the peasants enthusiastically sing, first as a quiet melody and later as an anthem. Doing what he does best, Jean Renoir provides a naturalistic, near-documentary portrait of the characters. In one sense, LA MARSEILLAISE is even something of a western, with its march paralleling the wagon train's trek. Released on the heels of the brilliant GRAND ILLUSION, this picture suffered from the critical prejudice that a director *can't* make two masterpieces in a row. A vastly inferior 79-minute version was released in the US in 1939. In French with English subtitles.

d, Jean Renoir; w, Jean Renoir, Carl Koch, N. Martel Dreyfus, Mme. Jean-Paul Dreyfus; ph, Jean Bourgoin, Alain Douarinou, Jean-Marie Maillols, Jean-Paul Alphen, J. Louis; ed, Marguerite Renoir, Marthe Huguet; m, Jean Philippe Rameau, Johann Sebastian Bach, Wolfgang Amadeus Mozart, Rouget de l'Isle.

Historical **(PR:A MPAA:NR)**

LA NUIT DE VARENNES***

(1982, Fr./It.) 135m Gaumont-COL/Triumph c

Marcello Mastroianni *(Casanova),* Jean-Louis Barrault *(Nicolas Edme Restif),* Hanna Schygulla *(Countess Sophie de la Borde),* Harvey Keitel *(Thomas Paine),* Jean-Claude Brialy *(Mons. Jacob),* Daniel Gelin *(De Wendel),* Jean-Louis Trintignant *(Mons. Sauce),* Michel Piccoli *(King Louis XVI),* Eleonore Hirt *(Queen Marie-Antoinette),* Andrea Ferreol *(Mme. Adelaide Gagnon),* Michel Vitold *(De Florange),* Laura Betti *(Virginia Capacelli),* Enzo Jannacci *(Italian Barker),* Pierre Malet *(Emile Delage),* Hugues Quester *(Jean-Louis Romeuf),* Dora Doll *(Nanette Precy),* Caterina Boratto *(Mme. Faustine),* Didi Porego *(Mme. Sauce),* Evelyne Dress *(Agnes Restif),* Aline Messe *(Marie Madeleine),* Patrick Osmond *(National Guard Commander),* Jacques Peyrac *(Outrider),* Yves Collignon *(Drouet),* Agnes Nobecourt *(Hubertine),* Claude LeGors, Vernon Dobtcheff, Ugo Fangareggi.

This good, often bizarre, historical drama begins with a basis in fact and runs wild with imaginative possibilities. King Louis XVI (Michel Piccoli) and his queen (Eleonore Hirt) flee Paris for the safety of Varennes at the height of the French Revolution. Close behind in a pursuing coach, bickering about life and politics, are Casanova (Marcello Mastroianni, in an excellent performance) and American revolutionary Thomas Paine (Harvey Keitel). All the while, the revolution spreads like wildfire. As with other recent films by Italian director Ettore Scola—LE BAL; MACARONI; THE FAMILY—the exploration of the past becomes a vehicle for understanding today's problems and those of the future. Besides the pluses of the lush photography and elegant costumes, Scola again works with an excellent cast that reads as a virtual Who's Who of European cinema—Mastroianni, Piccoli, Jean-Louis Barrault, Hanna Schygulla, Jean-Claude Brialy, Jean-Louis Trintignant, Andrea Ferreol, Daniel Gelin. In Italian with English subtitles.

p, Renzo Rossellini; d, Ettore Scola; w, Ettore Scola, Sergio Amidei; ph, Armando Nannuzzi; ed, Raimondo Crociani; m, Armando Trovaioli.

Historical/Comedy **(PR:O MPAA:R)**

LA PASSANTE***

(1982, Fr./Ger.) 115m Elephant-Films A2-CCC-COKG/ Cinema 5 c (LA PASSANTE DU SANS-SOUCI; Trans: The Passer-by of the "Sans Souci" Cafe)

Romy Schneider *(Elsa Weiner/Lina Baumstein),* Michel Piccoli *(Max Baumstein),* Wendelin Werner *(Max, as a Child),* Helmut Griem *(Michel Weiner),* Gerard Klein *(Maurice Bouillard),* Dominique Labourier *(Charlotte Maupas),* Mathieu Carriere *(Ruppert von Leggaert /Federico Lego),* Maria Schell *(Anna Hellwig).*

This complex French-German coproduction features Romy Schneider in a dual role as a German living in Occupied Paris and as the present-day wife of a human rights activist. The activist, Max Baumstein (Michel Piccoli), kills the Paraguayan ambassador when he learns that the politician is not only a former Nazi, but the general who ordered the death of his adoptive parents. In flashback, the young Max is taken to Paris by Elsa Weiner (Schneider), whose husband, Michel (Helmut Griem), is sent to a concentration camp because of his anti-Fascist publications. As a result, Elsa is forced to support herself as a singer in Pigalle, eventually giving up her body to a Nazi general who promises to arrange for Michel's release. The familiar story of former SS men altering their identities and rising in the South American political ranks is intelligently handled in LA PASSANTE, though the obviousness of director Jacques Rouffio sometimes undermines the subject matter's inherent power. This was the final screen appearance for Romy Schneider, who died just days before the film's release. In French with English subtitles.

p, Raymond Danon; d, Jacques Rouffio; w, Jacques Rouffio, Jacques Kirsner (based on the novel by Joseph Kessel); ph, Jean Penzer; ed, Anna Ruiz; m, Georges Delerue.

Drama **(PR:C MPAA:NR)**

LA RONDE****

(1950, Fr.) 97m Commercial bw

Anton Walbrook *(Raconteur),* Simone Signoret *(Leocadie the Prostitute),* Serge Reggiani *(Franz, the Soldier),* Simone Simon *(Marie, the Maid),* Daniel Gelin *(Alfred),* Danielle Darrieux *(Emma Breitkopf),* Fernand Gravey *(Charles, Emma's Husband),* Odette Joyeux *(The Grisette),* Jean-Louis Barrault *(Robert Kuhlenkampf),* Isa Miranda *(The Actress),* Gerard Philipe *(The Count),* Robert Vattier *(Prof. Schuller).*

Max Ophuls' merry-go-round of romance episodically presents a series of characters, drifting from one sequence to the next as they switch from one lover to another. Leocadie (Simone Signoret), a young prostitute, meets Franz (Serge Reggiani), a soldier who leaves her for housemaid Marie (Simone Simon). Marie then meets Alfred (Daniel Gelin), who seduces the married Emma (Danielle Darrieux), whose husband is involved with a young worker (Odette Joyeux). She loves the poet Robert (Jean-Louis Barrault), who in turn loves the actress Charlotte (Isa Miranda), who gives her affections to a count (Gerard Philippe). Love comes full circle when the count calls on Leocadie, the hooker from the first episode. Each segment is held together by a master of ceremonies (Anton Walbrook), who appears with a symbolic carousel in each of his scenes. Set in the fairy-tale world of turn-of-the-century Vienna, LA RONDE is a dazzling and dizzying account of lovers loved and lovers lost, an eternal merry-go-round of unreciprocated emotion. Ophuls' first production after returning to French soil, marking the end of his spotty career in Hollywood, LA RONDE was the first of four superb films he completed before his death in 1957. Like the never-ending circular merry-go-round journey with which he represents the inevitability of love, Ophuls' direction is perfect and seamless. In French with English subtitles.

p, Sacha Gordine; d, Max Ophuls; w, Max Ophuls, Jacques Natanson (based on the play "Der Reigen" by Arthur Schnitzler); ph, Christian Matras; ed, Leonide Azar; m, Oscar Strauss.

Drama **(PR:O MPAA:NR)**

LA STRADA*****

(1954, It.) 115m Trans-LUX bw (AKA: THE ROAD)

Anthony Quinn *(Zampano),* Giulietta Masina *(Gelsomina Di Costanzo),* Richard Basehart *(Il Matto, "The Fool"),* Aldo Silvani *(Colombaioni),* Marcella Rovere *(The Widow),* Livia Venturini *(The Nun).*

Federico Fellini was at the top of his form here, as was his wife and frequent star, Giulietta Masina, whose pantomime in LA STRADA caused her to dubbed a female Chaplin. Zampano (Anthony Quinn), a traveling strongman, "buys" the dim-witted but pure of heart Gelsomina (Masina) to help him with his act. The two travel together, with Gelsomina beating the drum and playing a trumpet to herald Zampano's act, becoming mistress and slave to the strongman. Eventually, the pair hooks up with a tiny circus in which they meet *il Matto* ("The Fool," played by Richard Basehart), a clown and high-wire artist who treats Gelsomina kindly. When the ethereal Fool is accidentally killed by the brutish Zampano, Gelsomina is devastated and suffers an emotional breakdown, and the strongman abandons her. Many years later, still traveling, he learns that she has died, and only then realizes his need for her. Perhaps the simplest and one of the most powerful of all Fellini's films, LA STRADA established his international fame while marking a distinct break from Neo-Realism for the director in its lyricism; its poetic, deeply personal imagery (especially the "Felliniesque" circus motif); and its religious symbolism. While Masina's unforgettable performance, perfectly combining comedy and pathos, caused the greatest stir, Quinn and Basehart are also excellent, and Nino Rota's music became famous worldwide. The film won numerous awards, including a Best Foreign-

Language Film Oscar, the Grand Prize at Venice, and the New York Film Critics Award. The videocassette is available in both dubbed and subtitled (Italian into English) versions.

p, Carlo Ponti, Dino De Laurentiis; d, Federico Fellini; w, Federico Fellini, Tullio Pinelli, Ennio Flaiano (based on a story by Federico Fellini, Tullio Pinelli); ph, Otello Martelli; ed, Leo Catozzo, Lina Caterini; m, Nino Rota.

Drama **(PR:A-C MPAA:NR)**

LA TERRA TREMA****

(1947, It.) 165m Universalia/Mario De Vecchi bw (AKA: THE EARTH TREMBLES)

Luchino Visconti, Antonio Pietrangeli *(Narrators),* Antonio Arcidiacono *('Ntoni),* Giuseppe Arcidiacono *(Cola),* Giovanni Greco *(Grandfather),* Nelluccia Giammona *(Mara),* Agnese Giammona *(Lucia),* Nicola Castorina *(Nicola),* Rosario Galvagno *(Don Salvatore),* Lorenzo Valastro *(Lorenzo),* Rosa Costanzo *(Nedda).*

With a lyrical quality that subtly combines photographic beauty with the cruel plight of its subjects, LA TERRA TREMA is one of the finest films to emerge from the Italian Neo-Realist movement. Set in Aci-Trezza, a small Sicilian fishing village, with the entire cast consisting of locals—their weather-beaten faces lending a sense of realism—the film involves the villagers' victimization by the entrepreneurs who control the fishing market. One young man, 'Ntoni (Antonio Arcidiacono), returns home from WW II convinced that the villagers need no longer be subject to such unfairness, that by pulling together they can alter the system and eventually overcome their imposed poverty. LA TERRA TREMA is a powerful picture that exposes the injustice inherent in a society where the privileged are allowed to ride roughshod over their inferiors. Despite its social import, the film was a terrible failure at the Italian theaters. It's historical significance, however, is immense. The use of non-professionals, cinema-verite and deep-focus photography, and direct sound recording, while rarely seen in Italian films of the day, were all integral to LA TERRA TREMA—products undoubtedly of Visconti's work with Jean Renoir. Serving as assistant directors on this picture were Francesco Rosi and Franco Zeffirelli, both of whom would eventually become leading directors. For his next film, BELLISSIMA, Visconti would discover a style which combined Neo-Realistic photography and dramatic stylization. In French with English subtitles.

p, Salvo D'Angelo; d, Luchino Visconti; w, Luchino Visconti (based on the novel *I Malavoglia* by Giovanni Verga); ph, G.R. Aldo; ed, Mario Serandrei; m, Luchino Visconti, Willy Ferrero.

Drama **(PR:A MPAA:NR)**

LA TRAVIATA****

(1982, It.) 105m Accent-R.A.I./UNIV c

Teresa Stratas *(Violetta Valery),* Placido Domingo *(Alfredo Germont),* Cornell MacNeil *(Giorgio Germont),* Alan Monk *(Baron),* Axelle Gall *(Flora Betvoix),* Pina Cei *(Annina),* Maurizio Barbacini *(Gastone),* Robert Sommer *(Doctor Grenvil),* Ricardo Oneto *(Marquis d'Obigny),* Luciano Brizi *(Giuseppe),* Tony Ammirati *(Messenger),* Russell Christopher, Charles Antony, Geraldine Decker, Michael Best, Ferruccio Furlanetto, Ariel Bybee, Richard Vernon, Ekaterina Maksimova, Vladimir Vassiljev, Gabriella Borni.

Franco Zeffirelli's version of the classic Verdi opera stars Teresa Stratas as Violetta and Placido Domingo as her lover Alfredo. Zeffirelli outdoes himself this time, offering no less than the cinema's finest opera adaptation. LA TRAVIATA boasts not only the presence of Domingo and Stratas (Lotte Lenya's heir as interpreter of Kurt Weill) but some truly amazing camerawork. Cameraman Ennio Guarnieri and art director Gianni Quaranta have combined to deliver a flowing, sparkling set that is an elaborate feast for the eyes—a worthy accompaniment to the brilliant score. And the camera dollies, zooms, cranes, and pans relentlessly showcase the gigantic, elaborately constructed set. After watching this film (opera lover or not) you'll wonder what possessed director Zeffirelli to make ENDLESS LOVE. LA TRAVIATA was an Academy Award nominee for Best Set Design and Best Costumes. In Italian with English subtitles.

p, Tarak Ben Ammar; d, Franco Zeffirelli; w, Franco Zeffirelli (based on the libretto by Francesco Maria Piave from the novel by Alexandre Dumas entitled *The Lady of the* Camelias); ph, Ennio Guarnieri; ed, Peter Taylor, Franca Sylvi; m, Giuseppe Verdi.

Musical **(PR:A MPAA:G)**

LA TRUITE (THE TROUT)***

(1982, Fr.) 104m Gaumont-TFI-SFPC/Triumph c

Isabelle Huppert *(Frederique),* Jean-Pierre Cassel *(Rambert),* Jeanne Moreau *(Lou),* Daniel Olbrychski *(Saint-Genis),* Jacques Speisser *(Galuchat),* Isao Yamagata *(Daigo Hamada),* Lisette Malidor *(Mariline),* Jean-Paul Roussillon *(Pere Verjon),* Roland Bertin *(The Count),* Craig Stevens *(Carter),* Alexis Smith *(Gloria),* Ruggero Raimondi *(Himself),* Lucas Delvaux *(Young Employee).*

The adventures of a French country girl-turned-entrepreneur are chronicled in this, Joseph Losey's penultimate film (STEAMING, 1985, was his last). Isabelle Huppert stars as Frederique, who, as the film opens, works on her father's trout farm and exploits her male coworkers' lust, on a look-but-don't-touch basis, for money. She marries Galuchat (Jacques Speisser), a latent homosexual with whom she has a close but unconsummated relationship. The pair falls in with some rich friends, and Frederique goes off with one of them to Japan, where, again, the promise of an affair is never fulfilled. After Galuchat tries to kill himself, she returns home, and the couple is taken in by the wealthy Rambert (Jean-Pierre Cassel) and his wife, Lou (Jeanne Moreau), in a strange menage that ends as Rambert, frustrated by Frederique's sexual indifference, kills Lou. Finally, Frederique settles down with Galuchat, now an alcoholic, to run a highly lucrative Japanese trout farm. Losey had wanted to film

Roger Vailland's novel for years, and the director's familiar concern with sex and class as expressions of power, egotism vs. love, and spiritual corruption are in place. These themes are somewhat undercut, however, by his ever-stylish direction and the gorgeous visuals from cinematographer Henri Alekan and production designer Alexandre Trauner. Huppert's character is essentially a mystery, and she gives an appropriately enigmatic performance, keeping the audience at an emotional distance. Losey's self-described "most open-ended" film, LA TRUITE is intriguing and beautiful to watch, but ultimately unsatisfying as either social comedy or allegory. In French with English subtitles.

p, Yves Rousset-Rouard; d, Joseph Losey; w, Joseph Losey, Monique Lange (based on the novel by Roger Vailland); ph, Henri Alekan (Eastmancolor); ed, Marie Castro-Vasquez; m, Richard Hartley.

Drama **(PR:O MPAA:R)**

L'ADDITION***

(1984, Fr.) 85m Swanie-TF1-UGC/NW c

Richard Berry *(Bruno Winkler),* Richard Bohringer *(Albert Lorca),* Farid Chopel *(Jose),* Fabrice Eberhard *(Minet),* Daniel Sarky *(Constantini),* Simon Reggiani *(Lenuzza),* Jacques Sereys *(Prison Guard),* Riton Liebman *(Jeannot),* Luc Florian *(Supermarket Security Man),* George Blaness, Julien Bukowski, Gerard Gaillaud, Yvone Daoudi, Serge Feuillard, Alain Frerot.

At the center of this curious and brutal prison drama is Bruno (Richard Berry), an unemployed actor who is arrested as an accomplice when he comes to the aid of beautiful shoplifter (Victoria Abril). While serving a short sentence, he inadvertently gets involved in a prison break during which guard Lorca (Richard Bohringer) is shot in the knee. When apprehended, Bruno becomes the victim of the now-crippled Lorca's psychotic terrorism. Doing his best to emulate Hollywood, director Denis Amar has come up with a compelling picture that pits two intense personalities in a violent, existential battle. Like the main character in Robert Bresson's 1984 film L'ARGENT (which is, in all ways, vastly superior to L'ADDITION), Bruno is caught in a Dostoyevskian swirl of fate that begins with a minor infraction and builds to murder. Unfortunately, all three of the main characters in this film are hollow shells who exist only as cogs in Amar's filmmaking machinery. Nonetheless, the always impressive Bohringer creates a mysterious, dangerous monster, and while not his best performance, it did manage to earn him a Cesar as Best Supporting Actor. Beware that the voices in the dubbed videocassette version are all unnervingly American.

p, Norbert Saada; d, Denis Amar; w, Jean Curtelin (based on the story by Jean-Pierre Bastid, Jean Curtelin, Denis Amar); ph, Robert Fraisse; ed, Jacques Witta; m, Jean-Claude Petit.

Prison **(PR:O MPAA:R)**

LADY CHATTERLEY'S LOVER**

(1955, Fr.) 102m Regie du Film-Orsay/Kingsley bw
(L'AMANT DE LADY CHATTERLEY)

Danielle Darrieux *(Constance Chatterley),* Erno Crisa *(Oliver Mellors),* Leo Genn *(Sir Clifford Chatterley),* Berthe Tissen *(Mrs. Bolton),* Janine Crispin *(Hilda),* Jean Murat *(Winter),* Gerard Sety *(Michaelis),* Jacqueline Noelle *(Bertha).*

D.H. Lawrence's *Lady Chatterley's Lover* was banned in the US for more than 30 years, and this tame film version of the novel met a similar fate. The familiar story revolves around the torrid affair between Constance Chatterley (Danielle Darrieux), the young wife of an impotent aristocrat (Leo Genn) and the estate's gamekeeper (Erno Crisa). Although the controversy surrounding Lawrence's book stemmed from its graphic sexual descriptions, the film eschews steamy depiction, cutting instead to shots of burning embers in the fireplace at the appropriate moments. For some reason New York censors felt that this was enough to warrant reediting before LADY CHATTERLEY'S LOVER was allowed to be released in that state. The film, as they put it, "presented adultery as a desirable, acceptable, and proper pattern of behavior." However, the case went to the Supreme Court, which ruled against the ban. Tame by 1950s standards, LADY CHATTERLEY'S LOVER is even less likely to raise any eyebrows today. But in 1981, soft-core pornography director Just Jaeckin (EMMANUELLE) and soft-core star Sylvia Kristel attempted a racier adaptation of the novel, which, if nothing else, looks good. In French with English subtitles.

p, Gilbert Cohn-Seat; d, Marc Allegret; w, Marc Allegret (based on the novel by D.H. Lawrence and the play by Gaston Bonheur, Philippe de Rothschild); ph, Georges Perinal; ed, Suzanne Troeye; m, Joseph Kosma.

Drama **(PR:A MPAA:NR)**

L'AGE D'OR*****

(1930, Fr.) 60m Corinth bw (AKA: AGE OF GOLD;
Trans: The Golden Age)

Lya Lys *(The Woman),* Gaston Modot *(The Man),* Max Ernst *(Bandit Chief),* Pierre Prevert *(Peman, a Bandit),* Caridad de Labaerdesque, Lionel Salem, Madame Noizet, Jose Artigas, Jacques B. Brunius, Liorens Artigas, Duchange, Ibanez, Pancho Cossio, Valentine Hugo, Marie Berthe Ernst, Simone Cottance, Paul Eluard, Manuel Angeles Ortiz, Juan Esplandio, Pedro Flores, Juan Castane, Joaquin Roa, Pruna, Xaume de Maravilles.

One of the most controversial films of all time, L'AGE D'OR is a surreal inquiry into the traditions and standards of modern culture that have kept true passion and instinct from being freely expressed. Lya Lys and Gaston Modot, simply called The Man and The Woman, are the lovers who allow nothing to prevent them from demonstrating their feelings for each other. They want to make love, but in order to do so they must overcome a number of seemingly insurmountable obstacles, the church, bourgeois social etiquette, and their own psychological handicaps. This love is demonstrated through surreal images that are both funny (a cow lying on a bed and a frustrated man kicking a socialite's obnoxious poodle into the air) and disturbing (a helpless young boy being brutally shot to death), but the overall impact is an expression of love's transcendent power. L'AGE D'OR, like all other Surrealist and Dadaist works, is more than a piece of art, it is a manifesto. It is not an entertainment but a model by which Bunuel, Dali, and their contemporaries expected humankind to live. As the accompanying program for the film read: "It is LOVE that brings about the transition from pessimism to action; Love, denounced in the bourgeois demonology as the root of all evil. For love demands the sacrifice of every other value: status, family, and honor." Although Dali is listed as co-writer, L'AGE D'OR, like UN CHIEN ANDALOU, truly belongs to Bunuel. In French with English subtitles.

p, Charles Vicomte de Noailles; d, Luis Bunuel; w, Luis Bunuel, Salvador Dali; ph, Albert Duverger; ed, Luis Bunuel; m, Van Parys, Wolfgang Amadeus Mozart, Richard Wagner, Felix Mendelssohn, Ludwig van Beethoven, Claude Debussy.

Drama **(PR:C MPAA:NR)**

L'ANNEE DES MEDUSES zero

(1984, Fr.) 110m T-FR3-Parafrance/European c (Trans: The Year of the Jellyfish)

Valerie Kaprisky *(Chris),* Bernard Giraudeau *(Romain),* Caroline Celier *(Claude),* Jacques Perrin *(Vic),* Beatrice Agenin *(Marianne),* Philippe Lemaire *(Lamotte),* Pierre Vaneck *(Pierre),* Barbara Nielsen *(Barbara),* Charlotte Kadi, Betty Assenza.

This worthless exploitation picture was released in France in 1984 but masqueraded as a "French art film" in the US in 1987. The attractive Valerie Kaprisky, who received her "Warholian" moment of fame in 1983's BREATHLESS, plays Chris, an 18-year-old *femme fatale* who spends her summers on the beach at St. Tropez with her 38-year-old mother (Caroline Celier). Both mother and daughter are sexual icons, which breeds something of a rivalry between them. Chris, like everyone else in St. Tropez, disrobes more times than a runway model on amphetamines, proudly parading her bronze body. In time she falls for Romain (Bernard Giraudeau), a local pimp who conducts business from his yacht, but matters are complicated when Mom is also attracted to Giraudeau and tries to keep their rendezvous secret from her disapproving daughter. L'ANNEE DES MEDUSES exists for one reason only—to show countless half-nude women on the beaches of St. Tropez. When this is a film's sole *raison d'etre*, not much can be said about the art of the filmmaking. In contrast, Eric Rohmer has made a career out of filming beautiful young women vacationing on the beaches yet has never resorted to the sort of banalities Christopher Frank employs here. The film tries to cloak its emptiness in some silly metaphors equating the deadly sting of a jellyfish with the treachery of Chris's love, but it's a weak attempt. In French with English subtitles.

p, Alain Terzian; d, Christopher Frank; w, Christopher Frank; ph, Renato Berta; ed, Nathalie Lafaurie; m, Alain Wisniak.

Drama **(PR:O MPAA:NR)**

LAST EMPEROR, THE****

(1987, It./Hong Kong/US) 160m COL c

John Lone *(Aisin-Gioro "Henry" Pu Yi as an Adult),* Joan Chen *(Wan Jung, "Elizabeth"),* Peter O'Toole *(Reginald Johnston, "R.J."),* Ying Ruocheng *(The Governor),* Victor Wong *(Chen Pao Shen),* Dennis Dun *(Big Li),* Ryuichi Sakamoto *(Masahiko Amakasu),* Maggie Han *(Eastern Jewel),* Ric Young *(Interrogator),* Wu Jun Mei *(Wen Hsiu),* Cary Hiroyuki Tagawa *(Chang),* Jade Go *(Ar Mo),* Fumihiko Ikeda *(Yoshioka),* Richard Vuu *(Pu Yi, Age 3),* Tijger Tsou *(Pu Yi, Age 8),* Wu Tao *(Pu Yi, Age 15),* Fan Guang *(Pu Chieh),* Henry Kyi *(Pu Chieh, Age 7),* Alvin Riley III *(Pu Chieh, Age 14),* Lisa Lu *(Tzu Hsui, The Empress Dowager),* Hideo Takamatsu *(Gen. Ishikari),* Hajime Tachibana *(Japanese Translator),* Basil Pao *(Prince Chun),* Jian Xireng *(Lord Chamberlain),* Chen Kai Ge *(Captain of Imperial Guard),* Zhang Liangbin *(Big Foot),* Huang Wenjie *(Hunchback),* Liang Dong *(Lady Aisin-Gioro),* Dong Zhendong *(Old Doctor),* Dong Jiechen *(Doctor),* Constantine Gregory *(Oculist),* Soong Huaikuei *(Lung Yu),* Xu Chunqing *(Grey Eyes),* Zhang Tianmin *(Old Tutor),* Yang Baozong *(Gen. Yuan Shikai),* Cai Hongxiang *(Scarface),* Wu Jun *(Wen Hsiu, Age 12).*

After a six-year absence, Italian director Bernardo Bertolucci returned to the screen with this grand and powerful biography of Aisin-Gioro "Henry" Pu Yi, who in 1908, at the age of three, was named emperor of China and by the end of his life was quietly working as a gardener at Peking's Botanical Gardens. Told in an intricate flashback/flashforward narrative that uses Pu Yi's communist "remolding" period as its fulcrum, the film opens in 1950 as Pu Yi, and thousands of others, are returned to their now-Communist homeland to face rehabilitation. From that point the story moves to Pu Yi's childhood, his imprisonment in the Forbidden City, his term as Japan's puppet emperor of Manchukuo, and his release into the population of China in 1959. Combining the command of the historical epic he displayed in 1900 with the political intrigue and melodrama of THE CONFORMIST, Bertolucci has, in THE LAST EMPEROR, constructed a beautiful film about the transformation of both a man and a country. A storyteller and not a historian, Bertolucci offers two tales in THE LAST EMPEROR—that of China's change, told through a selective sampling of events; and that of Pu Yi's change, told with an emphasis on myth rather than on fact. Moreover, Vittorio Storaro's carefully constructed lighting schemes and moving camera are unmatched by any cinematographer working today. John Lone, as the adult Pu Yi, is wholly credible, and Wu Tao, as the adolescent Pu Yi, is every bit Lone's equal. Both actors convey the emperor's innocence, ignorance, and veiled sadistic streak. Joan Chen demonstrates her skill by playing both a radiant teen bride and a rotting opium-addict. Peter O'Toole shows more restraint than usual and simply *becomes* his character, as if he, like Reginald Johnston, would have made an excellent tutor for the emperor. Also worthy of note is the film's score, which combines lush romanticism with traditional Chinese melodies and was written chiefly by Ryuichi Sakamoto (who also scored MERRY CHRISTMAS, MR. LAWRENCE) and David Byrne (of Talking Heads' fame). THE LAST EMPEROR made a clean sweep at the Academy Awards, winning an Oscar in every category in which it was nominated: Best Film, Director, Adapted Screenplay, Cinematography, Original Score, Editing, Art Direction, Costumes, and Sound. In English.

p, Jeremy Thomas; d, Bernardo Bertolucci; w, Mark Peploe, Bernardo Bertolucci, Enzo Ungari; ph, Vittorio Storaro (Technovision, Technicolor); ed, Gabriella Cristiani; m, Ryuichi Sakamoto, David Byrne, Cong Su.

Historical/Biography (PR:C MPAA:PG-13)

LAST LAUGH, THE*****

(1924, Ger.) 74m UFA bw (DER LETZTE MANN)

Emil Jannings *(The Doorman),* Maly Delschaft *(His Daughter),* Max Hiller *(Her Fiance),* Emilie Kurz *(The Doorman's Aunt),* Hans Unterkirchen *(Hotel Manager),* Olaf Storm *(Young Guest),* Hermann Vallentin *(Corpulent Guest),* Emma Wyda *(Thin Neighbor),* George John *(Night Watchman).*

One of the masterpieces of German silent film, THE LAST LAUGH solidified the international reputations of its director, F.W. Murnau, and its star, Emil Jannings. Jannings gives one of his greatest screen performances as the unnamed hotel doorman who, at the film's beginning, couldn't be more self-satisfied. Resplendent in his opulent uniform, the elderly man lords it over family and neighbors in paternalistic pride—until, one day, he is demoted to lavatory attendant, causing the loss of his social status and the uniform that is its symbol, with tragically demoralizing results. THE LAST LAUGH is perhaps the perfect example of pure cinema, in that it tells its story in completely visual terms, without the use of a single title. Murnau and cinematographer Karl Freund's subjective, moving camera—most famously in the opening traveling shot that sweeps through the hotel lobby to the revolving door attended by Jannings—represented a milestone in silent film technique, beautifully complementing the simplicity of Carl Mayer's (THE CABINET OF DR. CALIGARI) story. Jannings beautifully conveys his everyman's pathetic decline from pomposity to decrepitude, and is utterly convincing as a broken old man—although he was only 39 when THE LAST LAUGH was made. The film's improbably happy epilog was tacked on at the behest of its producer (who feared a downbeat ending would drive away audiences), and its merits have been much debated. The film's greatness, however, has never been in dispute.

p, Erich Pommer; d, F.W. Murnau; w, Carl Mayer; ph, Karl Freund; m, Giuseppe Becce.

Drama (PR:A MPAA:NR)

LAST METRO, THE***½

(1980, Fr.) 128m Carrosse-SEDIF-TF 1/MGM-UA c (LE DERNIER METRO)

Catherine Deneuve *(Marion Steiner),* Gerard Depardieu *(Bernard Granger),* Jean Poiret *(Jean-Loup Cottins),* Heinz Bennent *(Lucas Steiner),* Andrea Ferreol *(Arlette Guillaume),* Paulette Dubost *(Germaine Fabre),* Sabine Haudepin *(Nadine Marsac),* Jean-Louis Richard *(Daxiat),* Maurice Risch *(The Stage Manager),* Marcel Berbert *(Merlin),* Richard Bohringer *(Gestapo Officer),* Jean-Pierre Klein *(Christian Leglise),* Master Franck Pasquier *(Jacquot [Eric]),* Renata *(German Nightclub Singer),* Jean-Jose Richer *(Rene Bernardini),* Martine Simonet *(The Thief),* Laszlo Szabo *(Lt. Bergen),* Henia Ziv *(The Chambermaid),* Jessica Zucman *(Rosette Goldstern),* Alain Rasma *(Marc),* Rene Dupre *(Valentin),* Pierre Belot *(Desk Clerk),* Christian Baltauss *(Bernard's Replacement).*

A precise and oddly restrained picture set during the German Occupation of France, THE LAST METRO takes place almost entirely in a theater building. Marion (Catherine Deneuve in an arresting performance) is the wife of top stage director Lucas Steiner (Heinz Bennent), who is forced to go underground to avoid Nazi anti-Semitism. Instead of fleeing Paris, however, Lucas hides in the cellar of the theater, secretly observing rehearsals of his new play costarring Marion and Bernard Granger (Gerard Depardieu). As time passes, the lives of the theater company members become more open and strained, especially those of Marion and Bernard, who fight their attraction to each other. Politics and romance are placed on parallel tracks as Marion tries to remain as loyal to her husband as she is to her country. After being frequently scolded for not addressing political issues in his pictures, director Francois Truffaut finally found a suitable vehicle in THE LAST METRO—which deals with the Occupation in romantic terms. More than just presenting a realistic portrait of the Occupation, Truffaut has invested his Paris of the 1940s with the mythic qualities of wartime films he grew up watching. In French with English subtitles.

d, Francois Truffaut; w, Francois Truffaut, Suzanne Schiffman, Jean-Claude Grumberg (based on a story by Truffaut, Schiffman); ph, Nestor Almendros; ed, Martine Barraque; m, Georges Delerue.

War/Romance (PR:C-O MPAA:R)

LAST TANGO IN PARIS*****

(1973, Fr./It.) 125m UA c

Marlon Brando *(Paul),* Maria Schneider *(Jeanne),* Jean-Pierre Leaud *(Tom),* Massimo Girotti *(Marcel),* Maria Michi *(Rosa's Mother),* Veronica Lazare *(Rosa),* Gitt Magrini *(Jeanne's Mother),* Darling Legitimus *(Concierge),* Catherine Sola *(TV Script Girl),* Mauro Marchetti *(TV Cameraman),* Dan Diament *(TV Sound Engineer),* Peter Schommer *(TV Assistant Cameraman),* Catherine Allegret *(Catherine),* Marie-Helene Breillat *(Monique),* Catherine Breillat *(Mouchette),* Stephane Kosiak *(Small Mover),* Gerard Lepennec *(Tall Mover),* Luce Marquand *(Olympia),*

Michel Delahaye *(Bible Salesman),* Laura Betti *(Miss Blandish),* Giovanna Galletti *(Prostitute).*

Shattering the facade of social and sexual convention with the intensity of a jack-hammer, LAST TANGO IN PARIS is simply one of the finest examples of film art ever. Marlon Brando plays Paul, a confused middle-aged American living in Paris whose wife has just, inexplicably, committed suicide. Paul is obsessed with the thought that his wife's death, and her whole life, is a mystery to him. He knew nothing about her, nothing of the secret affair she carried on for years with Marcel (Massimo Girotti). Maria Schneider plays Jeanne, a 20-year-old from a wealthy Parisian family who is engaged to Tom (Jean-Pierre Leaud), a New Wave filmmaker who documents his fiancee's life in an attempt to discover the truth about her. While hunting for an apartment, Jeanne meets Paul. Moments later, the two strangers are wildly making love. Shortly afterwards they leave the empty apartment. When they meet again, it is under Paul's ground rules: "You and I are going to meet here without knowing anything that goes on outside here. We are going to forget everything we knew—Everything." All the elements are perfectly synthesized in this film masterpiece—Bernardo Bertolucci's direction; the raw, brave performances of Brando and Schneider; Storaro's lush camerawork; the sexual politics; and the psychoanalytic philosophy. If Bertolucci had made only this one film, he would still be remembered forever, but this, thankfully, is only one of his great achievements. It is a film not to be missed and one that should be seen and seen again. In French and English with English subtitles.

p, Alberto Grimaldi; d, Bernardo Bertolucci; w, Bernardo Bertolucci, Franco Arcalli (based on a story by Bernardo Bertolucci); ph, Vittorio Storaro; ed, Franco Arcalli; m, Gato Barbieri.

Drama **(PR:O MPAA:X)**

LAST YEAR AT MARIENBAD*****

(1961, Fr./It.) 94m Terra-Societe Nouvelle des Films Comoran-Argos-Precitel-Como-Les Films Tamara-Cinetel-Silver-Cineriz/Astor bw (L'ANEE DERNIERE A MARIENBAD; L'ANNO SCORSO A MARIENBAD)

Delphine Seyrig *(A),* Giorgio Albertazzi *(X),* Sacha Pitoeff *(M),* Francoise Bertin, Luce Garcia-Ville, Helena Kornel, Francois Spira, Karin Toeche-Mittler, Pierre Barbaud, Wilhelm von Deek, Jean Lanier, Gerard Lorin.

One of the most avant-garde of all feature films, LAST YEAR AT MARIENBAD stretches the limits of film language to the extreme. Based on a screenplay by Alain Robbe-Grillet, the film introduces us to four main characters—A (Delphine Seyrig), an attractive and well-dressed woman; X (Giorgio Albertazzi), a handsome stranger; M (Sacha Pitoeff), a man who might be A's husband; and a luxurious estate (important enough to be considered a character) with long sterile hallways and perfectly manicured grounds. The deliberately obscure plot focuses on X's attempt to convince A that they met last year at a resort hotel in Marienbad, where she promised to run away with him this year. A, however, has no recollection of the meeting. The viewer soon comes to suspect that the meeting never took place, that it is merely a hopeful fantasy X has concocted, or, perhaps, that he really believes it did happen. It is not for its emotions or characterization that LAST YEAR AT MARIENBAD is hailed as a masterpiece, but because of Robbe-Grillet and director Alain Resnais' manipulation of time—the past, present, future—in relation to the subjective realities of the film's characters. One of the great works of 20th-century art, LAST YEAR AT MARIENBAD can be viewed as a cubist film, offering a number of surfaces simultaneously, or even a surrealist film that presents a world in which more than one reality exists. Whatever one's reading of the film, its unique brilliance in undeniable. In French with English subtitles.

p, Pierre Courau, Raymond Froment; d, Alain Resnais; w, Alain Robbe-Grillet; ph, Sacha Vierny (Dyaliscope); ed, Henri Colpi, Jasmine Chasney; m, Francis Seyrig.

Drama **(PR:C MPAA:NR)**

L'ATALANTE*****

(1934, Fr.) 89m JL Nounez/Arqui bw (AKA: LE CHALAND QUI PASSE)

Michel Simon *(Pere Jules),* Jean Daste *(Jean),* Dita Parlo *(Juliette),* Gilles Margaritis *(Peddler),* Louis Lefevre *(Cabin Boy),* Fanny Clar *(Juliette's Mother),* Raphael Diligent *(Juliette's Father),* Maurice Gilles *(Office Manager),* Rene Bleck *(Best Man),* Charles Goldblatt *(Thief).*

Jean Vigo's poetic tale centers on Jean (Jean Daste), captain of the barge *L'Atalante*, who marries country girl Juliette (Dita Parlo). Bored with life on the barge, Juliette longs to see the bright lights of Paris. Jean finally gives in to his wife's request and takes her to a Paris cabaret, where a peddler flirts with the girl. The next day, an angry and jealous Jean leaves the ship without his wife. She is visited by the peddler, who entertains her and then is promptly thrown off the barge upon Jean's return. Juliette then sneaks off to Paris, and Jean purposefully sets sail without her, leaving the penniless girl to take a job in town. The film then concentrates on the lovers' pain before *L'Atalante* again sails on. Vigo made only four films (A PROPOS DE NICE, 1930; TARIS CHAMPION DE NATATION, 1931; ZERO DE CONDUITE, 1933; and L'ATALANTE) before his death at age 29. In L'ATALANTE, he treats his simple story both realistically and surrealistically, combining and contrasting styles. Thus, in one scene, Jean dives into the water and sees an image of a smiling Juliette swimming in her wedding gown; in another, a seaman played by Michel Simon (in perhaps the best role of his career) displays his odd collection of curios, including a pair of severed hands in a jar. (Surrealist poet Jacques Prevert and his brother, filmmaker Pierre, also make cameo appearances.) L'ATALANTE was poorly received at its initial 1934 screening, prompting its distributors to insert a popular song and re-edit nearly all the scenes. The result was a box-office disaster, and three weeks later Vigo was dead. Years later, a complete version was finally constructed thanks to the Cinematheque Francais and Henri Langlois. After the negative response to ZERO DE CONDUITE, Vigo reassured himself, remarking, "I knew I hadn't made a real film, like the others." L'ATALANTE *isn't* a film like the others—it's a masterpiece. In French with English subtitles.

p, Jacques-Louis Nounez; d, Jean Vigo; w, Jean Vigo, Albert Riera (based on a scenario by R.); ph, Boris Kaufman; ed, Louis Chavance.

Romance **(PR:C MPAA:NR)**

L'AVVENTURA*****

(1959, It./Fr.) 145m Duca-Produzioni Cinematografiche Europee-Lyre/Janus bw (Trans: The Adventure)

Monica Vitti *(Claudia),* Gabriele Ferzetti *(Sandro),* Lea Massari *(Anna),* Dominique Blanchar *(Giulia),* James Addams *(Corrado),* Renzo Ricci *(Anna's Father),* Esmeralda Ruspoli *(Patrizia),* Lelio Luttazi *(Raimondo),* Dorothy De Poliolo *(Gloria Perkins),* Giovanni Petrucci *(Young Prince),* Joe, fisherman from Panarea *(Old Fisherman on Island),* Professor Cucco *(Ettore),* Enrico Bologna, Franco Cimino.

A group of wealthy Italians embarks on a yachting excursion to a rocky island near Sicily. After arriving, they notice that Anna (Lea Massari) is missing, and everyone joins the search, scouring the wave-battered cliffs and endless crevices that may have swallowed her. Her best friend, Claudia (Monica Vitti), teams with Anna's lover, Sandro (Gabriele Ferzetti), in the search, which is eventually abandoned in the belief that Anna may simply have left the island. Back in town, inquiries are made as to her whereabouts, and occasionally someone who thinks they might know her is encountered. In the process, Sandro becomes increasingly involved with Claudia, who soon becomes his lover and substitute for Anna. Often cited as one of the greatest films of all time, L'AVVENTURA is not only Michelangelo Antonioni's masterpiece, but one of cinema's most important films, especially in terms of the (de) evolution of narrative forms. The pressing question the plot raises—"What happened to Anna?"—is simply ignored. Moreover, the plot itself becomes irrelevant; the adventure the title alludes to does not exist. Instead, the biggest adventure the picture offers is the changing lives of Claudia and Sandro, or perhaps what will happen to them after the film ends. As with all of Antonioni's films, the photography and composition are unsurpassed, providing the viewers with their own visual adventure. In Italian with English subtitles.

p, Cino Del Duca; d, Michelangelo Antonioni; w, Michelangelo Antonioni, Elio Bartolini, Tonino Guerra (based on the story by Antonioni); ph, Aldo Scavarda; ed, Eraldo Da Roma; m, Giovanni Fusco.

Drama **(PR:A MPAA:NR)**

LAW OF DESIRE½**

(1987, Sp.) 100m El Deseo-Laurenfilm/Cinevista c (LA LEY DEL DESEO)

Eusebio Poncela *(Pablo Quintero),* Carmen Maura *(Tina Quintero),* Antonio Banderas *(Antonio Benitez),* Miguel Molina *(Juan Bermudez),* Manuela Velasco *(Ada, Child),* Bibi Andersson *(Ada, Mother),* Fernando Guillen *(Inspector),* Nacho Martinez *(Dr. Martin),* Helga Line *(Antonio's Mother),* Fernando G. Cuervo *(Policeman, Child),* German Cobos *(Priest),* Maruchi Leon *(Maruchi),* Marta Fernandez Muro *(Groupie),* Marta Fernandez Muro *(Sergeant),* Tinin Almodovar *(Lawyer),* Lupe Barrado *(Nurse),* Roxy Von Donna *(Woman on Telephone),* Jose Manuel Bello *(Young Guard),* Jose Ramon Fernandez *(Pimp).*

Spain's acclaimed comedy director Pedro Almodovar, who scored a huge international success with 1988's WOMEN ON THE VERGE OF A NERVOUS BREAKDOWN, has stated he wants to reach audiences through "their hearts, their minds, and their genitals." In LAW OF DESIRE, he concentrates on the last, offering an occasionally fun romp detailing the erotic adventures of Pablo (Eusebio Poncela), a gay filmmaker; his bisexual lover, Juan (Miguel Molina); his transsexual "sister," Tina (Carmen Maura), the mother of a teenager *fathered* by her when she was a he; and Antonio (Antonio Banderas), who becomes involved with both Pablo and Tina as the story winds to its bizarre finale. The problem with LAW OF DESIRE is that it tries too hard to be eccentric, its humor becoming so forced that its satire falls flat. Though Almodovar directs with great energy, he is more interested in showing sexual orientation as character development than in taking real chances with the material. The fine acting helps to compensate for some of these deficiencies, and Poncela, in particular, turns in an enjoyable tongue-in-cheek performance. However, the real driving force in LAW OF DESIRE is the wonderfully zany Maura (star of WOMEN). Had Almodovar concentrated on her character instead of a series of liaisons, he might have really arrived at something unique. In Spanish with English subtitles.

p, Miguel A. Perez Campos; d, Pedro Almodovar; w, Pedro Almodovar; ph, Angel Luis Fernandez (Eastmancolor); ed, Jose Salcedo; m, Igor Stravinsky, Dmitri Shostakovich.

Comedy **(PR:O MPAA:NR)**

LE BAL½**

(1983, Fr./It./Algeria) 112m Cineproduction-Films A2-Massfilm-ONCIC/Almi c

Etienne Guichard, Regis Bouquet, Francesco de Rosa, Arnault Lecarpentier, Liliane Delval, Martine Chauvin, Danielle Rochard, Nani Noel, Azis Arbia, Marc Berman, Genevieve Rey-Penchenat, Michel Van Speybroeck, Rossana Di Lorenzo, Michel Toty, Raymonde Heudeline, Anita Picchiarini, Olivier Loiseau, Monica Scattini.

One of the most unique European films to play American screens in quite some time, LE BAL is set entirely in a French ballroom, spans a half-decade, and contains not a word of dialog. The result is a fabulously photographed tableaux history of France through the music and dance of the day—the 1936 Popular Front society, the German Occupation, the Liberation, the carefree 1950s, the rebellious atmosphere of May 1968, and the present day. The actors play an assortment of unrealistic characters throughout the decades, with their movements choreographed in a most exaggerated fashion. Based on a play that was a smash success in France, LE BAL doesn't attempt to reproduce the stage experience but instead uses the camera as a selective tool to highlight particularly interesting characters. LE BAL is sometimes boring (but never for long), sometimes frustrating (why can't these characters just say a few words?), and sometimes outrageously funny (as in the scene wherein the swinging Acapulco Boys play "Brazil"). Not surprisingly, LE BAL includes a plethora of musical numbers from Edith Piaf to The Glenn Miller Orchestra to The Beatles.

p, Giorgio Silvagni; d, Ettore Scola; w, Ettore Scola, Ruggero Maccari, Jean-Claude Penchenat, Furio Scarpelli (based on an idea by Penchenat); ph, Ricardo Aronovich (Fujicolor); ed, Raimondo Crociani; m, Vladimir Cosma.

Musical **(PR:A MPAA:NR)**

LE BEAU MARIAGE****

(1982, Fr.) 97m Losanger-Carosse/UA c (AKA: A GOOD MARRIAGE; THE WELL-MADE MARRIAGE)

Beatrice Romand *(Sabine),* Andre Dussollier *(Edmond),* Feodor Atkine *(Simon),* Huguette Faget *(Antique Dealer),* Arielle Dombasle *(Clarisse),* Thamila Mezbah *(Mother),* Sophie Renoir *(Lise),* Herve Duhamel *(Frederic),* Pascal Greggory *(Nicolas),* Virginie Thevenet *(The Bride),* Denise Bailly *(The Countess),* Vincent Gauthier *(Claude),* Ann Mercier *(Secretary),* Catherine Rethi *(Client),* Patrick Lambert *(Traveler).*

The second installment in Eric Rohmer's "Comedies and Proverbs" series, LE BEAU MARIAGE is the charming tale of Sabine (Beatrice Romand), a university student with a Paris flat who decides one day, quite arbitrarily, to get married. All she is lacking is a husband, a minor detail. She leaves her painter boy friend, quits her antique-store job, and begins pursuing Edmond (Andre Dussollier), a busy lawyer who is friendly to Sabine but clearly not interested in romancing her. This thoroughly enjoyable picture is carried by the spunky, idiosyncratic performance of Romand, who appeared 12 years earlier in Rohmer's "Moral Tale," CLAIRE'S KNEE. Two of her costars in this film would also be rewarded with lead roles in subsequent Rohmer films—Arielle Dombasle, who appears in PAULINE AT THE BEACH, and Sophie Renoir (cast here as Romand's pesty little sister), who stars in Rohmer's final "Comedies and Proverbs" entry, BOYFRIENDS AND GIRLFRIENDS. There's also a fine synthesized pop score that you may find yourself humming long after the film's end. In French with English subtitles.

p, Margaret Menegoz; d, Eric Rohmer; w, Eric Rohmer; ph, Bernard Lutic, Romain Winding, Nicolas Brunet; ed, Cecile Decugis, Lisa Heredia; m, Ronan Gure, Simon Des Innocents.

Drama/Comedy **(PR:C-O MPAA:PG)**

LE BEAU SERGE***½

(1958, Fr.) 97m United Motion Picture bw (AKA: HANDSOME SERGE)

Gerard Blain *(Serge),* Jean-Claude Brialy *(Francois),* Bernadette Lafont *(Marie),* Edmond Beauchamp *(Glomaud),* Michelle Meritz *(Yvonne),* Jeanne Perez, Claude Cerval, Andre Dino.

Generally considered the film that put the French New Wave in the history books (though Jacques Rivette's PARIS BELONGS TO US was the first to go into production), LE BEAU SERGE received overwhelming critical approval of its use of non-professional actors, raw black-and-white photography (masterfully executed by Henri Decae), and personal vision. It is the tale of two old friends, Francois (Jean-Claude Brialy), a city dweller who returns to the provincial French village of his childhood, and Serge (Gerard Blain), a successful architect-turned-drunkard. After the birth of a malformed son, Serge's life and marriage go into a tailspin as he collapses under the weight of tremendous guilt. Unfortunately, the film is cluttered with a surfeit of Catholicism, which director Claude Chabrol had the good sense to deemphasize as his career developed. Though highly acclaimed, LE BEAU SERGE was quickly overshadowed by the subsequent success of Francois Truffaut's 400 BLOWS, Jean-Luc Godard's BREATHLESS, and Alain Resnais' HIROSHIMA MON AMOUR. LES COUSINS, a companion piece to LE BEAU SERGE that also starred Brialy and Blain, appeared the following year to an equally enthusiastic reception. In French with English subtitles.

d, Claude Chabrol; w, Claude Chabrol; ph, Henri Decae; ed, Jacques Gaillard; m, Emile Delpierre.

Drama **(PR:C-O MPAA:NR)**

LE CAVALEUR (PRACTICE MAKES PERFECT)**

(1979, Fr.) 104m Les Films Ariane-Mondex-FR3/Quartet c (Trans: The Skirt Chaser)

Jean Rochefort *(Edouard Choiseul),* Nicole Garcia *(Marie-France),* Annie Girardot *(Lucienne),* Danielle Darrieux *(Suzanne Taylor),* Catherine Alric *(Murielle),* Lila Kedrova *(Olga),* Jean Dessailly *(Charles-Edmond),* Carole Lixon *(Pompom),* Catherine Leprince *(Valentine),* Jacques Jouanneau *(Le Goff),* Jean-Claude Ventura *(Railway Station Manager),* Lucienne Legrand *(Mother-in-law),* Philippe Castelli *(Marcel),* Dominique Probst *(Orchestra Conductor),* Raoul Guylad, Thomas Hnevsa, Oleg Oboldouieff *(Leningrad Trio),* Peggy Besson, Julie Besson, Anna-Emelie Roy *(Little Girls).*

A less-than-brilliant comedy from Philippe de Broca, LE CAVALEUR centers on classical pianist Edouard Choiseul (Jean Rochefort), a childish man with a monstrous ego who believes that the world revolves around him and his whims. Despite the fact that he has a beautiful wife (Nicole Garcia), a friendly ex-wife (Annie Girardot), a devoted agent (Lila Kedrova), a sexy mistress (Catherine Alric), charming children, and a successful career, Edouard is not content, and treats everyone with contempt. He leaves his mistress waiting for him at the train station, lies to his wife about his affairs, and awakens his ex-wife and her husband in the middle of the night by barging into their apartment to play the piano. His family and friends finally agree that he has pushed them too far for too long, and eventually Edouard is left without any female companionship. It takes this drastic turn of events to shock Edouard into changing his life, transforming him from a skirt chaser into the devoted teacher of a gifted young pianist. De Broca has assembled a superb cast that also includes a brief appearance by Danielle Darrieux as the woman with whom Edouard has his first affair during the Liberation. Unfortunately, Edouard is such a despicable character and his comeuppance so predictable that one hardly becomes enamored of him or the film. In French with English subtitles.

p, Georges Dancigers, Alexandre Mnouchkine; d, Philippe de Broca; w, Philippe de Broca, Michel Audiard; ph, Jean-Paul Schwartz; ed, Henri Lanoe; m, Johann Sebastian Bach, Ludwig van Beethoven, Robert Schumann, Jacques Offenbach, Georges Delerue.

Comedy **(PR:C MPAA:NR)**

LE CHAT**½

(1971, Fr.) 88m Green c (Trans: The Cat)

Jean Gabin *(Julien),* Simone Signoret *(Clemence),* Annie Cordy *(Nelly),* Jacques Rispal *(Doctor).*

The chief reason for watching this otherwise heavy-handed effort from writer-director Pierre Granier-Deferre is to witness the star turns of aging French film veterans Jean Gabin and Simone Signoret. Based on Georges Simenon's psychological novel, LE CHAT studies the deteriorating relationship between Julien (Gabin) and Clemence (Signoret). Once very much in love, they have grown to hate each other, the evil turn in their romance symbolized by Clemence's killing of Julien's cat. Julien leaves Clemence, and though he eventually returns to their decrepit house on the edge of Paris, they stop speaking and do their best to make each other miserable. When Clemence dies, however, Julien is left to face a loss far greater than that of his cat. Not surprisingly, Gabin and Signoret are superb, their every gesture an essay in contempt. In French with English subtitles.

d, Pierre Granier-Deferre; w, Pierre Granier-Deferre, Pascal Jardin (based on a novel by Georges Simenon); ph, Walter Wottitz (Eastmancolor); ed, Jean Ravel; m, Philippe Sarde.

Drama **(PR:C MPAA:NR)**

LE DERNIER COMBAT***

(1983, Fr.) 92m Loup/Triumph (AKA: THE LAST BATTLE)

Pierre Jolivet *(The Man),* Jean Bouise *(The Doctor),* Fritz Wepper *(The Captain),* Jean Reno *(The Brute),* Maurice Lamy *(The Dwarf),* Petra Muller *(The Woman in the Cell),* Pierre Carrive, Bernard Havet, Jean-Michel Castanie, Michel Doset, Marcel Berthomier, Garry Jode *(Captain's Men),* Christiane Kruger *(Captain's Concubine).*

The feature film debut of Luc Besson, who went on to achieve a measure of fame with SUBWAY and the French blockbuster THE BIG BLUE, LE DERNIER COMBAT is a masterfully directed—albeit somewhat empty and boring—picture that successfully tells its story without the aid of dialog or voice-over. The setting is the post-apocalyptic future, in which the few humans remaining are unable to speak. One of these is The Man (Pierre Jolivet), who lives in a half-buried skyscraper and spends his spare time building an airplane. Desiring freedom more than anything, The Man passes time by reading, struggling in vain to make his devolved throat produce words. When he finally gets his plane functioning, The Man is able to escape his post-apocalyptic hell by flying over the vast wasteland. Eventually, he falls from the sky to set up a new home in a dilapidated old Paris hotel. Also living in the ghost town are a huge brute (Jean Reno) who seems to be driven only by greed, hunger, and violence; and a doctor and aspiring painter (Jean Bouise) who has barricaded himself in a hospital with an endless supply of rations and . . . an imprisoned woman, to whom he devotes himself and his art. Besson's debut effort is witty, exciting, and frightening all at once, and its creation of a blasted, blighted landscape of half-recognizable, half-buried buildings is an amazing feat (especially on a nothing budget). Unfortunately, it's a bit slow-going in spots, and is saddled with a wretched electronic jazz score from Eric Serra. Besson would make essentially the same film in SUBWAY, another look at an alternate civilization, this time set in the Paris Metro.

p, Luc Besson, Pierre Jolivet; d, Luc Besson; w, Luc Besson, Pierre Jolivet; ph, Carlo Varini (Panavision); ed, Sophie Schmit; m, Eric Serra.

Science Fiction **(PR:O MPAA:R)**

LE DOULOS****

(1963, Fr.) 108m Rome-Paris-Champion/Lux bw (AKA: THE FINGERMAN; THE STOOLIE)

Jean-Paul Belmondo *(Silien),* Serge Reggiani *(Maurice),* Monique Hennessy *(Therese),* Rene Lefevre *(Gilbert),* Jean Desailly *(Inspector Clain),* Michel Piccoli *(Nuttheccio),* Carl Studer *(Kern),* Fabienne Dali *(Fabienne),* Jacques de Leon *(Armand),* Philippe Nahon *(Remy),* Aime de March *(Jean),* Marcel Cuvelier, Jack Leonard *(Inspectors),* Christian Lude *(Doctor),* Paulette Breil *(Anita),* Charles Bayard *(Old Man),* Daniel Crohem *(Inspector Salignari).*

Like so many of Jean-Pierre Melville's films, LE DOULOS pays homage to the American gangster films. Here Melville takes a romantic look at wet pavements, overcoats with up-turned collars, tough guys and sexy dames, danger that lies in dark shadows, and that most hated figure in all *film noir*—the stool pigeon. Silien (Jean-Paul Belmondo) is a Bogartesque burglar who keeps his contacts in the criminal underworld while maintaining a friendship with police inspector Salignari (Daniel Crohem). Because Silien regularly offers tips to the police, he is allowed to operate without much restriction. When his closest friend, the cat burglar Maurice (Serge Reggiani), guns down Salignari, Silien is forced to play both ends against the middle. In the meantime, the vengeful Maurice, thinking Silien has informed on him, sends a hit man after the burglar. Like his one-time collaborator Jean Cocteau (LES ENFANTS TERRIBLES), Melville is a mythmaker. His characters are archetypes of the cinema, specifically American cinema, though his outlook is unmistakably French, tinged with romanticism. A beautifully directed, photographed, and acted gangster film, LE DOULOS is the equal of many Hollywood-produced entries in the genre. Future directors Volker Schlondorff and Bertrand Tavernier served as an assistant director and publicity director, respectively. In French with English subtitles.

p, Carlo Ponti, Georges de Beauregard; d, Jean-Pierre Melville; w, Jean-Pierre Melville (based on the novel by Pierre Lesou); ph, Nicholas Hayer; ed, Monique Bonnot; m, Paul Misraki, Jacques Loussier.

Crime **(PR:C MPAA:NR)**

LE GRAND CHEMIN½**

(1988, Fr.) 107m Flach-Selena-TF 1/Miramax c (AKA: THE GRAND HIGHWAY)

Anemone *(Marcelle),* Richard Bohringer *(Pello),* Antoine Hubert *(Louis),* Vanessa Guedj *(Martine),* Christine Pascal *(Claire),* Raoul Billeray *(Priest),* Pascale Roberts *(Yvonne),* Marie Matheron *(Solange),* Daniel Rialet *(Simon),* Jean-Francois Derec.

Praised to the high heavens in France, where it was the No. 1 French-produced film of the year and the recipient of six Cesar nominations, LE GRAND CHEMIN (released in the US as THE GRAND HIGHWAY) has been compared to the films of Jean Renoir and Marcel Pagnol for its portrayal of provincial life and to those of Francois Truffaut for its handling of childhood. Unfortunately, the film is an uninventive, calculated look at the charm, innocence, and simplicity of country life that falls flat in all but a few scenes. Louis (Antoine Hubert) is a high-strung nine-year-old Parisian who is taken to the country for a few weeks while his pregnant mother (Christine Pascal) has her baby. He soon finds the peaceful village where he is staying with his mother's friend Marcelle (Anemone) to be a living hell of boredom. Marcelle, who gleefully skins rabbits and plucks out their eyes, horrifies Louis, but even more terrifying is her gruff, hulking monster of a husband, Pello (Richard Bohringer). The boy's only escape is his new-found friend Martine (Vanessa Guedj), a 10-year-old country girl who wanders around barefoot and willingly shows him her underwear. A loud, precocious youngster, this walking encyclopedia of taboos tells Louis about menstruation, gonorrhea, toilet habits, and funerals. Not surprisingly, Louis is frightened by his new friend, but he is also fascinated. While the film was widely praised for the escapades of the young stars, the most interesting and complex characters are Marcelle and Pello, whose lives have been in a state of suspended animation since the death of their child. One can't help but be moved by their situation and the rediscovery of life that they experience through Louis. Fortunately, both Anemone and the exceptional Bohringer were awarded Cesars for their efforts. In French with English subtitles.

p, Pascal Hommais, Jean-Francois Lepetit; d, Jean-Loup Hubert; w, Jean-Loup Hubert; ph, Claude Lecomte (Eastmancolor); ed, Raymonde Guyot; m, Georges Granier.

Drama **(PR:O MPAA:NR)**

LE JOUR SE LEVE*****

(1939, Fr.) 88m Signa/AFE bw (AKA: DAYBREAK)

Jean Gabin *(Francois),* Jules Berry *(M. Valentin),* Jacqueline Laurent *(Francoise),* Arletty *(Clara),* Rene Genin *(Concierge),* Mady Berry *(Concierge's Wife),* Bernard Blier *(Gaston),* Marcel Peres *(Paulo),* Jacques Baumer *(The Inspector),* Rene Bergeron *(Cafe Proprietor),* Gabrielle Fontan *(Old Woman),* Arthur Devere *(M. Gerbois),* Georges Douking *(Blind Man),* Germaine Lix *(Singer).*

A superb example of French poetic realism, LE JOUR SE LEVE is certainly one of the finest French films of the 1930s. Jean Gabin, in perhaps the finest performance of his career, is Francois, a tough, romantic loner who barricades himself in his apartment after committing a crime of passion, the murder of the lecherous Valentin (Jules Berry). While police surround his Normandy home, Francois remembers (in flashback) the two women he loved—Francoise (Jacqueline Laurent) and Clara (Arletty)—and Valentin, the man who wooed both. Every facet of the film's production values is expertly realized, but perhaps the most awe-inspiring is the set design of Alexandre Trauner—a re-creation of a city street corner decorated with Dubonnet posters that is one of the most memorable ever filmed. More poetic than realistic, LE JOUR SE LEVE is very much a film of a mood, but despite the optimism of its ironic title ("Daybreak" in English), melancholy and despair predominate. This inherent irony was then mirrored by real-life events as the film was released not long before Paris became an occupied city, and its citizens, like Francois, left with no way out. Recognizing the similarities, the Vichy government banned the picture as "demoralizing." Remade in Hollywood as THE LONG NIGHT. In French with English subtitles.

d, Marcel Carne; w, Jacques Prevert, Jacques Viot; ph, Curt Courant; ed, Rene Le Henaff; m, Maurice Jaubert.

Drama **(PR:A MPAA:NR)**

LE MAGNIFIQUE½**

(1973, Fr./It.) 93m Arian-Mondex-Cerito-Oceania Rizzolo/Cine III c (AKA: THE MAGNIFICENT ONE)

Jean-Paul Belmondo *(Bob St. Claire/Francois Mering),* Jacqueline Bisset *(Tatiana/Christine),* Vittorio Capprioli *(Charron/Karpoff),* Monique Tarbes *(Mme. Berger),* Raymond Gerome *(Gen. Pontaubert),* Hans Mayer *(Col. Collins),* Jean Lefebvre *(Electrician),* Andre Weber *(Plumber),* Rodrigo Puebla *(Benson),* Bruno Gargin *(Pilus),* Rene Barrera *(The Chinese/The Bride),* Etienne Assena *(Jean),* Raoul Guilad *(The Albanian),* Hubert Deschamps *(The Salesman),* Jean-Pierre Rambal *(The Lecturer),* Thalie Fruges *(Publishing House Hostess).*

Philippe de Broca teams again with his THAT MAN FROM RIO star Jean-Paul Belmondo for this spoof of James Bond flicks. Francois (Belmondo) is a dim-witted spy novelist who lives in a Paris apartment and is the subject of a paper being written by an English sociology student (Jacqueline Bisset). Intercut with their relationship is the fantasy world of Bob St. Clair (Belmondo again), a master spy who is everything that Francois is not, and his pretty assistant, Tatiana (Bisset again). Of course, the spy's arch enemy is, in real-life, the novelist's demanding publisher. Due primarily to Belmondo's performance and Bisset's charming presence, LE MAGNIFIQUE is a fairly likable comedy, though ultimately a pointless exercise. Francis Veber, who wrote the script—and whose screenplays have been better served by director Yves Robert in the similar TALL BLONDE MAN WITH ONE BLACK SHOE and its sequel—was so displeased with the film that he had his name removed from the credits. The videocassette has been dubbed into English.

p, Alexandre Mnouchkine, Georges Dancigers; d, Philippe de Broca; w, Francis Veber, Philippe de Broca; ph, Rene Mathelin (Panavision, Eastmancolor); ed, Henri Lanoe; m, Claude Bolling.

Comedy **(PR:A MPAA:NR)**

LE MILLION*****

(1931, Fr.) 90m Tobis bw (AKA: THE MILLION)

Annabella *(Beatrice),* Rene Lefevre *(Michel),* Paul Olivier *(Crochard, alias Le Pere La Tulipe),* Louis Allibert *(Prosper),* Constantin Stroesco *(Sopranelli),* Odette Talazac *(Mme. Ravallini, the Soprano),* Vanda Greville *(Vanda),* Raymond Cordy *(Raymond, the Cabbie),* Jane Pierson *(Grocer),* Andre Michaud *(Butcher),* Pitouto *(Stage Manager).*

One of the string of superb films Rene Clair made in the 1920s and 1930s, LE MILLION is a nonstop comic chase through a studio set of Paris (designed by Clair's collaborator Lazare Meerson) to find a winning lottery ticket left in the pocket of a discarded jacket. Generally considered Clair's masterpiece (though A NOUS LA LIBERTE also has its supporters), the film is a comic delight that sustains its tone throughout its entirety. As in the previous UNDER THE ROOFS OF PARIS and his subsequent A NOUS LA LIBERTE, Clair creates a wholly original world of song and sound that completely defies realism. One of the truly great early sound films, LE MILLION, despite being extremely French, was an international success both critically and commercially. In French with English subtitles.

p, Hans Haenkel; d, Rene Clair; w, Rene Clair (based on a the play by Georges Berr, Marcel Guillemaud); ph, Georges Perinal, Georges Raulet; ed, Rene Le Henaff; m, Armand Bernard, Philippe Pares, Georges Van Parys.

Comedy **(PR:A MPAA:NR)**

LE PLAISIR*½**

(1952, Fr.) 95m Stera-CCFC/Meyer-Kingsley bw (AKA: HOUSE OF PLEASURE)

"The Mask": Claude Dauphin *(The Doctor),* Jean Galland *(Ambroise),* Gaby Morlay *(Denise, His Wife),* Gaby Bruyere *(Frimousse),* "The Model": Daniel Gelin *(Jean),* Simone Simon *(Josephine),* Jean Servais *(The Friend),* Michel Vadet *(Journalist),* "The House of Madame Tellier": Madeleine Renaud *(Mme. Tellier),* Jean Gabin *(Joseph Rivet),* Danielle Darrieux *(Rosa),* Pierre Brasseur *(Julien Ledentu),* Ginette Leclerc *(Flora),* Paulette Dubost *(Fernande),* Mira Parely *(Raphaele),* Louis Seigner *(Mr. Tourneveau),* Rene Blanchard *(Mayor),* Michel Vadet *(Sailor),* Joe Dest *(The German),* Claire Olivier *(Mme. Tourneveau),* Georges Vitray *(The Captain),* Peter Ustinov *(Voice of Guy de Maupassant).*

Following the success of LA RONDE, Max Ophuls decided to adapt three stories by Guy de Maupassant in this film. The first, "The Mask," concerns an aging roue who, with his wife's compliance, wears a mask to a dance hall in order to hide his wrinkles. The second story, "The House of Madame Tellier," centers on a madame's closing of her brothel so that she and her girls can go to her niece's first communion. In the final episode, "The Model," the title character, who is in love with a painter, throws herself from a window to express her feelings. The painter marries the girl and devotes his life to her care, for she is now crippled for life. Ophuls' goal was to show the pain of pleasure in people's lives—pleasure and old age in "The Mask;' pleasure and purity in "Madame Tellier," and pleasure and marriage in "The Model." It's hard to imagine a more perfect cinematic adapter of Maupassant's writings—his breezy, simple, flowing narrative is wonderfully complemented by Ophuls' floating camera and delicate touch. This use of the moving camera, which has become synonymous with Ophuls' name, is evident from the film's first episode, when the camera waltzes through a ballroom with all the grace and fluidity of the best of dancers. In French with English subtitles.

p, Max Ophuls; d, Max Ophuls; w, Max Ophuls, Jacques Natanson (based on three stories by Guy de Maupassant); ph, Christian Matras, Philippe Agostini; ed, Leonide Azar; m, Joe Hajos, Maurice Yvain.

Drama **(PR:C-O MPAA:NR)**

LE SEX SHOP***

(1972, Fr./Ger./It.) 95m Renn-Allied-PEA-Regina c

Jean-Pierre Marielle *(Lucien),* Claude Berri *(Claude),* Juliet Berto *(Isabelle),* Nathalie Delon *(Jacqueline),* Francesca Romana Coluzzi *(Prostie),* Jacq.Martin *(Friend),* Gregoire Aslan *(Father),* Claude Pieplu *(Officer),* Beatrice Romand *(Karen),* Jacques Legras, Luisa Colpeyn, Jean Tissier, Catherine Allegret, Juliette Mills, Elisabeth Volkmann.

A long time before Claude Berri directed his international art house hits JEAN DE FLORETTE and MANON OF THE SPRING, he made this unique, sensitive, and often very funny picture about a bookstore owner, Claude (played by Berri), whose business is on the brink of failure. His wife, Isabelle (Juliet Berto), spends money carelessly and doesn't seem to enjoy being married, or being mother to their two children. Not only is Claude facing financial ruin, but his life is sexually and romantically bankrupt. Then, one day, he is given the opportunity to convert his bookstore into a Sex Shop that sells instructional manuals, films, leather outfits, and a variety of rubber novelties. Business booms, and Claude soon becomes friendly with Jacqueline (Nathalie Delon), a customer who leads a free, sexually open life with her swinger husband Lucien (Jean-Pierre

Marielle). Before long, Claude discovers a wild sexuality he has long suppressed. Isabelle, however, is less enthusiastic, unwillingly agreeing to be seduced in Claude's presence—first by a man (though Claude interferes and is beaten up) and then by a young woman (again Claude intervenes). While some might dismiss LE SEX SHOP as simply as lewd and immoral, it is really a film about tolerance and personal freedom. A less intelligent director would have turned this into a voyeuristic and exploitative film, but Berri treats the sexuality with an unglamorous frankness and concentrates on the social and psychological implications of carefree sex, building up to a very sweet and honest finale. The film's chief fault, however, is the male chauvinism that underlies Berri's direction—as he fills the screen with lesbians and female nudity. The videocassette is dubbed in English.

p, Claude Berri; d, Claude Berri; w, Claude Berri; ph, Pierre Lhomme (Eastmancolor); ed, Sophie Coussein; m, Serge Gainsbourg, Jane Birkin.

Comedy/Drama **(PR:O MPAA:R)**

LES CARABINIERS***½

(1963, Fr./It.) 80m Rome-Paris-Laetitia/New Yorker bw (GB: THE SOLDIERS)

Marino Mase *(Ulysse),* Albert Juross *(Michel-Ange),* Genevieve Galea *(Venus),* Catherine Ribero *(Cleopatre),* Gerard Poirot, Jean Brassat, Alvaro Gheri *(Carabiniers),* Barbet Schroeder *(Car Salesman),* Odile Geoffroy *(Young Communist Girl),* Roger Coggio, Pascale Audret *(Couple In Car),* Jean Gruault *(Bebe's Father),* Jean-Louis Comolli *(Soldier With The Fish).*

Jean-Luc Godard's fifth film is an ultraimpersonal exercise on the subject of war. A pair of soldiers (Albert Juross and Marino Mase) are called up to fight for the King. Promised great riches in return for their soldiering, they leave their wives behind and set off, sending their spouses letters detailing their activities—saluting the Statue of Liberty, endlessly executing a woman, buying a Masarati, going to the cinema. Back home, they display their great conquests: a massive collection of postcards of various sites, including the Grand Canyon, the Eiffel Tower, the Empire State Building, and the Egyptian pyramids. But the men wind up on the wrong end of the war, go in search of the King to collect their booty, and are gunned down. LES CARABINIERS was a tremendous box-office and critical bomb, and for the first hour it *is* a difficult viewing experience. Godard goes to great length to develop unsympathetic characters, distancing the audience from the on-screen proceedings. He purposely shot the film on a grainy film stock, then made it even grainier in the processing, yielding an old-newsreel effect and even incorporating actual stock footage into the final film. After the first hour, however, comes a remarkable Eisensteinian montage, consisting of 12 minutes of "conquests"—the postcard sequence. In LES CARABINIERS, Godard succeeded in portraying war as an ugly and ignoble atrocity, in a manner entirely different from what he has called "the beautiful Zanuck-ian style." If LES CARABINIERS cannot be called a compelling dramatic work, the film does represent a liberating step beyond cinematic convention. In French with English subtitles.

p, Georges de Beauregard, Carlo Ponti; d, Jean-Luc Godard; w, Jean-Luc Godard, Jean Gruault, Roberto Rossellini (based on the play "I Carabinieri" by Benjamino Joppolo); ph, Raoul Coutard; ed, Agnes Guillemot, Lila Lakshmanan; m, Philippe Arthuys.

War **(PR:O MPAA:NR)**

LES COMPERES***½

(1983, Fr.) 92m Fideline-Efve-DD/European c

Pierre Richard *(Francois Pignon),* Gerard Depardieu *(Jean Lucas),* Anne Duperey *(Christine Martin),* Michel Aumont *(Paul Martin),* Stephane Bierry *(Tristan Martin),* Jean-Jacques Scheffer *(Ralph),* Philippe Khorsand *(Milan),* Roland Blanche *(Jeannot),* Jacques Frantz *(Verdier),* Maurice Barrier *(Raffart),* Charlotte Maury *(Mme. Raffart),* Gisella Pascal *(Louise),* Patrick Blondel *(Stephane),* Florence Moreau *(Michele Raffart),* Bruno Allain, Francois Bernheim, Philippe Brigaud, Pulchier Castan, Robert Dalban, Luc-Antoine Duquiero, Natacha Güinaudeau, Sonia Laroze, Patrick Laurent, Jean-Claude Martin, Guy Matchoro, Charlotte Maury.

Tristan Martin (Stephane Bierry) is a 16-year-old runaway who leaves Paris and hitchhikes to Nice with Michele (Florence Moreau), a tough young girl who hangs out with degenerate bikers. Tristan's middle-class parents (Anne Duperey and Michel Aumont) inform the authorities but receive only the feeble assurance that their son will turn up sooner or later, "like a stolen car." Tristan's mother decides to phone newspaperman and old flame Jean (Gerard Depardieu), convincing him that he is Tristan's real father, hoping that he will offer to find the boy. When he refuses, she tries the same scheme on another past lover, Francois (Pierre Richard), a suicidal manic-depressive, who is thrilled by the request and agrees to help. In the meantime, Jean has reconsidered. Both men eventually meet and discover they have a mutual interest—finding a missing son—but it takes a while for them to realize that they are both looking for the *same* son. Naturally, the question of the boy's real parentage is raised, with both men claiming to be the father. A delightful film, LES COMPERES combines healthy doses of comedy, drama, and crime with three superbly sketched characters. Jean's and Francois's reactions to the possibility of fatherhood are fascinating, as is the interaction between them. LES COMPERES is a film that depends on the chemistry between the actors and thankfully there is not a moment where it fails. Depardieu and Richard are both superb, reminiscent of Laurel and Hardy—the hulkish Depardieu playing Hardy to Richard's whimpering Laurel—in their affectionate dislike for each other. The result is a thoroughly enjoyable, entertaining, funny, and touching celebration of fatherhood. In French with English subtitles.

d, Francis Veber; w, Francis Veber (based on his story); ph, Claude Agostini; ed, Marie Sophie Dubus; m, Vladimir Cosma.

Comedy/Drama **(PR:A MPAA:PG)**

LES ENFANTS TERRIBLES***

(1950, Fr.) 107m Melville bw (AKA: THE STRANGE ONES)

Nicole Stephane *(Elisabeth),* Edouard Dermit *(Paul),* Jacques Bernard *(Gerard),* Renee Cosima *(Dargelos, Agathe),* Roger Gaillard *(Gerard's Uncle),* Melvyn Martin *(Michael),* Maurice Revel *(Doctor),* Adeline Aucoc *(Mariette),* Maria Cyliakus *(The Mother),* Jean-Marie Robain *(Headmaster),* Emile Mathis *(Vice-Principal),* Jean Cocteau *(Narrator).*

Two seemingly disparate filmmakers—Jean-Pierre Melville, best known for his dark black-and-white ventures into the criminal underworld, and Jean Cocteau, the poet of the mythical underworld—came together to bring Cocteau's celebrated play of love, death, and incest to the screen. Paul (Edouard Dermit), a young Parisian, is severely injured when hit by a snowball thrown by Dargelos (Renee Cosima), the school bully whom he idolizes. He is cared for by his sister Elisabeth (Nicole Stephane), with whom he shares a bedroom, though both are in their teens. The near-incestuous pair is brought closer together by the death of their ailing mother and are joined by Paul's friend Gerard (Jacques Bernard), who is infatuated with Elisabeth. The trio eventually becomes a quartet when Paul meets a his sister's friend Agathe (Cosima, in a dual, cross-gender role). As the relationships intertwine, Elisabeth is forced admit her attraction to her brother. Melville, who was given the chance to direct this prestigious property after Cocteau saw one of his early 16mm films, shot LES ENFANTS TERRIBLES in his own apartment, which he rented with the intention of using it as a location, though his wife was reportedly somewhat less enthusiastic. The film also unmistakably bears Cocteau's stamp, and he even directed one scene (at the beach) when Melville fell ill. In French with English subtitles.

p, Jean-Pierre Melville; d, Jean-Pierre Melville; w, Jean-Pierre Melville, Jean Cocteau (based on the novel *The Holy Terrors* by Jean Cocteau); ph, Henri Decae; ed, Monique Bonnot; m, Johann Sebastian Bach, Antonio Vivaldi.

Drama **(PR:A-C MPAA:NR)**

LESSON IN LOVE, A***

(1954, Swed.) 95m Svensk/Janus bw (EN LEKITON I KARLEK)

Eva Dahlbeck *(Marianne Erneman),* Gunnar Bjornstrand *(Dr. David Erneman),* Yvonne Lombard *(Suzanne),* Harriet Andersson *(Nix),* Ake Gronberg *(Carl Adam),* Olof Winnerstrand *(Prof. Henrik Erneman),* Renee Bjorling *(Svea Erneman),* Birgitte Reimers *(Lise),* John Elfstrom *(Sam),* Dagmar Ebbesen *(Nurse),* Helge Hagerman *(Travelling Salesman),* Sigge Furst *(Pastor),* Gosta Pruzelius *(Train Guard),* Carl Strom *(Uncle Axel),* Arne Lindblad *(Hotel Manager),* Torsten Lilliecrona *(Porter),* Yvonne Brosset *(Ballerina),* Georg Adelly *(Bartender),* Ingmar Bergman *(Man on Train Reading Paper).*

Ingmar Bergman has a reputation as a creator of dark, complex films, but this popular early comedy shows an often overlooked side of the director that is both playful and comic. Told in an inexhaustible series of flashbacks, the film opens with David (Gunnar Bjornstrand), a middle-aged gynecologist, breaking off his affair with Suzanne (Yvonne Lombard), a cute, desirable, and married 21-year-old patient. Because of his own infidelities, David risks losing his wife, Marianne (Eva Dahlbeck), who has begun an affair with Carl-Adam (Ake Gronberg), a drunken sculptor she left standing at the altar some 16 years before. The beginning of David and Marianne's romance, their visits to his parents' estate, discussions about love and infidelity, and their efforts to raise their children (tomboyish daughter Harriet Andersson shocks her father when she requests a sex change operation) are all seen in flashback as David and Marianne travel by train to Copenhagen, where she has agreed to marry Carl-Adam. Subtitled "A Comedy for Grown-ups," A LESSON IN LOVE is a fine mix of compassion and humor that plays like a fairy tale (even a little Cupid appears at the finale). While the film could at any point become a tragedy, it instead follows the path of a delightful romantic comedy, because, as the narrator explains, "the gods were kind." Bergman wrote and shot the film in a relatively short time, with the idea of creating a frivolous story. He later stated that A LESSON IN LOVE was made only for the passing moment, though it is filled with genuine love and caring. In Swedish with English subtitles.

p, Ingmar Bergman; d, Ingmar Bergman; w, Ingmar Bergman; ph, Martin Bodin; ed, Oscar Rosander; m, Dag Wiren.

Comedy **(PR:C MPAA:NR)**

LIFE OF OHARU****

(1952, Jap.) 146m Shin Toho/Toho Intl. bw (SAIKAKU ICHIDAI ONNA; AKA: DIARY OF OHARU)

Kinuyo Tanaka *(Oharu),* Tsukie Matsura *(Tomo),* Ichiro Sugai *(Shonzaemon),* Toshiro Mifune *(Katsunosuke),* Toshiaki Konoe *(Lord Tokitaka Matsudaira),* Hisako Yamane *(Lady Matsudaira),* Jukichi Uno *(Yakichi Senya),* Eitaro Shindo *(Kohei Sasaya),* Akira Oizumi *(Fumikichi),* Toranosuke Ogawa *(Yataemon Isobei),* Eijiro Yanagi *(Daimo Enaka).*

LIFE OF OHARU is a later film in the long and brilliant career of masterful director Kenji Mizoguchi. The plot details the painful life of Oharu (Kinuyo Tanaka), a 50-year-old 17th-century prostitute. In flashback, Oharu's life unfolds, beginning when she, the young daughter of a samurai, falls in love with a lower-class man, Katsunosuke (Toshiro Mifune). As punishment, her lover is decapitated and her family banished from the Kyoto. After a failed suicide, Oharu becomes the mistress of a prince, who sends her away after she bears him a son. She is then sold by her father and put to work as a prostitute. A wealthy client buys her, but he is discovered to be a criminal, and she is again forced to sell herself. In time Oharu meets and marries a merchant and lives with him until his death, once again, at age 50, forced to turn to prostitution. In LIFE OF OHARU, Mizoguchi concentrates on the formal style he developed so successfully in his earlier work—extremely long takes of meticulously composed shots with a minimal amount of cutting. Kinuyo Tanaka is superb as the prostitute whose unceasing degradation Mizoguchi uses to criticize feudal Japan and its treatment of women. The winner of the Silver Lion at the Venice Film Festival. In Japanese with English subtitles.

d, Kenji Mizoguchi; w, Yoshikata Yoda, Kenji Mizoguchi (based on the novel *Koshuku Ichidai Onna* by Saikaku Ibara); ph, Yoshimi Kono, Yoshimi Hirano; ed, Toshio Goto; m, Ichiro Saito.

Drama **(PR:C MPAA:NR)**

LOLA MONTES*****

(1955, Fr./Ger.) 110m Gamma-Florida-Union/Brandon c (AKA: THE SINS OF LOLA MONTES; GB: THE FALL OF LOLA MONTES)

Martine Carol *(Maria Dolores Porriz y Montez, Countess of Lansfeld, "Lola Montes"),* Peter Ustinov *(Circus Master),* Anton Walbrook *(Ludwig I),* Ivan Desny *(Lt. James),* Will Quadflieg *(Franz Liszt),* Oskar Werner *(Student),* Lise Delamare *(Mrs. Craigie),* Henri Guisol *(Maurice),* Paulette Dubost *(Josephine),* Helena Manson *(James' Sister),* Willy Eichberger *(Doctor),* Jacques Fayet *(Steward),* Daniel Mendaille *(Captain).*

One of the masterpieces of French cinema, LOLA MONTES is certainly director Max Ophuls' greatest film. In flashback, the picture takes a fascinating look at the life and loves of the passionate Lola Montes (Martine Carol). Introduced by a New Orleans circus master (Peter Ustinov), the aging Lola does her pantomime act and answers personal questions from the audience in exchange for a quarter. The ringmaster relates her story to the audience—both circus and film. He tells of her encounters with men in France, Italy, Russia, and Poland, of her early affair with Franz Liszt, and finally of her romance with the king of Bavaria. In the final scene, Lola (who throughout the film has performed various circus acts) stands at the top of a high platform preparing for a dangerous jump and requests that the safety net be removed. Photographed in Eastmancolor and CinemaScope, the film is breathtaking visually, even though Ophuls tried to lessen the effect of the wide screen by placing pillars and curtains on both sides of the frame. It also displays the brilliant camera choreography that is Ophuls' trademark, and has rarely been equalled. A wonderful film, which, despite much criticism of Martine Carol's wooden performance, is the epitome of craft and technique. Pure elegance. The videocassette (in French with English subtitles) is letterboxed in its original format—for it is a sin to see it any other way.

p, Ralph Baum; d, Max Ophuls; w, Max Ophuls, Jacques Natanson, Franz Geiger, Annette Wademant (based on the unpublished novel *La Vie Extraordinaire de Lola Montes* by Cecil Saint-Laurent); ph, Christian Matras (CinemaScope, Eastmancolor); ed, Madeleine Gug; m, Georges Auric.

Drama **(PR:C MPAA:NR)**

LOS OLVIDADOS*****

(1950, Mex.) 88m Estudios Cinematograficos Del Tepeyac-Ultramar/Mayer-Kingsley bw (AKA: THE YOUNG AND THE DAMNED)

Estela Inda *(Marta, Pedro's Mother),* Alfonso Mejia *(Pedro),* Roberto Cobo *(Jaibo),* Jesus Navarro *(The Lost Boy),* Miguel Inclan *(Don Carmelo, the Blind Man),* Alma Delia Fuentes *(Meche),* Francisco Jambrina *(Farm School Director),* Mario Ramirez *(Big-Eyes),* Efrain Arauz *(Pockface),* Javier Amezcua *(Julian),* Jesus Garcia Navarro *(Julian's Father),* Jorge Perez *("Pelon"),* Sergio Villareal.

Set in the slums of Mexico City, this ruthless account of "Reckless Youth," whose dismal and directionless existence has become a vicious web from which they cannot escape, marked Luis Bunuel's reemergence, after an 18-year absence, as a prominent international filmmaker. At the film's core is the relationship between Pedro (Alfonso Mejia) and Jaibo (Roberto Cobo), two youths who live in Mexico's most disease-ridden urban slum. Jaibo, the older of the two, is already set in his ways, his selfish, vicious nature leading him to take advantage of those less fortunate than himself. As the film opens, he has just been released from jail, and immediately returns to take control of the gang of boys who hang out in the streets and commit senseless acts of violence—not for money but for the pleasure of seeing the less fortunate suffer. They pull a legless man off his cart and leave him lying helpless in the street; throw stones at a blind man who strums his guitar in the plaza to make a few pesos. The boy most eager to follow and please Jaibo is the childlike Pedro, whose innocent eyes reveal a spark of goodness lacking in the others. With the roots of this film stretching back to LAS HURDES, Bunuel's devastating 1932 document of the wretched living conditions in Spain's poorest region, and with an obvious nod to the Italian Neo-Realists, LOS OLVIDADOS is, as Andre Bazin called it, "a film that lashes the mind like a red-hot iron and leaves one's conscience no opportunity for rest." Rarely has such squalor and savagery been displayed so unsentimentally, for Bunuel, who has a deep love for his characters, refuses to judge or pity them. His presentation of his subject is not easy to watch or to accept as reality, but he forces his audience to experience the horrors of society without the thrill of entertainment. As a result, Bunuel was named Best Director at the 1951 Cannes Film Festival. In Spanish with English subtitles.

p, Oscar Dancigers; d, Luis Bunuel; w, Luis Bunuel, Luis Alcoriza, Oscar Dancigers; ph, Gabriel Figueroa; ed, Carlos Savage; m, Rodolfo Halfter.

Drama **(PR:O MPAA:NR)**

LOST HONOR OF KATHARINA BLUM, THE***

(1975, Ger.) 106m WDR-Bioskop/Cinema Intl. c (DIE VERLORENE EHRE DER KATHARINA BLUM)

Angela Winkler *(Katharina Blum),* Mario Adorf *(Insp. Beizmenne),* Dieter Laser *(Werner Toetgess),* Heinz Bennent *(Dr. Hubert Blorna),* Hannelore Hoger *(Trude Blorna),* Harald Kuhlmann *(Walter Moedig),* Karl-Heinz Vosgerau

(Prof. Alois Straubleder), Jurgen Prochnow *(Ludwig Goetten),* Rolf Becker *(Staatsanwalt Hach),* Regine Lutz *(Else Woltersheim),* Werner Eichhorn *(Konrad Beiters),* Herbert Fux *(Journalist Weniger),* Henry von Lyck *(Scheich Karl).*

Codirected by Volker Schlondorff and Margarethe von Trotta, this adaptation of the Heinrich Boll novel capably transfers the author's themes and structure to the screen. Katharina Blum (Angela Winkler) is a waitress and model citizen who suddenly finds herself the victim of an unorthodox police investigation and media assault after a brief affair with a man wanted by the police because of his political affiliations. Before her troubles began, Katharina had been respected by her employers for her efficiency, and by her friends for her level head. Her calm and uneventful life is made a shambles, however, by one particularly ruthless reporter who stops at nothing (including a grueling interview with her sickly mother) to find *something* behind the simple facts, going so far as to label her a Communist conspirator. The story unfolds in a series of bits of information gathered about the suspect, providing various conflicting viewpoints of her character. While this method may be too cold and distancing to evoke much audience empathy, it is effective in creating the oppressive atmosphere the story requires. Winkler's performance is equally cool, exposing a woman who seems incapable of revealing her emotions. An Americanized made-for-TV version appeared in 1984; titled THE LOST HONOR OF KATHRYN BECK, it starred Marlo Thomas and Kris Kristofferson. In German with English subtitles.

p, Willim Benninger, Eberhard Junkersdorf; d, Volker Schlondorff, Margarethe von Trotta; w, Volker Schlondorff, Margarethe von Trotta (based on the novel by Heinrich Boll); ph, Jost Vacano (Eastmancolor); ed, Peter Przygodda; m, Hans Werner Henze.

Drama (PR:C MPAA:R)

LOVE AFFAIR; OR THE CASE OF THE MISSING SWITCHBOARD OPERATOR****

(1967, Yugo.) 70m Avala-Brandon bw (LJUBAVNI SLUCAJ ILI TRAGEDIJA SLUZBENICE PTT; AKA: AN AFFAIR OF THE HEART)

Eva Ras *(Izabela),* Slobodan Aligrudic *(Ahmed),* Ruzica Sokic *(Ruza, Izabela's colleague),* Miodrag Andric *(Mica, the Postman),* Dr. Aleksandar Kostic *(Sexologist),* Dr. Zivojin Aleksic *(Criminologist),* Dragan Obradovic.

It is with great economy that Dusan Makavejev directs this 70-minute feature—his second—which contains a love story, a criminal investigation, lectures by both a sexologist (Dr. Aleksandar Kostic) and a criminologist (Dr. Zivojin Aleksic), a short documentary and a poem about killing rats, an autopsy, a *cinema-verite* scene on how to install a shower, documentary footage of Soviet citizens destroying churches, a lesson in how to make strudel, a Hungarian folk song ("A Man Isn't Made of Wood"), a Communist party anthem ("Crush to Dust the Rotten Vermin"), and a tender and erotic lovemaking scene. Amidst all this is the story, set in Yugoslavia, of a Hungarian switchboard operator, Izabela (Eva Ras), who falls in love with an Arabian rat exterminator, Ahmed (Slobodan Aligrudic). As their affair blossoms, the happy, playful footage of them together is intercut with *cinema-verite*-styled shots of a female corpse being extracted from a deep well and the subsequent autopsy. Our fear that this corpse is Izabela is quickly confirmed, and all we can do is await the signs of why and how she died. This, however, seems to concern Makavejev less than the juxtaposition of scenes and sounds. For example, he places the lovemaking next to documentary footage of the destruction of churches, paralleling (as in his WR: MYSTERIES OF AN ORGANISM and SWEET MOVIE) sexuality with politics. He also shocks his audience into a strange distance by comparing, though less obviously, the nude body of Izabela lying on her bed with that of the cold corpse lying in the morgue. Makavejev's cinema is very much a dialectic one, though LOVE AFFAIR is a tender, sweet, and ultimately very sad film. In Serbian with English subtitles.

d, Dusan Makavejev; w, Dusan Makavejev; ph, Aleksandar Petkovic; ed, Katarina Stojanovic; m, Hans Eisler.

Comedy (PR:O MPAA:NR)

LOVE AND ANARCHY***

(1973, It.) 108m Euro-Steinmann-Baxter/Peppercorn-Wormser c (FILM D'AMORE E D'ANARCHIA)

Giancarlo Giannini *(Tunin),* Mariangela Melato *(Salome),* Lina Polito *(Tripolina),* Eros Pagni *(Spatoletti),* Pina Cei *(Madame Aida),* Elena Fiore *(Donna Carmela),* Giuliana Calandra, Isa Bellini.

Lina Wertmuller's film about the two subjects most dear to her—the relationships between men and women, and the power struggle between opposing political factions—opens with a wonderful visual prolog, a photo montage of Mussolini that sets the historic mood of the picture. The scene then shifts to the Italian countryside where Tunin (Giancarlo Giannini), a humble, unattractive farmer, meets an aging anarchist who is on his way to assassinate Mussolini. Shortly afterwards, the anarchist is captured and killed, but not before the seed of revolutionary change is planted in Tunin's otherwise thick skull. He arrives in Rome at a brothel and meets Salome (Mariangela Melato), a vulgar but likable whore who has managed to extract information on Mussolini's itinerary from some of her more talkative Fascist clients. Together she and Tunin plot an assassination attempt, but in the meantime Tunin falls in love with Tripolina (Lina Polito), a working-class prostitute. Much of the success of LOVE AND ANARCHY stems from Wertmuller's unlikely hero Tunin. A shy, diminutive, unhealthy-looking commoner, he seems a most unlikely candidate to assassinate an immensely powerful world leader, and since we know that Mussolini was not assassinated, we also know that Tunin will fail. In cataloging the factors that lead Tunin to become an anarchist, Wertmuller concentrates not on his wrestling with ideology but on his naive romanticism, which cannot help but falter when confronted with the reality of the situation. Although LOVE AND ANARCHY is an insightful, complex look at the impact of politics on the romantic, it is filled with too many of Wertmuller's Felliniesque excesses (her grotesque portrayal of brothel life fast becomes annoying) to be totally effective. The videocassette is in Italian with English subtitles, though the image seems to have been compressed to fit the subtitles into the television format, and in spots they are still partially buried below the frame line.

p, Romano Cardarelli; d, Lina Wertmuller; w, Lina Wertmuller; ph, Giuseppe Rotunno (Technicolor); ed, Franco Fraticelli, Fima Noveck; m, Nino Rota.

Drama/Political **(PR:O MPAA:R)**

LOVE IN GERMANY, A**½

(1984, Fr./Ger.) 110m CCC-Gaumont-TF 1-FP Stand Art/Triumph c (UN AMOUR EN ALLEMAGNE; EINE LIEBE IN DEUTSCHLAND)

Hanna Schygulla *(Paulina Kropp),* Marie-Christine Barrault *(Maria Wyler),* Armin Mueller-Stahl *(Mayer),* Elisabeth Trissenaar *(Elsbeth Schnittgens),* Daniel Olbrychski *(Wiktorczyk),* Piotr Lysak *(Stanislaw Zasada),* Gerard Desarthe *(Karl Wyler),* Bernhard Wicki *(Dr. Borg),* Ralf Wolter *(Schultze),* Otto Sander *(Narrator),* Ben Becker *(Klaus),* Thomas Ringelmann *(Herbert),* Friedrich Beckhaus *(Zinngruber the Mayor),* Gernot Duda *(Stackmann),* Sigfrit Steiner *(Melchior),* Erika Wackernagel *(Mrs. Melchior),* Serge Merlin *(Alker),* Rainer Basedow *(Stackmann's Son),* Jutta Kloppel *(Stepdaughter),* Heidi Joschko *(Mrs. Zinngruber),* Jurgen Von Alten *(Old Zinngruber),* Ilse Bahrs *(Old Schnittgens).*

Hanna Schygulla stars as Paulina Kropp, a German shopkeeper in the village of Brombach during WW II. With her husband away at war, she falls in love with Stanislaw (Piotr Lysak), a Polish laborer, disregarding the law that strictly forbids relationships between Germans and prisoners of war. The lovers go to great lengths to keep their romance secret but are discovered by a snoopy neighbor (Marie-Christine Barrault) who wants to take over Paulina's shop. To avoid gossipmongers and discovery by the Nazis, Paulina tries to visit her husband in Bavaria. But the Nazis finally learn of the affair after intercepting one of Paulina's letters to Stanislaw and apprehend the Pole. Out of respect for Paulina, the Nazi officials in Brombach attempt to Aryanize Stanislaw, thus saving her from a charge of criminal misconduct. Intercut with the wartime story is a mysterious stranger's modern-day search for what really happened between Paulina and Stanislaw. Based on a nonfiction best-seller that documents their real-life affair (including the Nazis' embarrassing failure to Aryanize the Pole and their botched attempt to execute him in a stone quarry), A LOVE IN GERMANY is less concerned with the "love" of the title than with the political climate in which it flourished. Andrzej Wajda, who has turned out some of the cinema's most provocative political statements, does so again here. In German and Polish with English subtitles.

p, Arthur Brauner; d, Andrzej Wajda; w, Andrzej Wajda, Boleslaw Michalek, Agnieszka Holland (based on the book by Rolf Hochhuth); ph, Igor Luther; ed, Halina Prugar-Ketling; m, Michel Legrand.

Romance/War **(PR:O MPAA:R)**

LOVE ON THE RUN***½

(1979, Fr.) 94m Les Films Du Carrosse/NW bw (L'AMOUR EN FUITE)

Jean-Pierre Leaud *(Antoine Doinel),* Marie-France Pisier *(Colette),* Claude Jade *(Christine),* Dani *(Liliane),* Dorothee *(Sabine),* Rosy Varte *(Colette's Mother),* Marie Henriau *(Divorce Judge),* Daniel Mesguich *(Bookseller),* Julien Bertheau *(M. Lucien),* Jean-Pierre Ducos *(Christine's Lawyer),* Pierre Dios *(M. Renard),* Alain Ollivier *(Judge in Aix),* Monique Dury *(Mme. Ida),* Emmanuel Clot *(Emmanuel),* Christian Lentretien *(Man on Train),* Roland Thenot *(Angry Telephone Operator),* Julien Dubois *(Alphonse Doinel),* Alexandre Janssen, Chantal Zaugg *(Children in Dining Car).*

LOVE ON THE RUN is the fifth and final entry in Francois Truffaut's "Antoine Doinel" series, which began in 1959 with THE 400 BLOWS. By now the young, unpredictable Antoine (Jean-Pierre Leaud) has grown into a man of 34, able to reminisce about his past loves and put them into his new book. The picture opens with the unshaven Antoine and his newest love, Sabine (Dorothee, in a wonderful debut performance), awakening to a sunny morning—the morning that he is to get a divorce from his wife, Christine (Claude Jade, from 1971's BED AND BOARD). Before the day is over Antoine also encounters his first love, Colette (Marie-France Pisier, who appeared years before in Truffaut's episode of LOVE AT TWENTY). There is actually very little in LOVE ON THE RUN that resembles a story. Its chief purpose is simply to look back at the women Antoine has loved. Like so many of Truffaut's characters, Antoine is obsessed with the desire to love, and here he tells how he found a ripped-up, discarded picture of Sabine in a phone booth and set out to find her. In the process, clips are shown from THE 400 BLOWS; LOVE AT TWENTY; STOLEN KISSES; and BED AND BOARD, amounting to an overview of the life of Doinel (as well as those of both Leaud and Truffaut). For those who haven't seen any of the previous "Doinel" pictures, LOVE ON THE RUN will probably be a difficult picture to sit through, but for those who have followed the growth of these characters, the film is a true charmer. In keeping with other Truffaut films, LOVE ON THE RUN includes a superb score from Georges Delerue and a perfectly hummable title song from Alain Souchon. In French with English subtitles.

d, Francois Truffaut; w, Francois Truffaut, Marie-France Pisier, Jean Aurel, Suzanne Schiffman; ph, Nestor Almendros (Eastmancolor); ed, Martine Barraque; m, Georges Delerue.

Drama/Comedy **(PR:A-C MPAA:PG)**

LOVE SONGS*½

(1984, Fr./Can.) 107m 7 Films

Catherine Deneuve *(Margaux),* Richard Anconina *(Michel),* Christopher Lambert *(Jeremy),* Jacques Perrin *(Yves),* Nick Mancuso *(Peter),* Dayle Haddon *(Corinne),* Charlotte Gainsbourg *(Charlotte),* Frank Ayas *(Elliot),* Dominique Lavanant *(Florence),* Nelly Borgeaud *(Julie),* Lazslo Szabo *(Alain),* Inigo Lezzi *(JeanPaul),* Julie Ravix

(Claire), Lionel Rocheman *(Gruber),* Yuni Fujimori *(Switchboard Operator).*

The French rock'n'roll scene serves as the backdrop for this rather bland tale of modern-day relationships. Margaux (Catherine Deneuve) is a talent agent whose marriage has hit a dry spot. The tension between her and husband Peter (Nick Mancuso), the archetypal writer suffering from a creative block, has grown so high that they have decided to separate. Hoping to find inspiration, Peter relocates to Montreal, leaving Margaux to raise her two children while pursuing a career. When she discovers a new pop music duo—Jeremy (Christopher Lambert) and Michel (Richard Anconina)—her life becomes even more hectic. She falls in love with Jeremy, he ignores Michel, and the rest of this sad song plays like the B-side of a broken record. On the plus side, LOVE SONGS features a great cast, and Deneuve (who alone almost makes this worth watching), Lambert, and Anconina momentarily overshadow the banality of the script and direction. Worst of all is the music, insufferable, third-rate fluff from Michel Legrand. The videocassette is poorly dubbed French into English.

p, Elie Chouraqui, Robert Baylis; d, Elie Chouraqui; ph, Robert Alazraki; ed, Noelle Boisson; m, Michel Legrand.

Musical **(PR:C MPAA:NR)**

LOVES OF A BLONDE*½**

(1965, Czech.) 88m Barrandov-Ceskoslovensky/ Prominent bw (LASKY JEDNE PLAVOVLASKY; AKA: A BLONDE IN LOVE)

Hana Brejchova *(Andula),* Vladimir Pucholt *(Milda),* Vladimir Mensik *(Vacovsky),* Ivan Kheil *(Manas),* Jiri Hruby *(Burda),* Milada Jezkova *(Milda's Mother),* Josef Sebanek *(Milda's Father),* Marie Salacova *(Marie),* Jana Novakova *(Jana),* Jana Crkalova *(Jaruska),* Zdenka Lorencova *(Zdena),* Tana Zelinkova *(Girl with Guitar),* Jan Vostrcil *(Colonel),* Josef Kolb *(Pokorny),* Antonin Blazejovsky *(Tonda),* M. Zednickova *(Educator).*

This charming and frequently touching romantic comedy directed by Milos Forman concerns Andula (Hana Brejchova), a young woman who works in a shoe factory and dreams of love. Dissatisfied with the men in her town, she is forced to suffer the attentions of Tonda (Antonin Blazejovsky), an ardent admirer, but less than what she perceives to be her ideal man. When their plant manager arranges for a dance to be held in honor of group of soldiers, Andula looks forward to meeting a handsome military man. To her disappointment, however, the soldiers all turn out to be middle-aged reservists, and she next sets her sights on the piano player, Milda (Vladimir Pucholt). After some uneasy introductions, Andula spends the night with Milda. Now in love, she travels to his parents' home in Prague, where her stay is anything but blissful. An international success, LOVES OF A BLONDE was an important film not only in the career of Forman (who would eventually go to America and direct ONE FLEW OVER THE CUCKOO'S NEST), but also as one of the films (along with THE SHOP ON MAIN STREET and CLOSELY WATCHED TRAINS) that helped push Czech cinema into the worldwide spotlight. In Czech with English subtitles.

d, Milos Forman; w, Jaroslav Papousek, Ivan Passer, Milos Forman, Vaclav Sasek; ph, Miroslav Ondricek; ed, Miroslav Hajek; m, Evzen Illin.

Comedy **(PR:A MPAA:NR)**

LOWER DEPTHS, THE***

(1936, Fr.) 92m Albatros/Mayer-Burstyn bw (LES BAS-FONDS)

Jean Gabin *(Pepel),* Louis Jouvet *(The Baron),* Suzy Prim *(Vassilissa),* Jany Holt *(Nastia),* Vladimir Sokoloff *(Kostylev),* Junie Astor *(Natacha),* Robert Le Vigan *(The Actor),* Camille Bert *(The Count),* Rene Genin *(Luka),* Paul Temps *(Satine),* Robert Ozanne *(Jabot),* Henri Saint-Iles *(Kletsch),* Maurice Baquet *(Allochka),* Andre Gabreillo *(The Inspector),* Leon Larive *(Felix),* Nathalie Alexieff *(Anna),* Lucien Mancini *(Owner of Cafe).*

Jean Renoir's adaptation of the famed Gorky play moves the action from its original pre-Revolution Russian setting to the streets of Paris. Louis Jouvet is a baron who has lost his fortune and has nowhere to turn until he meets Pepel (Jean Gabin), a lower-class thief who gains the nobleman's respect. After an all-night card game, the baron and Pepel become great friends, and Pepel offers his "partner" a chance to escape and live in a doss house with a horde of thieves, drunks, and prostitutes. The slum quarters are run by the old, miserly Kostyley (Vladimir Sokoloff), who lives there with his young mistress Vassilissa (Suzy Prim). Vassalissa is also Pepel's mistress, though Pepel really loves her sister Natacha (Junie Astor), whom Kostyley is trying to marry off to a nasty police inspector. While THE LOWER DEPTHS is perhaps only mediocre Renoir (its supporting characters and slum world conventionally one-dimensional instead of complex), the relationship between Gabin's Pepel and Jouvet's Baron is a brilliant one—Renoir pointing to their internal similarities by stressing their external differences. Reportedly, Gorky saw the original script by Eugene Zamiatine and Jacques Companeez, and gave his approval before his death in 1936. In French with English subtitles.

p, Alexandre Kamenka; d, Jean Renoir; w, Jean Renoir, Charles Spaak, Eugene Zamyatin, Jacques Companeez (based on the play by Maxim Gorky); ph, Fedote Bourgas, Jean Bachelet; ed, Marguerite Renoir; m, Jean Wiener.

Drama **(PR:C MPAA:NR)**

LOWER DEPTHS, THE***

(1957, Jap.) 125m Toho/Brandon bw (DONZOKO)

Toshiro Mifune *(Sutekichi),* Isuzu Yamada *(Osugi),* Ganjiro Nakamura *(Rokubei),* Kyoko Kagawa *(Okayo),* Bokuzen Hidari *(Kahei),* Minoru Chiaki *(The Ex-Samurai),* Kamatari Fujiwara *(The Actor),* Eijiro Tono *(Tomekichi),* Eiko Miyoshi *(Asa, his Wife),* Akemi Negishi *(Osen),* Koji Mitsui *(Yoshisaburo),* Nijiko Kiyokawa *(Otaki),* Haruo Tanaka *(Tatsu).*

With THE LOWER DEPTHS, Akira Kurosawa once again looked to Russian drama for source material. Based on a 1902 play by Gorky and set in 19th-century Japan, it is an ensemble film filled with fine performances (though Toshiro Mifune, as usual, stands out). The action takes place in a small hostel that houses an odd assortment of eccentric, loquacious characters. The landlady, Osugi (Isuzu Yamada), hates her boarders and treats them shabbily, except for Sutekichi (Mifune), the thief she loves. Sutekichi, however, is in love with Osugi's sister, and when the landlady learns of this, she kills her husband in a jealous rage. It is Sutekichi, however, who is arrested and charged with the murder. While Jean Renoir's 1936 adaptation of the play stresses its social importance, Kurosawa found himself attracted to the material's inherent black comedy, though it is the performance of Mifune, with his wildly vulgar and comic style, that is the chief contributor to the film's irreverent humorous tone. In Japanese with English subtitles.

p, Sojiro Motoki, Akira Kurosawa; d, Akira Kurosawa; w, Hideo Oguni, Akira Kurosawa, Shinobu Hashimoto (based on the play *Nadne* by Maxim Gorky); ph, Ichio Yamazaki; m, Masaru Sato.

Drama/Comedy **(PR:C MPAA:NR)**

LUMIERE½**

(1976, Fr.) 95m Orphee-FR 3-Gaumont/NW c

Jeanne Moreau *(Sarah Dedieu),* Francine Racette *(Juliene),* Lucia Bose *(Laura),* Caroline Cartier *(Caroline),* Marie Henriau *(Flora),* Monique Tarbes *(Claire),* Keith Carradine *(David Foster),* Bruno Ganz *(Heinrich Grun),* Francois Simon *(Gregoire),* Francis Huster *(Thomas),* Niels Arestrup *(Nano),* Georges Wod *(Liansko),* Patrice Alexsandre *(Petard),* Rene Feret *(Julien),* Anders Holmquist *(Anders),* Jacques Spiesser *(Saint-Loup),* Cloe Caillat *(Marie),* Hermine Karagheuz *(Camilla),* Carole Lange *(Carole),* Gunilla Persson *(Swedish Woman),* Melusine Schamber *(Berthe),* Laurence Schuman *(Gisele).*

Jeanne Moreau's first self-directed effort tells the story of a group of actresses and the special friendship they share, opening as they gather at the estate of the eldest and most successful of their number, Sarah Dedieu (Moreau). Each of them is beset with her own romantic and career troubles: Laura (Lucia Bose) gave up acting to become wife and mother; Caroline (Caroline Cartier) is just beginning her career while attempting to work through problems with her lover (Niels Arestrup); and Juliene (Francine Racette), who is trying to choose between family and theatrical success, ends up in a one-night stand with American rocker David Foster (Keith Carradine). For her part, Sarah is ending a long affair with Thomas (Francis Huster), a writer-director, in order to move on to novelist Heinrich Grun (Bruno Ganz), yet she clings to old friend Gregoire (Francois Simon), a research scientist. It should come as no surprise that Moreau's directorial debut revolves around actresses, nor should it surprise anyone that Moreau's strength lies in her writing and direction of the cast. Her stylish command of camera movement and arrangement of elements within the frame are less expected, but it is LUMIERE's story and characters that are its raison d'etre. In French with English subtitles.

p, Claire Duval; d, Jeanne Moreau; w, Jeanne Moreau; ph, Ricardo Aronovich (Eastmancolor); ed, Albert Jurgenson; m, Astor Piazzola.

Drama **(PR:O MPAA:R)**

M

M*****

(1931, Ger.) 117m Nero-Star/PAR bw

Peter Lorre *(Franz Becker),* Otto Wernicke *(Inspector Karl Lohmann),* Gustav Grundgens *(Schraenker),* Theo Lingen *(Bauernfaenger),* Theodore Loos *(Police Commissioner Groeber),* Georg John *(Blind Peddler),* Ellen Widmann *(Mme. Becker),* Inge Landgut *(Elsie),* Ernst Stahl-Nachbaur *(Police Chief),* Paul Kemp *(Pickpocket),* Franz Stein *(Minister),* Rudolf Blumner *(Defense Attorney),* Karl Platen *(Watchman),* Gerhard Bienert *(Police Secretary),* Rosa Valetti *(Servant),* Hertha von Walter *(Prostitute),* Fritz Odemar *(The Cheater),* Fritz Gnass *(Burglar),* Heinrich Gretler, Lotte Lobinger, Isenta, Leonard Steckel, Karchow, Edgar Pauly, Kepich, Gunther Neumann, Leeser, Behal, Rosa Lichenstein, Carell, Mascheck, Else Ehser, Matthis, Elzer, Mederow, Faber, Margarete Melzer, Ilse Furstenberg, Trude Moss, Gelingk, Hadrian M. Netto, Goldstein, Nied, Anna Goltz, Klaus Pohl, Heinrich Gotho.

Fritz Lang's first sound film is also unquestionably his most chilling and provocative work, and contains Peter Lorre's greatest performance as the title child molester and murderer. As the film opens, Berlin is gripped by terror: a child molester is killing little girls, while the police's frantic search has so far turned up no clues to his identity. Frenzied citizens inform on their neighbors; police raids net scores of criminals, but none that can be linked to the killings. To stop this trend, the underworld's leading members resolve to catch the killer themselves, ordering the criminal community to find the murderer and bring him to a tribunal—and the trap to catch the desperate man is set in thrilling motion. Lang tells his grim tale in murky, expressive shadow, and (keeping the murders offscreen) achieves chilling effects through brilliant opticals—distorted camera angles; weird, unnatural images and setups; even crude symbols. He makes the most of the frenzy among the Berliners, cross-cutting into wholly different worlds to suggest their mutual fear, and uses the city in its entirety, its antiquity and squalor, to suggest a deep-seated corruption. Lang's debut in sound is also notable, the new medium used to extremely evocative effect (as in the killer's characteristic whistle). While M offers a truly sinister image of its killer, however, it is all the more effective for its psychological subtlety, effectively suggesting the psychopathic killer's guilt, despair, and compulsiveness. Lorre was so effective in the role of the repulsive—but oddly pathetic and abject—killer that he would be cast as grotesque psychopaths for the rest of his days. By the same token, Lang's distinctive images would influence many a filmmaker to come. In German with English subtitles.

p, Seymour Nebenzahl; d, Fritz Lang; w, Fritz Lang, Thea von Harbou, Paul Falkenberg, Adolf Jansen, Karl Vash (based on an article by Egon Jacobson); ph, Fritz Arno Wagner, Gustav Rathje; ed, Paul Falkenberg; m, Edvard Grieg.

Crime/Horror **(PR:O MPAA:NR)**

MACARONI**

(1985, It.) 104m Filmauro-Massfilm/PAR c (MACCHERONI)

Jack Lemmon *(Robert Traven),* Marcello Mastroianni *(Antonio Jasiello),* Daria Nicolodi *(Laura Di Falco),* Isa Danieli *(Carmelina Jasiello),* Marie Luisa Santella *(Door Keeper),* Patrizia Sacchi *(Virginia),* Bruno Esposito *(Giulio Jasiello),* Orsetta Gregoretti *(Young Actress in Theater),* Marc Berman, Jean Francois Perrier *(French Record Producers),* Fabio Tenore *(Pasqualino theLittle Monk),* Giovanna Sanfilippo *(Maria),* Marta Bifano *(Luisella),* Aldo De Martino *(Cottone the Theater Manager),* Clotilde De Spirito *(Villain's Mistress),* Carlotta Ercolino *(TV Journalist),* Vincenza Gioioso *(Donna Amalia),* Ernesto Mahieux *(Young Actor in Theater),* Giovanni Mauriello *(Driver),* Alfredo Mingione *(Aeritalia Manager),* Daniela Novak *(Giulio's Fiancee).*

After completing LE BAL, a wordless musical history of an Italian ballroom, director Ettore Scola turned to this potentially interesting, dialog-heavy dramatic comedy, which pairs one of America's most successful actors, Jack Lemmon, with one of Europe's, Marcello Mastroianni. Robert Traven (Lemmon), a brash American in Naples on business, is spotted by Antonio Jasiello (Mastroianni), an energetic and eccentric Italian. The encounter reminds Antonio of the past: in 1946, Traven was engaged to Antonio's sister Maria (Giovanna Sanfilippo), then broke her heart by returning to America and deserting her for good. Scola has crafted a potentially wonderful film about nostalgia and friendship in MACARONI, but the film often lapses into comedy that isn't funny, and the heavy plot distracts from its honesty. Mastroianni is predictably excellent, while Lemmon's performance runs hot and cold, falling on occasion into his own peculiar brand of hamming. Scola would follow in 1987 with the much more successful THE FAMILY. The dialog is mostly in English, with subtitles added for the occasional Italian lines.

p, Luigi De Laurentiis, Aurelio De Laurentiis, Franco Committeri; d, Ettore Scola; w, Ruggero Maccari, Furio Scarpelli, Ettore Scola; ph, Claudio Ragona (Eastmancolor); ed, Carla Simoncelli; m, Armando Trovaioli.

Comedy/Drama **(PR:C MPAA:PG)**

MACARTHUR'S CHILDREN***

(1985, Jap.) 120m Harold Ace/Orion bw

Takaya Yamauchi *(Ryuta Ashigara),* Yoshiyuki Omori *(Saburo Masaki),* Shiori Sakura *(Mume Hatano),* Masako Natsume *(Komako Nakai),* Shuji Otaki *(Tadao Ashigara),* Haruko Kato *(Haru Ashigara),* Ken Watanabe *(Tetsuo Nakai),* Naomi Chiaki *(Miyo),* Shinsuke Shimada *(Jiro Masaki),* Taketoshi Naito *(Ginzo Nakai),* Miyuki Tanigawa *(Setsuko),* Chiharu Shukuri *(Yoko Masaki),* Bill Jensen *(Lt. Anderson),* Howard Mohett *(G.I.).*

An attempt to bring about an understanding of how the Japanese reacted to the humiliating defeat of their troops in WW II, MACARTHUR'S CHILDREN approaches the subject in microcosm and, instead of concerning itself with the whole of Japan, centers on a small, remote island called Awaji Shima. Set just after the defeat, the film depicts events through the eyes of children, especially Ryuta Ashigara (Takaya Yamauchi), a young boy whose father was killed in battle and who is being raised by his grandfather, the local police chief. Ryuta's best friend, the rebellious Saburo (Yoshiyuki Omori), refuses to admit national dishonor and instead threatens to run away and become a gangster, or *baraketsu*. Although the children cannot fully comprehend what has happened to their country, they can see the changes in the people around them. Then come the Americans. With their candy bars and gum, baseball, and Glenn Miller records, they easily win over the children, but at the same time corrupt the once-pure Japanese culture with their unconscious imperialism. Like fellow Japanese director Nagisa Oshima, Masahiro Shinoda's talents blossomed in the 1960s with subjects pertaining chiefly to the passions of youth. Here, Shinoda places these passions in a historical context and a highly westernized narrative style, but the result is a mannered film lacking the urgency one might expect from a depiction of the powerful clash of prewar and postwar Japanese cultures. In Japanese with English subtitles.

p, You-No-Kai, Masato Hara; d, Masahiro Shinoda; w, Takeshi Tamura (based on the novel by Yu Aku); ph, Kazuo Miyagawa; ed, Sachiko Yamaji; m, Shinichiro Ikebe, Glenn Miller.

Drama **(PR:C MPAA:PG)**

MACBETH*½**

(1971, Brit.) 140m Playboy/COL c

Jon Finch *(Macbeth),* Francesca Annis *(Lady Macbeth),* Martin Shaw *(Banquo),* Nicholas Selby *(Duncan),* John Stride *(Ross),* Stephan Chase *(Malcolm),* Paul Shelley *(Donalbain),* Terence Bayler *(Macduff),* Andrew Laurence *(Lennox),* Frank Wylie *(Mentieth),* Bernard Archard *(Angus),* Bruce Purchase *(Caithness),* Keith Chegwin *(Fleance),* Noel Davis *(Seyton),* Noelle Rimmington *(Young Witch),* Maisie Farquhar *(Blind Witch),* Vic Abbott *(Cawdor),* Elsie Taylor *(1st Witch),* Bill Drysdale *(1st King's Groom),* Roy Jones *(2nd King's Groom),* Patricia Mason *(Gentlewoman),* Ian Hogg *(1st Minor Thane),* Geoffrey Reed *(2nd Minor Thane),* Nigel Ashton *(3rd Minor Thane),* Mark Dignam *(Macduff's Son),* Diane Fletcher *(Lady Mac-*

duff), Richard Pearson *(Doctor),* Sydney Bromley *(Porter),* William Hobbs *(Young Seyward),* Alf Joint *(Old Seyward),* Michael Balfour, Andrew McCulloch *(Murderers),* Howard Lang, David Ellison *(Old Soldiers),* Terence Mountain *(Soldier).*

Roman Polanski's graphically violent version of the classic Shakespeare play casts Jon Finch and Francesca Annis as the murderously obsessed couple in debt to witchcraft and prophecies. Polanski's first film after the murder of his wife, Sharon Tate, MACBETH could be read as an attempt to exorcise real-life demons. In any case, this version, if not the best Shakespearean adaptation, is certainly the most faithful to the original time reference. The vulgarity and gore on the screen is neither exploitative nor irresponsible, but a faithful interpretation that is not shaped by conventional theatrical techniques. While Annis' nude sleepwalking scene has been criticized as a result of Playboy Enterprises' involvement (in fact, the script was written before Playboy agreed to produce the film), it is true to the period. The project was originally offered to Allied Artists, then to Universal, but both deals fell through, and Hugh Hefner, who was anxious to get into film, felt this would be the perfect vehicle for the growing Playboy Enterprises. It turned out to be his first major failure instead. Polanski originally intended to cast Tuesday Weld as Lady Macbeth, but she declined after learning about the nude scene. Photographed in Wales during incessant downpours and fog, the picture was completed way behind schedule and lost about $3.5 million dollars. The original cut received an "X" rating. In English.

p, Andrew Braunsberg, Roman Polanski; d, Roman Polanski; w, Roman Polanski, Kenneth Tynan (based on the play by William Shakespeare); ph, Gilbert Taylor (Todd AO 35, Technicolor); ed, Alastair McIntyre; m, The Third Ear Band.

Drama **(PR:O MPAA:R)**

MADAME ROSA***½

(1977, Fr.) 105m Lira/WB-COL-New Line c (LA VIE DEVANT SOI)

Simone Signoret *(Mme. Rosa),* Claude Dauphin *(Dr. Katz),* Samy Ben Youb *(Mohammed "Momo"),* Gabriel Jabbour *(Mr. Hamil),* Michal Bat Adam *(Nadine),* Costa Gavras *(Ramon),* Stella Anicette *(Mme. Lola),* Bernard La Jarrige *(Mr. Charmette),* Mohammed Zineth *(Kadir Youssef),* Genervievre Fontanel *(Maryse).*

An aging survivor of Auschwitz, Madame Rosa (Simone Signoret) is a Parisian ex-streetwalker who cares for prostitutes' children in the city's poor Arab-Jewish section. Although she is slowly losing her memory, she is still able to care for her charges, especially Momo (Samy Ben Youb), an unruly Arab Muslim boy who, although he tends to be rebellious, reciprocates her love. When Madame Rosa has delusions that the Gestapo is going to come for her and makes the boy promise to hide her, he does so, sending the doctor away and maintaining the dying woman has gone to Israel. MADAME ROSA handles its underlying conflicts—between Arabs and Jews, between Naziism and Jews—well, and explores its mixed racial and cultural milieu with grace, sensitivity, and subtlety. The film is the first pairing of director-writer Moshe Mizrahi, a Moroccan-born Israeli, and the great Simone Signoret, who won a Cesar for her marvelous and unglamorous performance here. The two would team again for the bittersweet 1981 drama I SENT A LETTER TO MY LOVE. Film director Costa-Gavras has a supporting role in MADAME ROSA, which won the Best Foreign Film Oscar in 1977. The videocassette is dubbed in English.

p, Raymond Danon, Roland Girard, Jean Bolary; d, Moshe Mizrahi; w, Moshe Mizrahi (based on the novel *Momo* by Romain); ph, Nestor Almendros (Eastmancolor); ed, Sophie Coussein; m, Philippe Sarde, Dabket Loubna.

Drama **(PR:O MPAA:PG)**

MAEDCHEN IN UNIFORM****

(1931, Ger.) 110m Deutsche Film-Gemeinschaft bw (AKA: GIRLS IN UNIFORM)

Emila Unda *(The Principal),* Dorothea Wieck *(Fraulein von Bernburg),* Hedwig Schlichter *(Fraulein von Kesten),* Hertha Thiele *(Manuela von Meinhardis),* Ellen Schwannecke.

Late Weimar Germany produced a number of fine anti-authoritarian films, perhaps the best of which was MAEDCHEN IN UNIFORM, the story of a girl's struggles within the rigid discipline of a boarding school for daughters of poor military officers. New student Manuela (Hertha Thiele) is homesick, introspective, and alienated. The headmistress (Emilia Unda) disapproves of such individualism, and rules her students with the Prussian dictum, "Through discipline and hunger, hunger and discipline, we shall rise again." Manuela becomes attached to one teacher (Dorothea Wieck), who sees in the sensitive new student a reflection of her former, nonconformist self. But Manuela's dependence on her mentor grows into obsessive love, testing the headmistress' tolerance. Though MAEDCHEN IN UNIFORM's symbolism can seem heavy-handed (like Murnau's THE LAST LAUGH, it invests much in the uniform as an image of German social consciousness), it is a film of emotional, narrative, and visual assurance, sensitive in its treatment of a lesbian relationship. It was written (by Christa Winsloe and F.D. Andam, from the former's play) and directed (Leontine Sagan) by women, with an all-female cast. Historically, it represents a finality: within a few years the Nazis would control the film studios, replacing the messages of films like MAEDCHEN IN UNIFORM with propaganda. In German with English subtitles.

p, Carl Froelich; d, Leontine Sagan; w, Christa Winsloe, F.D. Andam (based on the play "Gestern und Heute" by Christa Winsloe).

Drama **(PR:C MPAA:NR)**

MAGICIAN, THE***

(1958, Swed.) 100m Svensk/Janus bw (ANSIKTET; AKA: THE FACE)

Max von Sydow *(Albert Emanuel Vogler),* Ingrid Thulin *(Manda Aman),* Gunnar Bjornstrand *(Dr. Vergerus),* Naima

Wifstrand *(Grandmother),* Bengt Ekerot *(Spegel),* Bibi Andersson *(Sara),* Gertrud Fridh *(Mrs. Ottilia Egerman),* Lars Ekborg *(Stinson),* Toivo Pawlo *(Police Chief Starbeck),* Erland Josephson *(Consul Egerman),* Ake Fridell *(Tubal),* Sif Ruud *(Sofia Garp),* Oscar Ljung *(Antonsson),* Ulla Sjoblom *(Mrs. Henrietta Starbeck),* Axel Duberg *(Rustan),* Birgitta Pettersson *(Sanna),* Frithiof Bjarne, Arne Martensson, Tor Borong *(Customs Officials).*

In THE MAGICIAN, Ingmar Bergman takes two favorite motifs—masks and magic—and explores them on a number of different levels. Albert Emanuel Vogler (Max Von Sydow), a 19-century magician, brings a troupe of traveling illusionists to a small Swedish town where the people don't believe in magic. Led by Vogler, the troupe proceeds to play with the townspeople's minds, and director Bergman, in turn, makes imaginative use of editing, lighting, and special effects to toy with audience expectations. Things are never quite what they seem, either narratively or cinematically. And the film's mysterious nature is further enhanced by the dark, rich, gothic look of Bergman's mise-en-scene. Though at times the story is overwhelmed by its theme and symbols, THE MAGICIAN is still fascinating, presenting a myriad of challenging ideas about magic, reality, and the nature of film itself. The videocassette is available in both dubbed and subtitled (Swedish into English) versions.

p, Carl-Henry Cagarp; d, Ingmar Bergman; w, Ingmar Bergman; ph, Gunnar Fischer, Rolf Halmquist; ed, Oscar Rosander; m, Erik Nordgren.

Drama **(PR:C MPAA:NR)**

MAKE ROOM FOR TOMORROW**½

(1979, Fr.) 105m Drouette-la Tour/Quartet c (AU BOUT DU BOUT DU BANC; Trans: At The End Of The End Of The Bench)

Victor Lanoux *(Ben),* Jane Birkin *(Peggy),* George Wilson *(Elie),* Henri Cremieux *(Isaac),* Mathieu Kassovitz *(Mathias),* Francoise Bertin, Chloe Caillat, Patrick Chesnais, Yvonne Clech, Jean Pierre Coffe, Florence Giorgetti, Nathalie Guerin, Odette Laure.

Too symbolic and charming for its own good, MAKE ROOM FOR TOMORROW manages to be entertaining without providing much insight into its story about four generations of Jewish males, ranging from 90-year-old Isaac (Henri Cremieux) to 10-year-old Mathias (Mathieu Kassovitz). The film takes place in the suburban Paris home of Ben (Victor Lanoux, who also produced) and Peggy (Jane Birkin), during a family gathering with Ben's father Elie (Georges Wilson), who is visiting from Israel, and Ben's grandfather, Isaac, who has traveled from Nice for the occasion. Intended as a metaphor for 20th-century Jewish existence, survival for these representatives of four generations has been difficult: Isaac has been jilted by his young female companion, Elie isn't as orthodox as one might expect, Ben is trying unsuccessfully to keep his marriage together, and Mathias does his best to make sense of the whole scene. Moreover, Ben's house is literally and symbolically falling apart—its walls and roof damaged by gradual shifts that have occurred over the years. Although the film is not as important as it would like to be, it does boast some nice performances, especially by Cremieux as the dapper old man who still has an eye on the young ladies. In French with English subtitles.

p, Victor Lanoux; d, Peter Kassovitz; w, Peter Kassovitz, Elie Pressmann, Chantal Remy; ph, Etienne Szabo; ed, Chantal Remy; m, Georges Moustaki.

Drama **(PR:O MPAA:NR)**

MALICIOUS***

(1973, It.) 98m Cineriz/PAR c (MALIZIA; AKA: MALICE)

Laura Antonelli *(Angela),* Turi Ferro *(Don Ignazio),* Alessandro Momo *(Nino),* Tina Aumont *(Luciana),* Lilla Brignone *(Nonna, Grandmother),* Pino Caruso *(Don Cirillo),* Angela Luce *(Widow Corallo),* Gianluigi Chirizzi *(Antonio),* Massimilano Filoni *(Enzino),* Stefano Amato *(Porcello),* Grazia Di Marza *(Adelina).*

What a surprise . . . Laura Antonelli in an Italian sex comedy. Don Ignazio (Turi Ferro), a Sicilian widower, hires the attractive Angela (Antonelli) to serve as housekeeper for him and his three sons. Unknowingly, Angela captivates the adolescent boys with her natural sensuality, causing 14-year-old Nino (Alessandro Momo) to try to manipulate her. The boy's blackmailing takes some cruel twists; however, Angela seductively outwits him. This Italian slice-of-life sex comedy works chiefly because of Antonelli. Conveying both innocence and sensuality, imbuing her role with intelligence and wit, she carries the story through its underdeveloped moments of cheap sexual humiliation. The film also offers some deft satirical jabs at life in 1950s Sicily. Despite some occasionally mean-spirited humor, MALICIOUS in an entertaining example of a popular Italian genre, photographed by one of the masters, Vittorio Storaro. The videocassette is dubbed in English.

p, Silvio Clementelli; d, Salvatore Samperi; w, Salvatore Samperi, Ottavio Jemma, Alessandro Parenzo (based on a story by Salvatore Samperi); ph, Vittorio Storaro (Technicolor); ed, Sergio Montanari; m, Fred Bongusto.

Comedy **(PR:O MPAA:R)**

MALOU***

(1981, Ger.) 93m Ziegler/Quartet c

Ingrid Caven *(Malou),* Grischa Huber *(Hannah),* Helmut Griem *(Martin),* Ivan Desny *(Paul),* Marie Colbin *(Lotte),* Peter Chatel *(Albert),* Margarita Calahorra *(Lucia),* Lo Van Hensbergen *(Paul's Father),* Liane Saalborn *(Paul's Mother),* Cordula Riedel *(Hannah at 12),* Jim Kain *(Uncle Max),* Peer Raben, Winnetou Kampmann, Estrongo Nahama, Carl Duering, Antonio Skarmeta, Constanza Lira, Angela Villroel, Michael Boehme.

This impressive debut feature by Jeanine Meerapfel benefits from the efforts of several members of R.W. Fassbinder's stock company—actress Ingrid Caven, cinematographer Michael Ballhaus, and composer Peer Raben. Hannah (Grischa Huber), a young married woman, sets out from Germany to find out the truth about her mother,

Malou (Caven). She learns that Malou left Strasbourg during the rise of Naziism, married an aristocratic German Jew, fled to Argentina, and was eventually abandoned by the man for whom she gave up her life and German roots. Constructed through flashbacks, MALOU creates a rich portrait of two women—a mother whose life and death were dictated by her dependence on a man, and a daughter who refuses to accept the same fate. The videocassette is available in both dubbed and subtitled (German into English) versions.

p, Regina Ziegler; d, Jeanine Meerapfel; w, Jeanine Meerapfel; ph, Michael Ballhaus; ed, Dagmar Hirtz; m, Peer Raben.

Drama **(PR:C MPAA:R)**

MAN AND A WOMAN, A***½

(1966, Fr.) 102m Les Films 13 c (UN HOMME ET UNE FEMME)

Anouk Aimee *(Anne Gauthier),* Jean-Louis Trintignant *(Jean-Louis Duroc),* Pierre Barouh *(Pierre Gauthier),* Valerie Lagrange *(Valerie Duroc),* Simone Paris *(Head Mistress),* Antoine Sire *(Antoine Duroc),* Souad Amidou *(Francoise Gauthier),* Yane Barry *(Mistress of Jean-Louis),* Paul Le Person *(Garage Man),* Henri Chemin *(Jean-Louis Codriver),* Gerard Sire *(Announcer).*

Effusively romantic and visually stunning, A MAN AND A WOMAN has been condemned by some as an exercise in style for style's sake and by others for its lack of emotional complexity. Yet for many viewers this Claude Lelouch-directed film is as magical a love story as any brought to the screen. Widowed film studio script girl Anne Gauthier (Anouk Aimee) and auto racer Jean-Louis Duroc (Jean-Louis Trintignant), whose wife has committed suicide, meet at the boarding school attended by his son and her daughter. When Jean-Louis gives Anne a ride back to Paris, friendship and then love blossom, though the specter of her much-loved late husband confuses their romance. It looks like the end, but Lelouch still has a dazzling scene on the beach at Deauville up his sleeve. Pulling out all the stops, Lelouch employs a wide variety of filmmaking techniques (swirling cameras, slow motion, switches from color to black and white, flashforwards and flashbacks) to tell his simple but effective love story. Although not the equal of the work of Lelouch's French contemporaries, A MAN AND WOMAN demonstrated that a wide American audience was interested in stylish films, provided their stories hit home. The film won Academy Awards for Best Story/Screenplay and Best Foreign-Language Film, and Aimee was nominated as Best Actress and Lelouch as Best Director, but for many viewers Francis Lai's catchy score remains their dominant memory. Lelouch has continued to get mileage out of A MAN AND A WOMAN—in 1972, he opened his HAPPY NEW YEAR with a clip from the film; in 1977, he remade it as ANOTHER MAN, ANOTHER CHANCE, setting it in the American West in 1870; and in 1986 he returned to his original characters for the sequel A MAN AND A WOMAN: 20 YEARS LATER. The videocassette is dubbed in English.

p, Claude Lelouch; d, Claude Lelouch; w, Claude Lelouch, Pierre Uytterhoeven (based on a story by Claude Lelouch); ph, Claude Lelouch (Eastmancolor); ed, Claude Lelouch, G. Boisser, Claude Barrois; m, Francis Lai.

Drama **(PR:A-C MPAA:NR)**

MAN AND A WOMAN: 20 YEARS LATER, A***

(1986, Fr.) 108m Films 13/WB c (UN HOMME ET UNE FEMME: VINGT ANS DEJA)

Anouk Aimee *(Anne Gauthier),* Jean-Louis Trintignant *(Jean-Louis Duroc),* Evelyne Bouix *(Francoise),* Marie-Sophie Pochat *(Marie-Sophie),* Philippe Leroy-Beaulieu *(Prof. Thevenin),* Charles Gerard *(Charlot),* Antoine Sire *(Antoine),* Andre Engel *(Film Director),* Robert Hossein, Tanya Lopert, Nicole Garcia, Jacques Weber, Richard Berry *(Themselves).*

Two decades after the smashing success of A MAN AND A WOMAN (see above), director Claude Lelouch, stars Anouk Aimee and Jean-Louis Trintignant, and Francis Lai's unforgettable theme song came together again for this relatively satisfying sequel. Twenty years older, no longer racing, and involved with a considerably younger woman (Marie-Sophie Pochat), Jean-Louis (Trintignant) organizes a Paris-to-Dakar rally; Anne (Aimee), on the other hand, has risen from script girl to producer and, searching for a hit, has chosen to make a musical about her affair with Jean-Louis starring Richard Berry (playing himself). As the film continues, several stories interweave, including the real-life reunion between Jean-Louis and Anne; the on-screen tale she is filming; the rally, during which Jean-Louis and his young girl friend are stranded in the desert; and a seemingly unrelated subplot about a madman who escapes from a mental hospital. Despite Lelouch's attempt to cram too many stories into one movie, A MAN AND A WOMAN: 20 YEARS LATER is an enjoyable, often funny effort, though those who've seen and liked the original are bound to appreciate this more than other viewers. Trintignant and Aimee, who look older and wiser, give fine performances, and the feeling of being with old friends is heightened by the presence of Antoine Sire, who played Jean-Louis' son in the original and does so again here, and by Lelouch's liberal use of footage from the first film. In French with English subtitles.

p, Claude Lelouch; d, Claude Lelouch; w, Claude Lelouch, Pierre Uytterhoeven, Monique Lange, Jerome Tonnerre; ph, Jean-Yves Le Mener (Eastmancolor); ed, Hugues Darmois; m, Francis Lai.

Romance **(PR:C MPAA:PG)**

MAN FACING SOUTHEAST****

(1986, Arg.) 105m Cinequanon/Film Dallas c (HOMBRE MIRANDO AL SUDESTE; AKA: MAN LOOKING SOUTHEAST)

Lorenzo Quinteros *(Dr. Dennis),* Hugo Soto *(Rantes),* Ines Vernengo *(Beatriz),* Cristina Scaramuzza *(Nurse),* Rubens W. Correa *(Dr. Prieto),* David Edery, Rodolfo Rodas, Jean Pierre Requeraz.

Argentine director Eliseo Subiela takes an allegorical approach to the story of Christ in this enigmatic parable. A jaded mental asylum psychiatrist, Dr. Dennis (Lorenzo Quinteros), becomes fascinated with Rantes (Hugo Soto), who suddenly appears in his ward. Upon questioning, Rantes explains he is a holographic being from another planet, which transmits to him from the southeast. As the two men grow closer, it begins to appear that Rantes' mission is something beyond an intergalactic visit; eventually, his inexplicable influence on the other patients incurs the displeasure of authorities who demand that Dennis take severe measures to counteract his friend and patient's delirium. Writer-director Subiela incorporates a wide variety of influences to create a fascinating, multifaceted work of art. The reworking of the Gospels is evident, but the biblical references are a basis for convincing contemporary characters and open questions, and the film clearly participates in the mystical tradition in Latin American literature. Subiela also incorporates a variety references to paintings in the film's design. Soto's performance is remarkable, Quinteros an excellent counterpart. Their natural, often affectionate, and unique relationship becomes the heart of this profound and highly personal film. In Spanish with English subtitles.

p, Lujan Pflaum; d, Eliseo Subiela; w, Eliseo Subiela; ph, Ricardo de Angelis; ed, Luis Cesar D'Angiolillo; m, Pedro Aznar.

Drama **(PR:O MPAA:R)**

MAN IN LOVE, A***½

(1987, Fr.) 108m Camera One-Alexandre-JMS/Cinecom c (UN HOMME AMOUREUX)

Greta Scacchi *(Jane Steiner),* Peter Coyote *(Steve Elliott),* Peter Riegert *(Michael Pozner),* Claudia Cardinale *(Julia Steiner),* John Berry *(Harry Steiner),* Vincent Lindon *(Bruno Schlosser),* Jamie Lee Curtis *(Susan Elliott),* Jean Pigozzi *(Dante Pizani),* Elia Katz *(Sam),* Constantin Alexandrov *(De Vitta),* Michele Melega *(Paolo),* Jean-Claude de Goros *(Dr. Sandro).*

A MAN IN LOVE is romantic melodrama on a grand, international scale. Set mostly in Italy's Cinecitta film studio, it stars Peter Coyote as Steve Elliott, a temperamental American actor playing the lead in a film biography of Cesare Pavese, the Italian Communist writer who committed suicide in 1950 at age 41. The film's stereotypically obsessive director (Jean Pigozzi) has cast a relatively unknown English-speaking actress, Jane Steiner (Greta Scacchi), in a minor role as one of the many women Pavese loved, and her first visit to the set results in an explosive confrontation with the difficult star, offering a hint of things to come. An unpredictable, sexually charged romance develops between the two actors both on- and off-screen, putting Steve's acting ability and his feelings for his wife (Jamie Lee Curtis) to the test. Diane Kurys' first film in English transcends borders. Displaying remarkable adroitness, she interweaves various languages and locales, shows her characters to be a unique group of people involved in a fiction-making process that overlaps with and confuses real life, and maintains a complex plot in which the simple act of choosing a supporting actress nearly sinks the film-within-the-film and upsets two relationships. Badly underrated by critics, especially in comparison with Kurys' ENTRE NOUS (1983), A MAN IN LOVE establishes even more firmly than that film that Kurys is one of the most compelling filmmakers to emerge from France in recent years.

p, Marjorie Israel, Armand Barbault, Roberto Guissani; d, Diane Kurys; w, Diane Kurys, Olivier Schatzky, Israel Horovitz; ph, Bernard Zitzermann (Eastmancolor); ed, Joele Van Effenterre; m, Georges Delerue.

Romance **(PR:O MPAA:R)**

MAN WHO LOVED WOMEN, THE***

(1977, Fr.) 118m Les Films du Carrosse-Les Productions Artistes/Cinema 5 c (L'HOMME QUI AIMAIT LES FEMMES)

Charles Denner *(Bertrand Morane),* Brigitte Fossey *(Genevieve Bigey, Editor),* Nelly Borgeaud *(Delphine Grezel),* Leslie Caron *(Vera, the Ghost),* Genevieve Fontanel *(Lingerie Saleswoman),* Nathalie Baye *(Martine Desdoits),* Sabine Glaser *("Midi Car" Employee),* Valerie Bonnier *(Fabienne),* Martine Chassaing *(Denise),* Roselyne Puyo *(Movie Usherette),* Anna Perrier *(Babysitter),* Monique Dury *(Mme. Duteil),* Nella Barbier *(Liliane),* Frederique Jamet *(Juliette),* Marie-Jeanne Montfajon *(Christine Morane),* Jean Daste *(Doctor),* Roger Leenhardt *(Editor),* Henri Agel, Henri-Jean Servat *(Readers),* Michel Marti *(Bertrand, as a Child),* Christian Lentretien *(Inspector),* Rico Lopez *(Joker in Restaurant),* Carmen Sarda-Canovas *(Laundress),* Philippe Lievre *(Bertrand's Colleague),* Marcel Berbert *(Delphine's Husband),* Michel Laurent, Pierre Gompertz, Roland Thenot *(Naval Officers),* Josiane Couedel *(Operator).*

Francois Truffaut's swiftly paced, light-hearted exercise concerns a man whose very existence is devoted to women—a man perhaps not unlike Truffaut himself. Bertrand (Charles Denner) is the amorous title male, a well-off researcher who is surely one of the most woman-crazy men ever to appear on film. He can't keep his mind off women; a mere glance at one *femme* dressed in black silk stockings sends him on a long journey towards love. All the while that Bertrand chases skirts, he remains charming and innocent, never believing he is doing anything wrong or harmful. Unlike those men who abuse women, Bertrand adores them—all of them. THE MAN WHO LOVED WOMEN is filled with Truffaut's ironic sense of humor, is always charming, and never in any way offending. As in all of Truffaut's romantic comedies, what appears as flippant and sugary is actually a cover for some very complex statements about the nature of love, Truffaut himself, and the cinema. In this sense THE MAN WHO LOVED WOMEN can be viewed, along with THE STORY OF ADELE H. and THE GREEN ROOM, as part of a trilogy about unrequited love and frustrating obsessions. A Hollywood remake of this film was made in 1983, directed by Blake Edwards and starring Burt Reynolds. In French with English subtitles.

d, Francois Truffaut; w, Francois Truffaut, Michel Fermaud, Suzanne Schiffman; ph, Nestor Almendros; ed, Martine Barraque; m, Maurice Jaubert.

Drama/Comedy (PR:O MPAA:NR)

MANON OF THE SPRING*½**

(1986, Fr.) 113m Renn-Films A2-RAI 2-DD/Orion c (MANON DES SOURCES; AKA: JEAN DE FLORETTE 2)

Yves Montand *(Cesar "Le Papet" Soubeyran),* Daniel Auteuil *(Ugolin Soubeyran),* Emmanuelle Beart *(Manon Cadoret),* Hippolyte Girardot *(Bernard Olivier),* Elizabeth Depardieu *(Aimee Cadoret),* Gabriel Bacquier *(Victor),* Armand Meffre *(Philoxene),* Andre Dupon *(Pamphile),* Pierre Nougaro *(Casimir),* Jean Maurel *(Anglade),* Roger Souza *(Ange),* Didier Pain *(Eliacin),* Pierre-Jean Rippert *(Cabridan),* Marc Betton *(Martial),* Yvonne Gamy *(Delphine),* Chantal Liennel *(Amandine),* Lucien Damiani *(Belloiseau).*

The continuation of JEAN DE FLORETTE resumes the story and brings its characters to their tragic ends. Ten years have passed and Manon (played by newcomer Emmanuelle Beart), the daughter of the hunchbacked farmer Jean (Gerard Depardieu in part one), has grown into a beautiful young shepherdess who tends her flock deep in the hills of Provence. In the years since her father's death, Le Papet (Yves Montand) and his nephew, Ugolin (Daniel Auteuil), have worked Jean's land into a profitable carnation farm by unplugging the underground spring they had kept secret from the hard-working farmer. Ugolin's vibrant red carnations now blossom in full glory, enabling him to save a small fortune. Le Papet, now old and withered, pushes his nephew toward marriage. Unless Ugolin takes a wife and begins a family, the name of Soubeyran (once the most-powerful family in the region) will cease to exist. Ugolin, however, has no desire to marry—until, one day, he sees Manon bathing in a small spring and falls instantly in love. Like its predecessor, MANON OF THE SPRING is filled with marvelous photography, gorgeous rolling landscapes, and spectacular performances. While part one favored Depardieu's character and his struggles against both man and nature, part two concentrates on the tragic end of Montand and his final reconciliation with the higher forces of fate. Montand, who is always brilliant, turns in a performance that surely ranks with his best work; Auteuil is also excellent as the manipulated young fool. (Beart, while lovely to look at, is given very little to do besides play the object of desire.) Much of the film is terribly traditional, though it is still an admirable piece of entertainment. MANON surpasses JEAN DE FLORETTE in its portrayal of the villagers, a necessary element virtually absent from part one. Taken as a whole, JEAN DE FLORETTE and MANON OF THE SPRING earned a total of eight Cesars: Best Film, Best Director, Best Actor (Auteuil), Best Actress, Best Screenplay, Best Score, Best Cinematography, and Best Sound (Pierre Gamet, Dominique Hennequin). In French with English subtitles. (SEE: JEAN DE FLORETTE.)

p, Pierre Grunstein; d, Claude Berri; w, Claude Berri, Gerard Brach (based on the novel by Marcel Pagnol); ph, Bruno Nuytten (Technovision, Eastmancolor); ed, Genevieve Louveau, Herve de Luze; m, Jean-Claude Petit, Giuseppe Verdi.

Drama (PR:C MPAA:R)

MARIUS*½**

(1931, Fr.) 103m Joinville/PAR bw

Raimu *(Cesar Olivier),* Orane Demazis *(Fanny),* Pierre Fresnay *(Marius),* Fernand Charpin *(Honore Panisse),* Alida Rouffe *(Honorine Cabanis),* Robert Vattier *(Mon. Brun),* Paul Dullac *(Felix Escartefigue),* Alexandre Mihalesco *(Piquoiseau),* Edouard Delmont *(2nd Mate),* Milly Mathis *(Aunt Claudine Foulon),* Callamand *(Le Goelec),* Maupi *(Stoker),* V. Ribe *(Customer),* Oueret *(Felicite),* Vassy *(Arab).*

MARIUS is the first of the "Marseilles Trilogy" penned by Marcel Pagnol, and was followed by FANNY and CESAR. Marius (Pierre Fresnay), toils at the Bar de la Marine in Marseilles and yearns for the sea. The bar is owned by his father, Cesar (Raimu), a widower who prates about Marius' lack of drive, though he truly adores the boy. Cesar spends his time consorting with his patrons—the wealthy Panisse (Fernand Charpin), ferry captain Felix Escartefigue (Paul Dullac), and customs inspector Brun (Robert Vattier). Marius loves Fanny (Orane Demazis), though he is unable to make a lasting commitment to her—the call of the sea is too strong. When the elder Panisse asks for Fanny's hand, Fanny sees this as her opportunity to work on Marius' jealousy, a ploy which works and results in their eventually becoming engaged. But despite her powerful love for Marius, Fanny is aware that he loves only the sea and cannot be happy as long as he lives in Marseilles. MARIUS is a touching and deeply affecting movie with an excellent cast (Raimu, a stage actor and silent screen comedian, is wonderful as Cesar and carried his role to even higher levels in the sequels), a rich record of life in Marseilles. Writer and producer Marcel Pagnol stayed on the set and watched carefully, then allowed Marc Allegret to direct FANNY and took over that chore himself for CESAR. (SEE: FANNY, 1932; and CESAR, 1936). In French with English subtitles.

p, Marcel Pagnol; d, Alexander Korda; w, Marcel Pagnol (based on the play by Marcel Pagnol); ph, Ted Pahle; ed, Roger Spiri Mercanton; m, Francis Gromon.

Drama (PR:C MPAA:NR)

MARRIAGE OF MARIA BRAUN, THE****

(1979, Ger.) 120m Albatros-Trio-Westdeutscher-Rudfunk-Filmverlog der Autoren/New Yorker c (DIE EHE DER MARIA BRAUN)

Hanna Schygulla *(Maria Braun),* Klaus Lowitsch *(Herman Braun),* Ivan Desny *(Oswald),* Gottfried John *(Willi),* Gisela Uhlen *(Mother),* Gunter Lamprecht *(Hans),* Hark Bohm *(Senkenberg),* George Byrd *(Bill),* Elisabeth Trissenaar *(Betti),* Rainer Werner Fassbinder *(Peddler),* Isolde Barth *(Vevi),* Peter Berling *(Bronski),* Sonja Neudorfer *(Red Cross Nurse),* Lieselotte Eder *(Frau Ehmcke),* Volker Spengler *(Conductor),* Karl-Heinz von Hassel *(Lawyer),*

Michael Ballhaus *(Anwalt),* Christine Hopf de Loup *(Notary),* Dr. Horst-Dieter Klock *(Gentleman With Car),* Gunther Kaufmann, Bruce Low *(American G.I.s),* Claus Holm *(Doctor),* Anton Schirsner *(Grandpa Berger),* Hannes Kaetner *(Justice of the Peace).*

The first in Rainer Werner Fassbinder's trilogy about women in post-WW II Germany (followed by VERONIKA VOSS and LOLA), this was the film that solidified Fassbinder's reputation both abroad and in Germany. The opening sequence shows a German city being torn apart by Allied bombs while a wedding takes place between Maria (Hanna Schygulla) and her soldier fiance, Hermann Braun (Klaus Lowitsch). Immediately afterwards the new husband is sent to the Russian front, leaving Maria Braun in poverty with her mother and sister. She waits for her husband, visiting the train station every day in the hope of hearing news about him. After receiving word that he has died, Maria takes work as a barmaid in a cafe that caters to American soldiers. There she meets Bill (George Byrd), a hefty black soldier who, despite the fact that they can barely converse, becomes her lover. She has nearly forgotten about her husband, until the starving and emasculated Hermann turns up as Maria and Bill are beginning to make love. The highly stylized, deliberate structure of THE MARRIAGE OF MARIA BRAUN owes much to the inspiration of Douglas Sirk's 1950s Hollywood melodramas, films such as IMITATION OF LIFE and WRITTEN ON THE WIND. With both Sirk and Fassbinder, the director remains distanced from the heart-wrenching dramatics that are taking place, in order to comment on certain social ills. Fassbinder, however, is even more removed from the material than Sirk—reflecting the alienation prevalent in a postwar Germany striving to rebuild itself into an industrial power, yet failing to take into account the human bonds that make a society healthy. The effect upon the heroine is one of great pathos; we can only watch helplessly as this beautiful young woman places herself in an emotional vacuum. Schygulla is quite powerful in this role, perhaps the best of her career, remaining cold and aloof yet evoking a strong sense of pity. Though THE MARRIAGE OF MARIA BRAUN is not always an easy film to understand, the stark atmosphere, icy performances, and poignant revelations make it one of the most important films to emerge from Germany in the 1970s, and one of Fassbinder's best. In German with English subtitles.

p, Michael Fengler; d, Rainer Werner Fassbinder; w, Peter Marthesheimer, Pia Frohlich, Rainer Werner Fassbinder (based on an idea by Fassbinder); ph, Michael Ballhaus; ed, Juliane Lorenz, Franz Walsch; m, Peer Raben.

Drama **(PR:O MPAA:R)**

MARRIED WOMAN, THE****

(1964, Fr.) 94m Anouchka-Orsay/Royal bw (UNE FEMME MARIEE; GB: A MARRIED WOMAN)

Macha Meril *(Charlotte Giraud),* Bernard Noel *(Robert, the Lover),* Philippe Leroy *(Pierre, the Husband),* Rita Maiden *(Mme. Celine),* Margaret Le Van, Veronique Duval *(Girls in Swimming Pool),* Chris Tophe *(Nicolas),* Georges Liron *(The Physician),* Roger Leenhardt *(Himself),* Jean-Luc Godard *(Narrator).*

Charlotte (Macha Meril) is a Parisian housewife with both a husband, airplane pilot Pierre (Philippe Leroy), and a lover, Robert (Bernard Noel). When she becomes pregnant, she realizes either man could be the father. She debates whether she should stay with her husband or leave him for Robert—then she gets no help from either in making her decision. Subtitled "Fragments of a film made in 1964," THE MARRIED WOMAN is a fragmented, distanced film that dissects Charlotte's character and morally situates her between the two men in her life. Even at the film's opening, Charlotte is represented as a disembodied figure—in separate shots we are shown, against a white bed sheet, her hands, legs, feet, torso. Taking place over a 24-hour period, even THE MARRIED WOMAN's time frame is cut apart into almost Resnaisian divisions. Heavily under the influence of the distancing devises of Brecht, director Jean-Luc Godard makes use of the written word, magazine advertisements and billboards, allusions to other arts (Racine, Apollinaire, Hitchcock, Resnais, Beethoven), visual references to film technique (the use of negative film images), and interviews in a *cinema-verite* mode. In French with English subtitles.

d, Jean-Luc Godard; w, Jean-Luc Godard; ph, Raoul Coutard; ed, Agnes Guillemot, Francoise Collin; m, Claude Nougaro.

Drama **(PR:C MPAA:NR)**

MASCULINE FEMININE*****

(1966, Fr./Swed.) 103m Anouchka-Argos-Svensk-Sandrews/Royal bw (MASCULIN FEMININ)

Jean-Pierre Leaud *(Paul),* Chantal Goya *(Madeleine),* Marlene Jobert *(Elisabeth),* Michel Debord *(Robert),* Catherine-Isabelle Duport *(Catherine),* Eva-Britt Strandberg *(Lavinia),* Birger Malmsten *(Actor),* Elsa Leroy *(Miss 19),* Francoise Hardy *(Woman with the American Officer),* Chantal Darget *(Woman on Metro),* Brigitte Bardot, Antoine Bourseiller *(Themselves).*

This is Jean-Luc Godard's inquiry into the generation he refers to as the "children of Marx and Coca-Cola," the 1960s youth culture. Paul (Jean-Pierre Leaud), a confused young romantic in search of perfect love, meets pop singer Madeleine (Chantal Goya) in a cafe, and eventually they move in together. Paul copes with his changing views by taking a job for a market research firm, gathering data, and interviewing people (including a young woman voted "Miss 19'). While Madeleine pursues her career, Paul tries to coexist with her and her two roommates, Elisabeth and Catherine (Marlene Jobert and Catherine-Isabelle Duport). Leaud's character—practically an extension of the Antoine Doinel character he played for Francois Truffaut (he even adopts the name Doinel at one point in the film)—wants to live for love, but the ideal becomes problematic in a detached and increasingly consumer-oriented society. With MASCULINE FEMININE, Godard began a string of increasingly political pictures, leading eventually to his self-imposed exile from commercial cinema. His interest in the synthesis of fiction and documentary is fully evident here, with long static shots of people being interviewed included as a means of bringing to the screen an everyday chronicle of Parisian youth in the winter of 1965. (Contrary to the director's intentions, the picture was banned in France for those under 18.) Charming, innovative, provocative, and prophetic, MASCULINE FEMININE is one of Godard's masterpieces. In French with English subtitles.

d, Jean-Luc Godard; w, Jean-Luc Godard (based on the stories "The Signal" and "Paul's Mistress" by Guy de Maupassant); ph, Willy Kurant; ed, Agnes Guillemot, Marguerite Renoir; m, Francis Lai, Jean-Jacques Debout.

Drama **(PR:C-O MPAA:NR)**

MAYERLING****

(1936, Fr.) 96m Nero/Pax bw

Charles Boyer *(Archduke Rudolph of Austria),* Danielle Darrieux *(Marie Vetsera),* Suzy Prim *(Countess Larisch),* Jean Dax *(Emperor Franz Joseph),* Gabrielle Dorziat *(Empress Elizabeth),* Jean Debucourt *(Count Taafe),* Marthe Regnier *(Baroness Vetsera),* Yolande Laffon *(Stephanie),* Vladimir Sokoloff *(Chief of Police),* Andre Dubosc *(Loschek the Valet),* Gina Manes *(Marinka),* Rene Bergeron *(Szeps),* Odette Talazac, Nane Germon.

MAYERLING is one of the greatest love stories ever brought to the screen, the bittersweet, painfully poignant romance between the star-crossed Crown Prince Rudolph of Austria and his adoring mistress, Marie Vetsera. Charles Boyer, in a riveting performance, is Rudolph, son of the powerful Franz Joseph, Emperor of Austria-Hungary. A free spirit who associates with radicals and gypsies, Rudolph is also a prisoner of his royal blood. Everywhere there are court spies assigned to track and trail the errant heir to the throne. Eluding his followers at a fair, he meets 17-year-old Marie Vetsera (Danielle Darrieux), and it's love at first sight, although Marie has no idea that her prince is *the* prince as the couple enjoys such little pleasures as tossing rings around a swan's neck and watching a puppet show. The following night, Marie attends the opera and is startled to see the handsome young man from the fair sitting in the royal box. Though she comes from an aristocratic family, she has no hope to reach so high. Instead, Rudolph reaches out to *her*, meeting secretly with the beautiful young woman. Only in Marie's presence does Rudolph find joy and peace; she responds to him with an innocence he has never encountered. When their liaison is discovered, however, the lovers must depart to a country hunting lodge from which they will never return. Based on fact, this story of an impossible love is told on a grand, exquisite scale by Anatole Litvak, and represents one of the high points of the director's spotty career. Filled with dreamy dissolves and fluid, nearly waltzlike camera movements, the film is a brilliant technical achievement, further enhanced by the wonderful performances of the two leads—the debonair Boyer and the ravishing Darrieux, who was then just 21 years old. The videocassette is in French, with the easy-to-read English subtitles placed against a black bar background.

d, Anatole Litvak; w, Joseph Kessel, Irma Von Cube (based on the novel *Idyl's End* by Claude Anet); ph, Armand Thirard; ed, Henri Rust; m, Arthur Honegger.

Historical/Romance **(PR:A-C MPAA:NR)**

MEN***½

(1985, Ger.) 99m Olga-ZDF/New Yorker c (MANNER)

Heiner Lauterbach *(Julius Armbrust),* Uwe Ochsenknecht *(Stefan Lachner),* Ulrike Kriener *(Paula Armbrust),* Janna Marangosoff *(Angelika),* Marie-Charlott Schuler *(Marita Strass),* Dietmar Bar *(Lothar),* Edith Volkmann *(Frau Lennart),* Louis Kelz *(Florian),* Cornelia Schneider *(Caro),* Sabine Wegener *(Juliane Zorn),* Monika Schwarz *(Woman in Bar),* Gabriel Pakleppa *(Boy in the House),* Bjorn Banhardt *(Boy in the Bathtub),* Werner Albert Puthe *(Sales Clerk),* Ulrich Gunther *(Sausage Man),* Astrid Pilling *(Woman in Car).*

Taking an age-old situation and turning it on its head, this wonderful farce is brimming with unique twists, wit, and style. Julius Armbrust (Heiner Lauterbach) is an advertising executive about to celebrate his 12th year of wedded bliss with wife Paula (Ulrike Kriener). His world suddenly falls apart, however, when he discovers she has been cheating on him with Stefan Lachner (Uwe Ochsenknecht), a young, long-haired bohemian who bandies about town on his bicycle. Julius decides on revenge, not through blackmail or murder, but in a manner he knows will bring Paula back to him. After ingratiating himself with Stefan on the sly, Julius begins work on his scheme, transforming Paula's artist lover into a carbon copy of himself. MEN is a sharp satire, playing off gender roles and male bonding with some real insight. Helmed by female director Doris Dorrie, the film wisely carries no obtrusive social message that might undermine the wonderful humor. Dorrie does rely rather heavily on slapstick (there is a silly bit involving a gorilla suit), but fortunately her inventive storytelling overcomes the film's lesser elements. Shot in 25 days on a budget of only $360,000, MEN grossed in excess of $15 million in international box-office receipts. The videocassette is dubbed in English.

d, Doris Dorrie; w, Doris Dorrie; ph, Helge Weindler; ed, Raimund Barthelmes; m, Claus Bantzer.

Comedy **(PR:O MPAA:NR)**

MEPHISTO****

(1981, Ger.) 144m Mafilm-Durniok/Cinegate-Analysis c

Klaus Maria Brandauer *(Hendrik Hofgen),* Krystyna Janda *(Barbara Bruckner),* Ildiko Bansagi *(Nicoletta Von Niebuhr),* Karin Boyd *(Juliette Martens),* Rolf Hoppe *(The General),* Christine Harbort *(Lotte Lindenthal),* Gyorgy Cserhalmi *(Hans Miklas),* Christiane Graskoff *(Cesar Von Muck),* Peter Andorai *(Otto Ulrichs),* Ildiko Kishonti *(Dora Martin),* Tamas Major *(Oskar H. Kroge),* Maria Bisztrai, Sandor Lukacs, Agnes Banfalvi, Judit Hernadi, Vilmos Kun, Ida Versenyi, Istvan Komlos, Sari Gencsy, Zdzislaw Mrozewski, Stanislava Strobachova, Karoly Ujlaky,

Professor Martin Hellberg, Katalin Solyom, Gyorgy Banffy, Josef Csor.

The winner of 1982's Academy Award for Best Foreign-Language Film, MEPHISTO is an inspired update of the Faust legend, with a marvelous starring performance by Klaus Maria Brandauer. A critically acclaimed stage actor, Hendrik Hofgen (Brandauer) tires of the usual diversionary forms of theater and attempts something more revolutionary, more Brechtian. Although his ideas are groundbreaking, he does not rise to fame—they can't even spell his name correctly on posters. Desperate Hendrik sells his soul, not to the Devil, but to the Nazis—his desire for fame more urgent than his hatred for the oppressor. It is only later, after he is indebted to the Third Reich, that he realizes his mistake. Based on a novel by Klaus Mann, son of Thomas, and exquisitely photographed, MEPHISTO is bubbling over with the energy of Brandauer's bravura performance—one that would quickly attract the attention of Hollywood. Brandauer and director Istvan Szabo would team again to make COLONEL REDL. The videotape version is atrociously dubbed, making Brandauer sound like some suburban dinner-theater actor.

p, Manfred Durniok; d, Istvan Szabo; w, Istvan Szabo, Peter Dobai (based on the novel by Klaus Mann); ph, Lajos Koltai (Eastmancolor); ed, Zsuzsa Csekany; m, Zdenko Tamassy.

War/Drama **(PR:O MPAA:NR)**

MERRY CHRISTMAS, MR. LAWRENCE****

(1983, Jap./Brit./New Zealand) 124m Recorded-Cineventure TV-Asahi-Oshima/UNIV c

David Bowie *(Jack Celliers),* Tom Conti *(Col. John Lawrence),* Ryuichi Sakamoto *(Capt. Yonoi),* Takeshi *(Sgt. Hara),* Jack Thompson *(Hicksley-Ellis),* Johnny Okura *(Kanemoto),* Alistair Browning *(DeJong),* James Malcolm *(Celliers' Brother),* Chris Brown *(Celliers at Age 12),* Yuya Uchida, Ryunosuke Kaneda, Takashi Naito, Tamio Ishikura, Rokko Toura, Kan Mikami, Yuji Honma, Daisuke Iijima, Hideo Murota, Barry Dorking.

Nagisa Oshima's first film in English stars Tom Conti as the title character, a British colonel in a Japanese-run POW camp during WW II. Col. Lawrence is an astute observer of cultural codes among both his fellow Britishers and his Japanese captors, and even forms a sort of friendship with one Japanese officer (Takeshi). Lawrence is also witness to the strange dynamics between new camp commandant Capt. Yoni (Ryuichi Sakamoto) and new prisoner Jack Celliers (David Bowie), an intrepid soldier Lawrence served with in Libya. Yoni is fascinated by Celliers, and plans to make him the prisoners' CO, replacing Hicksley-Ellis (Jack Thompson), whose Britishisms Yoni construes as signs of weakness. When Yoni calls for Hicksley-Ellis' execution, however, Celliers performs an act that upsets and exposes the film's precarious balance of national codes, personal relationships, and individual psychologies. Oshima's ambitious film is not without faults, but they are overshadowed by its emotional power. Many of the characters' actions and impulses are contradictory or not overtly explained, but the answers for this can generally be found buried in Oshima's complex story (the Yoni-Celliers relationship, which needs greater development, is a notable exception). The fine performances of Conti, Takeshi (brilliant in his first dramatic role), Sakamoto (a Japanese pop star in his film acting debut, he also contributes the memorable score), and Bowie enhance this provocative film. In English.

p, Jeremy Thomas; d, Nagisa Oshima; w, Nagisa Oshima, Paul Mayersberg (based on the novel *The Seed And The Sower* by Laurens Van Der Post); ph, Toichiro Narushima (Eastmancolor); ed, Tomoyo Oshima; m, Ryuichi Sakamoto.

Prison/War **(PR:O MPAA:R)**

METROPOLIS*****

(1927, Ger.) 120m UFA bw

Alfred Abel *(Joh Fredersen),* Gustav Frolich *(Freder),* Rudolf Klein-Rogge *(Rotwang),* Brigitte Helm *(Maria/Robot),* Fritz Rasp *(Slim),* Theodor Loos *(Josaphat/Joseph),* Erwin Biswanger *(Georg, No. 11811),* Heinrich George *(Grot, the Foreman),* Olaf Storm *(Jan),* Hans Leo Reich *(Marinus),* Heinrich Gotho *(Master of Ceremonies),* Margarete Lanner *(Woman in Car),* Max Dietze, Georg John, Walter Kuhle, Arthur Reinhard *(Workers),* Ellen Frey, Lisa Gray, Rose Lichtenstein, Helene Weigel *(Female Workers).*

METROPOLIS was inspired by Fritz Lang's first sight of the skyscraper landscape of New York City. At his suggestion, his wife, Thea von Harbou, wrote a tale from which Lang eventually filmed the silent era's biggest production. Approximately two million feet of film were shot, and tens of thousands comprised the cast. The special effects astound to this day, much to the credit of Eugene Schufftan's "Schufftan Process"—an ingenious device that made miniatures look like enormous buildings and that could combine these images with real people. Set in 2000, METROPOLIS concerns a mighty city ruled by Fredersen (Alfred Abel), a heartless capitalist whose son, Freder (Gustav Frolich), falls in love with Maria (Brigitte Helm), the saintly figure who proselytizes to the drones who toil in the workers' city, a nightmarish, mechanized netherworld where the wheels of industry are kept in constant, grinding motion. Freder deserts his class to become one with the downtrodden and the Christ-like Maria, who implores the rebellious workers to turn the other cheek. His father, however, encourages mad scientist Rotwang (brilliantly played by Rudolf Klein-Rogge) to abduct Maria, create a robot anti-Christ in her image, and program it to lead the workers in a revolt that can be put down in a definitive, crushing fashion. As the lower city is flooded—in some truly spectacular footage—it's up to the idealistic Freder to save the day. METROPOLIS is a visual work of art whose at times silly narrative is really only Lang's excuse to overwhelm us. His masses of extras forming incredible geometric patterns, expressionistic moods, and art nouveau sets and futuristic creations all leave the viewer stunned, and there are enough additional melodramatic thrills to satisfy any devotee of the matinee western. This monumental film no longer exists in its original 17-reel form; even on its initial English release, it was severely edited, with whole subplots excised for fear of censorship. In 1984, Giorgio Moroder rereleased METROPOLIS with new tintings, new title cards, and a repulsive rock score. Morodor must be given credit for bringing added life to this classic and initiating a new audience of teenagers to the film, but he should have stuck with his own synthesized score.

d, Fritz Lang; w, Fritz Lang, Thea von Harbou (based on her novel); ph, Karl Freund, Gunther Rittau.

Fantasy/Science Fiction (PR:A MPAA:NR)

MEXICAN BUS RIDE***½

(1951, Mex.) 85m Isla bw (SUBIDA AL CIELO; Trans: Ascent To Heaven)

Lilia Prado *(Raquel),* Carmelita Gonzalez *(Oliviero's wife),* Esteban Marquez *(Oliviero),* Manuel Donde, Roberto Cobo, Luis Acevez Castaneda.

One of Luis Bunuel's simplest, most straightforward films is this peasant tale of a young newlywed, Oliviero (Esteban Marquez), whose exotic honeymoon evening is abbreviated when his greedy, lazy brothers inform him of their mother's impending death. Fearing that his two elder brothers will profit unfairly from the old woman's demise, Oliviero journeys via bus to a distant village in order to return with a lawyer. Along the way, the bus gets stuck in a muddy river, a pregnant woman gives birth, the driver makes unscheduled stops to attend his own mother's birthday gala and to pay respects at a young girl's funeral, and the busty seductress Raquel (Lilia Prado) makes a man out of Oliviero. By the time he returns to his village, Oliviero is an innocent no more. While it initially appears to be little more than a light popular entertainment, MEXICAN BUS RIDE is completely surreal in tone, Bunuel taking quiet swipes at family, church, and technology. Visually, the film is simply photographed, though it is filled with numerous Bunuelian touches, as in Oliviero's fantasy in the back of a bus (overgrown with vegetation straight out of the Garden of Eden) in which he succumbs to the temptations of Raquel (dressed in his bride's wedding dress) while eating an umbilically unwinding apple peel. Bunuel's more subtle jokes include the obviously fake boulders and rainstorms that threaten the bus, and a peg-legged character played by a two-legged actor whose supposedly missing limb is clearly visible behind his wooden leg. The videocassette is in Spanish with barely legible English subtitles.

p, Manuel Altolaguirre; d, Luis Bunuel; w, Manuel Altolaguirre; ph, Alex Phillips; m, Gustavo Pittaluga.

Comedy/Drama (PR:A-C MPAA:NR)

MILKY WAY, THE***½

(1969, Fr./It.) 105m Greenwich-Fraia c (LA VOIE LACTEE; LA VIA LATTEA)

Paul Frankeur *(Pierre),* Laurent Terzieff *(Jean),* Alain Cuny *(Man with Cape),* Edith Scob *(Virgin Mary),* Bernard Verley *(Jesus),* Francois Maistre *(French Priest),* Claude Cerval *(Brigadier),* Muni *(Mother Superior),* Julien Bertheau *(Maitre d'Hotel),* Ellen Bahl *(Mme. Garnier),* Michel Piccoli *(The Marquis),* Agnes Capri *(Lamartine Institution Directress),* Michel Etcheverry *(The Inquisitor),* Pierre Clementi *(The Devil),* Georges Marchal *(The Jesuit),* Jean Piat *(The Jansenist),* Denis Manuel *(Rodolphe),* Daniel Pilon *(Francois),* Claudio Brook *(Bishop),* Julien Guiomar *(Spanish Priest),* Marcel Peres *(Spanish Innkeeper),* Delphine Seyrig *(Prostitute),* Jean-Claude Carriere *(Priscillian),* Christine Simon *(Therese),* Augusta Carriere *(Sister Francoise).*

The most overtly religious film in Luis Bunuel's *oeuvre,* THE MILKY WAY is an allegorical journey through the history of Catholicism that follows a pair of travelers—the somewhat pious Pierre (Paul Frankeur) and the younger, more skeptical Jean (Laurent Terzieff)—as they undertake a pilgrimage across Spain to the tomb of Saint James. En route, they meet any number of religious figures, including a caped, God-like figure (Alain Cuny) with a midget, the Virgin Mary (Edith Scob), Jesus (Bernard Verley), a bishop (Jean-Claude Carriere, Bunuel's screenwriting collaborator), a sadistic Marquis (Michel Piccoli), a prostitute (Delphine Seyrig), and even the Devil (Pierre Clementi). This comical film will make any viewer question their beliefs—from religious fanatic to rabid atheist. While it may seem strange that Bunuel, a lifetime surrealist and professed atheist, would produce such a work, the filmmaker remarked in his autobiography, *My Last Sigh,* that THE MILKY WAY "evokes the search for truth, as well as the necessity of abandoning it as soon as you've found it." If that doesn't shed some light on Bunuel's intent, then perhaps his most famously ambiguous statement will: "Thank God I'm an atheist." In French with English subtitles.

p, Serge Silberman; d, Luis Bunuel; w, Luis Bunuel, Jean-Claude Carriere; ph, Christian Matras (Eastmancolor); ed, Louisette Hautecoeur; m, Luis Bunuel.

Religious (PR:C MPAA:PG)

MIRACLE IN MILAN****

(1951, It.) 100m ENIC/Joseph Burstyn bw (MIRACOLO A MILANO)

Branduani Gianni *(Little Toto at Age 11),* Francesco Golisano *(Good Toto),* Paolo Stoppa *(Bad Rappi),* Emma Gramatica *(Old Lolatta),* Guglielmo Barnabo *(Mobbi the Rich Man),* Brunella Bovo *(Little Edvige),* Anna Carena *(Signora Marta Altezzosa),* Alba Arnova *(The Statue),* Flora Cambi *(Unhappy Sweetheart),* Virgilio Riento *(Sergeant),* Arturo Bragaglia *(Alfredo).*

The writing-directing team of Cesare Zavattini and Vittorio De Sica produced this picture shortly after they received international acclaim for THE BICYCLE THIEF. Though not as popular as that masterwork, MIRACLE IN MILAN is an equally touching look into human nature that concentrates on the plight of the poor in post-WW II Italy. The story is essentially a fairy tale, packed with a strong moral implications. The Good Toto (Francesco Golisano), a young orphan, finds refuge in a colony of beggars and helps to organize them, generating happiness among the otherwise distressed members of the group. When a wealthy landowner decides to kick the beggars off his land, Toto is given a magic dove by a fairy. Not only are the landowner's attempts thwarted, but the magical powers of the dove also allow Toto to grant wishes to the beggars. Unable to deny them anything, he grants their greedy requests, until eventually the dove is stolen. As in other Neo-Realist films, the performers in MIRACLE IN MILAN are a combination of professional actors and actual denizens of the street, and all the players give realistic and humane portrayals. De Sica handles his fantastic material subtly and with simplicity, yielding an original mix of sharp satire and poetic fable that extended the limits of the Neo-Realist style. In Italian with English subtitles.

p, Vittorio De Sica; d, Vittorio De Sica; w, Cesare Zavattini, Vittorio De Sica, Suso Cecchi D'Amico, Mario Chiari, Adolfo Franci (based on the story "Toto Il Buono" by Zavattini); ph, G.R. Aldo; ed, Eraldo Da Roma; m, Alessandro Cicognini.

Fantasy **(PR:A MPAA:NR)**

MISHIMA*½**

(1985, US) 120m Zoetrope-Filmlink-Lucasfilm/WB c

"November 25, 1970": Ken Ogata *(Yukio Mishima),* Masayuki Shionoya *(Morita),* Hiroshi Mikami *(Cadet No. 1),* Junya Fukuda *(Cadet No. 2),* Shigeto Tachihara *(Cadet No. 3),* Junkichi Orimoto *(Gen. Mashita),* "Flashbacks": Naoko Otani *(Mother),* Go Riju *(Mishima, Age 18-19),* Masato Aizawa *(Mishima, Age 9-14),* Yuki Nagahara *(Mishima, Age 5),* Kyuzo Kobayashi *(Literary Friend),* Haruko Kato *(Grandmother),* Kimiko Ito *(Grandmother's Nurse),* Hideo Fukuhara *(Military Doctor),* "Temple of the Golden Pavilion": Yasosuke Bando *(Mizoguchi),* Hisako Manda *(Mariko),* Imari Tauji *(Madame),* "Kyoko's House": Kenji Sawada *(Osamu),* Reisen Lee *(Kiyomi),* Setsuko Karasuma *(Mitsuko),* Tadanori Yokoo *(Natsuo),* Yasuaki Kurata *(Takei),* Sachiko Hidari *(Osamu's Mother),* Tsutomu Harada *(Romeo),* Mami Okamoto *(Juliet),* "Runaway Horses": Toshiyuki Nagashima *(Isao),* Ryo Ikebe *(Interrogator),* Shoichiro Sakata *(Isao's Classmate),* Roy Schieder *(English Narration).*

"Never in physical action had I discovered the chilling satisfaction of words. Never in words had I experienced the hot darkness of action. Somewhere there must be a higher principle which reconciles art and action. That principle, it occurred to me, was death." These words, written by Japanese author Yukio Mishima and spoken in a voice-over narration by Roy Scheider, eloquently state what writer-director Paul Schrader tried to convey in this ambitious, unique undertaking. Though MISHIMA contains much biographical material, it doesn't claim to be a definitive biography of the controversial writer. Instead, the film concentrates on Mishima's art, attempting to piece together a complicated puzzle by examining his work and its relation to his personal obsessions. Perhaps Japan's best-known author, Mishima wrote 35 novels, 25 plays, 200 short stories, and 8 volumes of essays before his ritual suicide at age 45. One of his driving concerns was his perception of Japan's post-WW II rejection of its rich history of tradition, ritual, honor, and religion in favor of the western world's pursuit of money. He formed his own private army, called the Shield Society, whose purpose was to restore Japan to the emperor. Schrader approaches his subject with taste and intelligence, juxtaposing Mishima's suicide with flashbacks from his life and dramatizations of his novels *Temple of the Golden Pavilion*, *Kyoko's House*, and *Runaway Horses*. Separated into four chapters ("Beauty," "Art," "Action," and "Harmony of Pen and Sword"), the film skillfully integrates the novels and real events, slowly dissecting Mishima's obsessions. MISHIMA's most stunning aspect is the visual style employed in the dramatizations of the novels. With colorful, theatrical sets by famed Japanese designer Eiko Ishioka, the sequences are quite unique and impressive in their own right, and the entire film is photographed beautifully by John Bailey. The visuals are enhanced by Philip Glass' haunting score. In Japanese with English subtitles and narration.

p, Mata Yamamoto, Tom Luddy; d, Paul Schrader; w, Paul Schrader, Leonard Schrader (conceived in collaboration with Jun Shiragi); ph, John Bailey (Technicolor); ed, Michael Chandler, Tomoyo Oshima; m, Philip Glass.

Biography **(PR:O MPAA:R)**

MISS MARY**

(1986, Arg.) 100m GEA/NW c

Julie Christie *(Miss Mary Mulligan),* Sofia Viruboff *(Carolina),* Donald McIntire *(Johnny),* Barbara Bunge *(Teresa as a Child),* Nacha Guevara *(Mecha),* Eduardo [Tato] Pavlovsky *(Alfredo),* Guillermo Battaglia *(Uncle Ernesto),* Iris Marga *(Aunt),* Luisina Brando *(Perla),* Nora Zinsky *(Teresa as an Adult),* Gerardo Romano *(Ernesto),* Regina Lam, Anne Henry, Sandra Ballesteros, Anita Larronde, Alfredo Quesada, Osvaldo Flores, Tessie Gilligan, Carlos Usay, Oscar Lopez, Susana Veron, Alberto Marty, Beatriz Thibaudin, Laura Feal, Lidia Cortinez, Juan Palomina.

Maria Luisa Bemberg's follow-up to her Oscar-nominated CAMILA (1985) stars Julie Christie as Mary Mulligan, the spinsterish but attractive English governess of three in 1938 Argentina. Told in flashback, the story opens in 1930, as two girls are put to bed by Miss Mary's predecessor while their parents prepare to attend a celebration of the coming to power of a military faction that will oppressively rule the country for 15 years. The upper class has "wholeheartedly supported this break of constitutional rule." Later, in 1945 Buenos Aires, as this era is about to end and Juan Peron's is about to begin, Miss Mary reflects on her life at the estate of the archconservative patriarch Alfredo (Eduardo Pavlovsky), his frail wife (Nacha Guevara), and their children. The film cuts between past and present, detailing the effect the sexual codes underlying the sumptuous life of the bourgeoisie have on the new governess and her charges. Christie does well in her role, but her character is underwritten, and, while the nuances of her stultifying environs are conveyed with a precise sense of the period, the travails of the patrician family are never very compelling. This was something of an autobiographical film for director-cowriter Bemberg, the feminist product of a rich family and a restrictive upbringing by foreign governesses.

Unfortunately, MISS MARY never shows the means by which its victimized characters arrive at their unhappy states with much force or complexity, making for a fairly uninvolving drama. In Spanish and English with English subtitles.

p, Lita Stantic; d, Maria Luisa Bemberg; w, Jorge Goldenberg, Maria Luisa Bemberg (based on a story by Maria Luisa Bemberg, Beda Docampo Feijoo, Juan Batista Stagnaro); ph, Miguel Rodriguez (Eastmancolor); ed, Luis Cesar D'Angiolillo; m, Luis Maria Serra, Erik Satie.

Drama **(PR:O MPAA:R)**

MR. HULOT'S HOLIDAY*****

(1953, Fr.) 85m Cady-Discina/Gaumont-Images bw (LES VACANCES DE MONSIEUR HULOT; AKA: MONSIEUR HULOT'S HOLIDAY)

Jacques Tati *(M. Hulot),* Nathalie Pascaud *(Martine),* Louis Perrault *(Fred),* Michele Rolla *(Martine's Aunt),* Andre Dubois *(Commandant),* Suzy Willy *(Commandant's Wife),* Valentine Camax *(Englishwoman),* Lucien Fregis *(Hotel Proprietor),* Marguerite Gerard *(Strolling Woman),* Rene Lacourt *(Strolling Man),* Raymond Carl *(The Boy).*

Director Jacques Tati turned his attention to those French who wrongly believe that a coastal holiday will be a time of rest and relaxation with this delightful film. Featuring the first appearance of Mons. Hulot (played by Tati himself, in the tradition of the great silent comedians), MR. HULOT'S HOLIDAY takes place at a coastal resort in Brittany. Chaos seems to follow Hulot wherever he goes, but he somehow makes it through life without ever really noticing. Like all vacationers, Hulot (and director Tati) spends a great deal of time observing *other* vacationers. There is the comely Martine (Nathalie Pascaud), whom Hulot would like to get to know better, but is too shy to make a direct assault on her sensibilities; the workaholic businessman (Jean-Pierre Zola, later seen in MY UNCLE) who cannot stop to relax; the burly British old maid (Valentine Camax); the besieged waiter (Raymond Carl); the former military man who still thinks he's leading a battalion (Andre Dubois); the beachcombing couple (Rene Lacourt and Marguerite Gerard), and countless other unidentified persons who are equally important to the scenery. There is no plot (as the prolog warns us), only a seemingly endless stream of events—with and without Hulot—that carry the film through to the end. With very little dialog and a creative use of sound, Tati (the actor and director) gives us an entirely new way of looking at a very familiar landscape. In French with English subtitles.

p, Fred Orain; d, Jacques Tati; w, Jacques Tati, Henri Marquet, Pierre Aubert, Jacques Lagrange; ph, Jacques Mercanton, Jean Mousselle; ed, Suzanne Baron, Charles Bretoneiche, Jacques Grassi; m, Alain Romans.

Comedy **(PR:A MPAA:NR)**

MR. KLEIN****

(1976, Fr.) 122m FOX-Lira/Quartet c

Alain Delon *(Mr. Klein),* Jeanne Moreau *(Florence),* Suzanne Flon *(Concierge),* Michel Lonsdale *(Pierre),* Juliet Berto *(Janine),* Jean Bouise *(Man),* Francine Berge *(Nicole),* Massimo Girotti *(Mr. Charles).*

Joseph Losey's first film in French is a meticulously constructed psychological thriller about a bourgeois antique dealer who lives in a plush Parisian apartment during the Nazi Occupation in 1942. Robert Klein (Alain Delon) makes his living by purchasing antiques from Jews who need quick money, desperate people who have no time to negotiate. His disregard for their plight comes back to haunt him, however, when he finds a Jewish newspaper delivered to his house addressed to a "Mr. Robert Klein." Certain there must be some mistake—he is, after all, an Alsatian French Catholic whose bloodline extends as far back as Louis XIV—Klein reports the other Mr. Klein to the somewhat suspicious police. When his namesake begins to get the best of him, Klein goes to his antagonist's apartment, hoping to find some answers, but becomes even more enmeshed in a mystery of duplicates, reflections, and negative images. After causing quite a stir in France, where audiences and critics alike were angered by American Losey's unflattering portrait of French anti-Semitism during WW II, MR. KLEIN won Cesars for Best Film and Best Director. Although Delon does not have the strength of frequent Losey collaborator Dirk Bogarde, the script (by Franco Solinas—THE BATTLE OF ALGIERS and STATE OF SIEGE), art direction (Alexandre Trauner), and direction are so perfectly realized that the film's minor weaknesses are easily overlooked. The videocassette is dubbed in English.

p, Raymond Danon, Alain Delon, Jean-Pierre Labrande, Robert Kupferberg; d, Joseph Losey; w, Franco Solinas; ph, Gerry Fisher (Eastmancolor); ed, Henri Lanoe; m, Egisto Macchi, Pierre Porte.

Drama **(PR:C MPAA:PG)**

MON ONCLE D'AMERIQUE****

(1978, Fr.) 125m Andrea-TF 1/NW c (AKA: LES SOMNAMBULES)

Gerard Depardieu *(Rene Ragueneau),* Nicole Garcia *(Janine Garnier),* Roger-Pierre *(Jean Le Gall),* Nelly Borgeaud *(Arlette Le Gall),* Marie Dubois *(Therese Ragueneau),* Pierre Arditi *(Zambeaux),* Gerard Darrieu *(Leon Veestrate),* Philippe Laudenbach *(Michael Aubert),* Alexandre Rignault *(Jean's Grandfather),* Guillaume Boisseau *(Jean as a Child),* Jean Daste *(Mons. Louis),* Laurence Badie *(Mme. Veestrate),* Helena Manson *(Mme. Crozet),* Dorothee *(Narrator),* Prof. Henri Laborit *(Himself).*

Alain Resnais' greatest, and most unlikely, commercial success is an offbeat, humorous case study of three characters—manager Rene (Gerard Depardieu), actress Janine (Nicole Garcia), and executive Jean (Roger-Pierre). Their pasts are quickly, and simultaneously, accounted for, allowing the focus to be placed on the pursuit of their careers. This action is intercut with segments of a lecture from Prof. Henri Laborit, a behavioral scientist speaking in a pure documentary fashion (Resnais had, in fact, attempted to do a short documentary project with Laborit), who contributes his theories on memory. Resnais also intercuts footage from other movies, featuring the film personae that serve as inspiration for the three main characters—for Rene, Jean Gabin; for Janine, Jean Marais; for Roger-Pierre, Danielle Darrieux. The (somewhat inexplicable) commercial and (less baffling) critical success of this film experiment was phenomenal, for it defies viewer pigeonholing. If you're interested in films that stretch the limits of narrative structure, MON ONCLE D'AMERIQUE is essential viewing. It won numerous awards, including six French Cesars and an Academy Award nomination for screenwriter Jean Gruault. In French with English subtitles.

p, Philippe Dussart; d, Alain Resnais; w, Jean Gruault (based on the works of Prof. Henri Laborit); ph, Sacha Vierny (Eastmancolor); ed, Albert Jurgenson; m, Arie Dzierlatka.

Drama **(PR:C MPAA:PG)**

MONTENEGRO***

(1981, Brit./Swed.) 96m Viking-Europa-Smart Egg/New Realm-Atlantic c (AKA: MONTENEGRO—OR PIGS AND PEARLS)

Susan Anspach *(Marilyn Jordan),* Erland Josephson *(Martin Jordan),* Jamie Marsh *(Jimmy),* Per Oscarsson *(Dr. Pazardjian),* Bora Todorovic *(Alex),* Marianne Jacobi *(Cookie),* John Zacharias *(Grandpa),* Svetozar Cvetkovic *(Montenegro),* Patricia Gelin *(Tirke),* Lisbeth Zachrisson *(Rita Rossignol),* Marina Zindahl *(Secretary),* Nikola Janic *(Moustapha),* Lasse Aberg *(Customs Inspector),* Dragan Ilic *(Hassan),* Milo Petrovic *(Zanzibar Customer),* John Parkinson *(Piano Player),* Jan Nygren *(Police Officer).*

A comic and perverse social commentary on the animalistic nature of man from Dusan Makavejev (WR: MYSTERIES OF THE ORGANISM), MONTENEGRO tells the story of Marilyn (Susan Anspach), a dejected American housewife living in Sweden with a wealthy husband Martin (Erland Josephson), their two children, and a grandfather who thinks he's Buffalo Bill. When Martin goes on another business trip (his 23rd that year), Marilyn rushes to meet him at the airport. Detained by customs, she meets a young girl from Yugoslavia who is smuggling alcohol and a dead pig into the country. The pair become friendly and, when Marilyn can't locate Martin, she goes off with the girl. Along the way they pick up a man with a knife in his forehead and drive on to a small village, where they visit the club Zanzibar. There Marilyn witnesses a brawl in which two men hit each other with shovels; comes to the aid of the loser, Montenegro (Svetozar Cvetkovic); sings a torch song; and watches an erotic dancer perform with a radio-operated army tank. This funny and subversive film is by no means as unwatchable as some people have made Makavejev's work out to be. Makavejev, like Luis Bunuel, is brilliant in assailing the upper class, severely attacking the repression that festers underneath elegant facades. This was Makavajev's first step into the commercial art-film arena, followed by THE COCA-COLA KID and MANIFESTO. In English.

p, Bo Jonsson; d, Dusan Makavejev; w, Dusan Makavejev, Bo Jonsson, Donald Arthur, Arnie Gelbert, Branko Vucicevic, Bojana Marijan; ph, Tomislav Pinter (Eastmancolor); ed, Sylvia Ingemarsson; m, Kornell Kovach.

Drama **(PR:O MPAA:NR)**

MOON IN THE GUTTER, THE***

(1983, Fr./It.) 126m Gaumont-TFI-Opera-SFPC/COL-Triumph c (LA LUNE DANS LE CANIVEAU)

Gerard Depardieu *(Gerard),* Nastassia Kinski *(Loretta),* Victoria Abril *(Bella),* Vittorio Mezzogiorno *(Newton Channing),* Dominique Pinon *(Frank),* Bertice Reading *(Lola),* Gabriel Monnet *(Tom),* Milena Vukotic *(Frieda),* Bernard Farcy *(Jesus),* Anne-Marie Coffinet *(Dora),* Katia Berger, Jacques Herlin, Rudo Alberti, Rosa Fumeto, Grasiano Giusti, Fred Ulysse, Victor Cavallo, Jean-Roger Milo, Jean-Pierre Laurent, Claudia Pola.

Jean-Jacques Beineix's much-awaited follow-up to DIVA is an obscure, poetic, dreamlike mystery based on a novel by cult favorite David Goodis. This visually awe-inspiring production tells the story of Gerard (Gerard Depardieu), a riverfront dock worker tormented by the need to find out who raped his sister, a calamity that caused her to commit suicide while lying in a gutter. During his search, Gerard becomes attracted to Loretta (Nastassia Kinski), the stunning mystery woman who cruises the waterfront in her blazing red convertible. The billboard in front of Gerard's house reads "Try Another World," and that is precisely what he decides to do. Where DIVA overpowered with bright romanticism, MOON IN THE GUTTER stuns with damp obsession. The script is often embarrassingly indulgent, not because of Beineix's ignorance but as a result of his tunnel vision in creating a wholly personal, poetic endeavor. For every failed line, action, and camera swirl, however, there is another that is astoundingly effective. This underrated wonder will certainly find its due praise as Beineix's career continues. In French with English subtitles.

p, Lise Fayolle; d, Jean-Jacques Beineix; w, Jean-Jacques Beineix, Olivier Mergault (based on the novel by David Goodis); ph, Philippe Rousselot, Dominique Brenguier (Panavision, Eastmancolor); ed, Monique Prim, Yves Deschamps; m, Gabriel Yared.

Drama **(PR:O MPAA:R)**

MOONLIGHTING****

(1982, Brit.) 97m Miracle/UNIV c

Jeremy Irons *(Nowak),* Eugene Lipinski *(Banaszak),* Jiri Stanislav *(Wolski),* Eugeniusz Haczkiewicz *(Kudaj),* Dorothy Zienciowska *(Lot Airline Girl),* Edward Arthur *(Immigation Officer),* Denis Holmes *(Neighbor),* Renu Setna *(Junk Shop Owner),* David Calder *(Supermarket Manager),* Judy Gridley *(Supermarket Supervisor),* Claire Toeman *(Supermarket Cashier),* Catherine Harding *(Lady Shoplifter),* Jill Johnson *(Haughty Supermarket Customer),* David Square *(Supermarket Assistant),* Mike Sarne *(Builder's Merchant),* Lucy Hornak, Robyn Mandell *(Wrangler Shop Assistants),* Ann Tirard *(Lady In Tele-*

phone Box), Christopher Logue *(Workman),* Hugh Harper *(Newspaper Boy),* Julia Chambers *(Chemist's Assistant),* Fred Lee Own *(Chinese Man),* Kenny Ireland *(Timber Man),* Trevor Cooper, Ian Ormsby-Knox *(Hire Shop Men).*

One month after martial law was declared in Poland in the wake of the Solidarity uprising, Jerzy Skolimowski began work on this political allegory about a group of four Polish workers in London. Led by the only English speaker among them, the foreman Nowak (Jeremy Irons), the group arrives to renovate a flat for their Polish boss. Working illegally at what by English standards are cut rates, they must live on the site under uncomfortable living arrangements. When Soviet troops roll into Warsaw, Nowak learns of the events, but, driven by private anxieties and determined to avoid dissent, schemes to conceal the news from his men. As budgetary and scheduling pressures mount, he must take increasingly drastic and draconian measures to do so. MOONLIGHTING contains no manifestos or crude symbols. Its politics are almost entirely limned in the actions and thoughts of Nowak, who is beautifully portrayed by Irons in the performance that made him one of the most respected actors of the decade. The better-educated and -paid Nowak is sympathetically characterized even as he mirrors the actions of the Polish authorities, cutting off his men's access to information and family ties, the workers' hierarchy (including the bosses back home) serving as a microcosm of Polish society. Director-cowriter Skolimowski never fails to truly *dramatize* his themes, however—creating that rarity, a "political film" that is also deeply personal, true to life, and morally and emotionally complex. In English.

p, Mark Shivas, Jerzy Skolimowski; d, Jerzy Skolimowski; w, Jerzy Skolimowski, Boleslaw Sulik, Barry Vince, Danuta Witold Stok; ph, Tony Pierce Roberts; ed, Barry Vince; m, Stanley Myers, Hans Zimmer.

Drama **(PR:C MPAA:PG)**

MOSCOW DOES NOT BELIEVE IN TEARS***

(1979, USSR) 148m Mosfilm-Intl. Film Exchange c (MOSKVA SLYOZAM NE VERIT; GB: MOSCOW DISTRUSTS TEARS)

Vera Alentova *(Katya),* Alexei Batalov *(Gosha),* Irina Muravyova *(Lyuda),* Raissa Rjasanova *(Tonya),* Yuri Vasilyev *(Rudolf/Rodion),* Alexander Fatyushin *(Gurin),* Boris Smorchkov *(Nikolai),* Natalya Vavilova *(Alexandra),* Oleg Tabakov *(Volodya),* Yevgeniya Khanayeva, Valentina Ushakova, Viktor Uralsky.

Winner of the 1981 Oscar for Best Foreign-Language Film, this nostalgic blend of comedy and drama is one of the most accessible Soviet films ever to reach US screens. Divided into two parts, the film begins in 1958 with the arrival in Moscow of three provincial girls—Lyuda (Irina Muravyova), on the lookout for a husband with big prospects; Tonya (Raisa Ryazanova), who already has a serious boy friend; and Katya (Vera Alentova), who falls for self-assured TV cameraman Rudolf (Yuri Vasilyev). After a little high jinks (including Katya and Lyuda's masquerade as the daughters of a professor) and a lot of shared meals, Tonya marries her longtime sweetheart, Lyuda becomes the wife of a well-known hockey player (Alexander Fatyushin), and Katya becomes pregnant with a baby Rudolf disowns. Part Two picks up the story 20 years later, with Tonya settled in marriage; Lyuda divorced and still searching for the man of her dreams; and Katya a single mother, factory administrator, and lover of a machinist (Alexsei Batalov) who thinks she is just another worker. When Rudolf appears again on the scene things get very complex indeed for Katya. Deceptively simple, funny, and touching, MOSCOW DOES NOT BELIEVE IN TEARS is neither innovative nor technically dazzling, but its familiar characters have a resonance that transcends national borders and its bittersweet humor addresses the human condition in a language that needs little translation. The videocassette is available in both dubbed and subtitled versions.

p, V. Kuchinsky; d, Vladimir Menshov; w, Valentin Yornykh; ph, Igor Slabnevich (Sovcolor); ed, Yelyena Miklaylovna; m, Sergei Nikitin.

Comedy/Drama **(PR:A MPAA:NR)**

MOTHER***½

(1952, Jap.) 98m Shintoho bw (OKASAN)

Kinuyo Tanaka *(Mother),* Massao Mishima *(Husband),* Akihiko Katayama *(Son),* Kyoko Kagawa *(Daughter),* Eiji Okada *(Baker).*

One of Mikio Naruse's portraits of Japanese women, MOTHER is based on a story written by an adolescent girl for a contest that had mothers as its topic. In the years following WW II, a husband (Massao Mishima) and wife (Kinuyo Tanaka) labor long and hard to reopen their laundry business while trying to raise their four children. When their eldest son dies of fever, and exhaustion claims the life of the husband, the wife is left to rebuild the laundry with her three surviving children. A look at the determination of the working class, MOTHER is an unspectacularly photographed, almost naive, film told through the eyes of the family's eldest daughter. Its art lies in its simplicity, and Naruse not only serves his source material well, but also presents his tale in a commercial, popular style that makes the film accessible to the very people it is about. Yet despite the light touch of Naruse's direction, one cannot overlook the dark, hopelessness of the characters' situation. Although the name Mikio Naruse is known to devotees of foreign film, his works are only rarely screened, making this videocassette (in Japanese with English subtitles) a very special release.

d, Mikio Naruse; w, Yoko Mizuki; ph, Hiroshi Suzuki; ed, Masatoshi Kato; m, Ichiro Saito.

Drama **(PR:A MPAA:NR)**

MURIEL****

(1963, Fr./It.) 116m Argos-Alpha-Eclair-Les Films de la Pleiade-Dear/Lopert c (MURIEL, OU LE TEMPS D'UN RETOUR)

Delphine Seyrig *(Helene Aughain),* Jean-Pierre Kerien *(Alphonse),* Nita Klein *(Francoise),* Jean-Baptiste Thieree

(Bernard Aughain), Claude Sainval *(Roland De Smoke),* Laurence Badie *(Claudie),* Jean Champion *(Ernest),* Jean Daste *(The Goat Man),* Martine Vartel *(Marie-Dominique),* Philippe Laudenbach *(Robert),* Robert Bordenave *(The Croupier),* Gaston Joly *(Antoine, the Tailor),* Catherine de Seynes *(Angele),* Julien Verdier *(The Stableman),* Gerard Lorin, Francoise Bertin, Wanda Kerien, Jean-Jacques Lagarde, Yves Vincent, Nelly Borgeaud.

Alain Resnais' third feature and first color film once again concerns memory. Helene (Delphine Seyrig) is a widow who sells antiques from her Boulogne-sur-Mer apartment. She shares the place with her eccentric filmmaker stepson, Bernard (Jean-Baptiste Thierree), a 22-month veteran of the Algerian War, during which he took part in the torture and murder of a young woman named Muriel. Bernard is haunted by the memory of Muriel, spending much time watching a grainy 8mm film of her and filming the surroundings in his neighborhood. He talks of Muriel to Helene, who assumes the woman is a girl friend she has yet to meet. Helene, meanwhile, is reunited with a past lover, Alphonse (Jean-Pierre Kerien), another veteran of Algeria, but they cannot recapture what they once had, if they had anything at all. Alphonse arrives at Helene's with his mistress, Francoise (Nita Klein), whom he introduces as his niece. While Helene; her present lover, de Smoke (Claude Sainval); and Alphonse try to sort out their emotions, Francoise shows an attraction to Bernard, who is involved with Marie-Dominique (Martine Vatel). MURIEL marked the second time Resnais worked with screenwriter Jean Cayrol, who previously contributed the commentary for Resnais' short documentary masterpiece NIGHT AND FOG. Their collaboration here produced a technical masterpiece that makes brilliant and confounding use of montage, sound construction and overlapping dialog, and color photography. With MURIEL, Resnais' true filmmaking style had finally begun to emerge, employing characters who are real people (not named after cities or designated by letters) with memories that cut deeply into their personalities and relationships. The videotape is in French with English subtitles—though, like most of the washed-out prints of the film, the reportedly excellent use of color is hardly evident.

p, Anatole Dauman; d, Alain Resnais; w, Jean Cayrol (based on the story by Cayrol); ph, Sacha Vierny (Eastmancolor); ed, Kenout Peltier, Eric Pluet, Claudine Merlin; m, Hans Werner Henze.

Drama **(PR:A MPAA:NR)**

MY BEST FRIEND'S GIRL***

(1983, Fr.) 99m Renn-Sara/European c (LA FEMME DE MON POTE)

Coluche *(Micky),* Isabelle Huppert *(Viviane),* Thierry Lhermitte *(Pascal),* Farid Chopel *(Hoodlum),* Francois Perrot *(Doctor),* Daniel Colas *(Flirt),* Frederique Michot.

Set against the backdrop of a Courcheval ski resort, this tale of sexual morality is relatively tame in comparison to Bertrand Blier's more anarchic 1970s Gerard Depardieu-Patrick Dewaere pairings, GOING PLACES and GET OUT YOUR HANDKERCHIEFS. This time out, Blier's *menage a trois* is more polished and comfortable than before, a reflection of both its 1980s sensibilities and of the film's snow-white setting. Viviane (Isabelle Huppert) is a perky young woman with a predilection for stripping off her bulky ski clothes and wandering around in red lingerie. While on holiday, she has a one-night stand with dullard Pascal (Thierry Lhermitte), owner of the resort's ski shop. The next morning, Pascal brings his best pal, Mickey (Coluche) —a cynical bear of a man whose friendship with Pascal is the only thing he values in this world—into the bedroom to have a look at his latest conquest, the nude, sleeping Viviane. Naturally, since this is both a French film *and* a Blier film, Mickey and Viviane make love, putting the latter in a terrible predicament. Blier's great talent is to somehow convert misogynistic situations such as this into warm and charming pictures. While the characters may have questionable sexual morals, their deeper concerns are for strong bonds of friendship—all three lament their inability to be friends without the interference of sex. Although Lhermitte plays a less than personable character, the ebullient Huppert and the portly Coluche (a super-popular French comedian who died tragically in 1986) more than make up for the casting imbalance. In French with English subtitles.

p, Alain Sarde; d, Bertrand Blier; w, Bertrand Blier, Gerard Brach; ph, Jean Penzer (Eastmancolor); ed, Claudine Merlin; m, J.J. Cale.

Comedy **(PR:O MPAA:NR)**

MY LIFE AS A DOG***

(1985, Swed.) 101m Svensk-AB c (MITT LIV SOM HUND)

Anton Glanzelius *(Ingemar Johansson),* Anki Liden *(His Mother),* Tomas von von Bromssen *(Uncle Gunnar),* Manfred Serner *(Erik, His Brother),* Melinda Kinnaman *(Saga),* Ing-Marie Carlsson *(Berit),* Kicki Rundgren *(Aunt Ulla),* Lennart Hjulstrom *(Konstnaren),* Leif Ericsson *(Farbor Sandberg),* Christina Carlwind *(Fru Sandberg),* Ralph Carlsson *(Harry),* Didrik Gustavsson *(Mr. Arvidsson),* Vivi Johansson *(Mrs. Arvidsson),* Jan-Philip Hollstrom *(Manne),* Arnold Alfredsson *(Manne's Grandfather),* Fritz Elofsson *(Glassworks Master),* Per Ottosson *(Tommy),* Johanna Udehn *(Lilla Grodan),* Susanna Wetterholm *(Karin).*

This critically acclaimed Swedish film, which also won kudos for its talented star, Anton Glanzelius, is a tragicomic, sensitive portrayal of adolescence set in 1959. The film centers on 12-year-old Ingemar Johansson (Glanzelius), who lives with his abusive brother (Manfred Serner) and terminally ill mother (Anki Liden). He is not discouraged, however—sure, he has it bad, but not as bad as Laika, the Soviet spacedog who starved to death while in orbit and whose fate haunts the boy. Ingemar's life has begun to spin out of control, and, like Laika, there's little he can do to stop it. When Ingemar is sent away for the summer to stay with relations, he meets a menage of eccentric—and sexually intimidating—villagers; eventually, these experiences give him a sustaining inner strength. Writer-director

Lasse Hallstrom's tale, like most films that look at childhood, is an episodic rite of passage, a story in which the emotions are touching but never sappy, the main character has the integrity and complexity of a real child with real troubles, and the glimpse of village life is rich and unique. MY LIFE AS A DOG is not just another charming film about growing up, but an expertly directed tale that takes a small, simple subject and colors it with invention and inspiration. The videocassette is available in both dubbed and subtitled (Swedish into English) versions.

p, Waldemar Bergendahl; d, Lasse Hallstrom; w, Lasse Hallstrom, Reidar Jonsson, Brasse Brannstrom, Per Berglund (based on the novel by Reidar Jonsson); ph, Jorgen Persson, Rolf Lindstrom (Fujicolor); ed, Christer Furubrand, Susanne Linnman; m, Bjorn Isfalt.

Comedy/Drama **(PR:C MPAA:PG-13)**

MY LIFE TO LIVE*****

(1962, Fr.) 85m Pleiade/Union-Pathe bw (VIVRE SA VIE; GB: IT'S MY LIFE)

Anna Karina *(Nana),* Saddy Rebbot *(Raoul),* Andre S. Labarthe *(Paul),* Guylaine Schlumberger *(Yvette),* Gerard Hoffman *(The Cook),* Monique Messine *(Elizabeth),* Paul Pavel *(A Journalist),* Dimitri Dineff *(A Youth),* Peter Kassowitz *(A Young Man),* Eric Schlumberger *(Luigi),* Brice Parain *(Himself),* Henri Attal *(Arthur),* Gisele Hauchecorne *(Concierge),* Jean-Luc Godard *(Voice).*

Jean-Luc Godard's fourth feature stars his then-wife, Anna Karina, as Nana, a Parisian sales clerk who, after separating from her husband, Paul (Andre S. Labarthe), tries to make it as an actress. After seeing Dreyer's silent classic THE PASSION OF JOAN OF ARC, she abandons the idea and turns to prostitution. The film is divided into 12 tableaux, which take place in cafes, in a record store, at a police station, and on the streets of Paris. The scenes and the issues raised range from prostitution (with quoted facts and figures on the subject), experiments with narration and autobiographical elements (Godard narrating, Karina starring), allusions to films and literature (Renoir's NANA, Zola's *Nana*, Truffaut's JULES AND JIM, Dreyer and Falconetti, and Edgar Allen Poe's "The Oval Portrait"), and philosophical discussions (with linguistic philosopher Brice Parain). For the first time, Godard successfully combined the facets that define him as a filmmaker—the genre elements of BREATHLESS, the politics of LE PETIT SOLDAT, and the narrative experimentation of A WOMAN IS A WOMAN. Technically MY LIFE TO LIVE was (and perhaps still is) far ahead of its time, knocking down the traditional walls of sound recording. Godard refused to mix the sound in the studio (except for Michel Legrand's barely used score), instead applying the same rule for sound and image—to capture life directly—and amended his "jump-cut" style of editing by allowing shots to last from six to eight minutes as the camera wandered through the set. MY LIFE TO LIVE also contains one of Godard's greatest and most personal scenes—a reading of Charles Baudelaire's translation of "The Oval Portrait," the story of an artist whose wife dies just as he finishes her portrait. Although Godard does not play Nana's lover in this scene, he does provide the character's voice. As we hear Godard reading Poe's words, we see the face of his wife, Anna Karina as Nana, and realize that, like Poe, Godard is painting a portrait of his wife. In French with English subtitles.

p, Pierre Braunberger; d, Jean-Luc Godard; w, Jean-Luc Godard; ph, Raoul Coutard; ed, Agnes Guillemot; m, Michel Legrand.

Drama **(PR:A MPAA:NR)**

MY NAME IS IVAN****

(1962, USSR) 97m Mosfilm/Sig Shore bw (IVANOVO DETSTVO; AKA: IVAN'S CHILDHOOD)

Kolya Burlyayev *(Ivan),* Valentin Zubkov *(Capt. Kholin),* Ye. Zharikov *(Lt. Galtsev),* S. Krylov *(Col. Katasonych),* Nikolai Grinko *(Col. Grygznov),* D. Milyutenko *(Old Man),* V. Malyavtina *(Masha),* I. Tarkovskaya *(Ivan's Mother),* A. Konchalovsky, Ivan Savkin, V. Marenkov, Vera Miturich.

This first feature from Andrei Tarkovsky is an intense cinematic poem on war and childhood, and the most horrific account of war's effects on the innocence of children since Roberto Rossellini's GERMANY, YEAR ZERO. Like Edmund in the Rossellini film, Ivan (Kolya Burlyayev) is a 12-year-old man/boy who has known little else in life but war, which has forced him to become an adult and (as reflected in the ironic actual translated title) robbed him of his childhood. As the film opens, Ivan seems an average youngster. Then he is shown trekking, neck-deep, through a murky swamp at the enemy front line, where Ivan is a member of a Russian military intelligence unit, sent to gather information on troop movements. Ivan has only a cause and a country, for his town has been overrun by Nazis, his father murdered, his mother shot and killed, and his sister blown apart by a bomb. Although his superiors are pleased with his efforts, they are protective of him and transfer him to the rear. Ivan rebels against this, however, and is allowed to go on one more mission. Much more than the story of a young boy at war, MY NAME IS IVAN is a pure film experience. Tarkovsky fills the frame with beautiful images, composed in extreme high, low, or tilted angles; uses an unpredictable editing style that alternates between rapid jarring cuts and carefully composed long takes; employs a stark black-and-white contrast that often turns natural scenery into abstract imagery; and constructs a soundtrack that is as inventive as the visuals. Complementing Tarkovsky's vision is the performance of Burlyayev, a young boy whose face expresses both determination and tenderness. Highly praised upon its release—it won awards at the Venice Film Festival for Best Film, Director, and Actor—MY NAME IS IVAN has found a new audience with the increasing international recognition of Tarkovsky's stature. The videocassette is in Russian with English subtitles, though the subtitles are often out of frame.

d, Andrei Tarkovsky; w, Vladimir Osipovich Bogomolov, Mikhail Papava, E. Smirnov (based on the short story "Ivan" by Vladimir Osipovich Bogomolov); ph, Vadim Yusov; ed, L. Feyginova; m, Vyacheslav Ovchinnikov.

Drama **(PR:O MPAA:NR)**

MY NEW PARTNER½**

(1984, Fr.) 107m Film 7/Orion c (LES RIPOUX)

Philippe Noiret *(Rene),* Thierry Lhermitte *(Francois),* Regine *(Simone),* Grace de Capitani *(Natacha),* Julien Guiomar *(Commissioner Bloret),* Claude Brosset *(Inspector Vidal),* Albert Simono *(Inspector Leblanc),* Bernard Bilaoul *(Camoun),* Pierre Frag *(Pierrot),* Jacques Santi *(Inspector del'I.G.S.).*

This standard police comedy-drama was such a crowd-pleaser in France that it walked away with the Cesar for Best Picture and Best Director. All the awards in the world, however, won't save this one from being anything but run-of-the-mill. Rene (Philippe Noiret) is a disheveled plain-clothes policeman who has long ago thrown away the rule-book. With the majority of his income consisting of bribes, he lives comfortably with Simone (Regine), a former prostitute, and relaxes by playing the horses. A monkey wrench is thrown into Rene's scheme, however, when he is assigned a new partner—Francois (Thierry Lhermitte), a rookie cop who knows all the rules. It's not long before Rene has corrupted Francois by fixing him up with Natacha (Grace de Capitani), a lovely call girl whose expensive tastes quickly empty the rookie's pocketbook, and when Francois' meager police salary can no longer satisfy his sweetheart's desires, he follows Rene's path. MY NEW PARTNER's success lies entirely in its casting; Noiret and Lhermitte provide a charged chemistry that carries the film despite its predictable script. It's not a bad film, but a forgettable one. In French with English subtitles.

p, Claude Zidi; d, Claude Zidi; w, Claude Zidi, Didier Kaminka (based on a story idea by Simon Mickael); ph, Jean-Jacques Tarbes (Eastmancolor); ed, Nicole Saulnier; m, Francis Lai.

Comedy/Crime **(PR:O MPAA:R)**

MY NIGHT AT MAUD'S****

(1969, Fr.) 105m FFP-Losange-Carrosse-Renn-Deux Mondes-Gueville-Simar Films de la Pleiade/Pathe-Corinth bw (MA NUIT CHEZ MAUD; AKA: MY NIGHT WITH MAUD)

Jean-Louis Trintignant *(Jean-Louis),* Francoise Fabian *(Maud),* Marie-Christine Barrault *(Francoise),* Antoine Vitez *(Vidal),* Leonide Kogan *(Concert Violinist),* Anne Dubot *(Blonde Friend),* Guy Leger *(Priest),* Marie Becker *(Marie, Maud's Daughter),* Marie-Claude Rauzier *(Student).*

The third of Eric Rohmer's "Six Moral Tales," MY NIGHT AT MAUD'S stars Jean-Louis Trintignant as Jean-Louis, a devout Catholic in love with Francoise (Marie-Christine Barrault), a pretty student he sees in church but is too shy to approach. When Jean-Louis runs into Vidal (Antoine Vitez), an old friend, Vidal invites him to dinner at the home of his bohemian lover, Maud (Francoise Fabian). There, Maud, Vidal (a Marxist professor), and Jean-Louis become involved in a lively conversation about the philosophy of Pascal and freedom of choice. In light of the bad snowstorm outside and the heavy drinking inside, Jean-Louis is persuaded to stay overnight at Maud's, but despite his hostess' advances does not make love to her. Later, he finally meets, and then marries, Francoise, only to find years later that she is the former mistress of Maud's husband. As in all of Rohmer's films, there is little "action" in MY NIGHT AT MAUD'S, but there is a great deal of intelligent and fascinating conversation as the characters question, expose, and explain their motivations and feelings (hence the "morality" of the tale). In Jean-Louis' case, his belief in premarital chastity is at issue. Photographed in black and white by Nestor Almendros, the film nicely captures the snowbound mood of the Christmas season, and the ensemble acting is excellent. The film was nominated for Best Foreign-Language Film and Best Original Screenplay Oscars, and won the New York Film Critics Best Screenwriting award. In French with English subtitles.

p, Pierre Cottrell, Barbet Schroeder; d, Eric Rohmer; w, Eric Rohmer; ph, Nestor Almendros; ed, Cecile Decugis.

Drama **(PR:A MPAA:GP)**

MY OTHER HUSBAND**

(1983, Fr.) 110m Marcel Dassault/Triumph c (ATTENTION! UNE FEMME PEUT EN CACHER UNE AUTRE)

Miou-Miou *(Alice),* Roger Hanin *(Philippe),* Eddy Mitchell *(Vincent),* Dominique Lavanant *(Solange),* Charlotte de Turckheim *(Cynthia),* Renee Saint-Cyr *(Mme. Le Boucau),* Venantino Venantini *(Nino),* Philippe Khorsand *(Raphael),* Rachid Ferrache *(Simon),* Ingrid Lurienne *(Pauline),* Vincent Barazzoni *(Jean),* Marcus Shopke *(Child Orchestra Leader),* Francois Perrot *(Surgeon),* Andre Valardy *(Interpreter),* Jean Rougerie *(Mr. Santaluccia),* Roland Giraud *(Jeff Belhome),* Lionel Rocheman *(Orchestra Leader's Father),* Patrick Floersheim *(Truck Driver),* Florence Giorgetti *(Zelda),* Martena Galli *(Mme. Belhome),* Dimitri Radochevitch *(Clarinettist),* Bobby Fehari, Julien Escale, Frank Beaujour *(Young Visitors),* Claude Leonardi *(Footballer),* Jean Pameja *(Mayor),* Max Fournal *(Pharmacist),* Robert Dalban *(Waiter at Restaurant).*

Alice (Miou-Miou) is a spunky coquette who, with great difficulty, manages to juggle two jobs in two cities, as well as two husbands and two families. In Paris, she holds a part-time nursing job and lives with her husband Philippe (Roger Hanin), a lovable airline pilot, and a 10-year-old son with an insatiable interest in Marxism. Because of Philippe's schedule, it's easy for Alice to get away to Deauville, where she works as a physical therapist and lives with Vincent (Eddy Mitchell), a fun-loving companion she's had two children with but has not married. With the help of her friends, Alice keeps her dual life a secret from both men, until one day both of them meet her at an airport restaurant. Had MY OTHER HUSBAND decided whether or not it wanted to be a comedy or a drama, it might have been a great film. Alice's dilemma is presented in a thoughtful and serious manner, but a number of scenes are better suited for a television situation comedy. The film has elements of inexplicable quirkiness throughout (for some reason, Alice has given both "husbands" very distinct sweaters—one with a large question mark on the front, the other with a large exclamation point, causing both men to do a double take when they meet), adding a nice touch to the film's dramatics. The gags often take over the story, however, and one senses that director George Lautner's main concern was to get himself (and Miou-Miou's character) out of the corner he paints the film into without forcing the audience to think too much. In French with English subtitles.

p, Alain Poire; d, Georges Lautner; w, Jean-Loup Dabadie; ph, Henri Decae (Eastmancolor); ed, Michelle David; m, Philippe Sarde.

Drama/Comedy **(PR:C MPAA:PG-13)**

MY UNCLE*****

(1958, Fr.) 110m Specta-Gray-Alter-Cady/Continental c (MON ONCLE)

Jacques Tati *(M. Hulot),* Jean-Pierre Zola *(M. Arpel),* Adrienne Servantie *(Mme. Arpel),* Alain Becourt *(Gerald Arpel),* Lucien Fregis *(Pichard),* Betty Schneider *(Betty, Landlord's Daughter),* Yvonne Arnaud *(Georgette, Arpel's Maid),* Dominique Marie *(Neighbor),* J.F. Martial *(Walter),* Andre Dino *(The Sweeper),* Claude Badolle *(The Junkman),* Nicolas Bataille *(The Workman),* Regis Fontenay *(The Suspenders Salesman),* Adelaide Danielli *(Mme. Pichard),* Denise Peronne *(Mlle. Fevrier),* Michel Goyot *(Car Salesman),* Dominique Derly *(M. Arpel's Secretary),* Max Martel *(The Drunkard),* Francomme *(The Painter),* Claire Rocca *(Mme. Arpel's Friend),* Loriot and the Inhabitants of the old Saint-Maur district of Paris.

Like Chaplin (MODERN TIMES) and Rene Clair (A NOUS LA LIBERTE) before him, Jacques Tati delivered here a comic satire on the ills of the technological age, its gadgetry, and the people who devote their lives to modern conveniences. Tati again casts himself in the role of Mons. Hulot, a lanky fellow with a raincoat and umbrella who stumbles through life, but just barely. Content to live in his neglected quarters, Hulot in direct contrast to the very modern Arpel family, comprising his sister (Adrienne Servantie), brother-in-law (Jean-Pierre Zola), and nephew, Gerald (Alain Becourt). The Arpels live in a stylized, modernized, desensitized suburb, their angular brick-and-glass house hidden from the street by a clanging metal gate, and fronted by a fountain with an obscene upright metal fish spurting water from its mouth. Inside are a number of gadgets that are meant to save time but do nothing but waste it—and make noise. Hulot's humble, simple life attracts young Gerald, whose mischievous enthusiasm has no place in the modern world. As much as Hulot and Gerald would like to escape from their high-tech environment, however, they cannot; it's here to stay, and they must contend with it. Less a condemnation of technology than of its worshippers, MY UNCLE is (like all of Tati's work) a rare example of comedy that is simultaneously entertaining, intelligent, and technically inventive. Of all Tati's films, it is the most accessible—the Hulot character taking center stage here instead of remaining in the background. MY UNCLE also contains one of the greatest shots in all of film, as Mme. and Mons. Arpel are each seen, from outside, walking back and forth in before their round bedroom windows, giving the impression that the house is rolling its eyes. In French with English subtitles.

p, Fred Orain; d, Jacques Tati; w, Jacques Tati, Jacques Lagrange, Jean L'Hote; ph, Jean Bourgoin (Eastmancolor); ed, Suzanne Baron; m, Franck Barcellini, Alain Romans.

Comedy **(PR:A MPAA:NR)**

MYSTERY OF ALEXINA, THE**½

(1985, Fr.) 86m Cineastes-TF1 c (MYSTERE ALEXINA)

Vuillemin *(Alexina/Camille Barbin),* Valerie Stroh *(Sara),* Veronique Silver, Bernard Freyd, Marianne Basler, Pierre Vial, Philippe Clevenot, Isabelle Gruault, Lucienne Hamon, Claude Bouchery, Olivier Sabran, Michel Amphoux.

When a young teacher of 22, Alexina (Vuillemin), arrives in the French town of La Rochelle in the mid-1800s, the townsfolk accept her with familial love and warmth. Sara (Valerie Stroh), another young teacher, helps her get adjusted, treating her as a sister and sharing a bedroom with her. It's soon apparent that Alexina has taken more than sisterly interest in Sara—long glances in the classroom, an occasional touch, and the torment of watching her undress in silhouette through the drapery that divides their bedroom—though what soon develops into a lesbian affair takes a strange turn when Sara observes that Alexina "makes love like a man." The locals are disgusted by the thought of lesbianism, especially among schoolteachers, but a medical examination of Alexina turns them rabid. Alexina is a hermaphrodite, who, raised in a convent by nuns, was told not to look "down there" and therefore took his-her gender to be female. Sure, it may be a little tough to believe, but the story is based on an actual celebrated case. The movie's interesting concept, unfortunately, suffers from weak execution—since the only mystery it concerns itself with is the nature of Alexina's gender, a search that takes up over half the film's 86 minutes. More intriguing is the question of how Alexina dealt with hermaphroditism, gender limitations, and romantic passion. The script by Jean Gruault (whose list of credits include Francois Truffaut's most obsessive movies—JULES AND JIM; THE STORY OF ADELE H.; THE GREEN ROOM) has promise, director Rene Feret is unable to adapt Gruault's words with anything like the brilliance of Truffaut. In French with English subtitles.

d, Rene Feret; w, Rene Feret, Jean Gruault; ph, Bernard Zitzermann; ed, Ariane Boeglin; m, Anne-Marie Deschamps.

Biography **(PR:O MPAA:NR)**

N

NAPOLEON*****

(1927, Fr.) 235m Gaumont/Metro-Goldwyn bw

Albert Dieudonne *(Napoleon Bonaparte),* Wladimir Roudenko *(Bonaparte as a Child),* Gina Manes *(Josephine de Beauharnais),* Nicolas Koline *(Tristan Fleuri),* Suzanne Charpentier *(Violine Fleuri),* Serge Freddykarll *(Marcellin Fleuri),* Edmond Van Daele *(Maximilien Robespierre),* Alexandre Koubitzky *(Danton),* Antonin Artaud *(Marat),* Abel Gance *(Saint-Just),* Max Maxudian *(Barras),* Philippe Heriat *(Salicetti),* Acho Chakatouny *(Pozzo di Borgo),* Eugenie Buffet *(Laetizia Bonaparte),* Yvette Dieudonne *(Elisa Bonaparte),* Georges Lampin *(Joseph Bonaparte),* Sylvio Cavicchia *(Lucien Bonaparte),* Simone Genevois *(Pauline Bonaparte),* Louis Sance *(Louis XVI),* Suzanne Bianchetti *(Marie-Antoinette),* Pierre Batcheff *(Gen. Lazare Hoche),* Philippe Rolla *(Massena),* Alexandre Bernard *(Dugommier),* W. Percy Day *(Adm. Hood),* Genica Missirio *(Capt. Joachim Murat),* Robert de Ansorena *(Capt. Desaix),* Harry-Krimer *(Rouget de l'Ilse),* Marguerite Gance *(Charlotte Corday),* Roger Blum *(Talma),* Jean Henry *(Sgt. Andoche Junot),* Maryse Damia *(La Marseillaise),* Henri Baudin *(Santo-Ricci),* Georges Henin *(Eugene de Beauharnais).*

A true motion picture legend, Abel Gance's amazing epic has been shown in no less than 19 versions since its 1927 Paris premiere. Filled with stunning technical innovations, the height of which is the explosion of the frame into a triptych (three screens of images that at times meld into one giant shot), NAPOLEON was distributed briefly in several truncated versions with and without the triptych, then disappeared entirely. Gance made a sound version in 1934, but his original masterpiece seemed lost forever—until 1980, when a restored NAPOLEON was given triumphant screenings in the US and Europe, accompanied by a full orchestra playing a score composed and conducted by Carmine Coppola, whose son, Francis Ford Coppola, provided financial support for the project. (Another restoration, by British film historian Kevin Brownlow, is also extant, and the differences between the "reconstructions" of Gance's original footage have raised some knotty questions as to cinematic aesthetics, authorship, and research.) Treating Napoleon as a romantic hero, the film charts his rise—from a childhood snowball fight to his early army career to his imprisonment during the Terror, defense of Paris against the Royalists, courtship of Josephine, and the invasion of Italy—in a rich blend of individual biography and French history. The film's climax is a wonderful spectacle, the triptych changing from one panoramic shot into three separate images and back again for more stunning, wide-screen views; then, as the army marches into Italy, the three screens are tinted blue, white, and red, making a giant French tricolor. It is a breathtaking moment in cinema history, but NAPOLEON is filled with such moments. The opening snowball fight; the "Double Tempest" sequence, in which Napoleon sails to France through a storm while a political hurricane blows in the Paris Convention Hall; the young soldier's "meeting" with the ghosts of the Revolution; the three-screen montages—all attest to Gance and his crew's amazing virtuosity and the greatness of the director's personal vision. Gance was convinced that the triptych—rendered, as best it can be, on videocassette in letterbox form—would revolutionize the film industry forever. Unfortunately, the arrival of sound soon after NAPOLEON's release caused such a sensation that Gance's film, burdened with distribution problems, suffered a 50-year eclipse.

p, Abel Gance; d, Abel Gance; w, Abel Gance; ph, Jules Kruger, Leonce-Henry Burel; ed, Marguerite Beauge, Henriette Pinson; m, Arthur Honegger, Carmine Coppola.

Biography/Historical **(PR:A MPAA:NR)**

NEST, THE**½

(1980, Sp.) 97m ELSA-Premier c (EL NIDO)

Hector Alterio *(Alejandro),* Ana Torrent *(Goyita),* Luis Politti *(Eladio),* Agustin Gonzalez *(Sargento),* Patricia Adriani *(Marisa),* Maria Luisa Ponte *(Amaro),* Mercedes Alonso *(Mercedes),* Luisa Rodrigo *(Gumer),* Amparo Baro *(Fuen),* Ovidi Montllor, Mauricia Calvo, Bernabe Arantza.

Hector Alterio (CAMILLA; THE OFFICIAL STORY) and the 12-year-old Ana Torrent (CRIA!; SPIRIT OF THE BEEHIVE) costar in this touching story of the passionate but chaste love an aging gentleman in the Spanish province of Castille feels for a young schoolgirl who shares his love of nature. Alejandro (Alterio) spends his days horseback riding and pretending to conduct Haydn's "Creation" in the woods. His life of solitude is essentially an empty one until he is befriended by the young Goyita (Torrent) and rediscovers a passion for life, loosening his ties to his past and to his dead wife and devoting himself to his new friend. Underneath the innocence and paternalism of the relationship lies a hint of sexuality, which leads to an eternal romantic vow. Nominated for an Oscar in 1981 as Best Foreign-Language Film, THE NEST has been called one of the best Spanish films to emerge since Franco's death. While the direction and photography are perhaps too glossy and romantic and the characters somewhat unbelievable, the view of father-as-provider versus father-as-oppressor is interesting in the context of Spanish post-Franco cinema. And while THE NEST has its faults, the performances are not among them. The chemistry between the two main characters is remarkable, with Torrent able to express volumes with her face. The videocassette is available in both dubbed and subtitled (Spanish into English) versions.

d, Jaime de Arminan; w, Jaime de Arminan; ph, Teodoro Escamilla (Eastmancolor); ed, Jose Luis Matesanz; m, Franz Joseph Haydn.

Drama **(PR:A MPAA:NR)**

NEVER ON SUNDAY***

(1960, Gr.) 97m Melina/UA-Lopert bw (POTE TIN KYRIAKI)

Melina Mercouri *(Ilya),* Jules Dassin *(Homer),* Georges Foundas *(Tonio),* Titos Vandis *(Jorgo),* Mitsos Liguisos *(The Captain),* Despo Diamantidou *(Despo),* Dimos Starrenios *(Poubelle),* Dimitri Papamikail *(A Sailor),* Alexis Salomos *(Noface).*

A colorful art-house comedy, filmed in Greece for a pittance (under $200,000), that broke through and made a ton of money when mass audiences flocked to see it, NEVER ON SUNDAY is the brainchild of Jules Dassin, an American writer-director who ran afoul of Red-baiters in the 1950s and had to go to Europe to earn a living. He helmed RIFIFI, then went to Greece, where he met and married Melina Mercouri, NEVER ON SUNDAY's star. Although the film is a standard "hooker with a heart of gold" story, audiences found its locale made it look different enough from any predecessor. Dassin not only wrote, produced, and directed, but also costarred as Homer, a tweedy American Grecophile who comes to Piraeus and encounters the local peasantry, who are slightly taken aback by his open ways. Homer loves Greece and everything about it. He soon meets Ilya (Mercouri), a prostitute with pride in her work who sees nothing immoral about the way she earns her living. Ilya takes all customers six days a week and reserves Sunday for seeing the great Greek plays, none of which she actually comprehends. Homer intends to reform Ilya, but old habits are hard to break. The title song won an Oscar, and nominations also went to Dassin's script and direction and Mercouri's performance (Mercouri fared a bit better at Cannes, where she won top honors). Most of the dialog is in English with a few speeches in Greek with titles.

p, Jules Dassin; d, Jules Dassin; w, Jules Dassin; ph, Jacques Natteau; ed, Roger Dwyre; m, Manos Hadjidakis.

Comedy/Drama (PR:O MPAA:NR)

NIGHT OF THE SHOOTING STARS, THE***

(1982, It.) 106m RAI-Ager-Premier/UA c (LA NOTTE DI SAN LORENZO; GB: THE NIGHT OF SAN LORENZO)

Omero Antonutti *(Galvano),* Margarita Lozano *(Concetta),* Claudio Bigagli *(Corrado),* Massimo Bonetti *(Nicole),* Norma Martelli *(Ivana),* Enrica Maria Modugno *(Mara),* Sabina Vannucchi *(Rosanna),* Dario Cantarelli *(Priest),* Sergio Dagliana *(Olinto),* Giuseppe Furia *(Requiem),* Paolo Hendel *(Dilvo),* Laura Mannucchi, Rinaldo Mirannalti, Donata Piacentini, Franco Piacentini, Antonio Prester, David Riondino, Gianfranco Salemi, Massimo Sarchielli, Mario Spallino.

On the night of San Lorenzo (a magical evening during which Europeans believe wishes may become fulfilled), a shooting star darts across the sky, sending a grown woman into a recollection of her childhood. As the star passes her window, she relates the events that took place in her small town during the last days of WW II: With the advancing Allies pushing the last remnants of the German army out of Italy, the Nazis enact a sick and desperate revenge on the townsfolk by staging vicious attacks on the old men, women, and children left in the villages. The members of the small town of San Miniato are divided in their opinions as to whether to remain in their village and risk dealing with the Nazis, or to attempt traveling across the back roads, dodging attacks from the sadistic Blackshirts, in an effort to meet the advancing Allies. One group made up of various segments of the town's population sets out on the journey, with all the old prohibitions breaking down as the people pull together in an effort to survive. An elderly peasant man with a natural ability to lead is chosen to guide the group to safety. Despite a few voices of dissent, the old man brings a clever ingenuity to his assignment and keeps the group's spirits up by showing a humane concern for all and encouraging them to watch out for one another. During the journey, he develops a romantic friendship with an aristocratic woman who had always admired him, but could never let him know because of their difference in class. Once he has guided the group out of danger, however, the townspeople immediately resume the societal roles that previously divided them. The Taviani brothers, who previously gained international attention with 1977 Cannes Film Festival Golden Pal winner PADRE PADRONE, approached this film in much the same way—using an imaginative combination of events and showing them as remembered by the narrator as she reminisces about the magical moments of her childhood—and came up with a dazzling, immensely popular import that earned them the Special Jury Prize at Cannes. In Italian with English subtitles.

p, Giuliani G. De Negri; d, Paolo Taviani, Vittorio Taviani; w, Vittorio Taviani, Paolo Taviani, Giuliani G. De Negri, Tonino Guerra; ph, Franco di Giacomo (Agfacolor); ed, Roberto Perpignani; m, Nicola Piovani.

Drama/War (PR:O MPAA:R)

NIGHT PORTER, THE½**

(1973, It./US) 117m Edwards-Esae De Simone/AE c (IL PORTIERE DI NOTTE)

Dirk Bogarde *(Max),* Charlotte Rampling *(Lucia),* Philippe Leroy *(Klaus),* Gabriele Ferzetti *(Hans),* Giuseppe Addobbati *(Stumm),* Isa Miranda *(Countess Stein),* Nino Bignamini *(Adolph),* Marino Mase *(Atherton),* Amedeo Amodio *(Bert),* Piero Vida *(Day Porter),* Geoffrey Copleston *(Kurt),* Manfred Freiberger *(Dobson),* Ugo Cardea *(Mario),* Hilda Gunther *(Greta),* Nora Ricci *(The Neighbor),* Piero Mazzinghi *(Concierge),* Kai S. Seefield *(Jacob),* Claudio Steiner *(Dobson).*

Filmmaker Liliana Cavani visited a Nazi concentration camp after WW II and interviewed a woman who had been involved in a sado-masochistic relationship with a guard, then made the story the basis for this powerful, sometimes ponderous film starring Dirk Bogarde as Max, the night porter in a Viennese hotel in 1958. Max's duties go far beyond the usual for a man in his position, since the hotel guests—former Nazis—and the proprietress enjoy being sadistically "dealt with" by the night porter, an ex-storm trooper. All believe they have managed to eliminate any witnesses to their war crimes, and though Max himself is about to go on trial, he too thinks he's safe, until Lucia (Charlotte Rampling) and her husband check in. Max recognizes Lucia as a former concentration camp prisoner of whom he took photographs while pretending to be a physician. That's not all, however; the picture flashes forward and back to show past episodes of rape, sodomy, and torture between Max and Lucia—episodes Lucia apparently enjoyed. Max and Lucia rekindle their strange love, but the other hotel residents are determined to stop them. A strange and unforgettable picture that questions the psyches of torturers and tortured, THE NIGHT PORTER presents its pschoanalytically provocative material without exploitation, but the subject was apparently too strong for most audiences and the film never caught fire with the public. In English.

p, Robert Gordon Edwards; d, Liliana Cavani; w, Liliana Cavani, Italo Moscati (based on a story by Cavani, Barbara Alberti, Amedeo Pagani); ph, Alfio Contini (Technicolor); ed, Franco Arcalli; m, Daniele Paris.

Drama **(PR:O MPAA:R)**

NIGHTS OF CABIRIA, THE***

(1957, Fr./It.) 110m Les Films Marcea-De Laurentiis/ Lopert bw (LE NOTTI DI CABIRIA; AKA: CABIRIA)

Giulietta Masina *(Cabiria),* Francois Perier *(Oscar D'Onofrio, Accountant),* Amedeo Nazzari *(Alberto Lazzari, Movie Star),* Aldo Silvani *(Hypnotist),* Franca Marzi *(Wanda Cabiria's Friend),* Dorian Gray *(Jessy Lazzari's Girl Friend),* Mario Passante *(Cripple in the "Miracle" Sequence),* Pina Gualandri *(Matilda the Prostitute),* Polidor *(The Monk),* Ennio Girolami, Christian Tassou, Jean Molier, Ricardo Fellini.

As in LA STRADA, Fellini directed his wife (Giulietta Masina) as an innocent woman thrust into the middle of a cold and cruel world in this film. NIGHTS OF CABIRIA lacks the lyrical simplicity that made LA STRADA such a magical experience, but was an impressive enough display of Fellini's fascinating visual style to warrant the Academy Award for Best Foreign-Language Film. Set in a district on the outskirts of Rome, the film focuses on Cabiria (Masina), a near-perfect embodiment of the prostitute with a heart of gold. She's the type who understands misfortune to be part and parcel of life, but never loses faith in the value of life itself. When misfortune does come her way, Cabiria shrugs it off and continues walking the streets for money, as when a handsome movie star picks her up during a brawl with his girl friend. He takes her to his fabulous home, but quickly discards her when he is through with her services. Eventually someone does fall in love with Cabiria—the shy and withdrawn Oscar D'Onofrio (Francois Perier)—or at least she believes this to be the case. Perhaps the most difficult aspect of NIGHTS OF CABIRIA is accepting Masina as a prostitute: this sweet and naive-looking woman, who stole audiences' hearts with her childlike innocence in LA STRADA, just doesn't seem likely as a woman selling herself on the streets, but does express the dismal point that fate makes no exceptions. As in the majority of Fellini's films, the emphasis here is on visual elements instead of on straight narrative form, relying on small details and eccentricities to breathe life into Cabiria. In Italian with English subtitles.

p, Dino De Laurentiis; d, Federico Fellini; w, Federico Fellini, Ennio Flaiano, Tullio Pinelli, Pier Paolo Pasolini; ph, Aldo Tonti, Otello Martelli; ed, Leo Catozzo; m, Nino Rota.

Drama **(PR:C MPAA:NR)**

1900****

(1976, It./Fr./Ger.) 248m PEA-Artistes Associes-Artemis/PAR c (NOVECENTO)

Burt Lancaster *(Alfredo Berlinghieri, Sr.),* Robert De Niro *(Alfredo Berlinghieri, his Grandson),* Sterling Hayden *(Leo Dalco),* Gerard Depardieu *(Olmo Dalco),* Dominique Sanda *(Ada Fiastri Paulhan),* Romolo Valli *(Giovanni Berlinghieri),* Anna-Maria Gherardi *(Eleonora),* Francesca Bertini *(Desolata),* Ellen Schwiers *(Amelia),* Pippo Campanini *(Don Tarcisio),* Paolo Branco *(Orso Dalco),* Giacomo Rizzo *(Rigoletto),* Antonio Piovanelli *(Turo Dalco),* Liu Bosisio *(Nella Dalco),* Maria Monti *(Rosina Dalco),* Anna Henkel *(Anita),* Tiziana Senatore *(Regina as a Child),* Jose Quaglio *(Aranzini),* Edoardo Dallagio *(Oreste Dalco),* Stefania Cassini *(Neve),* Salvator Mureddu *(Chief of Guards),* Allen Midgette *(Vagabond).*

The quintessential Bernardo Bertolucci film, 1900 captures everything that characterizes the director—his concern with the class dialectic and the battle between Marxism and Fascism, his painterly images of Italy, his historical scope, and his "divided hero" (to borrow from critic Robin Wood). While it may be a masterpiece at its original length of 320 minutes, 1900's American, British, and videocassette release is a shortened, somewhat erratic 245-minute version. The plot is about as grand and baroque as one can get—entailing the history of the Italian people and politics in the first half of the 1900s, from the organization of the peasant class to the rise of socialism to the fall of Fascism. This political dialectic is personified in Bertolucci's two central characters (the "divided hero")—Alfredo (Robert De Niro), born into a bourgeois clan of landowners, and Olmo (Gerard Depardieu), born into a peasant family—who share the same birthday, January 27, 1901. Although they grow up the best of friends, their friendship transforms into a love/hate relationship. As an adult, the weak Alfredo is put in charge of his family's property, but is merely a puppet controlled by his evil foreman, Attila (Donald Sutherland), while the Marxist Olmo becomes a leading union organizer. Even in its shortened version, 1900 is an achievement of great cinematic genius, directed by Bertolucci but made possible by the combined efforts of collaborator-cinematographer Vittorio Storaro, composer Ennio Morricone, art director Enzo Frigerio, costumer Gitt Magrini, and a phenomenal cast that includes an international Who's-Who of performers. Bertolucci's clearly left-wing politics have made him a subject of controversy, precisely because of the populism of his directing style—an interesting and important contrast to the radical techniques of Jean-Luc Godard, whose looming genius has long haunted Bertolucci.

p, Alberto Grimaldi; d, Bernardo Bertolucci; w, Franco Arcalli, Bernardo Bertolucci, Giuseppe Bertolucci; ph, Vittorio Storaro (Technicolor); ed, Franco Arcalli; m, Ennio Morricone.

Drama **(PR:O MPAA:R)**

NOSFERATU*****

(1922, Ger.) 63m Prana-Film bw (NOSFERATU, EINE SYMPHONIE DES GRAUENS; AKA: NOSFERATU, A SYMPHONY OF HORROR)

Max Schreck *(Nosferatu),* Alexander Granach *(Jonathan Knock),* Gustav von Wangenheim *(Hutter),* Greta Schroeder *(Nina),* G.H. Schnell *(Harding),* Ruth Landshoff *(Annie Harding),* John Gottowt *(Prof. Bulwer),* Gustav Botz *(Prof. Sievers),* Max Nemetz *(Captain of the "Demeter"),* Wolfgang Heinz, Albert Venohr *(Seamen),* Guido Hersfeld *(Innkeeper),* Hardy von Francois *(Doctor).*

The first cinematic "Dracula" (the title was changed to avoid copyright problems) is a wonderfully atmospheric work, made more eerie by virtue of its authentic location shooting. Hutter (Gustav von Wangenheim), a real estate clerk in the city of Bremen, must leave his bride to conduct a little business in the distant Carpathian mountains with an "eccentric" client, Graf Orlok (Max Schreck). The journey is filled with ominous warnings, especially the fact that the mysterious coach that finally delivers the young man to the Graf's castle is shot by director F.W. Murnau in fast motion and on negative stock. At the castle, Murnau's splendid sense of composition establishes a mood of creepy neoreality guaranteed to make the skin of the most devoted horror fan crawl. After a few evenings of bloodletting, the weakened but finally wise Hutter manages to escape Nosferatu's clutches. But the vampire follows him home, bringing terror and pestilence with him. Murnau's visualization of the Dracula saga makes the Tod Browning-Bela Lugosi 1931 adaptation look like Walt Disney, and the disconcerting, almost ratlike appearance of the appropriately named Schreck (whose surname is also the German word for "fright") greatly enhances the film's considerable present-day power.

d, F.W. Murnau; w, Henrik Galeen (based on the novel *Dracula* by Bram Stoker); ph, Fritz Arno Wagner, Gunther Krampf; m, Hans Erdmann.

Horror **(PR:C MPAA:NR)**

O

ODD OBSESSION***

(1959, Jap.) 96m Daiei/Harrison c (KAGI; AKA: THE KEY)

Machiko Kyo *(Ikuko Kenmochi),* Ganjiro Nakamura *(Mr. Kenji Kenmochi),* Junko Kano *(Toshiko Kenmochi),* Tatsuya Nakadai *(Kimura),* Tanie Kitabayashi *(Hana),* Ichiro Sugai *(Masseur),* Jun Hamamura *(Dr. Soma),* Mantaro Ushio *(Dr. Kodama),* Kyu Sazanka *(Curio Dealer).*

This strange black comedy revolves around an elderly art critic, Mr. Kenmochi (Ganjiro Nakamura), who has problems with his virility. Without telling his young wife, Ikuko (Machiko Kyo), he takes injections to improve his sex life, but they don't seem to have any effect. Turning to voyeurism, he finds that he is most aroused when in the throes of jealousy, and maneuvers his daughter's boy friend (Tatsuya Nakadai), a young intern, into an affair with his wife. When all of this becomes too much for Kenmochi, his life is threatened, then ended, by a stroke. Even more striking than the film's flagrant sexuality and its disconcerting, absurdly comic twists is Kon Ichikawa's stylistic flair—his use of freeze-frames, distancing insert shots, and unrealistic color. In Japanese with English subtitles.

p, Hiroaki Fujii; d, Kon Ichikawa; w, Natto Wada, Keiji Hasebe, Kon Ichikawa (based on the novel *Kagi* by Junichiro Tanizaki); ph, Kazuo Miyagawa (DaieiScope, Daiei-Agfa Color); ed, Hiroaki Fujii, Kon Ichikawa; m, Yasushi Akutagawa.

Drama **(PR:O MPAA:NR)**

OFFICIAL STORY, THE***½

(1985, Arg.) 112m Historias-Cinemania/Almi c (LA HISTORIA OFICIAL; AKA: THE OFFICIAL HISTORY; GB: THE OFFICIAL VERSION)

Hector Alterio *(Roberto),* Norma Aleandro *(Alicia),* Chela Ruiz *(Sara),* Chunchuna Villafane *(Ana),* Hugo Arana *(Enrique),* Patricio Contreras *(Benitez),* Guillermo Battaglia *(Jose),* Maria-Luisa Robledo *(Nata),* Analia Castro *(Gaby),* Jorge Petraglia *(Macci),* Augusto Larreta *(General),* Leal Rey *(Father Ismael).*

The first important film to emerge from Argentina after the fall of its military regime, THE OFFICIAL STORY, set in 1983, is a deeply moving drama examining one of the saddest chapters in that country's history. The tranquil lives of Alicia (Norma Aleandro), a history professor; her husband, Roberto (Hector Alterio), a high-powered businessman; and their five-year-old daughter, Gaby (Analia Castro), are thrown into turmoil when an old friend who was tortured and exiled by the military reveals that, under the junta, babies were taken from political prisoners and sold to well-connected adoptive parents. Realizing that Gaby may be one of these children, Alicia begins an investigation into her daughter's background, and meets Sara (Chela Ruiz), one of the woman who march each day at the Plaza de Mayo to protest the disappearance of loved ones in the junta's "dirty war." Coming to grips with her political naivete, Alicia confronts Alterio, who proves to be deeply involved with the reprehensible junta. The impressive feature film directorial debut by Luis Puenzo, who invests his scenes with tremendous emotional impact, THE OFFICIAL STORY won the 1986 Oscar for Best Foreign-Language Film. Poignantly political, its power comes not from an exhaustive indictment of the atrocities of the junta, but from its depiction of its tragic effect on individual lives. The screenplay was written with Aleandro (a political exile who returned to her native Argentina after the change of government) in mind, and she delivers a tour de force performance that won her the Best Actress Award at Cannes, as well as an Academy Award nomination. Originally, Puenzo intended to shoot the film in secret, using hidden 16mm cameras, but the junta was voted out of office just after cowriter Aida Bortnik completed the screenplay. The videocassette is available in both dubbed and subtitled (Spanish into English) versions.

p, Marcelo Pineyro; d, Luis Puenzo; w, Luis Puenzo, Aida Bortnik; ph, Felix Monti; ed, Juan Carlos Macias; m, Atilio Stampone.

Drama **(PR:O MPAA:NR)**

ONE DEADLY SUMMER**

(1983, Fr.) 130m SNC-CAPAC-TFI/UNIV c (L'ETE MEURTRIER)

Isabelle Adjani *(Elaine/Elle),* Alain Souchon *(Pin Pon),* Suzanne Flon *(Cognata),* Jenny Cleve *(Pin Pon's Mother),* Francois Cluzet *(Mickey),* Manuel Gelin *(Boubou),* Michel Galabru *(Gabriel),* Maria Machado *(Elle's Mother),* Roger Carel *(Henry IV),* Jean Gaven *(Leballech),* Max Morel *(Touret),* Cecile Vassort *(Josette),* Martin LaMotte *(Georges),* Jacques Nolot *(Fiero),* Raymond Meunier *(Brochard),* Jacques Dynam *(Ferraldo),* Evelyne Didi *(Calamite),* Yves Alfonso *(Rostollan).*

With ONE DEADLY SUMMER the French Cesars once again proved to be a kiss of death for a picture on American shores. And, indeed, though the film received a handful of Cesars, it amounts to little more than a convoluted tale of the emotionally unfit Eliane (Isabelle Adjani), who searches for the three men who years ago battered, raped, and impregnated her mother. Convinced that one of these rapists is her father, she tracks down the family of one of the men and ensnares his son, Pin-Pon (Alain Souchon). Eliane is a full-blown tart, wandering around town without underwear, flashing her breasts, and teasing anyone who looks her way. For some reason, Pin-Pon falls in love with her, lets her move into his family's home, and asks her to marry him. She, however, is keeping her true motives a secret. She also does not tell him that she is mentally disturbed, has a lesbian lover, fought off childhood sexual advances by her father, and still suckles at her mother's breast. Directed by Jacques Becker's son Jean, ONE DEADLY SUMMER is wildly unbelievable, cliched, and overlong, though it does make some interesting use of voice-over techniques. Adjani, who here bares all and does so often, turns in a histrionic performance that earned raves, though it is French pop star Souchon who carries the picture. Yves Montand sings "Trois Petites Notes De Musique." The excellent subtitles deserve a special mention and should serve as a model to all. Cesars went to Adjani (Best Actress), Suzanne Flon (Best Supporting Actress), Sebastien Japrisot (Best Adapted Screenplay), and Jacques Witta (Best Editing). In French with English subtitles.

p, Christine Beytout; d, Jean Becker; w, Jean Becker, Sebastien Japrisot (based on the novel by Sebastien Japrisot); ph, Etienne Becker (Panavision, Eastmancolor); ed, Jacques Witta; m, Georges Delerue.

Thriller **(PR:O MPAA:R)**

OPEN CITY*****

(1945, It.) 105m Excelsea-Mayer/Burstyn bw (ROMA, CITTA APERTA; AKA: ROME, OPEN CITY)

Anna Magnani *(Pina),* Aldo Fabrizi *(Don Pietro Pellegrini),* Marcello Pagliero *(Giorgio Manfredi),* Maria Michi *(Marina),* Harry Feist *(Maj. Bergmann),* Francesco Grandjacquet *(Francesco),* Giovanna Galletti *(Ingrid),* Vito Annichiarico *(Marcello Pina's Son),* Carla Revere *(Lauretta),* Nando Bruno *(Agostino),* Carlo Sindici *(Police Superintendent),* Joop Van Hulzen *(Hartmann).*

One of the most important achievements in the history of cinema, OPEN CITY is the first great fusion of documentary and melodrama. Filmed on the streets, without the use of sound recorders (dialog was dubbed in later), during the months just after the Allies liberated Italy from the grip of Fascism, the film has the appearance of documentary. The actors, except for Anna Magnani (then a some-time dance hall girl), were all nonprofessionals. The backgrounds were not constructions in a Cinecitta, but actual apartments, shops, and streets—a change for those used to sets and costumes. Set in Rome, 1943-44, the story brings together two enemy forces—the Communists and the Catholics—and unites them in the fight for their country's liberation. Manfredi (Marcello Pagliero) is a Resistance leader wanted by the Nazis who must deliver some money to his compatriots. Hiding out in the apartment block of Francesco (Francesco Grandjacquet) and his pregnant fiancee, Pina (Magnani), Manfredi's plan is to let a Catholic priest, Don Pietro (Aldo Fabrizi), make the delivery. When their building is raided, Francesco is arrested and hauled away. Pina chases after him, screaming, and is gunned down in the middle of the street. Manfredi takes refuge in the apartment of his mistress, Marina (Maria Michi), a lesbian drug addict who, unknown to him, is an informant whose drug supplier is a female Gestapo agent (Giovanna Galleti). As excellent as OPEN CITY is, it has often been criticized for its black-and-white division of characters into Good and Evil, and the emotional manipulation of Renzo Rossellini's score and its use of comic devices—these attributes apparently weakening the objective aims of Neo-Realist cinema. Director Roberto Rossellini, however, cannot be criticized for stirring emotions rather than intellect, since objectivity is not possible here. In OPEN CITY one can see, above all else, the honesty and morality of Rossellini's direction, and, while his result may not wholly comply with the accepted definition of Neo-Realism, his intent—to bring reality to the screen—most certainly does. Most videotape copies offer prints of mediocre quality and often unreadable subtitles.

p, Roberto Rossellini; d, Roberto Rossellini; w, Sergio Amidei, Federico Fellini, Roberto Rossellini (based on a story by Amidei, Alberto Consiglio); ph, Ubaldo Arata; m, Renzo Rossellini, Pietro Di Donato, Herman G. Weinberg.

War/Drama **(PR:O MPAA:NR)**

ORDET****

(1955, Den.) 126m Palladium/Kingsley bw (AKA: THE WORD)

Henrik Malberg *(Morten Borgen),* Emil Hass Christensen *(Mikkel Borgen),* Preben Lerdorff-Rye *(Johannes Borgen),* Cay Kristiansen *(Anders Borgen),* Birgitte Federspiel *(Inger Mikkel's Wife),* Ejner Federspiel *(Peter Skraedder),* Ove Rud *(Pastor),* Ann Elisabeth Rud *(Maren Borgen Mikkel's Daughter),* Susanne Rud *(Lilleinger Borgen Mikkel's Daughter),* Gerda Nielsen *(Anne Skraedder).*

Based on the play by Kaj Munk, this inspirational drama of Christian faith comes from Carl Theodor Dreyer, perhaps the most profoundly religious of cinema directors. Set in a staunchly God-fearing Danish village, ORDET tells the story of Morten Borgen (Henrik Malberg) and his three sons—Mikkel (Emil Hass Christensen), who is filled with religious doubt; Anders (Cay Kristiansen), who is involved in a romance complicated by differences of faith; and the central character, Johannes (Preben Lerdorff-Rye), who believes he is Christ, and whose extreme faith is viewed as madness—until he is visited by the Holy Spirit and Mikkel's wife is resurrected at her funeral. ORDET is an overwhelming intellectual experience, if only in its powerful subject matter. Dreyer successfully simplifies both the religious-metaphysical themes of the film and its visual style (the film contains only 114 shots in 126 minutes) to create a meditative and genuinely inspirational mood. The picture shows Dreyer's superb control of *mise-en-scene*, and is not to be missed by anyone who loved his great THE PASSION OF JOAN OF ARC. In Danish with English subtitles.

p, Carl Theodor Dreyer; d, Carl Theodor Dreyer; w, Carl Theodor Dreyer (based on the play by Kaj Munk); ph, Henning Bendtsen; ed, Edith Schussel; m, Poul Schierbeck.

Drama **(PR:A-C MPAA:NR)**

ORPHEUS*****

(1950, Fr.) 112m Productions Andre Paulve-Les Films du Palais-Royal/Discina bw (ORPHEE)

Jean Marais *(Orpheus),* Maria Casares *(The Princess),* Marie Dea *(Eurydice),* Francois Perier *(Heurtebise),* Juliette Greco *(Aglaonice),* Edouard Dermit *(Cegeste),* Henri Cremieux *(Friend in Cafe),* Pierre Bertin *(Police Commissioner),* Roger Blin *(Writer),* Jacques Varennes, Andre Carnege, Rene Worms *(Judges).*

This modernization of an ancient myth is a perfect example of Jean Cocteau's poetry—proof, if such is needed, that he was one of the great artists of the 20th century. Updating the story with an autobiographical element—the poet lives in contemporary Paris—Cocteau casts his longtime companion Jean Marais as Orpheus, a famous poet married to Eurydice (Marie Dea). When a fellow poet, the handsome young Cegeste (Edouard Dermit), is hit by a passing motorcyclist in front of a popular cafe, Orpheus is invited by an elegant and mysterious Princess (Maria Casares) to accompany her and the dead poet to her chalet.

There, the Princess brings Cegeste "back to life" (by ingeniously running the film backwards for that one shot, Cocteau was able to perform such magic) and disappears through a liquescent mirror into the Underworld. Later, after being chauffeured home by the Princess' servant, the angel Heurtebise (Francois Perier), Orpheus devotes himself to his poetry, scribbling down indecipherable messages transmitted to him over a car radio. He ignores everything but the radio, and fails to even notice when Eurydice is killed. Heurtebise, who has fallen in love with Eurydice during Orpheus' preoccupation with poetry, comes to suspect that the Princess overstepped her authority as an Angel of Death by killing Eurydice in order to make room for herself in Orpheus' life. Together, Heurtebise and Orpheus pass through the mirror and journey into the Underworld to find the Princess and Eurydice. Awarded the top prize at the 1950 Venice Film Festival, ORPHEUS was instantly heralded as a masterpiece. It was blessed with perfect casting (though Cocteau had considered both Greta Garbo and Marlene Dietrich for Casares' role), photographic innovation, and an exceptional score by Georges Auric. In French with English subtitles.

p, Emil Darbon; d, Jean Cocteau; w, Jean Cocteau (based on the play by Jean Cocteau); ph, Nicholas Hayer; ed, Jacqueline Sadoul; m, Georges Auric, Christophe Willibald Gluck.

Fantasy **(PR:A MPAA:NR)**

OSSESSIONE***

(1942, It.) 112m ICI Roma/Brandon bw

Clara Calamai *(Giovanna),* Massimo Girotti *(Gino),* Juan de Landa *(The Husband),* Elio Marcuzzo *(The Spaniard),* Dhia Cristiani *(Anita),* Vittorio Duse *(The Lorry Driver),* Michele Riccardini *(Don Remigio),* Michele Sakara *(Child).*

The first directorial effort in the brilliant, though sporadic, career of Luchino Visconti was made in 1942 but not shown outside Italy for several years because of copyright problems. Based on the James M. Cain novel *The Postman Always Rings Twice*, the film is a sizzling love story, set against a background of murder and adultery along the backroads of the Italian countryside. The nomadic Gino (Massimo Girotti), a man living under the illusion that attachments only act as a hindrance, happens upon the roadside inn run by Giovanna (Clara Calamai) and her older, grotesque-looking husband (Juan de Landa). One look at this couple tells their entire story: she is young, beautiful, and full of passion, married to a man unequal to her in all areas except one—money. Giovanna soon takes a romantic interest in the visitor, discovering the spark that never ignited with her husband. Often cited as the first film to show Neo-Realist tendencies, OSSESSIONE was shot in the Italian countryside (as opposed to the studios—a technique favored by Jean Renoir, with whom Visconti apprenticed) and showed the Italian people living in their natural environs. In Italian with English subtitles.

p, Libero Solaroli; d, Luchino Visconti; w, Mario Alicata, Antonio Pietrangeli, Gianni Puccini, Giuseppe De Santis, Luchino Visconti (based on the novel *The Postman Always Rings Twice* by James M. Cain); ph, Aldo Tonti, Domenico Scala; ed, Mario Serandrei; m, Giuseppe Rosati.

Drama **(PR:C MPAA:NR)**

P

PADRE PADRONE***½

(1977, It.) 114m Radio Italiano/Cinema V c (AKA: FATHER MASTER; MY FATHER, MY MASTER)

Omero Antonutti *(Gavino's Father),* Saverio Marconi *(Gavino),* Marcella Michelangeli *(Gavino's Mother),* Fabrizio Forte *(Gavino as a Child),* Marino Cenna *(Servant/Shepherd),* Stanko Molnar *(Sebastiano),* Nanni Moretti *(Cesare).*

This is the simple story of a boy's growth into manhood under the despotism of his father. At age six, Gavino (played as a child by Fabrizio Forte) is pulled out of school and taken by his father (Omero Antonutti) into the mountains to become a shepherd. His father tries to control his son's life in every respect, with a comportment bordering on the sadistic. As he grows to manhood, Gavino (played as a young man by Saverio Marconi) begins to discover things for himself and rebel against his father's authority, eventually escaping from the patriarch's rule, but encountering his changed father one last time in the film's denouement. Originally filmed by the Taviani brothers for Italian television, PADRE PADRONE is a fine example of a strong ensemble telling a story naturally, without intrusion by the directors. Using both professional actors and untrained locals from the Sardinian countryside, this story of the virtual imprisonment of young Sardinians by the sheep and pastures of their land unfolds simply and yet with great power. The winner of the grand prize at the Cannes Film Festival of 1977, the tale is based in truth: the real-life Gavino underwent similar experiences before escaping at age 20, going on to become a linguistics professor, and writing a book about his experiences. In Italian with English subtitles.

p, Giuliani G. De Negri; d, Vittorio Taviani, Paolo Taviani; w, Vittorio Taviani, Paolo Taviani (based on a book by Gavino Ledda); ph, Mario Masini (Eastmancolor); ed, Roberto Perpignani; m, Egisto Macchi.

Drama **(PR:C MPAA:NR)**

PAISAN*****

(1946, It.) 120m Oragnization-Foreign/Mayer-Burstyn bw (PAISA)

Carmela Sazio *(Carmela),* Robert Van Loon *(Joe from Jersey),* Alfonsino Pasca *(Boy),* Maria Michi *(Francesca),* Renzo Avanzo *(Massimo),* Harriet White *(Harriet),* Dots M. Johnson *(Black MP),* Bill Tubbs *(Capt. Bill Martin Chaplain),* Dale Edmonds *(Dale O.S.S. Man),* Carlo Piscane *(Peasant in Sicily Story),* Mats Carlson *(Soldier in Sicily Story),* Gar Moore *(Fred American Soldier),* Gigi Gori *(Partisan),* Cigolani *(Cigolani Partisan),* Lorena Berg *(Maddalena),* Benjamin Emmanuel, Raymond Campbell, Albert Heinz, Harold Wagner.

PAISAN is one of those rare segmented films that never loses steam as it moves through six chronologically ordered sequences beginning with the Allied invasion of Sicily in 1943 and concluding with the liberation in 1945. In addition to as moving across time, the film transports the viewer throughout Italy—from Sicily to Naples to Rome to Florence to Romagna to Po—each episode observing a slice of regional life. A film unlike any other the world had seen, PAISAN is OPEN CITY without the melodrama, though, despite its re-created scenes from life, it is anything but a flat, uninvolving newsreel. It is instead a portrait of life during wartime filled with humor, pathos, adventure, romance, tension, and warmth that are as tangible in the film as they are in the real world. Perhaps the straightforward nature of Roberto Rossellini's portrayal of the events is best reflected in the Naples segment: a young boy meets a drunken GI who is on the verge of passing out, but before he nods off, the boy warns him, "If you fall asleep, I'll steal your boots." The GI falls asleep and the boy steals his boots. PAISAN is a film about truth—truth stated and truth observed. Collaborating on the script was future director Federico Fellini, who was at the time also employed as Rossellini's full-time assistant. In Italian with English subtitles.

p, Roberto Rossellini, Rod E. Geiger, Mario Conti; d, Roberto Rossellini; w, Sergio Amidei, Federico Fellini, Roberto Rossellini, Annalena Limentani (based on stories by Victor Haines, Marcello Pagliero, Amidei, Fellini, Rossellini, Klaus Mann, Vasco Pratolini); ph, Otello Martelli; ed, Eraldo Da Roma, Herman G. Weinberg; m, Renzo Rossellini.

War **(PR:C MPAA:NR)**

PANDORA'S BOX*****

(1929, Ger.) 110m Nero Film A.G.-Moviegraphs bw (DIE BUECHSE DER PANDORA)

Louise Brooks *(Lulu),* Fritz Kortner *(Dr. Peter Schon),* Franz Lederer *(Alwa Schon, His Son),* Carl Gotz *(Schigolch/Papa Brommer),* Alice Roberts *(Countess Anna Geschwitz),* Daisy d'Ora *(Marie de Zarniko),* Krafft Raschig *(Rodrigo Quast),* Michael von Newlinsky *(Marquis Casti-Piani),* Siegfried Arno *(The Stage Manager),* Gustav Diessl *(Man/Jack the Ripper).*

If the close-up hadn't already existed in film, the presence of Louise Brooks would have necessitated its discovery. Here, in the role that made her internationally famous, Brooks—with her familiar short haircut—plays Lulu, a sexually free young woman who bubbles over with energy, celebrating life to a fuller extent than might a dozen other women combined. Although her wealthy lover and benefactor, Dr. Peter Schon (Fritz Kortner), is engaged to marry a high-ranking official's daughter, Lulu lures him into marrying her, over the objections of Schon's son, Alwa (Franz Lederer), a handsome young composer. On the night of their wedding, Schon and Lulu slip off to the bedroom, leaving a roomful of guests to sip champagne and dance. After a misunderstanding, Lulu accidentally fires a bullet into her husband. As Lulu holds the smoking pistol, Schon tries to speak before he dies, perhaps to warn Alwa of Lulu's dangerous ways. Alwa, however, runs off with Lulu. Fate is not kind to the young woman, but, despite the wicked turn of events, she remains full of life, finding a reason to celebrate even when faced with a murder charge, blackmail, poverty, and death. The film is a testament to both G.W. Pabst's talent as a visual storyteller and Brooks' ability as a physical storyteller. There are title cards, but they are not needed—one simply has to watch Brooks' face, lively mannerisms, and erotic bursts into dance or laughter, and to feel Pabst's control of the pace and atmosphere, to understand PANDORA'S BOX.

p, George C. Horsetzky; d, G.W. Pabst; w, Ladislaus Vajda (based on the plays "Erdgeist" and "Die Buechse der Pandora" by Franz Wedekind); ph, Gunther Krampf; ed, Joseph R. Fliesler.

Drama

(PR:C MPAA:NR)

PARDON MON AFFAIRE***½

(1976, Fr.) 105m Gaumont-La Gueville/First Artists c (UN ELEPHANT CA TROMPE ENORMEMENT; Trans: An Elephant Can Be Extremely Deceptive)

Jean Rochefort *(Etienne),* Claude Brasseur *(Daniel),* Guy Bedos *(Simon),* Victor Lanoux *(Bouly),* Daniele Delorme *(Marthe),* Anny Duperey *(Charlotte),* Martine Sarcey *(Esperanza),* Marthe Villalonga *(Mouchy).*

Yves Robert, the director responsible for THE TALL BLONDE MAN WITH ONE BLACK SHOE and its sequel, struck again with this pleasant, enjoyable mixture of comedy and drama about husbands and their affairs. Etienne (Jean Rochefort) is a Parisian civil servant who, while in his company parking lot, gazes at the bright red dress of a pretty young woman (Anny Duperey) as it is blown up above her waist by a rush of air. Although he is happily married to Marthe (Daniele Delorme, wife of director Robert) and has never even thought of having an affair, Etienne becomes enamored of this mystery woman. In the meantime, he and his three best friends witness the result of years of dalliances when one of them, Bouly (Victor Lanoux), comes home one day to find that his wife has left him, taking along his children and every last possession. Robert successfully creates a number of believable characters with honest emotions and places them in lightly humorous situations, and the result falls somewhere between broad comedy (one memorable scene has a character pretending to be blind and causing havoc in an elegant restaurant) and heartfelt drama (Bouly's reaction to his wife's departure), as if Robert was attempting a farcical French version of John Cassavetes' HUSBANDS. Many of the same names reunited for the less successful sequel, PARDON MON AFFAIRE, TOO! Remade in Hollywood as THE WOMAN IN RED. In French with English subtitles.

p, Alain Poire, Yves Robert; d, Yves Robert; w, Jean-Loup Dabadie (based on a story by Dabadie, Yves Robert); ph, Rene Mathelin; ed, Gerard Pollicand; m, Vladimir Cosma.

Comedy/Romance

(PR:A-C MPAA:PG)

PARIS, TEXAS****

(1984, Ger./Fr.) 145m Road-Argos-Westdeutscher-Channel 4-Pro-Ject/FOX c

Harry Dean Stanton *(Travis Clay Henderson),* Nastassia Kinski *(Jane),* Dean Stockwell *(Walt Henderson),* Aurore Clement *(Anne),* Hunter Carson *(Hunter),* Bernhard Wicki *(Dr. Ulmer),* Viva Auder *(Woman on TV),* Socorro Valdez *(Carmelita),* Tom Farrell *(Screaming Man),* John Lurie *(Slater),* Jeni Vici *(Stretch),* Sally Norvell *(Nurse Bibs),* Sam Berry *(Gas Station Attendant),* Claresie Mobley *(Car Rental Clerk),* Justin Hogg *(Hunter, age 3).*

Epic but intimate, PARIS, TEXAS combines the European sensibility of director Wim Wenders with the expansive locations of the American West. Amidst the desert and brilliant sky of Big Bend, Texas, Travis Clay Henderson (Harry Dean Stanton) aimlessly wanders under the boiling sun. He stops in a tavern and promptly collapses, awakening in the care of a German doctor (Bernhard Wicki). Assuming the catatonic Travis is mute, the doctor calls a number in his wallet and reaches Travis' brother, Walt (Dean Stockwell), who lives in Los Angeles with his French wife (Aurore Clement) and Hunter (Hunter Carson), Travis' seven-year-old son by his estranged wife, Jane (Nastassia Kinski). It turns out Travis has been missing and assumed dead for four years. Walt brings him back to LA for a reunion with Hunter, who subsequently joins his father on a quixotic quest for family, true love, and Jane. PARIS, TEXAS features neither sweeping themes, grandiose sets, nor a cast of thousands, but from its opening shots one senses its uniquely epic quality. The vast landscapes recall those of John Ford, but instead of John Wayne it's Stanton who wanders across the frame, a modern American father in suit and tie, displaced, aimless, and emotionally dead, on an odyssey to find himself. He knows where he began—in Paris, Texas—but not where he is going. Although based on stories by Sam Shepard, PARIS, TEXAS' vision of America is wholly that of Wenders, a German director deeply fascinated by Americana, and (as the title suggests) Wenders' America is a byproduct of the European imagination. Superbly scripted, the film features wonderful performances from all its major players. Equally brilliant, especially in a film that emphasizes script and character, is the cinematography by Robby Muller, perfectly capturing that indelible notion, "America." A final factor in PARIS, TEXAS' success is the remarkably haunting score by Ry Cooder.

p, Don Guest; d, Wim Wenders; w, Sam Shepard (based on a story adapted by L.M. Kit Carson); ph, Robby Muller; ed, Peter Przygodda; m, Ry Cooder.

Drama

(PR:C-O MPAA:R)

PASSENGER, THE****

(1975, It.) 123m Concordia-CIPI-Champion/MGM-UA c (AKA: PROFESSION: REPORTER)

Jack Nicholson *(David Locke),* Maria Schneider *(Girl),* Jennie Runacre *(Rachel Locke),* Ian Hendry *(Martin Knight),* Stephen Berkoff *(Stephen),* Ambroise Bia *(Achebe),* Jose Maria Cafarel *(Hotel Keeper),* James Campbell *(Witch Doctor),* Manfred Spies *(German Stranger),* Jean Baptiste Tiemele *(Murderer),* Angel Del Pozo *(Police Inspector),* Chuck Mulvehill *(Robertson).*

THE PASSENGER is a visually stunning adventure, rooted in philosophical meanderings, about a character literally and symbolically stuck in a sand trap from which he is miraculously handed a way out. David Locke (Jack Nicholson) is a reporter sent to North Africa on a mission to interview a band of guerrillas. After a battle with a Jeep that refuses to travel through sand, Locke winds up in a blisteringly hot, rundown hotel. There he is confused with another hotel guest, Robertson (Chuck Mulvehill), to whom he bears a striking resemblance. When he discovers Robertson dead in his room, Locke is presented with a perfect opportunity to escape his hell of a life. He switches passport photos and personal belongings and places the corpse in his own room. Looking through "his" daily planner, he finds a number of women's names and various appointments. Curious, he decides to keep a rendezvous and discovers that Robertson was a gun runner who supplied foreign governments with plans and documents. In the meantime he meets an enigmatic young woman (Maria Schneider) to whom he is magnetically drawn, causing him to ignore and avoid the efforts of his wife and best friend to locate him. THE PASSENGER could probably be analyzed until the end of time, each viewing uncovering a different path to understanding the film as a whole. What is more interesting than the Why and How of the film is the Where and When. Locke and The Girl are very much a part of their environment, whether the sandy wastelands of North Africa or the exquisitely organic Gaudi architecture of Barcelona. The Girl has no history—she just is—a state of being to which Locke also aspires. In English.

p, Carlo Ponti; d, Michelangelo Antonioni; w, Mark Peploe, Peter Wollen, Michelangelo Antonioni (based on a story by Mark Peploe); ph, Luciano Tovoli (Metrocolor); ed, Franco Arcalli, Michelangelo Antonioni.

Drama

(PR:C MPAA:PG)

PASSION OF BEATRICE, THE***

(1988, Fr./It.) 128m Clea-TF 1-la Tour-AMLF-Scena-Little Bear/Goldwyn c (LA PASSION BEATRICE)

Bernard-Pierre Donnadieu *(Francois de Cortemare),* Julie Delpy *(Beatrice),* Nils Tavernier *(Arnaud),* Monique Chaumette *(Francois' Mother),* Robert Dhery *(Raoul),* Maxime Leroux *(Richard),* Jean-Claude Adelin *(Bertrand Lemartin),* Claude Duneton *(The Priest),* Albane Guilhe *(Recluse),* Michele Gleizer *(Helene),* Jean-Luc Rivals *(Jehan).*

Bertrand Tavernier's follow-up to the internationally successful ROUND MIDNIGHT is the director's most challenging work in a career that has included such brilliant, idiosyncratic films as SUNDAY IN THE COUNTRY and the Oscar-nominated COUP DE TORCHON. Continuing Tavernier's interest in generational conflict and his predilection for placing timeless stories in very specific historical periods, BEATRICE, set in 14th-century France, tells the story of the relationship between Francois (Bernard-Pierre Donnadieu), a feudal lord who returns from the One Hundred Years War a bitter, sadistic man, and his pure-hearted daughter, Beatrice (Julie Delpy). For four long years Beatrice has anxiously awaited her father's return, but instead of showing his daughter fatherly kindness, Francois brutally (and sexually) abuses her until, finally, she refuses to take anymore. Difficult to watch, and more difficult to enjoy, BEATRICE alternates between Bruno de Keyzer's stunning photography of the French countryside and assaultive images of ugly violence. Tavernier's medieval world is not the stuff of Hollywood movies, but a raw, realistic portrayal of a society in which woman are treated abominably and children ignored. An anomaly in this world is the pure Beatrice—powerfully played by the radiant, 18-year-old Delpy, in her first starring role after appearances in Godard's DETECTIVE and KING LEAR and Leos Carax's BAD BLOOD. Donnadieu (THE RETURN OF MARTIN GUERRE) also delivers a strong performance as the frightening but not unsympathetic Francois. Unfortunately, while BEATRICE is an accomplished work and Tavernier a director in command of his vision, the film is never as compelling as it would like to be. A film about inner strength and purity of soul, it, regrettably, *tells* rather than *shows* us its meaning, at least partly because of the weak script by Tavernier's ex-wife, Colo Tavernier O'Hagan. The videocassette is in French with English subtitles.

p, Adolphe Viezzi; d, Bertrand Tavernier; w, Colo Tavernier O'Hagan; ph, Bruno de Keyzer (Eastmancolor); ed, Armand Psenny; m, Ron Carter, Lili Boulanger.

Historical

(PR:O MPAA:R)

PASSION OF JOAN OF ARC, THE****

(1928, Fr.) 114m Societe Generale Des Films bw

Renee (Marie) Falconetti *(Joan of Arc),* Eugene Silvain *(Bishop Pierre Cauchon),* Maurice Schultz *(Nicholas Loyseleur),* Michel Simon *(Jean Lemaitre),* Antonin Artraud *(Jean Massieu),* Louis Ravet *(Jean Beaupere),* Andre Berley *(Jean d'Estivet),* Jean d'Yd *(Guillaume Erard).*

Viewing this film, one might very nearly believe that the cinema existed in the 1400s, and that THE PASSION OF JOAN OF ARC is the only surviving document of that period—in effect, this masterpiece is cinema history's Shroud of Turin. Almost exclusively through close-ups, director Carl Theodor Dreyer brings to life the trial of military hero Joan of Arc. Responsible for a number of military triumphs, including the siege of Orleans in 1429, Joan was tried for heresy and burnt at the stake. Dreyer's version of the story is divided into three sections—an introduction to the judges and the tribunal; the trial, the sentence, and the torture;

and the execution—each of them uniquely constructed. Although Dreyer's genius is clear, it is the face of Renee (Marie) Falconetti that lends the film its deep spirituality. There has never been a face on film so radiant, so pained, so much that of a martyred saint. Further adding to Falconetti's aura is the fact that she never before or since appeared in another film—making the actress as great a legend as Joan. Although Dreyer's art as a filmmaker (his framing, closeups, distorted angles) can be analyzed, his greater achievement is in creating a world that exists beyond film. It is as if no artifice exists in THE PASSION OF JOAN OF ARC—no camera, no lighting, no actors, no screen. All that is visible is real life.

d, Carl Theodor Dreyer; w, Carl Theodor Dreyer; ph, Rudolph Mate; ed, Carl Theodor Dreyer; m, Victor Alix, Leo Pouget.

Drama

(PR:A MPAA:NR)

PATHER PANCHALI*½**

(1955, India) 112m West Bengal Government/Edward Harrison bw (AKA: THE SONG OF THE ROAD; THE SAGA OF THE ROAD; THE LAMENT OF THE PATH)

Kanu Banerji *(Harihar the Father),* Karuna Banerji *(Sarbojaya the Mother),* Subir Banerji *(Apu),* Runki Banerji *(Durga as a child),* Umas Das Gupta *(Durga as a young girl),* Chunibala Devi *(Indirtharkun the Old Aunt),* Reva Devi *(Mrs. Mookerji),* Rama Gangopadhaya *(Ranu Mookerji),* Tulshi Chakraborty *(Schoolmaster),* Harimoran Nag *(Doctor).*

Director Satyajit Ray's debut feature and the first installment of his "Apu Trilogy" tells the tale of a poverty-stricken family living in a Bengal village. The father, a struggling writer, leaves for the city, letting his wife take care of the children and an elderly relative. The old woman is driven to the countryside, where she dies, and by the time the mother returns home, her daughter has also died. The remaining two films of the trilogy—APARAJITO and THE WORLD OF APU—follow the son, Apu (here played by Subir Banerji), into manhood and fatherhood. Based on a popular two-volume novel, the "Apu Trilogy" proved Ray to be not only a great Indian director, but one of the world's finest. Commissioned in 1945 to illustrate a children's version of *Pather Panchali*, Ray became interested in bringing the novel to the screen, even though he had no previous film experience (nor did most of his crew). The production began sporadically on weekends, and was often interrupted by cash shortages before the Bengal government helped finish the picture. Inspired by Jean Renoir (Ray visited the set of THE RIVER during its production in India) and the classics of western cinema, Ray's films are perhaps better suited for the West than for his native land, where far more speak Hindi than Bengali. In Bengali with English subtitles.

p, Satyajit Ray; d, Satyajit Ray; w, Satyajit Ray (based on the novel by Bibhutibhusan Bandopadhaya); ph, Subrata Mitra; ed, Dulal Dutta; m, Ravi Shankar.

Drama

(PR:A MPAA:NR)

PAULINE AT THE BEACH*½**

(1983, Fr.) 94m Losange-Ariane/Orion c (PAULINE A LA PLAGE)

Amanda Langlet *(Pauline),* Arielle Dombasle *(Marion),* Pascal Greggory *(Pierre),* Feodor Atkine *(Henry),* Simon De La Brosse *(Sylvain),* Rosette *(Louisette).*

For the third in Eric Rohmer's series of "Comedies and Proverbs," the director moves from Paris and its surrounding suburbs to the coast of Normandy. Pauline (Amanda Langlet), a teenager blossoming into womanhood, is on vacation with her older, more fully developed, recently divorced cousin, Marion (Arielle Dombasle). These two get involved with three men during a beachside vacation. Marion carries on with writer Henry (Feodor Atkine) and tries to ignore the advances of old friend Pierre (Pascal Gregory), while Pauline meets a boy her own age, Sylvain, and has her first sexual experiences. Along the way, however, a situation arises that confuses the romances and the partners. Closer in spirit than usual here to Jean Renoir, Rohmer confines much of his film to the beach and a vacation home, turning his directorial attention to the interplay among the five main characters as they move in and out of rooms, are spied through windows and doors, and are forced to become masters of romantic deception. Detractors may think that all Rohmer films are alike, but there is a subtle difference in PAULINE AT THE BEACH. Instead of following one determined character along his or her journey to love, Rohmer here intertwines his characters and lets their paths overlap. Pauline herself, though singled out in the title as the main character, tends to function more as an observer caught in the whirlwind of love and romance. Rohmer was named Best Director at the Berlin Film Festival for PAULINE. In French with English subtitles.

p, Margaret Menegoz; d, Eric Rohmer; w, Eric Rohmer; ph, Nestor Almendros; ed, Cecile Decugis; m, Jean-Louis Valero.

Drama/Comedy

(PR:O MPAA:R)

PEDESTRIAN, THE*½**

(1974, Ger.) 97m Seitz-ALFA-MFG c (DER FUSSGANGER)

Gustav Rudolf Sellner *(Heinz Alfred Giese),* Ruth Hausmeister *(Inge Maria Giese),* Maximilian Schell *(Andreas Giese),* Manuel Sellner *(Hubert Giese),* Elsa Wagner *(Elsa Giese),* Dagmar Hirtz *(Elke Giese),* Michael Weinert *(Michael Giese),* Peter Hall *(Rudolf Hartmann),* Alexander May *(Alexander Markowitz),* Christian Kohlund *(Erwin Gotz),* Franz Seitz *(Dr. Karl Peters),* Herbert Mensching, Peter Moland *(Reporters),* Gertrud Bald *(Henriette Markowitz),* Walter Kohut *(Dr. Rolf Meineke),* Margarethe

Schell von Noe *(Frau Buchmann),* Sigfrit *(Auditor),* Gila von Weitershausen *(Karin).*

A powerful and revealing film about death, guilt, and Germany's involvement in wartime atrocities, THE PEDESTRIAN focuses on an aging industrialist, Heinz Alfred Giese (Gustav Rudolf Sellner), who prefers not to remember the events of WW II. In fact he prefers to be involved with life as little as possible. Since the death of his son, Andreas (Maximilian Schell), in an auto accident in which Giese was driving (resulting in the loss of his license, hence the title), his whole life has centered around his grandson, Hubert (Manuel Sellner). Although Giese would rather forget his past, Alexander Markowitz (Alexander May), the senior editor of a newspaper, begins a probe into Giese's involvement in the massacre of a Greek village. With the help of two witnesses—a survivor of the attack (Fani Fotinou) and a former German soldier (Walter von Varndal)—Markowitz discovers that Giese was involved in the massacre and could have prevented it had he tried. When the story is printed, Giese becomes the target of moral outrage and personal violence. This strong indictment of his generation's complacency is especially damning because its villain is not a monster but a well-respected businessman and a loving grandfather. Produced, directed, and written by Maximilian Schell, THE PEDESTRIAN received an Oscar nomination for Best Foreign-Language Film. The videocassette is dubbed in English.

p, Maximilian Schell, Zev Braun; d, Maximilian Schell; w, Maximilian Schell; ph, Wolfgang Treu, Klaus Koenig (Eastmancolor); ed, Dagmar Hirtz; m, Manos Hadjidakis.

Drama **(PR:C MPAA:PG)**

PEPE LE MOKO*****

(1937, Fr.) 90m Hakim-Paris/Mayer & Burtsyn/ Commercial bw

Jean Gabin *(Pepe le Moko),* Mireille Balin *(Gaby Gould),* Line Noro *(Ines),* Lucas Gridoux *(Inspector Slimane),* Gabriel Gabrio *(Carlos),* Fernand Charpin *(Regis),* Saturnin Fabre *(Grandfather),* Gilbert Gil *(Pierrot),* Roger Legris *(Max),* Gaston Modot *(Jimmy),* Marcel Dalio *(L'Arbi),* Frehel *(Tania),* Olga Lord *(Aicha).*

Based on the life of a real criminal who hid in the Casbah under the protection of his pals, PEPE LE MOKO stars Jean Gabin as the title thief, brigand, and charmer, who has surrounded himself with loyal gang members and keeps them in line through the sheer force of his personality, never resorting to violence. Tired of life with his moll, Ines (Line Noro), and of being on the run, Pepe yearns for his old days in Paris. He falls in love with a gorgeous tourist, Gaby Gould (Mireille Balin), but in the process lets his guard down and gives Algerian police inspector Slimane (Lucas Gridoux) the opportunity to finally nab him. PEPE LE MOKO owes a great deal of its inspiration to the early Hollywood gangster films, most notably Howard Hawks' SCARFACE, but director Julien Duvivier took the conventional mix of love and bullets and added a particular poetry of his own. The camerawork is as smooth as oil, the actors don't seem to be acting, and the lack of sentimentality deserves special praise. The film's success and the universality of its themes can be attested to by the fact that a Hollywood version, ALGIERS, was made immediately after PEPE LE MOKO and released in the States before the original could be imported. Charles Boyer turned the part of Pepe down when it was offered by Duvivier, then starred in the US version when Gabin refused to make the trip to Hollywood, explaining that he, like French wine, "didn't travel well." When the WW II started, the French government banned the film as too depressing and demoralizing, especially since the news from the front was also bleak. The Germans took over and their puppet government retained the ban, but the moment the war ended, PEPE LE MOKO was again shown and hailed as a classic. In French with English subtitles.

p, Robert Hakim, Raymond Hakim; d, Julien Duvivier; w, Julien Duvivier, Henri Jeanson, Roger d'Ashelbe, Jacques Constant (based on the book by d'Ashelbe); ph, Jules Kruger, Marc Fossard; ed, Marguerite Beauge; m, Vincent Scotto, Mohamed Yguerbouchen.

Crime/Romance **(PR:C MPAA:NR)**

PERIL½**

(1985, Fr.) 100m Gaumont-Elefilm-TF 1/Triumph c (PERIL EN LA DEMEURE)

Christophe Malavoy *(David Aurphet),* Nicole Garcia *(Julia Tombsthay),* Michel Piccoli *(Graham Tombsthay),* Anemone *(Edwige Ledieu),* Anais Jeanneret *(Vivian Tombsthay),* Richard Bohringer *(Daniel Forest),* Jean-Claude Jay *(Father),* Helene Roussel *(Mother),* Elisabeth Vitali *(Waitress),* Frank Lapersonne *(Guitar Salesman),* Daniel Verite *(Assailant).*

Heavy on style and thin on content, this French thriller revolves around David (Christophe Malavoy), a guitar teacher who takes on a new student, pretty young Vivian Tombsthay (Anais Jeanneret), at the request of her parents, Julia (Nicole Garcia) and Graham (Michel Piccoli). A frequent visitor to the Tombsthay estate, David is soon sleeping with both Julia and the Tombsthay's nosy neighbor Edwige Ledieu (Anemone). At about the same time, in a seemingly unrelated incident, he is attacked by a stranger who tries to smash his hands. Coming to his rescue is yet another stranger, Daniel Forest (Richard Bohringer), who befriends David and then reveals his secret—he is a hit man in town to do a job. As the days pass, David finds himself caught in a whirlwind of seduction, deceit, blackmail, and murder. For the most part the characters and situations are incomprehensible, but what the film lacks in logic it makes up for in its performances and style. The most notable aspect of PERIL is its unique editing approach, which distorts the viewer's sense of time and place, overlaps sound and dialog from one scene to the next, and makes use of optical effects such as mattes and iris shots. In French with English subtitles.

p, Emmanuel Schlumberger; d, Michel Deville; w, Michel Deville (based on the novel *Sur la Terre Comme au Ciel* by Rene Belletto); ph, Martial Thury; ed, Raymonde Guyot; m, Johannes Brahms, Franz Schubert, Enrique Granados.

Thriller **(PR:O MPAA:R)**

PERSONA****

(1966, Swed.) 84m Svensk-Lopert bw (AKA: MASKS)

Bibi Andersson *(Nurse Alma),* Liv Ullmann *(Elisabeth Vogler, the Actress),* Gunnar Bjornstrand *(Mr. Vogler),* Margareta Krook *(Dr. Lakaren),* Jorgen Lindstrom *(The Boy).*

Demanding repeated viewing, this complex, challenging film is one of Ingmar Bergman's masterworks. Opening with a sequence that includes a bare bulb projected onto a screen, the countdown leader of the first reel, and short film clips from slapstick comedies and cartoons, Bergman constantly reminds us that we are in the act of watching a film. Gradually, however, the story gets under way. Actress Elisabeth Vogler (Liv Ullmann) mysteriously stops speaking after a performance of "Electra" and is sent by a psychiatrist to a seaside cottage, where she is looked after by Alma (Bibi Andersson), a nurse. Using light and shadow masterfully, Bergman and his gifted cinematographer, Sven Nykvist, accentuate the resemblance between the two women, drawing the viewer into a psychodrama that is more the nurse's story than the patient's, as Alma pours her soul out to the silent Elisabeth. Slowly, she is shown to be just as troubled as her patient, whose personality she seems to be taking on. In a memorable and revealing sequence, Elisabeth and Alma's faces are superimposed, melting together into one visage. Finally, the movie comes full circle: film is shown slipping out of the projector and once more we are left with the bare bulb. Defying easy analysis, PERSONA has variously been interpreted as an exploration of the role of the artist, as an embodiment of the psychoanalytic process, and as a meditation on Bergman's standard existential themes—reality, life, and death. In any case, it is a film of great emotional intensity that benefits from the superlative performances of Ullmann—who reacts only with facial and body gestures—and Andersson, who speaks for both of them as she slips subtly into a kind of madness. In Swedish with English subtitles.

p, Ingmar Bergman; d, Ingmar Bergman; w, Ingmar Bergman; ph, Sven Nykvist; ed, Ulla Ryghe; m, Lars Johan Werle, Johann Sebastian Bach.

Drama **(PR:O MPAA:NR)**

PHANTOM OF LIBERTY, THE****

(1974, Fr.) 104m Greenwich-FOX c (LE FANTOME DE LA LIBERTE; THE SPECTER OF FREEDOM; AKA: THE SPECTER OF FREEDOM)

Jean-Claude Brialy *(Mr. Foucauld),* Monica Vitti *(Mrs. Foucauld),* Milena Vukotic *(Nurse),* Michel Lonsdale *(Hatter),* Michel Piccoli *(2nd Prefect),* Claude Pieplu *(Commissioner),* Paul Frankeur *(Innkeeper),* Julien Bertheau *(1st Prefect),* Adriana Asti *(Prefect's Sister),* Adolfo Celi *(Dr. Legendre),* Pierre Maguelon *(Policeman Gerard),* Francois Maistre *(Professor),* Helen Perdriere *(Aunt),* Jean Rochefort *(Mr. Legendre).*

THE PHANTOM OF LIBERTY is an illogical collection of incidents that jumps from place to place and time to time in a manner that follows the logic of dreams, and any attempt to summarize the plot would be feeble and miss the film's point—which seems to suggest that there isn't one. The film opens on a firing squad in Napoleonic times who shout "Down with Liberty." Following this is a scene of a maid reading to a child the story we have just witnessed. Again the direction switches, to a man selling supposedly pornographic postcards of French tourist attractions that are not pornographic at all. A nurse then makes the mistake of wandering into a poker game played by a group of monks. A man with a rifle kills passersby from the top of a Montparnasse building and is hailed as a hero. A missing girl helps the police fill out a report on her disappearance. And, in perhaps the most memorable sequence, a group of dinner guests sit on toilet seats and must raise their hands in order to go to the dining room. A crazy, uproariously funny film—for those who are not devoutly religious or part of the upper class. It is a joy to see that Luis Bunuel could still ruffle as many feathers at age 75 as he did in 1928 and 1930 with UN CHIEN ANDALOU and L'AGE D'OR. In French with English subtitles.

p, Serge Silberman; d, Luis Bunuel; w, Luis Bunuel, Jean-Claude Carriere; ph, Edmond Richard (Eastmancolor); ed, Helene Plemiannikov.

Drama **(PR:O MPAA:R)**

PICNIC ON THE GRASS***

(1959, Fr.) 91m Jean Renoir/Kingsley c (LE DEJEUNER SUR L'HERBE; GB: LUNCH ON THE GRASS)

Paul Meurisse *(Etienne)*, Catherine Rouvel *(Nenette)*, Fernand Sardou *(Nino)*, Jacqueline Morane *(Titine)*, Jean-Pierre Granval *(Ritou)*, Robert Chandeau *(Laurent)*, Micheline Gary *(Madeleine)*, Frederic O'Brady *(Rudolf)*, Ghislaine Dumont *(Magda)*, Ingrid Nordine *(Marie-Charlotte)*, Andre Brunot *(The Old Curate)*, Helene Duc *(Isabelle)*, Jacques Dannoville *(Mons. Paignant)*, Marguerite Cassan *(Mme. Paignant)*, Charles Blavette *(Gaspard)*, Jean Claudio *(Rousseau)*, Raymond Jourdan *(Eustache)*, Francis Miege *(Barthelemy)*.

One of director Jean Renoir's oddest films, PICNIC ON THE GRASS is visually influenced by the Impressionist paintings of his father, Auguste Renoir, and Edouard Manet (who painted "Le Dejeuner Sur L'Herbe"), but its plot could almost be considered science fiction. Etienne (Paul Meurisse) is a scientist running for the presidency of the United States of Europe on a platform of artificial insemination. He is engaged to Marie-Charlotte (Ingrid Nordine), with whom he communicates chiefly via television. To boost his earthy image, the candidate decides to have a "picnic on the grass." Before long Etienne is literally blown into the arms of a perky peasant girl, Nenette (Catherine Rouvel). Taken by Nenette's vivaciousness, he reevaluates his scientific approach to love, declaring that the old-fashioned method is superior to the artificial one. Filmed almost exclusively at Auguste Renoir's Les Collettes estate, PICNIC ON THE GRASS held a special place in Jean Renoir's affections. In his autobiography, *My Life and My Films*, Renoir wrote, "I had the immense pleasure of filming the olive trees my father had so often painted. That film was like a bath of purity and optimism. We felt, in its making, that we had been transformed into fauns and nymphs." Some critics were less enthusiastic about Renoir's idyll, thinking it a trite and infantile choice of subject matter, and many people just refused to accept the fact that in PICNIC ON THE GRASS Renoir was simply trying to make a charming, and somewhat silly, picture about love. The 63-year-old Renoir was enjoying himself and, perhaps, revelling in a glorious second childhood, where he found complexity in simple themes. In French with English subtitles.

p, Ginette Doynel; d, Jean Renoir; w, Jean Renoir; ph, Georges Leclerc (Eastmancolor); ed, Renee Lichtig, Francois London; m, Joseph Kosma.

Drama **(PR:C MPAA:NR)**

PIXOTE****

(1981, Braz.) 127m Embrafilm-Palace c

Fernando Ramos da Silva *(Pixote)*, Marilia Pera *(Sueli)*, Jorge Juliao *(Lilica)*, Gilberto Moura *(Dito)*, Jose Nilson dos Santos *(Diego)*, Edilson Lino *(Chico)*, Zenildo Oliveira Santos *(Fumaca)*, Claudio Bernardo *(Garatao)*, Tony Tornado *(Cristal)*, Jardel Filho *(Sapatos Brancos)*, Rubens de Falco *(Juiz)*.

This grim, disturbing, and engrossing Brazilian film set in the slums of Sao Paulo tells the disheartening tale of Pixote (Fernando Ramos da Silva), a boy abandoned by his parents who becomes a street-wise pimp and murderer by the age of 10. One of the best entries of the genre of films about children in the city, PIXOTE depicts a life of unrelenting violence and hopelessness. Whether focusing on the streets of Brazil, as in this film, or the streets of Germany (GERMANY YEAR ZERO), Mexico (LOS OLVIDADOS), or Paris (THE 400 BLOWS), the lives of these children are all related, the youngsters' innocence in effect stripped from their very beings. Here, director Hector Babenco successfully mixes the Neo-Realist style of taking the camera into the streets with a somewhat surreal visual context. The tragedy of PIXOTE is that the film is not make believe: In 1986, the film's star, da Silva, was killed in a shootout with police after allegedly resisting arrest following an assault. In Portuguese with English subtitles.

p, Paulo Francini; d, Hector Babenco; w, Hector Babenco, Jorge Duran (based on the novel *Infancia Dos Martos* by Jose Louzeiro); ph, Rodolfo Sanchez; ed, Luiz Elias; m, John Neschling.

Drama **(PR:O MPAA:NR)**

PLACE OF WEEPING***

(1986, South Africa) 90m NW c

James Whyle *(Philip Seago)*, Gcina Mhlophe *(Gracie)*, Charles Comyn *(Tokkie Van Rensburg)*, Norman Coombes *(Father Eagen)*, Michelle Du Toit *(Maria Van Rensburg)*, Ramolao Makhene *(Themba)*, Patrick Shai *(Lucky)*, Siphiwe Khumalo *(Joseph)*, Kernels Coertzen *(Prosecutor Dick Van Heerden)*, Doreen Mazibuko *(Ana)*, Thoko Ntshinga *(Joseph's Widow)*, Jeremy Taylor *(Tokkie's Son Pieter)*, Nicole Jourdan *(Tokkie's Daughter Elize)*.

On a South African farm, Joseph (Siphiwe Khumalo), a poor black worker, asks his white employer Tokkie Van Rensburg (Charles Comyn) if he can have an increase in weekly rations. Van Rensburg, a brutal individual who hates the blacks, responds by destroying Joseph's sack of flour and telling the man to leave. That evening Joseph sneaks back to the farm to steal a chicken for his family. When Van Rensburg hears a noise outside, he finds Joseph and savagely beats him to death. The next morning, when the workers find the corpse, Van Renburg accuses them of killing one of their own. The laborers are too frightened to speak out but one woman, Gracie (Gcina Mhlophe), refuses to bow under Tokkie's power, and enlists the aid of a white journalist (James Whyle) to help bring Van Rensburg to trial. As the film's stoic center, Gracie is a portrait of dignity in the face of violent retaliation that looms over her search for the truth. She brings a quiet but assured presence to the character which overcomes the weak, stereotypes of some of the other characters, particularly the relentlessly cruel farm boss. Writer/director Darryl Roodt emphasizes the human factor within Gracie's harsh story without giving a preachy anti-apartheid message. Instead, he wisely lets the characters and their situation speak for themselves, allowing the inherent political message to surface only in the viewers mind. Shot in 16mm, then blown up to 35mm, Roodt makes an effective use of his filmmaking tools—portraying violence in a stylized manner which utilizes distorted camera angles, closeups, and rapid editing to heighten the emotional impact. In English.

p, Anant Singh; d, Darrell Roodt; w, Darrell Roodt, Les Volpe; ph, Paul Witte; ed, David Heitner.

Drama **(PR:C-O MPAA:PG)**

PLAYTIME*****

(1967, Fr.) 108m Specta/Continental c

Jacques Tati *(M. Hulot),* Barbara Dennek *(Young Tourist),* Jacqueline Lecomte *(Her Friend),* John Abbey *(M. Luce),* Valerie Camille *(M. Luce's Secretary),* France Rumilly *(Eyeglass Saleswoman),* France Delahalle *(Shopper),* Laure Paillette, Colette Proust *(Women at the Lamp),* Georges Montant *(M. Giffard),* Erika Dentzler *(Mme. Giffard),* Yvette Ducreux *(Hat Check Girl),* Rita Maiden *(M. Schultz's Companion),* Nicole Ray *(Singer),* Jack Gauthier *(The Guide),* Henri Piccoli *(Important Gentleman),* Leon Doyen *(Doorman),* Billy Kearns *(M. Schultz),* Francois Viaur *(Unlucky Waiter),* Reinhart Kolldehoff *(German Businessman),* Gregory Katz *(German Salesman),* Marc Monjou *(The False Hulot),* Yves Barsacq *(The Friend),* Tony Andal *(Page Boy at the Royal Garden),* Andre Fouche *(The Manager),* Georges Faye *(The Architect),* Michel Fancini *(Headwaiter),* Gilbert Reeb *(Another Waiter).*

Jacques Tati's fourth feature was 10 years in the making and he risked everything on it, even going so far as to sell off rights to his previous three films in order to raise the needed money for the immense modernistic set he used here. Released in France at 145 minutes, the result was an instant failure. Tati soon cut the film to 108 minutes, then to 93, but the damage had already been done. As in Tati's other movies, PLAYTIME has almost no plot to speak of, just a series of incidents that Mons. Hulot (Tati) gets into and out of without comment, just with boundless energy and incurable optimism. It's a satire of the glass-and-steel world that was coming to pass in the 1960s, and Tati spent all his money building a set to capture his vision of what Paris would come to. Photographed in 70mm and recorded in Dolby stereo, PLAYTIME is not only a remarkable comic achievement, but a brilliant filmmaking achievement as well. Whether or not one finds humor in Tati's unique brand of comedy, one cannot deny the modernity of his cinematic style. With a narrative as unconventional as anything Alain Resnais has ever done, PLAYTIME delivers its point without even a main character. Instead, everyone and everywhere is the star. Without pointing to a comic moment, Tati the director opens up his frame and pulls his camera back, letting the viewer's eye wander through the frame to watch whatever pleases. His unparalleled directing style gives the audience complete freedom and, in a sense, transforms the viewer into the director, while Tati the actor slips into obscurity on the screen.

p, Rene Silvera; d, Jacques Tati; w, Jacques Tati, Jacques Lagrange, Art Buchwald; ph, Jean Badal, Andreas Winding (Eastmancolor); ed, Gerard Pollicand; m, Francis Lemarque, James Campbell, David Stein.

Comedy **(PR:A MPAA:NR)**

POIL DE CAROTTE***

(1932, Fr.) 80m Films Legrand Majestic bw (AKA: THE RED HEAD)

Harry Baur *(Mons. Lepic),* Robert Lynen *(Francois, ""Poil de Carotte"),* Catherine Fontenay *(Mme. Lepic),* Louis Gouthier *(Uncle),* Simone Aubry *(Ernestine Lepic),* Maxime Fromiot *(Felix Lepic),* Colette Segall *(Mathilde),* Marthe Marty *(Honorine),* Christiane Dor *(Annette).*

Julien Duvivier's second attempt to film the popular stories of Jules Renard, which he first brought to the screen in a 1925 silent, is a lyrical story of the unhappy childhood of the preadolescent Francois (Robert Lynen). Better known as "Poil de carotte," the red-haired Francois is a victim of the hatred between his mother (Catherine Fontenay) and her husband (Harry Baur)—a marriage that exists only for appearances' sake. Francois is actually his mother's illegitimate child, the result of an affair with a man who has the same glowing red hair as the boy. The mother treats her son with spite and cruelty, blaming him for her isolation; the stepfather, for the most part, treats Francois with indifference, but through the course of the film the two develop a close friendship based on mutual respect. One of the prolific Duvivier's most memorable films (he made 19 in the 1930s alone), POIL DE CAROTTE succeeds chiefly because of the characterization of Francois, who is a victim of other people's inconsiderateness, but is never idealized or treated as a saint. Rather, he is a normal child—at times irrational, at times loving, and often mischievous. Much credit goes to young Lynen, who was encountered by Duvivier while walking along a street. After appearing in a number of films in the 1930s, Lynen was killed by the Nazis for his involvement in the French underground. In French with English subtitles.

d, Julien Duvivier; w, Julien Duvivier (based on the novels *Poil de Carotte* and *La Bigote* by Jules Renard); ph, Armand Thirard; ed, Marthe Poncin; m, Alexandre Tansman.

Drama **(PR:A MPAA:NR)**

PORT OF CALL**½

(1948, Swed.) 100m Svensk/Janus bw (HAMNSTAD)

Nine-Christine Jonsson *(Berit),* Bengt Eklund *(Gosta),* Berta Hall *(Berit's Mother),* Erik Hell *(Berit's Father),* Mimi Nelson *(Gertrud),* Birgitta Valberg *(Welfare Worker),* Stig Olin *(Thomas),* Sif Ruud *(Mrs. Krona),* Hans Straat *(Engineer Vilander),* Nils Dahlgren *(Gertrud's Father),* Nils Hallberg *(Gustav).*

An early, minor work by Ingmar Bergman, interesting mainly in the general context of the great director's career, PORT OF CALL touches upon many themes that Bergman would continually return to, including his focus on the difficulties of breaking with traditional Swedish culture. As in nearly all of Bergman's films, an oppressive atmosphere prevails, and the conclusion projects a cloudy future. After the love affair between Gosta (Bengt Eklund), a young dock worker in Goteborg, and Berit (Nine-Christine Jonsson) is almost ended because of the young man's discomfort with Berit's past, the two decide they really need each other and reunite, making plans to begin a new life for themselves by moving to Stockholm. In the end, however, the couple must compromise their dreams. Originally produced in 1948, PORT OF CALL was not shown in the US until the early 1960s, when recognition of the director's stature made it a must-see for Bergman's fans and scholars. The videocassette is available in both dubbed and subtitled (Swedish into English) versions.

p, Allan Ekelund; d, Ingmar Bergman; w, Ingmar Bergman (based on the story by Olle Lansberg); ph, Gunnar Fischer; ed, Oscar Rosander; m, Erland von Koch.

Drama **(PR:C MPAA:NR)**

PROVIDENCE****

(1977, Fr.) 104m Action-SFP/Cinema 5 c

John Gielgud *(Clive Langham),* Dirk Bogarde *(Claude Langham),* Ellen Burstyn *(Sonia Langham),* David Warner *(Kevin Woodford),* Elaine Stritch *(Helen Weiner/Molly Langham),* Denis Lawson *(Dave Woodford),* Cyril Luckham *(Dr. Mark Eddington),* Kathryn Leigh-Scott *(Miss Boon),* Milo Sperber *(Mr. Jenner),* Anna Wing *(Karen),* Peter Arne *(Nils),* Tanya Lopert *(Miss Lister),* Samson Fainsilber *(Old Hairy Man),* Joseph Pittoors *(Old Man).*

PROVIDENCE takes place on the eve of the 78th birthday of Clive Langham (John Gielgud), a dying novelist. He lives alone in his country estate in Providence, Rhode Island, battling alcoholism, the memory of his dead wife, and a chronic rectal disorder. At night, he struggles to write what appears to be his last novel, basing the characters on his own children. His son, Claude (Dirk Bogarde), and daughter-in-law, Sonia (Ellen Burstyn), are unhappily married and constantly—if wittily—sparring. Another, illegitimate son (David Warner) is a former soldier on trial, and prosecuted by Claude, for killing an old man who turned into a werewolf. The defendant is acquitted, and soon falls in love with Sonia. As the increasingly drunken Clive's plot begins to reflect his inebriation, he decides to give Claude a mistress, but the character he creates (Elaine Stritch) is the image of his dead wife—an older woman with a terminal disease, whom Clive continually mistakes for her prototype. As he labors to complete his novel, characters disintegrate further and further, delivering each other's dialog and hopelessly confusing the story. Settings, too, change inexplicably. Then Clive's children pay a birthday visit, and prove a far cry from the ailing novelist's representations of them. PROVIDENCE is truly a breakthrough film, an attempt to synthesize literature and film into one fascinating work comprising two interdependent halves. Director Alain Resnais—who collaborated with novelists Marguerite Duras in HIROSHIMA MON AMOUR (1960); Alain Robbe-Grillet in LAST YEAR AT MARIENBAD (1962); and Jorge Semprun in LA GUERRE EST FINIE (1966) and STAVISKY (1974)—worked again here with another writer, playwright David Mercer, best known for his "A Suitable Case for Treatment" (filmed by Karel Reisz in 1965 as MORGAN!). The film should (but won't) put those who attack Resnais for being pretentious and cold at ease, especially in light of Gielgud's virtuoso performance. Filled with brilliant wit, PROVIDENCE is a superb instance of inventive filmmaking with a comic touch and an intellectual theme. In English.

p, Yves Gasser, Yves Peyrot, Klaus Hellwig; d, Alain Resnais; w, David Mercer; ph, Ricardo Aronovich (Panavision, Eastmancolor); ed, Albert Jurgenson; m, Miklos Rozsa.

Drama **(PR:O MPAA:R)**

Q

QUERELLE***

(1983, Ger./Fr.) 106m Planet Albatros/Triumph c

Brad Davis *(Querelle),* Franco Nero *(Lt. Seblon),* Jeanne Moreau *(Lysiane),* Laurent Malet *(Roger),* Nadja Brunkhorst *(Paulette),* Hanno Poschl *(Robert/Gil),* Gunther Kaufmann *(Nono),* Burkhard Driest *(Mario),* Dieter Schidor *(Vic),* Roger Fritz *(Marcellin),* Michael McLernon *(Matrose),* Neil Bell *(Theo),* Harry Baer *(Armenier),* Volker Sprengler, Isolde Barth, Y Sa Lo, Robert van Ackeren, Wolf Gremm, Frank Ripploh, Rainer Will.

Rainer Werner Fassbinder's final film is appropriately an adaptation of Jean Genet's infamous novel *Querelle de* Brest, which deals with the passions of a sailor coming to terms with his homosexuality. Querelle (Brad Davis, star of MIDNIGHT EXPRESS), a self-absorbed young man in search of his identity, slits the throat of his opium-smuggling partner, Vic (Dieter Schidor), when their ship docks at Brest. In the meantime, another murder is committed by Gil (Hanno Poschl), a man who looks very much like Querelle's brother, Robert (also played by Poschl). In a bar-whorehouse run by Lysiane (Jeanne Moreau), Querelle meets a number of the regulars, including Lysiane's husband, Nono (Gunther Kaufmann), a burly, intimidating black man who plays games of chance and sodomizes the losers. While trying to find himself, Querelle must, to use Fassbinder's phrase, "become identical with himself." To do this he confronts himself mentally and physically in his relationship with Gil/Robert. An extremely complex film, both philosophically and structurally, QUERELLE appeared to mark the beginning of a new era of filmmaking for Fassbinder. With it he began his attempt to liberate film from its inherent objective reality and to involve the viewer in a subjective imaginative experience more akin to reading a novel. As a result his Brest is a stylistic dream world of brilliant colors, harsh lighting, phallic architecture, black leather, and a painted sky—his own subjective conjuring. Because the film is an experiment, it often seems disjointed or incomprehensible, but more than anything it marks a radical turning point in narrative filmmaking. Unfortunately, Fassbinder died just after QUERELLE's completion. In English.

p, Dieter Schidor; d, Rainer Werner Fassbinder; w, Rainer Werner Fassbinder (based on the novel *Querelle de Brest* by Jean Genet); ph, Xaver Schwarzenberger, Josef Vavra (CinemaScope/Eastmancolor); ed, Juliane Lorenz, Franz Walsch; m, Peer Raben.

Drama **(PR:O MPAA:WR)**

QUESTION OF SILENCE***½

(1983, Neth.) 92m Sigma/Quartet c (DE STILTE ROND CHRISTINE M. . .; Trans: The Silence Of Christine M.)

Cox Habbema *(Dr. Janine Van Den Bos),* Edda Barends *(Christine M., the Housewife),* Nelly Frijda *(Annie, the Waitress),* Henriette Tol *(Andrea, the Secretary),* Eddy Brugman *(Rudd),* Dolf De Vries *(Boutique Manager),* Kees Coolen *(Police Inspector),* Onno Molenkamp *(Pathologist),* Hans Croiset *(Judge),* Eric Plooyer, Anna van Beers, Eric Besseling, Noa Cohen, Edgar Danz, Diana Dobbelman, Miranda Frijda, Frederik de Groot.

This controversial film focuses on three women—housewife Christine M. (Edda Barends), waitress Annie (Nelly Frijda), and secretary Andrea (Henriette Tol)—who, though unacquainted, spontaneously kill a male boutique owner when he catches one of them shoplifting. They are arrested and assigned a female psychiatrist, Dr. Janine Van Den Bos (Cox Habbema), who prepares a plea of insanity. Christine appears to be the most deeply affected of the threesome, slipping into a state of shock and refusing to utter a word. As Dr. Van Den Bos talks with Annie and Andrea, she begins to have her doubts about the insanity plea, and the murder makes increasingly more sense to her. Each of the three women was dealing with her own frustrations with men: the housewife was a slave to housekeeping duties and a victim of a thoughtless husband; the waitress subjected to rude comments by male customers; and the secretary constantly treated as a subordinate at the executive office where she worked. Instead of confirming the expected insanity pleas, Dr. Van Den Bos tells the courtroom that the women are fully responsible for the crime against the patronizing shopkeeper. But to the surprise of the males in the courtroom, all the women present unite in a grand show of female solidarity. QUESTION OF SILENCE is the first feature from writer-director Marleen Gorris, who hit upon the idea after reading an article about a working-class woman's arrest for shoplifting. Instead of putting three murderesses on trial, this superb, disturbing feminist film turns the tables and puts male society on the stand—which will undoubtedly anger as many viewers as it thrills. The videocassette is available in both dubbed and subtitled (Dutch into English) versions.

p, Matthijs van Heijningen; d, Marleen Gorris; w, Marleen Gorris; ph, Frans Bromet; ed, Hans van Dongen; m, Lodewijk De Boer, Martijn Hasebos.

Crime **(PR:O MPAA:R)**

R

RAN*****

(1985, Jap./Fr.) 160m Herald Ace-Nippon-Herald Greenwich/Orion c

Tatsuya Nakadai *(Lord Hidetora Ichimonji),* Akira Terao *(Tarotakatora Ichimonji),* Jinpachi Nezu *(Jiromasatora Ichimonji),* Daisuke Ryu *(Saburonaotora Ichimonji),* Mieko Harada *(Lady Kaede),* Yoshiko Miyazaki *(Lady Sue),* Kazuo Kato *(Ikoma),* Masayuki Yui *(Tango),* Peter *(Kyoami),* Hitoshi Ueki *(Fujimaki),* Hisashi Ikawa

(Kurogane), Takeshi Nomura *(Tsurumaru),* Jun Tazaki *(Ayabe),* Norio Matsui *(Ogura).*

At age 75, Akira Kurosawa, Japan's greatest living director, created one more magnificent work that will surely stand the test of time. In RAN, Kurosawa turned to Shakespeare for inspiration—as he had in THRONE OF BLOOD nearly 30 years before—and chose to film a Japanese adaptation of "King Lear." Set in 16th-century Japan, RAN (the Japanese character for fury, revolt, and madness—chaos) begins as Hidetora Ichimonji (Tatsuya Nakadai), an aging warlord who has acquired power through 50 years of ruthless bloodshed, announces his intention to divide his kingdom among his three sons, each of whom will live at one of three outlying castles. While the elder sons thank him for the honor, the youngest calls his father senile and mad, noting—prophetically—that it will only be a matter of time until the ambitious brothers begin battling for possession of the whole domain. In the process, Hidetora and his kingdom are consigned to a tragic and spectacular end. Kurosawa wanted desperately to make RAN for more than 10 years before, on the strength of KAGEMUSHA's success, he was finally able to obtain funding for this, the most expensive film ever made in Japan (though the $11 million budget is small by Hollywood standards). Partly shot at two of that country's most revered landmarks (the ancient castles at Himeji and Kumamoto; the third castle was constructed of plastic and wood on the slopes of Mount Fuji), RAN is a visually stunning epic, containing some of the most beautiful, colorful, breathtaking imagery ever committed to celluloid. As he grew older, Kurosawa began to shoot his films in a more traditionally Japanese style (static takes, little camera movement, no flamboyant editing). Here, especially in the battle scenes, he adopts a detached, impassive camera, heightening the tragedy by giving the audience a godlike, but powerless, perspective on all the madness and folly unfolding on-screen. At the same time, Kurosawa infuses the film with deep human emotion, aided by uniformly superb performances. The work of a mature artist in complete control of his medium, RAN is a true cinematic masterwork of sight, sound, intelligence, and—most importantly—passion. In Japanese with English subtitles.

p, Masato Hara, Serge Silberman; d, Akira Kurosawa; w, Akira Kurosawa, Hideo Oguni, Masato Ide (based on *King Lear* by William Shakespeare); ph, Takao Saito, Masaharu Ueda, Asakazu Nakai; ed, Akira Kurosawa; m, Toru Takemitsu.

Historical (PR:O MPAA:R)

RASHOMON*****

(1950, Jap.) 90m Daiei/RKO bw (AKA: IN THE WOODS)

Toshiro Mifune *(Tajomaru, the Bandit),* Machiko Kyo *(Masago),* Masayuki Mori *(Takehiro, the Samurai),* Takashi Shimura *(Woodcutter),* Minoru Chiaki *(Priest),* Kichijiro Ueda *(Commoner),* Fumiko Homma *(Medium),* Daisuke Kato *(Police Agent).*

One of the most brilliantly constructed films of all time, RASHOMON is a monument to Akira Kurosawa's greatness, combining his well-known humanism with an experimental narrative style that has become a hallmark of film history. The central portion of the film revolves around four varying points-of-view of the rape of a woman and death of her husband in a forest. Set in the 11th century, the film opens with a framing device, the conversation between three men—a woodcutter (Takashi Shimura), a priest (Minoru Chiaki), and a commoner (Kichijiro Ueda)—who have taken refuge from a rainstorm under the ruins of the stone Rashomon gate. The priest relates the details of a trial he witnessed in a prison courtyard involving the rape of Masago (Machiko Kyo) and the murder of her samurai husband Takehiro (Masayuki Mori). As he explains, the audience is shown the four main defendants: Masago; the bandit Tajomaru (Toshiro Mifune); the spirit of Takehiro, which has been conjured by a medium; and the woodcutter, who admits that he witnessed the murder. Each of their viewpoints is depicted, the "truth" changing with each new defendant's explanation. Based on two short stories by Japanese author Ryunosuke Akutagawa ("In the Grove," the inspiration for the central crime story, and "Rashomon," the basis for the framing scenes), RASHOMON is a reflection of Kurosawa at his most Eisensteinian. Here he uses a juxtaposition of shots and a varying sequence of events to tell an essentially visual story. Although the film has been described by some as being about the search for truth, it is much more than that, as the framing story hints. Like the ruins of the Rashomon Gate (the film is after all named RASHOMON and not IN THE GROVE), the humanity Kurosawa depicts is crumbling and in danger of completely collapsing. While philosophers contend there are many truths, logic asserts there is only one, and, therefore, three of the four testifying characters in his film must be lying. Since Kurosawa's interests lie chiefly in human nature (and not philosophy or narrative structure), it follows that RASHOMON is not about truth but human fallibility, dishonesty, and selfishness. Like so many Kurosawa films, RASHOMON also contains some of the most amazing performances you are likely to find anywhere, especially that of the wildly fascinating Toshiro Mifune as the bandit. The videocassette is available in both dubbed and subtitled (Japanese into English) versions.

p, Jingo Minoru, Masaichi Nagata; d, Akira Kurosawa; w, Shinobu Hashimoto, Akira Kurosawa (based on the stories "In A Grove" and "Rashomon" by Ryunosuke Akutagawa); ph, Kazuo Miyagawa; m, Fumio Hayasaka.

Drama (PR:A-C MPAA:NR)

RED BEARD****

(1965, Jap.) 185m Kurosawa/Toho bw (AKAHIGE)

Toshiro Mifune *(Dr. Kyojio Niide, "Red Beard"),* Yuzo Kayama *(Dr. Noboru Yasumoto),* Yoshio Tsuchiya *(Dr. Handayu Mori),* Terumi Niki *(Otoyo),* Tsutomu Yamazaki *(Sahachi),* Yoko Naito *(Masae),* Reiko Dan *(Osugi),* Akemi Negishi *(Okuni),* Kyoko Kagawa *(The Mad Woman),* Kamatari Fujiwara *(Rokusuke),* Miyuki Kuwano *(Onaka),* Takashi Shimura *(Tokubei Izumiya),* Eijiro Tono *(Goheiji),* Tatsuyoshi Ehara *(Genzo Tsugawa),* Haruko Sugimura *(Kin),* Ken Mitsuda *(Masae's Father).*

This lengthy film details the transformation of a young intern from a greedy idealist into pragmatic but caring physician. In early 19th-century Japan, Dr. Kyojo Niide (Toshiro Mifune), better known as "Red Beard," is the head of a poverty stricken public health clinic, whose latest intern, Dr. Noboru Yasumoto (Yuzo Kayama), has his own ideas about practicing medicine. However, despite initial signs of revolt, including excessive drinking and unorthodox dress, by film's end, Yasumoto learns that being a good doctor requires much sacrifice, his new awareness due largely to the patience and dedication of the aging Red Beard. A powerful tale of morality and human decency this monumental film took two years to complete and runs over three hours. While its scope would initially seem better suited to a SEVEN SAMURAI or a RAN, Kurosawa brings a battlefieldlike intensity to a different arena—the public health clinic. Here the wise Red Beard is faced with the same tragedies, dilemmas, and fears that confront Kurosawa's brave samurai—even his name sounds like that of a warrior. Mifune is as great here as he ever has been. In Japanese with English subtitles.

p, Tomoyuki Tanaka, Ryuzo Kikushima; d, Akira Kurosawa; w, Masato Ide, Hideo Oguni, Ryuzo Kikushima, Akira Kurosawa (based on the novel *Akahige Shinryo Tan* by Shugoro Yamamoto); ph, Asakazu Nakai, Takao Saito (Tohoscope); m, Masaru Sato.

Historical **(PR:C-O MPAA:NR)**

RED DESERT*½**

(1964, Fr./It.) 116m Duemila-Federiz-Francoriz/Rizzoli c (IL DESERTO ROSSO; LE DESERT ROUGE)

Monica Vitti *(Giuliana),* Richard Harris *(Corrado Zeller),* Carlo Chionetti *(Ugo),* Xenia Valderi *(Linda),* Rita Renoir *(Emilia),* Aldo Grotti *(Max),* Valerio Baroleschi *(Valerio),* Giuliano Missirini *(Workman),* Lili Rheims *(Workman's Wife),* Emanuela Paola Carboni *(Girl in Fable),* Bruno Borghi, Beppe Conti, Giulio Cotignoli, Hiram Mino Madonia.

A masterpiece of color cinematography, RED DESERT uses its carefully rendered color scheme to heighten the emotional impact of Michelangelo Antonioni's portrayal of the alienating effect of the modern world on one woman. Giuliana (Monica Vitti) lives in the northern Italian town of Ravenna with her husband, Ugo (Carlo Chionetti), a factory engineer who fails to appreciate the depth of her despair, and Valerio (Valerio Bartoleschi), the young son upon whom she dotes. The city's grim industrial landscape weighs heavily on Giuliana. Corrado (Richard Harris), who has come to recruit workers for a South American project, is attracted to her, and understands her depression, realizing that the an auto accident ostensibly responsible for her malaise was really a suicide attempt. Giuliana's struggle to come to terms with her environment is not easily resolved, but as the film ends, and her son asks her why birds don't fly through the poisonous yellow smoke of factory, she is able to tell him it's "because they have learned to fly around it," illustrating the separate peace she must make with technology. An extremely disturbing film, RED DESERT captures a rare beauty that extends the boundaries of film art in its use of color and setting. In attempting to depict Giuliana's perception of the destructive influence of technology on the natural environment, Antonioni went so far as to enhance the bleakness of his industrial wasteland by literally painting the marshlands gray, and Giuliana's sense of isolation is further reenforced by a frightening electronic soundtrack. In Italian with English subtitles.

p, Antonio Cervi; d, Michelangelo Antonioni; w, Michelangelo Antonioni, Tonino Guerra; ph, Carlo Di Palma (Eastmancolor); ed, Eraldo Da Roma; m, Giovanni Fusco, Vittorio Gelmetti.

Drama **(PR:O MPAA:NR)**

REPENTANCE****

(1987, USSR) 150m Gruziafilm/Cannon c (POKAYANIYE)

Avtandil Makharadze *(Varlam Aravidze/Abel Aravidze),* Iya Ninidze *(Guliko, Varlam's Daughter-in-Law),* Merab Ninidze *(Tornike, Varlam's Grandson),* Zeinab Botsvadze *(Katevan Barateli),* Ketevan Abuladze *(Nino Baratelli),* Edisher Giorgobiani *(Sandro Baratelli),* Kakhi Kavsadze *(Mikhail Korisheli),* Nino Zakariadze *(Elena Korisheli),* Nato Otijigava *(Ketevan as a Child),* Dato Kemkhadze *(Abel as a Child),* Veriko Anjaparidze, Boris Tsipuria, Akaki Khidasheli, Leo Antadze, Rezo Esadze, Amiran Amiranashvili, Amiran Buadze.

As the 1980s draw to a close, it seems likely that Tengiz Abuladze's REPENTANCE will emerge as the decade's most significant Soviet film, a historically important document of the springtime of Mikhail Gorbachev's *glasnost* policy. Written in 1981 and okayed under the Brezhnev administration by Eduard Shevardnadze, REPENTANCE was filmed in Soviet Georgia, the homeland of Stalin, as a television project. It was shelved from 1984 until 1987, when, under Gorbachev, the Union of Cinematographers liberated it from state censorship. Before 1987 came to a close, REPENTANCE had won a Special Jury Prize at the Cannes Film Festival and was named as the Soviet Union's official entry in the Academy Awards' Foreign-Language Film category. As the film opens, Ketevan Barateli (Zejnab Botsvadze), a cake decorator, learns of the death of the aged Varlam Aravidze (brilliantly played by Avtandil Makharadze, who also plays the deceased man's son), a highly revered Georgian mayor whose physical appearance and personality is a composite of Stalin, Mussolini, Hitler, and Lavrenti Beria, Stalin's chief of secret police. Later that evening, after the dignitary's funeral, the freshly buried corpse keeps reappearing in his family's garden, despite all attempts at reinterment. The grave robber turns out to be the cake decorator, who is apprehended and tried. As she explains her actions to the court, the film flashes back to the Stalinist era, and a terrible history for which the living are still culpable is laid bare. A powerful, intelligent, and visually poetic picture, REPENTANCE condemns not only Stalinism but those who try to bury it. The film is also a plea for religious freedom, filled with religious iconography. Many of its dreamy images (such as that of the painter and his wife buried, except for the faces, under a pile of rocks while the mayor sings an aria) are unforgettable, although Abuladze's use of them sometimes becomes too generous. Still, REPENTANCE stands as one of the finest films to be released as a result of *glasnost*. The videocassette is subtitled in English.

d, Tengiz Abuladze; w, Nana Djanelidze, Tengiz Abuladze, Rezo Kveselava; ph, Mikhail Agranovich (Orwo Color); ed, Guliko Omadze; m, Nana Djanelidze.

Drama/Fantasy/Political (PR:C MPAA:PG)

REPULSION*****

(1965, Brit.) 104m Compton-Tekli/Royal bw

Catherine Deneuve *(Carol Ledoux),* Ian Hendry *(Michael),* John Fraser *(Colin),* Patrick Wymark *(Landlord),* Yvonne Furneaux *(Helen Ledoux),* Renee Houston *(Miss Balch),* Helen Fraser *(Bridget),* Valerie Taylor *(Mme. Denise),* James Villiers *(John),* Hugh Futcher *(Reggie),* Mike Pratt *(Workman),* Monica Merlin *(Mrs. Rendlesham),* Imogen Graham *(Manicurist),* Roman Polanski *(Spoons Player).*

REPULSION is one of the most frightening pictures ever made. It has often been compared to Hitchcock's PSYCHO (1960), but Roman Polanski's film, rather than presenting a portrait of a psychotic killer, pulls the audience into the crazed individual's mind. Catherine Deneuve plays Carol, a Belgian manicurist working in London and living in an apartment with her sister (Yvonne Furneaux). Carol becomes increasingly unhinged, apparently due to her feelings about sex, which simultaneously repulses and attracts her, and which she is constantly reminded of by the presence of her sister's lover. When her sister goes on holiday, Carol is left to fend for herself, and becomes the victim of terrifying and destructive hallucinations within the confines of the apartment. REPULSION tells a simple story, but Polanski turns it into something undeniably brilliant. The director-writer took great pains in creating the proper composition and details for his nightmarish black-and-white visuals, extracting maximum hallucinatory effect from the apartment set. A powerfully engrossing film, which owes much to the realistic, nearly silent performance of Deneuve, REPULSION was Polanski's first English-language feature. The director makes a cameo appearance as a spoons player.

p, Gene Gutowski; d, Roman Polanski; w, Roman Polanski, Gerard Brach, David Stone; ph, Gilbert Taylor; ed, Alastair McIntyre; m, Chico Hamilton.

Horror (PR:O MPAA:NR)

RETURN OF MARTIN GUERRE, THE***½

(1982, Fr.) 111m La Societe Francais-FR3-La Societe de Production des Films Marcel Dassault/European Intl. c

Gerard Depardieu *(Martin Guerre),* Bernard Donnadieu *(Martin Guerre),* Nathalie Baye *(Bertrande de Rols),* Roger Planchon *(Jean de Coras),* Maurice Jacquemont *(Judge Rieux),* Isabelle Sadoyan *(Catherine Boere),* Rose Thierry *(Raimonde de Rols),* Maurice Barrier *(Pierre Guerre),* Stephane Peau *(Young Martin),* Sylvie Meda *(Young Bertrande),* Chantal Deruaz *(Jeanne),* Valerie Chassigneux *(Guillemette),* Tcheky Karyo *(Augustin),* Dominique Pinon *(Antoine),* Adrien Duquesne *(Sanxi),* Andre Chaumeau *(The Cure),* Philippe Babin *(Jacques),* Francis Arnaud, Axel Bogousslavsky, Neige Dolsky, Gilbert Gilles, Jean-Claude Perrin, Alain Recoing, Rene Bouloc, Alain Frerot, Andre Delon.

Set in 16th-century France, this engrossing period piece is based on existing records of an actual court case tried in a small peasant village. Two youngsters, Martin Guerre and Bertrande de Rols, enter into a marriage of convenience at the behest of their peasant families. After a number of years, the strangely distant Martin disappears from the village, leaving behind his chaste, love-starved wife (Nathalie Baye). When Martin (Gerard Depardieu) returns, nine years later, he receives a warm welcome from the townsfolk and Bertrande, who has remained faithful to him. However, when Martin experiences occasional lapses of memory and fails to recognize faces, accusations fly—some of the villagers accusing him of being an impostor in the belief that the real Martin lost a leg in combat. Bertrande grows increasingly confused, at times defending her husband, who has discovered a new-found affection for her, and on other occasions condemning him with her silence. The matter becomes even more confused when another man claiming to be Martin Guerre (Bernard Donnadieu) arrives in the village. One of the most successful art house films of the 1980s, THE RETURN OF MARTIN GUERRE relies on two powerful performers—Depardieu, who is perfectly cast as the mysterious peasant, and Baye, whose demanding role calls for carefully measured silence and reserve. In his second theatrical outing, television director Daniel Vigne realized that the facts and details of this elaborate historical drama (shaped by Jean-Claude Carriere's script) are fascinating enough in themselves that he needed only stick to them to create a captivating film. The videocassette is available in both dubbed and subtitled (French into English) versions.

p, Daniel Vigne; d, Daniel Vigne; w, Daniel Vigne, Jean-Claude Carriere; ph, Andre Neau (Fujicolor); ed, Denise de Casabianca; m, Michel Portal.

Historical (PR:C MPAA:NR)

RETURN OF THE TALL BLOND MAN WITH ONE BLACK SHOE, THE***

(1974, Fr.) 80m Gaumont-La Gueville/Brenner c (LE RETOUR DU GRAND BLOND)

Pierre Richard *(Francois Perrin),* Jean Carmet *(Maurice),* Mireille Darc *(Christine),* Jean Rochefort *(Louis Toulouse),* Jean Bouise *(Minister),* Paul Le Person *(Perrache),* Colette Castel *(Paulette),* Henri Guybet, Herve Sand, Jean Amos, Antoine Baud, Andre Bollet, Paul Bonifas, Michel Francini, Jacques Giraud, Louis Navarre, Jeannette Pico, Michel Duchaussoy.

This sequel to THE TALL BLOND MAN WITH ONE BLACK SHOE begins three months after the tall blond Francois Perrin (Pierre Richard) has departed for Rio with Christine (Mireille Darc), a pretty blonde agent, as once again Francois becomes the target of the French Secret Service. Because of his "heroic" exploits in the previous film, Francois is to honored by the government. Inspector Toulouse (Jean Rochefort), however, knows that Francois is not a spy but a hapless innocent who survives by sheer chance. He sends his agents to Rio to liquidate Francois in order to avoid any embarrassment. Of course, Francois proves just as difficult a target as in the previous film. Not quite as entertaining as the original—it's joke beginning to wear thin—but the performances, especially Richard's, are worth seeing. The videocassette is dubbed in English.

p, Alain Poire, Yves Robert; d, Yves Robert; w, Yves Robert, Francis Veber; ph, Rene Mathelin; ed, Ghislaine Desjonqueres, Francois London; m, Vladimir Cosma.

Comedy/Spy **(PR:A-C MPAA:NR)**

REVOLT OF JOB, THE***½

(1983, Hung./Ger.) 98m Mafilm Tarsulas-Starfilm-ZDF-Macropus-Hungarian TV/Teleculture c (JOB LAZADASA)

Ferenc Zenthe *(Job)*, Hedi Temessy *(Roza)*, Gabor Feher *(Lacko)*, Peter Rudolf *(Jani)*, Leticia Caro *(Ilka)*.

Set in a small East Hungarian farming village in 1943, THE REVOLT OF JOB stars Ferenc Zenthe and Hedi Temessy as Job and Roza, an elderly Jewish couple who have outlived all their children. Wishing for an heir, the couple schemes with an adoption center to gain custody of a seven-year-old Christian boy, Lacko (Gabor Feher), by trading two calves for him. Lacko is at first rebellious and cannot be reached by his loving "parents," choosing instead to play with a dog he has befriended, but eventually he warms to Job and Roza. All the while, the advance of Hitler's troops threatens Job and Roza's safety, and the couple prepare for the worst, arranging for a Gentile family to take care of their bewildered, now-loving adopted son while teaching him all they can about their own, endangered culture. Wisely concentrating its examination of religious and historical themes in a simple, small story, THE REVOLT OF JOB is a moving and intelligent film. As told from the boy's point of view, the film is dependent on Feher's performance as Lacko, and, thankfully, he is superb in his debut role. The script and direction by Imre Gyongyossy and Barna Kabay are fine, but it is the young star—selected from more than 4,000 hopefuls by the filmmakers—who remains the film's brightest point. The film received a Best Foreign-Language Film Oscar nomination. In Hungarian with English subtitles.

d, Imre Gyongyossy, Barna Kabay; w, Imre Gyongyossy, Barna Kabay, Katalin Petenyi; ph, Gabor Szabo (Eastmancolor); ed, Katalin Petenyi; m, Zoltan Jeny.

Drama **(PR:O MPAA:NR)**

RIFIFI*****

(1955, Fr.) 117m Indus-Pathe-Prima/UMP bw (AKA: DU RIFIFI CHEZ DES HOMMES)

Jean Servais *(Tony le Stephanois)*, Carl Mohner *(Jo Le Suedois)*, Robert Manuel *(Mario)*, Jules Dassin *(Cesar)*, Magali Noel *(Viviane)*, Marie Sabouret *(Mado)*, Janine Darcy *(Louise)*, Pierre Grasset *(Louis Grutter)*, Robert Hossein *(Remi Grutter)*, Marcel Lupovici *(Pierre Grutter)*, Dominique Maurin *(Tonio)*, Claude Sylvain *(Ida)*.

This landmark caper film shows the robbery of a Parisian jewelry store and the complications that follow for the thieves—mastermind Tony (Jean Servais), a recently released ex-con who may or may not have a terminal respiratory problem; Jo (Carl Mohner), whom Tony served time to protect; safecracker Cesar (the film's director, Jules Dassin, acting under the pseudonym Perlo Vita), and Mario (Robert Manuel)—all of them surprisingly decent men. The film's centerpiece is a 28-minute sequence that captures the robbery itself in fascinating detail, employing neither dialog nor music, allowing only the actual sounds of the thieves at work to be heard. Once the heist is accomplished, life doesn't get any easier for the crooks, as Tony's gangster rival (Marcel Lupovici) and cohorts get violently greedy after learning about the robbery through Cesar's indiscretion. The kidnaping of Jo's son and plenty of shooting follow before RIFIFI (French slang for "trouble") is over. This was the second European-made film for writer-director-actor Dassin, an American who plied his trade abroad after the House Un-American Activities Committee made life difficult at home. Dassin, whose wonderful you-are-there direction won him a share of the Best Director award at Cannes, also manages to inject more than a little humor into this tension-filled genre classic, preceded by the likes of THE ASPHALT JUNGLE (1950) and followed by films like BIG DEAL ON MADONNA STREET (1958) and Dassin's own TOPKAPI (1964). In French with English subtitles.

p, Rene G. Vuattoux; d, Jules Dassin; w, Jules Dassin, Rene Wheeler, Auguste Le Breton (based on the novel by Le Breton); ph, Philippe Agostini; ed, Roger Dwyre; m, Georges Auric.

Crime **(PR:A-C MPAA:NR)**

RISE TO POWER OF LOUIS XIV, THE*****

(1966, Fr.) 100m O.R.T.F./Brandon c (LA PRISE DE POUVOIR PAR LOUIS XIV; AKA: THE RISE OF LOUIS XIV)

Jean-Marie Patte *(Louis XIV)*, Raymond Jourdan *(Colbert)*, Silvagni *(Mazarin)*, Katherina Renn *(Anne of Austria)*, Dominique Vincent *(Mme. du Plessis)*, Pierre Barrat *(Fouquet)*, Fernand Fabre *(Le Tellier)*, Francoise Ponty *(Louise de la Valliere)*, Joelle Langeois *(Marie Therese)*, Jacqueline Corot *(Mme. Henrietta)*, Maurice Barrier *(D'Artagnan)*, Andre Dumas *(Father Joly)*, Francois Mirante *(Mons. de Brienne)*, Pierre Spadoni *(Noni)*, Roger Guillo *(Pharmacist)*, Louis Raymond *(1st Physician)*, Maurice Bourdon *(2nd Physician)*, Michel Ferre *(Mons. de Gesvres)*, Raymond Pelissier *(Pomponne)*, Guy Pintat *(Master Chef)*, Michele Marquais *(Mme. de Motteville)*, Jean-Jacques Daubin *(Mons. de Vardes)*, Georges Goubert *(Mons. de Soyecourt)*, Pierre Pernet *(Monsieur)*, Claude Rio *(Vardes)*, Daniel Dubois *(Lionne)*, Ginette Barbier *(Pierrette Dufour)*, Jean Obe *(Le Vau)*.

This is Roberto Rossellini's sparse, near-documentary

look at the young Sun King (Jean-Marie Patte) and at how he codified and choreographed an empire, framing fashions to ensure absolute obedience. No detail of the artful young king's designs and graces—which culminated in the structured elegance of the court at Versailles—is too small to be captured by the camera, while the big *events*, the executions and rebellions, are, quite properly, trivialized. What won obeisance for playboy Louis was *fashion*, carefully crafted for conquest. Rossellini's pans and zooms follow these strategies of manners and mores intimately: Louis' dying mentor Mazarin (Silvagni) rouges his pallid cheeks prior to his audience with the young king; Louis demands more height to his wigs to enhance his stature and more lace to his jacket to gain attention; the king choreographs the rituals attendant on funerals, cabinet meetings, banquets. The complexities of Louis' life-structurings consolidate his previously shaky power—all eyes are on the young king, hoping to spot each new nuance, each fad-to-be—and intrigues and plots are forgotten in this atmosphere of utter attendance: the Sun King is all-powerful. A revival of sorts for Rossellini, this picture would set the standard for its genre, playing as important a part in film history as did his earliest Neo-Realist films. Like PAISAN, its predecessor of 20 years, THE RISE TO POWER OF LOUIS XIV is constructed of episodes, each giving the observer a chance to bear witness to a reality, a view of history not of battles and bravado, but of guile, manipulation, and role-playing charisma. In French with English subtitles.

d, Roberto Rossellini; w, Philippe Erlanger, Jean Gruault; ph, Georges Leclerc (Eastmancolor); ed, Armand Ridel.

Historical **(PR:A MPAA:G)**

ROUND MIDNIGHT*****

(1986, Fr./US) 133m PECF-Little Bear/WB c

Dexter Gordon *(Dale Turner),* Francois Cluzet *(Francis Borier),* Gabrielle Haker *(Berangere),* Sandra Reaves-Phillips *(Buttercup),* Lonette McKee *(Darcey Leigh),* Christine Pascal *(Sylvie),* Herbie Hancock *(Eddie Wayne),* Bobby Hutcherson *(Ace),* Pierre Trabaud *(Francis's Father),* Frederique Meininger *(Francis's Mother),* Liliane Rovere *(Mme. Queen),* Hart Leroy Bibbs *(Hershell),* Ged Marlon *(Beau),* Benoit Regent *(Psychiatrist),* Victoria Gabrielle Platt *(Chan),* Arthur French *(Booker),* John Berry *(Ben),* Martin Scorsese *(Goodley),* Philippe Noiret *(Redon),* Alain Sarde *(Terzian),* Eddy Mitchell *(A Drunk),* Billy Higgins *(Drums),* Bobby Hutcherson *(Vibes),* Eric Le Lann *(Trumpet),* John McLaughlin *(Guitar),* Pierre Michelot *(Bass),* Wayne Shorter *(Tenor Saxophone),* Ron Carter *(Bass),* Billy Higgins *(Drums),* Palle Mikkelborg *(Trumpet),* Wayne Shorter *(Soprano Saxophone),* Mads Vinding *(Bass),* Cheikh Fall *(Percussion),* Michel Perez *(Guitar),* Mads Vinding *(Bass),* Tony Williams *(Drums),* Ron Carter *(Bass),* Freddie Hubbard *(Trumpet),* Cedar Walton *(Piano).*

ROUND MIDNIGHT might easily be called the best jazz film ever made, and not only because, aside from 1988's BIRD, the competition is so weak. The film's greatness lies not just in its vivid portrayal of the bebop milieu, but also in its sensitive examination of the turbulent forces within an artist compelled to create on a nightly basis, despite personal consequences. Dedicated to jazz greats Lester Young and Bud Powell, the film begins in 1959 as black bebop jazzman Dale Turner (Dexter Gordon), "the greatest tenor saxophone player in the world," leaves New York City for Paris. Alcoholic, ill, and apparently a former heroin addict, Turner plays nightly at Paris' famous Blue Note club to adoring fans, who appreciate his and his fellow expatriates' music. One of his most fervent admirers, Francis (Francois Cluzet), forms a close friendship with Turner, who moves in with him. Together the two try to bring Turner's self-destructive impulses under control, until Turner decides to risk a return to the US. The irony of ROUND MIDNIGHT—a sadly familiar one recognized in the plot—is that it took a Frenchman, director-cowriter and jazz lover Betrand Tavernier, to make this most accurate and intelligent film about the distinctly American art of jazz. Casting musicians (including Wayne Shorter, Tony Williams, Ron Carter, and Herbie Hancock, who did the Oscar-winning score) as his actors and insisting that the music be recorded live on the set with cameras rolling, Tavernier captures the complex relations among the players at work; the process has never been shown so well in a narrative film. Turner (an amalgam of various figures, including Young, Powell, and Gordon himself) is brilliantly *played* by the great Gordon, who contributed much of the dialog, suggested changes in the script, and eventually received a Best Actor Oscar nomination. With Gordon's performance and the wonderful musical numbers providing the heart of his film, Tavernier captures not only jazz, but passion—for music, for art, for life itself.

p, Irwin Winkler; d, Bertrand Tavernier; w, Bertrand Tavernier, David Rayfiel (based on incidents in the lives of Francis Paudras, Bud Powell); ph, Bruno de Keyzer (Panavision, Eastmancolor); ed, Armand Psenny; m, Herbie Hancock.

Drama **(PR:C MPAA:R)**

RULES OF THE GAME, THE*****

(1939, Fr.) 110m NEF/Janus bw (LA REGLE DU JEU)

Marcel Dalio *(Robert de la Chesnaye),* Nora Gregor *(Christine de la Chesnaye),* Roland Toutain *(Andre Jurieu),* Jean Renoir *(Octave),* Mila Parely *(Genevieve de Marrast),* Paulette Dubost *(Lisette),* Gaston Modot *(Schumacher),* Julien Carette *(Marceau),* Odette Talazac *(Charlotte de la Plante),* Pierre Magnier *(The General),* Pierre Nay *(M. de Saint-Aubin),* Richard Francoeur *(M. La Bruyere),* Claire Gerard *(Mme. La Bruyere),* Anne Mayen *(Jackie),* Roger Forster *(Effeminate Guest),* Nicolas Amato *(The South American),* Tony Corteggiani *(Berthelin),* Eddy Debray *(Corneille),* Leon Larive *(The Cook),* Jenny Helia *(The Servant).*

One of cinema's most monumental achievements, Jean Renoir's THE RULES OF THE GAME passionately tackles the pre-WW II French class system, and succeeds in bringing forth the human complexities and frailties that underlie bourgeois civility. When aviator Andre Jurieu (Roland Toutain) is met by his friend Octave (director Renoir) and ecstatic reporters after a record-setting flight, he tells the radio audience that he undertook the adventure the for the love of a woman—who failed to greet him at the airport. This woman, Christine (Nora Gregor), is in the meantime preparing for an evening out with her husband, Robert de la Chesnaye (Marcel Dalio), who knows of his wife's affair and doesn't want to lose her, but continues to dally with his adoring mistress (Mila Parely). Octave, the character with the clearest understanding of his environment, admits to Andre that he too cares for Christine (although, like the others, he has difficulty distinguishing love from "friendship"), and maintains that Andre will never win her because he doesn't heed "the rules" of society. When the two men are included among the guests in a weekend shooting party at de la Chesnaye's country estate (a remarkably beautiful location that recalls the works of the director's father, Auguste Renoir, and that is greatly enhanced by the crystal clear, deep-focus photography), everyone, servants included, brings along their own little drama, to be played out during and after the hunt—a brutal game complete with its own rigid rules that threatens to spill over into the domestic, "civilized" sphere. A labor of love and passion, THE RULES OF THE GAME was borne of Renoir's discontent with the complacency of his French contemporaries as the country faced occupation. Relentlessly booed at its 1939 Paris premiere and banned by both the French and Vichy governments, the film is a classic example of audience revulsion to a truthful portrayal of their world, in which Renoir aimed to create "an exact description of the bourgeoisie of our time." Renoir tried to appease his critics by whittling the picture from its original 113 to 85 minutes, then the masterwork was pulled from distribution by the Germans and stored in a warehouse that was later bombed, making the dream of a complete version seem impossible. It wasn't until 1959 that the film was restored to its nearly original form at 110 minutes, thanks to Jean Gaborit and Jacques Durand, who gathered up hundreds of cans of original footage and pieced the film together again with help from Renoir. The Venice Film Festival premiere of the restored version quickly put the film onto nearly every "top 10" list imaginable, a position it has justly retained.

d, Jean Renoir; w, Jean Renoir (in collaboration with Carl Koch, Camille Francois); ph, Jean Bachelet; ed, Marguerite Renoir; m, Camille Saint-Saens, Salabert, E. Rose, Vincent Scotto, Wolfgang Amadeus Mozart, Johann Strauss.

Drama **(PR:C MPAA:NR)**

S

SACRIFICE, THE****

(1986, Fr./Swed.) 145m Swedish Film Institute-Argos-Film Four-Josephson & Nykvist-Swedish TV-Sandrew-French Ministry of Culture/Orion c (OFFRET-SACRIFICATIO)

Erland Josephson *(Alexander),* Susan Fleetwood *(Adelaide),* Valerie Mairesse *(Julia),* Allan Edwall *(Otto),* Gudrun Gisladottir *(Maria),* Sven Wollter *(Victor),* Filippa Franzen *(Marta),* Tommy Kjellqvist *(Little Man).*

The final film from one of Russia's greatest filmmakers, Andrei Tarkovsky, was also his first to receive any widespread recognition in the US. Like all of Tarkovsky's work, it tackles complex themes and concerns that most directors would never approach. THE SACRIFICE is about a number of things, none obvious and none remaining wholly consistent from viewing (or viewer) to the next; it is a poetic vision, filled with the symbolism peculiar to Tarkovsky's imagination. It is also a visually stunning, hauntingly beautiful, brilliant piece of art. THE SACRIFICE opens as Alexander (Erland Josephson) and his six-year-old son are busily planting a tree along the sandy, barren shore of the small island where the family is vacationing. During this vacation, it is announced on the radio that WW III has begun—and the complete destruction of Europe by nuclear arms is certain. Later, when Alexander is alone, he gets down on his hands and knees to ask forgiveness from his creator, begging for the terrible events that are transpiring to be undone. He promises to do anything—give up all his possessions, even part with his son—if only things will be returned to normal. More than a beautiful film, THE SACRIFICE is a hopeful message to future generations to live in harmony with nature and with one another (which only gains in power by virtue of its dedication to the filmmaker's son). By December 29, 1986, less than a year after this movie was completed, Tarkovsky would fall victim to the cancer that he already knew would kill him. Aware that this would probably be his last film, Tarkovsky makes a conscious plea that we consider the damage done to the planet before it's too late, and seems to be saying that for all the modern world's astounding scientific progress, there is nothing to compensate for the loss of our spiritual essence—creating a dangerous gap between human consciousness and the natural world. While perhaps not the most typical of Tarkovsky's works (the Swedish cast, Sven Nykvist's photography, and the Faro location occasionally lend it a Bergmanesque quality), THE SACRIFICE is a brilliant picture that should not be missed. In Swedish with English subtitles.

p, Katinka Farago; d, Andrei Tarkovsky; w, Andrei Tarkovsky; ph, Sven Nykvist (Eastmancolor); ed, Andrei Tarkovsky, Michal Leszczylowski; m, Johann Sebastian Bach, Watazumido Shuoo.

Drama **(PR:C MPAA:PG)**

SAMURAI TRILOGY, THE***½

(1954, Jap.) 300m Toho/Toho International-FA c (ICHIJOJI NO KETTO; ZOKU MIYAMOTO MUSASHI; KETTO GANRYU JIMA; AKA: THE LEGEND OF MUSASHI; MASTER SWORDSMAN; DUEL AT GANRYU ISLAND)

Toshiro Mifune *(Miyamoto Musashi),* Kaoru Yachigusa *(Otsu),* Rentaro Mikuni *(Matahachi),* Mariko Okada *(Akemi),* Kuroemon Onoe *(Takuan),* Mitsuko Mito *(Oko),* Eiko Miyoshi *(Osugi),* Koji Tsurata *(Sasaki Kojiro),* Sachio Sakai *(Matahachi Honiden),* Akihiko Hirata *(Seijuro*

Yoshioka), Yu Fujiki *(Denshichiro Yoshioka),* Daisuke Kato *(Toji Gion),* Ko Mihashi *(Koetsu),* Kenjin Iida *(Jotaro),* Michiyo Kogure *(Yoshino Dayu),* Eijiro Tono *(Baiken Shishido),* Kuninori Kodo *(Old Priest Nikkan),* Michiko Saga *(Omitsu),* Takashi Shimura *(Court Official),* William Holden *(Narrator).*

Based on the exploits of a legendary Japanese hero, THE SAMURAI TRILOGY stars Toshiro Mifune as Miyamoto Musashi, a celebrated swordsman, artist, and teacher who wandered the country, battling his enemies and discovering the secrets of life, in the first half of the 17th century. Aiming to elevate himself from his low caste in a poor village, where he is known as Takeso, to the high status of the powerful samurai warriors, the adventurer is faced with numerous temptations and setbacks, but sticks to his goal and becomes a great samurai by the end. This beautifully photographed color costume epic (Toho Studios' first) is easily accessible to Western audiences, since it is—at least superficially—a western, with swords and samurais instead of rifles and cowboys. Its sweeping visuals and long shots, along with its three part structure and five-hour length, truly makes this one of cinema's grandest experiences. The American release of Part One, in 1955, gained a special Academy Award. The video release is in three separate cassettes (Part One, 93 minutes; Part Two, 102 minutes; Part Three, 105 minutes) and is in Japanese with English subtitles.

p, Kazuo Takimura; d, Hiroshi Inagaki; w, Tokuhei Wakao, Hiroshi Inagaki, Hideji Hojo (based on the novel *Miyamoto Musashi* by Eiji Yoshikawa); ph, Jun Yasumoto, Asushi Atumoto, Kazuo Yamada (Eastmancolor); ed, Robert Homel; m, Ikuma Dan.

Adventure/Historical (PR:C MPAA:NR)

SANJURO***

(1962, Jap.) 96m Toho bw (TSUBAKI SANJURO)

Toshiro Mifune *(Sanjuro),* Tatsuya Nakadai *(Muroto),* Takashi Shimura *(Kurofuji),* Yuzo Kayama *(Iori Izaka),* Reiko Dan *(Koiso),* Masao Shimizu *(Kukui),* Yunosuke Ito *(Mutsuta the Chamberlain),* Takako Irie *(Chamberlain's Wife),* Kamatari Fujiwara *(Takebayashi),* Keiju Kobayashi *(Spy),* Akihiko Hirata, Kunie Tanaka, Hiroshi Tachikawa, Tatsuhiko Hari, Tatsuyoshi Ehara, Kenzo Matsui, Yoshio Tsuchiya, Akira Kubo *(Young Samurai).*

Along with its predecessor, YOJIMBO, SANJURO represents Akira Kurosawa at his most commercial and entertaining, with both films revolving around the eccentric—practically choreographed—mannerisms of Toshiro Mifune. Mifune again plays a renegade samurai here, Sanjuro, who becomes involved with a group of young samurai determined to end the graft and corruption overrunning their land. When Iori Izaka (Yuzo Kayama), the nephew of a powerful chamberlain, suspects his uncle of fomenting political unrest, the samurai enlist Sanjuro's aid in helping them fight their battle. Directed by Kurosawa after the success of YOJIMBO, SANJURO is a essentially a rehashing, albeit a highly entertaining one, of the previous film. While the script and direction display Kurosawa's usual expertise, the real reason to watch is Mifune's wild performance. Offering more proof that he is one of film's great physical actors, Mifune goes through the entire film grimacing, scratching, yawning, and stretching—mannerisms, like his toothpick chewing in YOJIMBO, in direct contrast to his character's phenomenal skill as a swordsman. One of the most remarkable scenes in any Kurosawa film, notable for its special-effects bloodletting, occurs at the end of this SANJURO as the hero faces his rival, Muroto (Tatsuya Nakadai), in battle, they draw their swords, and, in an instant, Sanjuro strikes. The stunned Muroto wavers and falls, a geyser of blood erupting from his slashed heart. In Japanese with English subtitles.

p, Ryuzo Kikushima, Tomoyuki Tanaka; d, Akira Kurosawa; w, Ryuzo Kikushima, Akira Kurosawa, Hideo Oguni (based on the short story "Hibi Heian" by Shugoro Yamamoto); ph, Fukuzo Koizumi, Kozo Saito (Tohoscope); ed, Akira Kurosawa; m, Masaru Sato.

Adventure (PR:C MPAA:NR)

SANSHO THE BAILIFF*****

(1954, Jap.) 125m Daiei-Kyoto/Brandon bw (SANSHO DAYU; AKA: THE BAILIFF)

Yoshiaki Hanayagi *(Zushio),* Kyoko Kagawa *(Anju),* Kinuyo Tanaka *(Tamaki),* Eitaro Shindo *(Sansho),* Akitake Kono *(Taro),* Masao Shimizu *(Masauji Taira),* Ken Mitsuda *(Prime Minister Morozane Fujiwara),* Chieko Naniwa *(Ubatake),* Kikue Mori *(Priestess),* Kazukimi Okuni *(Norimura),* Yoko Kosono *(Kohagi),* Kimiko Tachibana *(Namiji),* Ichiro Sugai *(Minister Of Justice),* Masashiko Tsugawa *(Zushio as a Boy),* Naoki Fujiwara *(Zushio as an Infant),* Keiko Enami *(Anju as a Girl),* Ryosuke Kagawa *(Ritsushi Kumotake),* Kanji Koshiba *(Kaikudo Naiko),* Shinobu Araki *(Sadaya).*

A classic of Japanese and world cinema, SANSHO THE BAILIFF, set in the 11th century, tells the story of Zushio (Yoshiaki Hanayagi) and his struggle within the limits of feudal society. The film begins as a family—mother Tamaki (Kinuyo Tanaka), sister Anju (Kyoko Kagawa), and Zushio—travel through the woods in search of their exiled patriarch. They are soon assaulted by kidnapers, and Tamaki is sold into prostitution and exiled to Sado Island while the children are sold as slaves to a powerful and cruel bailiff, Sansho (Eitaro Shindo). Ten years pass, and Zushio has become as evil as Sansho, for whom he now works as an overseer at a labor compound. Haunted by thoughts of his dead father and his exiled mother, Zushio prepares his escape, planning to leave with Anju. She, however, in order to keep from burdening her brother or from revealing his whereabouts, drowns herself. When Zushio reaches his destination, Kyoto, he discovers that his father is a folk legend immortalized in song. In recognition of his father's prestige, Zushio is granted the post of governor, and he takes it upon himself to abolish slavery and banish Sansho the bailiff from his land. Perhaps Kenji Mizoguchi's greatest achievement, SANSHO THE BAILIFF is a visually mesmerizing picture that pays great and careful attention to the smallest details of nature and environment, highlighted by Mizoguchi's use of the long take and deep-focus shots. In an attempt to film life as he sees it, Mizoguchi and his cinematographer, Kazuo Miyagawa, capture images in a painterly way—using the entire palette of contrasts and movements to create a richly textured atmosphere. In Japanese with English subtitles.

p, Masaichi Nagata; d, Kenji Mizoguchi; w, Yahiro Fuji, Yoshikata Yoda (based on the story "Sansho Dayu" by Ogai Mori); ph, Kazuo Miyagawa; ed, Mitsuji Miyata; m, Fumio Hayasaka, Kanahichi Odera, Tamekichi Mochizuki.

Drama **(PR:C MPAA:NR)**

SAWDUST AND TINSEL***

(1953, Swed.) 92m Sandrews/Baumanfilm-Times-Janus bw (GYCKLARNAS AFTON; AKA: THE NAKED NIGHT; SUNSET OF A CLOWN)

Harriet Andersson *(Anne),* Ake Groenberg *(Albert Johansson),* Hasse Ekman *(Frans),* Anders Ek *(Teodor Frost),* Annika Tretow *(Agda, Albert's wife),* Kiki *(The Dwarf),* Gudrun Brost *(Alma Frost),* Gunnar Bjornstrand *(Mr. Sjuberg),* Erik Strandmark *(Jens),* Ake Fridell *(Officer),* Curt Lowgren *(Blom),* Olav Riego, John Starck, Erna Groth, Agda Hilin *(Theater Actors).*

One of a handful of Bergman pictures sent to the US after the success of THE SEVENTH SEAL and the onset of "Bergmania," SAWDUST AND TINSEL subscribes to all the then-held theories of what an "art film" should be, especially a "Swedish art film." Filled with depressing images, self-consciously intellectual dialog, and psychoanalytic and religious symbolism, it lacks only what almost all Bergman films lack—subtlety and hope. Albert Johannson (Ake Groenberg) is the owner of a traveling circus who leaves his mistress (Harriet Andersson) and tries to reunite with his wife (Annika Tretow). Hailed by some at the time of its release as Bergman's masterpiece, SAWDUST AND TINSEL is proof of the director's maturing visual and thematic style, and perhaps more importantly, it was the first of the Bergman's films photographed by the great Sven Nykvist, thereafter his frequent collaborator. In Swedish with English subtitles.

p, Rune Waldecranz; d, Ingmar Bergman; w, Ingmar Bergman; ph, Sven Nykvist, Hilding Bladh, Goran Strindberg; ed, Carl-Olov Skeppstedt; m, Karl-Birger Blomdahl.

Drama **(PR:O MPAA:NR)**

SCENE OF THE CRIME***

(1986, Fr.) 90m T.-Films A2/Kino c (LE LIEU DU CRIME)

Catherine Deneuve *(Lili),* Danielle Darrieux *(Grandmother),* Wadeck Stanczak *(Martin),* Nicolas Giraudi *(Thomas),* Victor Lanoux *(Maurice),* Jean Bousquet *(Grandfather),* Claire Nebout *(Alice),* Jacques Nolot *(Father Sorbier),* Jean-Claude Adelin.

This French provincial upper-class thriller (of the sort usually directed by Claude Chabrol) revolves around the rebellious 13-year-old Thomas (Nicolas Giraudi) and his beautiful mother, Lili (Catherine Deneuve), whose lives are transformed by the arrival of Martin (Wadeck Stanczak), a handsome, disheveled criminal. When Martin accosts the boy in a cemetery and threatens to hurt him if he doesn't return before nightfall with some money, Thomas complies. Martin's accomplice tries to kill the boy, however, wrongly believing that he informed on them, and Martin, in turn, kills his own partner. Eventually, Lili, who feels a bond with Martin since he saved Thomas' life, falls in love with the criminal, viewing this love as a chance to finally act in her own interest and start life anew. But a third accomplice, a frightened young woman (Claire Nebout), is determined not to lose Martin to Lili. A thriller with an uneasy sexual tension, SCENE OF THE CRIME functions on many levels, concentrating on the interdependent relationships among the characters. Deneuve, whose excellence as an actress is superceded only by her beauty, is a marvel to watch as she casts aside (as best as nature will allow) her elegant looks to portray a plain, provincial woman. Not since THE LAST METRO in 1980 has she had a role of such depth, erasing the unpleasant memories of THE HUNGER and 1988's LOVE SONGS. Danielle Darrieux, the *grande dame* of French cinema (she appeared in such great films as MAYERLING; THE EARRINGS OF MADAME DE . . .; LE PLAISIR; and THE YOUNG GIRLS OF ROCHEFORT in 1968 with Deneuve), is also excellent as the family matriarch. Making a lasting impression in a small role is Nebout, whose intense, glassy-eyed gaze is haunting and unforgettable. In French with English subtitles.

p, Alain Terzian; d, Andre Techine; w, Andre Techine, Pascal Bonitzer, Olivier Assayas; ph, Pascal Marti (Eastmancolor); ed, Martine Giordano; m, Philippe Sarde.

Thriller **(PR:C-O MPAA:NR)**

SCENES FROM A MARRIAGE***

(1973, Swed.) 155m Cinematograph AB Sweden/ Cinema 5-Donald Rugoff c (SCENER UR ETT AKTENSKAP)

Liv Ullmann *(Marianne),* Erland Josephson *(Johan),* Bibi Andersson *(Katarina),* Jan Malmsjo *(Peter),* Anita Wall *(Mrs. Palm),* Gunnel Lindblom *(Eva),* Bertil Nordstrom *(Arne).*

One of the finest of Ingmar Bergman's late-period films, SCENES FROM A MARRIAGE was in its original form a six-episode, 300-minute Swedish television series, and was cut by Bergman for US release. Here the director-writer again proves that he is one of film's best, and most theatrical, directors of actresses, giving the inimitable Liv Ullmann a superb script that casts her in the role of Marianne, the abandoned wife forced to deal with her weak husband Johan's (Erland Josephson) involvement with a younger woman. Filmed almost entirely in extreme close-ups by the masterful Sven Nykvist, Ullmann's face conveys a variety of expressions reminiscent of Renee Falconetti in Carl Dreyer's silent THE PASSION OF JOAN OF ARC. The film is not without its faults, especially a certain choppiness resulting from the editing down of the TV version. (Its made-for-TV visual content, however, should be admirably suited to videocassette). There is little plot to speak of, the film's chief force lying in its dramatization of marital trauma, but viewers will be deeply moved by the marvelous acting and the honesty of Bergman's screenplay. The videocassette is dubbed in English.

p, Ingmar Bergman; d, Ingmar Bergman; w, Ingmar Bergman; ph, Sven Nykvist (Eastmancolor); ed, Siv Lundgren.

Drama **(PR:C-O MPAA:PG)**

SECRETS OF WOMEN*½**

(1952, Swed.) 107m Svensk/Janus bw (KVINNORS VANTAN; GB: WAITING WOMEN)

Anita Bjork *(Rakel),* Karl-Arne Holmsten *(Eugen Lobelius),* Jarl Kulle *(Kaj, Rakel's lover),* Maj-Britt Nilsson *(Marta Lobelius),* Eva Dahlbeck *(Karin Lobelius),* Gunnar Bjornstrand *(Fredrik Lobelius),* Birger Malmsten *(Martin Lobelius),* Gerd Andersson *(Maj, Marta's sister),* Bjorn Bjelvenstam *(Henrik),* Aino Taube *(Annette),* Hakan Westergren *(Paul),* Naima Wifstrand *(Old Mrs. Lobelius),* Ingmar Bergman *(Street Character),* Kjell Nordenskold *(American Pilot),* Carl Strom *(Doctor).*

This mostly light-hearted comedy, made by Ingmar Bergman in 1952 but not released in the US until nine years later, was written by the director during what he considered a dark time in his life—which seems strange, considering how much fun the film is. Divided into three parts, SECRETS OF WOMEN is told in flashback as the wives of the Lobelius brothers converse about past romantic experiences. The first section (based on a Bergman play) relates the tale of Rakel's (Anita Bjork) infidelity with an old lover, the second depicts Marta's (Maj-Britt Nilsson) Parisian affair and subsequent marriage to Martin (Birger Malmsten), and the last takes place in a broken elevator that strands Karin (Eva Dahlbeck) and husband Fredrik (Gunnar Bjornstrand). At the conclusion of these three stories, a fourth Lobelius wife (Aino Taube) decides to keep her story to herself. Although this is one of several well-received comedies that Bergman somewhat grudgingly turned out at the request of the Swedish film industry in the 1950s, it still shows a deliberate attempt on the director's part to advance his filmic style. In the elevator sequence, especially, Bergman, under the influence of Alfred Hitchcock, tried primarily to let images tell his story, keeping the dialog to a minimum. The videocassette is available in dubbed and subtitled (Swedish into English) versions.

p, Allan Ekelund; d, Ingmar Bergman; w, Ingmar Bergman; ph, Gunnar Fischer; ed, Oscar Rosander; m, Erik Nordgren.

Drama/Comedy **(PR:C MPAA:NR)**

SEDUCED AND ABANDONED**

(1964, Fr./It.) 118m Lux-Ultra-Vides-CCF/CD bw (SEDUITE ET ABANDONNEE; SEDOTTA E ABBANDONATA)

Stefania Sandrelli *(Agnese Ascalone),* Aldo Puglisi *(Peppino Califano),* Saro Urzi *(Vincenzo Ascalone),* Lando Buzzanca *(Antonio Ascalone),* Leopoldo Trieste *(Baron Rizieri),* Rocco D'Assunta *(Orlando Califano),* Lola Braccini *(Amalia Califano),* Paola Biggio *(Matilde Ascalone),* Umberto Spadaro *(Cousin Ascalone),* Oreste Palella *(Police Chief Potenza),* Lina La Galla *(Francesca Ascalone),* Roberta Narbonne *(Rosaura Ascalone),* Rosetta Urzi *(Consolata the Maid),* Adelino Campardo *(Bisigato),* Vincenzo Licata *(Profumo the Undertaker),* Italia Spadaro *(Aunt Carmela).*

Complications aplenty arise when Peppino (Aldo Puglisi) seduces Agnese (Stefania Sandrelli), the 15-year-old sister of his fiancee, Matilde (Paola Biggio). The girls' father, Vincenzo (Saro Urzi), puts an end to Peppino's engagement to his older daughter and demands that the unscrupulous lothario marry the younger when it is revealed that she is pregnant. When Peppino has other ideas, the angry father decides do away with this plague on his kin, but the police intercede and give Peppino their own ultimatum: marry Agnese or serve time for seducing a minor. Reluctantly, Peppino chooses a figurative ball and chain instead of a literal one, although Agnese has some thoughts of her own on the matter. Meanwhile, Vincenzo has found a new fiancee for Matilde, the ne'er-do-well Baron Rizieri (Leopoldo Trieste). Mixing fantasy and reality, shifting from present to past, and moving in and out of his characters' minds, director Pietro Germi (whose script for DIVORCE ITALIAN STYLE was nominated for an Oscar) creates an occasionally amusing but generally undistinguished slice of Sicilian life here. In Italian with English subtitles.

p, Franco Cristaldi; d, Pietro Germi; w, Pietro Germi, Luciano Vincenzoni, Age, Scarpelli (based on an idea by Germi, Vincenzoni); ph, Aiace Parolin; ed, Roberto Cinquini; m, Carlo Rustichelli.

Drama **(PR:C MPAA:NR)**

SEDUCTION OF MIMI, THE*½**

(1972, It.) 92m Bera-Euro-International/New Line c (MIMI METALLURGICO FERITO NELL'ONORE)

Giancarlo Giannini *(Carmelo "Mimi" Mardocheco),* Mariangela Melato *(Fiore),* Agostina Belli *(Rosalia),* Elena Fiore *(Signora Finocchiaro),* Turi Ferro *(Tricarico),* Agostina Belli, Luigi Diberti, Tuccio Musumeci, Ignazio Pappalardo, Rosaria Rapisarda.

This early film by Lina Wertmuller earned her the Best Director prize at the Cannes Film Festival and stars Giancarlo Giannini as a Sicilian metallurgist named Mimi. After refusing to vote for the Mafia candidate in a local election, Mimi loses his factory job and decides to head north for work. Although professing to be communist, he is eager to get rich, enjoy a life of luxury, and step on his fellow workers. Leaving behind his wife, Rosalia (Agostina Belli), whom he cruelly dominates and castigates for her infertility, Mimi finds work in Turin. There, he falls in love with Fiore (Mariangela Melato), a virgin anarchist who bears him a child. Mimi's idyllic life in the north is sabotaged, however, by the menacing Mafia-controlled authorities who transfer him back to Sicily. Returning with his mistress and child, Mimi finds that his wife has not only taken a lover and become pregnant, but has also begun to form her own political opinions, leaving Mimi no choice but to restore his hometown honor. A clever examination of the bonds between sexual and political power, and the differences between the "civilized" northern Italians and the "barbaric" southerners, Wertmuller's film comes to life through Giannini's bravura performance; a macho brute and philistine, his Mimi is still a sympathetic character, more victim than victimizer. The videocassette is dubbed in English though, as in LOVE AND ANARCHY, the image appears to have been squeezed into the television format.

p, Daniele Senatore, Romano Cardarelli; d, Lina Wertmuller; w, Lina Wertmuller; ph, Dario Di Palma; ed, Franco Fraticelli; m, Piero Piccioni.

Drama **(PR:O MPAA:R)**

SERPENT'S EGG, THE**

(1977, Ger./US) 119m Rialto-De Laurentiis/PAR c (DAS SCHLANGENEI)

Liv Ullmann *(Manuela Rosenberg),* David Carradine *(Abel Rosenberg),* Gert Frobe *(Inspector Bauer),* Heintz Bennent *(Dr. Hans Vergerus),* James Whitmore *(The Priest),* Toni Berger *(Mr. Rosenberg),* Christian Berkel *(Student),* Paula Braend *(Mrs. Hemse),* Edna Bruenell *(Mrs. Rosenberg),* Paul Buerks *(Cabaret Comedian),* Gaby Dohm *(Woman with Baby),* Emil Feist *(Cupid),* Hans Eichler *(Max),* Toni Berger *(Mr. Rosenberg),* Erna Brunnell *(Mrs. Rosenberg),* Georg Hartmann *(Hollinger),* Edith Heerdegen *(Frau Holle),* Lis Mangold *(Mikaela),* Grischa Huber *(Stella),* Hans Quest *(Dr. Silbermann),* Fritz Strassner *(Dr. Soltermann),* Glynn Turman *(Negro).*

Set in poverty-stricken Berlin in 1923, Ingmar Bergman's first film made outside of Sweden is a dark tale of murder, alcoholism, and inhumanity. At the center of the story are Abel Rosenberg (David Carradine) and his former sister-in-law, Manuela (Liv Ullmann), who once participated in a circus act together with her husband (his brother), Max. She now makes ends meet as a prostitute, and he comes looking for her after Max kills himself. Other familiar corpses also end up in the morgue before Manuela and the alcoholic David, who has been questioned by the police, take up residence at a clinic run by David's childhood friend, Dr. Hans Vergerus (Heinz Bennent), who conducts cruel experiments on human subjects. A heavy film, but lacking the insight of much of Bergman's other work, THE SERPENT'S EGG was a failure both at the box office and with the critics. Visually, however, it bears the distinctive stamp of Bergman and his frequent collaborator, famed cinematographer Sven Nykvist. In English.

p, Dino De Laurentiis; d, Ingmar Bergman; w, Ingmar Bergman; ph, Sven Nykvist (Eastmancolor); ed, Petra von Oelffen; m, Rolf Wilhelm.

Drama **(PR:O MPAA:R)**

SEVEN BEAUTIES***½

(1976, It.) 115m Medusa/Cinema 5 c (PASQUALINO SETTEBELLEZZE; AKA: PASQUALINO: SEVEN BEAUTIES)

Giancarlo Giannini *(Pasqualino Frafuso),* Fernando Rey *(Pedro),* Shirley Stoler *(Commandant),* Elena Fiore *(Concettina),* Enzo Vitale *(Don Raffaele),* Mario Conti *(Totonno),* Piero Di Orio *(Francesco),* Ermelinda De Felice *(Mother),* Francesca Marciano *(Carolina),* Lucio Amelio *(Lawyer),* Roberto Herlitzka *(Socialist),* Doriglia Palmi *(Doctor).*

The grotesque casting, surreal images, and the entire production of SEVEN BEAUTIES might lead one to think that Federico Fellini was in charge of this movie, but it was Lina Wertmuller who wrote and directed (and garnered Oscar nominations for both). Pasqualino (Giancarlo Giannini, who received a well-deserved Oscar nomination himself) is a small-time crook in Naples during the dark days of WW II. He has seven ugly sisters, none of whom will probably ever get married, and he is busily supporting them, doing whatever he can do to keep their substantial bodies and souls together. Pasqualino is subjected to the terrors of a German prison camp, where the commandant (Shirley Stoler) forces him to do unspeakable things to her gross form. In an all-out attempt to survive, Pasqualino does whatever is necessary to keep from being killed. A picture of great scope, SEVEN BEAUTIES is filled with many memorable, horrific scenes that linger in the mind long after the film has ended. Stoler, whose portrayal of the grotesque commandant is the *piece de resistance* of the film's visual horrors, has since become a regular on Saturday morning's "Pee-wee's Playhouse." In Italian with English subtitles.

p, Lina Wertmuller, Giancarlo Giannini, Arrigo Colombo; d, Lina Wertmuller; w, Lina Wertmuller; ph, Tonino Delli Colli (Eastmancolor); ed, Franco Fraticelli; m, Enzo Iannacci.

Comedy/Drama **(PR:O MPAA:R)**

SEVEN SAMURAI, THE*****

(1954, Jap.) 200m Toho/COL-Landmark bw (SHICHININ NO SAMURAI; AKA: THE MAGNIFICENT SEVEN)

Takashi Shimura *(Kambei),* Toshiro Mifune *(Kikuchiyo),* Yoshio Inaba *(Gorobei),* Seiji Miyaguchi *(Kyuzo),* Minoru Chiaki *(Heihachi),* Daisuke Kato *(Shichiroji),* Ko Kimura *(Katsushiro),* Kunihori Kodo *(Gisaku),* Kamatari Fujiwara *(Manzo),* Yoshio Tsuchiya *(Rikichi),* Bokuzen Hidari *(Yohei),* Yoshio Kosugi *(Mosuke),* Keiji Sakakida *(Gosaku),* Jiro Kumagai *(Gisaku's Son),* Haruko Toyama *(Gisaku's Daughter-in-Law),* Fumiko Homma *(Peasant Woman),* Ichiro Chiba *(Priest),* Tsuneo Katagiri, Yasuhisa Tsutsumi *(Peasants),* Keiko Tsushima *(Shino),* Toranosuke Ogawa *(Grandfather),* Noriko Sengoku *(Wife from Burned House),* Yu Akitsu *(Husband from Burned House),* Gen Shimizu *(Masterless Samurai),* Jun Tasaki *(Big Samurai),* Isao Yamagata *(Samurai),* Jun Tatari *(Laborer),* Atsushi Watanabe *(Vendor),* Yukiko Shimazaki *(Rikichi's Wife),* Sojin Kamiyama *(Minstrel),* Shimpei Takagi *(Bandit Chief).*

Simply one of the best movies ever made, THE SEVEN SAMURAI covers so much ground, assaults so many emotions, and is so totally satisfying that it emerges as a picture that can be viewed over and over again. The film is set in the 1600s during the Sengoku era, when the once-powerful samurai were coming to the end of their rule. A small, unprotected village, which is regularly pillaged by murderous thieves, comes under the protection of a band of these samurai. Kambei (Takashi Shimura) is a veteran warrior who has fallen on hard times and who answers the villager's appeal for help by gathering six comrades to help defend the town. (Each of the samurai is quickly limned to show us who they are, what they do, and whatever personal quirks they may have.) In return for three small meals daily, the men drill the town on how to fight, but the parties are battling for different reasons—the townspeople desperate to keep lives and property intact, the warriors in it for honor alone. The last of the samurai to join is Kikuchiyo (Toshiro Mifune), a loudmouth who pretends that he is qualified but who is, in reality, a farmer's son who hopes to be accepted by the others. The bandits arrive and a huge battle takes place. In the end, only three of the warriors survive. Akira Kurosawa's classic tells a simple tale, but one so rich with underlying meaning and cinematic technique that no synopsis can do justice to the film's power. Those viewers under the misconception that foreign films are boring should be thrilled by the staging of this film's brutal action sequences, such as the raid on the town, the violent hand-to-hand combat in the pouring rain, and the epic horseback battles. The action is never shown strictly for its own sake, however. All the characters are so carefully etched that we sincerely grieve when they are killed. One of the most successful of all Japanese films, and surely the most accessible. In Japanese with English subtitles.

p, Sojiro Motoki; d, Akira Kurosawa; w, Shinobu Hashimoto, Hideo Oguni, Akira Kurosawa; ph, Asakazu Nakai; ed, Akira Kurosawa; m, Fumio Hayasaka.

Drama **(PR:C MPAA:NR)**

SEVENTH SEAL, THE****

(1956, Swed.) 95m Svensk/Janus bw (DET SJUNDE INSEGLET; RIDDAREN OCH DODEN [THE KNIGHT AND DEATH])

Max von Sydow *(Antonius Block),* Gunnar Bjornstrand *(Squire Jons),* Nils Poppe *(Jof),* Bibi Andersson *(Mia),* Bengt Ekerot *(Death),* Ake Fridell *(Blacksmith Plog),* Inga Gill *(Lisa, Plog's wife),* Maud Hansson *(Tyan, the Accused Witch),* Gunnel Lindgren *(Mute Girl),* Inga Landgre *(Block's Wife),* Bertil Anderberg *(Raval),* Anders Ek *(Doomsday Monk),* Gunnar Olsson *(Church Painter),* Erik Strandmark *(Skat),* Ulf Johansson *(Leader of the Soldiers),* Bengt-Ake Benktsson *(Merchant in Tavern).*

The film that gained Ingmar Bergman an international reputation, THE SEVENTH SEAL is a all-out religious allegory addressing that most-contemplated question, "Does God exist?" Set during a single day in the Middle Ages, the film concerns the philosophical quandary of a knight, Antonius Block (Max von Sydow), who returns from the Crusades to find his country at the mercy of plague and witchhunts. In the midst of his moral and religious confusion, Antonius is visited by Death (Bengt Ekerot), a black-cloaked figure who is ready to call the knight from this earth. Antonius strikes a deal with Death, winning a brief reprieve by inviting him to play a game of chess. Since Death apparently has a soft spot for chess, he agrees. Over the next several hours, Antonius is confronted by some who are unconvinced of God's existence (the Knight's agnostic squire, played by Gunnar Bjornstrand) and some who are (a wandering band of performers). Long hailed as a masterpiece of cinema, the status of THE SEVENTH SEAL (and, more generally, Bergman's place in the pantheon of great filmmakers) has steadily declined over the years, though there can be no doubt that the film's imagery is among the most memorable ever put on film. Whatever one thinks of Bergman's philosophical debates on good and evil and on God and the Devil, his image of Ekerot's Death wandering the countryside will never be forgotten. In Swedish with English subtitles.

p, Allan Ekelund; d, Ingmar Bergman; w, Ingmar Bergman (based on his play "Tramalning"); ph, Gunnar Fischer; ed, Lennart Wallen; m, Erik Nordgren.

Drama **(PR:C MPAA:NR)**

SHADOWS OF FORGOTTEN ANCESTORS***

(1965, USSR) 100m Dovzhenko/Artkino bw (TINI ZABUTYKH PREDKIV; AKA: WILD HORSES OF FIRE)

Ivan Mikolaychuk *(Ivan),* Larisa Kadochnikova *(Marichka),* Tatyana Bestayeva *(Palagna),* Spartak Bagashvili *(Yurko),* N. Grinko *(Batag),* L. Yengibarov *(Miko),* Nina Alisova, A. Gay *(Paliychuks),* N. Gnepovskaya, A. Raydanov *(Gutenyuks),* I. Dzyura *(Ivan as a child),* V. Glyanko *(Marichka as a child).*

A victory of visuals over narrative, this fiercely directed tale of love, set in the western Ukrainian region of Ruthenia some time in the late 1800s, follows Ivan (played as a child by I. Dzyura and as an adult by Ivan Mikolaichuk) who, from the outset, is the victim of fate: his older brother is killed while trying to save the young boy from a falling tree, and his father is bludgeoned by an axe-wielding neighbor. It is also Ivan's fate to fall in love with Marichka (Larisa Kadochnikova), the daughter of his father's murderer. The two young lovers romp through the forests, and swim naked in a watering hole. When Marichka accidentally falls to her death, Ivan is destroyed; eventually, however, he marries Palagna (Tatyana Bestayeva), in the hope that she will be able to bring him a family and happiness. Clearly preferring to tell his story abstractly rather than concretely, director Sergey Paradzhanov assails viewers' eyes with streaks of color and rushes of camera movement, while simultaneously stimulating the ears with sounds best described as revolutionary and industrial—some coming from the *trembita*, an elongated, trumpet-like folk instrument. This was the third film directed (he codirected another) by the Georgian-born Paradzhanov, and it is quite unlike most other Soviet films of the day—a nonpolitical, poetic study of emotions, mysticism, and love. After winning numerous international prizes for this film, Paradzhanov was allowed to make one more, THE COLOR OF POMEGRANATES, before spending a number of years in Soviet labor camps, returning in 1985 with THE LEGEND OF SURAM FORTRESS. The videocassette is subtitled in English.

d, Sergey Paradzhanov; w, Sergey Paradzhanov, Ivan Chendey (based on the story "Tini Zabutykh Predkiu" by Mikhaylo Mikhaylovich Koysyubinskiy); ph, V. Ilyenko (Sovcolor); ed, M. Ponomarenko; m, M. Skorik.

Drama **(PR:A MPAA:NR)**

SHOESHINE***

(1946, It.) 93m Societa Cooperativa Alfa-Lopert bw (SCIUSCIA)

Rinaldo Smordoni *(Giuseppe Filippucci),* Franco Interlenghi *(Pasquale Maggi),* Aniello Mele *(Raffaele),* Bruno Ortensi *(Arcangeli),* Pacifico Astrologo *(Vittorio),* Francesco de Nicola *(Ciriola),* Antonio Carlino *(L'Abruzzese),* Enrico de Silva *(Giorgio),* Antonio Lo Nigro *(Righetoo),* Angelo D'Amico *(Siciliano),* Emilio Cigoli *(Staffera),* Giuseppe Spadaro *(Attorney Bonavino),* Leo Garavaglia *(Commissario),* Luigi Saltamerenda *(Il Panza),* Maria Campi *(La Chiromante),* Irene Smordoni *(Giuseppe's Mother),* Anna Pedoni *(Nannarella).*

Along with THE BICYCLE THIEF and UMBERTO D, this film is one of the three Neo-Realist masterpieces produced through the collaborative efforts of director Vittorio De Sica and screenwriter Cesare Zavattini. Like so many of the films of the Neo-Realist movement, SHOESHINE is simply real life projected on a screen. After spying on a pair of shoeshine boys for a year in war-torn Rome, De Sica and Zavattini decided to bring their story to the screen with two nonprofessionals in the lead roles. Giuseppe (Rinaldo Smordoni) and Pasquale (Franco Interlenghi) are waifs who survive by harassing American soldiers—the only ones in postwar Italy with spare change—into spending a few lire to have their boots cleaned. Despite their bleak surroundings, these shoeshine boys still have innocent dreams and hopes, and, in fact, are saving their earnings to buy a handsome white horse. When Giuseppe's brother approaches them with a black market opportunity to make some quick money, they jump at the chance, buy their dream horse, and refuse to let it out of their sight, even going so far as to sleep in the stable with it. This brief moment in paradise is short-lived, however, and they are arrested, taken to a reformatory, and locked away. The longer they stay in their damp, vermin-infested cells, the more hardened the youngsters become. A powerful indictment of the Italian penal system and, on a larger scale, the brutal inevitability of the loss of innocence. In Italian with English subtitles.

p, Paolo W. Tamburella; d, Vittorio De Sica; w, Cesare Zavattini, Sergio Amidei, Adolfo Franci, Cesare Giulio Viola, Vittorio De Sica (based on a story by Zavattini); ph, Anchise Brizzi; ed, Nicolo Lazzari; m, Alessandro Cicognini.

Prison **(PR:C MPAA:NR)**

SHOOT THE PIANO PLAYER***

(1960, Fr.) 85m Les Films de la Pleiade/Astor bw (TIREZ SUR LE PIANISTE; GB: SHOOT THE PIANIST)

Charles Aznavour *(Charlie Kohler/Edouard Saroyan),* Marie Dubois *(Lena),* Nicole Berger *(Theresa),* Michele Mercier *(Clarisse),* Catherine Lutz *(Mammy),* Albert Remy *(Chico Saroyan),* Jean-Jacques Aslanian *(Richard Saroyan),* Richard Kanayan *(Little Fido Saroyan),* Claude Mansard *(Momo),* Daniel Boulanger *(Ernest),* Serge Davri *(Plyne),* Claude Heymann *(Lars Schmeel),* Alex Joffe *(Stranger),* Boby Lapointe *(Singer),* Alice Sapritch *(Concierge).*

For his follow-up to THE 400 BLOWS (1959), Francois Truffaut chose not to deliver another episode of his autobiography, nor to study childhood, but to pay homage to Hollywood gangster films. Deciding to adapt David Goodis' pulp novel *Down There*, Truffaut chose Charles Aznavour, one of France's most popular singers and songwriters, to play the role of Charlie Kohler, a honky-tonk cafe piano player who has given up his life as the famed concert pianist Edouard Saroyan. He becomes mixed up in the underworld affairs of his brother Chico (Albert Remy), and fears not only for his own safety, but for that of his adolescent brother, Fido (Richard Kanayan). In the process he falls in love with Lena (Marie DuBois) but has trouble mustering the courage to court her. As he gets entangled deeper and deeper in the underworld and in romance, Charlie reveals who he really is, how he got "down there," and why he doesn't ever want to go back. SHOOT THE PIANO PLAYER is a magnificent picture, not because of its debt to the gangster genre, but because of Truffaut's personal approach to that genre. Truffaut doesn't concern himself with plot mechanisms—since those have been provided for him countless times by Hollywood—but instead uses the conventions as a frame upon which to hang his own ideas (in much the same way the science-fiction genre served him in FAHRENHEIT 451). Said Truffaut, "The idea behind SHOOT THE PIANO PLAYER was to make a film without a subject, to express all I wanted to say about glory, success, downfall, failure, women, and love by means of a detective story. It's a grab bag." More than anything, it is a collection of beautifully scripted and photographed moments, many of which do nothing to further the narrative, but give the film a soul. One such moment lasts only a split second: A heartless club owner swears that he is telling the truth and proclaims, "If I am lying, may my mother drop dead." At that instant, Truffaut cuts to a shot of a decrepit old woman dropping to the floor. The casting of Aznavour is brilliant, the actor combining the proper blend of cafe piano man and classical pianist—a figure who loses everything he has ever loved, except his music. Available in a standard format and in its original wide-screen version. In French with English subtitles.

p, Pierre Braunberger; d, Francois Truffaut; w, Francois Truffaut, Marcel Moussy (based on the novel *Down There* by David Goodis); ph, Raoul Coutard (Dyaliscope); ed, Cecile Decugis, Claudine Bouche; m, Georges Delerue.

Crime **(PR:C MPAA:NR)**

SHOP ON MAIN STREET, THE**

(1965, Czech.) 128m Barrandov/Prominent bw (OBCH OD NA KORZE; AKA: THE SHOP ON HIGH STREET)

Jozef Kroner *(Tono Brtko),* Ida Kaminska *(Rosalie Lautmann),* Hana Slivkova *(Evelina Brtko),* Frantisek Zvarik

(Marcus Kolkotsky), Helena Zvarikov *(Rose Kolkotsky),* Martin Holly *(Imro Kuchar),* Martin Gregory *(Katz),* Adam Matejka *(Piti Baci),* Mikulas Ladizinsky *(Marian Peter),* Eugen Senaj *(Blau),* Frantisek Papp *(Andoric),* Gita Misurova *(Andoricova),* Luise Grossova *(Eliasova),* Alojz Kramar *(Balko Baci),* Tibor Vadas *(Tobacconist).*

One of the best-known and most highly praised Eastern European films of the 1960s, THE SHOP ON MAIN STREET is a profoundly moving tragicomedy set against a WW II backdrop of racial hatred and fascism. Tono Brtko (Jozef Kroner) is a carpenter who seems to go through life without any morals or principles to guide him. He is content to just get by, do some carpentry work, and soak his feet, though his domineering wife, Evelina (Hana Slivkova), who longs for a more comfortable existence, tries to force him into a more financially lucrative endeavor—like working for her fascist brother-in-law, Marcus Kolkotsky (Frantisek Zvarik). One evening, Marcus and Evelina's sister, Rose (Helena Zvarikov), pay an unexpected visit. They bring a bagful of food, wine, and gifts, thrilling Evelina but leaving Tono indifferent. Marcus also brings news that Tono has been appointed Aryan comptroller of a Jewish button shop. Evelina is ecstatic at the thought of the money and status the shop will bring, and Marcus is pleased that he is recruited another soldier to their cause. When Tono visits the shop the next day to assume his new position, he informs the aged, rheumatic proprietress, Rozalie Lautmannova (Ida Kaminska), that he is now in charge, but she is too deaf to understand and too blind to read his authorization. Only after a regular customer comes into the shop does Tono learn that the business is completely bankrupt and that the old woman is supported by her fellow Jewish merchants. With no other choice, Tono agrees to the charade of working as Rozalie's assistant, and forms a strong friendship with her that transcends racial, religious, and political conflicts. Codirected by Jan Kadar and Elmar Klos, THE SHOP ON MAIN STREET is a relatively straightforward narrative without the stylistic virtuosity of so many other films by young Eastern European filmmakers. What it lacks in style, however, it makes up for in craftsmanship, intelligence, and universality. By treating a tragic subject with a comic tone, THE SHOP ON MAIN STREET enforces the point that the greatest, most inhumane of disasters can strike anyone, anywhere, at any time. While one cannot help but be charmed by the white-haired Rozalie and her friendship with the well-intentioned Tono, the underlying, historical tragedy of their situation is never forgotten. The film received a Best Foreign-Language Film Oscar in 1965, and a Best Actress nomination for Ida Kaminska in 1966. In Czech with English subtitles.

p, Ladislav Hanus, Jaromir Lukas, Jordan Balurov; d, Jan Kadar, Elmar Klos; w, Jan Kadar, Elmar Klos, Ladislav Grossman (based on the story "Obchod No Korze" by Grossman); ph, Vladimir Novotny; ed, Jaromir Janacek, Diana Heringova; m, Zdenek Liska.

War/Drama **(PR:C-O MPAA:NR)**

SIEGFRIED****

(1924, Ger.) 100m UFA bw (SIEGFRIEDS TOD; AKA: SIEGFRIED'S DEATH)

Paul Richter *(Siegfried),* Margarethe Schon *(Kriemhild),* Theodor Loos *(King Gunther),* Hanna Ralph *(Brunhild),* Georg John *(Mime the Smith/Alberich),* Gertrud Arnold *(Queen Ute),* Hans Carl Muller *(Gerenot),* Erwin Biswanger *(Giselher),* Bernhard Goetzke *(Volker von Alzey),* Hans Adalbert von Schlettow *(Hagen Tronje),* Hardy von Francois *(Dankwart),* Hubert Heinrich *(Werbel).*

Part I of Fritz Lang's two-part DIE NIBELUNGEN, SIEGFRIED, opens as a minstrel sings of the adventures of the title hero (Paul Richter). In flashback, Siegfried is shown forging swords with his master, the smith Mime (Georg John), then venturing forth to make his name and fortune. On a white horse, bearing a magic sword, Siegfried meets and slays a fierce dragon. Told that he will become invulnerable if he bathes in its blood, he does just that, but fails to notice the leaf that falls on his back, leaving one area untouched by the gore. Next, in the realm of the Nibelungs, Siegfried kills the dwarf Alberich (John again) and acquires a helmet that renders its wearer invisible. Bearing the Nibelung riches, Siegfried arrives at the court of King Gunther (Theodor Loos) and falls in love with the king's sister, the beautiful Kriemhild (Margarethe Schon). Before Gunther will consent to a marriage, however, Siegfried must help him win the Icelandic Amazon queen, Brunhild (Hanna Ralph). All seems ready for a romantic happy ending, until court intrigue sets the stage for Siegfried's downfall and KRIEMHILD'S REVENGE, Part II of Lang's version of the *Nibelungenlied.* While Lang, by 1924, was no stranger to big-budget magnificence, nothing he had done yet approached the scope of this epic. The wonderfully composed visuals, filled with pomp and pageantry, with extras and actors used architecturally in perfect balance with the massive set constructions and background dioramas, rival any D.W. Griffith or Cecil B. DeMille spectacle. The sets were real constructions; Lang had not yet joined forces with Eugen Schufftan, the special-effects expert who was to prove so instrumental to the success of the film with which Lang followed DIE NIBELUNGEN, METROPOLIS. Fans of the "Ring" cycle should note that Lang disliked Richard Wagner's music and does not incorporate the composer's reworking of the Siegfried legend here. (SEE: KRIEMHILD'S REVENGE.)

p, Erich Pommer; d, Fritz Lang; w, Thea von Harbou (based on the anonymous poem "Das Nibelungenlied" and various traditional Nordic legends); ph, Carl Hoffmann, Gunther Rittau.

Drama **(PR:C MPAA:NR)**

SILENCE, THE***

(1963, Swed.) 95m Svensk/Janus bw (TYSTNADEN)

Ingrid Thulin *(Ester),* Gunnel Lindblom *(Anna),* Jorgen Lindstrom *(Johan),* Hakan Jahnberg *(Hotel Waiter),* Birger Malmsten *(Restaurant Waiter),* The Eduardini *(The Seven Dwarfs),* Eduardo Gutierrez *(Dwarf Manager),* Lissi Alandh *(Girl in Cabaret),* Leif Forstenberg *(Man in Cabaret),* Nils

Waldt *(Cashier in Cinema),* Birger Lensander *(Usher in Cinema).*

Bergman's final film in his trilogy about faith (following THROUGH A GLASS DARKLY and WINTER LIGHT) is typical of his filmic style: stark, mystic, and loaded with hidden meanings and symbolism. Ester (Ingrid Thulin) is a lesbian intellectual who is strongly attracted to her younger sister Anna (Gunnel Lindblom), the sexually active mother of the ten-year-old Johan (Jorgen Lindstrom). As the threesome are traveling home to Sweden, they are forced to stop in an unnamed country because of Ester's tubercolosis. While Ester gets drunk in her hotel room and masterbates, her sister Anna wanders through the foreign city, spies a couple making love, and finds a companion in the hotel waiter. In the meantime, Johan meets a troupe of midgets staying in the hotel who dress him in women's clothing. Like so many of Bergman's films, this work wanders between the pretentious and the profound. The miniscule dialog and absence of music leave much of the work to the actors who do a fine job projecting the story's drama. As in THROUGH A GLASS DARKLY and WINTER LIGHT, the overriding question in this film has to do with God's existence, though here the ways of the spirit are contrasted with the ways of the flesh. The videocassette is available in both dubbed and subtitled versions.

p, Allan Ekelund; d, Ingmar Bergman; w, Ingmar Bergman; ph, Sven Nykvist; ed, Ulla Ryghe; m, Bo Nilsson, Johann Sebastian Bach.

Drama **(PR:O MPAA:NR)**

SINCERELY CHARLOTTE***

(1986, Fr.) 92m Les Films de la Tour-FR3/New Line c (SIGNE CHARLOTTE)

Isabelle Huppert *(Charlotte),* Niels Arestrup *(Mathieu),* Christine Pascal *(Christine),* Nicolas Wostrikoff *(Freddy),* Jean-Michel Ribes *(Roger),* Philippe Delevingne *(Mathieu's Friend),* Laurence Mercier *(Christine's Mother),* Frederic Bourboulon *(Workman),* Berangere Gros *(Marie-Cecile),* Chantal Bronner *(Marie),* Justine Heynemann *(Emilie),* Baptiste Heynemann *(Vincent).*

In her directorial debut, Caroline Huppert, the older sister of actress Isabelle, has fashioned an entertaining tale of romantic temptation and crumbled memories. Charlotte (Isabelle Huppert) is a chanteuse who, after discovering her lover's fresh corpse, turns for help to Mathieu (Niels Arestup), a former lover she lived with for six years, but has not seen in four. Mathieu is now happily engaged to Christine (Christine Pascal), a pretty-but-safe schoolteacher and mother. Upon seeing Charlotte, Mathieu rediscovers long-forgotten feelings. He wrestles with his desire for Charlotte and his devotion to his Christine, but agrees to help Charlotte prove that she is innocent of her lover's murder. Despite the set-up, SINCERELY CHARLOTTE is not a mystery, but a mature examination of a man who must make a choice between the security of family life and his attachment to the memories of a past lover. Unfortunately, each decision he makes takes him further away from the happiness he seeks. With lesser actors than Huppert and Arestup the film could have been a disaster; as it is, the film teeters on the verge of becoming a ridiculous sexual romp. Fortunately, there is enough talent involved to carry it off. Huppert, one of the best actresses working today, manages to make the deceitful, unloving, destructive Charlotte into the type of woman every man would want as a lover. Although dangerous, she is full of life, impulsive energy, and sensuality. Arestup is also excellent, making the audience sympathize with his wayward character. Many films show man's attraction to the femme fatale, but few capture the victim's emotions as well as SINCERELY CHARLOTTE does. In French with English subtitles.

p, Adolphe Viezzi, Jean Ardy; d, Caroline Huppert; w, Caroline Huppert, Luc Beraud, Joelle Goron; ph, Bruno de Keyzer; ed, Anne Boissel, Jacqueline Thiedot; m, Philippe Sarde.

Drama/Comedy **(PR:C-O MPAA:NR)**

SISTERS OF THE GION****

(1936, Jap.) 70m Daiichi Eiga bw (GION NO SHIMAI)

Isuzu Yamada *(Umekichi, the Elder Sister),* Yoko Umemura *(O-Mocha, the Younger Sister),* Eitaro Shindo, Benkei Shiganoya, Namiko Kawahima, Fumio Okura, Taizo Fukami, Reido Aoi.

This is one of two excellent films (the other being THE OSAKA ELEGY) that director Kenji Mizoguchi made in 1936. Both were made possible by Daiichi Eiga, the failing studio for whom the director was employed, which gave him complete control before it was shuttered. Like so many of Mizoguchi's works, SISTERS OF THE GION focuses on female characters, in this case two sisters, both of whom are *geisha*. Umekichi (Isuzu Yamada) is the elder, an experienced prostitute who has become romantically involved with one of her former clients, a bankrupt merchant. Omocha (Yoko Umemura), the younger sister, has different ideas about men and relationships. Having seen the way men treat women, especially her sister, she decides to take the upper hand, deciding to manipulate, and ultimately to destroy, a young kimono clerk. In a twist of fate that seems to suggest that gender roles are irreversible, both sisters are victimized by the film's end. This elegant, carefully directed tale shows Mizoguchi's early talents. He manages to pull to beautiful performances from his actresses, already establishing himself as one of the great directors of women, and embarking on his career as the greatest cinematic interpreter of the lives of Japanese women. From SISTERS OF THE GION's very beginning, with its rollicking jazz score, Mizoguchi demonstrates his unique mastery of the film frame, moving through the expansive space of a merchant's home in which every last piece of furniture is auctioned off—a masculine material defeat that neatly contrasts with the female romantic defeat at the film's end. In Japanese with English subtitles.

p, Masaichi Nagata; d, Kenji Mizoguchi; w, Yoshikata Yoda (based on a story by Kenji Mizoguchi); ph, Minoru Miki.

Drama **(PR:A-C MPAA:NR)**

SKYLINE***

(1983, Sp.) 83m La Salamandre P.C./Kino c (LA LINEA DEL CIELO)

Antonio Resines *(Gustavo Fernandez),* Beatriz Perez-Porro *(Pat),* Jaime Nos *(Jaime Bos),* Roy Hoffman *(Roy),* Patricia Cisarano *(Elizabeth),* Irene Stillman *(Irene),* Whit Stillman *(Thornton).*

This refreshing comedy follows a Spanish photographer, Gustavo Fernandez (Antonio Resines), as he travels to Manhattan dreaming of fame, but realizing quickly that a camera and famous skyline aren't all that's necessary to assure his success. Gustavo loves New York, but has a hard time fitting and, trying to overcome the language barrier, he enrolls in an English class, in which, unfortunately, he learns nothing of real importance. But while hanging out with the Greenwich Village art crowd, he becomes friends with a southern novelist (Roy Hoffman) infatuated with a woman from Barcelona (Beatriz Perez-Porro). SKYLINE's most notable success is its depiction of Gustavo's interaction with his new friends—Resines perfectly conveying a likable foreigner's attempts to adjust his new surroundings. Yet it is not only his struggle that is fascinating, but also the "customs" that Americans take for granted, which, seen from his perspective, are, indeed, a little strange. Honestly and economically directed by Fernando Colomo, SKYLINE was filmed on a microscopic budget in style that is as simple as its central character, allowing the audience to *feel* the city that nearly envelops the Spaniard. In Spanish and English with English subtitles.

d, Fernando Colomo; w, Fernando Colomo; ph, Angel Luis Fernandez; ed, Miguel Angel Santamaria; m, Manzanita.

Comedy **(PR:C MPAA:R)**

SMALL CHANGE****

(1976, Fr.) 104m Les Films du Carrosse-Les Productions Artistes/NW c (L'ARGENT DE POCHE)

Geory Desmouceaux *(Patrick Desmouceaux),* Philippe Goldmann *(Julien Leclou),* Claudio Deluca *(Mathieu Deluca),* Franck Deluca *(Franck Deluca),* Richard Golfier *(Richard),* Laurent Devlaeminck *(Laurent Riffle),* Bruno Staab *(Bruno Rouillard),* Sebastien Marc *(Oscar),* Sylvie Grezel *(Sylvie),* Pascale Bruchon *(Martine),* Corinne Boucart *(Corinne),* Eva Truffaut *(Patricia),* Jean-Francois Stevenin *(Jean-Francois Richet),* Jean-Francois Gondre *(Oscar's Father),* Chantal Mercier *(Chantal Petit),* Francis Devlaeminck *(M. Riffle),* Christian Lentretien *(M. Golfier),* Laura Truffaut *(Madeleine Doinel),* Francois Truffaut *(Martine's Father),* Yvon Boutina *(Oscar, as an Adult),* Marcel Berbert *(School Principal),* Vincent Touly *(Concierge),* Christine Pelle *(Mme. Leclou),* Nicole Felix *(Gregory's Mother).*

Chiefly a collection of vignettes, this sentimental homage to children and their innocent ways focuses on two young boys, Patrick (Geory Desmouceaux) and Julien (Philippe Goldman). Patrick is a shy, slightly plump boy who looks after his paralyzed father and who is infatuated with a schoolmate's mother. His desire for romance is finally satisfied by the film's end, when he gets his first kiss from schoolgirl Martine (Pascale Bruchon). Julien's life is the polar opposite of Patrick's. Long-haired and neglected, he is a present-day "wild child" (see Truffaut's 1972 THE WILD CHILD) living in a hovel with his hateful mother and grandmother, who are not beyond physically abusing him. At the center of the children's lives is a schoolteacher (Jean-Francois Stevenin), a thoughtful, fatherly man who eventually becomes a parent himself. The film is filled with adorable youngsters: Sylvie, a seven-year-old with two pet fish and a fuzzy elephant purse that her parents won't let her bring to a restaurant; the Deluca brothers, who offer to play barber to save a classmate some money; and little Gregory, a mischievous tyke too charming to incur ire. Director Francois Truffaut worked his screenplay around the children, using them as his inspiration rather than forcing a script on them. The result is a collection of some of the most natural sequences ever filmed. Although the cast is made up of children, parent will appreciate SMALL CHANGE far more than kids will. In French with English subtitles.

d, Francois Truffaut; w, Francois Truffaut, Suzanne Schiffman; ph, Pierre-William Glenn (Eastmancolor, Panavision); ed, Yann Dedet, Martine Barraque; m, Maurice Jaubert.

Drama/Comedy **(PR:C MPAA:PG)**

SMILES OF A SUMMER NIGHT***

(1955, Swed.) 108m Svensk/Rank bw (SOMMARNATTENS LEENDE)

Ulla Jacobsson *(Anne Egerman),* Eva Dahlbeck *(Desiree Armfeldt),* Margit Carlqvist *(Charlotte Malcolm),* Harriet Andersson *(Petra),* Gunnar Bjornstrand *(Fredrik Egerman),* Jarl Kulle *(Count Malcolm),* Ake Fridell *(Frid, the Groom),* Bjorn Bjelvenstam *(Henrik Egerman),* Naima Wifstrand *(Mrs. Armfeldt),* Jullan Kindahl *(Beata),* Gull Natorp *(Malla),* Birgitta Valberg, Bibi Andersson *(Actresses),* Anders Wulff *(Desiree's Son),* Svea Holst *(Dresser),* Hans Straat *(Almgen),* Lisa Lundholm *(Mrs. Almgren).*

One of Ingmar Bergman's finest films, easily his best comedy, SMILES OF A SUMMER NIGHT is set in turn-of-the-century Sweden and takes place primarily at an old country estate, where love permeates the summer air. As a result of the scheming of actress Desiree Armfeldt (Eva Dahlbeck), a group of former, present, and would-be lovers gathers at her mother's country home, including Desiree's one-time lover Fredrik Egerman (Gunnar Bjornstrand); Anne (Ulla Jacobsson), his 20-year-old, still-virgin wife of two years; Fredrik's son, Henrik (Bjorn Bjelvenstam), a theology student little younger than his stepmother; Desiree's current lover, Count Malcolm (Jarl Kulle); and his wife, Charlotte (Margit Carlquist). In the course of this midsummer's eve, Anne runs off with her stepson, Fredrik rekindles his romance with Desiree, and Count Malcolm and Charlotte reconcile their marriage—while the maid, Petra (Harriet Andersson), literally rolls in the hay with a coachman. SMILES OF A SUMMER NIGHT is a delightful comedy, full of blithe spirits, brilliantly evoked. Though Bergman's staging of the affair occasionally suggests a proscenium is just beyond the frame, the ensemble brings joyful veracity to the romantic complications and well-drawn characters. Influenced by Shakespeare's "A Midsummer Night's Dream," Bergman's film provided the inspiration for the Broadway musical "A Little Night Music" and Woody Allen's A MIDSUMMER NIGHT'S SEX COMEDY (1982). In Swedish with English subtitles.

p, Allan Ekelund; d, Ingmar Bergman; w, Ingmar Bergman; ph, Gunnar Fischer; ed, Oscar Rosander; m, Erik Nordgren.

Comedy **(PR:A MPAA:NR)**

SOFT SKIN, THE***½

(1964, Fr.) 116m Les Films du Carrosse-SEDIF/Cinema 5 bw (LA PEAU DOUCE; GB: SILKEN SKIN)

Jean Desailly *(Pierre Lachenay),* Francoise Dorleac *(Nicole Chomette),* Nelly Benedetti *(Franca Lachenay),* Daniel Ceccaldi *(Clement),* Laurence Badie *(Ingrid),* Jean Lanier *(Michel),* Paule Emanuele *(Odile),* Philippe Dumat *(Rheims Cinema Manager),* Pierre Risch *(Canon),* Dominique Lacarriere *(Pierre's Secretary),* Sabine Haudepin *(Sabine),* Maurice Garrel *(Bookseller),* Gerard Poirot *(Franck),* Georges de Givray *(Nicole's Father),* Charles Lavialle *(Night Porter),* Carnero *(Lisbon Organizer),* Catherine Duport *(Young Girl),* Maximilienne Harlaut *(Mme. Leloix).*

One of Truffaut's least successful, most derivative films, THE SOFT SKIN came in reaction to the resounding impact of JULES AND JIM. While the latter concentrates on love in the country, Truffaut's aim in THE SOFT SKIN was, as he put it, "a violent answer to JULES AND JIM. It's as though someone else had made JULES AND JIM . . . [THE SOFT SKIN shows] a truly modern love; it takes place in planes, in elevators; it has all the harassments of modern life." From its opening, THE SOFT SKIN surely does not seem like a Truffaut film. It is distant, restrained—as the title implies, a surface film in which emotions run only skin deep. The story concerns Pierre Lechenay (played by Jean Desailly and named after Truffaut's friend Robert Lechenay), a literary critic with a wife (Nelly Benedetti) and child who falls in love with stewardess Nicole (Francoise Dorleac) after a trip to Lisbon. While THE SOFT SKIN is perhaps Truffaut's weakest film, it can also be considered his most daring. Rather than presenting a conventionally melodramatic love triangle, Truffaut gives us a common, albeit bookish, man whose life is not nearly as romantic as are those of the characters in the Balzac novels he reads. When fate intervenes and Pierre gets his beautiful dream girl, he begins his downward Hitchcockian spiral, an innocent caught up in a situation he cannot control. In THE SOFT SKIN Balzac meets Hitchcock, and the film frame becomes an arena in which Truffaut's two greatest influences do battle. In French with English subtitles.

d, Francois Truffaut; w, Francois Truffaut, Jean-Louis Richard; ph, Raoul Coutard; ed, Claudine Bouche; m, Georges Delerue.

Drama **(PR:C-O MPAA:NR)**

SOLDIER OF ORANGE***½

(1977, Neth.) 165m Rank-Intl. Picture Show c

Rutger Hauer *(Erik),* Jeroen Krabbe *(Gus),* Peter Faber *(Will),* Derek De Lint *(Alex),* Eddy Habbema *(Robby),* Lex Van Delden *(Nico),* Edward Fox *(Col. Rafelli),* Belinda Meuldijk *(Esther),* Susan Penhaligon *(Susan),* Andrea Domburh *(Queen Wilhelmina),* Huib Rooymans *(John),* Dolf De Vries *(Jacques),* Rijk De Gooyer *(Breitner).*

Carefully crafted by veteran Dutch director Paul Verhoeven (ROBOCOP; THE FOURTH MAN), this WW II drama details the effects of Nazi occupation on a group of Dutch students. Erik (well played by Rutger Hauer, familiar to US audiences from such films as NIGHTHAWKS and WANTED: DEAD OR ALIVE) is hesitant to join the resistance effort at first, but once he escapes to England he becomes deeply involved, courageously transporting supplies to his comrades in Holland. After the war, Erik returns to his homeland to find that most of his fellow students and resistance fighters have been killed, including one-time student leader Gus (Jeroen Krabbe, the heavy in NO MERCY and Barbara Hershey's husband in A WORLD APART), while others have come through the war barely affected. An exceptional character study, SOLDIER OF ORANGE is also beautifully photographed Peter De Bont, and the shots of Hauer on the supply boat's windy prow as he travels between Britain and Holland linger in memory long after the film is over. Verhoeven would again work with Krabbe and screenwriter Gerard Soeteman in his haunting THE FOURTH MAN. In Dutch with English subtitles.

p, Rob Houwer; d, Paul Verhoeven; w, Paul Verhoeven, Gerard Soeteman, Kees Holierhoek (based on the autobiography of Erik Hazelhoff Roelfzema); ph, Peter De Bont, Jost Vacano (Eastmancolor); ed, Jane Sperr; m, Rogier Van Otterloo.

War/Drama **(PR:O MPAA:R)**

SOTTO. . .SOTTO**½

(1984, It.) 105m Intercapital/Triumph c

Enrico Montesano *(Oscar),* Veronica Lario *(Ester),* Luisa de Santis *(Adele),* Massimo Wertmuller *(Ginetto),* Mario Scarpetta *(Amilcare),* Isa Danieli *(Rosa),* Elena Fabrizi *(Sora Ines),* Antonia Dell'Atte *(Bellissima),* Renato D'Amore *(Mario),* Alfredo Bianchini *(The Priest).*

This forgettable film from Wertmuller failed to make the impression that SEVEN BEAUTIES and SWEPT AWAY did years earlier. This time Wertmuller's sexist male lead (taking over from Giancarlo Giannini) is the superb Enrico Montesano, playing Oscar, the moderately intelligent, hard-working husband of young and beautiful Ester (Varonica Lario). Their romance is long gone, and Ester has discovered an attraction for her best friend, Adele (Luisa de Santis). Ester confesses to an erotic dream—a reenactment of the famous kissing scene in Alfred Hitchcock's NOTORIOUS in which Ester was Ingrid Bergman to Adele's Cary Grant. Although they hesitate to consummate their love, the women begin a dangerous game that drives the confused and insulted Oscar off the deep end. SOTTO . . . SOTTO (which translates roughly as "subtly" or "softly"—an ironic description of male sexuality) is a well-acted, well-written farce, and is occasionally quite powerful and humorous in its examination of the sexual expectations and traditions underlying the battle of the sexes. Unfortunately, Wertmuller assumes that all her characters are cretins. Oscar is shown as a person of some intelligence, but his reactions to Ester's lesbian desires are far from credible, reducing his character to a dummy for the director instead of a real person as Wertmuller, far less subtly than before, drives home her belief that the male animal is not equipped to understand or appreciate the superior nature of the female. In Italian with English subtitles.

p, Mario Gori, Vittorio Cecchi Gori; d, Lina Wertmuller; w, Lina Wertmuller, Enrico Oldoini (based on a story by Wertmuller); ph, Dante Spinotti; ed, Luigi Zita; m, Paolo Conte.

Drama/Comedy **(PR:O MPAA:R)**

SPETTERS***

(1980, Neth.) 109m VSE/EM c

Toon Agterberg *(Eve),* Maarten Spanjer *(Hans),* Hans Van Tongeren *(Reen),* Marianne Boyer *(Maya),* Renee Soutendijk *(Fientje),* Jeroen Krabbe *(Henkhof),* Rutger Hauer *(Witkamp),* Peter Tuinman, Saskia Ten Batenburg, Yvonne Valkenberg, Rudi Falkenhagen, Albert Abspoel, Hans Veerman, Ben Aerden, Margot Keune.

A flashy, fast-paced drama, SPETTERS is the story of Dutch teenage motorcycle enthusiasts Eve (Toon Agterberg), Hans (Maarten Spanjer), and Reen (Hans Van Tongeren)—all of whom dream of being as tough and successful as motorcycle champ Witkamp (Rutger Hauer). Their youthful rebellion is an empty one, however, and ends tragically for both Reen, who is crippled in an accident, and Eve, who is raped, beaten, and killed by a gang of violent homosexuals. Providing a sexual outlet for the teenagers, and just about every other biker on the wharf, is Fientje (Renee Soutendijk), a conniving creature who runs a greasy spoon with her gay brother. SPETTERS is a violent, action-packed assault on the sensibilities of all but the most hardened filmgoers, not surprising given that it was directed by Paul Verhoeven, who would go on to score a major success in the US with his ultraviolent ROBOCOP (1987). Here he demonstrates his penchant for startling visuals, explicit sex, and graphic violence, though his intelligent direction is anything but careless or irresponsible. The beautiful blonde Soutendijk and Jeroen Krabbe would later costar again in another Verhoeven film, THE FOURTH MAN. The videocassette is available in both dubbed and subtitled (Dutch into English) versions.

p, Joop Van Den Ende; d, Paul Verhoeven; w, Gerard Soeteman; ph, Jost Vacano (Eastmancolor); ed, Ine Schenkkan; m, Ton Scherpenzeel.

Drama **(PR:O MPAA:R)**

SPIES****

(1928, Ger.) 130m UFA/MGM bw (SPIONE; AKA: THE SPY)

Rudolf Klein-Rogge *(Haighi),* Willy Fritsch *(Det. Donald Tremaine),* Gerda Maurus *(Sonia),* Lupu Pick *(Dr. Masimoto),* Fritz Rasp *(Colonel Jellusic),* Lien Deyers *(Kitty),* Craighall Sherry *(Police Chief),* Julius Falkenstein *(Hotel Manager),* Georg John *(Train Conductor),* Paul Rehkopf *(Strotch),* Paul Horbiger *(Franz),* Louis Ralph *(Hans Morrier),* Hertha von Walther *(Lady Leslane),* Hermann Vallentin, Grete Berger.

Fritz Lang followed his astonishing METROPOLIS with this independently produced, tightly edited, rapidly paced thriller about a London spy hunt. When an vital secret document is stolen, Burton Jason (Craighall Sherry) calls in his best man, Agent 326, Donald Tremaine (Willy Fritsch). Meanwhile, the man behind the heist, Haghai (Rudolf Klein-Rogge), who directs an international spy ring, sends Sonia (Gerda Maurus), a Russian emigre, to keep tabs on Agent 326. In the process of carrying out her assignment, however, Sonia falls for Tremaine, and he for her, leading to some special 326 heroics when Haghai holds Sonia prisoner. In perhaps the film's most memorable scene, Haghai, who has taken to disguising himself as a clown, is trapped by Tremaine on a music-hall stage in front of an audience, and chooses to end the whole affair with a bang, bringing down the house. A thriller to its core, SPIES has all of the standard espionage twists and techniques well in place, including chase scenes, secret papers, and even a smash-up of the European Express. The beautiful Maurus does a nice turn as Sonia and Lupu Pick gives an admirable performance as a Japanese envoy involved in the intrigue.

p, Fritz Lang; d, Fritz Lang; w, Thea von Harbou, Fritz Lang (based on a novel by Harbou); ph, Fritz Arno Wagner; m, Werner R. Heymann.

Spy **(PR:A MPAA:NR)**

SPIRIT OF THE BEEHIVE, THE*½**

(1976, Sp.) 98m Querejeta/Kino-Janus c (EL ESPIRITU DE LA COLMENA)

Ana Torrent *(Ana),* Isabel Telleria *(Isabel),* Fernando Fernan Gomez *(Fernando),* Teresa Gimpera *(Teresa),* Jose Villasante *(The Monster),* Lally Soldavilla *(Milagros),* Juan Margallo *(The Fugitive),* Miguel Picazo *(The Doctor).*

Praised by some as the greatest movie ever to come out of Spain, THE SPIRIT OF THE BEEHIVE is a haunting, atmospheric film that focuses on a young girl's obsession with the Frankenstein monster. Ana (Ana Torrent), a charming eight-year-old, lives in a Castillian village in 1940, just after the end of the Spanish Civil War. Although the village has been spared the destruction of battle, the after-effects of war are still felt, and the villagers buckle under Francoist repression. Ana's mother (Teresa Gimpera) shares a dream world with an imaginary lover; her father (Fernando Fernan Gomez) tends a beehive and ponders existence in ongoing work he calls "The Spirit of the Beehive." After watching the 1931 James Whale-Boris Karloff FRANKENSTEIN, Ana begins to worry about the monster, and returns daily to the old house where her 10-year-old sister (Isabel Telleria) says he can be found. Eventually, an escaped convict becomes a surrogate for the monster, but though he is killed, Ana continues to cling to the idea that the monster's spirit exists, holding on to the power of imagination. Slow-moving but lyrical, Victor Erice's stunning feature-film directorial debut carefully recreates the post-Civil War period, but much more is at work here than appears at first glance. SPIRIT OF THE BEEHIVE is a thought-provoking, highly symbolic work about the isolation engendered by Franco's stultifying reign, made by one of a generation of Spanish filmmakers forced to cloak their political messages in allegory. In Spanish with English subtitles.

p, Elias Querejeta; d, Victor Erice; w, Francisco J. Querejeta (based on an idea by Erice, Angel Fernandez Santos); ph, Luis Cuadrado (Eastmancolor); ed, Pablo G. del Amo; m, Luis de Pablo.

Drama (PR:C MPAA:NR)

SPRING SYMPHONY**½

(1983, Ger./E. Ger.) 103m Allianz-Schamoni-ZDF-DEFA/Greentree c (FRUHLINGSSINFONIE)

Nastassia Kinski *(Clara Wieck),* Herbert Gronemeyer *(Robert Schumann),* Rolf Hoppe *(Friedrich Wieck),* Anja-Christine Preussler *(Clara as a Child),* Edda Seippel *(Schumann's Mother),* Andre Heller *(Felix Mendelssohn),* Gidon Kremer *(Nicolo Paganini),* Bernhard Wicki *(Baron von Fricken),* Sonja Tuchmann *(Baroness von Fricken),* Margit Geissler *(Christerl),* Uwe Muller *(Becker),* Gunter Kraa *(Karl Banck),* Inge Marschall *(Clemenza Wieck),* Helmut Oskamp *(Alwien Wieck),* Wolfgang Greese *(Presiding Judge),* Gesa Thoma *(Nanni),* Kitty Mattern *(Princess Starnitz),* Walter Schuster *(Professor Fischhof),* Peter Schamoni *(Publisher Hartel),* H.G. Rohrig *(Music Director Dorn).*

SPRING SYMPHONY treats with fatal reverence the love affair between Robert Schumann and Clara Wieck (one of the most highly praised pianists of her day, she became both Schumann's wife and a major interpreter of his compositions). As the picture opens in Germany in the early 1800s, both the teenage Schumann and the prepubescent Wieck are being touted as virtuosos. Although Clara's father (Schumann's instructor) is perversely possessive of her, the developing daughter (played in adulthood by Nastassja Kinski) becomes attracted to Schumann, and he to her. Most of her time is spent traveling to recitals throughout Europe, earning praise from everyone from Goethe to Mendelssohn to Paganini to Chopin. Meanwhile, Schumann, who has partially crippled his hands through overly strenuous practicing, spends his days composing brilliant works that mainstream music critics fail to appreciate. As Clara gains fame, she regularly includes Schumann's compositions in her repertoire, including his declaration of love for her, the "Spring Symphony" (Symphony No. 1 in B Flat, Op. 38). While the romance between Schumann and Wieck was especially interesting and intense, Peter Schamoni's direction of their story is less than inspired. His reverence may please the Schumann devotees who will hunt this film out, but it does not make for a very interesting picture, and one never senses the excitement of genius that must have existed in the characters' lives. Instead, SPRING SYMPHONY is as staid as the music scene that Schumann et al. fought to reshape. In German with English subtitles.

d, Peter Schamoni; w, Peter Schamoni; ph, Gerard Vandenberg (Fujicolor); ed, Elfie Tillack; m, Robert Schumann.

Biography/Musical (PR:A-C MPAA:PG-13)

STATE OF SIEGE***½

(1972, Fr./US/It./Ger.) 120m Reggana-Cinema 10-Unidis-Euro-Dieter Geissler/Cinema 5 (ETAT DE SIEGE)

Yves Montand *(Philip Michael Santore),* Renato Salvatori *(Capt. Lopez),* O.E. Hasse *(Carlos Ducas),* Jacques Weber *(Hugo),* Jean Luc Bideau *(Este),* Evangeline Peterson *(Mrs. Santore),* Maurice Teynac *(Minister of Internal Security),* Yvette Etievant *(Woman Senator),* Harald Wolff *(Minister of Foreign Affairs),* Nemesio Antunes *(President of the Republic),* Andre Falcon *(Deputy Fabbri),* Mario Montilles *(Fontant),* Jerry Brouer *(Anthony Lee),* Jean-Francois Boggi *(Journalist),* Eugenio Guzman *(Spokesman),* Maurice Jacquemont *(Dean),* Roberto Navarette *(Romero),* Gloria Lass *(Tortured Student),* Alejandro Cohen *(Manuel),* Martha Contreras *(Alicia),* Jacques Perrin *(Telephonist),* Gerard Manneveau *(Bardes),* Aldo Francia *(Dr. Francia),* Gilbert Brandini *(Journalist).*

Taking aim at the repressive right-wing government of a Latin American country (a thinly veiled Uruguay) and the support it received from at least one employee of the US Agency for International Development (AID), Costa-Gavras offers here another tightly knit political thriller along the lines of his Z; MISSING; and THE CONFESSION. Set in the 1970s, STATE OF SEIGE chronicles the kidnaping of AID "traffic expert" Philip Santore (Yves Montand, star of Z and THE CONFESSION) by *Tupamaro*-like left-wing guerrillas, who are determined to prove he is behind the introduction of sophisticated torture methods in their country and in others as well—an international criminal. As they try to extract a confession from the wounded but cool Santore, the government's search begins to zero in on their location, with tension mounting as the guerrilla's demand for a prisoner exchange is refused. When Santore confesses, his captors are left with the difficult decision of whether or not to execute him. Told mostly in flashback and allegedly based on the case of real-life AID officer Daniel Mitrione, STATE OF SIEGE was banned from the American Film Institute theater in Washington upon its release, its opponents arguing that it glorified assassination and was violently anti-American while others cited the first amendment. Never one to pull political punches, Costa-Gavras delivers yet another impassioned, intensely dramatic indictment of the abuse of power. As he is occasionally wont to do, the writer-director stacks the deck in favor of the Leftists, but even you if don't carry Marx with you wherever you go, it will be difficult not to be gripped by STATE OF SIEGE's tense development or to remain unshaken by its underlying allegations and assumptions. In English.

p, Jacques Perrin; d, Constantine Costa-Gavras; w, Franco Solinas, Constantine Costa-Gavras; ph, Pierre-William Glenn (Eastmancolor); ed, Francoise Bonnot; m, Mikis Theodorakis.

Political/Thriller **(PR:C MPAA:PG)**

STATE OF THINGS, THE***½

(1982, US/Ger.) 123m Gray City-Road Movies-V.O. Films/Artificial Eye bw (DER STAND DER DINGE)

Isabelle Weingarten *(Anna),* Rebecca Pauly *(Joan),* Jeffrey Kime *(Mark),* Geoffrey Carey *(Robert),* Camila Mora *(Julia),* Alexandra Auder *(Jane),* Patrick Bauchau *(Friedrich),* Paul Getty III *(Dennis),* Viva Auder *(Kate),* Samuel Fuller *(Joe),* Arturo Samedo *(Production Manager),* Francisco Baiao *(Soundman),* Robert Kramer *(Camera Operator),* Allen Goorwitz *(Gordon),* Roger Corman *(Jerry, a Lawyer),* Martine Getty *(Secretary).*

THE STATE OF THINGS is the innovative and exciting saga of a filmmaker and his crew shooting a movie (a remake of the Hollywood B movie THE MOST DANGEROUS MAN ON EARTH) on the outer edges of Spain. They are stranded with no money and, worse, no film. The adventure begins as the director searches to find an elusive American producer. More interesting than the film itself is its reflection of the real-life situation of director Wim Wenders. Having spent a couple of years on HAMMETT, Wenders turned to Francis Ford Coppola to lend him the necessary funds to keep the production afloat. After a stint in filmmaking limbo, HAMMETT finally emerged, but bearing little resemblance to Wenders' original conception. Wenders' debt to Hollywood movies is once again acknowledged (his first payment was the Nick Ray documentary LIGHTNING OVER WATER in 1978) in the casting of Sam Fuller as a cameraman and Roger Corman as a lawyer. Exquisitely photographed in crisp black and white by Henri Alekan, the veteran cinematographer who would go on to shoot Wenders' WINGS OF DESIRE. In German and English with English subtitles.

p, Chris Sievernich; d, Wim Wenders; w, Wim Wenders, Robert Kramer; ph, Henri Alekan, Fred Murphy; ed, Barbara von Weitershausen, Peter Przygodda; m, Jurgen Knieper.

Drama **(PR:A MPAA:NR)**

STAY AS YOU ARE**

(1978, It./Sp.) 118m San Francisco-Roma-Alex/New Line c (COSI COME SEI)

Marcello Mastroianni *(Giullo),* Nastassia Kinski *(Francesca),* Francisco Rabal *(Lorenzo),* Monica Randal *(Luisa),* Giuliana Calandra *(Teresa),* Ana Pieroni *(Cecilia),* Barbara de Rossi *(Ilaria).*

Nastassia Kinski and Marcello Mastroianni star in this frothy but erotic tale of incest contemplated and committed. He plays 50-year-old Giulio, and she is 18-year-old Francesca, who, he discovers after they've begun an affair, is the daughter of the woman who left him sitting in a movie theater 18 years earlier—meaning that he may or may not be Francesca's father. Giulio agonizes over the moral ramifications of their coupling, while the effervescent Francesca is more interested in getting down to monkey business. Despite the limitations of the script, Mastroianni delivers a well-rounded portrayal of man who is as troubled as he is titillated, but except for Kinski fans always anxious to see *more* of her, STAY AS YOU ARE doesn't have much appeal. The videocassette is dubbed in English.

p, Giovanni Bertolucci; d, Alberto Lattuada; w, Enrico Oldoini, Alberto Lattuada; ph, Luis Alcaine; m, Ennio Morricone.

Comedy/Drama **(PR:O MPAA:NR)**

STOLEN KISSES****

(1968, Fr.) 90m Les Films Du Carrosse-Les Productions Artistes/Almi c (BAISERS VOLES)

Jean-Pierre Leaud *(Antoine Doinel),* Delphine Seyrig *(Fabienne Tabard),* Michel Lonsdale *(M. Tabard),* Claude Jade *(Christine Darbon),* Harry Max *(M. Henri),* Daniel Ceccaldi *(M. Darbon),* Claire Duhamel *(Mme. Darbon),* Catherine Lutz *(Mme. Catherine),* Andre Falcon *(M. Blady),* Paul Pavel *(Julien),* Serge Rousseau *(Stranger),* Christine Pelle *(Secretary),* Marie-France Pisier *(Colette Tazzi),* Jean-Francois Adam *(Albert Tazzi),* Jacques Robiolles *(Unemployed TV Writer),* Martine Ferriere *(Manager of Show Shop),* Simono *(M. Albani),* Roger Trapp *(Hotel Manager),* Jacques Delord *(Magician).*

STOLEN KISSES is the installment in the life of Antoine Doinel (Jean-Pierre Leaud), which began in THE 400 BLOWS and continued through the LOVE AT TWENTY episode entitled "Antoine and Colette." The film picks up as Doinel is discharged from the army at age 20. Unable to make Christine (Claude Jade) love him, he continues his search for the perfect woman. In the process, Doinel lands a job with a detective agency, where the rookie Sherlock Holmes bungles every case he investigates. He finally gets a simple assignment in a shoe store after displaying his "technical proficiency" by wrapping a shoe box. Doinel is supposed to discover why the store's owner, Mons. Tabard (Michel Lonsdale), feels hated and whether there is a conspiracy against him, but while working late one night, he begins an affair with Tabard's wife, Fabienne (Delphine Seyrig). Dismissed, as Truffaut's work often is, as overly charming and simplistic, STOLEN KISSES was oddly enough made during a time of extremely intense political crisis in Paris, with a sidebar of artistic controversy. Dedicated to Henri Langlois and his Cinematheque Francaise, STOLEN KISSES was made while Truffaut worked with a defense committee that fought for the reinstatement of the Cinematheque director. Langlois, who in his lifetime was probably responsible for the film education of every aspiring director in France, was ordered removed by Minister of Culture Andre Malraux—a move met with opposition by the entire international film community. Truffaut stated, "If STOLEN KISSES is good, it will be thanks to Langlois." As violence erupted in the streets of Paris, Truffaut continued his filming, but, instead of making the political film one might expect to emerge from a period of revolt, the director chose to reaffirm his belief in cinema. In French with English subtitles.

p, Marcel Berbert; d, Francois Truffaut; w, Francois Truffaut, Bernard Revon, Claude de Givray; ph, Denys Clerval (Eastmancolor); ed, Agnes Guillemot; m, Antoine Duhamel.

Romance/Comedy **(PR:O MPAA:R)**

STORY OF ADELE H., THE****

(1975, Fr.) 96m Les Films du Carrosse-Les Productions Artistes/NW c (L'HISTOIRE D'ADELE H.)

Isabelle Adjani *(Adele Hugo),* Bruce Robinson *(Lt. Albert Pinson),* Sylvia Marriott *(Mrs. Saunders),* Reuben Dorey *(Mr. Saunders),* Joseph Blatchley *(Mr. Whistler),* Mr. White *(Col. White),* Carl Hathwell *(Lt. Pinson's Orderly),* Ivry Gitlis *(The Magician),* Sir Cecil De Sausmarez *(M. Lenoir),* Sir Raymond Falla *(Judge Johnstone),* Roger Martin *(Dr. Murdock),* Madame Louise *(Mme. Baa),* Jean-Pierre Leursse *(The Scribe),* Louis Bourdet *(Victor Hugo's Servant),* Clive Gillingham *(Keaton),* Francois Truffaut *(Officer On Ramparts),* Ralph Williams *(Canadian),* Thi Loan N'Guyen *(Chinese Woman),* Edward J. Jackson *(O'Brien).*

Truffaut's hauntingly poetic tale of obsession stars the beautiful Isabelle Adjani as Adele Hugo, daughter of France's most beloved author, Victor Hugo. The picture opens in Halifax, Nova Scotia, in 1863, after Adele has left her father's Guernsey home in order to seek out her fiance, Albert Pinson (Bruce Robinson), a young English lieutenant who wants nothing to do with the determined girl. Although her obsession with Pinson grows to the point that she announces a pending engagement to her father, Adele's only real "contact" with him is from a distance—spying on him while he makes love to another woman, following him (or those she believes to be him) in the streets. Adele is obsessed not only with the lieutenant, but also with her own writing, paying frequent visits to a local bookstore where she buys reams of paper and then retreating to her room to scrawl indecipherable coded messages in her journal. One of Truffaut's most complex films, a love story that shows only one half of an affair, THE STORY OF ADELE H. combines the fascination with obsessive women that fills his films (Catherine from JULES AND JIM, Julie Kohler from THE BRIDE WORE BLACK, Camille Bliss from SUCH A GORGEOUS KID LIKE ME) with his love of books, diaries, and the process of writing (FAHRENHEIT 451 and THE WILD CHILD). The true story of Adele Hugo is already engrossing—unable to live up to her father's expectations, she felt she could not fill the void in his heart after his favorite daughter, Leopoldine, drowned—and Truffaut's disturbing film on the subject is as difficult to walk away from as it is to watch. An Academy Award nomination for Best Actress went to Adjani. Truffaut makes a cameo appearance as a man Adele mistakes for her lover. In French and English with English subtitles.

p, Marcel Berbert; d, Francois Truffaut; w, Francois Truffaut, Jean Gruault, Suzanne Schiffman, Jan Dowson (based on the book *Le Journal d'Adele Hugo* by Frances V. Guille); ph, Nestor Almendros (Eastmancolor); ed, Yann Dedet, Martine Barraque; m, Maurice Jaubert.

Biography **(PR:C-O MPAA:PG)**

STRAY DOG***½

(1949, Jap.) 122m Shintoho-Toho bw (NORA INU)

Toshiro Mifune *(Murakami),* Takashi Shimura *(Sato),* Ko Kimura *(Yuro),* Keiko Awaji *(Harumi),* Reisaburo Yamamoto *(Hondo),* Noriko Sengoku *(Girl).*

This gripping, but somewhat flawed, Akira Kurosawa film details the efforts of young police detective Murakami (Toshiro Mifune) to recover his pistol after it is stolen from him on a crowded bus. Murakami becomes obsessed with finding the gun, taking personal responsibility for all the crimes committed with it—including murder—chasing his own criminal impulses by vicariously experiencing the killer's deeds. Kurosawa has indicated that he considers STRAY DOG a failure in its concern with technique over character. While the analysis is debatable, technical lapses do mar the film more than the script or performances. A sloppy pace; indifferent narration; and an unbearably long montage sequence comprising nearly 10 minutes of dissolves, double-exposures, etc., distract from the fascinating character study and threaten to collapse the whole film under a ponderous weight. Despite this, STRAY DOG is a powerful film and well worth seeing. In Japanese with English subtitles.

p, Sojiro Motoki; d, Akira Kurosawa; w, Ryuzo Kikushima, Akira Kurosawa (based on a novel by Kurosawa); ph, Asakazu Kakai; ed, Yoshi Sugihara; m, Fumio Hayasaka.

Crime **(PR:A-C MPAA:NR)**

STROMBOLI**

(1949, It.) 81m Be-Ro/RKO bw

Ingrid Bergman *(Karin Bjiorsen),* Mario Vitale *(Antonio),* Renzo Cesana *(The Priest),* Mario Sponza *(The Lighthouse Keeper).*

The film that began the pairing of Roberto Rossellini and Ingrid Bergman on and off the screen, STROMBOLI was also the first and last picture that the great Italian director would make for Hollywood. Funded by Howard Hughes, who recognized Bergman's box-office appeal and who had designs on the actress himself, STROMBOLI was photographed on the title volcanic island. Although it was reportedly severely mangled in the editing, compelling Rossellini to denounce the US version (the only one available), it remains a pivotal film in the director's career—a meeting of the documentary and the Hollywood tradition, as represented by Bergman's star quality. So as not to distract from Bergman's beauty or of the ashen surroundings, the plot is kept simple: Karin (Bergman) is a Lithuanian war refugee whose only means of escaping from an internment camp is to wed Antonio (Mario Vitale), a fisherman from Stromboli. She lives on the island with him, but cannot fit in with the locals, and the island becomes nothing more to her than another internment camp, from which escape seems impossible. In English.

p, Roberto Rossellini; d, Roberto Rossellini; w, Roberto Rossellini, Art Cohn, Renzo Cesana, Sergio Amidei, C.P. Callegari; ph, Otello Martelli; ed, Roland Gross, Jolanda Benvenuti (uncredited, Alfred Werker, U.S. version); m, Renzo Rossellini.

Drama **(PR:C-O MPAA:NR)**

SUBWAY**

(1985, Fr.) 104m Gaumont-Films du Loup-TEF-TF1/ Island Alive c

Isabelle Adjani *(Helena),* Christopher Lambert *(Fred),* Richard Bohringer *(The Florist),* Michel Galabru *(Inspector Gesberg),* Jean-Hugues Anglade *(The Roller Skater),* Jean-Pierre Bacri *(Batman),* Jean Bouise *(Station Master),* Pierre-Ange Le Pogam *(Jean),* Jean Reno *(The Drummer),* Arthur Simms *(The Singer),* Constantin Alexandrov *(The Husband),* Jean-Claude Lecas *(Robin),* Eric Serra *(The Bassist),* Benoit Regent *(Salesman).*

SUBWAY is DIVA with no brains—a film of all style and little substance. Ah, but what style! At the tender age of 26, Luc Besson had already directed LE DERNIER COMBAT and shown that he possessed a wondrous eye and the ability to make a good-looking film for a pittance. Next, Besson infused SUBWAY with his great visual flair and delivered a funny film that no one could take seriously. Fred (Christopher Lambert) is a punkishly coiffed, mysterious blonde who sets up a plan to extort money from Helena (Isabelle Adjani), the young, bored wife of a wealthy businessman. An interesting thing about Fred is that he lives in the winding, hidden tunnels beneath the Paris Metro, along with numerous other colorful characters: The Florist (Richard Bohringer), a florist who specializes in shifty deals; Roller (Jean-Hugues Anglade), a roller-skating purse snatcher; and a rock'n'roll band that Fred eventually manages. The slim plot is mostly a setup for dazzling visuals (the great Alexandre Trauner was the film's designer) and breakneck chases underground, giving the impression that SUBWAY is nothing but an extended rock video. The most impressive visual of the film is not a technical achievement, however, but the face of Adjani, who gets little chance to act but who does get numerous opportunities to traipse around in fancy costumes. The films salutory opening epigram reads: "To Be Is To Do . . .—Sartre, To Do Is To Be . . .—Camus, Do Be Do Be Do . . .,—Sinatra." SUBWAY did win some praise from the French film industry, garnering a much-deserved Cesar for Art Direction and a thoroughly incomprehensible Best Actor award to Lambert, who gives what is essentially a stylish nonperformance. The videocassette is dubbed in English.

p, Luc Besson, Francois Ruggieri; d, Luc Besson; w, Luc Besson, Pierre Jolivet, Alain Le Henry, Marc Perrier, Sophie Schmit; ph, Carlo Varini; ed, Sophie Schmit; m, Eric Serra, Rickie Lee Jones.

Crime **(PR:C-O MPAA:R)**

SUGAR CANE ALLEY***

(1983, Fr./Martinique) 103m Sumafa-Orca-N.E.F. Diffusion/Orion-Artifical Eye c (LA RUE CASES NEGRES; Trans: Street Of Black Shacks)

Garry Cadenat *(Jose),* Darling Legitimus *(M'Man Tine),* Douta Seck *(Medouze),* Joby Bernabe *(M. Saint-Louis),* Francisco Charles *(Le Gereur),* Marie-Jo Descas *(Leopold's Mother),* Marie-Ange Farot *(Mme. Saint-Louis),* Henri Melon *(M. Roc),* Eugene Mona *(Douze Orteils),* Joel Palcy *(Carmen),* Laurent St. Syr *(Leopold),* Mathieu Crico, Virgine Delaunay-Belleville, Tania Hamel, Maite Marquet, Dominique Arfi, Emilie Blameble, Norita Blameble.

Set in the French colony of Martinique in the 1930s, this film—both stark and charming—takes a look at life in "Rue Cases Negres," a wooden shack community isolated in the middle of a sugar plantation. While the adults toil in the fields, the children romp the "alley," but for many of the youngsters this will be their last summer on the plantation. The brightest among them will find better jobs or go on to school, while the less fortunate will remain to assist their parents in the fields. Most prominently featured is Jose (Garry Cadenat), a frolicsome 11-year-old who earns a prestigious scholarship to a high school at Fort-de-France. This well-acted film is an unexpected delight, showing that a ray of hope can materialize amidst the despondency of shantytown. SUGAR CANE ALLEY was a double prize winner at the Venice Film Festival, the film taking a Silver Lion and Darling Legitimus garnering a Best Actress award. In French with English subtitles.

p, Michel Loulergue, Alix Regis; d, Euzhan Palcy; w, Euzhan Palcy (based on the novel *La Rue Cases Negres* by Joseph Zobel); ph, Dominique Chapius (Fujicolor); ed, Marie-Josephe Yoyotte; m, Groupe Malavoi, Roland Louis, V. Vanderson, Brunoy Tocnay, Max Cilla, Slap Cat.

Drama **(PR:C MPAA:PG)**

SUGARBABY***½

(1985, Ger.) 86m Pelemele/Kino c (ZUCKERBABY)

Marianne Sagebrecht *(Marianne),* Eisi Gulp *(Huber 133),* Toni Berger *(Old Subway Driver),* Manuela Denz *(Huber's Wife),* Will Spindler *(Funeral Director),* The Paul Wurges Combo *(Dance Hall Band),* Hans Stadlbauer.

SUGARBABY is the dynamic and delightful story of Marianne (Marianne Sagebrecht), a hugely overweight mortuary attendant who, while going to work one morning on the subway, becomes infatuated with the conductor, Huber 133 (Eisi Gulp), a handsome, blonde young man in a tight-fitting uniform. She is determined to win him over, but must go to great lengths to find him, since route numbers and schedules change on a complicated basis. In the meantime, she prepares herself for her future lover, buying sexy lingerie (which must be specially ordered in her size), flashy high heels, and pink satin sheets. Although it seems likely that all this preparation will backfire, Huber, nicknamed *Zuckerbaby* by Marianne, accepts her invitation to dinner. SUGARBABY is a lighthearted, fun, energetic, and fresh addition to German film, but is not a piece of fluff. Unlike so many other German film characters (Don Lope de

Aguirre in Werner Herzog's AGUIRRE, THE WRATH OF GOD, for example), Sagebrecht's "Marianne" is a lovable person with whom you could enjoy spending time in the real world. Director Percy Adlon combines the free-spirited energy of his characters with technique to match, fashioning a magnificent lighting scheme that relies heavily on color effects, a minimalist set reduced to barest essentials, and a frantic camera style that allows the camera to wander, sway, and zig-zag through the set. Adlon's direction is fun—he lets no barriers stand in his way and, as a result, the entire picture is an engaging, intelligent entertainment. In German with English subtitles.

d, Percy Adlon; w, Percy Adlon; ph, Johanna Heer; ed, Jean-Claude Piroue.

Drama/Comedy (PR:C-O MPAA:NR)

SUMMER***½

(1986, Fr.) 98m Losange/Orion c (LE RAYON VERT; GB: THE GREEN RAY)

Marie Riviere *(Delphine),* Lisa Heredia *(Manuella),* Beatrice Romand *(Beatrice),* Rosette *(Francoise),* Eric Hamm, *(Edouard),* Vincent Gauthier *(Jacques),* Carita *(Lena),* Joel Comarlot *(Joel),* Amira Chemakhi, Sylvia Richez, Basile Gervaise, Virginie Gervaise, Rene Hernandez, Dominique Riviere, Claude Jullien, Alaric Jullien, Laetitia Riviere, Isabelle Riviere, Marcello Pezzutto, Irene Skobline, Gerard Quere, Brigitte Poulain, Gerard Leleu, Liliane Leleu, Vanessa Leleu, Huger Foote.

SUMMER is the fifth in Eric Rohmer's series of "Comedies and Proverbs" begun with THE AVIATOR'S WIFE (1981), a film that also starred the lovely Marie Riviere. It's August in Paris, and the natives have gone on holiday, leaving the city to the throngs of tourists. Delphine (Riviere), however, has nowhere to go, having missed out on a planned trip to Greece when her girl friend decided to go with her new lover instead. Depressed, lonely, and loveless, Delphine is determined to take a vacation before the start of her fall term at college. After accepting an invitation to stay in a friend's vacated Biarritz apartment, Delphine meets Lena (Carita), a blonde Swedish playgirl who makes every effort to pull her out of her melancholy, although ultimately Delphine must gain insight on her own. Since his rise to prominence in the late 1950s, director-writer Rohmer has consistently delivered small but wonderful romantic episodes. Rather than filming events or spectacles, he films people—usually lovelorn Parisians on a stubborn quest. Here Delphine is the stubborn one—determined not to be stuck in Paris and to find a lover who will bring her happiness, even if her determination makes her unhappy. Riviere remarked that Rohmer "had seen some women alone on the beach on holiday and he noticed sometimes that women were looking for men in newspaper advertisements. He wanted to explore this loneliness of young women who are not ugly, who have nothing wrong with them, but who are still alone." Filming with a typically small crew, shooting on 16mm film, and allowing his cast to improvise, Rohmer made one of his most refreshing and natural films to date in SUMMER. The film won the Golden Lion at the Venice Film Festival, although the French Cesars mysteriously overlooked it in all categories. In French with English subtitles.

p, Margaret Menegoz; d, Eric Rohmer; w, Eric Rohmer; ph, Sophie Maintigneux; ed, Maria-Luisa Garcia; m, Jean-Louis Valero.

Drama (PR:O MPAA:R)

SUMMER INTERLUDE***

(1951, Swed.) 96m Svensk/Gaston Hakim bw (SOMMARLEK; AKA: ILLICIT INTERLUDE; SUMMERPLAY)

Maj-Britt Nilsson *(Marie),* Alf Kjellin *(David Nystrom),* Birger Malmsten *(Henrik),* Georg Funkquist *(Uncle Erland),* Renee Bjorling *(Aunt Elisabeth),* Mimi Pollack *(Black-clad Woman),* Anna Lisa Ericsson *(Kaj),* Stig Olin *(Ballet Master),* Gunnar Olsson *(Clergyman),* John Botvid *(Karl),* Douglas Hage *(Nisse),* Julia Caesar *(Maja),* Carl Strom *(Sandell),* Torsten Lilliecrona *(Lighting Man),* Marianne Schuler *(Kerstin),* Ernst Bruman *(Capt. on Steamer),* Olav Riego *(Doctor).*

During a dress rehearsal of "Swan Lake," Marie (Maj-Britt Nilsson), a ballerina, receives a diary she had written many years before, when she was involved in a romance with Henrik (Birger Malmsten), a young student. While she reads the diary, the film slips into three flashbacks, showing the courtship and love affair between the two. One of Bergman's favorites among his own films, SUMMER INTERLUDE (strangely retitled ILLICIT INTERLUDE for its US release) has a complex episodic structure and makes fine use of lighting to create an effective ambience for the flashback sequences. In Swedish with English subtitles.

p, Allan Ekelund; d, Ingmar Bergman; w, Ingmar Bergman, Herbert Grevenius (based on a story by Ingmar Bergman); ph, Gunnar Fischer, Bengt Jarnmark; ed, Oscar Rosander; m, Erik Nordgren, Pyotr Ilich Tchaikovsky.

Drama (PR:O MPAA:NR)

SUNDAY IN THE COUNTRY, A****

(1984, Fr.) 94m Sara-A2/MGM-UA c (UN DIMANCHE A LA CAMPAGNE)

Louis Ducreux *(Mons. Ladmiral),* Sabine Azema *(Irene),* Michel Aumont *(Gonzague/Edouard),* Genevieve Mnich *(Marie-Therese),* Monique Chaumette *(Mercedes),* Claude Winter *(Mme. Ladmiral),* Thomas Duval *(Emile),* Quentin Ogier *(Lucien),* Katia Wostrikoff *(Mireille),* Valentine Suard, Erika Faivre *(Little Girls),* Marc Perrone *(Accordionist).*

This beautiful film details a day in the life of an elderly painter, Ladmiral (Louis Ducreux), a holdover from the days of the French Impressionists. On one average Sunday in 1912, Ladmiral entertains his son (Michel Aumont) and the latter's family. They walk through the picturesque grounds of Ladmiral's country estate, prepare dinner, and tell wonderful stories about life and art. Unexpectedly, Ladmiral's daughter Irene (Sabine Azema) also pays a rare visit. Although Irene is the troubled outcast of the family, she is still her father's favorite, making this otherwise average Sunday exciting and worthwhile. The story line may appear simple and undramatic, but the film's beauty lies in this simplicity. The old painter's Sunday is serene. An old man who has lived a quiet life and enjoys reminiscing, his surroundings are bathed in a peaceful light, his canvas quietly awaits his artistic touch. The sum of these simple parts is a rich view of life. Betrand Tavernier, named Best Director at the Cannes Film Festival for this film, successfully evokes the essence of French life in the early 20th century. "I wanted to make a film that would be based entirely on feelings," Tavernier has said, "a film where emotions could reach a peak simply because a young woman leaves her father a bit early on a Sunday afternoon—that's the only dramatic moment in the film. I found it irresistible." Tavernier and cinematographer Bruno de Keyzer have made a conscious effort to attain, on film, the appearance of French Impressionist painting. In fact, A SUNDAY IN THE COUNTRY is nothing short of a painting come to life. In French with English subtitles.

p, Alain Sarde; d, Bertrand Tavernier; w, Bertrand Tavernier, Colo Tavernier (based on the novella *Monsieur Ladmiral Va Bientot Mourir* by Pierre Bost); ph, Bruno de Keyzer (Eastmancolor); ed, Armand Psenny; m, Gabriel Faure, Louis Ducreux, Marc Perrone.

Drama **(PR:A MPAA:G)**

SUNDAYS AND CYBELE***

(1962, Fr.) 110m Terra-Fides-Orsay-Trocadero/Davis-Royal COL bw (LES DIMANCHES DE VILLE D'AVRAY; CYBELE)

Hardy Kruger *(Pierre)*, Patricia Gozzi *(Francoise)*, Nicole Courcel *(Madeleine)*, Daniel Ivernel *(Carlos)*, Michel de Re *(Bernard)*, Andre Oumansky *(Nurse)*, Anne-Marie Coffinet, Alain Bouvette, Rene Clermont, Malka Ribovska, Jocelyne Loiseau, Renee Duchateau, Raymond Pelissier, Martine Ferriere, Maurice Garrel, France Anglade, Albert Hugues.

After accidentally killing a young girl on a bombing mission in the Indochinese War, Pierre (Hardy Kruger) returns to France and takes up residence in a small town near Paris, becoming friendly with a 12-year-old girl (Patricia Gozzi) who lives in a nearby convent orphanage. Pretending to be her father, Pierre, who suffers from bouts of amnesia as a result of war trauma, begins spending Sundays with the precocious child. A close, warm friendship builds between them, and they decide to spend Christmas together. However, friends of the woman with whom Pierre lives (Nicole Courcel) take a dark view of his relationship with the girl and call the police, who arrive on the scene just as "Francoise" has revealed to Pierre, as a Christmas gift, her real name, Cybele. Director-cowriter Serge Bourguignon treats a sensitive subject with grace here, and the result is in a warm, often poignant film, although his presentation tends to call attention to the film's style at the expense of substance. The true heart of the picture is the marvelous chemistry between Kruger and Gozzi, with the added benefit of Henri Decae's fine photography. The film won an Oscar as Best Foreign-Language Film of 1962.

p, Romain Pines; d, Serge Bourguignon; w, Serge Bourguignon, Antoine Tudal, Bernard Eschasseriaux (based on the novel *Les Dimanches de Ville d'Avray* by Eschasseriaux); ph, Henri Decae; ed, Leonide Azar; m, Maurice Jarre.

Drama **(PR:C MPAA:NR)**

SWANN IN LOVE**½

(1984, Fr./Ger.) 110m Orion c (UN AMOUR DE SWANN)

Jeremy Irons *(Charles Swann)*, Ornella Muti *(Odette De Crecy)*, Alain Delon *(Baron De Charlus)*, Fanny Ardant *(Duchesse de Guermantes)*, Marie-Christine Barrault *(Mme. Verdurin)*, Ann Bennent *(Chloe)*, Nathalie Juvent *(Mme. Cottard)*, Charlotte Kerr *(Sous-Maitresse)*, Humbert Balsan *(Head of Protocol)*, Jean Aurenche *(Mons. Vinteuil)*, Veronique Dietschy *(Mlle. Vinteuil)*, Philippine Pascale *(Mme. De Gallardon)*, Charlotte de Turckheim *(Mme. de Cambremer)*, Jean-Francoise Balmer *(Mons. Cottard)*, Jean-Louis Richard *(Mons. Verdurin)*, Jacques Boudet *(Duc De Guermantes)*, Bruno Thost *(Saniette)*, Roland Toper *(Biche)*, Nicolas Baby *(Juif)*, Catherine Lachens *(Mme. V.'s Guest)*.

It took four writers, several production companies, and the French Ministry of Culture to make this adaptation of the beginning of Marcel Proust's monumental *Remembrance of Things Past*. Jeremy Irons is Charles Swann, a wealthy Jewish intellectual who has overcome anti-Semitism in 19th-century Paris and managed to become part of *le haute monde*. The film shows his courtship and socially suicidal marriage to the courtesan Odette (Ornella Muti), condensing part of Proust's seven-volume work into a single day in the life of Swann. The couple's affair is shown in flashback as recalled by Swann, revealing that he has married this woman, his complete opposite, without benefit of really loving (much less liking) her. Paralleling this story is that of Swann's friend, the aesthete homosexual Baron de Charlus (Alain Delon), and his effort to seduce an unwilling young man. Directed by Volker Schlondorff, who made THE TIN DRUM and the Dustin Hoffman TV film of "Death of a Salesman," SWANN IN LOVE reflects a similar dedication to bringing great literature to the screen, but Schlondorff's style is more suited to Gunther Grass and Arthur Miller than to the unhurriedly subtle Proust. The film does lavishly re-create the period milieu and features some beautiful location settings shot by the great Sven Nykvist, as well as a top cast, but the filmmakers seem to have been too intimidated by the original material to have come up with the kind of truly satisfying, original cinematic work that would have justified the effort. In English.

p, Margaret Menegoz; d, Volker Schlondorff; w, Volker Schlondorff, Peter Brook, Jean-Claude Carriere, Marie-Helene Estienne (based on the novel *Un Amour de Swann* by Marcel Proust); ph, Sven Nykvist; ed, Francoise Bonnot; m, Hans Werner Henze, David Graham, Gerd Kuhr, Marcel Wengler.

Drama **(PR:C-O MPAA:R)**

SWEET COUNTRY**

(1987, US/Gr.) 120m Playmovie-Greek Film Centre/ Cinema Group c

Jane Alexander *(Anna Willing),* John Cullum *(Ben Willing),* Carole Laure *(Eva Maria Araya),* Franco Nero *(Paul Dumont),* Joanna Pettet *(Monica Araya),* Randy Quaid *(Juan),* Irene Papas *(Mrs. Araya),* Jean-Pierre Aumont *(Mr. Araya),* Pierre Vaneck *(Father Venegas),* Katia Dandoulaki *(Sister Mathilda),* Yannis Voglis *(Max),* Ann Coleman *(Dorothy),* Dimitris Poulikakos *(Torturer),* Betty Valassi *(Sara),* Saun Ellis *(Evelyn),* Yula Gavala *(Pauline),* Lea Hatzopoulou-Karavia *(Angry Woman),* Marianna Toli *(Ira),* Aspa Nakopoulou *(Mrs. Ortega),* Alexis Revidis *(Mr. Ortega),* Myrto Liati *(Jane),* Emily Rose Yiaxi *(Maria Paz),* Yannis Kakleas *(Jose),* Alexandros Mylonas *(Search Officer),* Ann Hodgson *(Kay),* Penelope Pitsouli *(Waitress),* Spyros Mavidis *(Rebellious Soldier).*

Set in Chile against the backdrop of the September 1973 Rightist military coup that followed the assassination of President Salvador Allende, SWEET COUNTRY explores the emotional turmoil that befalls an American couple living under military rule. Beginning in New York at the screening of a smuggled documentary, the story flashes back to Chile in 1973, after Anna Willing (Jane Alexander), an American who lived in Chile during the political upheaval, is injured by a bomb that goes off in the theater. The film then depicts the intrigue that she and her university professor husband, Ben (John Cullum), became involved in when they begin taking sides against the junta. A talky, uninvolving movie, SWEET COUNTRY has more than its share of problems and never approaches the level of intensity attained by such films as Costa-Gavras' STATE OF SIEGE (which also deals with the Chilean situation); Z; or MISSING. While the story (scripted by director Michael Cacoyannis from a novel by Caroline Richards) is potentially explosive, the film's uneven pacing and the over-the-top histrionics of the horribly miscast performers undermine its value. Randy Quaid, who plays his leering military policeman with all the subtlety of a "Saturday Night Live" sketch, is simply in the wrong movie, though Alexander fares better. In English.

p, Michael Cacoyannis, Costas Alexakis; d, Michael Cacoyannis; w, Michael Cacoyannis (based on a novel by Caroline Richards); ph, Andreas Bellis; Dinos Katsourides; ed, Michael Cacoyannis; m, Stavros Xarhakos.

Drama **(PR:O MPAA:R)**

SWEPT AWAY. . .BY AN UNUSUAL DESTINY IN THE BLUE SEA OF AUGUST*½**

(1974, It.) 116m Medusa/Cinema 5 c (AKA: SWEPT AWAY)

Giancarlo Giannini *(Gennario Carunchio),* Mariangela Melato *(Raffaella Pancetti).*

On a chartered yacht, a group of wealthy northern Italians discuss a variety of topics while basking in the sun. The snobbish Raffaella (Mariangela Melato) takes particular delight in taunting Gennario (Giancarlo Giannini), a Sicilian deckhand, ridiculing his smelly shirt and communist ideology. Surely, Gennario is the last man on earth Raffaella would ever want to be shipwrecked with on a deserted isle . . . SWEPT AWAY is a wild romp, and certainly lives up to its elongated title. When destiny does indeed shipwreck the two, none of Raffaella's arrogance can keep this two-person war between the sexes and classes from taking some passionately amorous turns. Director-screenwriter Lina Wertmuller's 11th film (the fourth to gain a US release) provoked much controversy for what many perceived as a reactionary, sexist treatment of Raffaella by Wertmuller, a self-described feminist. The argument has merit, although it ignores the broadness of Wertmuller's treatment here of some of her favorite themes. Gender and class politics are ever-present throughout the story, but laced with a delightfully satiric bite that provokes laughter as well as thought. Giannini and Melato are perfectly matched as the combatants/lovers, providing a chemistry that lends Wertmuller's parable naturalism and honesty. With lesser actors, the story might never have worked, and certainly wouldn't have made such a splash at the box office. The videocassette is dubbed in English.

p, Romano Cardarelli; d, Lina Wertmuller; w, Lina Wertmuller; ph, Giulio Battiferri, Giuseppe Fornari, Stefano Ricciotti; m, Piero Piccioni.

Drama/Comedy **(PR:O MPAA:R)**

SWORD OF DOOM, THE***

(1966, Jap.) 122m Toho bw (DAIBOSATSU TOGE)

Tatsuya Nakadai *(Ryunosuke Tsukue),* Toshiro Mifune *(Toranosuke Shimada),* Yuzo Kayama *(Hyoma Utsuki),* Michiyo Aratama *(Ohama),* Ichiro Nakaya *(Bunnojo Utsuki).*

At the center of this compelling picture is Tsukue, an unceasingly violent samurai who habitually kills by the sword to prove his own existence. Driven by this need, he seeks out opponents to prove himself against; however, he is not beyond killing the innocent, such as the old man he slays at the beginning of the film. Interwoven with Tsukue's story is the tale of another samurai, Hyoma Utsuki (Yuzo Kayama), who takes up the sword to avenge the murder of his brother, one of Tsukue's victims. Although Toshiro Mifune is billed as Nakadai's costar, his appearance here is a brief one.

p, Sanezumi Fujimoto; d, Kihachi Okamoto; w, Shinobu Hashimoto (based on the novel *Daibosatsu Toge* by Kaizan Nakazato); ph, Hiroshi Murai (Tohoscope); m, Masaru Sato.

Drama **(PR:O MPAA:NR)**

SYLVIA AND THE PHANTOM½**

(1945, Fr.) 90m DIF bw (SYLVIE ET LE FANTOME; GB: SYLVIA AND THE GHOST)

Odetta Joyeux *(Sylvie),* Francois Perier *(Ramure),* Louis Salou *(Anicet),* Julien Carette *(Hector),* Pierre Larquey *(The Baron),* Jean Desailly *(Frederick),* Rognoni *(Antique Dealer),* Jacques Tati *(Alain de Francigny),* Paul Demange

(Counsellor), Claude Marcy *(Countess),* Gabrielle Fontan *(Mariette),* Marguerite Cassan *(Marthe).*

Directed by Claude Autant-Lara before he made the immensely successful DEVIL IN THE FLESH, but released in the US in the wake of that film's popularity, SYLVIA AND THE PHANTOM is an enchanting, though minor, film about ghosts and young love. Best remembered today as one of the few films to feature a pre-Mr. Hulot Jacques Tati in a supporting role, SYLVIA AND THE PHANTOM stars teenaged Odetta Joyeux as Sylvie, a young French aristocrat who is in love with the image of her grandmother's nobleman lover, long since killed in a duel. In the castle where Sylvie lives hangs a huge portrait of the handsome young man upon which she gazes lovingly, despite having been told that his ghost haunts the castle. When her father, an impoverished baron, sells the painting to raise money for his daughter's 16th birthday celebration, Sylvie is overcome with sadness. During her party, her father arranges a surprise, hiring a ghost, or, more correctly, a man in a white sheet. However, matters are further confused when it turns out there are actually three men playing specter, which only serves to make Sylvie suspicious of the ghost's authenticity. All the while, the real ghost (Tati) watches over the affair, unable to communicate with Sylvie. The result is a light-hearted tale with little to distinguish it, except the pleasant Joyeux, the silent Tati, and some well-executed special effects. In French with English subtitles.

p, Andre Paulve; d, Claude Autant-Lara; w, Jean Aurenche (based on the play by Alfred Adam); ph, Philippe Agostini; ed, Madeleine Gug; m, Rene Cloerec.

Comedy/Drama (PR:A MPAA:NR)

T

TALL BLOND MAN WITH ONE BLACK SHOE, THE***½

(1972, Fr.) 90m Gaumont-Gueville-Madeleine/Cinema 5 c (LE GRAND BLOND AVEC UNE CHAUSSURE NOIRE)

Pierre Richard *(Francois Perrin),* Bernard Blier *(Bernard Milan),* Jean Rochefort *(Louis Toulouse),* Mireille Darc *(Christine),* Jean Carmet *(Maurice),* Colette Casel *(Paulette),* Paul Le Person *(Perrache),* Jean Obe *(Botrel),* Robert Castel *(Georghiu),* Roger Caccia *(Mons. Boudart),* Robert Dalban *(Faux Livreur),* Jean Saudray *(Poucet),* Arlette Balkis *(Mme. Boudart),* Yves Robert *(Orchestra Conductor).*

Filled with dry humor and featuring an understated comic performance by the expressionless Pierre Richard, this French farce concentrates on the silly aspects of the espionage world. Because of infighting in the French Secret Service, chief Louis Toulouse (Jean Rochefort) sets a trap for an ambitious underling, Bernard Milan (Bernard Blier), who is after his job. As a result, the innocent Francois Perrin (Richard), a tall blonde with one black shoe, is randomly chosen as a decoy to trap Milan, who immediately puts his men to work on Francois' past, his contacts, his mission, and his real identity, convinced that he is a "superagent." In the classic tradition of the silent comics, Francois walks through this danger zone of espionage completely oblivious to the gangs of assassins out to kill him. What is especially funny about the film is its send-up of the genre. Milan and his top agents assume that every one of Francois' actions has a double meaning: If he goes to the dentist, they think it is to meet a contact; when he plays the violin, they think it is a secret signal. They even try to decode an innocent message inscribed on a photo from his mistress. A sequel followed in 1974 titled, appropriately enough, RETURN OF THE TALL BLOND MAN WITH ONE BLACK SHOE. The original was remade in 1985 as THE MAN WITH ONE RED SHOE, starring Tom Hanks. The videocassette is dubbed in English.

p, Alain Poire, Yves Robert; d, Yves Robert; w, Yves Robert, Francis Veber; ph, Rene Mathelin (Eastmancolor); ed, Ghislaine Desjonqueres; m, Vladimir Cosma.

Comedy/Spy (PR:A-C MPAA:PG)

TAMPOPO***½

(1986, Jap.) 114m Itami c (Trans: Dandelion)

Ken Watanabe, Tsutomu Yamazaki, Nobuko Miyamoto, Koji Yakusho, Rikiya Yasuoka, Kinzo Sakura, Shuji Otaki.

A hilarious comedy from Japan concerned exclusively with food, TAMPOPO begins in a movie theater as we (the viewing audience) sit watching the audience in the film. In walks a suave *yakuza* attended by his girl friend and an entourage of goons. Gangster and moll sit down in the front row, while the henchmen set up a table filled with delectable food. As the gangster eats, he suddenly notices us watching him, leans forward into the camera, and asks, "What are you eating?" He then informs us that he hates noise in movie theaters—especially people who crinkle wrappers and eat loudly. Of course, a man behind him *is* eating too noisily, and the gangster angrily threatens to kill the confused moviegoer if he continues. He then sits down to enjoy the show, urging us to do the same. Now TAMPOPO proper begins, a string of rollicking comic vignettes concerning food that—more or less—tells the story of a heroic truck driver and his sidekick's attempts to help a young widow improve her noodle-shop business. The second feature by director Juzo Itami (preceded by THE FUNERAL, 1984), TAMPOPO is a wonderfully funny and creative film with a cornucopia of comical characters in absurd situations. These loony elements combine to offer some perceptive observations about human joy, fear, and passion for food. TAMPOPO also satirizes filmmaking (with references to THE SEVEN SAMURAI, American westerns, Steven Spielberg, and Japanese *yakuza* films), though Itami's film is itself heavily indebted to Luis Bunuel. With his first two films (his "Taxing Woman" entries, unfortunately, have less bite), Itami moved to the forefront of the irreverent young Japanese directors who have recently put a comedic spotlight on Japanese society, finding some very funny and disturbing truths about life in that enigmatic nation. In Japanese with English subtitles.

p, Yasushi Tamaoki, Seigo Hosogoe; d, Juzo Itami; w, Juzo Itami; ph, Masaki Tamura; ed, Akira Suzuki; m, Kunihiko Murai.

Comedy (PR:C-O MPAA:NR)

TAXING WOMAN, A***½

(1987, Jap.) 127m Itami-New Century/Japanese c (MARUSA NO ONNA)

Nobuko Miyamoto *(Ryoko Itakura, Tax Inspector),* Tsutomu Yamazaki *(Hideki Gondo),* Masahiko Tsugawa *(Assistant Chief Inspector Hanamura),* Hideo Murota *(Ishii, Motel President),* Shuji Otaki *(Tsuyuguchi, Tax Office Manager),* Daisuke Yamashita *(Taro Gondo),* Shinsuke Ashida, Keiju Kobayashi, Mariko Okada, Kiriko Shimizu, Kazuyo Matsui, Yasuo Daichi, Kinzo Sakura, Hajimeh Asoh, Shiro Ito, Eitaro Ozawa.

Continuing his series of hilariously incisive examinations of modern Japanese culture (burial rites in THE FUNERAL, food in TAMPOPO), director Juzo Itami turns his unique cinematic gaze on that most sacred of current Nipponese obsessions—money. Part social satire, part procedural drama, A TAXING WOMAN takes its title from spunky, dedicated tax agent Ryoko Itakura (wonderfully acted by Nobuko Miyamoto, Itami's wife), who uses her demure looks to lull tax cheats into false confidence before she lowers the boom. Most of the film details her determined attempt to get the goods on suave "adult motel" tycoon Hideki Gondo (Tsutomu Yamazaki), who launders his money through the *yakuza* (gangsters), phony corporations, real estate, and his mistress. He's sharp, but Ryoko's sharper, and by the end, not only are the interests of the Japanese Tax Office served, but love (though unrequited) makes an appearance. More traditionally structured than the Bunuelian TAMPOPO, A TAXING WOMAN is reminiscent of such classic Kurosawa procedural dramas as STRAY DOG; HIGH AND LOW; and THE BAD SLEEP WELL, yet despite focusing on the fascinating step-by-step detail of the investigation, Itami still manages to leave plenty of room for his trademark bit players to contribute delightfully vivid performances. Although not as out-and-out loopy as TAMPOPO, Itami's portrait of money-mad Japanese society has a biting satiric edge. The boundless energy of the Japanese seems to be what really fascinates Itami, who is well on his way to becoming the leading chronicler of life in modern-day Japan, though his 1988 sequel to this film, A TAXING WOMAN'S RETURN, is less satisfying than the original. In Japanese with English subtitles.

p, Yasushi Tamaoki, Seigo Hosogoe; d, Juzo Itami; w, Juzo Itami; ph, Yonezo Maeda; ed, Akira Suzuki; m, Toshiyuki Honda.

Comedy/Drama (PR:C-O MPAA:NR)

TCHAO PANTIN***½

(1983, Fr.) 94m Renn/European Classics c (Trans: So Long, Stooge)

Coluche *(Lambert),* Richard Anconina *(Bensoussan),* Agnes Sorai *(Lola),* Philippe Leotard *(Bauer),* Mahmoud Zemmouri *(Rachid),* Albert Dray, Ben Smail, Pierrick Mescam, Mickael Pichet, Michel Paul, Annie Kerani, Vincent Martin, La Horde.

Popular and irreverent French comic Coluche stars in this quiet but powerful psychological drama as Lambert, a 40ish Parisian gas station attendant who drowns his physical fatigue and sense of defeat in alcohol. A loner who works the night shift, he befriends a young Arab drug pusher, Bensoussan (Richard Anconina), and develops a fatherly relationship with him. Bensoussan comes every night to Lambert's station and the two talk about women and motorcycles while getting high—Lambert with booze, Bensoussan with marijuana. When Bensoussan's stash is stolen, he becomes the target of Arab cafe owner-drug kingpin Rachid (Mahmoud Zemmouri), whose young thugs murder Bensoussan at the gas station, and are killed by Lambert in the process. Shaken by Bensoussan's death, Lambert turns avenger and, with the help of Lola (Agnes Soral), a young blonde punk who barely knew Bensoussan, hunts down the young Arab's killers. Later, a police probe by sympathetic investigator Bauer (Philippe Leotard) reveals that Lambert is a former cop who has nothing left to lose. A multi-award winner at the French Cesars, TCHAO PANTIN is an honest, unglamorous, and understated drama rooted in *film noir* psychology, though it concentrates less on genre conventions than on characterization. Although Lambert is the standard "former cop who is "already dead' emotionally," Coluche invests the character with a flesh and blood reality that has little to do with movie heroes. One never doubts Lambert's motivations, or those of the people that surround him. Unfortunately, the script puts all the pieces of the puzzle into place far too neatly. In French with English subtitles.

d, Claude Berri; w, Claude Berri, Alain Paige (based on the novel by Paige); ph, Bruno Nuytten; ed, Herve de Luze; m, Charlelie Couture.

Crime/Drama (PR:O MPAA:NR)

TEN DAYS THAT SHOOK THE WORLD*****

(1928, USSR) 104m Sovkino/Artino bw (AKA: OCTOBER)

V. Nikandrov *(Lenin),* N. Popov *(Kerensky),* Boris Lianov *(Minister Tereshchenko),* Chibisov *(Minister Kishkin),* Smelsky *(Minister Verderevsky),* N. Podvoisky *(Bolshevik Podvoisky),* Eduard Tisse *(A German),* Soldiers of the Red Army, Sailors of the Red Navy, Citizens and Workers of Leningrad.

Commissioned by the Soviet government to celebrate the 10th anniversary of 1917 revolution, Sergei Eisenstein's TEN DAYS THAT SHOOK THE WORLD is a damaged masterwork, loaded with the director's spellbinding use of montage and visual symbols. Because the government cooperated completely, the many historical re-creations are spectacles equaled only in the largest Hollywood productions: the attack on the Winter Palace, for example, for which 11,000 soldiers and workers were provided along with weapons; while the whole of Leningrad was plunged into darkness in order to provide the needed current to light the night scenes in the city. In many ways, Eisenstein even exceeded his earlier triumph, BATTLESHIP POTEMKIN, with TEN DAYS THAT SHOOK THE WORLD (adapted from John Reed's book and other sources), and one can only speculate what the film would have been like had it been left untampered with. Alas, it was never shown in its original form. One of the main figures in the events Eisenstein and his collaborator, Grigori Alexandrov, had so skillfully re-created was Leon Trotsky, who, by the film's completion, had been expelled by the Communist party. Eisenstein was forced to excise any references to Trotsky from the original version, cutting nearly 1,000 feet from the film (only parts of which were actually ready for the anniversary commemoration). TEN DAYS is an early instance of the use of montage and visual metaphor that Eisenstein was to develop throughout his career.

d, Sergei Eisenstein, Grigori Alexandrov; w, Sergei Eisenstein, Grigori Alexandrov (based on the book by John Reed); ph, Eduard Tisse; ed, Sergei Eisenstein; m, Edmund Meisel.

Historical **(PR:C MPAA:NR)**

TENANT, THE***

(1976, Fr.) 124m PAR c (LE LOCATAIRE)

Roman Polanski *(Trelkovsky),* Isabelle Adjani *(Stella),* Shelley Winters *(Concierge),* Melvyn Douglas *(Mr. Zy),* Jo Van Fleet *(Mme. Dioz),* Bernard Fresson *(Scope),* Lila Kedrova *(Mme. Gaderian),* Claude Dauphin *(Husband),* Claude Pieplu *(Neighbor),* Rufus *(Badar),* Romain Bouteille *(Simon),* Jacques Monod *(Cafe Proprietor),* Patrice Alexandre *(Robert),* Josiane Balasko *(Viviane),* Jean Pierre Bagot *(Policeman),* Michel Blanc *(Scope's Neighbor),* Jacky Cohen *(Stella's Friend),* Florence Blot *(Mme. Zy),* Bernard Donnadieu *(Bar Waiter),* Alain Frerot *(Beggar),* Gerard Jugnot *(Office Clerk),* Raoul Guylad *(Priest),* Helena Manson *(Head Nurse),* Arlette Reinerg *(Tramp),* Eva Ionesco *(Mme. Gaderian's Daughter),* Gerard Pereira *(Drunk).*

Roman Polanski's psychological horror film stars Polanski himself as Trelkovsky, a Polish office clerk in Paris. He rents an apartment in a quiet building, whose elderly residents seem to feel malevolence toward the new tenant from the start. After he learns that Simone, the previous occupant, jumped from the apartment window, he visits the dying woman—who is covered head to toe in wrappings—in the hospital, and meets Stella (Isabelle Adjani), a friend of Simone's. Simone lets out a bloodcurdling scream and dies, an event that forms a bond between Trelkovsky and Stella, who nearly become lovers, but drift apart. ɘ, Trelkovsky grows more obsessed with uncovering the mystery of Simone and her fate, and becomes positive his neighbors are trying to kill him. As the film progresses, however, his paranoia seems less and less justified, his actions more and more insane. In many ways, THE TENANT is Polanski's REPULSION (1965) with the director in the Catherine Deneuve role. In both films, a character's vision of the world clashes with "reality" to the point at which no sense can be made of either, and in both the conflict leads to violence. We are never really sure if there is a plot against Polanski, even though logic suggests he is imagining everything, and this uneasy sense that maybe Polanski's character is *right* makes the film extremely, scarily effective (it is also surprisingly funny). Technically, THE TENANT is superb, with stunning camerawork by Sven Nykvist, an eerie score by Philippe Sarde, and thoroughly convincing performances from the entire cast. In English.

p, Andrew Braunsberg; d, Roman Polanski; w, Roman Polanski, Gerard Brach (based on the novel *Le Locataire Chimerique* by Roland Topor); ph, Sven Nykvist (Panavision, Eastmancolor); ed, Francoise Bonnot; m, Philippe Sarde.

Horror **(PR:O MPAA:R)**

TENDRES COUSINES*½

(1980, Fr.) 90m Stephan-Filmedis/Crown c (Trans: Tender Cousins)

Elisa Cervier *(Claire),* Jean-Yves Chatelais *(Charles),* Pierre Chantepie *(Mathieu),* Evelyne Dandry *(Adele),* Laure Dechasnel *(Clementine),* Valerie Dumas *(Poune),* Anne Fontaine *(Justine),* Jean-Louis Fortuit *(Antoine),* Anja Shute *(Julia),* Thierry Tevini *(Julien),* Pierre Vernier *(Edouard),* Macha Meril *(Agnes),* Catherine Rouvel *(Mme. LaCroix),* Jean Rougerie *(M. LaCroix),* Hannes Kaetner *(Professeur),* Gaelle Legrand *(Mathilde),* Fanny Meunire *(Angele),* Silke Rein *(Liselotte),* Jean-Pierre Rambal *(Le Facteur),* Carmen Weber *(Madeleine).*

Famed soft-core photographer David Hamilton's second foray into feature films (after 1976's BILITIS) is a silly soft-core sex tale with soft-focus photography and a bunch of barely pubescent nymphettes wandering through the countryside. Set for some reason in 1939, the film takes place at a country estate where a 15-year-old boy discovers sex and his own sexuality. It's mildy erotic, mildly funny, pretty to look at, acceptably acted (Macha Meril especially), and totally void of any real insight. We, the viewing audience, however, are supposed to believe that it's art. The videocassette is dubbed in English.

p, Vera Belmont; d, David Hamilton; w, Josiane Leveque, Pascal Laine, Claude D'Anna (based on a story by Laine); ph, Bernard Daillencourt; ed, Jean-Bernard Bonis; m, Jean-Marie Senia.

Romance **(PR:O MPAA:R)**

TESS***

(1979, Fr./Brit.) 170m Renn-Burrill/COL c

Nastassia Kinski *(Tess Durbeyfield),* Leigh Lawson *(Alec d'Urberville),* Peter Firth *(Angel Clare),* John Collin *(John Durbeyfield),* David Markham *(Rev. Mr. Clare),* Rosemary Martin *(Mrs. Durbeyfield),* Richard Pearson *(Vicar of Marlott),* Carolyn Pickles *(Marian),* Pascale de Boysson *(Mrs. Clare),* Tony Church *(Parson Tringham),* John Bett *(Felix Clare),* Tom Chadbon *(Cuthbert Clare),* Sylvia Coleridge

(Mrs. d'Urberville), Caroline Embling *(Retty),* Arielle Dombasle *(Mercy Chant),* Josine Comellas *(Mrs. Crick),* Patsy Smart *(Housekeeper),* Graham Weston *(Constable).*

Roman Polanski's delicate, visually rich adaptation of Thomas Hardy's classic novel places the supremely photogenic Nastassia Kinski in the title role. Peasant girl Tess Durbeyfield is sent to the estate of the wealthy d'Urbervilles by her desperate father after he learns that the two families are distantly related. It turns out, however, that the d'Urbervilles are not the d'Urbervilles after all, but a family who bought the noble line's name. Alec d'Urberville (Leigh Lawson), the cocky young master of the household, takes Tess as his lover, but later she returns home, disillusioned and pregnant. After the death of her baby, Tess is left to work on the dairy farm where she falls in love with Angel Clare (Peter Firth). Their romance leads to a marriage that ends abruptly on their wedding night when her outraged husband refuses to accept her past. With nowhere else to go, Tess returns to Alec, a decision that leads to a violent end. Visually TESS is a masterwork, capturing in amazing detail the scenery and atmosphere of the England of yore. The film's chief drawback, however, is its lack of vitality; instead of Hardy's passionate tale of ruin and disenchantment, TESS is a very cautious and reserved 170 minutes indeed. It was awarded Oscars for Best Cinematography (begun by Geoffrey Unsworth, who died midpoint, it was completed by Ghislain Cloquet), Best Costume Design, and Best Art Direction. Producer Claude Berri and coscreenwriter Gerard Brach later teamed on the Berri-directed JEAN DE FLORETTE and MANON OF THE SPRING, both of which are reminiscent of TESS. In English.

p, Claude Berri; d, Roman Polanski; w, Roman Polanski, Gerard Brach, John Brownjohn (based on the novel *Tess of the d'Urbervilles* by Thomas Hardy); ph, Geoffrey Unsworth, Ghislain Cloquet (Panavision, Eastmancolor); ed, Alastair McIntyre, Tom Priestly; m, Philippe Sarde.

Drama (PR:A-C MPAA:PG)

TESTAMENT OF DR. MABUSE, THE***½

(1933, Ger.) 122m Nero-Constantine-Deutsche/Janus bw (DAS TESTAMENT DES DR. MABUSE; LE TESTAMENT DU DR. MABUSE; AKA: THE LAST WILL OF DR. MABUSE; CRIMES OF DR. MABUSE)

Rudolf Klein-Rogge *(Dr. Mabuse),* Oskar Beregi *(Prof. Dr. Baum),* Karl Meixner *(Hofmeister),* Theodor Loos *(Dr. Kramm),* Otto Wernicke *(Commissioner Karl Lohmann),* Klaus Pohl *(Muller),* Wera Liessem *(Lilli),* Gustav Diesel *(Kent),* Camilla Spira *(Juwelen-Anna),* Rudolph Schundler *(Hardy),* Theo Lingen *(Hardy's Friend),* Paul Oskar Hocker *(Bredow),* Paul Henckels *(Lithographer),* Georg John *(Baum's Servant),* Ludwig Stossel *(Employee),* Hadrian M. Netto, Paul Bernd, Henry Pless, A.E. Licho, Gerhard Bienert, Josef Damen.

This haunting, suspenseful sequel to Fritz Lang's 1922 silent DR. MABUSE, THE GAMBLER picks up where the original left off—with Rudolf Klein-Rogge, reprising his role as the mad Dr. Mabuse, in a cell in an insane asylum. When Mabuse dies, Prof. Baum (Oskar Beregi), the director of the asylum, becomes possessed by the dead doctor's spirit and is compelled to carry out the madman's master plan to destroy the state through theft, violence, murder, and destruction. Although Baum engineers these chaotic acts, he manages to lead a double life, retaining his position at the asylum. Interwoven into this story is the tale of two lovers—Lilli (Wera Liessem) and Kent (Gustav Diesel), a member of Baum's gang who wants out and manages to prove the connection between Mabuse's plans and the chaos that is rocking Berlin. Filmed in 1932 and coscripted by Lang's wife, Thea von Harbou, THE TESTAMENT OF DR. MABUSE was made during the Nazi party's rise to power, and completed just before Lang fled, without von Harbou (who would become a top Nazi screenwriter), to the US. Whether or not it was Lang's intention, there are distinct parallels between THE TESTAMENT OF DR. MABUSE and the real-life events of the day—Prof. Baum symbolizing all those whose minds had become controlled by the thought of carrying out the "master plan." It should come as no surprise, then, that the film was banned, and nearly destroyed, by the Nazis. In German with English subtitles.

p, Fritz Lang; d, Fritz Lang; w, Fritz Lang, Thea von Harbou (based on the characters from the novel by Norbert Jacques); ph, Fritz Arno Wagner, Karl Vash; m, Hans Erdmann.

Crime (PR:C MPAA:NR)

TESTAMENT OF ORPHEUS, THE*****

(1959, Fr.) 79m Editions Cinegraphiques/Films Around the World-Brandon bw (LE TESTAMENT D'ORPHEE)

Jean Cocteau *(Himself, the Poet),* Edouard Dermit *(Cegeste),* Jean-Pierre Leaud *(The Schoolboy),* Henri Cremieux *(The Professor),* Francoise Christophe *(The Nurse),* Maria Casares *(The Princess),* Francois Perier *(Heurtebise),* Yul Brynner *(The Court Usher),* Daniel Gelin *(The Intern),* Nicole Courcel *(The Young Mother),* Jean Marais *(Oedipus),* Claudine Auger *(Minerva),* Philippe *(Gustave),* Alice Heyliger *(Isolde),* Brigitte Morissan *(Antigone),* Pablo Picasso, Jacqueline Picasso, Luis-Miguel Dominguin, Lucia Bose, Serge Lifar, Charles Aznavour, Francoise Arnoul, Francoise Sagan, Roger Vadim, Annette Stroyberg, Brigitte Bardot *(Themselves).*

Poet-filmmaker-sculptor-painter Jean Cocteau bade a fond farewell to cinema with this free-flowing, spirited collection of images and scenes that includes characters from his past films and a gathering of personal friends and admirers. What there is of a story retreads the ground of Cocteau's 1930 THE BLOOD OF A POET and 1949's ORPHEUS, bringing his cinematic career (which is difficult to separate from his other pursuits) full circle. For fans of Cocteau, everything in this picture will strike a familiar chord—a poet lives, must die, is resurrected, and must die again to qualify for immortality. Cocteau again employs some of the most inventive and beautiful photographic manipulations ever done in films, including the reverse motion techniques that never fail to bring a smile to his devotees. The cast reads like a cultural who's who—Pablo Picasso, Charles Aznavour, Francoise Sagan, Brigitte Bardot, Roger Vadim, Jean-Pierre Leaud, and, yes, Yul Brynner. Also making appearances are familiar faces from ORPHEUS, including Jean Marais, Maria Casares, Edouard Dermit, Francois Perier, and Henri Cremieux. Francois Truffaut, in honor of one of his masters, assisted with the production and financing of the picture. A pure, personal poem from one of the greats, THE TESTAMENT OF ORPHEUS allows Cocteau to continue to live on forever. In French with English subtitles.

p, Jean Thuillier; d, Jean Cocteau; w, Jean Cocteau; ph, Roland Pontoiseau; ed, Marie-Josephe Yoyotte; m, Christoph Gluck, Georges Auric, Martial Solal, George Frederick Handel, Johann Sebastian Bach, Richard Wagner.

Drama **(PR:C MPAA:NR)**

THAT OBSCURE OBJECT OF DESIRE****

(1977, Fr./Sp.) 100m Greenwich-Galaxie-Incine/First Artists c (CET OBSCUR OBJET DU DESIR)

Fernando Rey *(Mathieu),* Carole Bouquet, Angela Molina *(Conchita),* Julien Bertheau *(Judge),* Milena Vukotic *(Traveler),* Andre Weber *(Valet),* Pieral *(Psychologist),* Maria Asquerino, Ellen Bahl, Valerie Blanco, Auguste Carriere, Jacques Debary, Antonio Duque, Andre Lacombe, Lita Lluch-Piero, Annie Monange.

The final film from the 77-year-old Luis Bunuel shows the playful director in outrageous form as ever, casting two women—the graceful Carole Bouquet and the saucy Angela Molina—in the role of Conchita, a beautiful but elusive Spanish girl who becomes the object of obsession for Mathieu (Fernando Rey, his voice dubbed into French by Michel Piccoli), an upstanding French businessman. Widowed seven years ago, Mathieu regards love and sex moralistically, priding himself on his ability to count on one hand the number of times he has had sex with a woman he didn't love. When he sees Conchita, however, his mind overflows with thoughts of her. Although Conchita professes her love to Mathieu, she leaves him and flees to Switzerland, only to return later as his maid. When Mathieu finally manages to bed her, she is dressed in such an impenetrable outfit (a chastity belt of sorts) that he is unable to satisfy his uncontrollable sexual urge. This straightforward tale of obsessive love is colored with the always amazing Bunuelian touches. Mathieu's story is framed by a train trip in which he speaks of Conchita to his fellow passengers: a French official, a woman and her teenage daughter, and a dwarf psychologist. Also prevalent throughout the picture is a rash of bombings by a terrorist group that calls itself The Revolutionary Army of the Infant Jesus. The most fascinating aspect of THAT OBSCURE OBJECT OF DESIRE, however, is the character of Conchita, who is exactly what the title promises—so obscure that Bunuel chose to cast two actresses in her role. LAST TANGO IN PARIS star Maria Schneider was originally cast to play Conchita by herself, but was replaced early in the shooting. In a stroke of genius, Bunuel then cast two women in the same role—a completely logical dualism, since Conchita seems to vary greatly in her feelings for Mathieu, loving him one day and leaving him the next. The videocassette is available in a dubbed version and in French with English subtitles.

p, Serge Silberman; d, Luis Bunuel; w, Luis Bunuel, Jean-Claude Carriere (based on the novel *La Femme et la Pantin* by Pierre Louys); ph, Edmond Richard (Eastmancolor); ed, Helene Plemiannikov.

Drama **(PR:O MPAA:R)**

THERESE****

(1986, Fr.) 90m AFC-Films A2/Circle c

Catherine Mouchet *(Therese Martin),* Aurore Prieto *(Celine),* Sylvie Habault *(Pauline),* Ghislaine Mona *(Marie),* Helene Alexandridis *(Lucie),* Clemence Massart *(Prioress),* Nathalie Bernart *(Aimee),* Beatrice DeVigan *(The Singer),* Noele Chantre *(The Old Woman),* Anna Bernelat *(The Cripple),* Sylvaine Massart *(The Nurse),* M.C. Brown-Sarda *(The Gatekeeper),* M.L. Eberschweiler *(The Painter),* Jean Pelegri *(Father),* Michel Rivelin *(Pranzini),* Quentin *(Child in the Chorus),* Pierre Baillot *(The Priest),* Jean Pieuchot *(The Bishop),* Georges Aranyossy *(The Cardinal),* Armand Meppiel *(The Pope).*

In 1897 Therese Martin, a young French girl, died of tuberculosis in a Carmelite convent in Liseux. Twenty-eight years later, she was canonized and has since become known as "the Little Flower of Jesus." Her diaries, written in the convent, have been translated into numerous languages and served as the basis for this film directed by Alain Cavalier and cowritten with his daughter, Camille De Casabianca. Catherine Mouchet stars as Therese, a novice who faces the cold, hard life of the convent with great spiritual devotion, suffering in silent physical deterioration. Like all Carmelite nuns, she believes that she is the bride of Jesus Christ. Rather than viewing her "marriage" with Jesus in strictly spiritual terms, however, the schoolgirlish Therese views Him as something like a beau with whom she is infatuated. As her physical condition weakens, she is confined to bed under the care of her fellow nuns and novices—all of whom have come to love her deeply. In respect for this young saint whose simple and pure devotion led to her canonization, Cavalier and De Casabianca have fashioned a beautiful and sensitive film. Constructed in a series of tableaux, THERESE is sparse, with very little music, limited dialog, and, most strikingly, a set constructed in a minimal style. Rather than lose his fragile novice in an elaborate convent set, Cavalier places her against the plain grey backdrop of the sound stage, or in a simple pool of light. As Therese, Mouchet is to the film what Renee Falconetti was to Carl Dreyer's PASSION OF JOAN OF ARC: the film rests upon her face, which simply radiates with a saintly glow. Winner of the Jury Prize at the Cannes Film Festival and recipient of Cesars for Best Picture, Best Director, Best Young Female Hopeful (Mouchet), Best Script, and Best Editing (it also received nominations for cinematography, sound, and costumes). In French with English subtitles.

p, Maurice Bernart; d, Alain Cavalier; w, Alain Cavalier, Camille De Casabianca; ph, Philippe Rousselot (Eclair Color);

ed, Isabelle Dedieu.

Biography **(PR:C MPAA:NR)**

THERESE AND ISABELLE**

(1968, US/Ger.) 118m Amsterdam-Berolina/Audubon bw (THERESE UND ISABELL)

Essy Persson *(Therese),* Anna Gael *(Isabelle),* Barbara Laage *(Therese's Mother),* Anne Vernon *(Mlle. Le Blanc),* Maurice Teynac *(Mons. Martin),* Remy Longa *(Pierre),* Simone Paris *(The Madame),* Suzanne Marchellier *(Mlle. Germain),* Nathalie Nort *(Renee),* Darcy Pullian *(Agnes),* Martine Leclerc *(Martine),* Bernadette Stern *(Francoise),* Serge Geraert, Edith Ploquin, Alexander Kobes.

THERESE AND ISABELLE is a fairly sensitive, if somewhat exploitative, drama detailing a schoolgirl's foray into lesbianism. In a flashback triggered by a visit to her old school, Therese (Essy Persson) recalls being sent away to school by her indifferent mother, recently married to a man who dislikes children. Painfully lonely, the teenage Therese relies on fellow student Isabelle (Anna Gael) for solace. After both young women have brutal sexual encounters with men, they look to each other for sexual fulfillment. While neither the story nor the characters are especially interesting (and both Persson and Gael are at least a decade away from adolescence), THERESE AND ISABELLE does vary somewhat from the usual exploitation fare in quality—it's photographed in widescreen (which is lost on video) and in black and white, features a score by French composer Georges Auric (A NOUS LA LIBERTE; ORPHEUS; WAGES OF FEAR), and is based on a novel by Violette Leduc. The videocassette is dubbed in English.

p, Radley H. Metzger; d, Radley H. Metzger; w, Jesse Vogel (based on the novel *Therese et Isabelle* by Violette Leduc); ph, Hans Jura (Ultrascope); ed, Humphrey Wood; m, Georges Auric.

Drama **(PR:O MPAA:NR)**

THREE BROTHERS***

(1981, It.) 113m Iter-Gaumont/Artificial-NW c

Philippe Noiret *(Raffaele Giuranna),* Charles Vanel *(Donato Giuranna),* Michele Placido *(Nicola Giuranna),* Vittorio Mezzogiorno *(Rocco Giuranna/Young Donato),* Andrea Ferreol *(Raffaele's Wife),* Maddalena Crippa *(Giovanna),* Sara Tafuri *(Rosaria),* Marta Zoffoli *(Marta),* Tino Schipinzi *(Raffaele's Friend),* Simonetta Stefanelli *(Young Donato's Wife),* Pietro Biondi, Ferdinando Greco *(Judges),* Accursio DiLeo *(Friend at Bar),* Cosimo Milone *(Raffaele's Son),* Gina Pontrelli *(The Brother's Mother),* Girolamo Marzano *(Nicola's Friend).*

Directed by Francesco Rosi, whose films have long explored Italy's complex sociopolitical milieu, THREE BROTHERS delivers a symbolic state-of-the-society message. Three brothers, each representing a significant segment of the Italian body politic, return to the village of their youth to attend their mother's funeral. Raffaele (Philippe Noiret) is a Roman judge presiding over the trial of a terrorist whose life is consequently in constant danger; Rocco (Vittorio Mezzogiorno) is a self-sacrificing teacher; and Nicola (Michele Placido) is a factory worker and organizer. None of the brothers is as happy or at peace with the world as is their father (Charles Vanel), who has lived his life simply and close to the land. Though the talk periodically becomes a little ponderous, Rosi's mise-en-scene speaks volumes about the fragmented lives of his characters and an Italy on the brink of social disintegration. THREE BROTHERS was nominated for a Best Foreign-Language Film Oscar in 1981. In Italian with English subtitles.

p, Georgio Nocell, Antonio Macri; d, Francesco Rosi; w, Francesco Rosi (based on the story "The Third Son" by A. Platonov); ph, Pasqualino De Santis (Technicolor); ed, Ruggero Mastroianni; m, Piero Piccioni.

Drama **(PR:C MPAA:PG)**

THREE MEN AND A CRADLE*

(1985, Fr.) 100m Flach-TF 1-Soprofilm/Goldwyn c

Roland Giraud *(Pierre),* Michel Boujenah *(Michel),* Andre Dussollier *(Jacques),* Philippine Leroy Beaulieu *(Sylvia),* Dominque Lavanant *(Madame Rapons),* Marthe Villalonga *(Antoinette),* Annik Alane *(Pharmacist).*

THREE MEN AND A CRADLE is an insipid French comedy about three bachelors who find an abandoned baby at their door (a plot line direct from John Ford's THREE GODFATHERS). The jokes are stale, the story familiar, the style tedious, and the outcome predictable, yet the film went on to score an Oscar nomination as Best Foreign-Language Film (thankfully, it lost to the infinitely superior THE OFFICIAL STORY), and French Cesars for Best Picture, Best Screenplay, and Best Supporting Actor (Michel Boujenah). The film begins with the arrival of a baby in a basket before the closed door of goofy roommates Jacques (Andre Dussollier), Pierre (Roland Giraud), and Michel (Boujenah). The men become increasingly attached to the cute little bundle and soon become jealous of one another's paternalism. Things take an unbelievable turn for the worse (as if the screenwriters couldn't sustain their characters without an added device) when Jacques hides a smuggled cache of heroin in the baby's diapers, and the trio get drawn into a drug-dealing subplot. The most popular film in France during the 1985-86 film year (handily beating out such contenders as RAMBO II; OUT OF AFRICA; ROCKY IV; and BACK TO THE FUTURE), THREE MEN AND A CRADLE was also, of course, the film that inspired the Hollywood remake THREE MEN AND A BABY, which performed similar magic at the box office. The videocassette is available in both dubbed and subtitled (French into English) versions.

p, Jean-Francois Lepetit; d, Coline Serreau; w, Coline Serreau; ph, Jean-Yves Escoffier; ed, Catherine Renault; m, Franz Schubert.

Comedy **(PR:C MPAA:PG-13)**

THREEPENNY OPERA, THE***½

(1931, Ger./US) 113m Nero-Tobis Klandfilm/WB bw (DIE DREIGROSCHENOPER; L'OPERA DE QUAT'SOUS; BEGGARS' OPERA)

Rudolf Forster *(Mackie Messer)*, Carola Neher *(Polly)*, Reinhold Schunzel *(Tiger Brown)*, Fritz Rasp *(Peachum)*, Valeska Gert *(Mrs. Peachum)*, Lotte Lenya *(Jenny)*, Hermann Thimig *(Vicar)*, Ernst Busch *(Street-Singer)*, Vladimir Sokolov *(Smith)*, Paul Kemp, Gustav Puttjer, Oskar Hocker, Kraft Raschig *(Mackie's Gang)*, Herbert Grunbaum *(Filch)*.

Less revered today than the Bertolt Brecht play or the Kurt Weill songs, G.W. Pabst's film version of "The Threepenny Opera" is still a fine example of pre-Hitler German filmmaking. In the German version available on videocassette (a French version exists with a different cast, while the planned English version was never completed), Rudolf Forster plays the infamous Mackie Messer, or Mack the Knife, an underworld gangster of the 1890s whose territory is London. A dashing and respected criminal, Mackie is best of friends with the corrupt police chief, Tiger Brown (Reinhold Schunzel). After meeting Polly (Carola Neher), Mackie decides to marry her. In a dusty underground warehouse—the room lavishly prepared with goods stolen from London's top shops—the wedding is attended by a crowd of beggars and thieves, as well as Tiger Brown. Polly, however, is the daughter of Peachum (Fritz Rasp), the king of the beggars, who strongly opposes the marriage. He puts pressure on Tiger Brown to send Mackie to the gallows, threatening to organize a beggars' revolt to disrupt the queen's upcoming coronation if the police chief does not accede to his wishes. Based on the John Gay satire of 1728, "The Beggar's Opera," Pabst's film lacks the punch that made the Brecht-Weill collaboration so potent when it hit the stage in 1928. The sting of social criticism is lessened here, with greater emphasis placed on dramatics; in fact, Brecht was so disappointed with the director's interpretation that he ended his own work on the screenplay. What the film lacks in Brechtian qualities, however, it makes up for in the aesthetics of Pabst. Having previously exposed the seedier side of London in the silent PANDORA'S BOX (1929), Pabst once again brings it to the screen here in a unique mixture of realism and expressionism, taking great care to evoke the textures of London's underworld—populated by the lowest of lowlifes—in both his visuals and his soundtrack. Although there is a noticeable absence of some of Weill's tunes ("Ballad of Sexual Dependency," "The Ballad for the Hangman," and "The Tango Ballad"), the inimitable Lotte Lenya, as the prostitute Jenny, makes up for the omissions with her delivery of "Pirate Jenny." In German with English subtitles.

p, Seymour Nebenzahl; d, G.W. Pabst; w, Leo Lania, Bela Balasz, Ladislaus Vajda, Solange Bussi, Andre Mauprey, Ninon Steinhoff (based on the play by Bertolt Brecht, adapted from "The Beggar's Opera" by John Gay); ph, Fritz Arno Wagner; ed, Hans Oser, Henri Rust; m, Kurt Weill.

Musical **(PR:C MPAA:NR)**

THRONE OF BLOOD****

(1957, Jap.) 110m Toho bw (KUMONOSU-JO; AKA: COBWEB CASTLE; THE CASTLE OF THE SPIDER'S WEB)

Toshiro Mifune *(Taketoki Washizu)*, Isuzu Yamada *(Asaji)*, Takashi Shimura *(Noriyasu Odagura)*, Minoru Chiaki *(Yoshiaki Miki)*, Akira Kubo *(Yoshiteru)*, Takamaru Sasaki *(Kuniharu Tsuzuki)*, Yoichi Tachikawa *(Kunimaru)*, Chieko Naniwa *(Witch)*.

A truly remarkable film combining beauty and terror to produce a mood of haunting power, THRONE OF BLOOD was the brilliant fulfillment of Japanese master Akira Kurosawa's longtime ambition to bring Shakespeare's "Macbeth" to Japanese audiences. Kurosawa set the story in feudal Japan, and the transposition of cultures is surprisingly successful, with all the plot elements intact. After putting down a mutinous rebellion for their lord, warriors Taketoki Washizu (Toshiro Mifune) and Yoshaki Miki (Minoru Chiaki) are called to the main castle for an audience. Riding through the dense and foggy forest that protects the warlord's castle, they encounter a mysterious old woman bathed in white light and mist. When questioned, the woman prophesies that Washizu will be given command of a castle and soon become warlord, but his reign will be brief and his throne will be occupied by his friend's son thereafter. When it appears her predictions are coming true, Washizu grows increasingly corrupted by his own ambitions. THRONE OF BLOOD is filled with unforgettable, haunting imagery. Departing from his usual (very Western) fluid camera style and fast-paced editing, Kurosawa borrowed here from the conventions of Noh theater. While the visuals are gorgeous, the compositions are static and stagy, concentrating on the emotional moment as it seems to hang in the air—unaltered by editing or camera movement. The visual (and acting) styles work marvelously with the material, although the film is somewhat cold and detached, containing little of the exhilarating passion found in Kurosawa's other work. In Japanese with English subtitles.

p, Akira Kurosawa, Sojiro Motoki; d, Akira Kurosawa; w, Hideo Oguni, Shinobu Hashimoto, Ryuzo Kikushima, Akira Kurosawa (based on the play "Macbeth" by William Shakespeare); ph, Asaichi Nakai (Tohoscope); ed, Akira Kurosawa; m, Masaru Sato.

Drama **(PR:O MPAA:NR)**

THROUGH A GLASS DARKLY***

(1961, Swed.) 89m Svensk-Janus bw (SASOM I EN SPEGEL)

Harriet Andersson *(Karin, the Daughter)*, Gunnar Bjornstrand *(David, the Father)*, Max von Sydow *(Martin, the Husband)*, Lars Passgard *(Minus, the Brother)*.

The first in Bergman's trilogy of films examining man's futile search for God (followed by WINTER LIGHT and THE SILENCE) stars Harriet Andersson as Karin, a young schizophrenic recently released from a mental institution who spends the summer with her family in an isolated cabin on the Baltic coast. Her father, David (Gunnar Bjornstrand), is a writer who studies his disturbed daughter with a cold, intellectual detachment that only makes her condition worse. Her husband, Martin (Max von Sydow), is a doctor but is unable to assist Karin in her recovery. Minus (Lars Passgard), Karin's brother, is a youth on the verge of sexual awakening, and he, too, is occupied with his own troubled thoughts and emotions. Soon Karin is suffering from seizures, during which she hears voices from the walls telling her not to fear, God will come and save her. The usual fine performances from Bergman's regulars combined with a script that is not as ponderous as much of the director's other works earned THROUGH A GLASS DARKLY an Academy Award for Best Foreign Film of 1961. The videocassette is available in both dubbed and subtitled (Swedish into English) versions.

p, Allan Ekelund; d, Ingmar Bergman; w, Ingmar Bergman; ph, Sven Nykvist; ed, Ulla Ryghe; m, Erik Nordgren, Johann Sebastian Bach.

Drama **(PR:O MPAA:NR)**

TILL MARRIAGE DO US PART**

(1974, It.) 97m Dean/Franklin Media c (DIO MIO, COME SONO CADUTA IN BASSO; Trans: How Low Can You Fall?)

Laura Antonelli *(Eugenia),* Alberto Lionello *(Raimondo),* Michele Placido *(Pantasso),* Jean Rochefort *(Henry),* Karin Schubert *(Evelyn).*

Another in the series of Italian sex farces starring international sex symbol Laura Antonelli, TILL MARRIAGE DO US PART concerns newlyweds Eugenia (Antonelli) and Raimondo (Alberto Lionello), who discover that they are actually brother and sister. Luckily, this is revealed before the marriage is consummated, forcing the frustrated pair to seek satisfaction elsewhere. Raimondo begins to read the erotic novels of Gabriele D'Annunzio voraciously, while Eugenia finds refuge in the Bible. Fans of Antonelli and her anatomy will probably enjoy her virginal performance, and the jabs director Luigi Comencini takes at the upper class also elicit a few chuckles. This film is especially funny in light of Luchino Visconti's 1979 feature, THE INNOCENT, which stars Antonelli in an adaptation of a D'Annunzio novel. The videocassette is dubbed in English.

p, Pio Angeletti, Adriano de Micheli; d, Luigi Comencini; w, Luigi Comencini, Ivo Perilli; ph, Tonino Delli Colli (Technicolor); ed, Nino Baragli; m, Fiorenzo Carpi.

Comedy **(PR:O MPAA:R)**

TIN DRUM, THE***½

(1979, Ger./Fr./Yugo./Pol.) 142m Artemis-Hallelujah/NW c (DIE BLECHTROMMEL)

David Bennent *(Oskar Matzerath),* Mario Adorf *(Alfred Matzerath),* Angela Winkler *(Agnes Matzerath),* Daniel Olbrychski *(Jan Bronski),* Katharina Thalbach *(Maria),* Charles Aznavour *(Sigismund Markus),* Heinz Bennent *(Greff),* Andrea Ferreol *(Lina Greff),* Fritz Hakl *(Bebra),* Mariella Oliveri *(Raswitha Raguna),* Tina Engel *(The Young Anna Kollaiczek),* Berta Drews *(The Old Anna Kollaiczek),* Roland Beubner *(Joseph Kollaiczek),* Ernst Jacobi *(Gauleiter Lobsack),* Werner Rehm *(Scheffler the Baker),* Ilse Page *(Gretchen Scheffler),* Kate Jaenicke *(Mother Truczinski),* Wigand Witting *(Herbert Truczinski),* Schugger-Leo *(Marek Walczewski).*

Winner of the Academy Award for Best Foreign-Language Film and cowinner (along with APOCALYPSE NOW) of the top prize at the Cannes Film Festival, this adaptation of the Gunter Grass novel combines surreal imagery and straightforward storytelling. Oskar (David Bennent), born to a German rural family in the 1920s, becomes disgusted with the behavior of adults and decides, on his third birthday, not to grow any more, preferring instead to beat his tin drum (a birthday present) and shatter glass with his shrill scream. As he "ages," little Oskar continues to observe the hypocritical behavior of adults, beating out a constant tattoo on his tin drum to control the world around him. His small stature also makes for a very peculiar relationship with a teenage girl, Maria (Katharina Tahlbach), who is also mistress to a much older, and bigger, man. THE TIN DRUM is a disturbing film, rich with black humor, that takes a decidedly bitter and horrific look at the German people. Director Volker Schlondorff frames a piercing study of the origins of the German nightmare and the rise of Naziism through national complacency. Only Oskar, in his singularly demented way, is the voice of reason, proclaiming, "Once there was a credulous people who believed in Santa Claus, but Santa Claus turned out to be the gas man." The film is often difficult to watch and downright frightening, especially due to the haunting face of 12-year-old actor Bennent. In German with English subtitles.

p, Franz Seitz, Anatole Dauman; d, Volker Schlondorff; w, Franz Seitz, Volker Schlondorff, Jean-Claude Carriere, Gunter Grass (based on the novel *The Tin Drum* by Grass); ph, Igor Luther (Eastmancolor); ed, Suzanne Baron; m, Friedrich Meyer, Maurice Jarre.

Drama **(PR:O MPAA:R)**

TONI***½

(1934, Fr.) 90m d'Aujourd'hui/Pathe bw

Charles Blavette *(Antonio "Toni" Canova),* Celia Montalvan *(Josepha),* Jenny Helia *(Marie),* Edouard Delmont *(Fernand),* Andrex *(Gaby),* Andre Kovachevitch *(Sebastian),* Max Dalban *(Albert),* Paul Bozzi *(The Guitarist).*

TONI has often been called the first "Neo-Realist" film, preceding Luchino Visconti's OSSESSIONE by seven years, and since the Italian director was one of Jean Renoir's assistants on the project, its influence on his work seems clear. Basing his film on police files dealing with an incident that occurred in the small town of Les Martigues, Renoir, seeking authenticity, brought his crew to that town and used its citizens as characters. The story centers on Toni (Charles Blavette), an Italian laborer who falls in love with his landlady (Jenny Helia) and then with a Spanish woman, Josepha (Celia Montalvan). After receiving permission from Josepha's father to marry her, Toni discovers that she has been raped by a sleazy foreman, whom

Josepha ends up marrying, eventually deserts, and accidentally kills. Not surprisingly, Toni takes the blame. An insightful portrayal of male-female relationships and a skillful rendering its near-pulp novel plot (again predating Visconti's adaptation of James M. Cain), TONI is nonetheless far from perfect, riddled with numerous technical weaknesses and some seemingly improvised direction; still it is clearly one of Renoir's important technical experiments. In French with English subtitles.

p, Pierre Gault; d, Jean Renoir; w, Jean Renoir, Carl Einstein (based on material gathered by Jacques Levert); ph, Claude Renoir; ed, Marguerite Renoir, Suzanne de Troeye; m, Paul Bozzi.

Drama **(PR:C MPAA:NR)**

TONIO KROGER½**

(1964, Fr./Ger.) 90m Mondex-Procinex-Thalia/Pathe bw

Jean-Claude Brialy *(Tonio Kroger),* Nadja Tiller *(Lisaweta Iwanowna),* Werner Hinz *(Consul Kroger),* Anaid Iplicjian *(Frau Kroger),* Rudolf Forster *(Herr Seehaase),* Walter Giller *(Merchant),* Theo Lingen *(Knaak),* Adeline Wagner *(A Woman),* Beppo Brem *(Adalbert Prantl),* Rosemarie Lucke *(Inge Holm),* Elisabeth Klettenhauer *(Girl),* Mathieu Carriere *(Young Tonio Kroger).*

Based on Thomas Mann's 1903 novella of the same name, TONIO KROGER stars Jean-Claude Brialy as Tonio, a young writer who wanders through Bohemian circles in Europe grappling with his memories of childhood (Mathieu Carriere plays young Tonio) and his conflicting love of and alienation from his more bourgeois countrymen. The painter Lisaweta (Nadja Tiller) becomes Tonio's only confidante in his exile, an isolation that is the necessary condition of his creativity. Cowritten (along with Fellini scenarist Ennio Flajano) by Erika Mann, Thomas' daughter, TONIO KROGER is hampered by the novel's uncinematic form: much of the Mann original consists of Tonio's conversation with or letters to Lisaweta, and his character is very much more an observer than an actor. Consequently, the film is short on action, with Tonio's development presented in a few, essentially disconnected episodes. Still, the black-and-white visuals from director Rolf Thiele and cinematographer Wolf Wirth are highly evocative, and the film is a serious and thoughtful attempt to adapt the great Mann. In German with English subtitles.

d, Rolf Thiele; w, Erika Mann, Ennio Flaiano (based on the novella by Thomas Mann); ph, Wolf Wirth; m, Rolf Wilhelm.

Drama **(PR:C MPAA:NR)**

TORMENT*½**

(1944, Swed.) 101m Svensk/Oxford bw (HETS; GB: FRENZY)

Stig Jarrel *(Caligula),* Alf Kjellin *(Jan-Erick Widgren),* Mai Zetterling *(Bertha Olsson),* Olof Winnerstrand *(Headmaster),* Gosta Cederlund *(Pippi, the Teacher),* Hugo Bjorne *(Doctor),* Stig Olin *(Sandman, Jan-Erick's Friend),* Olav Riego *(Mr. Widgren),* Marta Arbiin *(Mrs. Widgren),* Jan Molander *(Pettersson),* Anders Nystrom *(Jan-Erik's Brother),* Nils Dahlgren *(Police Officer),* Gunnar Bjornstrand *(Teacher).*

One of the most popular Swedish films of its day, TORMENT is hailed by many as Alf Sjoberg's masterpiece. It was also the first script written by the then-26-year-old Ingmar Bergman and the film which brought Mai Zetterling international attention. It is the story of two young lovers—Jan-Erik (Alf Kjellin) and Bertha (Zetterling)—who are pitted against the wicked Caligula (Stig Jarrel), a professor at the boy's school Jan-Erik attends. Bertha, a tobacconist shop employee whom Jan-Erik had found drunk in the street, refuses to be completely open with him, causing Jean-Erik to suspect that someone else is involved. He soon discovers who that other person is when he finds Bertha dead, with Caligula hiding in the hallway outside her room. While the picture is somewhat dated, it does carry with it a certain innocence, a quality which has considerably diminished in Bergman's own films. Jarrel's professor was consciously modeled after the infamous Nazi Heinrich Himmler in the hope of identifying him with a most despicable evil. While much of the film's early success was due to Sjoberg's name and talent, and the film's harsh look at education, TORMENT is remembered today because of Bergman's involvement. The videocassette is in both dubbed and subtitled (Swedish into English) versions.

p, Harald Molander; d, Alf Sjoberg; w, Ingmar Bergman; ph, Martin Bodin; ed, Oscar Rosander; m, Hilding Rosenberg.

Drama **(PR:A MPAA:NR)**

TRANSPORT FROM PARADISE***

(1962, Czech.) 94m Barrandov/Ceskoslovensky-Impact bw (TRANSPORT Z RAJE)

Zdenek Stepanek *(Lowenbach),* Cestmir Randa *(Marmulstaub),* Ilja Prachar *(Moric Herz),* Jaroslav Rauser *(Von Holler),* Jiri Vrstala *(Binde),* Ladislav Pesek *(Roubicek),* Waltr Taub *(Spiegel),* Vlastimil Brodsky *(Mukl),* Josef Abrham *(Datel),* Josef Vinklar *(Vagus),* Jaroslav Rozsival *(A Smith),* Vaclav Lohnisky *(Man at the Smithy),* Jirina Stepnickova *(Feinerova),* Martin Gregor *(Geron),* Jindrich Narenta *(Gen. Knecht),* Jiri Nemecek *(Vlastimil Fiala),* Juraj Herz *(Mylord),* Helga Cockova *(Liza),* Marta Richterova *(Anna),* Jan Smid *(Stepan),* Ladislav Potmesil *(Kuzle),* Miroslav Svoboda *(Mayer).*

Set during WW II in the concentration camp at Theresienstadt, this award-winning Czech film details devastating Nazi inhumanity. Unlike the death camps, the "Terezin Ghetto" is a model facility situated in southeast Germany to which Jews from many countries are sent. Created by the Nazis as proof that they are treating their prisoners humanely, the "town" has banks, shops, and even a local administrative board. When the Nazis receive word that the International Red Cross will be inspecting the prison camp, the authorities even make a film to illustrate just how wonderful life is there. But underneath the decorative posters, are ones which read, in a variety of languages, "Death to Fascism." Despite the Nazis' attempts to make the camp pleasant, its residents live in fear of being shipped elsewhere. When the chairman of the Council of

Jewish Elders is faced with authorizing a transport to another camp equipped with gas chambers, he refuses to sign the order; however, the Nazis simply get rid of him and find someone who will comply. A group is rounded up, and in the haunting final scene, not realizing where they are headed, the transportees actually save places for loved ones on the death-bound train. This grim depiction of an unforgettable human ordeal reveals the awful brutality that can lurk behind a mask of human decency. Zbynek Brynych's direction concentrates on the *herding* of European Jews, especially those bound for death camps—their numbered suitcases piled high against a wall. An upbeat musical score serves to further underscore the horrible absurdity of the Nazi masquerade. In Czech, German, and French with English subtitles.

d, Zbynek Brynych; w, Arnost Lustig, Zbynek Brynych; ph, Jan Curik; ed, Miroslav Hajek; m, Jiri Sternwald.

Drama/War **(PR:A MPAA:NR)**

TWENTY-FOUR EYES****

(1954, Jap.) 158m Shochiku/Janus c (NIJUSHI NO HITOMI)

Hideko Takamine *(Miss Oishi),* Chishu Ryu, Toshiko Kobayashi, Shizue Natsukawa, Nijiko Kiyokawa, Yumeji Tsukioka, Ushio Akashi, Chieko Naniwa, Kumeko Urabe, Hideyo Tenmoto, Toshio Takanara.

The only film available on videotape from the masterful Keisuke Kinoshita, whose brilliance is practically unknown in the US, TWENTY-FOUR EYES chronicles 20 years in the lives of a loving teacher (Hideo Takemine, the star of 11 Kinoshita films) and 12 of her pupils in a small Inland Sea village. Concerned in many of his films with youth, purity, and innocence, the prolific Kinoshita has directed some of the most visually inventive and audacious movies to come out of Japan—from his early WOMAN (a 1948 romantic thriller that has the urgency of a Hollywood B-movie) to CARMEN COMES HOME (a wild 1951 musical satire about a bubbly stripper) to THE BALLAD OF NARAYAMA (his 1958 adaptation of the popular ballad about old age that contains some of the most remarkable lighting schemes and set designs ever put on film). Yet his most popular film in Japan is TWENTY-FOUR EYES, the touching account of a teacher who watches helplessly as her pupils are called to join the war effort, leading to much sorrow and the inevitable loss of innocence. An interesting complement to this film is Masahiro Shinoda's 1985 film MACARTHUR'S CHILDREN, a less impressive effort about the effect of the American presence on a group of schoolchildren at the close of WW II. The videocassette is in Japanese with English subtitles.

p, Ryotaro Kuwata; d, Keisuke Kinoshita; w, Keisuke Kinoshita (based on a novel by Sakae Tsuboi); ph, Hiroshi Kusuda; ed, Yoshi Sugiwara; m, Chuji Kinoshita.

Drama **(PR:A MPAA:NR)**

TWIST & SHOUT**½

(1984, Den.) 99m Holst-Palle Fogtdal-Danish Film Institute-Children's Film Council-Danmarks Radio/Miramax c (TRO, HAB OG KARLIGHED)

Adam Tonsberg *(Bjorn),* Lars Simonsen *(Erik),* Camilla Soeberg *(Anna),* Ulrikke Juul Bondo *(Kirsten),* Thomas Nielsen *(Henning),* Lone Lindorff *(Bjorn's Mother),* Arne Hansen *(Bjorn's Father),* Aase Hansen *(Erik's Mother),* Bent Mejding *(Erik's Father),* Malene Schwarz, Kurt Ravn, Grethe Mogensen, Troels Munk, Elga Olga, Helle Spaangard, Finn Gimlinge, Bent Brian, Rudolf Brink, Ingelise Ullner.

Reportedly the highest grossing film in Denmark's history, TWIST & SHOUT is set in that country in 1963, when the music of the Beatles filled the streets and teenagers found themselves growing up a bit too fast. Bjorn (Adam Tonsberg) and Erik (Lars Simonsen) are the closest of friends, standing by each other through good times and bad. Erik is the worse off—his mother is mentally ill, his father is perversely repressive—and, as a result, has been browbeaten into a pathetic excuse for a young man. The one girl Erik wants—the prissy, rich Kirsten (Ulrikke Juul Bondo)—is dead set on getting Bjorn to marry her. Bjorn, however, is infatuated with Anna (Camilla Soeberg), a vision of beauty, maturity, and intelligence. TWIST & SHOUT is so well-intentioned and honest that it seems cynical to find fault with it. In the first half of his film, director Bille August paints a charming but honest landscape of content, problem-free teenagers, a fantasy world in which nothing matters but getting a Beatles haircut, dancing to their songs, and forming a Beatles cover band. Life is easy and love is truly romantic. But when August begins to shout loud and clear his message that all is not a Beatles song and that everything has its dark side, he does so far too obviously, and the latter half of TWIST & SHOUT is pure convention. The young actors are excellent and manage to save the film, especially Simonsen, whose character walks a thin line and who displays much grace in his acting. August would later direct the international success PELLE THE CONQUEROR. The videotape has been excellently dubbed into English.

p, Ib Tardini; d, Bille August; w, Bille August, Bjarne Rather (based on Rather's novels); ph, Jan Weincke (Eastmancolor); ed, Janus Billeskov Jansen; m, Bo Holten.

Drama **(PR:O MPAA:R)**

TWO DAUGHTERS***

(1961, India) 114m Ray/Janus bw (TEEN KANYA)

"The Postmaster": Anil Chatterjee *(Nandalal),* Chandana Bannerjee *(Ratan),* Nripati Chatterjee *(Bishay),* Kagen Rathak *(Khagen),* "The Conclusion": Aparna Das Gupta *(Mrinmoyee),* Soumitra Chatterjee *(Amulya),* Sita Mukherji *(Jogmaya),* Gita Dey *(Nistarini),* Santosh Dutt *(Kishory),* Mihir Rakhal Chakravarty.

Released in India as the three-episode film TEEN KANYA, this Satyajit Ray picture was trimmed of its final episode ("Monihara"—a ghost story of sorts) for its US, and subsequently videocassette, release. In the first story, "The

Postmaster," Nandalal (Anil Chatterjee) is a city boy who goes to the country to take a job as postmaster. In the small village where he works, Ratan (Chandana Bannerjee), an orphan girl of 10, serves as his assistant. A real friendship develops between her and the new postmaster, who treats her far more kindly than her previous employer. However, rural life doesn't suit Nadalal, and after a bout with malaria, he decides to return to the city. The second tale, "The Conclusion" ("Samapti"), focuses on Amulya (Soumitra Chatterjee), an unmarried lawyer who refuses to wed the homely bride his mother has chosen and instead marries Mrinmoyee (Aparna Das Gupta), a carefree tomboy. On their wedding night, Mrinmoyee tells Amulya that she was forced into the marriage and now resents her loss of freedom. Satyajit Ray, who is still best known for his "Apu Trilogy," here delivers two beautifully textured tales of a young woman's discovery of love and affection, capturing the transition between childhood and adulthood. Ray contributes to the already inherent exoticism of the characters and rural locales by also composing the score, the first of many he has written for his films. In Bengali with English subtitles.

p, Satyajit Ray; d, Satyajit Ray; w, Satyajit Ray (based on the short stories "The Postmaster" and "The Conclusion" by Rabindranath Tagore); ph, Soumandu Roy; ed, Dulal Dutta; m, Satyajit Ray.

Comedy/Drama **(PR:A MPAA:NR)**

TWO ENGLISH GIRLS***½

(1972, Fr.) 132m Carosse-Cinetel/Janus c (LES DEUX ANGLAISES ET LE CONTINENT; GB: ANNE AND MURIEL)

Jean-Pierre Leaud *(Claude Roc),* Kika Markham *(Anne Brown),* Stacey Tendeter *(Muriel Brown),* Sylvia Marriott *(Mrs. Brown),* Marie Mansart *(Madame Claire Roc),* Philippe Leotard *(Diurka),* Irene Tune *(Ruta),* Mark Petersen *(Mr. Flint),* Marie Irakane *(Claire and Claude's maid),* Georges Delerue *(Claude's Business Agent),* Marcel Berbert *(Art Dealer),* Annie Miller *(Monique de Monferrand),* Jane Lobre *(Jeanne, the Concierge),* Anne Levaslot *(Muriel, as a Child),* Sophie Jeanne *(Clarisse),* Laura Truffaut, Eva Truffaut, Mathieu Schiffman, Guillaume Schiffman *(Children at the Seasaw),* Jean-Claude Dolbert *(Policeman),* Francois Truffaut *(Narrator).*

Francois Truffaut's TWO ENGLISH GIRLS is a three-sided love story examining the complications of a romance between one man and two women, in a reversal of JULES AND JIM (both films are based on novels by Henri-Pierre Roche). Set at the beginning of the 20th century, the film focuses on Claude (Jean-Pierre Leaud), a young art critic and aspiring author who charms his way through life. In Paris, he meets Anne Brown (Kika Markham), a liberated young woman who invites him to spend the summer at the seaside cottage she shares with her sister, Muriel (Stacey Tendeter). Although Anne shows some initial interest in Claude, it is her secret intention that he fall in love with the puritanical Muriel. Her plot works, but when she herself has a tryst with Claude, the situation becomes increasingly intense. One of Truffaut's darker films, TWO ENGLISH GIRLS is too exclusively compared to its companion piece, JULES AND JIM. Both films shine light on the personality of Roche (Truffaut had access to his unpublished diaries), mainly through the characters of Catherine (Jeanne Moreau in JULES AND JIM) and Claude, but TWO ENGLISH GIRLS is more interestingly viewed as a precursor to Truffaut's later film, THE STORY OF ADELE H., with Muriel bearing remarkable similarities to Adele Hugo. In French with English subtitles.

p, Claude Miller; d, Francois Truffaut; w, Francois Truffaut, Jean Gruault (based on the novel *Les Deux Anglaises et le Continent* by Henri-Pierre Roche); ph, Nestor Almendros (Eastmancolor); ed, Yann Dedet; m, Georges Delerue.

Drama **(PR:O MPAA:R)**

TWO OF US, THE****

(1967, Fr.) 86m Valoria-PAC-Renn/Cinema V bw (LE VIEIL HOMME ET L'ENFANT; THE OLD MAN AND THE BOY; AKA: CLAUDE)

Michel Simon *("Gramps"),* Alain Cohen *(Claude),* Luce Fabiole *("Granny"),* Roger Carel *(Victor),* Paul Preboist *(Maxime),* Charles Denner *(Claude's Father),* Zorica Lozic *(Claude's Mother),* Jacqueline Rouillard *(Teacher),* Aline Bertrand *(Raymonde),* Sylvine Delannoy *(Suzanne),* Marco Perrin *(The Priest),* Elisabeth Rey *(Dinou).*

Life's joys and sorrows are given a fine, sensitive treatment in this autobiographical first feature from Claude Berri, who was one of many Jewish children sent by Parisian parents to live in the French countryside during the Occupation. This film, an honest portrait of one such boy, was considered by Francois Truffaut to be one of the best films ever made about the Occupation. Ten-year-old Claude (Alain Cohen, in a touching, natural performance) is sent to live with the parents of his father's Catholic friends. "Gramps" (Michel Simon), the cranky old man who looks after Claude, takes an immediate liking to the boy and begins teaching him about anti-Semitism, not realizing that his young friend is a Jew. A warm friendship grows between the two, despite the their differences in age and religion. Some genuinely comic moments also arise, including Claude's accusation that the old man is Jew (he cites Gramps' big nose as evidence). Through everything, the two remain the best of friends, bound together by the trials of everyday living, the problems the war gives rise to, and the old man's aging dog, Kinou. Georges Delerue delivers a moving score, and, in his comeback performance, Simon, delivers one of the most memorable portrayals of his brilliant career. In French with English subtitles.

p, Paul Cadeac; d, Claude Berri; w, Claude Berri, Michel Rivelin, Gerard Brach; ph, Jean Penzer; ed, Sophie Coussein, Denise Charvein; m, Georges Delerue.

Drama/Comedy **(PR:A MPAA:NR)**

TWO WOMEN****

(1960, It./Fr.) 105m CC Champion-Marceau Cocinor-SGC/Embassy bw (LA CIOCIARA)

Sophia Loren *(Cesira),* Jean-Paul Belmondo *(Michele),* Eleanora Brown *(Rosetta),* Raf Vallone *(Giovanni),* Renato Salvatori *(Florindo),* Carlo Ninchi *(Michele's Father),* Andrea Checchi *(Fascist),* Pupella Maggio, Emma Baron, Bruna Cealti, Mario Frera, Luciana Coltellesi, Toni Calio, Elsa Mancini.

Sophia Loren won a Best Actress Oscar—the first to a non-American actress in a foreign-language film—for this Vittorio De Sica film, adapted by screenwriter Cesare Zavattini from an Alberto Moravia novel. Loren plays Cesira, a young widow in 1943 Italy who leaves her grocery store in San Lorenzo in the hands of her sometime lover (Raf Vallone), fleeing Allied bombing with her teenage daughter, Rosetta (Eleanora Brown), to return to her native village. There, after an arduous journey, she meets Michele (Jean-Paul Belmondo), the intellectual son of a local farmer with whom Rosetta falls in love, though he falls for her lovely mother. As the town grows increasingly besieged by bombing and shortages, Michele is forced to guide some fleeing Germans on an escape route, while Cesira and Rosetta go back to Rome for safety. Along the way, mother and daughter suffer a tragedy that changes both their lives forever, despite Cesira's best efforts to protect her child from the ravages of war. Loren also won the Best Actress Award at Cannes and the same honor from the British Film Academy; more importantly, she demonstrated in this film that she was a mature actress with talent to match her looks. De Sica (who also won an Oscar for the film) and Zavattini's previous collaborations included SHOESHINE; THE BICYCLE THIEF; and UMBERTO D, and while TWO WOMEN doesn't match the greatness or simplicity of those Neo-Realist masterworks, it remains a remarkably moving, humane vision of individual struggle in an inhumane world. In Italian with English subtitles.

p, Carlo Ponti; d, Vittorio De Sica; w, Cesare Zavattini, Vittorio De Sica (based on the novel by Alberto Moravia); ph, Gabor Pogany, Mario Capriotti (CinemaScope); ed, Adriana Novelli; m, Armando Trovaioli.

Drama/War **(PR:C-O MPAA:NR)**

U

UGETSU*****

(1953, Jap.) 96m Daiei-Harrison bw (UGETSU MONOGATARI)

Machiko Kyo *(Lady Wakasa),* Masayuki Mori *(Genjuro),* Kinuyo Tanaka *(Miyagi),* Sakae Ozawa *(Tobei),* Mitsuko Mito *(Ohama),* Sugisaku Aoyama *(Priest),* Ryosuke Kagawa *(Chief),* Kichijiro Tsuchida *(Merchant),* Mitsusaburo Ramon *(Captain),* Ichisaburo Sawamura *(Genichi),* Kikue Mori *(Ukan),* Syozo Nanbu *(Shinto Priest).*

Set in 16th-century Japan, this lyrical and enchanting film by Kenji Mizoguchi is one of the Japanese cinema's greatest masterpieces. As intense civil warfare ravages the land, brothers Genjuro and Tobei (Masayuki Mori and Sakae Ozawa), peasant potters, dream of finding glory. They devote themselves to producing pottery nonstop to sell at market, almost killing themselves in the process, then head for the big city. Genjuro leaves his wife behind, never to see her again, for she is killed by rampaging soldiers. He is taken in by a gorgeous noblewoman (Machiko Kyo), who is, in fact, a ghost who supplies the potter's every material desire in her beautiful estate, far from the sorrows of war. Tobei, on the other hand, becomes a soldier of fortune, also abandoning his wife, who is raped and forced into prostitution. UGETSU's combination of fantastic and realistic elements can make it rather difficult for Western audiences, particularly in its matter-of-fact treatment of ghosts and legends. Though many themes are interwoven in the simple tale (including strong parallels to the post-WW II plight of Japan), the film's real beauty lies in its magnificent, almost painterly images and the subtle combination of sound and visuals. The soundtrack is filled with background noises that produce a particularly eerie atmosphere, enhancing Mizoguchi's predilection for allowing environment to dominate his film and take control of the story.

p, Masaichi Nagata; d, Kenji Mizoguchi; w, Matsutaro Kawaguchi, Yoshikata Yoda (based on two tales by Akinari Ueda); ph, Kazuo Miyagawa; ed, Mitsuji Miyata; m, Fumio Hayasaka, Ichiro Saito.

Drama **(PR:A MPAA:NR)**

UMBERTO D*****

(1952, It.) 89m Amato-Rizzoli-Dear/Harrison-Davidson bw

Carlo Battisti *(Umberto Domenico Ferrari),* Maria Pia Casilio *(Maria),* Lina Gennari *(Landlady),* Alberto Albani Barbieri *(Fiance),* Elena Rea *(Sister),* Ileana Simova *(Surprised Woman).*

Simple on its surface but actually multi-layered and complex, this shattering portrait of an old man is an indictment of postwar Italy and its treatment of the aged. Umberto Domenico Ferrari (non-pro Carlo Battisti, a university professor) is a retired civil servant with no friends, family, or prospects, and only his dog, Flike, to keep him company. His meager pension does not provide enough for him to both eat and afford shelter, so Umberto is far behind on his rent for the room he has lived in for three decades. When he used to work during the day, his landlady (Lina Gennari) rented his room to lovers, but since his continual presence isn't adding to her income, she is planning to evict him. Umberto is one of many elderly people who voice their opposition to the way the government is treating pensionsers, but depressed by the lack of response, he determines there is no way out but suicide. He puts those thoughts aside, however, when he realizes that his dog would be at the mercy of the streets. One of the greatest films of all time and one of the handful of masterpieces to emerge from the Italian Neo-Realist period, UMBERTO D.

is as cerebral as it is emotional, as bleak as it is warm. There is no sentimentality or pandering for sympathy in De Sica's direction, because there simply isn't any need for it. The emotions one feels watching Umberto and Flike are real; in this remarkable collaboration between De Sica, Battista, and screenwriter Cesare Zavattini, the viewer is not guided by the filmmaking process, but by the actual sorrows and small joys that fill the screen. In Italian with English subtitles.

p, Vittorio De Sica; d, Vittorio De Sica; w, Cesare Zavattini, Vittorio De Sica (based on a story by Zavattini); ph, G.R. Aldo; ed, Eraldo Da Roma; m, Alessandro Cicognini.

Drama **(PR:C MPAA:NR)**

UMBRELLAS OF CHERBOURG, THE****

(1964, Fr./Ger.) 90m Madeleine-Parc-Beta-Laundau c (LES PARAPLUIES DE CHERBOURG)

Catherine Deneuve *(Genevieve Emery),* Nino Castelnuovo *(Guy),* Anne Vernon *(Mme. Emery),* Ellen Farner *(Madeleine),* Marc Michel *(Roland Cassard),* Mireille Perrey *(Aunt Elise),* Jean Champion *(Aubin),* Harald Wolff *(Dubourg),* Dorothee Blank *(Girl in Cafe).*

Although inspired by the Hollywood musical, Jacques Demy's vibrant, inventive film forgoes the familiar backdrop of a Broadway show or movie premiere to revel instead in the myth and magic of everyday romance, in all its sentimental and banal glory. Not quite a musical or an operetta, THE UMBRELLAS OF CHERBOURG is, as Demy has described it, "a film in color and song." What separates it from the Hollywood musical is Demy and composer Michel Legrand's decision to deliver all the dialog—every last meaningless word—in song form. Divided into three acts—Departure, Absence, Return—and set in Cherbourg on the coast of Normandy, the film begins with the blossoming romance of two young lovers: Genevieve (the beautiful 19-year-old Catherine Deneuve), who works in her mother's umbrella store, and Guy (Nino Castelnuovo), a service station attendant. They fall in love, have an evening of romantic bliss, and are then separated when Guy receives his draft notice. In the second act, Genevieve learns that she is pregnant and, after failing to hear from Guy, agrees to marry the acommodating Roland (Marc Michel) and move to Paris. Voila, Guy returns to Cherbourg. A feast of movement, color, and song, THE UMBRELLAS OF CHERBOURG transforms the quotidian into a celebration. By inflating the life of a common of shop girl into a musical spectacle, Demy succeeds in turning a tedious existence into a fantasy, yet he and cinematographer Jean Rabier and art director Bernard Evein do so without creating a false world. Instead they discover the "poetic realism" in Genevieve's world of umbrellas, chairs, and shop windows. This genuine international success was named Best Film at Cannes and earned a Oscar nomination in 1964 as Best Foreign-Language Film and three more in 1965 for screenplay, score, and song ("I Will Wait for You"). In French with English subtitles.

p, Mag Bodard; d, Jacques Demy; w, Jacques Demy; ph, Jean Rabier (Eastmancolor); ed, Anne-Marie Cotret; m, Michel Legrand.

Musical **(PR:A-C MPAA:NR)**

UNDER THE ROOFS OF PARIS****

(1930, Fr.) 96m Tobis/Images bw (SOUS LES TOITS DE PARIS)

Albert Prejean *(Albert),* Pola Illery *(Pola),* Edmond Greville *(Louis),* Gaston Modot *(Fred),* Paul Olivier *(Tippler),* Bill Bocket *(Bill),* Jane Pierson *(Woman),* Raymond Aimos *(Thief),* Thomy Bourdelle *(Francois).*

Billed upon its release as "The most beautiful film in the world," UNDER THE ROOFS OF PARIS may well have fit that description—at least at the time. In this first "100 percent French talking and singing film," Rene Clair was determined make sound and visuals equal partners. Instead of simply employing synchronous sound techniques, he chose to use sound only when needed, refusing to use dialog just for the sake of doing so. As he had done in ITALIAN STRAW HAT, Clair expressed the film's meaning "essentially in images with words used only when helpful and to avoid lengthy visual explanations." The story itself is a simple one. Street singer Albert (Albert Prejean) and Pola (Pola Illery) are lovers, though she enjoys flirting with his best friend, Louis (Edmond Greville). When Albert finds himself in prison for a crime he didn't commit, the door is open for Pola and Edmond to act upon their mutual attraction. Upon his release from prison, Albert is enraged by Pola and Edmond's coupling, but the final arrangement the three arrive at is unexpected indeed. In 1931, using practically the same set of technicians, Clair went on to make his two greatest films—LE MILLION and A NOUS LA LIBERTE, both of which continued his experiments with sound. Much of this film's visual style, however, can be attributed to the great art director Lazare Meerson, who collaborated with Clair on the director's greatest works.

p, Hans Haenkel; d, Rene Clair; w, Rene Clair; ph, Georges Perinal, Georges Raulet; ed, Rene Clair; m, Armand Bernard, R. Nazelles, R. Moretti.

Drama **(PR:A MPAA:NR)**

V

VAGABOND***½

(1985, Fr.) 105m Tamaris-Films A2-Ministere de la Culture/Intl. Film Exchange c (SANS TOIT NI LOI)

Sandrine Bonnaire *(Mona),* Macha Meril *(Madame Landier),* Stephane Freiss *(Jean-Pierre),* Laurence Cortadellas *(Elaine),* Marthe Jarnias *(Tante Lydie),* Yolande Moreau *(Yolande),* Joel Fosse *(Paulo),* Patrick Lepcynski, Yahiaoui Assouna, Setti Ramdane, Dominique Durand, Patrick Schmit, Daniel Bos.

Hauntingly atmospheric, cold and distancing, yet somehow engaging, VAGABOND combines a stylized documentary technique with the fictional vision of director Agnes Varda. The picture opens in the dead of winter, as a farmhand discovers a woman's frozen corpse in a ditch—long hair a tangle of knots, skin hidden beneath a well-worn leather jacket, and filthy blue jeans. This was Mona (Sandrine Bonnaire), a fiercely independent "vagabond" whose last weeks are reconstructed in flashback by Varda's camera and narration, and in "interviews" (both with actors and nonprofessionals Varda found during shooting) with people who met Mona—though it becomes clear that no one really knew her. Mona is not a character many will like or identify with, nor is one expected to. Varda presents her story without any sentiment, and in the process tells the stories of a number of different people whose lives were altered, perhaps permanently, by their contact with the vagabond. After working in the shadow of more popular French New Wave directors, the then-57-year-old Varda broke new ground in narrative film with her methods in VAGABOND. Equal credit for the film's success, however, must go to Bonnaire, who perfectly transforms herself into the filthy, aimless, and fascinatingly enigmatic wanderer called for by Varda. In French with English subtitles.

p, Oury Milshtein; d, Agnes Varda; w, Agnes Varda; ph, Patrick Blossier; ed, Agnes Varda, Patricia Mazuy; m, Joanna Bruzdowicz.

Drama **(PR:O MPAA:NR)**

VAMPYR*****

(1932, Fr./Ger.) 83m Dreyer-Tobis-Klangfilm bw (VAMPYR, OU L'ETRANGE AVENTURE DE DAVID GRAY; VAMPYR, DER TRAUM DES DAVID GRAY; AKA: THE STRANGE ADVENTURE OF DAVID GRAY; NOT AGAINST THE FLESH; CASTLE OF DOOM; THE VAMPIRE)

Julian West *(David Gray),* Henriette Gerard *(Marguerite Chopin),* Jan Hieronimko *(Doctor),* Maurice Schutz *(Lord of the Manor),* Rena Mandel *(His Daughter Gisele),* Sybylle Schmitz *(His Daughter Leone),* Albert Bras *(Servant),* N. Babanini *(The Girl),* Jane Mora *(The Religious Woman).*

Much to the dismay of his admirers, Danish director Carl Theodor Dreyer followed his silent masterpiece THE PASSION OF JOAN OF ARC (1927) with this horror film, his first foray into sound. The result was a masterpiece of subtle terror, the stuff of true nightmares. Loosely based on *In a Glass Darkly*, a collection of stories by Joseph Sheridan Le Fanu, the film begins as a young man (Julian West) arrives in a dark, mysterious European village and takes a room at the inn. That night a strange old man (Maurice Schutz) visits and gives him a package to be opened upon the old man's death, then disappears. The young visitor wanders the village, following a disembodied shadow of a one-legged man to a house where more shadows dance insanely to odd music. After observing various strange goings-on, the young man opens his package, which turns out to be a copy of *Strange Tales of Vampires*. As the story proceeds, it becomes apparent that the town is at the mercy of just such a creature. In VAMPYR, Dreyer conveys a deep sense of terror by suggesting evil, not showing it. There is no gore, but the film leaves a much more effective sense of unease and dread, moving slowly and with little cinematic trickery through its bizarre world. The director's use of sound is brilliant: Phrases are purposely muffled and half-heard from off-screen, giving the impression that something is going on that we can't quite comprehend. As in all of Dreyer's works, viewers must decelerate their normal narrative expectations and allow the film to wash over them; VAMPYR is a sensual film of mood and emotion rather than plot and thrills. Accordingly, the film did poorly at the box office worldwide. US distributors tried to cut footage from the film to pick up the pace, retitling it CASTLE OF DOOM and presenting it to audiences accustomed to the more visceral thrills of Universal's DRACULA and FRANKENSTEIN, and it failed miserably. Nonetheless, VAMPYR is one of the true classics of the horror genre. It cannot be described, but must be seen and savored as an example of filmmaking at its most evocative. In Danish with English subtitles.

p, Baron Nicolas de Gunzberg, Carl Theodor Dreyer; d, Carl Theodor Dreyer; w, Carl Theodor Dreyer, Christen Jul (based on stories from *In a Glass Darkly* by Joseph Sheridan Le Fanu); ph, Rudolph Mate, Louis Nee; m, Wolfgang Zeller.

Horror **(PR:O MPAA:NR)**

VARIETY****

(1925, Ger.) 104m UFA/PAR bw

Emil Jannings *("Boss" Huller),* Lya De Putti *(Berthe-Marie),* Warwick Ward *(Artinelli),* Georg John *(Sailor),* Kurt Gerron *(Docker),* Alex Hyde and His Original New York Jazz Orchestra.

E.A. Dupont's wonderful silent film concerns "Boss" Huller (Emil Jannings), who, as VARIETY opens, tells his prison warden the story of his crime. In flashback, we see Boss as an embittered, washed-up trapeze artist, forced by an accident to give up high-flying and now running a cheap dance act. After Boss hires young Berthe-Marie (Lya De Putti) for the show, he becomes completely enslaved by her sensuality, and runs off with her, abandoning his wife. The lovers put together an aerial act and play the carnival circuit until, finally, they join up with world-famous acrobat Artinelli (superbly played by Warwick Ward) to form The Three Artinellis. Before long, Berthe and Artinelli begin a torrid affair for which Boss takes a horrible revenge. VARIETY is a visual tour de force, with Karl Freund's camera constantly moving and seeking out unusual camera angles. The action is shown in reflections on eyeglasses, through binoculars, between blades of a whirling electric fan, and from the point of view of individual characters—including subjective views from a swinging trapeze. It was the most successful German film to play the US at the time of its release, and Jannings, De Putti, and director-writer Dupont were all offered work in Hollywood. Of the three, only the great Jannings found Stateside success—De Putti made a few American films but died in 1932 at age 30, while Dupont made only one American picture before going to England, where he made five films (including ATLANTIC, the first English talking picture), and later returned to the US to direct a string of cheapies in the 1950s. Judging on the basis of this technically innovative, atmospheric story of passion and betrayal, his talents were sadly wasted.

p, Erich Pommer; d, E.A. Dupont; w, E.A. Dupont, Leo Birinski (based on the novel *Der Eid des Stefan Huller* by Felix Hollander); ph, Karl Freund; m, Erno Rappdee.

Drama **(PR:C MPAA:NR)**

VERY CURIOUS GIRL, A**

(1969, Fr.) 107m Cythere/REG-UNIV c (LA FIANCEE DU PIRATE; AKA: DIRTY MARY; PIRATE'S FIANCEE)

Bernadette Lafont *(Marie),* Georges Geret *(Gaston Duvalier),* Michel Constantin *(Andre),* Julien Guiomar *(Le Duc),* Jean Paredes *(M. Paul),* Francis Lax *(Emile),* Claire Maurier *(Irene),* Henry Czarniak *(Julien),* Jacques Marin *(Felix Lechat),* Pascal Mazzotti *(Father Dard),* Marcel Peres *(Pepe),* Micha Bayard *(Melanie Lechat),* Fernand Berset *(Jeanjean),* Louis Malle *(Jesus),* Claude Makovski *(Victor).*

Nelly Kaplan's first feature chronicles the satiric exploits of Marie (Bernadette Lafont), a young country girl who sleeps with everyone in the local village, but gets nothing in return. When her mother is killed in a car accident and the priest denies her a proper burial, Marie goes on the offensive and learns to use her sexuality to her best advantage, charging her male callers and gradually becoming financially independent. She then turns her skills to blackmail, buying a tape recorder and secretly preserving some otherwise private conversations with her clients. A VERY CURIOUS GIRL was a minor art-house success, in part because Pablo Picasso, of all people, drew comparisons between Kaplan's style and that of Luis Bunuel. Kaplan had come to the great artist's attention after she directed the documentary LE REGARD PICASSO, which earned a Golden Lion at Venice. In French with English subtitles.

p, Claude Makovski; d, Nelly Kaplan; w, Nelly Kaplan, Claude Makovski, Jacques Serguine, Michel Fabre; ph, Jean Badal (Technicolor); ed, Nelly Kaplan; m, Georges Moustaki.

Drama **(PR:O MPAA:R)**

VERY PRIVATE AFFAIR, A**

(1962, Fr./It.) 95m Pro Ge Fi-CIPRA-Jacques Bar-CCM/MGM c (LA VIE PRIVEE; VITA PRIVATA)

Brigitte Bardot *(Jill),* Marcello Mastroianni *(Fabio),* Gregor von Rezzori *(Gricha),* Eleonore Hirt *(Cecile),* Ursula Kubler *(Carla),* Dirk Sanders *(Dick),* Paul Soreze *(Maxime),* Jacqueline Doyen *(Juliette),* Antoine Roblot *(Alain),* Nicolas Bataille *(Edmond),* Marco Naldi *(Italian Grocer),* Francois Marie *(Francois),* Elie Presman *(Olivier),* Gilles Queant *(Trovar),* Christian de Tillere *(Albert),* Stan Kroll *(Maxine's Chauffeur),* Jeanne Allard *(Charwoman),* Gloria France *(Anna),* Louis Malle *(Journalist),* Fred Surin *(Director),* Paul Apoteker *(Cameraman),* Claude Day *(Publicist),* Isarco Ravaioli, Simonetta Simeoni, Jacques Gheusi.

This early directorial effort by Louis Malle offers a look at the life of a glamorous movie queen supposedly patterned after that of its star, Brigitte Bardot. Jill (Bardot), an 18-year-old who lives with her mother on a huge estate overlooking Lake Geneva, is infatuated with Fabio (Marcello Mastroianni), an Italian magazine publisher and stage director who is married to Jill's friend Carla (Ursula Kubler). When Fabio takes little notice of Jill, she goes to Paris to become a ballerina. A switch to modeling makes her the talk of town, bringing the attention of a movie producer, and after three short years of jet-setting, she becomes an international star. Dissatisfied with the downside of fame, Jill returns to Lake Geneva to pursue a quiet life with Fabio, who has since shed his wife. Although they share some happy times together, the fans and papparazzi begin to take a toll on the fragile Jill, causing her to become increasingly depressed and reclusive. Despite the star appeal of the leads, and the talent of director Malle, A VERY PRIVATE AFFAIR is a barely satisfying film that stumbles along without purpose. Although Malle had proven himself to be a gifted stylist with interest in experimental narrative techniques in FRANTIC; THE LOVERS; and especially ZAZIE IN THE METRO, A VERY PRIVATE AFFAIR is a relatively tame film that employs its technical devices (freeze-frames, rear-projection) to no real effect. Photographed by Henri Decae, with art direction by Bernard Evein. The videocassette is dubbed in English.

p, Christine Gouse-Renal; d, Louis Malle; w, Louis Malle, Jean-Paul Rappeneau, Jean Ferry; ph, Henri Decae (Eastmancolor); ed, Kenout Peltier; m, Fiorenzo Carpi.

Drama **(PR:C MPAA:NR)**

VIRGIN SPRING, THE****

(1960, Swed.) 88m Svensk/Janus bw (JUNGFRUKALLAN)

Max von Sydow *(Herr Tore),* Birgitta Pettersson *(Karin Tore),* Birgitta Valberg *(Mareta Tore),* Gunnel Lindblom *(Ingeri),* Axel Duberg *(Shepherd/Rapist),* Tor Isedal *(Mute Herdsman),* Ove Porath *(Shepherd Boy),* Allan Edwall *(Beggar),* Gudrun Brost *(Frida),* Oscar Ljung *(Simon),* Axel Slangus *(Old Man at River Ford).*

The Best Foreign-Language Film Oscar awarded to THE VIRGIN SPRING was director Ingmar Bergman's first Academy Award, and the film still numbers among the director's classics. The story takes place in 13th-century Sweden, as Christianity and folklore vie for dominance in the popular belief. Karin (Birgitta Pettersson) the spoiled young virgin daughter of wealthy landowner Tore (Max von Sydow), is to go to church to light candles to the Virgin, and is allowed to wear a special gown, handmade by 15 virgins, on the occasion. Riding in the woods, Karin is raped, and then killed, by shepherds. The men take her gown, hoping to sell it, and move on, arriving at Tore's house, where they receive food and shelter. Their crime is discovered, however, moving Tore to enact bloody revenge and testing the bereaved father's faith. THE VIRGIN SPRING is based on a medieval ballad, and is full of the folk-tale oppositions (a good sister and a bad one) and motifs (the tell-tale gown, the trio of shepherds) so beloved by Bergman (the film is also true to its origins in its extreme violence). As always, those with little affinity for Bergman's preoccupations will find the film overlong and overdone. Most, however, will be rewarded by the depth of the director's moral and religious questioning, the emotional power of the story and acting, the haunting and symbolic imagery, and the excellent black-and-white photography of Sven Nykvist. The videocassette is available in both dubbed and subtitled (Swedish into English) versions.

p, Ingmar Bergman, Allan Ekelund; d, Ingmar Bergman; w, Ulla Isaksson (based on the medieval ballad "Tores Dotter I Vange"); ph, Sven Nykvist; ed, Oscar Rosander; m, Erik Nordgren.

Drama **(PR:C MPAA:NR)**

VIRIDIANA*****

(1961, Mex./Sp.) 90m Unici-Films 59-Gustavo Alatriste/ Kingsley bw

Silvia Pinal *(Viridiana),* Francisco Rabal *(Jorge),* Fernando Rey *(Don Jaime),* Margarita Lozano *(Ramona),* Victoria Zinny *(Lucia),* Teresa Rabal *(Rita),* Jose Calvo, Joaquin Roa, Palmira Guerra, Milagros Tomas, Alicia Jorge Barriga *(The Beggars).*

Luis Bunuel had been absent from his native land for 25 years when he was invited by the Franco government to produce a film in Spain. The result was VIRIDIANA. Ironically, it was never shown theatrically in Spain, having been banned by the Franco government immediately after its debut at the Cannes Film Festival, where it won the Golden Palm. Silvia Pinal plays the title young woman, a religious novitiate who, before taking her vows, makes a visit to her last remaining relative, the wealthy Don Jaime (Fernando Rey). Viridiana, firmly intent on resisting the corruption of her uncle's estate, is surprised to find him most gracious, kind, and gentle. He, however, is secretly obsessed with Viridiana's resemblance to his wife, who died 30 years earlier on their wedding night. After Don Jaime attempts to ravish the nun-to-be, who has obliged the lonely man by putting on his wife's wedding gown, he feels such remorse that he commits suicide. Viridiana inherits the estate, along with Don Jaime's son, Jorge (Francisco Rabal), and intends to use her new position to benefit the local poor. Once again, her virtuous intentions backfire. VIRIDIANA is filled with allegories concerning the general state of the world and Spain in particular, conveyed with the master surrealist's usual mix of black humor and stunning images—foremost among them the famous "Last Supper," in which a group of thoroughly degenerate beggars carouse drunkenly, in a visual parody of Da Vinci's painting, to the strains of Handel's "Messiah." Viridiana, who wishes to redeem these miscreants through her idealism, is mocked in the process—as is the Catholicism that Bunuel believed had to be overthrown if Spain was to avoid becoming a decaying mess like the Don's estate. Viridiana's ineffectual faith is contrasted with Jorge's more beneficial pragmatism; however, the changes he attempts to realize can also do but minimal good, as indicated in one of Bunuel's most famous jokes: just after Jorge has rescued a dog that was being dragged mercilessly from a cart by buying it from its owner, the director shows another cur in the same predicament, attached to another cart coming from the opposite direction. Immediately after the film was shot, it was shipped to Paris, where it was quickly edited in time for Cannes. Spanish authorities, who had not seen the final print before the festival screening, were shocked when it won the Golden Palm, and further scandal followed the film to Italy, where Bunuel was threatened with a prison sentence if he entered the country. Despite all this controversy, VIRIDIANA has a simple quality, stemming from the poetic formality with which Bunuel allows the picture to unfold. He steered away from complex and confusing images or camera movement, and created perhaps the greatest film of his magnificent career. In Spanish with English subtitles.

p, Ricardo Munoz Suay; d, Luis Bunuel; w, Luis Bunuel, Julio Alejandro (based on a story by Bunuel); ed, Pedro del Rey.

Drama **(PR:C-O MPAA:NR)**

W

WAGES OF FEAR, THE****

(1955, Fr./It.) 140m Filmsonor-CICC-Vera-Fono Roma/ Intl. Affiliates bw (LE SALAIRE DE LA PEUR)

Yves Montand *(Mario),* Charles Vanel *(Jo),* Vera Clouzot *(Linda),* Folco Lulli *(Luigi),* Peter Van Eyck *(Bimba),* William Tubbs *(Bill O'Brien),* Dario Moreno *(Hernandez),* Joe Dest *(Smerloff),* Centa *(Camp Chief),* Luis de Lima *(Bernardo),* Jeronimo Mitchell *(Dick).*

When the powerful oil company that controls the poverty-stricken Central American village of Las Piedras is faced with a well-fire disaster 300 miles away, they call for drivers to haul a load of highly volatile nitroglycerine across the dangerous terrain to the disaster site. Although it's a suicide mission, there are those in the village who feel the wages are worth the danger. After the driving skills of the applicants are tested, four men are chosen—Mario (Yves Montand), a French-raised Corsican; Luigi (Folco Lulli), his husky Italian roommate; Bimba (Peter Van Eyck), a cold and egotistical German; and Jo (Charles Vanel), a fifth choice who has conveniently gotten rid of the man before him. Maneuvering two trucks and driving at a snail's pace, they must overcome numerous obstacles to reach their destination, including a rickety wooden support suspended over a deep ravine; a giant boulder that blocks the road and must be detonated with a nitro charge; a swamp of oil; and their greatest natural danger—fear. A superb suspenser that eats at one's nerves for its entire last half, THE WAGES OF FEAR can almost be thought of as two movies. While director Henri Georges Clouzot, relying on visuals, devotes the final portion of the film to the safe passage of the trucks, he spends the first half building characters and atmosphere—the sweaty, dusty, hellish existence in Las Piedras, which is no better than death. It is this detailing of the human condition that proves essential to the film's success. From the opening shot—of four frantic beetles that have been strung together by a mischievous child—it is clear that the four characters are prisoners of Las Piedras. Remade in 1977 by William Friedkin as SORCERER. In French with English subtitles.

p, Henri-Georges Clouzot; d, Henri-Georges Clouzot; w, Henri-Georges Clouzot, Jerome Geronimi (based on the novel by Georges Arnaud); ph, Armand Thirard; ed, Henri Rust, Madeleine Gug, Etiennette Muse; m, Georges Auric.

Adventure **(PR:O MPAA:NR)**

WALL, THE*½**

(1983, Fr.) 117m MK2-Guney-TF1-Ministere de la Culture/Kino c (LE MUR)

Tuncel Kurtiz, Ayse Emel Mesci, Nicolas Hossein, Isabelle Tissandier, Malik Berrichi, Ahmet Ziyrek, Ali Berktay, Selahattin Kuzuoglu, Jean-Pierre Colin, Jacques Dimanche, Ali Dede Altuntas, Necdet Nakiboglu, Sema Kuray, Zeynep Kuray.

THE WALL is an unceasingly brutal film about life in a Turkish prison. Director Yilmaz Guney, who died in 1984, served three separate jail sentences (one for murder) before finally escaping in 1981. Filming from this first-hand experience in France (in an abbey converted to a jail for the production), Guney brings to the screen a film that stands up defiantly and violently for the rights of the imprisoned. The prison in the film, based on Turkey's Ankara prison, separates men, women, and children, but has no policy of separating violent offenders from political dissidents. In an indictment of the barbaric Turkish penal system, Guney recreates Ankara—an overcrowded prison with no windows, heat, hot water, or decent food, and inhumane visiting conditions—which was the sight of a inmate rebellion in 1976. The inmates (mostly children in the film) are beaten savagely: one is kicked in the eye, another is forced to swallow a louse found on his body, and yet another is savagely battered on the soles of his feet, while his bloodchilling screams are transmitted through the prison's public address system. These children pray to God, not to be released, but simply to be sent to another prison. While the subject has been brought to the screen before and certain elements of THE WALL have become cliches, this should not lessen the power of its message. THE WALL is perhaps not the most artful or poetic film (although it does contains one of the most amazingly photographed birth scenes in cinema), but is nonetheless one of the most necessary. In Turkish with English subtitles.

p, Marin Karmitz; d, Yilmaz Guney; w, Yilmaz Guney; ph, Izzet Akay (Fujicolor); ed, Sabine Mamou; m, Ozan Garip Sahin, Setrak Bakirel, Ali Dede Altuntas, Robert Kempler.

Prison **(PR:O MPAA:NR)**

WANNSEE CONFERENCE, THE***

(1987, Ger./Aust.) 87m Infafilm-Austrian TV-ORF-Bavarian Broadcasting/Rearguard c (DIE WANNSEEKONFERENZ)

Robert Artzorn *(Hofmann),* Friedrich Beckhaus *(Muller),* Gerd Bockmann *(Adolf Eichmann),* Jochen Busse *(Leibbrandt),* Hans W. Bussinger *(Luther),* Harald Dietl *(Meyer),* Peter Fitz *(Dr. Wilhelm Stuckart),* Reinhard Glemnitz *(Buhler),* Dieter Groest *(Neumann),* Martin Luttge *(Dr. Rudolf Lange),* Anita Mally *(Secretary),* Dietrich Mattausch *(Reinhard Heydrich),* Gerd Rigauer *(Schongarth),* Franz Rudnick *(Kritzinger),* Gunter Sporrle *(Klopfer),* Rainer Steffen *(Friesler).*

This is the startling re-creation of one of the most infamous events in history—the gathering of 14 Nazi officials on Jan. 20, 1942, in the Berlin suburb of Wannsee to discuss the "final solution," or the extermination of some 11 million Jews. Like the meeting, the film lasts 85 minutes and takes place almost entirely in the conference room. Organized by Reinhard Heydrich, chief of the Nazi security police and secret service, the meeting was held at the request of Adolf Hitler and Hermann Goering to secure and coordinate the cooperation of key figures in the Nazi hierarchy to institute the plan. As converts to the Nazi ideology, the conferees did not discuss the project's morality, only the most efficient means of achieving their goal, and the film follows their casual, at times petty discussion of genocide—ending as the group breaks for lunch. Made for German and Austrian TV and broadcast in 1984, THE WANNSEE CONFERENCE is not an exact re-creation, since no Wannsee transcript exists (only the minutes and other archival material, including conferee Adolf Eichmann's recollections of the meeting). Screenwriter Paul Mommertz and director Heinz Schirk reconstructed dialog and characters through research, then, without providing additional historical background, replayed the meeting in real time to eerie effect. The scene takes on an absurd quality, a "banality of evil," as if the participants were discussing marketing strategy for a new product line. The camera wanders around the room dispassionately, while the convincing performances nearly fool the audience into thinking the real event is unfolding before their eyes. The result is undeniably chilling. In German with English subtitles.

p, Manfred Korytowski; d, Heinz Schirk; w, Paul Mommertz; ph, Horst Schier; ed, Ursula Mollinger.

Historical **(PR:A-C MPAA:NR)**

WHERE THE GREEN ANTS DREAM***

(1984, Ger.) 100m Herzog-ZDF/Orion c (WO DIE GRUNEN AMEISEN TRAUMEN)

Bruce Spence *(Lance Hackett),* Wandjuk Marika *(Miliritbi),* Roy Marika *(Dayipu),* Ray Barrett *(Cole),* Norman Kaye *(Baldwin Ferguson),* Colleen Clifford *(Miss Strehlow),* Ralph Cotterill *(Fletcher),* Nicolas Lathouris *(Arnold),* Basil Clarke *(Judge Blackburn),* Ray Marshall *(Solicitor General Coulthard),* Dhungula Imarika *(Malila, "the Mute"),* Gary Williams *(Watson),* Tony Llewellyn-Jones *(Fitzsimmons),* Marraru Wunungmurra *(Daisy Barunga),* Robert Brissenden *(Prof. Stanner),* Susan Greaves *(Secretary).*

German director Werner Herzog seems to have an affinity for the environments of the socially outcast or the physically deformed, and in WHERE THE GREEN ANTS DREAM he has traveled to Australia to be at home with the

Aborigines. Obsessed with the notion that these outcasts are pure souls in touch with a superior spirituality, Herzog (like Peter Weir in THE LAST WAVE, Nicolas Roeg in WALKABOUT, and Dusan Makavejev in THE COCA-COLA KID) has given all his filmic energies to bringing these people and their stories to the screen. Set on the tribal lands of the Riratjingu, the story concerns a mining company that sends bulldozers and explosives to the land in preparation for opening a new uranium mine. The aboriginal people passively resist the encroachment, claiming that the area is the sacred place "where the green ants dream." Although one company employee, Lance Hackett (Bruce Spence), is sympathetic to the tribe's beliefs, his superiors bring the case before the Australian Supreme Court. While not Herzog's most original or compelling film, WHERE THE GREEN ANTS DREAM is further proof of his enlightened vision. More than simply an environmental, anthropological, or entomological study, the film realizes an environment created in Herzog's mind—in reality, there is no battle between miners and the Aborigines, nor is there a place where the green ants dream, nor are the "facts" about such ants based in reality. The film is not a real study of the contemporary situation in Australia, but a symbolic expose of the troubles that exist between imperialists and the lands they invade. The film is in English, the production team is German, the cast is made up of locals, and the photography was done in Melbourne and Coober Pedy.

p, Lucki Stipetic; d, Werner Herzog; w, Werner Herzog, Bob Ellis; ph, Jorge Schmidt-Reitwein; ed, Beate Mainka-Jellinghaus; m, Gabriel Faure, Richard Wagner, Klaus-Jochen Wiese, Ernst Bloch, Wandjuk Marika.

Drama **(PR:O MPAA:R)**

WHERE'S PICONE?**½

(1984, It.) 112m A.M.A.-Medusa-RAI-TV/Medusa-SACIS c (MI MANDA PICONE; Trans: Picone Sent Me)

Giancarlo Giannini *(Salvatore),* Lina Sastri *(Luciella),* Clelia Rondinella *(Teresa),* Carlo Croccolo *(Baron Armato),* Marzio C. Honorato *(Micione),* Armando Marra *(Troncone),* Mario Santella *(Severino),* Carlo Taranto *(Gallina),* Gerardo Scala *(Gennaro),* Nicola di Pinto *(Cametta),* Leo Gullotta *(Sgueglia),* Aldo Giuffre *(Coco).*

This clever, though not entirely successful, Italian black comedy opens during a public hearing on organized crime. One witness, Pasquale Picone, stuns the courtroom crowd by setting himself ablaze, then rushing out into the street. Though he's picked up by an ambulance, the man apparently disappears, with no hospital and morgue records bearing any record of him. Enter Salvatore (Giancarlo Giannini), a ragtag, homeless hustler who carries his belongings in a plastic shopping bag. Salvatore runs his own version of an office outside the doors of the morgue, where he meets Luciella (Lina Sastri), Picone's wife. Luciella is soon using the hapless hustler for her own purposes, and together they uncover the absent Picone's secret underworld life as a pimp, pusher, and explosives expert. Giannini, decked out in shabby clothing and mismatched footwear, gives a marvelous comic performance that more often than not strengthens the film's weak spots. Best known to American audiences as the star of numerous Lina Wertmuller films, he injects into his character some marvelous eccentricities. Unfortunately, WHERE'S PICONE? relies a little too much on slapstick humor and hysterical personalities, rather than letting the more gentle characters develop the story, and in doing so director Nanni Loy occasionally wears out the premise. In Italian with English subtitles.

p, Gianni Minervini; d, Nanni Loy; w, Nanni Loy, Elvio Porta (based on an idea by Nanni Loy); ph, Claudio Cirillo; ed, Franco Fraticelli; m, Tullio de Piscopo.

Comedy **(PR:O MPAA:NR)**

WHITE SHEIK, THE***

(1952, It.) 86m PDC-OFI/Janus-API bw (LO SCEICCO BIANCO)

Alberto Sordi *(Fernando Rivoli),* Brunella Bovo *(Wanda Cavalli),* Leopoldo Trieste *(Ivan Cavalli),* Giulietta Masina *(Cabiria),* Lilia Landi *(Felga),* Ernesto Almirante *(Director of "White Sheik" Strip),* Fanny Marchio *(Marilena Vellardi),* Gina Mascetti *("White Sheik's" Wife),* Enzo Maggio *(Hotel Concierge),* Ettore M. Margadonna *(Ivan's Uncle),* Jole Silvani, Anna Primula, Nino Billi, Armando Libianchi, Ugo Attanasio, Elettra Zago, Giulio Moreschi, Piero Antonucci, Aroldino the Comedian.

Federico Fellini's first solo directorial effort (he codirected VARIETY LIGHTS with Alberto Lattuada in 1951) is an enjoyable romp that shows the director's early promise. Newlyweds Wanda (Brunella Bovo) and Ivan Cavalli (Leopoldo Trieste) are honeymooning in Rome. The couple is mismatched: Ivan is conservative in nature, while his bride is full of spontaneity and eager to pursue her dreams. When Wanda learns that the popular photostrip comic book "The White Sheik" is being shot nearby, she heads off to ogle the "Sheik" (Alberto Sordi), sending Ivan on a frantic search for her all over Rome and jeopardizing their planned papal audience. When Wanda actually meets her idol, however, the sheik proves to be less than dashing. Already displaying his fascination with the romantic dreams of everyday people, Fellini orchestrates fantasy and reality deftly here as the newlyweds' perceptions of life and of each other change under the pressure of their unusual circumstances. The film falters in its pacing, however, which is somewhat too slow. Originally proposed as a project for Michelangelo Antonioni, THE WHITE SHEIK is not one of Fellini's masterworks (and uncharacteristically farcical), but it is a must-see for those interested in the director's *oeuvre* and an entertaining piece on its own.

p, Luigi Rovere; d, Federico Fellini; w, Federico Fellini, Tullio Pinelli, Ennio Flaiano (based on a story by Federico Fellini and Tullio Pinelli from an idea by Michelangelo Antonioni); ph, Arturo Galea; ed, Rolando Benedetti; m, Nino Rota.

Comedy **(PR:C MPAA:NR)**

WIFEMISTRESS½**

(1977, It.) 101m Vices/Quartet c (MOGLIAMANTE; AKA: LOVER, WIFE)

Laura Antonelli *(Antonia De Angelis),* Marcello Mastroianni *(Luigi De Angelis),* Leonard Mann *(Dr Dario Favella),* Olga Karlatos *(Dottoressa Pagano),* Annie Belle *(Clara),* Gastone Moschin *(Vincenzo),* William Berger *(Count Brandini),* Stefano Patrizi *(Clara's Fiance),* Helen Stollaroff *(Innkeeper).*

Antonia De Angelis (Laura Antonelli), a sequestered middle-class housewife, experiences a social and sexual awakening when her husband, Luigi (Marcello Mastroianni), is threatened with arrest for his political activities and forced to seek asylum with a neighbor. Looking over her absent husband's private papers and tracing his steps kindles the frail recluse's interest in his politics, his business activities, and, to her surprise, his philandering. The bosomy Antonia blossoms, virtually assuming the identity of her departed mate—writer of political tracts, philosopher, rakehell. She engages in casual sexual encounters and begins an affair with Dario Favella (Leonard Mann) a dedicated young doctor; meanwhile, closeted in an attic room in the adjacent house, Luigi, with a view of his wife's bedroom, turns unwilling voyeur, witnessing her sexual peccadiloes. Beautiful muted color photography characterizes this steamy story of a woman's awakening. Antonelli is gorgeous, but, as usual, offers little in the way of acting ability; the talented Mastroianni is wasted in his entirely reactive loneliness. The videocassette is dubbed in English.

p, Franco Cristaldi; d, Marco Vicario; w, Rodolfo Sonego; ph, Ennio Guarnieri (Technicolor); ed, Nino Baragli; m, Armando Trovaioli.

Drama **(PR:O MPAA:R)**

WILD STRAWBERRIES*****

(1957, Swed.) 90m Svensk/Janus bw (SMULTRONSTALLET)

Victor Seastrom *(Prof. Isak Borg),* Bibi Andersson *(Sara),* Ingrid Thulin *(Marianne Borg),* Gunnar Bjornstrand *(Evald Borg),* Jullan Kindahl *(Agda),* Folke Sundquist *(Anders),* Bjorn Bjelvenstam *(Victor),* Naima Wifstrand *(Isak's Mother),* Gunnel Brostrom *(Mrs. Berit Almann),* Gertrud Fridh *(Isak's Wife),* Ake Fridell *(Her Lover),* Sif Ruud *(Aunt at Breakfast Table),* Gunnar Sjoberg *(Alman),* Max von Sydow *(Akerman),* Yngve Nordwall *(Uncle Aron),* Per Sjostrand *(Sigfrid),* Gio Petre *(Sigbritt),* Gunnel Lindblom *(Charlotta).*

Ingmar Bergman's finest film and a staple in film history, WILD STRAWBERRIES not only serves as an example of one of Sweden's greatest directors' greatest works, but of how important a superb performance can be. Victor Sjostrom stars as Isak Borg, a medical professor on his way to accept an honorary degree on the 50th anniversary of his graduation from the university at Lund. He rides with his daughter-in-law, Marianne (Ingrid Thulin), who has decided to leave her husband. Animosity exists between the opinionated Isak (as she sees him) and Marianne, mainly because the old man reminds her so much of her husband. En route, they stop at Isak's childhood house, where he recalls his family in the days of his youth (although he is unseen by the characters and not present in the flashback). He sees his sweetheart, Sara (Bibi Andersson), picking wild strawberries and carrying on semi-innocently with his own brother, and later is awakened (in the present) by a teenage girl named Sara (again played by Andersson). She asks the old man for a ride, bringing two male friends and admirers along for the trip. This foray proves less than ideal, discolored by a car crash and Isak's disturbing nightmares. A fascinating, compelling picture, WILD STRAWBERRIES is viewed by many as Bergman's greatest achievement. Its most striking portion, which perhaps best illustrates Bergman's talents, is a dream sequence in which Isak walks through a desolate city, is approached by a man without a face, sees a clock without hands, and watches a funeral wagon crash and leave a coffin in the middle of the street. As he nears the coffin, it opens, and the corpse—again Isak—emerges and attempts to pull him into the afterlife. The visual and aural symbolism is chilling, and the entire scene is perfectly integrated into the "reality" of the rest of the picture. Sjostrom, in his final film, delivers the finest performance in any Bergman film—a major accomplishment considering the virtuosity Bergman's actors consistently display. The usual annoying Bergman traits—a deep concentration on symbols and psychoanalysis, over-intellectualizing, and the use of theater dramatics—also surface in this film, however. Bergmaniacs love these attributes, but time has not treated them so kindly. In Swedish with English subtitles.

p, Allan Ekelund; d, Ingmar Bergman; w, Ingmar Bergman; ph, Gunnar Fischer, Bjorn Thermenius; ed, Oscar Rosander; m, Erik Nordgren.

Drama **(PR:C MPAA:NR)**

WINGS OF DESIRE*****

(1987, Fr./Ger.) 130m Road-Argos-WDR/Orion Classics bw (DER HIMMEL UBER BERLIN)

Bruno Ganz *(Damiel),* Solveig Dommartin *(Marion),* Otto Sander *(Cassiel),* Curt Bois *(Homer),* Peter Falk *(Himself).*

With WINGS OF DESIRE, Wim Wenders created a visual poem about the walls that exist in our world—those that separate fiction from reality, Heaven from Earth, history from the present, those who observe from those who feel. Bruno Ganz and Otto Sander play two angels who circulate in a black-and-white Berlin, where they "observe, collect, testify, and preserve" the world around them, unseen by all but innocent children. The angels focus their attentions on three individuals—an octogenarian poet (Curt Bois); an American film and TV star (Peter Falk, playing himself); and a French trapeze artist (Solveig Dommartin). But, while helping these mortals, Ganz also struggles with his own desires to be able to feel, not just emotionally but physically as well. After his self-imposed exile in America, where he made HAMMETT; THE STATE OF THINGS; and PARIS, TEXAS; Wenders returned to his native West Germany to make WINGS OF DESIRE, his greatest film since 1976's KINGS OF THE ROAD. Although much of the influence on WINGS OF DESIRE can be traced to Cocteau's filmic depiction of angels or to German poet Rainer Maria Rilke's writings, the film's roots are perhaps closest to Walter Ruttmann's classic 1927 silent documentary SYMPHONY OF A CITY. WINGS OF DESIRE, too, is a symphony on Berlin, though under Wenders' direction the city limits (which have been bisected by the Wall) become fantastic, extending far above to include those angels who keep a watchful eye on the world below. One of the most curious aspects of WINGS OF DESIRE is the overwhelmingly positive reception it received, both at the box office, where it exceeded the success normally enjoyed by "arthouse" offerings, and critically. The jury of the 1987 Cannes Film Festival named Wenders Best Director. In German with English subtitles.

p, Wim Wenders, Anatole Dauman; d, Wim Wenders; w, Wim Wenders, Peter Handke; ph, Henri Alekan; ed, Peter Przygodda; m, Jurgen Knieper.

Fantasy **(PR:C MPAA:PG-13)**

WINTER LIGHT, THE**

(1962, Swed.) 80m Svensk/Janus bw (NATTVARDSGAESTERNA; Trans: The Communicants)

Ingrid Thulin *(Marta Lundberg),* Gunnar Bjornstrand *(Tomas Ericsson),* Max von Sydow *(Jonas Persson),* Gunnel Lindblom *(Karin Persson),* Allan Edwall *(Algot Frovik),* Kolbjorn Knudsen *(Knut Aronsson),* Olof Thunberg *(Fredrik Blom),* Elsa Ebbesen *(Magdalena Ledfors),* Tor Borong *(Johann Akerblom),* Bertha Sannell *(Hanna Appelblad),* Helena Palmgren *(Doris Appelblad),* Eddie Axberg *(Johan Strand),* Lars-Owe Carlberg *(Police Inspector).*

This is the second in an Ingmar Bergman trilogy that also includes THROUGH A GLASS DARKLY and THE SILENCE, all three films centering on the metaphysical question of man's place in God's scheme of things. The story takes place in rural Sweden, where pastor Tomas Ericsson (Gunnar Bjornstrand, the lead in THROUGH A GLASS DARKLY) finds the members of his congregation dwindling until there are only a few people left, including a woman who is blindly in love with him. Still he goes through the rituals of his office, less out of faith than his own inability to answer the ultimate question, "Why is God silent?" His doubts come to a head when he hears the confession of Jonas Persson (Max von Sydow), a fisherman obsessed with the thought of the Chinese using the atom bomb who comes to the pastor to express his fears and for guidance. Instead, all the pastor can offer is uncertainty. THE WINTER LIGHT presents a philosophical and moral puzzle without providing any definite answers—which, considering the subject matter, is probably the way it should be. The videocassette is available in both dubbed and subtitled versions.

p, Ingmar Bergman; d, Ingmar Bergman; w, Ingmar Bergman; ph, Sven Nykvist; ed, Ulla Ryghe.

Drama **(PR:C MPAA:NR)**

WOLF AT THE DOOR, THE½**

(1986, Fr./Den.) 102m Dagmar-Henning Dam Kargarrd-Cameras Continentales-Famous French-TF 1-Danish Film Institute-Danish Radio & TV-French Ministry of Culture/Manson c (OVIRI)

Donald Sutherland *(Paul Gauguin),* Valerie Morea *(Annah-la-Javanaise),* Max von Sydow *(August Strindberg),* Sofie Graboel *(Judith Molard),* Merete Voldstedlund *(Mette Gauguin),* Jorgen Reenberg *(Edward Brandes),* Yves Barsack *(Edgar Degas),* Thomas Antoni *(Jourdan),* Fanny Bastien *(Juliette Huet),* Jean Yanne *(William Molard),* Ghita Norby *(Ida Molard),* Kristina Dubin *(Aline Gauguin),* Henrik Larsen *(Julien Leclercq).*

An unexceptional film about an exceptional man, this respectful but tame portrait of Paul Gauguin fails to capture the artistic and personal ferocity that prompted Edgar Degas to say of the French artist that he "painted like a wolf." Focusing on a short period in Gauguin's life (1893-94) when he returned to Paris from Tahiti ready to rock the art world with his colorful, exotic paintings of native girls, only to be all but ignored, THE WOLF AT THE DOOR presents Gauguin (Donald Sutherland) as a stubborn iconoclast who also craves acceptance and companionship. At the center of the film is the painter's relationship with four women: the stoic Danish wife he left behind with their children (Merete Voldstedlund); a former mistress with whom he has had a child (Fanny Bastien); a young Javanese model (Valerie Morea); and a pretty 14-year-old neighbor (Sofie Graboel) who reminds Gauguin of his own daughter. Much is also made of Gauguin's friendship/rivalry with August Strindberg (Max von Sydow), their conversations taken from actual correspondence between the painter and the Swedish playwright. While director Henning Carlsen, working from a screenplay by playwright Christopher Hampton (from the original script by Carlsen and Bunuel collaborator Jean-Claude Carriere), fails to infuse his film with the necessary passion, that doesn't stop Sutherland from delivering an extraordinary performance. In a weather-beaten straw hat and ratty jacket, Sutherland doesn't act the role of Gauguin, he is possessed by it. He receives excellent support from the women (particularly the charming Graboel) in Gauguin's life, which has been brought to the screen twice before by Hollywood—with Anthony Quinn playing him in an Oscar-winning performance opposite Kirk Douglas' Vincent van Gogh in 1956's LUST FOR LIFE and George Sanders essaying a thinly veiled Gauguin in the MOON AND THE SIXPENCE, the 1942 adaptation of W. Somerset Maugham's novel. In English.

p, Henning Carlsen; d, Henning Carlsen; w, Christopher Hampton (based on a story by Henning Carlsen, Jean-Claude Carriere); ph, Mikael Salomon (Eastmancolor); ed, Janus Billeskov Jansen; m, Ole Schmidt.

Biography **(PR:C-O MPAA:R)**

WOMAN IN FLAMES, A***

(1983, Ger.) 106m Van Ackeren/Geissler/Almi c (DIE FLAMBIERTE FRAU; A WOMAN FLAMBEE)

Gudrun Landgrebe *(Eva),* Mathieu Carriere *(Chris),* Hanns

Zischler *(Kurt),* Gabriele Lafari *(Yvonne),* Matthias Fuchs, Christiane B. Horn, Rene Schonenberger, Magdalena Montezuma, Klaus Mikoleit, Georg Tryphon, Walther Busch, Carola Regnier, Johannes Grutzke, Salome.

This bizarre picture concerns a middle-class housewife, Eva (Gudrun Landgrebe), who leaves her husband and turns to prostitution. She is initially conservative in her choice of clients, but becomes more daring. Once she meets Chris (Mathieu Carriere), a bisexual prostitute who invites her to his luxurious apartment, the pair fall in love and share the flat, setting aside one room for their prostitution business—which rapidly becomes a highly organized chore of high-finance bookkeeping. Chris continues entertaining both male and female clients, while Landgrebe begins to favor johns with strange fetishes. After their work is done, Eva and Chris resume their romance. These conditions naturally put a strain on their relationship, which comes to a surprisingly surreal end. A very weird entry from the eccentric Robert Van Ackeren—who was once touted as the next Rainer Werner Fassbinder (he never fulfilled such a prophecy)—A WOMAN IN FLAMES became one of Germany's top-grossing films. The videocassette is dubbed in English.

p, Robert Van Ackeren; d, Robert Van Ackeren; w, Robert Van Ackeren, Catharina Zwerenz; ph, Jurgen Jurges; ed, Tanja Schmidtbauer; m, Peer Raben.

Drama **(PR:O MPAA:R)**

WOMAN IN THE DUNES*****

(1964, Jap.) 123m Teshigahara/Pathe bw (SUNA NO ONNA; AKA: WOMAN OF THE DUNES)

Eiji Okada *(Niki Jumpei),* Kyoko Kishida *(Woman),* Koji Mitsui, Hiroko Ito, Sen Yano, Ginzo Sekigushi, Kiyohiko Ichiha, Tamutsu Tamura, Hiroyuki Nishimo.

A profoundly moving parable of man's search for meaning in life and love, told with beautiful simplicity, WOMAN IN THE DUNES begins as Niki Jumpei (Eiji Okada), a reserved entomologist, collects specimens along a Japanese beach. He is met by some villagers, who offer him both a place to sleep and a woman, and is led to a shack located at the bottom of a sand pit, where he climbs down a rope ladder to the woman, Kyoko (Kyoko Kishida). The next morning, he notices that the ladder has been removed. A panicky urge to climb out of the pit is followed by a futile attempt to scale the sand walls, which cascade beneath his feet. Helpless, he watches as Kyoko endlessly shovels the sand into buckets, which are then hoisted by the villagers above. In return, food and water are sent down—no shoveling, no food. Niki soon realizes the necessity of the woman's work. He becomes accustomed to his new lifestyle and takes the woman as his lover. She becomes pregnant, and he must wrestle with his urge to escape and his growing devotion to Kyoko and his new life. Beautifully photographed and confined almost exclusively to a single set, WOMAN IN THE DUNES is a poetic affirmation of life. As frustrating and claustrophobic as the man's situation may first appear, the film becomes increasingly seductive as it lulls the audience into the woman's sandpit existence. Based on a novel by Kobo Abe, Hiroshi Teshigahara's emotionally draining picture was nominated for Best Foreign Film at the 1964 Academy Awards and the following year earned him a nomination for Best Director. In Japanese with English subtitles.

p, Kiichi Ichikawa, Tadashi Ohono; d, Hiroshi Teshigahara; w, Kobo Abe (based on the novel *Suna no Onna* by Kobo Abe); ph, Hiroshi Segawa; ed, F. Susui; m, Toru Takemitsu.

Drama **(PR:O MPAA:NR)**

WOMAN NEXT DOOR, THE*½**

(1981, Fr.) 106m Carrosse-TF 1/MGM-UA c (LA FEMME D'A COTE)

Gerard Depardieu *(Bernard Coudray),* Fanny Ardant *(Mathilde Bauchard),* Henri Garcin *(Philippe Bauchard),* Michele Baumgartner *(Arlette Coudray),* Veronique Silver *(Mme. Jouve),* Philippe Morier-Genoud *(Psychoanalyst),* Roger Van Hool *(Roland Duguet),* Jacques Preisach, Catherine Crassac *(Couple on Hotel Staircase).*

This dark entry from Francois Truffaut pairs French superstar Gerard Depardieu with newcomer Fanny Ardant as Bernard and Mathilde, former flames who have married other people and now live next door to each other. Bernard, who has been living a comfortable though joyless bourgeois existence with his wife and young son, tries to avoid Mathilde at all costs. However, a chance meeting at the supermarket opens a floodgate of buried emotions and they resume their romance. Gradually, Bernard and Mathilde's mutual obsession builds to a dangerous level that neither can control. As he did in JULES AND JIM and THE STORY OF ADELE H., Truffaut once again displays his interest in obsessive love and the pain and destruction it can cause; but as was the case with THE SOFT SKIN and THE BRIDE WORE BLACK, the shadow of Hitchcock looms large, leading Truffaut and his screenwriting collaborators to create a taut, psychological narrative that stifles the director's poetic impulse. Stage actress Ardant, who makes a stunning starring debut here as the woman obsessed, also appears again in Truffaut's final film, CONFIDENTIALLY YOURS. In French with English subtitles.

d, Francois Truffaut; w, Francois Truffaut, Suzanne Schiffman, Jean Aurel; ph, William Lubtchansky (Fujicolor); ed, Martine Barraque; m, Georges Delerue.

Drama **(PR:O MPAA:R)**

WOMAN WITHOUT LOVE, A*½**

(1951, Mex.) 90m Internacional Cinematografica/COL bw (UNA MUJER SIN AMOR)

Tito Junco, Rosario Granados, Julio Villarreal, Joaquin Cordero, Javier Loya, Elda Peralta, Jaime Calpe, Eva Calvo, Miguel Manzano.

Luis Bunuel's rarely seen adaptation of Guy de Maupassant's "Pierre et Jean" begins in an antique shop run by dealer Carlos Montero and Rosario, the working-class woman he saved from a life of poverty (along with her family) by marrying her. Although Rosario works in the shop, her husband runs the business just as he completely controls her home life. When Carlos is informed by the school principal that his son, Carlito, was caught stealing, he explodes with rage and plans the boy's punishment without even hearing his son's version of the story. Rosario objects, telling her husband that he can treat her without love, but not her son. The boy eventually runs away and is befriended by construction foreman Julio Mistral, who returns him to the shop, where Julio is welcomed as a friend and embraced by the boy's gracious father. Julio and Rosario exchange glances and later, when her husband has left the room, make their desires known. Eventually, unable to control their attraction to one another, they makes plans to escape to Brazil with the boy. Time passes, however, Rosario has another son, and life takes a perverse twist. As he did so successfully, if in varying degrees, during his Mexican period, Bunuel here again injects his own, surrealist obsession-with-obsessions into an otherwise routine melodrama (which bears little resemblance in tone to Maupassant's original). Love and passion control all, guiding the actions and twisting the fate of their victims, and assaulting the concept of family in the process. In Spanish with yellow English subtitles.

p, Oscar Dancigers; d, Luis Bunuel; w, Luis Bunuel, Jaime Salvador, Rodolfo Usigli (based on the story "Pierre Et Jean" by Guy De Maupassant); ph, Raul Martinez Solares; ed, Jorge Bustos; m, Raul Lavista.

Drama **(PR:C MPAA:NR)**

WORLD OF APU, THE***½

(1959, India) 103m Ray/Harrison bw (APUR SANSAR)

Soumitra Chatterjee *(Apu),* Sharmila Tagore *(Aparna),* Swapan Mukherji *(Pulu),* Aloke Chakravarty *(Kajol),* Shefalika *(Aparna's Mother),* Dhiresh Mazumder *(Aparna's Father),* Dhiren Ghosh *(Landlord),* Abhijit Chatterjee *(Aparna's Brother),* Belarni *(Apu's Neighbor),* Shanti Bhattacharjee *(Office Associate).*

THE WORLD OF APU is the third and final installment of Satyajit Ray's "Apu Trilogy," the most famous group of films to come out of India. After following the young character of Apu from his early years (PATHER PANCHALI) to his schooldays (APARAJITO), the trilogy picks up with Soumitra Chatterjee in the role of Apu as a young man. His desire is to become a writer, but a lack of finances has forced him to abandon his university studies. His life changes, however, when he meets again his old friend Pulu (Shapan Mukerji). Together, the two travel to the wedding of Pulu's cousin, Aparna (Sharmila Tagore). When the bridegroom turns out to be insane and the wedding is canceled, Apu agrees to marry Aparna to save her from ridicule return with her to his Calcutta apartment to start a new life, but destiny does not look kindly upon the newlyweds. In this final entry, Ray rounds out the life of Apu, charting his loss of innocence and painting a detailed and textured portrait of Indian life in the process. In Apu, Ray has brought to the screen a character who lives out his story, though he is never able to finally put it on paper. A rich and insightful picture, THE WORLD OF APU, despite being rooted deep in Indian culture, strikes a universal humanistic chord. In Bengali with English subtitles.

p, Satyajit Ray, Amiyanath Mukerjee; d, Satyajit Ray; w, Satyajit Ray (based on the novel *Aparajito* by Bibhutibhusan Bandopadhaya); ph, Subrata Mitra; ed, Dulal Dutta; m, Ravi Shankar.

Drama **(PR:A MPAA:NR)**

WRONG MOVE***½

(1975, Ger.) 103m Solaris-WDR/Bauer c (FALSCHE BEWEGUNG)

Rudiger Vogler *(Wilhelm Meister),* Hanna Schygulla *(Therese),* Hans Christian Blech *(Laertes),* Nastassia Kinski *(Mignon),* Peter Kern *(Bernhard Landau),* Marianne Hoppe *(Wilhelm's Mother),* Ivan Desny *(Industrialist),* Lisa Kreuzer *(Janine),* Adolf Hansen *(Conductor),* Wim Wenders *(Man in Dining Car).*

Scripted by Peter Handke—who cowrote Wim Wenders' THE GOALIE'S ANXIETY AT THE PENALTY KICK—this cool, distant film about unsympathetic characters is nonetheless engaging because of the special touch Wenders brings to it. WRONG MOVE centers on aspiring writer Wilhelm Meister (Rudiger Vogler), who sits in his apartment wondering how he can ever write when he despises people so intensely. At the insistence of his mother, Wilhelm goes out into the world, and during a train ride he meets the old Laertes (Hans Christian Blech), his teenage traveling companion, Mignon (Nastassia Kinski), and the attractive Therese Farner (Hanna Schygulla). Later, these four hook up with Bernhard Landau (Peter Kern) and wander the streets of Bonn, breaking up soon after Wilhelm discovers Laertes is a former concentration camp commandant. Like Joseph Bloch, the goalie in the earlier Handke-Wenders collaboration who can't even to attempt to block a shot, Wilhelm is incapable of taking action. But un like Bloch, Wilhelm is unable to do anything to change himself. Fearful of making a wrong move, he ends up doing nothing, hoping by the film's end that some miracle will alter his life. A challenging film that purposely lacks the charm found in Wenders' other pictures, WRONG MOVE received awards for Best Picture and Best Director at the Berlin Film Festival, as well as being honored for its script, editing, music, and cinematography. In German with English subtitles.

p, Peter Genee; d, Wim Wenders; w, Peter Hanke (based on the novel *Wilhelm Meister's Apprenticeship* by Johann Wolfgang von Goethe); ph, Robby Muller; ed, Peter Przygodda; m, Jurgen Knieper, Troggs.

Drama **(PR:C-O MPAA:NR)**

WUTHERING HEIGHTS****

(1953, Mex.) 90m Tepeyac bw (ABISMOS DE PASION; CUMBRES BORRASCOSAS)

Irasema Dilian *(Catalina),* Jorge Mistral *(Alejandro),* Lilia Prado, Ernesto Alonso, Luis Aceves Castaneda, Francisco Reiguera, Hortensia Santovena, Jaime Gonzalez.

Luis Bunuel's long-planned version of Emily Bronte's novel (the screenplay was written some 20 years before the film was made, but no backer could be found), a favorite work of the Surrealists, shifts the setting from the English moors to a small Mexican estate and turns Heathcliff into Alejandro (Jorge Mistral) and Cathy into Catalina (Irasema Dilian). As the Spanish title implies, the lovers fall into an "abyss of passion"—a place where love exists above and beyond all else. Unlike Hollywood's sanitized backlot version of Bronte, Bunuel's reworking is rooted in the darker aspects of love. The film opens with a slow-motion image of crows as they scatter from a twisted, leafless tree, frightened by an off-screen gunshot. This image of death and decay hangs over the film until the very end—a beautiful, but wholly amoral, final scene in which the distraught Alejandro violates Catalina's tomb, unearthing her corpse in order to be forever united with his love. The film is flawed (the acting is flatter than usual, the emphasis is overly literary), but it is one of the most passionate and expressionistic works of Bunuel's Mexican period, featuring an ending as brilliant as anything ever accomplished by a surrealist artist. In Spanish with yellow English subtitles.

p, Oscar Dancigers; d, Luis Bunuel; w, Luis Bunuel, Julio Alejandro, Dino Maiuri (based on the novel by Emily Bronte); ph, Agustin Jimenez; ed, Carlos Savage; m, Raul Lavista, Richard Wagner.

Romance **(PR:C MPAA:NR)**

XYZ

YESTERDAY, TODAY, AND TOMORROW***

(1963, It./Fr.) 119m CC Champion-Concordia/Embassy c (IERI, OGGI E DOMANI; GB: SHE GOT WHAT SHE ASKED FOR)

"Adelina-Naples": Sophia Loren *(Adelina),* Marcello Mastroianni *(Carmine),* Aldo Giuffre *(Pasquale Nardella),* Agostino Salvietti *(Lawyer Verace),* Lino Mattera *(Amadeo Scapece),* Tecla Scarano *(Bianchina Verace),* Silvia Monelli *(Elvira Nardella),* Carlo Croccolo *(Auctioneer),* Pasquale Cennamo *(Police Captian),* "Anna—Milan": Sophia Loren *(Anna),* Marcello Mastroianni *(Renzo),* Armando Trovajoli *(Other Man),* "Mara—Rome": Sophia Loren *(Mara),* Marcello Mastroianni *(Augusto Rusconi),* Tina Pica *(Grandmother),* Giovanni Ridolfi *(Umberto),* Gennaro Di Gregario *(Grandfather).*

This Italian sex trilogy teams up two of that country's biggest stars, Sophia Loren and Marcello Mastroianni, with director Vittorio De Sica. The first and most interesting episode, "Adelina," features Loren as the title Neopolitan, who is in trouble with the law, and Mastroianni as her husband, who discovers a legal loophole: pregnant women cannot be jailed until six months after the child's birth. Adelina duly gets pregnant, and pregnant again, and so on until her mate can no longer take it. "Anna" casts Loren as the Milanese wife of an industrialist who drops her lover (Mastroianni) after he nearly wrecks her beloved sports car. Lastly, in "Mara," the eponymous Roman prostitute (Loren) resists the temptation to seduce a young seminarian (Giovanni Ridolfi) who has fallen in love with her, and even takes a one-week vow of chastity herself, much to the frustration of her most devoted client (Mastroianni). Although YESTERDAY, TODAY AND TOMORROW won a Best Foreign-Language Film Academy Award, it's hardly representative of the best work of its stars, director (UMBERTO D; THE BICYCLE THIEF; SHOESHINE), or screenwriters (Cesare Zavattini, De Sica's frequent collaborator, contributes "Anna" and "Mara"). It is, however, an enjoyable romp, buoyed by the professionalism of all concerned.

p, Carlo Ponti; d, Vittorio De Sica; w, "Adelina," Eduardo De Filippo, Isabella Quarantotti, "Anna," Cesare Zavattini, Billa Billa Zanuso (based on the story "Troppo Ricca" by Alberto Moravia), "Mara," Zavattini; ph, Giuseppe Rotunno (Techniscope, Technicolor); ed, Adriana Novelli; m, Armando Trovajoli.

Comedy/Drama **(PR:O MPAA:NR)**

YOJIMBO***½

(1961, Jap.) 110m Toho-Kurosawa/Seneca bw

Toshiro Mifune *(Sanjuro Kuwabatake),* Eijiro Tono *(Gonji),* Seizaburo Kawazu *(Seibei),* Isuzu Yamada *(Orin),* Hiroshi Tachikawa *(Yoichiro),* Kyu Sazanka *(Ushitora),* Daisuke Kato *(Inokichi),* Tatsuya Nakadai *(Unosuke),* Kamatari Fujiwara *(Tazaemon),* Takashi Shimura *(Tokuemon),* Ikio Sawamura *(Hansuke),* Atsushi Watanabe *(Coffin Maker),* Yoshio Tsuchiya *(Kohei the Farmer),* Yoko Tsukasa *(Nui).*

Directed by Japanese master Akira Kurosawa, YOJIMBO is the spirited, strangely moralistic tale of Sanjuro Kuwabatake (Toshiro Mifune), a samurai who wanders into a town divided by a civil war. On one side stands silk merchant Tazaemon (Kamatari Fujiwara), on the other sake merchant Tokuemon (Takashi Shimura)—both equally evil. Sanjuro views their conflict as an opportunity to make some money, as well as secure food and lodging. Hired by Tazaemon as a *yojimbo* (bodyguard), Sanjro puts a devious plan of his own into effect, pretending to enter the employ of Tokuemon, then secretly killing some of his men. Sanjuro is caught, however, brutally beaten, and tossed in prison. He escapes, in time to witness the momentous battle between the two factions that ultimately brings peace to the war-ravaged village. Kurosawa's entertaining direction, Kazuo Miyagawa's beautiful widescreen photography, and Mifune's eccentric acting combined to make YOJIMBO such a box-office success that Toho Studios asked the director to make another film along similar lines. The result was SANJURO, which again starred Mifune as an unorthodox samurai. The videocassette is available in both dubbed and subtitled (Japanese into English) versions.

d, Akira Kurosawa; w, Akira Kurosawa, Ryuzo Kikushima, Hideo Oguni; ph, Kazuo Miyagawa (Tohoscope); m, Masaru Sato.

Action **(PR:O MPAA:NR)**

YOL*½**

(1981, Turk./Switz.) 111m Guney-Cactus-Maran/ Triumph-Artificial Eye c (AKA: THE ROAD; Trans: The Way)

Tarik Akan *(Seyit Ali),* Halil Ergun *(Mehmet Salih),* Necmettin Cobanoglu *(Omer),* Serif Sezer *(Zine),* Meral Orhonsoy *(Emine),* Semra Ucar *(Gulbahar),* Hikmet Celik *(Mevlut),* Sevda Aktolga *(Meral),* Tuncay Akca *(Yusuf).*

Five Turkish convicts are given a week's leave from prison to visit their loved ones in this extraordinarily painful drama. What has promised to be an emotionally uplifting period of freedom takes a disastrous and tragic turn for each of the prisoners, one of whom comes home to find that his brother has been murdered by police, while another learns of his wife's infidelity. A visually intense examination of Turkish mores and customs (the scene of the prisoner dragging his unfaithful wife into a snowy wasteland is both powerful and alien for Western audiences), YOL was written by actor-turned-director Yilmaz Guney while he was behind bars and directed by one of Guney's former assistants under his supervising instructions. Guney escaped from prison in 1981, and died three years later, after completing his final picture, THE WALL. YOL shared the top prize at Cannes with Costa-Gavras' MISSING, another grim tale of political oppression. In Turkish with English subtitles.

p, Edi Hubschmid, K.L. Puldi; d, Serif Goren; w, Yilmaz Guney; ph, Erdogan Engin (Fujicolor); ed, Yilmaz Guney, Elisabeth Waelchli; m, Sebastian Argol.

Drama **(PR:O MPAA:PG)**

Z****

(1969, Fr./Algeria) 127m Reggane-Office National Pour Le Commerce Et l'Industrie Cinematographique/Cinema V c

Yves Montand *(The Deputy),* Jean-Louis Trintignant *(The Examining Magistrate),* Irene Papas *(Helene),* Jacques Perrin *(Photojournalist),* Charles Denner *(Manuel),* Francois Perier *(Public Prosecutor),* Pierre Dux *(The General),* Julien Guiomar *(The Colonel),* Bernard Fresson *(Matt),* Renato Salvatori *(Yago),* Marcel Bozzuffi *(Vago),* Jean Bouise *(Deputy Pirou),* Georges Geret *(Nick),* Magali Noel *(Nick's Sister),* Jean Daste *(Coste),* Jean-Pierre Miquel *(Pierre),* Guy Mairesse *(Dumas),* Clotilde Joano *(Shoula),* Gerard Darrieu *(Baron),* Jose Artur *(The Newspaper Editor),* Van Doude *(The Hospital Director).*

Originally subtitled "The Anatomy of a Political Assassination," this intense political thriller is based on the real-life 1963 killing of Gregorios Lambrakis, a Greek liberal whose extreme popularity and advocacy of peace shook the stability of the government in power. Starring is Yves Montand, who, although referred to only as "the Deputy," is clearly Lambrakis. After his liberal organization, the Friends of Peace, loses a large meeting hall at the last moment, the Deputy is forced to find another venue. He appeals and is given a permit to hold the meeting in a small, 200-seat auditorium, although it is expected to draw over 4,000. During the meeting, the Deputy's supporters are taunted by a violent right-wing faction, while the police "protection" stands by passively. Later, the police do little to protect the Deputy from a truck that speeds by, from which one of the passengers ferociously clubs the Deputy in the head, killing him. In order to give the appearance of an investigation, the general in charge appoints an Examining Magistrate (Jean-Louis Trintignant), who is believed to be a pawn of the government, but soon surprises all by probing deep into a government conspiracy and cover-up. Rather than appealing only to a politically minded audience, Z found a great deal of enthusiastic support from almost everyone who saw it. At the Cannes Film Festival it received a unanimous vote for the Jury Prize, with Trintignant receiving Best Actor honors. The Academy Awards also responded, with Oscars for Best Foreign Film and Best Editing and nominations for Best Picture, Best Director, and Best Adapted Screenplay. Z succeeds where so many political pictures have failed because of its concentration on the thriller aspects of the story. Borrowing heavily from American conventions, Costa-Gavras' film contains many action-packed, high-tension scenes that help speed along the sometimes confusing politics. Rather than worrying about which right-wing general did what, the audience becomes wrapped up in whether or not a character will survive a beating, or be run down by a speeding car. Detractors complained that the film commercialized and simplified the Lambrakis incident and politics in general. Costa-Gavras responded: "That's the way it is in Greece. Black and White. No Nuances." The videocassette is dubbed in English.

p, Jacques Perrin, Hamed Rachedi; d, Constantine Costa-Gavras; w, Constantine Costa-Gavras, Jorge Semprun (based on the novel by Vassili Vassilikos); ph, Raoul Coutard (Technicolor); ed, Francoise Bonnot; m, Mikis Theodorakis.

Political **(PR:C-O MPAA:M)**

ZABRISKIE POINT**

(1970, US) 112m Trianon/MGM c

Mark Frechette *(Mark),* Daria Halprin *(Daria),* Rod Taylor *(Lee Allen),* Paul Fix *(Cafe Owner),* G.D. Spradlin *(Lee's Associate),* Bill Garaway *(Morty),* Kathleen Cleaver *(Kathleen).*

In his super-successful BLOW-UP, Antonioni made an attempt to understand the English youth movement of the 1960s. Here, in his first American film, Antonioni took his search for answers to America. Unfortunately, with this picture the director falls into two traps: employing endless "anti-Establishment" cliches and saddling himself with the underwhelming talents of Mark Frechette. The picture opens in documentary style, with a meeting of college radicals discussing the meaning of revolution. Mark (Frechette), disgusted with the students' stagnant ideals, declares that he is ready to die—but not of boredom—and walks out. Identified as a cop killer during a campus riot, Mark flees to a nearby airfield, steals a small private plane, flies through Death Valley, and meets Daria (Daria Halprin), a pretty, pot-smoking, meditative secretary. It's not long before they are holding hands at Zabriskie Point, a tourist spot marked by a small plaque explaining that a man named Zabriskie discovered mineral matter there. The psychedelic happenings plod along until the explosive, apocalyptic finale. On the basis of Antonioni's "art-house" following in America, MGM decided to jump on the bandwagon and give the director *carte blanche* for this film. The result is a critical but relatively accurate portrait of America in the late 1960s, which, however, now seems horribly dated. Antonioni concentrates chiefly on the gaps between student radicals and the establishment, naturalism and plasticity, free-spirited individualism and the restraints of modern life. While Antonioni's visual sense is once again in top form, his "mind-expanding" hippie dialog, as delivered by his amateur leads, is painful to experience. MGM hoped that a combination of art-house and hippie audiences would help return their $7 million investment. Instead the film was a box-office and critical bomb, surviving today as a nugget of the hippie culture. In English.

p, Carlo Ponti; d, Michelangelo Antonioni; w, Michelangelo Antonioni, Fred Gardner, Sam Shepard, Tonino Guerra, Clare Peploe (based on a story by Michelangelo Antonioni); ph, Alfio Contini (Panavision, Metrocolor); ed, Franco Arcalli.

Drama **(PR:O MPAA:R)**

ALTERNATE TITLE

Listed below are alternate, foreign, and Great Britain titles of films, followed by the title under which the film appears in this volume.

A

A BOUT DE SOUFFLE (SEE: BREATHLESS)
A HORA DA ESTRELA (SEE: HOUR OF THE STAR, THE)
ADIEU POULET (SEE: FRENCH DETECTIVE, THE)
ADVENTURES OF ST. FRANCIS OF ASSISI, THE (SEE: FLOWERS OF ST. FRANCIS, THE)
AH! LES BELLES BACCHANTES (SEE: FEMMES DE PARIS)
AKAHIGE (SEE: RED BEARD)
ALICE IN DEN STADTEN (SEE: ALICE IN THE CITIES)
ANNE AND MURIEL (SEE: TWO ENGLISH GIRLS)
ANSIKTET (SEE: MAGICIAN, THE)
ANXIETY OF THE GOLAIE AT THE PENALTY KICK (SEE: GOALIE'S ANXIETY AT THE PENALTY KICK, THE)
APA (SEE: FATHER)
APUR SANSAR (SEE: WORLD OF APU, THE)
ASCENSEUR POUR L'ECHAFAUD (SEE: FRANTIC)
ATTENTION! UNE FEMME PEUT EN CACHER UNE AUTRE (SEE: MY OTHER HUSBAND)
AUS DEM LEBEN DES MARIONETTEN (SEE: FROM THE LIFE OF THE MARIONETTES)
AUSTERLITZ (SEE: BATTLE OF AUSTERLITZ, THE)

B

BAILIFF, THE (SEE: SANSHO THE BAILIFF)
BAISERS VOLES (SEE: STOLEN KISSES)
BANDE A PART (SEE: BAND OF OUTSIDERS)
BEGGARS' OPERA (SEE: THREEPENNY OPERA, THE)
BETWEEN TWO WORLDS (SEE: DESTINY)
BEYOND THE WALL (SEE: DESTINY)
BIG DAY, THE (SEE: JOUR DE FETE)
BIG NIGHT, THE (SEE: JOUR DE FETE)
BIRDS OF A FEATHER (SEE: LA CAGE AUX FOLLES)
BIRUMANO TATEGOTO (SEE: BURMESE HARP, THE)
BLONDE IN LOVE, A (SEE: LOVES OF A BLONDE)
BOBO JACCO (SEE: JACKO AND LISE)
BOUDU SAUVE DES EAUX (SEE: BOUDU SAVED FROM DROWNING)
BRONENOSETS POTEMKIN (SEE: BATTLESHIP POTEMKIN)
BRUTE, THE (SEE: EL BRUTO)
BURNING HEARTS (SEE: KOLBERG)
BRUTTI, SPORCHI E CATTIVI (SEE: DOWN AND DIRTY)

C

CABIRIA (SEE: NIGHTS OF CABIRIA, THE)
CARMEN (SEE: BIZET'S CARMEN)
CASTLE OF DOOM (SEE: VAMPYR)
CASTLE OF THE SPIDER'S WEB, THE (SEE: THRONE OF BLOOD)
CAT, THE (SEE: LE CHAT)
CESAR ET ROSALIE (SEE: CESAR AND ROSALIE)
CET OBSCUR OBJET DU DESIRE (SEE: THAT OBSCURE OBJECT OF DESIRE)
CHE? (SEE: DIARY OF FORBIDDEN DREAMS)
CHERE INCONNUE (SEE: I SENT A LETTER TO MY LOVE)
CHRISTO SI E FERMATO A EBOLI (SEE: CHRIST STOPPED AT EBOLI)
CITY AND THE DOGS (SEE: LA CIUDAD Y LOS PERROS)
CLAUDE (SEE: TWO OF US, THE)
CLICKETYCLACK (SEE: DODES 'KA-DEN)
CLIO DE CINQ A SEPT (SEE: CLEO FROM 5 TO 7)
CLOSELY OBSERVED TRAINS (SEE: CLOSELY WATCHED TRAINS)
COBWEB CASTLE (SEE: THRONE OF BLOOD)
COMRADESHIP (SEE: KAMERADSCHAFT)
COUP DE FOUDRE (SEE: ENTRE NOUS)
COUP DE TORCHON (SEE: CLEAN SLATE)
CRIMES OF DR. MABUSE (SEE: TESTAMENT OF DR. MABUSE, THE)
CYBELE (SEE: SUNDAYS AND CYBELE)

D

DAIBOSATSU TOGE (SEE: SWORD OF DOOM, THE)
DAS BOOT (SEE: BOAT, THE)
DAS CABINETT DES DR. CALIGARI (SEE: CABINET OF DR. CALIGARI, THE)
DAS SCHLANGENEI (SEE: SERPENT'S EGG, THE)
DAS TAGEBUCH EINER VERLORENEN (SEE: DIARY OF A LOST GIRL)
DAS TESTAMENT DES DR. MABUSE (SEE: TESTAMENT OF DR. MABUSE, THE)
DAYBREAK (SEE: LE JOUR SE LEVE)
DE STILTE ROND CHRISTINE M. . . (SEE: QUESTION OF SILENCE)
DEATH—JAPANESE STYLE (SEE: FUNERAL, THE)
DEMANTY NOCI (SEE: DIAMONDS OF THE NIGHT)
DER BLAUE ENGEL (SEE: BLUE ANGEL, THE)
DER BULLE UND DAS MAEDCHEN (SEE: COP AND THE GIRL, THE)
DER FANGSCHUSS (SEE: COUP DE GRACE)
DER FUSSGANGER (SEE: PEDESTRIAN, THE)
DER HIMMEL UBER BERLIN (SEE: WINGS OF DESIRE)
DER LETZTE MANN (SEE: LAST LAUGH, THE)
DER MUDE TOD: EIN DEUTSCHES VOLKSLIED IN 6 VERSEN (SEE: DESTINY)
DER STAND DER DINGE (SEE: STATE OF THINGS, THE)
DET SJUNDE INSEGLET (SEE: SEVENTH SEAL, THE)

E

F

G

H

I

LE DERNIER METRO (SEE: LAST METRO, THE)
LE DESERT ROUGE (SEE: RED DESERT)
LE DIABLE AU CORPS (SEE: DEVIL IN THE FLESH, THE)
LE DIMANCHES DE VILLE DAVRAY (SEE: SUNDAYS AND CYBELE)
LE FANTOME DE LA LIBERTE (SEE: PHANTOM OF LIBERTY, THE)
LE GENOU DE CLAIRE (SEE: CLAIRE'S KNEE)
LE GRAND BLEU (SEE: BIG BLUE, THE)
LE GRAND BLOND AVEC UNE CHASSURE NOIRE (SEE: TALL BLOND MAN WITH ONE BLACK SHOE, THE)
LE JOURNAL D'UN CURE DE CAMPAGNE (SEE: DIARY OF A COUNTRY PRIEST)
LE JOURNAL D'UNE FEMME DE CHAMBRE (SEE: DIARY OF A CHAMBERMAID)
LE LIEU DU CRIME (SEE: SCENE OF THE CRIME)
LE LOCATAIRE (SEE: TENANT, THE)
LE MEPRIS (SEE: CONTEMPT)
LE MUR (SEE: WALL, THE)
LE NOTTI DE CABIRIA (SEE: NIGHTS OF CABIRIA, THE)
LE PAYS BLEU (SEE: BLUE COUNTRY, THE)
LE RAYON VERT (SEE: SUMMER)
LE REGLE DU JEU (SEE: RULES OF THE GAME, THE)
LE ROI DE COEUR (SEE: KING OF HEARTS)
LE SALAIRE DE LA PEUR (SEE: WAGES OF FEAR, THE)
LE SANG D'UN POETE (SEE: BLOOD OF A POET, THE)
LE TESTAMENT D'ORPHEE (SEE: TESTAMENT OF ORPHEUS, THE)
LE TESTAMENT DU DR. MABUSE (SEE: TESTAMENT OF DR. MABUSE, THE)
LE VIEIL HOMME ET L'ENFANT (SEE: TWO OF US, THE)
LEGEND OF MUSASHI (SEE: SAMURAI TRILOGY, THE)
LES BAS-FONDS (SEE: LOWER DEPTHS, THE)
LES DEUS ANGALISES ET LE CONTINENT (SEE: TWO ENGLISH GIRLS)
LES DIABOLIQUES (SEE: DIABOLIQUE)
LES JEUX INTERDIT (SEE: FORBIDDEN GAMES)
LES NUITS DE LA PLEINE LUNE (SEE: FULL MOON IN PARIS)
LES PARAPLUIES DE CHERBOURG (SEE: UMBRELLAS OF CHERBOURG, THE)
LES QUATRE CENTS COUPS (SEE: FOUR HUNDRED BLOWS, THE)
LES RIPOUX (SEE: MY NEW PARTNER)
LES SOMNAMBULES (SEE: MON ONCLE D'AMERIQUE)
LES VACANCES DE MONSIEUR HULOT (SEE: MR. HULOT'S HOLIDAY)
LES VALSEUSES (SEE: GOING PLACES)
L'ETERNEL RETOUR (SEE: ETERNAL RETURN, THE)
LETYAT ZHURAVLI (SEE: CRANES ARE FLYING, THE)
L'HORLOGER DE SAINT-PAUL (SEE: CLOCKMAKER, THE)
LIGHT WITHIN, THE (SEE: DESTINY)
LJUBAVNI SLUCAJ ILI TRAGEDIJA SLUZBENICE PTT (SEE: LOVE AFFAIR: OR THE CASE OF THE MISSING SWITCHBOARD OPERATOR)
LO SCEICCO BIANCO (SEE: WHITE SHEIK, THE)
L'OPERA DE QUAT'SOUS (SEE: THREEPENNY OPERA, THE)
LOS SANTOS INOCENTES (SEE: HOLY INNOCENTS, THE)
LOVE ETERNAL (SEE: ETERNAL RETURN, THE)
LOVE PLAY (SEE: PLAYTIME)
LOVER, WIFE (SEE: WIFEMISTRESS)
LOYAL 47 RONIN OF THE GENROKU ERA, THE (SEE: 47 RONIN, THE (PARTS I & II))
LUNCH ON THE GRASS (SEE: PICNIC ON THE GRASS)

M

MA NUIT CHEZ MAUD (SEE: MY NIGHT AT MAUD'S)
MACCHERONI (SEE: MACARONI)
MAD CAGE, THE (SEE: LA CAGE AUX FOLLES)
MADAME DE. . .THE DIAMOND EARRINGS (SEE: EARRINGS OF MADAME DE. . ., THE)
MAGNIFICENT ONE, THE (SEE: LE MAGNIFIQUE)
MAGNIFICENT SEVEN, THE (SEE: SEVEN SAMURAI, THE)
MALICE (SEE: MALICIOUS)
MAN LOOKING SOUTHEAST (SEE: MAN FACING SOUTHEAST)
MANNER (SEE: MEN)
MANON DES SOURCES (SEE: MANON OF THE SPRING)
MARUSA NO ONNA (SEE: TAXING WOMAN, A)
MASKS (SEE: PERSONA)
MASTER SWORDSMAN (SEE: SAMURAI TRILOGY, THE)
MEACHOREI HASORAGIM (SEE: BEYOND THE WALLS)
MIKAN NO TAIKYOKU (SEE: GO-MASTERS, THE)
MILLION, THE (SEE: LE MILLION)
MIRACOLO A MILANO (SEE: MIRACLE IN MILAN)
MITT LIV SOM HUND (SEE: MY LIFE AS A DOG)
MIYAMOTO MUSASHI (SEE: SAMURAI TRILOGY, THE)
MOGLIAMANTE (SEE: WIFEMISTRESS)
MON ONCLE (SEE: MY UNCLE)
MONSIEUR HULOT'S HOLIDAY (SEE: MR. HULOT'S HOLIDAY)
MONTENEGRO—OR PIGS AND PEARLS (SEE: MONTENEGRO)
MORT A VENISE (SEE: DEATH IN VENICE)
MOSCOW DISTRUSTS TEARS (SEE: MOSCOW DOES NOT BELIEVE IN TEARS)
MOSKVA SLYOZAM NE VERIT (SEE: MOSCOW DOES NOT BELIEVE IN TEARS)
MURIEL, OU LE TEMPS D'UN RETOUR (SEE: MURIEL)
MY FATHER, MY MASTER (SEE: PADRE PADRONE)
MYSTERE ALEXINA (SEE: MYSTERY OF ALEXINA, THE)
MYSTERY OF KASPAR HAUSER, THE (SEE: EVERY MAN FOR HIMSELF AND GOD AGAINST ALL)

N

NAGOOA (SEE: DRIFTING)
NAKED NIGHT, THE (SEE: SAWDUST AND TINSEL)
NAKED UNDER LEATHER (SEE: GIRL ON A MOTORCYCLE, THE)
NARK, THE (SEE: LA BALANCE)

NATTVARDSGAESTERNA
(SEE: WINTER LIGHT, THE)
NIGHT OF SAN LORENZO, THE
(SEE: NIGHT OF THE SHOOTING STARS, THE)
NO HABRA MAS PENAS NI OLVIDO (SEE: FUNNY, DIRTY LITTLE WAR, A)
NOBI (SEE: FIRES ON THE PLAIN)
NORA INU (SEE: STRAY DOG)
NOSFERATU, A SYMPHONY OF HORROR (SEE: NOSFERATU)
NOSFERATU EINE SYMPHONIE DES GRAUENS
(SEE: NOSFERATU)
NOT AGAINST THE FLESH
(SEE: VAMPYR)
NOVECENTO (SEE: 1900)
NOZ W WODZIE (SEE: KNIFE IN THE WATER)

O

OBCH OD NA KORZE (SEE: SHOP ON MAIN STREET, THE)
OBERST REDL (SEE: COLONEL REDL)
OCI CIORNIE (SEE: DARK EYES)
OCTOBER (SEE: TEN DAYS THAT SHOOK THE WORLD)
OFFICIAL VERSION, THE
(SEE: OFFICIAL STORY, THE)
OFFRET-SA CRIFICATIO
(SEE: SACRIFICE, THE)
OLD MAND AND THE BOY, THE
(SEE: TWO OF US, THE)
ON A VOLE LA CUISSE DE JUPITER (SEE: JUPITER'S THIGH)
ONLY THE FRENCH CAN
(SEE: FRENCH CANCAN)
ORFEU NEGRO (SEE: BLACK ORPHEUS)
ORPHEE (SEE: ORPHEUS)
OSOSHIKI (SEE: FUNERAL, THE)
OSTRE SLEDOVANE VLAKY
(SEE: CLOSELY WATCHED TRAINS)
OTTO E MEZZO (SEE: 8 1/2)
OUT OF ROSENHEIM
(SEE: BAGDAD CAFE)
OUTSIDERS, THE (SEE: BAND OF OUTSIDERS)
OVIRI (SEE: WOLF AT THE DOOR, THE)

P

PAISA (SEE: PAISAN)
PARIS DOES STRANGE THINGS
(SEE: ELENA AND HER MEN)
PASQUALINO SETTEBELLEZZE
(SEE: SEVEN BEAUTIES)
PASQUALINO: SEVEN BEAUTIES
(SEE: SEVEN BEAUTIES)
PAULINE A LA PLAGE
(SEE: PAULINE AT THE BEACH)
PEAU D'ANE (SEE: DONKEY SKIN)
PEEK-A-BOO (SEE: FEMMES DE PARIS)
PIRATE'S FIANCEE (SEE: VERY CURIOUS GIRL, A)
PLEIN SUD (SEE: HEAT OF DESIRE)
POKAYANIYE
(SEE: REPENTANCE)
POPIOL Y DIAMENT (SEE: ASHES AND DIAMONDS)
POTE TIN KYRIAKI (SEE: NEVER ON SUNDAY)
POTEMKIN (SEE: BATTLESHIP POTEMKIN)
POUVOIS INTIME (SEE: BLIND TRUST)
PREPAREZ VOS MOUCHOIRS
(SEE: GET OUT YOUR HANDKERCHIEFS)
PROFESSION: REPORTER
(SEE: PASSENGER, THE)

R

RED HEAD, THE (SEE: POIL DE CAROTTE)
REDL EZREDES (SEE: COLONEL REDL)
REHEARSAL FOR A CRIME
(SEE: CRIMINAL LIFE OF ARCHIBALDO DE LA CRUZ, THE)
RIDDAREN OCH DODEN
(SEE: SEVENTH SEAL, THE)
RISE OF LOUIS XIV, THE
(SEE: RISE TO POWER OF LOUIS XIV, THE)
ROAD, THE (SEE: LA STRADA)
ROMA, CITTA APERTA
(SEE: OPEN CITY)
ROMAN POLANSKI'S DIARY OF FORBIDDEN DREAMS
(SEE: DIARY OF FORBIDDEN DREAMS)
ROME, OPEN CITY (SEE: OPEN CITY)
ROSE IN THE MUD, THE
(SEE: BAD SLEEP WELL, THE)
RUE CASES NEGRES
(SEE: SUGAR CANE ALLEY)

S

SAGA OF THE ROAD, THE
(SEE: PATHER PANCHALI)
SAIKAKU ICHIDAI ONNA
(SEE: LIFE OF CHARU)
SANS TOIT NI LOI
(SEE: VAGABOND)
SANSHO DAYO (SEE: SANSHO THE BAILIFF)
SASOM I EN SPEGEL
(SEE: THROUGH A GLASS DARKLY)
SATYRICON (SEE: FELLINI SATYRICON)
SCENER UR ETT AKTENSKAP
(SEE: SCENES FROM A MARRIAGE)
SCHERZO DEL DISTINO IN AGGUATO DIETRO L'ANGLO COME UN BRIGANTE DI STRADA (SEE: JOKE OF DESTINY, A)
SCIUSCIA (SEE: SHOESHINE)
SECRET OF ANNA, THE
(SEE: CRIA!)
SEDOTTA E ABBANDONATA
(SEE: SEDUCED AND ABANDONED)
SEDUITE ET ABANDONNEE
(SEE: SEDUCED AND ABANDONED)
SEKKA TOMURAI ZASHI
(SEE: IREZUMI (SPIRIT OF TATTOO))
SHADOW WARRIOR, THE
(SEE: KAGEMUSHA)
SHICHININ NO SAMURAI
(SEE: SEVEN SAMURAI, THE)
SHINJO TEN NO AMIJIMA
(SEE: DOUBLE SUICIDE)
SHOOT THE PIANIST
(SEE: SHOOT THE PIANO PLAYER)
SHOP ON HIGH STREET, THE
(SEE: SHOP ON MAIN STREET, THE)
SIGNE CHARLOTTE
(SEE: SINCERELY CHARLOTTE)
SILKEN SKIN (SEE: SOFT SKIN, THE)
SMULTRONSTALLET (SEE: WILD STRAWBERRIES)
SOIL (SEE: EARTH)
SOLDIERS, THE (SEE: LES CARABINIERS)
SOMMARLEK (SEE: SUMMER INTERLUDE)
SOMMARNATTENS LEENDE
(SEE: SMILES OF A SUMMER NIGHT)
SONG OF THE ROAD
(SEE: PATHER PANCHALI)
SOUS LES TOITS DE PARIS
(SEE: UNDER THE ROOFS OF PARIS)
SPECTOR OF FREEDOM, THE
(SEE: PHANTOM OF LIBERTY, THE)

INDEX

Individuals listed in the Index are grouped by function as follows:

Actors (major players only)
Cinematographers
Directors
Editors
Music Composers
Producers
Screenwriters
Source Authors (authors of the original material or creators of the characters upon which the film is based)

Individual names are followed by an alphabetical listing of the films in which they were involved.

ACTORS (Major players)

Arnoul, Francoise
FRENCH CANCAN

Arquette, Rosanna
BIG BLUE, THE

Arski, N.N.
ALEXANDER NEVSKY

Artzorn, Robert
WANNSEE CONFERENCE, THE

Atkine, Feodor
LE BEAU MARIAGE

Atzorn, Robert
FROM THE LIFE OF THE MARIONETTES

Audran, Stephane
CLEAN SLATE (COUP DE TORCHON)
LA CAGE AUX FOLLES 3: THE WEDDING
DISCREET CHARM OF THE BOURGEOISIE, THE
BABETTE'S FEAST
BAD GIRLS

Auger, Claudine
ASSOCIATE, THE

Aumont, Jean-Pierre
CAT AND MOUSE
DAY FOR NIGHT
SWEET COUNTRY

Aumont, Michel
LES COMPERES
SUNDAY IN THE COUNTRY, A

Auteuil, Daniel
JEAN DE FLORETTE
MANON OF THE SPRING

Azema, Sabine
SUNDAY IN THE COUNTRY, A

Aznavour, Charles
EDITH AND MARCEL
SHOOT THE PIANO PLAYER

Baker, Frank
ARIA

Bakri, Muhamad
BEYOND THE WALLS

Balin, Mireille
PEPE LE MOKO

Balint, Andras
FATHER

Ban, Junzaburo
DODES 'KA-DEN

Banderas, Antonio
LAW OF DESIRE

Banerji, Kanu
PATHER PANCHALI

Banerji, Karuna
APARAJITO
PATHER PANCHALI

Banerji, Runki
PATHER PANCHALI

Banerji, Subir
PATHER PANCHALI

Bannerjee, Chandana
TWO DAUGHTERS

Bannerjee, Victor
HOME AND THE WORLD, THE

Bansagi, Ildiko
MEPHISTO

Bardot, Brigitte
AND GOD CREATED WOMAN
CONTEMPT
VERY PRIVATE AFFAIR, A

Barends, Edda
QUESTION OF SILENCE

Barjac, Sophie
HOLIDAY HOTEL

Barouh, Pierre
MAN AND A WOMAN, A

Barr, Jean-Marc
BIG BLUE, THE

Barrault, Jean-Louis
LA NUIT DE VARENNES

Barrault, Marie-Christine
MY NIGHT AT MAUD'S
SWANN IN LOVE

Barsky, Vladimir
BATTLESHIP POTEMKIN

Bartley, Janet
HARDER THEY COME, THE

Basehart, Richard
LA STRADA

Batalov, Alexei
CRANES ARE FLYING, THE
MOSCOW DOES NOT BELIEVE IN TEARS

Bates, Alan
KING OF HEARTS

Batti, Jeanette
FOUR BAGS FULL

Battisti, Carlo
UMBERTO D

Baur, Harry
POIL DE CAROTTE

Baviera, Jose
EXTERMINATING ANGEL, THE

Baye, Nathalie
BEAU PERE
LA BALANCE
GREEN ROOM, THE
RETURN OF MARTIN GUERRE, THE

Beart, Emmanuelle
MANON OF THE SPRING

Beckhaus, Friedrich
WANNSEE CONFERENCE, THE

Bedos, Guy
PARDON MON AFFAIRE

Belli, Agostina
SEDUCTION OF MIMI, THE

Belmondo, Jean-Paul
BREATHLESS
TWO WOMEN
LE DOULOS
LE MAGNIFIQUE

Bendova, Jitka
CLOSELY WATCHED TRAINS

Benedetti, Nelly
SOFT SKIN, THE

Bennent, David
TIN DRUM, THE

Bennent, Heinz
LOST HONOR OF KATHARINA BLUM, THE

Benrath, Martin
FROM THE LIFE OF THE MARIONETTES

Beregi, Oskar
TESTAMENT OF DR. MABUSE, THE

Berger, Helmut
GARDEN OF THE FINZI-CONTINIS, THE
DAMNED, THE

Berger, Nicole
SHOOT THE PIANO PLAYER

Berger, Toni
SUGARBABY

Berggren, Thommy
ELVIRA MADIGAN

Bergman, Ingmar
LESSON IN LOVE, A

Bergman, Ingrid
AUTUMN SONATA
FEAR
STROMBOLI
ELENA AND HER MEN

Bergonzi, Carlo
ARIA

Bernard, Jacques
LES ENFANTS TERRIBLES

Berri, Claude
LE SEX SHOP

Berry, Jules
LE JOUR SE LEVE

Berry, Richard
L'ADDITION
LA BALANCE

Berto, Juliet
LE SEX SHOP

Besnehard, Dominique
A NOS AMOURS

Besse, Ariel
BEAU PERE

Bestayeva, Tatyana
SHADOWS OF FORGOTTEN ANCESTORS

Bidonde, Hector
FUNNY, DIRTY LITTLE WAR, A

Bigagli, Claudio
NIGHT OF THE SHOOTING STARS, THE

Biral, Thelma
EL MUERTO

Birch, Peter
ARIA

Birkin, Jane
DUST
MAKE ROOM FOR TOMORROW

Birman, Serafima
IVAN THE TERRIBLE PART I AND II

Bischofova, Ilse
DIAMONDS OF THE NIGHT

Bisset, Jacqueline
DAY FOR NIGHT
LE MAGNIFIQUE

Bjoernstrand, Gunnar
FANNY AND ALEXANDER

Bjork, Anita
SECRETS OF WOMEN

Bjornstrand, Gunnar
AUTUMN SONATA
LESSON IN LOVE, A
DREAMS
MAGICIAN, THE
SECRETS OF WOMEN
SEVENTH SEAL, THE
SMILES OF A SUMMER NIGHT
PERSONA
WILD STRAWBERRIES
WINTER LIGHT, THE
THROUGH A GLASS DARKLY

Blain, Gerard
LE BEAU SERGE

Blanchar, Dominique
L'AVVENTURA

Blanche, Roland
DANTON

Blanck, Dorothee
CLEO FROM 5 TO 7

Blavette, Charles
TONI

Blier, Bernard
TALL BLOND MAN WITH ONE BLACK SHOE, THE

Blinnikov, S.K.
ALEXANDER NEVSKY

Bockmann, Gerd
WANNSEE CONFERENCE, THE

Bogarde, Dirk
DESPAIR
DEATH IN VENICE
PROVIDENCE
DAMNED, THE
NIGHT PORTER, THE

Bohringer, Richard
L'ADDITION
DIVA
SUBWAY
LE GRAND CHEMIN

Bonnaire, Sandrine
A NOS AMOURS
VAGABOND

Bosco, Maria
DOWN AND DIRTY

Bose, Lucia
LUMIERE

Bouise, Jean
LE DERNIER COMBAT

Bouix, Evelyne
EDITH AND MARCEL
MAN AND A WOMAN: 20 YEARS LATER, A

Boujenah, Michel
THREE MEN AND A CRADLE

Boulanger, Daniel
BREATHLESS

Bouquet, Carole
THAT OBSCURE OBJECT OF DESIRE

Bouquet, Regis
LE BAL

Bourseiller, Antoine
CLEO FROM 5 TO 7

Bourvil
FOUR BAGS FULL

Bovo, Brunella
WHITE SHEIK, THE

Bowie, David
MERRY CHRISTMAS, MR. LAWRENCE

Boyer, Charles
EARRINGS OF MADAME DE . . ., THE
MAYERLING

Boyer, Myriem
HOLIDAY HOTEL

Boyle, Peter
HAMMETT

Bradshaw, Carl
HARDER THEY COME, THE

Braga, Sonia
GABRIELA
DONA FLOR AND HER TWO HUSBANDS
KISS OF THE SPIDER WOMAN

Brandauer, Klaus Maria
COLONEL REDL
MEPHISTO

Brando, Marlon
LAST TANGO IN PARIS

Brasseur, Claude
BAND OF OUTSIDERS
LA BOUM
ELUSIVE CORPORAL, THE
PARDON MON AFFAIRE

Brasseur, Pierre
KING OF HEARTS
HORROR CHAMBER OF DR. FAUSTUS, THE

Brauss, Arthur
GOALIE'S ANXIETY AT THE PENALTY KICK, THE

Brazzi, Rossano
BATTLE OF AUSTERLITZ, THE

Brejchova, Hana
LOVES OF A BLONDE

Brialy, Jean-Claude
CLAIRE'S KNEE
KING OF HEARTS
PHANTOM OF LIBERTY, THE
TONIO KROGER
LE BEAU SERGE

Brightwell, Paul
ARIA

Brooks, Louise
PANDORA'S BOX
DIARY OF A LOST GIRL

Brosset, Colette
FEMMES DE PARIS

Brown, Eleonor
TWO WOMEN

Buchegger, Christine
FROM THE LIFE OF THE MARIONETTES

Buchholz, Horst
APHRODITE

Buchrieser, Franz
COP AND THE GIRL, THE

Bueno, Gustavo
LA CIUDAD Y LOS PERROS

Bujold, Genevieve
KING OF HEARTS

Bunster, Carmen
ALSINO AND THE CONDOR

Burlyayev, Kolya
MY NAME IS IVAN

Burstyn, Ellen
PROVIDENCE

Byrne, Gabriel
HANNAH K.
JULIA AND JULIA

Cadenat, Garry
SUGAR CANE ALLEY

Calamai, Clara
OSSESSIONE

Camero, Juan Jose
EL MUERTO

Campbell, Paul
GOLDEN COACH, THE

Cancellieri, Alba
JULIET OF THE SPIRITS

Cantafora, Antonio
GABRIELA

Capolicchio, Lino
GARDEN OF THE FINZI-CONTINIS, THE

Capprioli, Vittorio
LE MAGNIFIQUE

Caprioli, Vittorio
GENERAL DELLA ROVERE

Capucine
FELLINI SATYRICON
APHRODITE

Cardinale, Claudia
BATTLE OF AUSTERLITZ, THE
HENRY IV
GIFT, THE

8 1/2
MAN IN LOVE, A
FITZCARRALDO

Carell, Lianella
BICYCLE THIEF, THE

Carmet, Jean
BLACK AND WHITE IN COLOR
RETURN OF THE TALL BLOND MAN WITH ONE BLACK SHOE, THE
INVESTIGATION

Carol, Martine
BATTLE OF AUSTERLITZ, THE
LOLA MONTES

Caron, Leslie
DANGEROUS MOVES
MAN WHO LOVED WOMEN, THE

Carradine, David
SERPENT'S EGG, THE

Carras, Costa
IPHIGENIA

Carriere, Mathieu
WOMAN IN FLAMES, A

Cartaxo, Marcelia
HOUR OF THE STAR, THE

Carton, Pauline
BLOOD OF A POET, THE

Caruso, Margherita
GOSPEL ACCORDING TO ST. MATTHEW, THE

Casares, Maria
ORPHEUS

Casilio, Maria Pia
UMBERTO D

Caspar, Horst
KOLBERG

Cassel, Jean-Pierre
ELUSIVE CORPORAL, THE
LA TRUITE (THE TROUT)

Castel, Lou
EYES, THE MOUTH, THE

Castelnuovo, Nino
UMBRELLAS OF CHERBOURG, THE
CAMILLE 2000

Caven, Ingrid
MALOU

Ceccaldi, Daniel
CHLOE IN THE AFTERNOON
HOLIDAY HOTEL

Celi, Adolfo
KING OF HEARTS

Celier, Caroline
L'ANNEE DES MEDUSES

Cerdan, Marcel Jr.
EDITH AND MARCEL

Cervier, Elisa
TENDRES COUSINES

Chaplin, Geraldine
CRIA!

Charbit, Corynne
LA CHEVRE

Charpin, Fernand
CESAR

Chatelais, Jean-Yves
TENDRES COUSINES

Chatterjee, Anil
TWO DAUGHTERS

Chatterjee, Soumitra
HOME AND THE WORLD, THE
WORLD OF APU, THE

Chatterjee, Swatilekha
HOME AND THE WORLD, THE

Chen, Joan
LAST EMPEROR, THE

Chereau, Patrice
DANTON

Cherkassov, Nikolai
ALEXANDER NEVSKY
IVAN THE TERRIBLE PART I AND II

Chiaki, Minoru
HIDDEN FORTRESS, THE

Chiari, Walter
BELLISSIMA

Chionetti, Carlo
RED DESERT

Chopel, Farid
L'ADDITION

Christensen, Emil Hass
ORDET

Christie, Julie
FAHRENHEIT 451
MISS MARY

Clayburgh, Jill
HANNAH K.

Clement, Aurore
PARIS, TEXAS
INVITATION AU VOYAGE

Clementi, Pierre
CONFORMIST, THE

Cliff, Jimmy
HARDER THEY COME, THE

Clouzot, Vera
DIABOLIQUE
WAGES OF FEAR, THE

Cluzet, Francois
ROUND MIDNIGHT

Cobo, Roberto
LOS OLVIDADOS

Cocteau, Jean
TESTAMENT OF ORPHEUS, THE

Cohen, Alain
TWO OF US, THE

Collard, Paul
ARIA

Coluche
MY BEST FRIEND'S GIRL
TCHAO PANTIN

Comyn, Charles
PLACE OF WEEPING

Constantin, Michel
VERY CURIOUS GIRL, A

Constantine, Eddie
ALPHAVILLE

Conti, Tom
MERRY CHRISTMAS, MR. LAWRENCE

Cordy, Annie
LE CHAT

Cordy, Raymond
A NOUS LA LIBERTE

Corey, Isabel
BOB LE FLAMBEUR

Cornu, Aurora
CLAIRE'S KNEE

Cortese, Valentina
DAY FOR NIGHT

Courcel, Nicole
SUNDAYS AND CYBELE

Cox, Arthur
ARIA

Coyote, Peter
MAN IN LOVE, A

Crisa, Erno
LADY CHATTERLEY'S LOVER

Cruz, Ernesto Gomez
EL NORTE

Cullum, John
SWEET COUNTRY

Cuny, Alain
EMMANUELLE
MILKY WAY, THE

Curtis, Mickey
FIRES ON THE PLAIN

Curzi, Pierre
DECLINE OF THE AMERICAN EMPIRE, THE
BLIND TRUST

Cusack, Cyril
FAHRENHEIT 451

Cybulski, Zbigniew
ASHES AND DIAMONDS

D'Angelo, Beverly
ARIA

Dagover, Lil
DESTINY

Dahlbeck, Eva
LESSON IN LOVE, A
DREAMS
SECRETS OF WOMEN
SMILES OF A SUMMER NIGHT

Dalio, Marcel
GRAND ILLUSION
RULES OF THE GAME, THE

Dalle, Beatrice
BETTY BLUE

Dani
LOVE ON THE RUN

Danilova, A.S.
ALEXANDER NEVSKY

Dao-lin, Sun
GO-MASTERS, THE

Darc, Mireille
RETURN OF THE TALL BLOND MAN WITH ONE BLACK SHOE, THE
TALL BLOND MAN WITH ONE BLACK SHOE, THE

Darrieux, Danielle
EARRINGS OF MADAME DE . . ., THE
SCENE OF THE CRIME
MAYERLING
LADY CHATTERLEY'S LOVER

Dassas, Stella
HIROSHIMA, MON AMOUR

Dassin, Jules
NEVER ON SUNDAY

Daste, Jean
GREEN ROOM, THE
L'ATALANTE

Dauphin, Claude
MADAME ROSA
LE PLAISIR

Davis, Brad
QUERELLE

Dawn, Marpessa
BLACK ORPHEUS

Dax, Jean
MAYERLING

Day, Josette
BEAUTY AND THE BEAST

Dayan, Assi
BEYOND THE WALLS

de Almeida, Joaquim
GOOD MORNING BABYLON

de Funes, Louis
FEMMES DE PARIS

de Haviland, Consuelo
BETTY BLUE

de Landa, Juan
OSSESSIONE

de Lint, Derek
ASSAULT, THE

de Lucia, Paco
CARMEN

De Niro, Robert
1900

de Oliveira, Lourdes
BLACK ORPHEUS

De Putti, Lya
VARIETY

de Rosa, Francesco
LE BAL

de Santis, Luisa
SOTTO. . .SOTTO

De Sica, Vittorio
BATTLE OF AUSTERLITZ, THE
GENERAL DELLA ROVERE
EARRINGS OF MADAME DE . . ., THE

Dea, Marie
ORPHEUS

Debucourt, Jean
DEVIL IN THE FLESH, THE

Decombie, Guy
JOUR DE FETE

Decomble, Guy
BOB LE FLAMBEUR

Degermark, Pia
ELVIRA MADIGAN

del Sol, Laura
CARMEN
EL AMOR BRUJO

Delair, Suzy
GERVAISE

Delamare, Lise
LA MARSEILLAISE

Delofski, Sevilla
ARIA

Delon, Alain
ECLIPSE
MR. KLEIN
SWANN IN LOVE
GIRL ON A MOTORCYCLE, THE

Delpy, Julie
PASSION OF BEATRICE, THE

Delschaft, Mary
LAST LAUGH, THE

Deluca, Claudio
SMALL CHANGE

Demazis, Orane
CESAR
FANNY
MARIUS

Deneuve, Catherine
CHOICE OF ARMS
LAST METRO, THE
DONKEY SKIN
LOVE SONGS
SCENE OF THE CRIME
UMBRELLAS OF CHERBOURG, THE
REPULSION

Denis, Jacques
CLOCKMAKER, THE

Denner, Charles
AND NOW MY LOVE
Z
MAN WHO LOVED WOMEN, THE

Depardieu, Gerard
CHOICE OF ARMS
DANTON
LES COMPERES
LAST METRO, THE
GOING PLACES
GET OUT YOUR HANDKERCHIEFS
RETURN OF MARTIN GUERRE, THE
MON ONCLE D'AMERIQUE
MOON IN THE GUTTER, THE
1900
WOMAN NEXT DOOR, THE
JEAN DE FLORETTE
LA CHEVRE

Dermit, Edouard
TESTAMENT OF ORPHEUS, THE
LES ENFANTS TERRIBLES

Desailly, Jean
SOFT SKIN, THE

Desmouceaux, Geory
SMALL CHANGE

Desny, Ivan
MARRIAGE OF MARIA BRAUN, THE

Dewaere, Patrick
BEAU PERE
HEAT OF DESIRE
GET OUT YOUR HANDKERCHIEFS
FRENCH DETECTIVE, THE

Dhery, Robert
FEMMES DE PARIS

Dietrich, Marlene
BLUE ANGEL, THE

Dieudonne, Albert
NAPOLEON

Diffring, Anton
FAHRENHEIT 451

Dilian, Irasema
WUTHERING HEIGHTS

Dombasle, Arielle
PAULINE AT THE BEACH

Domingo, Placido
BIZET'S CARMEN
LA TRAVIATA

Dommartin, Solveig
WINGS OF DESIRE

Donnadieu, Bernard Pierre
RETURN OF MARTIN GUERRE, THE

Donnadieu, Bernard-Pierre
PASSION OF BEATRICE, THE

Dorleac, Francoise
SOFT SKIN, THE

Douglas, Melvyn
TENANT, THE

Doyle, Johnny
ARIA

DuBois, Marie
SHOOT THE PIANO PLAYER

Duchesne, Robert
BOB LE FLAMBEUR

Ducreux, Louis
SUNDAY IN THE COUNTRY, A

Dufilho, Jaques
BLACK AND WHITE IN COLOR

Dumont, Fernand
ARIA

Dumont, Jose
HOUR OF THE STAR, THE

Duperey, Anne
LES COMPERES

Dussollier, Andre
AND NOW MY LOVE
LE BEAU MARIAGE
THREE MEN AND A CRADLE

Ekberg, Anita
LA DOLCE VITA

Eklund, Bengt
PORT OF CALL

Ekman, Gosta
FAUST

Ekman, Hasse
SAWDUST AND TINSEL

Ergun, Halil
YOL

Ernst, Max
L'AGE D'OR

Ersbov, V.L.
ALEXANDER NEVSKY

Esposti, Piera Degli
JOKE OF DESTINY, A

Esquivel, Alan
ALSINO AND THE CONDOR

Eustache, Jean
AMERICAN FRIEND, THE

Faber, Peter
SOLDIER OF ORANGE

Fabian, Francoise
MY NIGHT AT MAUD'S
HAPPY NEW YEAR

Fabiole, Luce
TWO OF US, THE

Fabrizi, Aldo
OPEN CITY
FLOWERS OF ST. FRANCIS, THE

Fabrizi, Franco
GINGER & FRED
I VITELLONI

Faithfull, Marianne
GIRL ON A MOTORCYCLE, THE

Falconetti . Renee
PASSION OF JOAN OF ARC, THE

Falk, Peter
WINGS OF DESIRE

Faria, Betty
BYE-BYE BRAZIL

Farmer, Derek
ARIA

Fassbinder, Rainer Werner
KAMIKAZE '89

Feher, Friedrich
CABINET OF DR. CALIGARI, THE

Fejto, Raphael
AU REVOIR LES ENFANTS

Felix, Maria
FRENCH CANCAN

Fenin, L.A.
ALEXANDER NEVSKY

Fernandez, Wilhelmenia Wiggins
DIVA

Ferreol, Andrea
DESPAIR

Ferrer, Mel
ELENA AND HER MEN

Ferro, Turi
MALICIOUS

Ferzetti, Gabriele
L'AVVENTURA

Finch, Jon
MACBETH

Firth, Peter
TESS

Fischer, Kai
GOALIE'S ANXIETY AT THE PENALTY KICK, THE

Fitzgerald, Danny
ARIA

Fleetwood, Susan
SACRIFICE, THE

Flon, Suzanne
MR. KLEIN
ONE DEADLY SUMMER

Florelle
CRIME OF MONSIEUR LANGE, THE

Fontenay, Catherine
POIL DE CAROTTE

Forrest, Frederic
HAMMETT

Forster, Rudolf
THREEPENNY OPERA, THE

Fossey, Brigitte
BLUE COUNTRY, THE
LA BOUM
GOING PLACES
FORBIDDEN GAMES
MAN WHO LOVED WOMEN, THE

Foundas, Georges
NEVER ON SUNDAY

France, Rolla
A NOUS LA LIBERTE

Franciosa, Anthony
CRICKET, THE

Frankeur, Paul
JOUR DE FETE
MILKY WAY, THE

Fraser, John
REPULSION

Frechette, Mark
ZABRISKIE POINT

Freiss, Stephane
VAGABOND

Fresnay, Pierre
CESAR
GRAND ILLUSION
FANNY
MARIUS

Frey, Sami
BAND OF OUTSIDERS
CESAR AND ROSALIE

Frijda, Nelly
QUESTION OF SILENCE

Frisoni, Gianni
LA CAGE AUX FOLLES II

Fritsch, Willy
SPIES

Frobe, Gert
SERPENT'S EGG, THE

Froeling, Ewa
FANNY AND ALEXANDER

Frolich, Gustav
METROPOLIS

Fujio, Jerry
YOJIMBO

Fujita, Susumu
YOJIMBO

Fujiwara, Kamatari
YOJIMBO

Fuller, Samuel
AMERICAN FRIEND, THE

Funakoshi, Eiji
FIRES ON THE PLAIN

Gabin, Jean
LA BETE HUMAINE
GRAND ILLUSION
FRENCH CANCAN
FOUR BAGS FULL
PEPE LE MOKO
LE CHAT
LE PLAISIR
LE JOUR SE LEVE
LOWER DEPTHS, THE (1936)

Gabor, Miklos
FATHER

Gades, Antonio
BLOOD WEDDING
CARMEN
EL AMOR BRUJO

Gael, Anna
THERESE AND ISABELLE

Galabru, Michel
LA CAGE AUX FOLLES

Galea, Genevieve
LES CARABINIERS

Galland, Jean
LE PLAISIR

Ganz, Bruno
AMERICAN FRIEND, THE
WINGS OF DESIRE

Garcia, Nicole
MON ONCLE D'AMERIQUE
PERIL
LE CAVALEUR (PRACTICE MAKES PERFECT)

Garcin, Ginette
BLUE COUNTRY, THE

Garcin, Henri
WOMAN NEXT DOOR, THE

Gassman, Vittorio
FAMILY, THE
BIG DEAL ON MADONNA STREET, THE

Gaubert, Daniele
CAMILLE 2000

Gelin, Daniel
LE PLAISIR

Genevieve
BEAU PERE

Genn, Leo
LADY CHATTERLEY'S LOVER

Gennari, Lina
UMBERTO D

George, Heinrich
KOLBERG

Gerard, Charles
HAPPY NEW YEAR

Gerard, Henriette
VAMPYR

Gerardi, Brother Nazario
FLOWERS OF ST. FRANCIS, THE

Geret, Georges
DIARY OF A CHAMBERMAID
VERY CURIOUS GIRL, A

Gerron, Kurt
BLUE ANGEL, THE

Ghosal, Smaran
APARAJITO

Gianni, Branduani
MIRACLE IN MILAN

Giannini, Giancarlo
LOVE AND ANARCHY
INNOCENT, THE
SEVEN BEAUTIES
WHERE'S PICONE?
SEDUCTION OF MIMI, THE

Gianninni, Giancarlo
SWEPT AWAY. . .BY AN UNUSUAL DESTINY IN THE BLUE SEA OF AUGUST

Gielgud, John
PROVIDENCE

Girard, Remy
DECLINE OF THE AMERICAN EMPIRE, THE

Girardot, Annie
JUPITER'S THIGH
LE CAVALEUR (PRACTICE MAKES PERFECT)
JACKO AND LISE

Giraud, Roland
THREE MEN AND A CRADLE

Giraudeau, Bernard
L'ANNEE DES MEDUSES

Girotti, Massimo
OSSESSIONE

Giuffre, Aldo
YESTERDAY, TODAY, AND TOMORROW

Glanzelius, Anton
MY LIFE AS A DOG

Gobert, Boy
KAMIKAZE '89

Godard, Jean-Luc
BREATHLESS

Goetzke, Bernhard
DESTINY

Goldmann, Philippe
SMALL CHANGE

Goldsmith, Clio
GIFT, THE

Golisano, Francesco
MIRACLE IN MILAN

Gomez, Fernando Fernan
SPIRIT OF THE BEEHIVE, THE

Gonzalez, Carmelita
MEXICAN BUS RIDE

Gordon, Dexter
ROUND MIDNIGHT

Goya, Chantal
MASCULINE FEMININE

Gozzi, Patricia
SUNDAYS AND CYBELE

Granach, Alexander
KAMERADSCHAFT
NOSFERATU

Granados, Rosario
WOMAN WITHOUT LOVE, A

Grandval, Charles
BOUDU SAVED FROM DROWNING

Gregor, Nora
RULES OF THE GAME, THE

Greville, Edmond
UNDER THE ROOFS OF PARIS

Griem, Helmut
MALOU

Griffith, Hugh
DIARY OF FORBIDDEN DREAMS

Grist, Reri
ARIA

Groenberg, Ake
SAWDUST AND TINSEL

Gronemeyer, Herbert
SPRING SYMPHONY
BOAT, THE

Grundgens, Gustav
M

Guedj, Vanessa
LE GRAND CHEMIN

Guerra, Ruy
AGUIRRE, THE WRATH OF GOD

Guibert, Andre
DIARY OF A COUNTRY PRIEST

Guichard, Etienne
LE BAL

Guisol, Henri
CRIME OF MONSIEUR LANGE, THE

Gulp, Eisi
SUGARBABY

Gupta, Aparna Das
TWO DAUGHTERS

Gupta, Pinaki Sen
APARAJITO

Gutierrez, Zaide Silvia
EL NORTE

Guve, Bertil
FANNY AND ALEXANDER

Habault, Sylvie
THERESE

Habbema, Cox
QUESTION OF SILENCE

Habich, Matthias
COUP DE GRACE

Haggiag, Brahim
BATTLE OF ALGIERS, THE

Hagiwara, Kenichi
KAGEMUSHA

Hainia, Marcella
BOUDU SAVED FROM DROWNING

Haker, Gabrielle
ROUND MIDNIGHT

Hall, Berta
PORT OF CALL

Halliday, Ruth
ARIA

Hanayagi, Yoshiaki
SANSHO THE BAILIFF

Hanin, Roger
MY OTHER HUSBAND

Harris, Richard
RED DESERT

Hasegawa, Kazuo
GATE OF HELL

Hasse, O.E.
STATE OF SIEGE

Hauer, Rutger
SOLDIER OF ORANGE

Hausmeister, Ruth
PEDESTRIAN, THE

Hayden, Sterling
1900

Helia, Jenny
TONI

Hemmings, David
BLOW-UP

Hendry, Ian
REPULSION

Henner, Marilu
HAMMETT

Hennessy, Monique
LE DOULOS

Henry, Buck
ARIA

Heredia, Lisa
SUMMER

Hieronimko, Jan
VAMPYR

Hintz, Barbara
GERMANY, YEAR ZERO

Hinz, Werner
TONIO KROGER

Hoffman, Thom
FOURTH MAN, THE

Hoger, Hannelore
LOST HONOR OF KATHARINA BLUM, THE

Holmes, Dennis
ARIA

Hoppe, Rolf
SPRING SYMPHONY

Hopper, Dennis
AMERICAN FRIEND, THE

Horn, Camilla
FAUST

Hossein, Nicolas
WALL, THE

Hostetter, John
ARIA

Howard, Trevor
DUST

Hoyos, Christina
BLOOD WEDDING

Hoyos, Cristina
EL AMOR BRUJO

Huber, Grischa
MALOU

Hubert, Antoine
LE GRAND CHEMIN

Hubert, Lucien
FORBIDDEN GAMES

Hunter, Chris
ARIA

Huppert, Isabelle
CLEAN SLATE (COUP DE TORCHON)
GOING PLACES
ENTRE NOUS
SINCERELY CHARLOTTE
MY BEST FRIEND'S GIRL
LA TRUITE (THE TROUT)

Hurley, Elizabeth
ARIA

Hurt, John
ARIA

Hurt, William
KISS OF THE SPIDER WOMAN

Hyatt, Roy
ARIA

Illery, Pola
UNDER THE ROOFS OF PARIS

Inaba, Yoshio
SEVEN SAMURAI, THE

Inda, Estela
LOS OLVIDADOS

Interlenghi, Franco
SHOESHINE
I VITELLONI

Irazoqui, Enrique
GOSPEL ACCORDING TO ST. MATTHEW, THE

Irons, Jeremy
SWANN IN LOVE
MOONLIGHTING

Ivasbeva, V.S.
ALEXANDER NEVSKY

Ivashov, Vladimir
BALLAD OF A SOLDIER

Iwashita, Shima
DOUBLE SUICIDE

Izewska, Teresa
KANAL

Jacobsson, Ulla
SMILES OF A SUMMER NIGHT

Jacques, Yves
DECLINE OF THE AMERICAN EMPIRE, THE

Jade, Claude
LOVE ON THE RUN
STOLEN KISSES

Janczar, Tadeusz
KANAL

Janda, Krystyna
MEPHISTO

Jannings, Emil
LAST LAUGH, THE
BLUE ANGEL, THE
VARIETY
FAUST

Jansky, Ladislav
DIAMONDS OF THE NIGHT

Janssen, Walter
DESTINY

Jarrel, Stig
TORMENT

Jefford, Barbara
AND THE SHIP SAILS ON

Jimenez, Juan Antonio
BLOOD WEDDING

Jobert, Marlene
MASCULINE FEMININE

John, Gottfried
BERLIN ALEXANDERPLATZ

Johnson, Amy
ARIA

Jolivet, Pierre
LE DERNIER COMBAT

Jones, Freddie
AND THE SHIP SAILS ON

Jones, George Ellis
ARIA

Jonsson, Nine-Christine
PORT OF CALL

Josephson, Erland
AFTER THE REHEARSAL
AUTUMN SONATA
CRIES AND WHISPERS
MAGICIAN, THE
SACRIFICE, THE
SCENES FROM A MARRIAGE
MONTENEGRO
HOUR OF THE WOLF, THE

Jourdan, Catherine
APHRODITE

Jourdan, Raymond
RISE TO POWER OF LOUIS XIV, THE

Jouvet, Louis
LOWER DEPTHS, THE (1936)

Jouvet, youis
CARNIVAL IN FLANDERS

Joyeux, Odetta
SYLVIA AND THE PHANTOM

Julia, Raul
KISS OF THE SPIDER WOMAN

Juliao, Jorge
PIXOTE

Junco, Tito
WOMAN WITHOUT LOVE, A

Junior, Fabio
BYE-BYE BRAZIL

Jurado, Katy
EL BRUTO

Jurgens, Curt
AND GOD CREATED WOMAN

Juross, Albert
LES CARABINIERS

Kadochnikova, Larisa
SHADOWS OF FORGOTTEN ANCESTORS

Kagawa, Kyoko
SANSHO THE BAILIFF

Kamatsu, Hosei
DOUBLE SUICIDE

Kaminska, Ida
SHOP ON MAIN STREET, THE

Kampers, Fritz
KAMERADSCHAFT

Kaneko, Nobuo
IKIRU

Kaprisky, Valerie
L'ANNEE DES MEDUSES
APHRODITE

Karina, Anna
ALPHAVILLE
BAND OF OUTSIDERS
MY LIFE TO LIVE

Kasper, Gary
ARIA

Katayama, Akihiko
MOTHER

Kato, Daisuke
YOJIMBO

Kato, Takeshi
BAD SLEEP WELL, THE

Kaufmann, Gunther
KAMIKAZE '89

Kawaguchi, Hiroshi
FLOATING WEEDS

Kawarazaki, Chojuro
47 RONIN, THE (PARTS 1 & 2)

Kawarazaki, Kunitaro
47 RONIN, THE (PARTS 1 & 2)

Kawazu, Seizaburo
YOJIMBO

Kayama, Yuzo
RED BEARD

Kazakos, Costa
IPHIGENIA

Keitel, Harvey
LA NUIT DE VARENNES
DEATHWATCH

Kelin-Rogge, Rudolph
DR. MABUSE, THE GAMBLER, PART 1 & 2

Keller, Hiram
FELLINI SATYRICON

Keller, Marthe
AND NOW MY LOVE
DARK EYES

Ker, Evelyne
A NOS AMOURS

Kerien, Jean-Pierre
MURIEL

Kerr, Bill
COCA-COLA KID, THE

Kime, Jeffrey
STATE OF THINGS, THE

Kimura, Ko
STRAY DOG

Kinski, Klaus
AGUIRRE, THE WRATH OF GOD
FITZCARRALDO

Kinski, Nastassia
SPRING SYMPHONY
WRONG MOVE
MOON IN THE GUTTER, THE
PARIS, TEXAS
STAY AS YOU ARE
TESS

Kirschstein, Rudiger
COUP DE GRACE

Kishi, Keiko
KWAIDAN

Kishida, Kyoko
WOMAN IN THE DUNES

Kitaoji, Kinya
HIMATSURI

Kjellin, Alf
TORMENT
SUMMER INTERLUDE

Klein, Nita
MURIEL

Klein-Rogge, Rudolf
TESTAMENT OF DR. MABUSE, THE
SPIES
METROPOLIS

Kobayashi, Toshiko
TWENTY-FOUR EYES

Kolb, Josef
FIREMAN'S BALL, THE

Kortner, Fritz
PANDORA'S BOX

Kraaykamp, John
ASSAULT, THE

Krabbe, Jeroen
FOURTH MAN, THE
SOLDIER OF ORANGE

Krauss, Werner
CABINET OF DR. CALIGARI, THE

Kreuzer, Lisa
ALICE IN THE CITIES
KINGS OF THE ROAD

Kristel, Sylvia
EMMANUELLE

Kroner, Jozef
SHOP ON MAIN STREET, THE

Kruger, Franz
GERMANY, YEAR ZERO

Kruger, Hardy
SUNDAYS AND CYBELE

Krzyzewska, Eva
ASHES AND DIAMONDS

Kulle, Jarl
DEVIL'S EYE, THE

Kumbera, Antonin
DIAMONDS OF THE NIGHT

Kurtiz, Tuncel
WALL, THE

Kyle, Jackson
ARIA

Kyo, Machiko
RASHOMON
ODD OBSESSION
UGETSU
GATE OF HELL

Laage, Barbara
THERESE AND ISABELLE

Labarthe, Andre S.
MY LIFE TO LIVE

Lacoste, Philippe
HAIL, MARY

Ladengast, Walter
EVERY MAN FOR HIMSELF AND GOD AGAINST ALL

Lafont, Bernadette
VERY CURIOUS GIRL, A
LE BEAU SERGE

Lafont, Jean-Philippe
BABETTE'S FEAST

Lagutin, I.I.
ALEXANDER NEVSKY

Lamarr, Hedy
ECSTASY

Lambert, Christopher
LOVE SONGS
SUBWAY

Lamont, Duncan
GOLDEN COACH, THE

Lamprecht, Gunter
BERLIN ALEXANDERPLATZ

Lancaster, Burt
1900

Landa, Alfredo
HOLY INNOCENTS, THE

Landgrebe, Gudrun
COLONEL REDL
WOMAN IN FLAMES, A

Lane, Stephanie
ARIA

Lang, Fritz
CONTEMPT

Langlet, Amanda
PAULINE AT THE BEACH

Lanoux, Victor
COUSIN, COUSINE
MAKE ROOM FOR TOMORROW
INVESTIGATION
FRENCH DETECTIVE, THE

Laplace, Victor
FUNNY, DIRTY LITTLE WAR, A

Lario, Veronica
SOTTO. . .SOTTO

Larive, Leon
LA MARSEILLAISE

Laser, Dieter
LOST HONOR OF KATHARINA BLUM, THE

Laudenbach, Philippe
CONFIDENTIALLY YOURS!

Laure, Carole
DIRTY DISHES

Laurent, Jacqueline
LE JOUR SE LEVE

Lauterbach, Heiner
MEN

Lawson, Leigh
TESS

Laydu, Claude
DIARY OF A COUNTRY PRIEST

Leaud, Jean-Pierre
DAY FOR NIGHT
LOVE ON THE RUN
STOLEN KISSES
TESTAMENT OF ORPHEUS, THE
TWO ENGLISH GIRLS
FOUR HUNDRED BLOWS, THE
LAST TANGO IN PARIS
MASCULINE FEMININE

Leclerc, Ginette
BAKER'S WIFE, THE

Lederer, Franz
PANDORA'S BOX

Ledoux, Fernand
LA BETE HUMAINE

Lefebvre, Rene
MILLION, THE

Lefevre, Rene
CRIME OF MONSIEUR LANGE, THE

Legitimus, Darling
SUGAR CANE ALLEY

Legrand, Michel
CLEO FROM 5 TO 7

Leigh, Spencer
ARIA

Lemaitre, Arabella
FLOWERS OF ST. FRANCIS, THE

Lemmon, Jack
MACARONI

Leotard, Philippe
CAT AND MOUSE
LA BALANCE
TCHAO PANTIN

Lerdorff-Rye, Preben
ORDET

Leroy, Philippe
MARRIED WOMAN, THE
NIGHT PORTER, THE

Lhermitte, Thierry
MY BEST FRIEND'S GIRL
MY NEW PARTNER

Liden, Anki
MY LIFE AS A DOG

Linda, Boguslaw
DANTON

Lindblom, Gunnel
SILENCE, THE

Lindstrom, Jorgen
SILENCE, THE

Lipinski, Eugene
MOONLIGHTING

Lisi, Virna
CRICKET, THE

Livanov, Boris
TEN DAYS THAT SHOOK THE WORLD

Lombard, Yvonne
LESSON IN LOVE, A

Lone, John
LAST EMPEROR, THE

Lonsdale, Michael
ERENDIRA

Lonsdale, Michel
STOLEN KISSES
PHANTOM OF LIBERTY, THE

Loos, Theodor
KRIEMHILD'S REVENGE

Loren, Sophia
YESTERDAY, TODAY, AND TOMORROW
TWO WOMEN

Lorre, Peter
M

Lowitsch, Klaus
MARRIAGE OF MARIA BRAUN, THE

Lozano, Margarita
NIGHT OF THE SHOOTING STARS, THE

Luchini, Fabrice
FULL MOON IN PARIS

Luke, Benny
LA CAGE AUX FOLLES 3: THE WEDDING
LA CAGE AUX FOLLES II

Luppi, Federico
FUNNY, DIRTY LITTLE WAR, A

Lynen, Robert
POIL DE CAROTTE

Lys, Lya
L'AGE D'OR

Macedo, Rita
CRIMINAL LIFE OF ARCHIBALDO DE LA CRUZ, THE

McIntire, Donald
MISS MARY

McLoughlin, Marianne
ARIA

MacNeil, Cornell
LA TRAVIATA

Maggio, Pupella
AMARCORD

Maggiorani, Lamberto
BICYCLE THIEF, THE

Magnani, Anna
GOLDEN COACH, THE
OPEN CITY
BELLISSIMA

Maia, Marise
ITALIAN STRAW HAT, AN

Maille, Anne-Sophie
A NOS AMOURS

Mairesse, Valerie
SACRIFICE, THE
INVESTIGATION

Makharadze, Avtandil
REPENTANCE

Malanowicz, Zygmunt
KNIFE IN THE WATER

Malavoy, Christophe
PERIL

Malberg, Henrik
ORDET

Malet, Laurent
INVITATION AU VOYAGE
JACKO AND LISE

Malet, Pierre
BASILEUS QUARTET

Malmsten, Birger
SUMMER INTERLUDE

Manes, Gina
NAPOLEON

Manesse, Gaspard
AU REVOIR LES ENFANTS

Manfredi, Nino
IN THE NAME OF THE POPE KING
DOWN AND DIRTY

Mangano, Silvana
DARK EYES
DEATH IN VENICE

Mann, Leonard
WIFEMISTRESS

Mannhardt, Renate
FEAR

Manuel, Robert
RIFIFI

Marais, Jean
BATTLE OF AUSTERLITZ, THE
BEAUTY AND THE BEAST
ETERNAL RETURN, THE
DONKEY SKIN
ORPHEUS
ELENA AND HER MEN

Marceau, Sophie
LA BOUM

Marchand, Corinne
CLEO FROM 5 TO 7

Marchand, Guy
HEAT OF DESIRE
ENTRE NOUS

Marchand, Henri
A NOUS LA LIBERTE

Marconi, Saverio
PADRE PADRONE

Marie-Christine
COUSIN, COUSINE
LOVE IN GERMANY, A

Marielle, Jean-Pierre
CLEAN SLATE (COUP DE TORCHON)
LE SEX SHOP

Marika, Roy
WHERE THE GREEN ANTS DREAM

Marika, Wandjuk
WHERE THE GREEN ANTS DREAM

Markham, Kika
TWO ENGLISH GIRLS

Marquand, Christian
AND GOD CREATED WOMAN
PLAYTIME

Marsh, Jamie
MONTENEGRO

Martin, Jean
BATTLE OF ALGIERS, THE

Mase, Marino
LES CARABINIERS

Masina, Giulietta
LA STRADA
JULIET OF THE SPIRITS
GINGER & FRED
NIGHTS OF CABIRIA, THE
WHITE SHEIK, THE

Masokha, Pyotr
EARTH

Massalitinova, V.O.
ALEXANDER NEVSKY

Massari, Lea
L'AVVENTURA

Mastroianni, Marcello
DIARY OF FORBIDDEN DREAMS
DARK EYES
LA NUIT DE VARENNES

ETERNAL RETURN, THE

Muravyova, Irina
MOSCOW DOES NOT BELIEVE IN TEARS

Musaus, Hans
EVERY MAN FOR HIMSELF AND GOD AGAINST ALL

Muti, Ornella
SWANN IN LOVE

Mutton, Roger
GIRL ON A MOTORCYCLE, THE

Nakadai, Tatsuya
KAGEMUSHA
RAN
SANJURO
YOJIMBO
SWORD OF DOOM, THE
HIGH AND LOW

Nakamoto, Ryota
HIMATSURI

Nakamura, Ganjiro
ODD OBSESSION
FLOATING WEEDS
LOWER DEPTHS, THE (1957)

Nakamura, Kanemon
47 RONIN, THE (PARTS 1 & 2)

Nakamura, Kichiemon
DOUBLE SUICIDE

Natsuki, Yosuke
YOJIMBO

Navarro, Jesus
LOS OLVIDADOS

Nazzari, Amedeo
NIGHTS OF CABIRIA, THE

Neckar, Vaclav
CLOSELY WATCHED TRAINS

Negami, Jun
GOLDEN DEMON

Negro, Del
AGUIRRE, THE WRATH OF GOD

Neher, Carola
THREEPENNY OPERA, THE

Neiiendam, Sigrid
DAY OF WRATH

Nero, Franco
QUERELLE
SWEET COUNTRY

Nezu, Jinpachi
RAN

Nicholson, Jack
PASSENGER, THE

Niemczyk, Leon
KNIFE IN THE WATER

Nikandrof
TEN DAYS THAT SHOOK THE WORLD

Nilsson, Maj-Britt
SECRETS OF WOMEN
SUMMER INTERLUDE

Ninidze, Iya
REPENTANCE

Ninidze, Merab
REPENTANCE

Nishimura, Akira
YOJIMBO

Nissen, Aud Egede
DR. MABUSE, THE GAMBLER, PART 1 & 2

Noel, Bernard
MARRIED WOMAN, THE

Noel, Magali
AMARCORD

Noiret, Philippe
CLOCKMAKER, THE
CLEAN SLATE (COUP DE TORCHON)
MY NEW PARTNER
THREE BROTHERS
JUPITER'S THIGH

Norby, Ghita
BABETTE'S FEAST

Noro, Line
PEPE LE MOKO

Novikov, V.K.
ALEXANDER NEVSKY

O'Neill, Jennifer
INNOCENT, THE

O'Toole, Peter
LAST EMPEROR, THE

Ochoa, Juan Manuel
LA CIUDAD Y LOS PERROS

Ochsenknecht, Uwe
MEN

Ogata, Ken
MISHIMA

Ogier, Pascale
FULL MOON IN PARIS

Ohana, Claudia
ERENDIRA

Okada, Eiji
HIROSHIMA, MON AMOUR
WOMAN IN THE DUNES

Okhlopkov, N.P.
ALEXANDER NEVSKY

Olin, Lena
AFTER THE REHEARSAL

Oliver, Lucy
ARIA

Olivier, Paul
MILLION, THE

Omori, Yoshiyuki
MACARTHUR'S CHILDREN

Orimoto, Junkichi
MISHIMA

Orlov, D.N.
ALEXANDER NEVSKY

Orsini, Umberto
CESAR AND ROSALIE

Ousdal, Sverre Anker
FLIGHT OF THE EAGLE

Pagliero, Marcello
OPEN CITY

Palance, Jack
BATTLE OF AUSTERLITZ, THE
BAGDAD CAFE
CONTEMPT

Papas, Irene
IPHIGENIA
ERENDIRA
CHRIST STOPPED AT EBOLI
SWEET COUNTRY

Pappas, Irene
Z

Parlo, Dita
L'ATALANTE

Pasca, Alfonsino
PAISAN

Pascal, Christine
SINCERELY CHARLOTTE

Pascaud, Nathalie
MR. HULOT'S HOLIDAY

Pasolini, Susanna
GOSPEL ACCORDING TO ST. MATTHEW, THE

Patte, Jean-Marie
RISE TO POWER OF LOUIS XIV, THE

Pauly, Rebecca
STATE OF THINGS, THE

Pavez, Terele
HOLY INNOCENTS, THE

Pawlikowski, Adam
ASHES AND DIAMONDS

Pawlowa, Vera
DIARY OF A LOST GIRL

Pecoraro, Susu
CAMILA

Peng, Du
GO-MASTERS, THE

Pera, Marilia
PIXOTE

Perez, Conchita
CRIA!

Perez-Porro, Beatriz
SKYLINE

Perier, Francois
GERVAISE
SYLVIA AND THE PHANTOM
NIGHTS OF CABIRIA, THE

Perrault, Louis
MR. HULOT'S HOLIDAY

Perrin, Francis
JUPITER'S THIGH

Perrin, Jacques
DONKEY SKIN

Persson, Essy
THERESE AND ISABELLE

Peterson, Marion
ARIA

Pettersson, Birgitta
VIRGIN SPRING, THE

Philipe, Gerard
DEVIL IN THE FLESH, THE

Pialat, Maurice
A NOS AMOURS

Piccoli, Michel
CONTEMPT
DANGEROUS MOVES
EYES, THE MOUTH, THE
DIARY OF A CHAMBERMAID
PERIL
LA PASSANTE

Pierra, Francisco
GARDEN OF DELIGHTS, THE

Pietrangeli, Antonio
LA TERRA TREMA

Pinal, Silvia
EXTERMINATING ANGEL, THE
VIRIDIANA

Pisier, Marie-France
COUSIN, COUSINE
LOVE ON THE RUN

Pisu, Mario
JULIET OF THE SPIRITS

Pitoeff, Sacha
LAST YEAR AT MARIENBAD

Placido, Michele
THREE BROTHERS
TILL MARRIAGE DO US PART

Pluhar, Erika
GOALIE'S ANXIETY AT THE PENALTY KICK, THE

Poiret, Jean
LAST METRO, THE

Polanski, Roman
TENANT, THE

Poletti, Victor
AND THE SHIP SAILS ON

Polito, Lina
LOVE AND ANARCHY

Politti, Luis
NEST, THE

Poncela, Eusebio
LAW OF DESIRE

Popov, N.
TEN DAYS THAT SHOOK THE WORLD

Poppe, Nils
SEVENTH SEAL, THE

Potter, Martin
FELLINI SATYRICON

Poujouly, Georges
FORBIDDEN GAMES
FRANTIC

Pounder, CCH
BAGDAD CAFE

Prachar, Ilja
TRANSPORT FROM PARADISE

Prado, Lilia
WUTHERING HEIGHTS
MEXICAN BUS RIDE

Prejean, Albert
UNDER THE ROOFS OF PARIS
ITALIAN STRAW HAT, AN

Presle, Micheline
DEVIL IN THE FLESH, THE

Price, Voices of: Leontyne
ARIA

Prieto, Aurore
THERESE

Prim, Suzy
MAYERLING
LOWER DEPTHS, THE (1936)

Prochnow, Jurgen
BOAT, THE
COP AND THE GIRL, THE

Prokhorenko, Shanna
BALLAD OF A SOLDIER

Pszoniak, Wojciech
DANTON

Pucholt, Vladimir
LOVES OF A BLONDE

Puglisi, Aldo
SEDUCED AND ABANDONED

Puttjer, Gustav
KAMERADSCHAFT

Quaid, Randy
SWEET COUNTRY

Quinn, Anthony
LA STRADA
INHERITANCE, THE

Quinteros, Lorenzo
MAN FACING SOUTHEAST

Rabal, Francisco
HOLY INNOCENTS, THE
ECLIPSE
VIRIDIANA
STAY AS YOU ARE
EL MUERTO

Racette, Francine
AU REVOIR LES ENFANTS
LUMIERE

Raimondi, Ruggero
BIZET'S CARMEN

Raimu
BAKER'S WIFE, THE
CESAR
FANNY
MARIUS

Ralph, Hanna
KRIEMHILD'S REVENGE

Rampling, Charlotte
DAMNED, THE
NIGHT PORTER, THE

Randa, Cestmir
TRANSPORT FROM PARADISE

Ras, Eva
LOVE AFFAIR; OR THE CASE OF THE MISSING SWITCHBOARD OPERATOR

Ray, Nicholas
AMERICAN FRIEND, THE

Read, Michelle
ARIA

Rebbot, Saddy
MY LIFE TO LIVE

Redgrave, Vanessa
BLOW-UP

Reggiani, Serge
CAT AND MOUSE
LA RONDE
LE DOULOS

Regine
MY NEW PARTNER

Remy, Albert
FOUR HUNDRED BLOWS, THE

Renaud, Madeleine
LE PLAISIR

Renn, Katherina
RISE TO POWER OF LOUIS XIV, THE

Reno, Jean
BIG BLUE, THE

Renoir, Pierre
LA MARSEILLAISE

Resines, Antonio
SKYLINE

Rey, Fernando
DISCREET CHARM OF THE BOURGEOISIE, THE
SEVEN BEAUTIES
VIRIDIANA
THAT OBSCURE OBJECT OF DESIRE

Richard, Pierre
LES COMPERES
RETURN OF THE TALL BLOND MAN WITH ONE BLACK SHOE, THE
TALL BLOND MAN WITH ONE BLACK SHOE, THE
LA CHEVRE

Richter, Paul
SIEGFRIED

Riegert, Peter
MAN IN LOVE, A

Risch, Maurice
BEAU PERE

Riva, Emmanuelle
HIROSHIMA, MON AMOUR

Riveyre, Jean
DIARY OF A COUNTRY PRIEST

Riviere, Marie
SUMMER

Roberts, Eric
COCA-COLA KID, THE

Robinson, Bruce
STORY OF ADELE H., THE

Rochefort, Jean
CLOCKMAKER, THE
I SENT A LETTER TO MY LOVE

TALL BLOND MAN WITH ONE BLACK SHOE, THE
TILL MARRIAGE DO US PART
LE CAVALEUR (PRACTICE MAKES PERFECT)
PARDON MON AFFAIRE

Rode, Ebbe
GERTRUD

Rode, Nina Pens
GERTRUD

Rode, Thierry
HAIL, MARY

Roeg, Maximillian
ARIA

Roger-Pierre
MON ONCLE D'AMERIQUE

Rogoz, Zvonomir
ECSTASY

Rogozbin, N.A.
ALEXANDER NEVSKY

Rojo, Helena
AGUIRRE, THE WRATH OF GOD

Romand, Beatrice
CLAIRE'S KNEE
LE BEAU MARIAGE
SUMMER

Rome, Sydne
DIARY OF FORBIDDEN DREAMS

Rondinella, Clelia
WHERE'S PICONE?

Ronet, Maurice
FRANTIC

Roose, Thirkild
DAY OF WRATH

Rory, Rossana
BIG DEAL ON MADONNA STREET, THE

Rosay, Francoise
CARNIVAL IN FLANDERS

Ross, David
ARIA

Rossi-Drago, Eleanora
CAMILLE 2000

Rothe, Bendt
GERTRUD

Rottlander, Yella
ALICE IN THE CITIES

Roudenko, Wladimir
NAPOLEON

Roussel, Myriem
HAIL, MARY

Rouvel, Catherine
BLACK AND WHITE IN COLOR
PICNIC ON THE GRASS

Roveyre, Liliane
DIRTY DISHES

Ruiz, Chela
OFFICIAL STORY, THE

Runacre, Jennie
PASSENGER, THE

Russell, Theresa
ARIA

Ryu, Chishu
TWENTY-FOUR EYES

S., Bruno
EVERY MAN FOR HIMSELF AND GOD AGAINST ALL

Saadi, Yacef
BATTLE OF ALGIERS, THE

Sacristan, Jose
EL DIPUTADO

Sagalle, Jonathan
DRIFTING

Sagebrecht, Marianne
BAGDAD CAFE
SUGARBABY

Sakamoto, Ryuichi
MERRY CHRISTMAS, MR. LAWRENCE

Sakura, Shiori
MACARTHUR'S CHILDREN

Salmonova, Lyda
GOLEM, THE

Salou, Louis
SYLVIA AND THE PHANTOM

Salvatori, Renato
BIG DEAL ON MADONNA STREET, THE
CRICKET, THE
STATE OF SIEGE

Samberg, R.
DYBBUK, THE

Samoilova, Tatyana
CRANES ARE FLYING, THE

San Jose, Maria Luisa
EL DIPUTADO

Sanda, Dominique
CONFORMIST, THE
INHERITANCE, THE
GARDEN OF THE FINZI-CONTINIS, THE
1900

Sander, Otto
WINGS OF DESIRE

Sandrelli, Stefania
CONFORMIST, THE
FAMILY, THE
SEDUCED AND ABANDONED
1900

Santini, Pierre
DIRTY DISHES

Sardou, Fernand
PICNIC ON THE GRASS

Sarky, Daniel
EMMANUELLE

Sassard, Jaqueline
BAD GIRLS

Sastri, Lina
WHERE'S PICONE?

Savshenko, Semyon
EARTH

Sawamura, Ikio
YOJIMBO

Sazanka, Kyu
YOJIMBO

Sazio, Carmela
PAISAN

Scacchi, Greta
GOOD MORNING BABYLON
MAN IN LOVE, A
COCA-COLA KID, THE

Scarpitta, Carmen
IN THE NAME OF THE POPE KING

Schauer, Roger
INHERITORS, THE

Schell, Maria
GERVAISE

Schell, Maximilian
PEDESTRIAN, THE

Schlichter, Hedwig
MAEDCHEN IN UNIFORM

Schneider, Maria
PASSENGER, THE
LAST TANGO IN PARIS

Schneider, Romy
CESAR AND ROSALIE
DEATHWATCH
LA PASSANTE

Scho, Margarethe
SIEGFRIED

Schon, Margarethe
KRIEMHILD'S REVENGE

Schreck, Max
NOSFERATU

Schuendler, Rudolf
KINGS OF THE ROAD

Schunzel, Reinhold
THREEPENNY OPERA, THE

Schygulla, Hanna
LOVE IN GERMANY, A
LA NUIT DE VARENNES
WRONG MOVE
MARRIAGE OF MARIA BRAUN, THE
BERLIN ALEXANDERPLATZ

Scob, Edith
HORROR CHAMBER OF DR. FAUSTUS, THE

Scott, Nina
INVITATION AU VOYAGE

Seastrom, Victor
WILD STRAWBERRIES

Seberg, Jean
BREATHLESS
PLAYTIME

Seck, Douta
SUGAR CANE ALLEY

Seki, Kyoko
IKIRU

Sellner, Gustav Rudolf
PEDESTRIAN, THE

Selznick, Albie
ARIA

Serra, Pablo
LA CIUDAD Y LOS PERROS

Serrault, Michel
ASSOCIATE, THE
LA CAGE AUX FOLLES 3: THE WEDDING
LA CAGE AUX FOLLES II
LA CAGE AUX FOLLES
GET OUT YOUR HANDKERCHIEFS

Serre, Henri
JULES AND JIM

Serres, Jacques
BLUE COUNTRY, THE

Servais, Jean
RIFIFI

Servantie, Adrienne
MY UNCLE

Seyrig, Delphine
LAST YEAR AT MARIENBAD
I SENT A LETTER TO MY LOVE
DONKEY SKIN
DISCREET CHARM OF THE BOURGEOISIE, THE
STOLEN KISSES
MURIEL

Shaw, Martin
MACBETH

Shimura, Takashi
IKIRU
DRUNKEN ANGEL
SANJURO
SEVEN SAMURAI, THE
STRAY DOG
YOJIMBO
THRONE OF BLOOD

Shionoya, Masayuki
MISHIMA

Shkurat, Stepan
EARTH

Signoret, Simone
LA RONDE
I SENT A LETTER TO MY LOVE
DIABOLIQUE
LE CHAT

Signoret, Simore
MADAME ROSA

Silva, Fernando Ramos da
PIXOTE

Silvagni
RISE TO POWER OF LOUIS XIV, THE

Silvain, Eugene
PASSION OF JOAN OF ARC, THE

Silver, Veronique
MYSTERY OF ALEXINA, THE

Simon, Francois
BASILEUS QUARTET

Simon, Michel
BOUDU SAVED FROM DROWNING
TWO OF US, THE
L'ATALANTE

Simon, Simone
LA RONDE
LA BETE HUMAINE
LE PLAISIR

Simonsen, Lars
TWIST & SHOUT

Slivkova, Hana
SHOP ON MAIN STREET, THE

Smordoni, Rinaldo
SHOESHINE

Soderbaum, Kristina
KOLBERG

Soeberg, Camilla
TWIST & SHOUT

Sofonova, Elena
DARK EYES

Soler, Andres
EL BRUTO

Sologne, Madeleine
ETERNAL RETURN, THE

Solomine, Yuri
DERSU UZALA

Somr, Josef
CLOSELY WATCHED TRAINS

Sorai, Agnes
TCHAO PANTIN

Sordi, Alberto
I VITELLONI
WHITE SHEIK, THE

Soto, Hugo
MAN FACING SOUTHEAST

Soto, Luchy
GARDEN OF DELIGHTS, THE

Souchon, Alain
ONE DEADLY SUMMER

Soutendijk, Renee
FOURTH MAN, THE

Spanjer, Maarten
SPETTERS

Spano, Vincent
GOOD MORNING BABYLON

Spence, Bruce
WHERE THE GREEN ANTS DREAM

Spengler, Volker
DESPAIR

Spiesser, Jacques
BLACK AND WHITE IN COLOR

Staiola, Enzo
BICYCLE THIEF, THE

Stamp, Terence
DIVINE NYMPH, THE

Stanczak, Wadeck
SCENE OF THE CRIME

Stangertz, Goran
FLIGHT OF THE EAGLE

Stanislav, Jiri
MOONLIGHTING

Stanton, Harry Dean
DEATHWATCH
PARIS, TEXAS

Steinruck, Albert
GOLEM, THE

Stepanek, Zdenek
TRANSPORT FROM PARADISE

Stephane, Nicole
LES ENFANTS TERRIBLES

Stern, Miroslava
CRIMINAL LIFE OF ARCHIBALDO DE LA CRUZ, THE

Sting
JULIA AND JULIA

Stockel, Vaclav
FIREMAN'S BALL, THE

Stockwell, Dean
ALSINO AND THE CONDOR
PARIS, TEXAS

Stoeckl-Eberhard, Anneliese
INHERITORS, THE

Stoler, Shirley
SEVEN BEAUTIES

Stoppa, Paolo
MIRACLE IN MILAN

Stratas, Teresa
LA TRAVIATA

Stroh, Valerie
MYSTERY OF ALEXINA, THE

Sugai, Ichiro
LIFE OF OHARU

Sugai, Kin
DODES 'KA-DEN
FUNERAL, THE

Sugawara, Kenji
GOLDEN DEMON

Sugimura, Haruko
FLOATING WEEDS

Sukowa, Barbara
BERLIN ALEXANDERPLATZ

Sutherland, Donald
1900
WOLF AT THE DOOR, THE

Svet, Josef
FIREMAN'S BALL, THE

Swain, Nicola
ARIA

Swinton, Tilda
ARIA

Tachikawa, Hiroshi
YOJIMBO

Tagore, Sharmila
WORLD OF APU, THE

Taichi, Kiowako
HIMATSURI

Takamine, Hideko
TWENTY-FOUR EYES

Takeshi
MERRY CHRISTMAS, MR. LAWRENCE

Takita, Yusuke
IREZUMI (SPIRIT OF TATTOO)

Takizawa, Osamu
FIRES ON THE PLAIN

Talazac, Odette
BLOOD OF A POET, THE

Tamiroff, Akim
ALPHAVILLE

Tanaka, Kinuyo
SANSHO THE BAILIFF
UGETSU
LIFE OF OHARU
MOTHER

Tati, Jacques
MR. HULOT'S HOLIDAY
MY UNCLE
JOUR DE FETE

Taub, Walter
DAVID

Tavernier, Nils
PASSION OF BEATRICE, THE

Taxman, Tamara
HOUR OF THE STAR, THE

Telleria, Isabel
SPIRIT OF THE BEEHIVE, THE

Temessy, Hedi
REVOLT OF JOB, THE

Tendeter, Stacey
TWO ENGLISH GIRLS

Terao, Akira
RAN

Terzieff, Laurent
MILKY WAY, THE

Testi, Fabio
INHERITANCE, THE

Thulin, Ingrid
AFTER THE REHEARSAL
CRIES AND WHISPERS
MAGICIAN, THE
SILENCE, THE
WILD STRAWBERRIES
WINTER LIGHT, THE
DAMNED, THE

Tifo, Marie
BLIND TRUST

Tiller, Nadja
TONIO KROGER

Tognazzi, Ugo
LA CAGE AUX FOLLES 3: THE WEDDING
LA CAGE AUX FOLLES II
LA CAGE AUX FOLLES
JOKE OF DESTINY, A

Tono, Eijiro
YOJIMBO

Tonsberg, Adam
TWIST & SHOUT

Torrent, Ana
NEST, THE
CRIA!
SPIRIT OF THE BEEHIVE, THE

Toutain, Roland
RULES OF THE GAME, THE

Traub, Ami
DRIFTING

Trieste, Leopoldo
HENRY IV
WHITE SHEIK, THE

Trintignant, Jean Louis
MAN AND A WOMAN, A

Trintignant, Jean-Louis
AND GOD CREATED WOMAN
CONFIDENTIALLY YOURS!
CONFORMIST, THE
MAN AND A WOMAN: 20 YEARS LATER, A
MY NIGHT AT MAUD'S
Z
BAD GIRLS

Trissenaar, Elisabeth
LOVE IN GERMANY, A

Truffaut, Francois
DAY FOR NIGHT
GREEN ROOM, THE

Tschekowa, Olga
ITALIAN STRAW HAT, AN

Tselikovskaya, Ludmila
IVAN THE TERRIBLE PART I AND II

Tsuchiya, Yoshio
RED BEARD
YOJIMBO

Tsugawa, Masahiko
TAXING WOMAN, A

Tsukasa, Yoko
YOJIMBO

Turner, Kathleen
JULIA AND JULIA

Uehara, Misa
HIDDEN FORTRESS, THE

Ullmann, Liv
AUTUMN SONATA
CRIES AND WHISPERS
DANGEROUS MOVES
SCENES FROM A MARRIAGE
PERSONA
HOUR OF THE WOLF, THE
SERPENT'S EGG, THE

Umecka, Jolanta
KNIFE IN THE WATER

Umemura, Yoko
SISTERS OF THE GION

Unda, Emila
MAEDCHEN IN UNIFORM

Urzi, Saro
SEDUCED AND ABANDONED

Ustinov, Peter
LOLA MONTES

Utsunomiya, Tasayo
IREZUMI (SPIRIT OF TATTOO)

Vadim, Christian
FULL MOON IN PARIS

Valberg, Birgitta
VIRGIN SPRING, THE

Valli, Alida
HORROR CHAMBER OF DR. FAUSTUS, THE

Valli, Romolo
DIARY OF FORBIDDEN DREAMS
1900

Vallone, Raf
TWO WOMEN

van de Ven, Monique
ASSAULT, THE

Van Loon, Robert
PAISAN

Van Tongeren, Hans
SPETTERS

Vanel, Charles
DIABOLIQUE
WAGES OF FEAR, THE
THREE BROTHERS

Vazquez, Jose Luis Lopez
GARDEN OF DELIGHTS, THE

Veidt, Conrad
CABINET OF DR. CALIGARI, THE

Ventura, Lino
HAPPY NEW YEAR
FRENCH DETECTIVE, THE

Verley, Bernard
CHLOE IN THE AFTERNOON

Verley, Francoise
CHLOE IN THE AFTERNOON

Vernon, Anne
UMBRELLAS OF CHERBOURG, THE

Verrett, Shirley
ARIA

Villalpando, David
EL NORTE

Villarreal, Julio
WOMAN WITHOUT LOVE, A

Viruboff, Sofia
MISS MARY

Visconti, Luchino
LA TERRA TREMA

Vitale, Mario
STROMBOLI

Vitti, Monica
L'AVVENTURA
ECLIPSE
RED DESERT
PHANTOM OF LIBERTY, THE

Vogel, Nikolas
INHERITORS, THE

Vogler, Rudiger
ALICE IN THE CITIES
KINGS OF THE ROAD
WRONG MOVE

Volonte, Gian Maria
CHRIST STOPPED AT EBOLI

von Klier, Annette
COP AND THE GIRL, THE

von Rezzoni, Gregor
VERY PRIVATE AFFAIR, A

CINEMATOGRAPHERS

Anderson, Carl
DAY OF WRATH

Ando, Shohei
GO-MASTERS, THE

Androschin, Hans
ECSTASY

Arata, Ubaldo
OPEN CITY

Arnold, Peter
COUP DE GRACE

Aronovich, Ricardo
LE BAL
HANNAH K.
FAMILY, THE
LUMIERE
PROVIDENCE

Arribas, Fernando
CAMILA

Arvantis, Georges
IPHIGENIA

Asai, Shinpai
FUNERAL, THE

Atumoto, Asushi
SAMURAI TRILOGY, THE

Baberske, Robert
KAMERADSCHAFT

Babic, Milan
BATTLE OF AUSTERLITZ, THE

Bachelet, Jean
CRIME OF MONSIEUR LANGE, THE
RULES OF THE GAME, THE
LOWER DEPTHS, THE

Badal, Jean
PLAYTIME
VERY CURIOUS GIRL, A

Bailey, John
MISHIMA

Ballhaus, Michael
DESPAIR
MARRIAGE OF MARIA BRAUN, THE
MALOU

Battiferri, Giulio
SWEPT AWAY. . .BY AN UNUSUAL DESTINY IN THE BLUE SEA OF AUGUST

Bazzoni, Camillio
JOKE OF DESTINY, A

Becker, Etienne
ONE DEADLY SUMMER

Bellis, Andreas
SWEET COUNTRY

Bendtsen, Henning
GERTRUD
ORDET

Benoit, George
BAKER'S WIFE, THE

Benoit, Georges
FANNY

Beristain, Gabriel
ARIA

Berta, Renato
AU REVOIR LES ENFANTS
L'ANNEE DES MEDUSES
FULL MOON IN PARIS

Biroc, Joseph
HAMMETT

Bladh, Hilding
DREAMS
SAWDUST AND TINSEL

Blossier, Patrick
VAGABOND

Bodin, Martin
LESSON IN LOVE, A
TORMENT

Boffety, Jean
CESAR AND ROSALIE
EDITH AND MARCEL

Bourgas, Fedote
LOWER DEPTHS, THE

Bourgoin, Jean
BLACK ORPHEUS
LA MARSEILLAISE
MY UNCLE

Brenguier, Dominique
MOON IN THE GUTTER, THE

Brizzi, Anchise
SHOESHINE

Bromet, Frans
QUESTION OF SILENCE

Brunet, Nicolas
LE BEAU MARIAGE

Burel, Leonce-Henry
DIARY OF A COUNTRY PRIEST
NAPOLEON

Burmann, Hans
HOLY INNOCENTS, THE

Capriotti, Mario
TWO WOMEN

Cardiff, Jack
GIRL ON A MOTORCYCLE, THE

Carlini, Carlo
GENERAL DELLA ROVERE
FEAR
I VITELLONI

Champetier, Carolyn
ARIA

Chapius, Dominique
SUGAR CANE ALLEY

Charvein, Jean
INVESTIGATION

Cirillo, Claudio
WHERE'S PICONE?

Clerval, Denys
ERENDIRA
STOLEN KISSES

Cloquet, Ghislain
I SENT A LETTER TO MY LOVE
DONKEY SKIN
TESS

Colas, Rene
FEMMES DE PARIS

Colli, Tonino Delli
GOSPEL ACCORDING TO ST. MATTHEW, THE
GINGER & FRED
SEVEN BEAUTIES

Collomb, Jean
AND NOW MY LOVE
CAT AND MOUSE
HAPPY NEW YEAR
FRENCH DETECTIVE, THE

Contini, Alfio
NIGHT PORTER, THE
ZABRISKIE POINT

Courant, Curt
LA BETE HUMAINE
LE JOUR SE LEVE

Coutard, Raoul
ALPHAVILLE
BAND OF OUTSIDERS
BREATHLESS
CONTEMPT
DANGEROUS MOVES
JULES AND JIM
SHOOT THE PIANO PLAYER
SOFT SKIN, THE
Z
LES CARABINIERS
MARRIED WOMAN, THE
MY LIFE TO LIVE

Coutelain
FANNY

Cuadrado, Luis
GARDEN OF DELIGHTS, THE
SPIRIT OF THE BEEHIVE, THE

Cuevas, Antonio
EL DIPUTADO

Curik, Jan
TRANSPORT FROM PARADISE

Daillencourt, Bernard
APHRODITE
TENDRES COUSINES

Dantan, Andre
FANNY

de Angelis, Ricardo
MAN FACING SOUTHEAST

De Bont, Jan
FOURTH MAN, THE

De Bont, Peter
SOLDIER OF ORANGE

de Keyzer, Bruno
SINCERELY CHARLOTTE
SUNDAY IN THE COUNTRY, A
ROUND MIDNIGHT
PASSION OF BEATRICE, THE

De Santis, Pasquale
DEATH IN VENICE
DAMNED, THE

De Santis, Pasqualino
BIZET'S CARMEN
INNOCENT, THE

CHRIST STOPPED AT EBOLI
THREE BROTHERS

De Venanzo, Gianni
JULIET OF THE SPIRITS

De-an, Luo
GO-MASTERS, THE

Decae, Henri
SUNDAYS AND CYBELE
MY OTHER HUSBAND
FRANTIC
LE BEAU SERGE
LES ENFANTS TERRIBLES
FOUR HUNDRED BLOWS, THE
BOB LE FLAMBEUR
VERY PRIVATE AFFAIR, A

Delli Colli, Tonino
TILL MARRIAGE DO US PART

Demutsky, Danilo
EARTH

Desanzo, Juan Carlos
EL MUERTO

Desfassiaux, Maurice
ITALIAN STRAW HAT, AN

Desideri, Danilo
IN THE NAME OF THE POPE KING
CRICKET, THE

di Giacomo, Franco
DARK EYES
NIGHT OF THE SHOOTING STARS, THE

Di Palma, Carlo
GABRIELA
RED DESERT

di Palma, Carlo
BLOW-UP

Di Palma, Dario
SEDUCTION OF MIMI, THE
DOWN AND DIRTY

Di Venanzo, Gianni
8 1/2
ECLIPSE
BIG DEAL ON MADONNA STREET, THE

Dobronavov, Fyodor
DERSU UZALA

Douarinou, Alain
LA MARSEILLAISE

Dufaux, Guy
DECLINE OF THE AMERICAN EMPIRE, THE
BLIND TRUST

Duverger, Albert
L'AGE D'OR

Elmes, Frederick
ARIA

Ende, Walther Vanden
DUST

Engin, Erdogan
YOL

Escamilla, Teo
BLOOD WEDDING
CARMEN
EL AMOR BRUJO
CRIA!

Escamilla, Teodoro
NEST, THE

Escoffier, Jean-Yves
THREE MEN AND A CRADLE

Escorel, Lauro
BYE BYE BRAZIL

Fellous, Roger
DIARY OF A CHAMBERMAID

Fernandez, Angel Luis
SKYLINE
LAW OF DESIRE

Figueroa, Gabriel
LOS OLVIDADOS
EXTERMINATING ANGEL, THE

Fischer, Gunnar
DEVIL'S EYE, THE
MAGICIAN, THE
PORT OF CALL
SECRETS OF WOMEN
SEVENTH SEAL, THE
SMILES OF A SUMMER NIGHT
WILD STRAWBERRIES
SUMMER INTERLUDE

Fisher, Gerry
MR. KLEIN

Fornari, Giuseppe
SWEPT AWAY. . .BY AN UNUSUAL DESTINY IN THE BLUE SEA OF AUGUST

Fossard, Marc
PEPE LE MOKO

Foucard, Robert
BATTLE OF AUSTERLITZ, THE

Fraisse, Robert
L'ADDITION

Franchi, Marcel
JOUR DE FETE

Freund, Karl
LAST LAUGH, THE
VARIETY
GOLEM, THE
METROPOLIS

Frimann, Jacques
HAIL, MARY

Fujii, Hideo
IREZUMI (SPIRIT OF TATTOO)

Galea, Arturo
WHITE SHEIK, THE

Gantman, Yuri
DERSU UZALA

Gatti, Marcello
BATTLE OF ALGIERS, THE
DIARY OF FORBIDDEN DREAMS

Gaudry, Daniel
GIFT, THE
HOLIDAY HOTEL

Gavruvsjov, Mischa
FLIGHT OF THE EAGLE

Gennesseaux, Pascal
JACKO AND LISE

Glenn, Pierre-William
CHOICE OF ARMS
CLOCKMAKER, THE
CLEAN SLATE (COUP DE TORCHON)
DAY FOR NIGHT
DEATHWATCH
SMALL CHANGE
STATE OF SIEGE

Glennon, James
EL NORTE

Graziati [G.R. Aldo], Aldo
MIRACLE IN MILAN

Guarnieri, Ennio
INHERITANCE, THE
GINGER & FRED
GARDEN OF THE FINZI-CONTINIS, THE
WIFEMISTRESS
CAMILLE 2000
LA TRAVIATA

Guerra, Pili Flores
LA CIUDAD Y LOS PERROS

Halmquist, Rolf
MAGICIAN, THE

Hameister, Willy
CABINET OF DR. CALIGARI, THE

Harrison, Harvey
ARIA

Hayer, Nicholas
ORPHEUS
LE DOULOS

Heer, Johanna
SUGARBABY

Heinl, Bernd
BAGDAD CAFE

Herrera, Jorge
ALSINO AND THE CONDOR

Hirano, Yoshimi
LIFE OF OHARU

Hoffmann, Carl
SIEGFRIED
FAUST
DR. MABUSE, THE GAMBLER (PARTS I & II)
KRIEMHILD'S REVENGE

Hubert, Roger
ETERNAL RETURN, THE
FANNY

Hughes, Christopher
ARIA

Ilyenko, V.
SHADOWS OF FORGOTTEN ANCESTORS

Ito, Takeo
DRUNKEN ANGEL

Jarnmark, Bengt
SUMMER INTERLUDE

Jassop, Peter
HARDER THEY COME, THE

Jimenez, Agustin
WUTHERING HEIGHTS

Jimenez, Augustin
EL BRUTO
CRIMINAL LIFE OF ARCHIBALDO DE LA CRUZ, THE

Juillard, Rene
GERVAISE

Juillard, Robert
GERMANY, YEAR ZERO
FORBIDDEN GAMES

Jura, Hans
THERESE AND ISABELLE

Jurges, Jurgen
WOMAN IN FLAMES, A

Kakai, Asakazu
STRAY DOG

Kaufman, Boris
L'ATALANTE

Kelber, Michel
FRENCH CANCAN
DEVIL IN THE FLESH, THE

Klosinski, Edward
COP AND THE GIRL, THE

Kobayashi, Setsuo
FIRES ON THE PLAIN

Koenig, Klaus
PEDESTRIAN, THE

Koizumi, Fukuzo
SANJURO

Koltai, Lajos
COLONEL REDL
MEPHISTO

Kono, Yoshimi
LIFE OF OHARU

Krampf, Gunther
PANDORA'S BOX
NOSFERATU

Kristiansen, Henning
BABETTE'S FEAST

Kruger, Jules
PEPE LE MOKO
NAPOLEON

Kucera, Jaroslav
DIAMONDS OF THE NIGHT

Kurant, Willy
MASCULINE FEMININE

Kusuda, Hiroshi
TWENTY-FOUR EYES

L'Homme, Pierre
KING OF HEARTS

Lanci, Giuseppe
HENRY IV
GOOD MORNING BABYLON
EYES, THE MOUTH, THE

Lathrop, Philip
HAMMETT

Le Mener, Jean-Yves
MAN AND A WOMAN: 20 YEARS LATER, A

Leclerc, Georges
ELUSIVE CORPORAL, THE
PICNIC ON THE GRASS
RISE TO POWER OF LOUIS XIV, THE

Lecomte, Claude
LE GRAND CHEMIN

Lelouch, Claude
AND NOW MY LOVE
HAPPY NEW YEAR
MAN AND A WOMAN, A

Lendi, Georges
COUSIN, COUSINE

Lhomme, Pierre
LE SEX SHOP

Lindstrom, Rolf
MY LIFE AS A DOG

Lipman, Jerzy
KNIFE IN THE WATER
KANAL

Loiseleux, Jacques
A NOS AMOURS

Louis, J.
LA MARSEILLAISE

Lubtchansky, William
WOMAN NEXT DOOR, THE

Luther, Igor
COUP DE GRACE
DANTON
LOVE IN GERMANY, A
TIN DRUM, THE

Lutic, Bernard
LE BEAU MARIAGE
HEAT OF DESIRE
ENTRE NOUS

McDonald, David
HARDER THEY COME, THE

Maeda, Yonezo
FUNERAL, THE
TAXING WOMAN, A

Magasouba, Nanamoudou
BLACK AND WHITE IN COLOR

Maillols, Jean-Marie
LA MARSEILLAISE

Maintigneux, Sophie
SUMMER

Mannuzzi, Armando
LA CAGE AUX FOLLES

Martelli, Otello
LA STRADA
LA DOLCE VITA
STROMBOLI
PAISAN
I VITELLONI
FLOWERS OF ST. FRANCIS, THE
NIGHTS OF CABIRIA, THE

Martinez, Pablo
ALSINO AND THE CONDOR

Masini, Mario
PADRE PADRONE

Mate, Rudolph
VAMPYR
PASSION OF JOAN OF ARC, THE

Mathelin, Rene
TALL BLOND MAN WITH ONE BLACK SHOE, THE
PARDON MON AFFAIRE
LE MAGNIFIQUE
RETURN OF THE TALL BLOND MAN WITH ONE BLACK SHOE, THE

Matras, Christian
LA RONDE
GRAND ILLUSION
EARRINGS OF MADAME DE . . ., THE
LE PLAISIR
LOLA MONTES
MILKY WAY, THE

Mauch, Thomas
AGUIRRE, THE WRATH OF GOD
FITZCARRALDO

Menoud, Jean-Bernard
HAIL, MARY

Mercanton, Jacques
MR. HULOT'S HOLIDAY

Mercanton, Jean
JOUR DE FETE

Mignot, Pierre
ARIA

Miki, Minoru
SISTERS OF THE GION

Mitra, Subrata
PATHER PANCHALI
WORLD OF APU, THE

Mitra, Subroto
APARAJITO

Miyagawa, Kazuo
KAGEMUSHA
MACARTHUR'S CHILDREN
RASHOMON
SANSHO THE BAILIFF
ODD OBSESSION
UGETSU
YOJIMBO
FLOATING WEEDS

Miyajima, Yoshio
KWAIDAN

Mondi, Bruno
KOLBERG

Montanari, Sergio
CRICKET, THE

Monti, Felix
OFFICIAL STORY, THE

Montuori, Carlo
BICYCLE THIEF, THE

Moskvin, Andrei
IVAN THE TERRIBLE PART I AND II

Moura, Edgar
HOUR OF THE STAR, THE

Mousselle, Jean
MR. HULOT'S HOLIDAY

Muller, Robby
ALICE IN THE CITIES
AMERICAN FRIEND, THE

KINGS OF THE ROAD
PARIS, TEXAS
GOALIE'S ANXIETY AT THE PENALTY KICK, THE
WRONG MOVE

Murai, Hiroshi
SWORD OF DOOM, THE

Murphy, Fred
STATE OF THINGS, THE

Nakai, Asaichi
KAGEMUSHA
THRONE OF BLOOD

Nakai, Asakazu
IKIRU
DERSU UZALA
RAN
RED BEARD
SEVEN SAMURAI, THE

Nakai, Choichi
HIGH AND LOW

Nannuzzi, Armando
LA NUIT DE VARENNES
LA CAGE AUX FOLLES II
DAMNED, THE

Narushima, Toichiro
DOUBLE SUICIDE
MERRY CHRISTMAS, MR. LAWRENCE

Natteau, Jacques
FOUR BAGS FULL
NEVER ON SUNDAY

Neau, Andre
RETURN OF MARTIN GUERRE, THE

Nee, Louis
VAMPYR

Nikolayev, Vladimir
BALLAD OF A SOLDIER

Nitzschmann, Erich
DESTINY

Novotny, Vladimir
SHOP ON MAIN STREET, THE

Nuytten, Bruno
GOING PLACES
TCHAO PANTIN
JEAN DE FLORETTE
INVITATION AU VOYAGE
MANON OF THE SPRING

Nykvist, Sven
AFTER THE REHEARSAL
AUTUMN SONATA
CRIES AND WHISPERS
FROM THE LIFE OF THE MARIONETTES
FANNY AND ALEXANDER
SACRIFICE, THE
SCENES FROM A MARRIAGE
SILENCE, THE
PERSONA
VIRGIN SPRING, THE
WINTER LIGHT, THE
SWANN IN LOVE
TENANT, THE
THROUGH A GLASS DARKLY
SAWDUST AND TINSEL
HOUR OF THE WOLF, THE
SERPENT'S EGG, THE

Ondricek, Miroslav
FIREMAN'S BALL, THE
LOVES OF A BLONDE

Pahle, Ted
MARIUS

Parolin, Aiace
SEDUCED AND ABANDONED

Pascal Marti
SCENE OF THE CRIME

Penzer, Jean
GET OUT YOUR HANDKERCHIEFS
MY BEST FRIEND'S GIRL
TWO OF US, THE
LA PASSANTE

Perinal, Georges
A NOUS LA LIBERTE
BLOOD OF A POET, THE
LE MILLION
UNDER THE ROOFS OF PARIS
LADY CHATTERLEY'S LOVER

Persson, Jorgen
ELVIRA MADIGAN
MY LIFE AS A DOG

Petkovic, Aleksandar
LOVE AFFAIR; OR THE CASE OF THE MISSING SWITCHBOARD OPERATOR

Phillips, Alex
MEXICAN BUS RIDE
LA CHEVRE

Picon-Borel, R.
BATTLE OF AUSTERLITZ, THE

Pinter, Tomislav
MONTENEGRO

Pogany, Gabor
TWO WOMEN

Polak, Hanus
INHERITORS, THE

Pontoiseau, Roland
TESTAMENT OF ORPHEUS, THE

Popov, V.
BATTLESHIP POTEMKIN

Portalupe, Piero
BELLISSIMA

Protat, Francois
DIRTY DISHES

Rabier, Jean
CLEO FROM 5 TO 7
UMBRELLAS OF CHERBOURG, THE
BAD GIRLS

Ragona, Claudio
MACARONI

Rathje, Gustav
M

Raulet, Georges
LE MILLION
UNDER THE ROOFS OF PARIS

Renoir, Claude
GOLDEN COACH, THE
ELENA AND HER MEN
TONI

Ricciotti, Stefano
SWEPT AWAY. . .BY AN UNUSUAL DESTINY IN THE BLUE SEA OF AUGUST

Richard, Edmond
DISCREET CHARM OF THE BOURGEOISIE, THE
PHANTOM OF LIBERTY, THE
THAT OBSCURE OBJECT OF DESIRE

Rittau, Gunther
SIEGFRIED
BLUE ANGEL, THE
METROPOLIS
KRIEMHILD'S REVENGE

Roberts, Tony Pierce
MOONLIGHTING

Robin, Jean-Francois
BETTY BLUE

Rodriguez, Miguel
MISS MARY

Roeg, Nicholas
FAHRENHEIT 451

Ronald, H.
GOLDEN COACH, THE

Rotunno, Giuseppe
AMARCORD
AND THE SHIP SAILS ON
LOVE AND ANARCHY
FELLINI SATYRICON
DIVINE NYMPH, THE
JULIA AND JULIA
YESTERDAY, TODAY, AND TOMORROW

Roudakoff, Nicolas
ITALIAN STRAW HAT, AN

Rousselot, Philippe
DIVA
MOON IN THE GUTTER, THE
THERESE

Roy, Soumandu
HOME AND THE WORLD, THE
TWO DAUGHTERS

Ruban, Al
DAVID

Ruzzolini, Giuseppe
DIARY OF FORBIDDEN DREAMS

Saalfrank, Hermann
DESTINY

Saito, Kozo
SANJURO

Saito, Takao
KAGEMUSHA
DODES 'KA-DEN
RAN
RED BEARD
HIGH AND LOW

Salles, Maurilo
DONA FLOR AND HER TWO HUSBANDS

Salomon, Amnon
BEYOND THE WALLS

Salomon, Mikael
WOLF AT THE DOOR, THE

Sanchez, Rodolfo
PIXOTE
KISS OF THE SPIDER WOMAN

Sara, Sandor
FATHER

Savelyeva, Yera
BALLAD OF A SOLDIER

Scala, Domenico
OSSESSIONE

Scavarda, Aldo
L'AVVENTURA

Schafer, Martin
ALICE IN THE CITIES

Schier, Horst
WANNSEE CONFERENCE, THE

Schmidt-Reitwein, Jorge
EVERY MAN FOR HIMSELF AND GOD AGAINST ALL
WHERE THE GREEN ANTS DREAM

Schnackertz, Heinz
FEAR

Schneeberger, Hans
BLUE ANGEL, THE

Schwartz, Jean-Paul
JUPITER'S THIGH
LE CAVALEUR (PRACTICE MAKES PERFECT)

Schwarzenberger, Xaver
QUERELLE
BERLIN ALEXANDERPLATZ
KAMIKAZE '89

Sechan, Edmond
BLUE COUNTRY, THE
LA BOUM

Segawa, Hiroshi
WOMAN IN THE DUNES

Semler, Dean
COCA-COLA KID, THE

Serandrei, Mario
GOLDEN COACH, THE

Shuftan, Eugene
HORROR CHAMBER OF DR. FAUSTUS, THE

Slabnevich, Igor
MOSCOW DOES NOT BELIEVE IN TEARS

Sofr, Jaromir
CLOSELY WATCHED TRAINS

Solares, Raul Martinez
WOMAN WITHOUT LOVE, A

Solis, Leonardo Rodriguez
FUNNY, DIRTY LITTLE WAR, A

Southon, Mike
ARIA

Spinotti, Dante
BASILEUS QUARTET
SOTTO. . .SOTTO
ARIA

Stallich, Jan
ECSTASY

Stapleton, Oliver
ARIA

Storaro, Vittorio
CONFORMIST, THE
MALICIOUS
1900
LAST TANGO IN PARIS
LAST EMPEROR, THE

Stradling, Harry
CARNIVAL IN FLANDERS

Strindberg, Goran
SAWDUST AND TINSEL

Sugiyama, Kohei
GATE OF HELL
47 RONIN, THE (PARTS I & II)

Suzuki, Hiroshi
MOTHER

Suzuki, Richard
EMMANUELLE

Szabo, Etienne
ASSOCIATE, THE
MAKE ROOM FOR TOMORROW

Szabo, Gabor
REVOLT OF JOB, THE

Takahashi, Michio
HIROSHIMA, MON AMOUR
GOLDEN DEMON

Tamura, Masaki
HIMATSURI
TAMPOPO

Tarbes, Jean-Jacques
MY NEW PARTNER

Tattersall, Gale
ARIA

Taylor, Gilbert
MACBETH
REPULSION

Thermenius, Bjorn
WILD STRAWBERRIES

Thirard, Armand
AND GOD CREATED WOMAN
DIABOLIQUE
POIL DE CAROTTE
MAYERLING
WAGES OF FEAR, THE

Thury, Martial
PERIL

Tisse, Eduard
IVAN THE TERRIBLE PART I AND II
BATTLESHIP POTEMKIN
TEN DAYS THAT SHOOK THE WORLD
ALEXANDER NEVSKY

Tonti, Aldo
OSSESSIONE
NIGHTS OF CABIRIA, THE

Toporkoff, Nicolas
FANNY

Tovoli, Luciano
LA CAGE AUX FOLLES 3: THE WEDDING
PASSENGER, THE

Trasatti, Luciano
I VITELLONI

Treu, Wolfgang
PEDESTRIAN, THE

Troell, Jan
FLIGHT OF THE EAGLE

Ueda, Masaharu
RAN

Ueda, Shoji
KAGEMUSHA

Unsworth, Geoffrey
TESS

Urussevsky, Sergei
CRANES ARE FLYING, THE

Vacano, Jost
LOST HONOR OF KATHARINA BLUM, THE
SOLDIER OF ORANGE
SPETTERS
BOAT, THE

van de Sande, Theo
ASSAULT, THE

Vandenberg, Gerard
SPRING SYMPHONY

Varini, Carlo
SUBWAY
BIG BLUE, THE
LE DERNIER COMBAT

Vash, Karl
TESTAMENT OF DR. MABUSE, THE

Vavra, Josef
QUERELLE

Vierny, Sacha
BEAU PERE
LAST YEAR AT MARIENBAD
HIROSHIMA, MON AMOUR
MON ONCLE D'AMERIQUE
MURIEL

Wagner, Fritz Arno
M
TESTAMENT OF DR. MABUSE, THE
SPIES
DESTINY
NOSFERATU
THREEPENNY OPERA, THE
KAMERADSCHAFT

Wein, Yossi
DRIFTING

Weincke, Jan
TWIST & SHOUT

Weindler, Helge
MEN

Willy
CESAR

Winding, Andreas
PLAYTIME

Winding, Romain
LE BEAU MARIAGE

Wirth, Wolf
TONIO KROGER

Witte, Paul
PLACE OF WEEPING

Wojcik, Jerzy
ASHES AND DIAMONDS

Wottitz, Walter
LE CHAT

Wywerka, Albert
DYBBUK, THE

Yamada, Kazuo
SAMURAI TRILOGY, THE

Yamazaki, Ichio
LOWER DEPTHS, THE

Yamazaki, Kazuo
HIDDEN FORTRESS, THE

Yasumoto, Jun
SAMURAI TRILOGY, THE

Yokoyama, Minoru
BURMESE HARP, THE

Yusov, Vadim
MY NAME IS IVAN

Zitzermann, Bernard
LA BALANCE
MAN IN LOVE, A
MYSTERY OF ALEXINA, THE

DIRECTORS

Abuladze, Tengiz
REPENTANCE

Adlon, Percy
BAGDAD CAFE
SUGARBABY

Alexandrov, Grigori
TEN DAYS THAT SHOOK THE WORLD

Allegret, Marc
FANNY
LADY CHATTERLEY'S LOVER

Almodovar, Pedro
LAW OF DESIRE

Altman, Robert
ARIA

Amar, Denis
L'ADDITION

Amaral, Suzana
HOUR OF THE STAR, THE

Andre Techine
SCENE OF THE CRIME

Annaud, Jean-Jacques
BLACK AND WHITE IN COLOR

Antonioni, Michelangelo
L'AVVENTURA
ECLIPSE
RED DESERT
PASSENGER, THE
BLOW-UP
ZABRISKIE POINT

Arcand, Denys
DECLINE OF THE AMERICAN EMPIRE, THE

August, Bille
TWIST & SHOUT

Autant-Lara, Claude
FOUR BAGS FULL
DEVIL IN THE FLESH, THE
SYLVIA AND THE PHANTOM

Axel, Gabriel
BABETTE'S FEAST

Babenco, Hector
PIXOTE
KISS OF THE SPIDER WOMAN

Bal, Walter
JACKO AND LISE

Bannert, Walter
INHERITORS, THE

Barbash, Uri
BEYOND THE WALLS

Barreto, Bruno
GABRIELA
DONA FLOR AND HER TWO HUSBANDS

Becker, Jean
ONE DEADLY SUMMER

Beineix, Jean-Jacques
BETTY BLUE
DIVA
MOON IN THE GUTTER, THE

Bellocchio, Marco
HENRY IV
EYES, THE MOUTH, THE

Bemberg, Maria Luisa
CAMILA
MISS MARY

Beraud, Luc
HEAT OF DESIRE

Beresford, Bruce
ARIA

Bergman, Ingmar
AFTER THE REHEARSAL
AUTUMN SONATA
CRIES AND WHISPERS
LESSON IN LOVE, A
FROM THE LIFE OF THE MARIONETTES
FANNY AND ALEXANDER
DREAMS
DEVIL'S EYE, THE
MAGICIAN, THE
PORT OF CALL
SCENES FROM A MARRIAGE
SECRETS OF WOMEN
SEVENTH SEAL, THE
SMILES OF A SUMMER NIGHT
SILENCE, THE
PERSONA
VIRGIN SPRING, THE
WILD STRAWBERRIES
WINTER LIGHT, THE
THROUGH A GLASS DARKLY
SUMMER INTERLUDE
SAWDUST AND TINSEL
HOUR OF THE WOLF, THE
SERPENT'S EGG, THE

Berri, Claude
TWO OF US, THE
TCHAO PANTIN
JEAN DE FLORETTE
LE SEX SHOP
MANON OF THE SPRING

Bertolucci, Bernardo
CONFORMIST, THE
1900
LAST TANGO IN PARIS
LAST EMPEROR, THE

Besson, Luc
SUBWAY
BIG BLUE, THE
LE DERNIER COMBAT

Blier, Bertrand
BEAU PERE
GOING PLACES
GET OUT YOUR HANDKERCHIEFS
MY BEST FRIEND'S GIRL

Boese, Carl
GOLEM, THE

Bolognini, Mauro
INHERITANCE, THE

Bourguignon, Serge
SUNDAYS AND CYBELE

Bresson, Robert
DIARY OF A COUNTRY PRIEST

Bryden, Bill
ARIA

Brynych, Zbynek
TRANSPORT FROM PARADISE

Bunuel, Joyce
DIRTY DISHES

Bunuel, Luis
EL BRUTO
CRIMINAL LIFE OF ARCHIBALDO DE LA CRUZ, THE
LOS OLVIDADOS
EXTERMINATING ANGEL, THE
DISCREET CHARM OF THE BOURGEOISIE, THE
DIARY OF A CHAMBERMAID
WUTHERING HEIGHTS
PHANTOM OF LIBERTY, THE
WOMAN WITHOUT LOVE, A
VIRIDIANA
THAT OBSCURE OBJECT OF DESIRE
MEXICAN BUS RIDE
L'AGE D'OR
MILKY WAY, THE

Cacoyannis, Michael
IPHIGENIA
SWEET COUNTRY

Camus, Marcel
BLACK ORPHEUS

Camus, Mario
HOLY INNOCENTS, THE

Cardiff, Jack
GIRL ON A MOTORCYCLE, THE

Carlsen, Henning
WOLF AT THE DOOR, THE

Carne, Marcel
LE JOUR SE LEVE

Carpi, Fabio
BASILEUS QUARTET

Cavalier, Alain
THERESE

Cavani, Liliana
NIGHT PORTER, THE

Chabrol, Claude
LE BEAU SERGE
BAD GIRLS

Chouraqui, Elie
LOVE SONGS

Chukhrai, Grigori
BALLAD OF A SOLDIER

Clair, Rene
A NOUS LA LIBERTE
LE MILLION
UNDER THE ROOFS OF PARIS
ITALIAN STRAW HAT, AN

Clement, Rene
GERVAISE
FORBIDDEN GAMES

Clouzot, Henri-Georges
DIABOLIQUE
WAGES OF FEAR, THE

Cocteau, Jean
BEAUTY AND THE BEAST
BLOOD OF A POET, THE
ORPHEUS
TESTAMENT OF ORPHEUS, THE

Colomo, Fernando
SKYLINE

Comencini, Luigi
TILL MARRIAGE DO US PART

Corneau, Alain
CHOICE OF ARMS

Costa-Gavras, Constantin
HANNAH K.

Costa-Gavras, Constantine
Z
STATE OF SIEGE

Dassin, Jules
RIFIFI
NEVER ON SUNDAY

de Arminan, Jaime
NEST, THE

de Broca, Philippe
KING OF HEARTS
JUPITER'S THIGH
LE CAVALEUR (PRACTICE MAKES PERFECT)
LE MAGNIFIQUE

de la Iglesia, Eloy
EL DIPUTADO

De Sica, Vittorio
BICYCLE THIEF, THE
GARDEN OF THE FINZI-CONTINIS, THE
SHOESHINE
TWO WOMEN
UMBERTO D
MIRACLE IN MILAN
YESTERDAY, TODAY, AND TOMORROW

Del Monte, Peter
JULIA AND JULIA
INVITATION AU VOYAGE

Delannoy, Jean
ETERNAL RETURN, THE

Dembo, Richard
DANGEROUS MOVES

Demy, Jacques
DONKEY SKIN
UMBRELLAS OF CHERBOURG, THE

Deville, Michel
PERIL

Diegues, Carlos
BYE BYE BRAZIL

Dorrie, Doris
MEN

Dovzhenko, Alexander
EARTH

Dreyer, Carl Theodor
VAMPYR

Dreyer, Carl Theodor
DAY OF WRATH
GERTRUD
ORDET
PASSION OF JOAN OF ARC, THE

Dupont, E.A.
VARIETY

Duvivier, Julien
POIL DE CAROTTE
PEPE LE MOKO

Eisenstein, Sergei
IVAN THE TERRIBLE PART I AND II
BATTLESHIP POTEMKIN
TEN DAYS THAT SHOOK THE WORLD
ALEXANDER NEVSKY

Erice, Victor
SPIRIT OF THE BEEHIVE, THE

Fassbinder, Rainer Werner
DESPAIR
QUERELLE
MARRIAGE OF MARIA BRAUN, THE
BERLIN ALEXANDERPLATZ

Fellini, Federico
AMARCORD
AND THE SHIP SAILS ON
LA STRADA
LA DOLCE VITA
JULIET OF THE SPIRITS
GINGER & FRED
FELLINI SATYRICON
8 1/2
I VITELLONI
NIGHTS OF CABIRIA, THE
WHITE SHEIK, THE

Feret, Rene
MYSTERY OF ALEXINA, THE

Feyder, Jacques
CARNIVAL IN FLANDERS

Forman, Milos
FIREMAN'S BALL, THE
LOVES OF A BLONDE

Franju, Georges
HORROR CHAMBER OF DR. FAUSTUS, THE

Frank, Christopher
L'ANNEE DES MEDUSES

Fuest, Robert
APHRODITE

Gainville, Rene
ASSOCIATE, THE

Gance, Abel
BATTLE OF AUSTERLITZ, THE
NAPOLEON

Germi, Pietro
SEDUCED AND ABANDONED

Godard, Jean-Luc
ALPHAVILLE
BAND OF OUTSIDERS
BREATHLESS
CONTEMPT
LES CARABINIERS
HAIL, MARY
MARRIED WOMAN, THE
MASCULINE FEMININE
MY LIFE TO LIVE
ARIA

Goren, Serif
YOL

Gorris, Marleen
QUESTION OF SILENCE

Granier-Deferre, Pierre
LE CHAT
FRENCH DETECTIVE, THE

Gremm, Wolf
KAMIKAZE '89

Griffi, Giuseppe Patroni
DIVINE NYMPH, THE

Guerra, Ruy
ERENDIRA

Guney, Yilmaz
WALL, THE

Guttman, Amos
DRIFTING

Gyongyossy, Imre
REVOLT OF JOB, THE

Hallstrom, Lasse
MY LIFE AS A DOG

Hamilton, David
TENDRES COUSINES

Hansel, Marion
DUST

Harlan, Veit
KOLBERG

Henzell, Perry
HARDER THEY COME, THE

Herzog, Werner
AGUIRRE, THE WRATH OF GOD
EVERY MAN FOR HIMSELF AND GOD AGAINST ALL
WHERE THE GREEN ANTS DREAM
FITZCARRALDO

Hubert, Jean-Loup
LE GRAND CHEMIN

Huppert, Caroline
SINCERELY CHARLOTTE

Ichikawa, Kon
FIRES ON THE PLAIN
ODD OBSESSION
BURMESE HARP, THE

Inagaki, Hiroshi
SAMURAI TRILOGY, THE

Itami, Juzo
TAMPOPO
FUNERAL, THE
TAXING WOMAN, A

Jaeckin, Just
EMMANUELLE

Jarman, Derek
ARIA

Ji-shun, Duan
GO-MASTERS, THE

Kabay, Barna
REVOLT OF JOB, THE

Kadar, Jan
SHOP ON MAIN STREET, THE

Kalatozov, Mikhail
CRANES ARE FLYING, THE

Kaplan, Nelly
VERY CURIOUS GIRL, A

Kassovitz, Peter
MAKE ROOM FOR TOMORROW

Keglevic, Peter
COP AND THE GIRL, THE

Kinoshita, Keisuke
TWENTY-FOUR EYES

Kinugasa, Teinosuke
GATE OF HELL

Klos, Elmar
SHOP ON MAIN STREET, THE

Kobayashi, Masaki
KWAIDAN

Korda, Alexander
MARIUS

Kurosawa, Akira
KAGEMUSHA
IKIRU
HIDDEN FORTRESS, THE
DRUNKEN ANGEL
DODES 'KA-DEN
DERSU UZALA
RAN
RASHOMON
RED BEARD
SANJURO
SEVEN SAMURAI, THE
STRAY DOG
YOJIMBO
THRONE OF BLOOD
HIGH AND LOW
LOWER DEPTHS, THE
BAD SLEEP WELL, THE

Kurys, Diane
ENTRE NOUS
MAN IN LOVE, A

Lang, Fritz
SIEGFRIED
M
TESTAMENT OF DR. MABUSE, THE
SPIES
DR. MABUSE, THE GAMBLER (PARTS I & II)
DESTINY
METROPOLIS
KRIEMHILD'S REVENGE

Lang, Michel
GIFT, THE
HOLIDAY HOTEL

Lattuada, Alberto
CRICKET, THE
STAY AS YOU ARE

Lautner, Georges
LA CAGE AUX FOLLES 3: THE WEDDING
MY OTHER HUSBAND

Lelouch, Claude
AND NOW MY LOVE
CAT AND MOUSE
EDITH AND MARCEL
MAN AND A WOMAN: 20 YEARS LATER, A
HAPPY NEW YEAR
MAN AND A WOMAN, A

Lilienthal, Peter
DAVID

Littin, Miguel
ALSINO AND THE CONDOR

Litvak, Anatole
MAYERLING

Lombardi, Francisco J.
LA CIUDAD Y LOS PERROS

Losey, Joseph
MR. KLEIN
LA TRUITE (THE TROUT)

Loubignac, Jean
FEMMES DE PARIS

Loy, Nanni
WHERE'S PICONE?

Machaty, Gustav
ECSTASY

Magni, Luigi
IN THE NAME OF THE POPE KING

Makavejev, Dusan
COCA-COLA KID, THE
MONTENEGRO
LOVE AFFAIR; OR THE CASE OF THE MISSING SWITCHBOARD OPERATOR

Malle, Louis
AU REVOIR LES ENFANTS
FRANTIC
VERY PRIVATE AFFAIR, A

Meerapfel, Jeanine
MALOU

Melville, Jean-Pierre
LES ENFANTS TERRIBLES
LE DOULOS
BOB LE FLAMBEUR

Menshov, Vladimir
MOSCOW DOES NOT BELIEVE IN TEARS

Menzel, Jiri
CLOSELY WATCHED TRAINS

Metzger, Radley H.
CAMILLE 2000
THERESE AND ISABELLE

Mikhalkov, Nikita
DARK EYES

Mizoguchi, Kenji
SANSHO THE BAILIFF
UGETSU
LIFE OF OHARU
47 RONIN, THE (PARTS I & II)
SISTERS OF THE GION

Mizrahi, Moshe
I SENT A LETTER TO MY LOVE
MADAME ROSA

Molinaro, Edouard
LA CAGE AUX FOLLES II
LA CAGE AUX FOLLES

Monicelli, Mario
BIG DEAL ON MADONNA STREET, THE

Moreau, Jeanne
LUMIERE

Murnau, F.W.
LAST LAUGH, THE
FAUST
NOSFERATU

Naruse, Mikio
MOTHER

Nava, Gregory
EL NORTE

Nemec, Jan
DIAMONDS OF THE NIGHT

Okamoto, Kihachi
SWORD OF DOOM, THE

Olivera, Hector
FUNNY, DIRTY LITTLE WAR, A
EL MUERTO

Ophuls, Max
LA RONDE
EARRINGS OF MADAME DE . . ., THE
LE PLAISIR
LOLA MONTES

Oshima, Nagisa
MERRY CHRISTMAS, MR. LAWRENCE

Ozu, Yasujiro
FLOATING WEEDS

Pabst, G.W.
PANDORA'S BOX
DIARY OF A LOST GIRL
THREEPENNY OPERA, THE
KAMERADSCHAFT

Pagnol, Marcel
BAKER'S WIFE, THE
CESAR

Palcy, Euzhan
SUGAR CANE ALLEY

Paradzhanov, Sergey
SHADOWS OF FORGOTTEN ANCESTORS

Pasolini, Pier Paolo
GOSPEL ACCORDING TO ST. MATTHEW, THE

Perier, Etienne
INVESTIGATION

Petersen, Wolfgang
BOAT, THE

Pialat, Maurice
A NOS AMOURS

Pinoteau, Claude
LA BOUM

Polanski, Roman
DIARY OF FORBIDDEN DREAMS
KNIFE IN THE WATER
TENANT, THE
MACBETH
REPULSION
TESS

Pontecorvo, Gillo
BATTLE OF ALGIERS, THE

Puenzo, Luis
OFFICIAL STORY, THE

Rademakers, Fons
ASSAULT, THE

Ray, Satyajit
APARAJITO
HOME AND THE WORLD, THE
PATHER PANCHALI
WORLD OF APU, THE
TWO DAUGHTERS

Renoir, Jean
BOUDU SAVED FROM DROWNING
CRIME OF MONSIEUR LANGE, THE
LA MARSEILLAISE
LA BETE HUMAINE
GRAND ILLUSION
GOLDEN COACH, THE
FRENCH CANCAN
ELUSIVE CORPORAL, THE
RULES OF THE GAME, THE
ELENA AND HER MEN
PICNIC ON THE GRASS
TONI
LOWER DEPTHS, THE

Resnais, Alain
LAST YEAR AT MARIENBAD
HIROSHIMA, MON AMOUR
PROVIDENCE
MON ONCLE D'AMERIQUE
MURIEL

Robert, Yves
TALL BLOND MAN WITH ONE BLACK SHOE, THE
PARDON MON AFFAIRE
RETURN OF THE TALL BLOND MAN WITH ONE BLACK SHOE, THE

Roddam, Franc
ARIA

Roeg, Nicolas
ARIA

Rohmer, Eric
CHLOE IN THE AFTERNOON
CLAIRE'S KNEE
LE BEAU MARIAGE
FULL MOON IN PARIS
SUMMER
MY NIGHT AT MAUD'S
PAULINE AT THE BEACH

Roodt, Darrell
PLACE OF WEEPING

Rosi, Francesco
BIZET'S CARMEN
CHRIST STOPPED AT EBOLI
THREE BROTHERS

Rossellini, Roberto
GERMANY, YEAR ZERO
GENERAL DELLA ROVERE
FEAR
STROMBOLI
OPEN CITY
PAISAN
FLOWERS OF ST. FRANCIS, THE
RISE TO POWER OF LOUIS XIV, THE

Rouffio, Jacques
LA PASSANTE

Russell, Ken
ARIA

Sagan, Leontine
MAEDCHEN IN UNIFORM

Samperi, Salvatore
MALICIOUS

Sato, Junya
GO-MASTERS, THE

Saura, Carlos
BLOOD WEDDING
CARMEN
EL AMOR BRUJO
GARDEN OF DELIGHTS, THE
CRIA!

Sautet, Claude
CESAR AND ROSALIE

Schamoni, Peter
SPRING SYMPHONY

Schell, Maximilian
PEDESTRIAN, THE

Schirk, Heinz
WANNSEE CONFERENCE, THE

Schlondorff, Volker
COUP DE GRACE
LOST HONOR OF KATHARINA BLUM, THE
SWANN IN LOVE
TIN DRUM, THE

Schrader, Paul
MISHIMA

Scola, Ettore
LE BAL
LA NUIT DE VARENNES
FAMILY, THE
MACARONI
DOWN AND DIRTY

Serreau, Coline
THREE MEN AND A CRADLE

Shima, Koji
GOLDEN DEMON

Shinoda, Masahiro
DOUBLE SUICIDE
MACARTHUR'S CHILDREN

Simoneau, Yves
BLIND TRUST

Sjoberg, Alf
TORMENT

Skolimowski, Jerzy
MOONLIGHTING

Sturridge, Charles
ARIA

Subiela, Eliseo
MAN FACING SOUTHEAST

Swaim, Bob
LA BALANCE

Szabo, Istvan
COLONEL REDL
MEPHISTO
FATHER

Tacchella, Jean-Charles
BLUE COUNTRY, THE
COUSIN, COUSINE

Takabayashi, Yoichi
IREZUMI (SPIRIT OF TATTOO)

Tarkovsky, Andrei
SACRIFICE, THE
MY NAME IS IVAN

Tati, Jacques
PLAYTIME
MR. HULOT'S HOLIDAY
MY UNCLE
JOUR DE FETE

Tavernier, Bertrand
CLOCKMAKER, THE
CLEAN SLATE (COUP DE TORCHON)
DEATHWATCH
SUNDAY IN THE COUNTRY, A
ROUND MIDNIGHT
PASSION OF BEATRICE, THE

Taviani, Paolo
GOOD MORNING BABYLON
NIGHT OF THE SHOOTING STARS, THE
PADRE PADRONE

Taviani, Vittorio
GOOD MORNING BABYLON
NIGHT OF THE SHOOTING STARS, THE
PADRE PADRONE

Temple, Julien
ARIA

Teshigahara, Hiroshi
WOMAN IN THE DUNES

Thiele, Rolf
TONIO KROGER

Troell, Jan
FLIGHT OF THE EAGLE

Truffaut, Francois
CONFIDENTIALLY YOURS!
DAY FOR NIGHT
LOVE ON THE RUN
LAST METRO, THE
JULES AND JIM
GREEN ROOM, THE
SHOOT THE PIANO PLAYER
SMALL CHANGE
SOFT SKIN, THE
STOLEN KISSES
STORY OF ADELE H., THE
WOMAN NEXT DOOR, THE
TWO ENGLISH GIRLS
FAHRENHEIT 451
FOUR HUNDRED BLOWS, THE
MAN WHO LOVED WOMEN, THE

Vadim, Roger
AND GOD CREATED WOMAN

Van Ackeren, Robert
WOMAN IN FLAMES, A

Varda, Agnes
CLEO FROM 5 TO 7
VAGABOND

Vassiliev, Dmitri I.
ALEXANDER NEVSKY

Veber, Francis
LES COMPERES
LA CHEVRE

Verhoeven, Paul
FOURTH MAN, THE
SOLDIER OF ORANGE
SPETTERS

Vicario, Marco
WIFEMISTRESS

Vigne, Daniel
RETURN OF MARTIN GUERRE, THE

Vigo, Jean
L'ATALANTE

Visconti, Luchino
INNOCENT, THE
DEATH IN VENICE
OSSESSIONE
DAMNED, THE
LA TERRA TREMA
BELLISSIMA

von Sternberg, Josef
BLUE ANGEL, THE

von Trotta, Margarethe
LOST HONOR OF KATHARINA BLUM, THE

Wajda, Andrzej
DANTON
LOVE IN GERMANY, A
ASHES AND DIAMONDS
KANAL

Waszynski, Machael
DYBBUK, THE

Wegener, Paul
GOLEM, THE

Weine, Robert
CABINET OF DR. CALIGARI, THE

Wenders, Wim
ALICE IN THE CITIES
AMERICAN FRIEND, THE
KINGS OF THE ROAD
PARIS, TEXAS
HAMMETT
GOALIE'S ANXIETY AT THE PENALTY KICK, THE
STATE OF THINGS, THE
WINGS OF DESIRE
WRONG MOVE

Wertmuller, Lina
LOVE AND ANARCHY
JOKE OF DESTINY, A
SEVEN BEAUTIES
SOTTO. . .SOTTO
SEDUCTION OF MIMI, THE
SWEPT AWAY. . .BY AN UNUSUAL DESTINY IN THE BLUE SEA OF AUGUST

Widerberg, Bo
ELVIRA MADIGAN

Yanagimachi, Mitsuo
HIMATSURI

Zeffirelli, Franco
LA TRAVIATA

Zidi, Claude
MY NEW PARTNER

EDITORS

Abrahamson, Neil
ARIA

Alice, Mauro
KISS OF THE SPIDER WOMAN

Anderson, Seicland
HARDER THEY COME, THE

Antonioni, Michelangelo
PASSENGER, THE

Arcalli, Franco
CONFORMIST, THE
1900
PASSENGER, THE
LAST TANGO IN PARIS
NIGHT PORTER, THE
ZABRISKIE POINT

Asher, Tova
BEYOND THE WALLS

Auge, Jennifer
ARIA

Azar, Leonide
BATTLE OF AUSTERLITZ, THE
LA RONDE
SUNDAYS AND CYBELE
FRANTIC
LE PLAISIR

Balenci, Noelle
APHRODITE

Bannert, Walter
INHERITORS, THE

Baragli, Nino
GOSPEL ACCORDING TO ST. MATTHEW, THE
GINGER & FRED
WIFEMISTRESS
TILL MARRIAGE DO US PART

Baron, Suzanne
MR. HULOT'S HOLIDAY
MY UNCLE
TIN DRUM, THE

Barraque, Martine
CONFIDENTIALLY YOURS!
DAY FOR NIGHT
LOVE ON THE RUN
LAST METRO, THE
GREEN ROOM, THE
SMALL CHANGE
STORY OF ADELE H., THE
WOMAN NEXT DOOR, THE
MAN WHO LOVED WOMEN, THE

Barrois, Claude
MAN AND A WOMAN, A

Barthelmes, Raimund
MEN

Beauge, Marguerite
PEPE LE MOKO
NAPOLEON

Benedetti, Rolando
I VITELLONI
WHITE SHEIK, THE

Benvenuti, Jolanda
FEAR
STROMBOLI
FLOWERS OF ST. FRANCIS, THE

Biurrun, Jose Maria
HOLY INNOCENTS, THE

Blankett, Betsy
EL NORTE

Boeglin, Ariane
MYSTERY OF ALEXINA, THE

Boehm, Michele
BLACK AND WHITE IN COLOR

Boiche, Marie Therese
ARIA

Boissel, Anne
SINCERELY CHARLOTTE

Boisser, G.
MAN AND A WOMAN, A

Boisson, Noelle
LOVE SONGS
JEAN DE FLORETTE

Bonis, Jean-Bernard
DIRTY DISHES
TENDRES COUSINES

Bonnot, Francoise
BLACK AND WHITE IN COLOR
I SENT A LETTER TO MY LOVE
HANNAH K.
Z
SWANN IN LOVE
TENANT, THE
STATE OF SIEGE

Bonnot, Monique
LES ENFANTS TERRIBLES
LE DOULOS
BOB LE FLAMBEUR

Boos, Walter
FEAR

Bouche, Claudine
JULES AND JIM
SHOOT THE PIANO PLAYER
SOFT SKIN, THE
EMMANUELLE

Bradsell, Michael
ARIA

Bretoneiche, Charles
MR. HULOT'S HOLIDAY

Brillouin, Jacques
CARNIVAL IN FLANDERS

Bunuel, Luis
L'AGE D'OR

Bustos, Jorge
EL BRUTO
CRIMINAL LIFE OF ARCHIBALDO DE LA CRUZ, THE
WOMAN WITHOUT LOVE, A

Cacoyannis, Michael
IPHIGENIA
SWEET COUNTRY

Cartwright, Peter
ARIA

Castro, Emmanuelle
AU REVOIR LES ENFANTS
GABRIELA

Castro-Vasquez, Marie
LA TRUITE (THE TROUT)

Caterini, Lina
LA STRADA

Catozzo, Leo
LA STRADA
LA DOLCE VITA
8 1/2
NIGHTS OF CABIRIA, THE

Cavagna, Cesare
GENERAL DELLA ROVERE

Chandler, Michael
JULIA AND JULIA
MISHIMA

Charvein, Denise
TWO OF US, THE

Chasney, Jasmine
LAST YEAR AT MARIENBAD
HIROSHIMA, MON AMOUR

Chavance, Louis
L'ATALANTE

Cinquini, Roberto
SEDUCED AND ABANDONED

Clair, Rene
UNDER THE ROOFS OF PARIS
ITALIAN STRAW HAT, AN

Clarke, Frank
BLOW-UP

Cocteau, Jean
BLOOD OF A POET, THE

Collin, Francoise
BAND OF OUTSIDERS
MARRIED WOMAN, THE

Colpi, Henri
COUP DE GRACE
LAST YEAR AT MARIENBAD
HIROSHIMA, MON AMOUR

Condroyer, Valerie
A NOS AMOURS

Cook, Angus
ARIA

Corriveau, Andre
BLIND TRUST

Cotret, Anne-Marie
DONKEY SKIN
UMBRELLAS OF CHERBOURG, THE

Coussein, Sophie
A NOS AMOURS
TWO OF US, THE
LE SEX SHOP
MADAME ROSA

Cragg, Mike
ARIA

Cristiani, Gabriella
LAST EMPEROR, THE

Crociani, Raimondo
LE BAL
LA NUIT DE VARENNES
DOWN AND DIRTY

Csekany, Zsuzsa
COLONEL REDL
MEPHISTO

D'Angiolillo, Luis Cesar
CAMILA
MAN FACING SOUTHEAST
MISS MARY

Da Roma, Eraldo
BICYCLE THIEF, THE
L'AVVENTURA
GERMANY, YEAR ZERO
ECLIPSE
RED DESERT
PAISAN
UMBERTO D
MIRACLE IN MILAN

Darmois, Hugues
EDITH AND MARCEL
MAN AND A WOMAN: 20 YEARS LATER, A

David, Michelle
LA CAGE AUX FOLLES 3: THE WEDDING
MY OTHER HUSBAND

de Casabianca, Denise
RETURN OF MARTIN GUERRE, THE

de Luze, Herve
TCHAO PANTIN
JEAN DE FLORETTE
MANON OF THE SPRING

De Rossi, Ugo
GINGER & FRED

de Troeye, Suzanne
CESAR
LA BETE HUMAINE
TONI

de Troye, Suzanne
BAKER'S WIFE, THE
BOUDU SAVED FROM DROWNING

Decugis, Cecile
BREATHLESS
CHLOE IN THE AFTERNOON
CLAIRE'S KNEE
LE BEAU MARIAGE
FULL MOON IN PARIS
SHOOT THE PIANO PLAYER
MY NIGHT AT MAUD'S
PAULINE AT THE BEACH

Dedet, Yann
A NOS AMOURS
DAY FOR NIGHT
SMALL CHANGE
STORY OF ADELE H., THE
TWO ENGLISH GIRLS

Dedieu, Isabelle
THERESE

del Amo, Pablo
BLOOD WEDDING

del Amo, Pablo G.
GARDEN OF DELIGHTS, THE
CRIA!
SPIRIT OF THE BEEHIVE, THE

Del Rey, Pedro
CARMEN

del Rey, Pedro
EL AMOR BRUJO
VIRIDIANA

Derocles, Thierry
CHOICE OF ARMS

Deschamps, Yves
MOON IN THE GUTTER, THE

Desjonqueres, Ghislaine
TALL BLOND MAN WITH ONE BLACK SHOE, THE
RETURN OF THE TALL BLOND MAN WITH ONE BLACK SHOE, THE

Dorn, Anette
COUP DE GRACE

Dovzhenko, Alexander
EARTH

Dreyer, Carl Theodor
PASSION OF JOAN OF ARC, THE

Dubus, Marie Sophie
LES COMPERES

Dutta, Dulal
HOME AND THE WORLD, THE

PATHER PANCHALI
WORLD OF APU, THE
TWO DAUGHTERS

Dutta, Dulala
APARAJITO

Dwyre, Roger
FORBIDDEN GAMES
RIFIFI
NEVER ON SUNDAY

Eisenstein, Sergei
IVAN THE TERRIBLE PART I AND II
BATTLESHIP POTEMKIN
TEN DAYS THAT SHOOK THE WORLD
ALEXANDER NEVSKY

Elgood, Rick
ARIA

Elias, Luiz
PIXOTE

Ellis, Michael
DEATHWATCH

Falkenberg, Paul
M

Fauvel, Suzanne
ETERNAL RETURN, THE

Feix, Andree
BLACK ORPHEUS

Feyginova, L.
MY NAME IS IVAN

Finkelstein, Anna
DRIFTING

Fliesler, Joseph R.
PANDORA'S BOX

Fortier, Monique
DECLINE OF THE AMERICAN EMPIRE, THE

Fraticelli, Franco
LOVE AND ANARCHY
JOKE OF DESTINY, A
SEVEN BEAUTIES
SEDUCTION OF MIMI, THE
WHERE'S PICONE?

Fujii, Hiroaki
FIRES ON THE PLAIN
ODD OBSESSION

Furubrand, Christer
MY LIFE AS A DOG

Gaillard, Jacques
LE BEAU SERGE
BAD GIRLS

Garcia, Maria-Luisa
SUMMER

Garrone, Mirco
HENRY IV

Ginestet, Jeanette
CESAR

Goto, Toshio
LIFE OF OHARU

Grassi, Jacques
MR. HULOT'S HOLIDAY

Gross, Roland
STROMBOLI

Gug, Madeleine
FOUR BAGS FULL
DIABOLIQUE
DEVIL IN THE FLESH, THE
WAGES OF FEAR, THE
SYLVIA AND THE PHANTOM
LOLA MONTES

Guillemot, Agnes
ALPHAVILLE
BAND OF OUTSIDERS
BLUE COUNTRY, THE
CONTEMPT
COUSIN, COUSINE
DANGEROUS MOVES
STOLEN KISSES
LES CARABINIERS
INVITATION AU VOYAGE
MARRIED WOMAN, THE
MASCULINE FEMININE
MY LIFE TO LIVE

Guney, Yilmaz
YOL

Guyot, Raymonde
ASSOCIATE, THE
PERIL
LE GRAND CHEMIN

Hajek, Miroslav
DIAMONDS OF THE NIGHT
TRANSPORT FROM PARADISE
FIREMAN'S BALL, THE
LOVES OF A BLONDE

Hautecoeur, Louisette
DIARY OF A CHAMBERMAID
MILKY WAY, THE

Hawkins, David
GOLDEN COACH, THE

Heitner, David
PLACE OF WEEPING

Henriksen, Finn
BABETTE'S FEAST

Heredia, Lisa
LE BEAU MARIAGE

Heringova, Diana
SHOP ON MAIN STREET, THE

Herman, Lila
BREATHLESS

Herzner, Norbert
BAGDAD CAFE

Higino, Raimundo
DONA FLOR AND HER TWO HUSBANDS

Hinshelwood, Humphrey
CAMILLE 2000

Hirtz, Dagmar
PEDESTRIAN, THE
MALOU

Homel, Robert
SAMURAI TRILOGY, THE

Huguet, Marthe
LA MARSEILLAISE

Iberia, Claude
BEAUTY AND THE BEAST

Ichikawa, Kon
FIRES ON THE PLAIN
ODD OBSESSION

Ingemarsson, Sylvia
AFTER THE REHEARSAL
FANNY AND ALEXANDER
MONTENEGRO

Ingmarsdotter, Sylvia
AUTUMN SONATA

Isnardon, Monique
LA CAGE AUX FOLLES

Isnardon, Robert
LA CAGE AUX FOLLES II
LA CAGE AUX FOLLES

Iwatani, Keisuke
KAGEMUSHA

Jager, Siegrun
DAVID

Janacek, Jaromir
SHOP ON MAIN STREET, THE

Jansen, Janus Billeskov
WOLF AT THE DOOR, THE
TWIST & SHOUT

Javet, Francoise
LA BALANCE
KING OF HEARTS

Jurgenson, Albert
LUMIERE
PROVIDENCE
MON ONCLE D'AMERIQUE
LA CHEVRE

Kaplan, Nelly
VERY CURIOUS GIRL, A

Kato, Masatoshi
MOTHER

Katsourides, Dinos
SWEET COUNTRY

Klee, Walter
BLUE ANGEL, THE

Klotz, George
AND NOW MY LOVE

Klotz, Georges
CAT AND MOUSE
HAPPY NEW YEAR

Kurosawa, Akira
RAN
SANJURO
SEVEN SAMURAI, THE
THRONE OF BLOOD
BAD SLEEP WELL, THE

Lacreta, Ide
HOUR OF THE STAR, THE

Lafaurie, Nathalie
L'ANNEE DES MEDUSES

Lakshmanan, Lila
CONTEMPT
LES CARABINIERS

Lamy, Raymond
FANNY

Langmann, Arlette
JEAN DE FLORETTE

Lanoe, Henri
MR. KLEIN
JUPITER'S THIGH
LE CAVALEUR (PRACTICE MAKES PERFECT)
LE MAGNIFIQUE

Latini, Massimo
BASILEUS QUARTET

Laub, Marc
HAMMETT

Lawson, Tony
ARIA

Lazzari, Nicolo
SHOESHINE

Le Hanaff, Rene
A NOUS LA LIBERTE

Le Henaff, Rene
LE MILLION
LE JOUR SE LEVE

Lelouch, Claude
MAN AND A WOMAN, A

Leszczylowski, Michal
SACRIFICE, THE

Lewin, Borys
FRENCH CANCAN
EARRINGS OF MADAME DE . . ., THE
ELENA AND HER MEN

Lewin, Michel
JACKO AND LISE

Lichtig, Renee
ELUSIVE CORPORAL, THE
PICNIC ON THE GRASS
INVESTIGATION

Linnman, Susanne
MY LIFE AS A DOG

Linthorst, Kees
ASSAULT, THE

London, Francois
PICNIC ON THE GRASS
RETURN OF THE TALL BLOND MAN WITH ONE BLACK SHOE, THE

Longfellow, Matthew
ARIA

Lopez, Eduardo
FUNNY, DIRTY LITTLE WAR, A

Lorenz, Juliane
DESPAIR
QUERELLE
MARRIAGE OF MARIA BRAUN, THE
BERLIN ALEXANDERPLATZ

Louveau, Genevieve
MANON OF THE SPRING

Lovett, Robert Q.
HAMMETT

Lukesova, Jirina
CLOSELY WATCHED TRAINS

Lundgren, Siv
CRIES AND WHISPERS
SCENES FROM A MARRIAGE

Macias, Juan Carlos
OFFICIAL STORY, THE

McIntyre, Alastair
DIARY OF FORBIDDEN DREAMS
MACBETH
REPULSION
TESS

Mainka-Jellinghaus, Beate
AGUIRRE, THE WRATH OF GOD
EVERY MAN FOR HIMSELF AND GOD AGAINST ALL
WHERE THE GREEN ANTS DREAM
FITZCARRALDO

Malkin, Barry
HAMMETT

Mamou, Sabine
WALL, THE

Martin, Yvonne
BATTLE OF AUSTERLITZ, THE

Martine Giordano
SCENE OF THE CRIME

Mastroianni, Ruggero
AMARCORD
AND THE SHIP SAILS ON
BIZET'S CARMEN
JULIET OF THE SPIRITS
INNOCENT, THE
GINGER & FRED
FELLINI SATYRICON
CHRIST STOPPED AT EBOLI
DEATH IN VENICE
THREE BROTHERS
IN THE NAME OF THE POPE KING
DAMNED, THE

Matesanz, Jose Luis
NEST, THE

Mauffroy, Olivier
BIG BLUE, THE

Mavel, Jacques
FEMMES DE PARIS

Mazuy, Patricia
VAGABOND

Meniconi, Enzo
DARK EYES

Mercanton, Roger Spiri
MARIUS

Mercanton, Victoria
AND GOD CREATED WOMAN

Merlin, Claudine
BEAU PERE
GET OUT YOUR HANDKERCHIEFS
MY BEST FRIEND'S GIRL
MURIEL

Miklaylovna, Yelyena
MOSCOW DOES NOT BELIEVE IN TEARS

Miyata, Mitsuji
SANSHO THE BAILIFF
UGETSU

Mollinger, Ursula
WANNSEE CONFERENCE, THE

Montanari, Anna Maria
GENERAL DELLA ROVERE

Montanari, Sergio
MALICIOUS

Moreau, Marcel
JOUR DE FETE

Morra, Mario
BATTLE OF ALGIERS, THE

Muse, Etiennette
WAGES OF FEAR, THE

Musgrave, Peter
GIRL ON A MOTORCYCLE, THE

Nater, Thorsten
KAMIKAZE '89

Natot, Gilbert
HORROR CHAMBER OF DR. FAUSTUS, THE

Nawrocka, Halina
ASHES AND DIAMONDS
KANAL

Nikel, Hannes
BOAT, THE

Noble, Thom
FAHRENHEIT 451

Noveck, Fima
LOVE AND ANARCHY
INHERITANCE, THE

Novelli, Adriana
GARDEN OF THE FINZI-CONTINIS, THE
TWO WOMEN
BIG DEAL ON MADONNA STREET, THE
YESTERDAY, TODAY, AND TOMORROW

Nowarra, Karin
COP AND THE GIRL, THE

Nuti, Sergio
EYES, THE MOUTH, THE

Omadze, Guliko
REPENTANCE

Oser, Hans
THREEPENNY OPERA, THE
KAMERADSCHAFT

Oshima, Tomoyo
MISHIMA
MERRY CHRISTMAS, MR. LAWRENCE

Peltier, Kenout
GOING PLACES
ERENDIRA
MURIEL
VERY PRIVATE AFFAIR, A

Pena, Julio
EL DIPUTADO

Percy, Lee
KISS OF THE SPIDER WOMAN

Perpignani, Roberto
GOOD MORNING BABYLON
DIVINE NYMPH, THE
NIGHT OF THE SHOOTING STARS, THE
PADRE PADRONE

Petenyi, Katalin
REVOLT OF JOB, THE

Petersen, Anne Marie
DAY OF WRATH

Piaggo, Carlos
EL MUERTO

Pinson, Henriette
NAPOLEON

Piroue, Jean-Claude
SUGARBABY

Plemiannikov, Helene
DISCREET CHARM OF THE BOURGEOISIE, THE
PHANTOM OF LIBERTY, THE
THAT OBSCURE OBJECT OF DESIRE
HOLIDAY HOTEL

Pluet, Eric
MURIEL

Pollicand, Gerard
PLAYTIME
PARDON MON AFFAIRE

Poncin, Marthe
POIL DE CAROTTE

Ponomarenko, M.
SHADOWS OF FORGOTTEN ANCESTORS

Priestly, Tom
TESS

Prim, Monique
BETTY BLUE
DIVA
MOON IN THE GUTTER, THE

Prugar-Ketling, Halina
DANTON
LOVE IN GERMANY, A
KNIFE IN THE WATER

Przygodda, Peter
ALICE IN THE CITIES
AMERICAN FRIEND, THE
LOST HONOR OF KATHARINA BLUM, THE
KINGS OF THE ROAD
PARIS, TEXAS
GOALIE'S ANXIETY AT THE PENALTY KICK, THE
STATE OF THINGS, THE
WINGS OF DESIRE
WRONG MOVE

Psenny, Armand
CLOCKMAKER, THE
CLEAN SLATE (COUP DE TORCHON)
DEATHWATCH
SUNDAY IN THE COUNTRY, A
ROUND MIDNIGHT
PASSION OF BEATRICE, THE

Ravel, Jean
LE CHAT
FRENCH DETECTIVE, THE

Remy, Chantal
MAKE ROOM FOR TOMORROW

Renault, Catherine
THREE MEN AND A CRADLE

Renoir, Marguerite
BOUDU SAVED FROM DROWNING
CRIME OF MONSIEUR LANGE, THE
LA MARSEILLAISE
LA BETE HUMAINE
GRAND ILLUSION
RULES OF THE GAME, THE
TONI
LOWER DEPTHS, THE
MASCULINE FEMININE

Ridel, Armand
RISE TO POWER OF LOUIS XIV, THE

Robert, Paulette
DIARY OF A COUNTRY PRIEST

Roberts, Wendy
HAMMETT

Roland, George
DYBBUK, THE

Rooz, M.
BALLAD OF A SOLDIER

Rosander, Oscar
LESSON IN LOVE, A
DEVIL'S EYE, THE
MAGICIAN, THE
PORT OF CALL
SECRETS OF WOMEN
SMILES OF A SUMMER NIGHT
VIRGIN SPRING, THE
WILD STRAWBERRIES
TORMENT
SUMMER INTERLUDE

Rossberg, Susanna
DUST

Rozsa, Janos
FATHER

Ruiz, Anna
LA PASSANTE

Rust, Henri
GERVAISE
MAYERLING
WAGES OF FEAR, THE
THREEPENNY OPERA, THE

Ryghe, Ulla
SILENCE, THE
PERSONA
WINTER LIGHT, THE
THROUGH A GLASS DARKLY
HOUR OF THE WOLF, THE

Sadoul, Jacqueline
ORPHEUS

Safa, Amedeo
CAMILLE 2000

Sagara, Hisashi
KWAIDAN

Salcedo, Jose
LAW OF DESIRE

Santamaria, Miguel Angel
SKYLINE

Sarraute, Anne
HIROSHIMA, MON AMOUR

Saulnier, Nicole
MY NEW PARTNER

Savage, Carlos
LOS OLVIDADOS
EXTERMINATING ANGEL, THE
WUTHERING HEIGHTS

Schenkkan, Ine
FOURTH MAN, THE
SPETTERS

Schett, Susanne
COP AND THE GIRL, THE

Schlussel, Edith
DAY OF WRATH
GERTRUD

Schmidtbauer, Tanja
WOMAN IN FLAMES, A

Schmit, Sophie
SUBWAY
LE DERNIER COMBAT

Schussel, Edith
ORDET

Scola, Ettore
FAMILY, THE

Scott, John
COCA-COLA KID, THE

Semprun, Colette
BIZET'S CARMEN

Serandrei, Mario
BATTLE OF ALGIERS, THE
GOLDEN COACH, THE
OSSESSIONE
LA TERRA TREMA
BELLISSIMA

Simoncelli, Carla
MACARONI

Skeppstedt, Carl-Olav
DREAMS

Skeppstedt, Carl-Olov
SAWDUST AND TINSEL

Smith, John Victor
HARDER THEY COME, THE

Sperr, Jane
COUP DE GRACE
SOLDIER OF ORANGE

Stojanovic, Katarina
LOVE AFFAIR; OR THE CASE OF THE MISSING SWITCHBOARD OPERATOR

Sugihara, Yoshi
STRAY DOG

Sugiwara, Yoshi
TWENTY-FOUR EYES

Susui, F.
WOMAN IN THE DUNES

Suzuki, Akira
TAMPOPO
FUNERAL, THE
TAXING WOMAN, A

Sylvi, Franca
LA TRAVIATA

Talavera, Meriam
ALSINO AND THE CONDOR

EDITORS

Tarkovsky, Andrei
SACRIFICE, THE

Tavares, Mair
BYE BYE BRAZIL

Taylor, Peter
LA TRAVIATA

Thiedot, Jacqueline
CESAR AND ROSALIE
SINCERELY CHARLOTTE

Tillack, Elfie
SPRING SYMPHONY

Timofeyeva, M.
CRANES ARE FLYING, THE

Troell, Jan
FLIGHT OF THE EAGLE

Troeye, Suzanne
LADY CHATTERLEY'S LOVER

Tsujii, Masanori
BURMESE HARP, THE

van Dongen, Hans
QUESTION OF SILENCE

Van Effenterre, Joele
HEAT OF DESIRE
ENTRE NOUS
MAN IN LOVE, A

Varda, Agnes
VAGABOND

Verneau, Jeanne
CLEO FROM 5 TO 7

Vince, Barry
MOONLIGHTING

von Oelffen, Petra
FROM THE LIFE OF THE MARIONETTES
SERPENT'S EGG, THE

von Weitershausen, Barbara
STATE OF THINGS, THE

Waelchli, Elisabeth
YOL

Wallen, Lennart
SEVENTH SEAL, THE

Walsch, Franz
DESPAIR
QUERELLE
MARRIAGE OF MARIA BRAUN, THE

Weinberg, Herman G.
PAISAN
FANNY

Weitershausen, Barbara von
ALICE IN THE CITIES

White, Richard
HARDER THEY COME, THE

Widerberg, Bo
ELVIRA MADIGAN

Winston, Sam
BLUE ANGEL, THE

Witta, Jacques
L'ADDITION
ONE DEADLY SUMMER

Wood, Humphrey
THERESE AND ISABELLE

Yamaji, Sachiko
HIMATSURI
MACARTHUR'S CHILDREN

Yannopoulos, Takis
IPHIGENIA

Yoyotte, Marie-Josephe
LA BOUM
DIVA
SUGAR CANE ALLEY
TESTAMENT OF ORPHEUS, THE
FOUR HUNDRED BLOWS, THE

Zita, Luigi
SOTTO. . .SOTTO

MUSIC COMPOSERS

Abril, Anton Garcia
HOLY INNOCENTS, THE

Akutagawa, Yasushi
FIRES ON THE PLAIN
ODD OBSESSION
GATE OF HELL

Albinoni, Tomaso Giovanni
EVERY MAN FOR HIMSELF AND GOD AGAINST ALL

Alix, Victor
PASSION OF JOAN OF ARC, THE

Alphaville
COP AND THE GIRL, THE

Altuntas, Ali Dede
WALL, THE

Andriessen, Jurriaan
ASSAULT, THE

Anfosso, Gerard
BLUE COUNTRY, THE
COUSIN, COUSINE

Argol, Sebastian
YOL

Arthuys, Philippe
LES CARABINIERS

Auric, Georges
A NOUS LA LIBERTE
BEAUTY AND THE BEAST
BLOOD OF A POET, THE
GERVAISE
ETERNAL RETURN, THE
RIFIFI
ORPHEUS
WAGES OF FEAR, THE
TESTAMENT OF ORPHEUS, THE
LOLA MONTES
THERESE AND ISABELLE

Aznar, Pedro
MAN FACING SOUTHEAST

Bacalov, Luis
GOSPEL ACCORDING TO ST. MATTHEW, THE
ENTRE NOUS

Bach, Johann Sebastian
AUTUMN SONATA
BAGDAD CAFE
CRIES AND WHISPERS
LA MARSEILLAISE
GOSPEL ACCORDING TO ST. MATTHEW, THE
SACRIFICE, THE
SILENCE, THE
PERSONA
TESTAMENT OF ORPHEUS, THE
THROUGH A GLASS DARKLY
LES ENFANTS TERRIBLES
LE CAVALEUR (PRACTICE MAKES PERFECT)
HAIL, MARY

Bachelet, Pierre
BLACK AND WHITE IN COLOR

Badarou, Wally
KISS OF THE SPIDER WOMAN

Bakirel, Setrak
WALL, THE

Bantzer, Claus
MEN

Barber, Samuel
EL NORTE

Barbieri, Gato
LAST TANGO IN PARIS

Barcellini, Franck
MY UNCLE

Barclay, Eddie
BOB LE FLAMBEUR

Barry, John
HAMMETT

Baudry, Jacques
BAD GIRLS

Becaud, Gilbert
AND NOW MY LOVE

Becce, Giuseppe
LAST LAUGH, THE
ECSTASY

Beethoven, Ludwig van
DIARY OF FORBIDDEN DREAMS
DEATH IN VENICE
L'AGE D'OR
LE CAVALEUR (PRACTICE MAKES PERFECT)

Beethoven, Ludwig Von
BASILEUS QUARTET

Bell, Daniel
FANNY AND ALEXANDER

Bellini, Vincenzo
BASILEUS QUARTET

Bernard, Armand
LE MILLION
UNDER THE ROOFS OF PARIS

Beydts, Louis
CARNIVAL IN FLANDERS

Birkin, Jane
LE SEX SHOP

Bixio, C.A.
DIVINE NYMPH, THE

Bizet, Georges
BIZET'S CARMEN
CARMEN

Bjorlin, Ulf
ELVIRA MADIGAN

Bloch, Ernst
WHERE THE GREEN ANTS DREAM

Blomdahl, Karl-Birger
SAWDUST AND TINSEL

Bocquet, Roland
LA BALANCE

Bolling, Claude
LE MAGNIFIQUE

Bonfa, Luis
BLACK ORPHEUS

Bongusto, Fred
MALICIOUS

Boulanger, Lili
PASSION OF BEATRICE, THE

Boulze, Jean
BOUDU SAVED FROM DROWNING

Boyer, Jo
BOB LE FLAMBEUR

Bozzi, Paul
TONI

Brahms, Johannes
PERIL

Britten, Benjamin
FANNY AND ALEXANDER

Brower, Leo
ALSINO AND THE CONDOR

Bruzdowicz, Joanna
VAGABOND

Buarque, Chico
BYE BYE BRAZIL
DONA FLOR AND HER TWO HUSBANDS

Bunuel, Luis
MILKY WAY, THE

Buondonno, Fr. Enrico
FLOWERS OF ST. FRANCIS, THE

Buongusto, Fred
CRICKET, THE

Byrne, David
LAST EMPEROR, THE

Cale, J.J.
MY BEST FRIEND'S GIRL

Calvi, Gerard
FEMMES DE PARIS

Campbell, James
PLAYTIME

Can
ALICE IN THE CITIES

Carpi, Fiorenzo
TILL MARRIAGE DO US PART
VERY PRIVATE AFFAIR, A

Carter, Ron
PASSION OF BEATRICE, THE

Charpentier, Gustave
ARIA

Chopin, Frederic
AUTUMN SONATA
COLONEL REDL
CRIES AND WHISPERS
INNOCENT, THE

Cicognini, Alessandro
BICYCLE THIEF, THE
SHOESHINE
UMBERTO D
MIRACLE IN MILAN

Cilla, Max
SUGAR CANE ALLEY

Cliff, Jimmy
HARDER THEY COME, THE

Cloerec, Rene
FOUR BAGS FULL
DEVIL IN THE FLESH, THE
SYLVIA AND THE PHANTOM

Coltrane, John
HAIL, MARY

Constantin, Jean
FOUR HUNDRED BLOWS, THE

Conte, Paolo
JOKE OF DESTINY, A
SOTTO. . .SOTTO

Conti, Bill
BIG BLUE, THE

Cooder, Ry
PARIS, TEXAS

Coppola, Carmine
NAPOLEON

Cosma, Vladimir
LES COMPERES
LE BAL
LA BOUM
DIVA
TALL BLOND MAN WITH ONE BLACK SHOE, THE
LA CHEVRE
PARDON MON AFFAIRE
RETURN OF THE TALL BLOND MAN WITH ONE BLACK SHOE, THE

Costa, Gal
GABRIELA

Couture, Charlelie
TCHAO PANTIN

Crosby, Bing
BYE BYE BRAZIL

Dan, Ikuma
SAMURAI TRILOGY, THE

Daniderff, Leo
BOUDU SAVED FROM DROWNING

Davis, Miles
FRANTIC

De Boer, Lodewijk
QUESTION OF SILENCE

de Diego, Emilio
BLOOD WEDDING

de Falla, Manuel
EL AMOR BRUJO

de l'Isle, Rouget
LA MARSEILLAISE

de Lucia, Paco
CARMEN

de Pablo, Luis
GARDEN OF DELIGHTS, THE
SPIRIT OF THE BEEHIVE, THE

de Piscopo, Tullio
WHERE'S PICONE?

De Sica, Manuel
GARDEN OF THE FINZI-CONTINIS, THE

Debout, Jean-Jacques
MASCULINE FEMININE

Debussy, Claude
AND THE SHIP SAILS ON
BASILEUS QUARTET
L'AGE D'OR

Dekker, Desmond
HARDER THEY COME, THE

Delerue, Georges
CONFIDENTIALLY YOURS!
CONFORMIST, THE
CONTEMPT
DAY FOR NIGHT
LOVE ON THE RUN
LAST METRO, THE
KING OF HEARTS
JULES AND JIM
HIROSHIMA, MON AMOUR
GET OUT YOUR HANDKERCHIEFS
SHOOT THE PIANO PLAYER
SOFT SKIN, THE
MAN IN LOVE, A
ONE DEADLY SUMMER
TWO OF US, THE
WOMAN NEXT DOOR, THE
TWO ENGLISH GIRLS
LA PASSANTE
LE CAVALEUR (PRACTICE MAKES PERFECT)

Delpierre, Emile
LE BEAU SERGE

Demarsan, Eric
HEAT OF DESIRE

Des Innocents, Simon
LE BEAU MARIAGE

Deschamps, Anne-Marie
MYSTERY OF ALEXINA, THE

Di Donato, Pietro
OPEN CITY

Di Lasso, Orlando
EVERY MAN FOR HIMSELF AND GOD AGAINST ALL

Dikker, Loek
FOURTH MAN, THE

Ding-xian, Jiang
GO-MASTERS, THE

Djanelidze, Nana
REPENTANCE

Dockstader, Tod
FELLINI SATYRICON

Doldinger, Klaus
BOAT, THE

Dominguinhos
BYE BYE BRAZIL

Dominique, Carl-Axel
FLIGHT OF THE EAGLE

Dompierre, Francois
DECLINE OF THE AMERICAN EMPIRE, THE

Ducreux, Louis
SUNDAY IN THE COUNTRY, A

Duhamel, Antoine
DEATHWATCH
STOLEN KISSES

Dumoulin, Edouard
BOUDU SAVED FROM DROWNING

Dvorak, Anton
HAIL, MARY
APHRODITE

Dzierlatka, Arie
CHLOE IN THE AFTERNOON
MON ONCLE D'AMERIQUE

Eisler, Hans
LOVE AFFAIR; OR THE CASE OF THE MISSING SWITCHBOARD OPERATOR

Elli et Jacno
FULL MOON IN PARIS

Erdmann, Hans
TESTAMENT OF DR. MABUSE, THE
NOSFERATU

Everly Brothers, The
BYE BYE BRAZIL

Faure, Gabriel
SUNDAY IN THE COUNTRY, A
WHERE THE GREEN ANTS DREAM

Ferrero, Willy
LA TERRA TREMA

Folkloristas, The
EL NORTE

Frank, Cesar
APHRODITE

Froese, Edgar
KAMIKAZE '89

Fukai, Shiro
47 RONIN, THE (PARTS I & II)

Fusco, Giovanni
L'AVVENTURA
HIROSHIMA, MON AMOUR
ECLIPSE
RED DESERT

Gainsbourg, Serge
LE SEX SHOP

Galaxie Musique
DISCREET CHARM OF THE BOURGEOISIE, THE

Gelmetti, Vittorio
RED DESERT

Glass, Philip
MISHIMA

Gluck, Christoph
INNOCENT, THE
TESTAMENT OF ORPHEUS, THE

Gluck, Christophe Willibald
ORPHEUS

Gonda, Janos
FATHER

Graham, David
SWANN IN LOVE

Granados, Enrique
PERIL

Granier, Georges
LE GRAND CHEMIN

Grappelli, Stephane
GOING PLACES

Gregoire, Richard
BLIND TRUST

Grieg, Edvard
M

Gromon, Francis
MARIUS

Groupe Malavoi
SUGAR CANE ALLEY

Grunenwald, Jean-Jacques
DIARY OF A COUNTRY PRIEST

Gure, Ronan
LE BEAU MARIAGE

Hadjidakis, Manos
NEVER ON SUNDAY
PEDESTRIAN, THE

Hajos, Joe
LE PLAISIR

Halfter, Rodolfo
LOS OLVIDADOS

Hamilton, Chico
REPULSION

Hancock, Herbie
BLOW-UP
ROUND MIDNIGHT

Handel, George Frederick
TESTAMENT OF ORPHEUS, THE

Handel, George Frideric
AUTUMN SONATA

Hart, Lorenz
BASILEUS QUARTET

Hartley, Richard
LA TRUITE (THE TROUT)

Hasebos, Martijn
QUESTION OF SILENCE

Hatzinassios, George
JUPITER'S THIGH

Hayasaka, Fumio
IKIRU
DRUNKEN ANGEL
RASHOMON
SANSHO THE BAILIFF
SEVEN SAMURAI, THE
STRAY DOG
UGETSU

Hayashi, Hikaru
GO-MASTERS, THE

Haydn, Franz Joseph
BASILEUS QUARTET
NEST, THE

Helmerson, Frans
FANNY AND ALEXANDER

Henze, Hans Werner
LOST HONOR OF KATHARINA BLUM, THE
SWANN IN LOVE
MURIEL

Herrmann, Bernard
FAHRENHEIT 451

Heymann, Werner R.
SPIES

Hollander, Friedrich
BLUE ANGEL, THE

Holten, Bo
TWIST & SHOUT

Honda, Toshiyuki
TAXING WOMAN, A

Honegger, Arthur
MAYERLING
NAPOLEON

Iannacci, Enzo
SEVEN BEAUTIES

Ifukube, Akira
BURMESE HARP, THE

Ikebe, Shinichiro
KAGEMUSHA
MACARTHUR'S CHILDREN

Illin, Evzen
LOVES OF A BLONDE

Isfalt, Bjorn
MY LIFE AS A DOG

Jacobs, Marianne
FANNY AND ALEXANDER

Jansen, Pierre
BAD GIRLS

Jarre, Maurice
SUNDAYS AND CYBELE
TIN DRUM, THE
HORROR CHAMBER OF DR. FAUSTUS, THE
JULIA AND JULIA
DAMNED, THE

Jaubert, Maurice
GREEN ROOM, THE
SMALL CHANGE
STORY OF ADELE H., THE
LE JOUR SE LEVE
MAN WHO LOVED WOMEN, THE

Jeny, Zoltan
REVOLT OF JOB, THE

Jersild, Jorgen
GERTRUD

Jobim, Antonio Carlos
BLACK ORPHEUS
GABRIELA

Jones, Brynmor
COP AND THE GIRL, THE

Jones, Rickie Lee
SUBWAY

Kempler, Robert
WALL, THE

Kilar, Wojciech
DAVID

Kinoshita, Chuji
TWENTY-FOUR EYES

Knieper, Jurgen
AMERICAN FRIEND, THE
GOALIE'S ANXIETY AT THE PENALTY KICK, THE
STATE OF THINGS, THE
WINGS OF DESIRE
WRONG MOVE

Komeda, Krzysztof
KNIFE IN THE WATER

Kon, Henryk
DYBBUK, THE

Korngold, Erich Wolfgang
ARIA

Kosma, Joseph
LA BETE HUMAINE
GRAND ILLUSION
ELUSIVE CORPORAL, THE
ELENA AND HER MEN
PICNIC ON THE GRASS
LADY CHATTERLEY'S LOVER

Kovach, Kornell
MONTENEGRO

Kranz, George
COP AND THE GIRL, THE

Krenz, Jan
KANAL

Kuhr, Gerd
SWANN IN LOVE

Lai, Francis
AND NOW MY LOVE
CAT AND MOUSE
DARK EYES
EDITH AND MARCEL
MAN AND A WOMAN: 20 YEARS LATER, A
MY NEW PARTNER
HAPPY NEW YEAR
MAN AND A WOMAN, A
MASCULINE FEMININE

Lavista, Raul
EL BRUTO
WUTHERING HEIGHTS
WOMAN WITHOUT LOVE, A

Lecoeur, Maurice
ERENDIRA

Ledrut, Jean
BATTLE OF AUSTERLITZ, THE

Legrand, Michel
BAND OF OUTSIDERS
CLEO FROM 5 TO 7
LOVE IN GERMANY, A
GIFT, THE
DONKEY SKIN
LOVE SONGS
UMBRELLAS OF CHERBOURG, THE
MY LIFE TO LIVE

Lemarque, Francis
PLAYTIME

Leoncavallo, Ruggiero
ARIA

Linstadt, Axel
KINGS OF THE ROAD

Liska, Zdenek
SHOP ON MAIN STREET, THE

Liszt, Franz
COLONEL REDL
INNOCENT, THE

Loubna, Dabket
MADAME ROSA

Louis, Roland
SUGAR CANE ALLEY

Loussier, Jacques
LE DOULOS

Lovin' Spoonful, The
BLOW-UP

Lully, Jean Baptiste
ARIA

Macchi, Egisto
MR. KLEIN
PADRE PADRONE

Mahler, Gustav
ALICE IN THE CITIES
INHERITORS, THE
DEATH IN VENICE
EL NORTE
APHRODITE

Mannino, Franco
INNOCENT, THE
BELLISSIMA

Manzanita
SKYLINE

Mares, Karel
FIREMAN'S BALL, THE

Marika, Wandjuk
WHERE THE GREEN ANTS DREAM

Martinez, Melecio
EL NORTE

Meisel, Edmund
BATTLESHIP POTEMKIN
TEN DAYS THAT SHOOK THE WORLD

Mendelssohn, Felix
L'AGE D'OR

Menescal, Roberto
BYE BYE BRAZIL

Meyer, Friedrich
TIN DRUM, THE

Miller, Glenn
MACARTHUR'S CHILDREN

Miller, Roger
KINGS OF THE ROAD

Mimaroglu, Ilhan
FELLINI SATYRICON

Misraki, Paul
ALPHAVILLE
AND GOD CREATED WOMAN
INVESTIGATION
LE DOULOS

Mochizuki, Tamekichi
SANSHO THE BAILIFF

Mompoll, Federico
CRIA!

Montez, Chris
KINGS OF THE ROAD

Moretti, R.
UNDER THE ROOFS OF PARIS

Morricone, Ennio
BATTLE OF ALGIERS, THE
LA CAGE AUX FOLLES 3: THE WEDDING
LA CAGE AUX FOLLES II
LA CAGE AUX FOLLES
INHERITANCE, THE
DIVINE NYMPH, THE
1900
STAY AS YOU ARE

Motzing, William
COCA-COLA KID, THE

Moustaki, Georges
VERY CURIOUS GIRL, A
MAKE ROOM FOR TOMORROW

Mozart, Wolfgang Amadeus
DIARY OF FORBIDDEN DREAMS
LA MARSEILLAISE
INNOCENT, THE
GOSPEL ACCORDING TO ST. MATTHEW, THE
GET OUT YOUR HANDKERCHIEFS
EVERY MAN FOR HIMSELF AND GOD AGAINST ALL
ELVIRA MADIGAN
RULES OF THE GAME, THE
L'AGE D'OR
BABETTE'S FEAST

Murai, Kunihiko
TAMPOPO

Mussorgsky, Modest Petrovich
DEATH IN VENICE

Myers, Stanley
COUP DE GRACE
MOONLIGHTING

Nazelles, R.
UNDER THE ROOFS OF PARIS

Neschling, John
PIXOTE
KISS OF THE SPIDER WOMAN

Nikitin, Sergei
MOSCOW DOES NOT BELIEVE IN TEARS

Nilsson, Bo
SILENCE, THE

Nomi, Klaus
A NOS AMOURS

Nordgren, Erik
MAGICIAN, THE
SECRETS OF WOMEN
SEVENTH SEAL, THE
SMILES OF A SUMMER NIGHT
VIRGIN SPRING, THE
WILD STRAWBERRIES
THROUGH A GLASS DARKLY
SUMMER INTERLUDE

Norgard, Per
BABETTE'S FEAST

Nougaro, Claude
MARRIED WOMAN, THE

O'Brien, Linda
EL NORTE

Ocampo, Oscar Cardoza
FUNNY, DIRTY LITTLE WAR, A

Odera, Kanahichi
SANSHO THE BAILIFF

Offenbach, Jacques
LE CAVALEUR (PRACTICE MAKES PERFECT)

Ovchinnikov, Vyacheslav
MY NAME IS IVAN

Pachelbel, Johann
EVERY MAN FOR HIMSELF AND GOD AGAINST ALL

Paganini, Nicolo
BASILEUS QUARTET

Paradisi, Pietro Domenico
EXTERMINATING ANGEL, THE

Pares, Philippe
LE MILLION

Paris, Daniele
NIGHT PORTER, THE

Parys, Van
L'AGE D'OR

Perez, Jorge
CRIMINAL LIFE OF ARCHIBALDO DE LA CRUZ, THE

Perrone, Marc
SUNDAY IN THE COUNTRY, A

Petit, Jean-Claude
L'ADDITION
JEAN DE FLORETTE
MANON OF THE SPRING

Philip, Hans-Erik
FLIGHT OF THE EAGLE

Philippe Sarde
SCENE OF THE CRIME

Piazzola, Astor
HENRY IV
LUMIERE

Piccioni, Piero
CHRIST STOPPED AT EBOLI
SEDUCTION OF MIMI, THE
SWEPT AWAY. . .BY AN UNUSUAL DESTINY IN THE BLUE SEA OF AUGUST
THREE BROTHERS
CAMILLE 2000

Piovani, Nicola
GOOD MORNING BABYLON
GINGER & FRED
EYES, THE MOUTH, THE
NIGHT OF THE SHOOTING STARS, THE

Pittaluga, Gustavo
MEXICAN BUS RIDE

Plenixio, Gianfranco
AND THE SHIP SAILS ON

Pontecorvo, Gillo
BATTLE OF ALGIERS, THE

Popol Vuh [Florian Fricke]
AGUIRRE, THE WRATH OF GOD

Portal, Michel
RETURN OF MARTIN GUERRE, THE

Porte, Pierre
MR. KLEIN

Pouget, Leo
PASSION OF JOAN OF ARC, THE

Prodromides, Jean
DANTON

Prokofiev, Sergei
IVAN THE TERRIBLE PART I AND II
GOSPEL ACCORDING TO ST. MATTHEW, THE
ALEXANDER NEVSKY

Puccini, Giacomo
ARIA

Purcell, Henry
A NOS AMOURS

Raben, Peer
DESPAIR
QUERELLE
MARRIAGE OF MARIA BRAUN, THE
WOMAN IN FLAMES, A
BERLIN ALEXANDERPLATZ
MALOU

Rameau, Jean Philippe
LA MARSEILLAISE
ARIA

Ramirez, Ariel
EL MUERTO

Raphael
BOUDU SAVED FROM DROWNING

Rappdee, Erno
VARIETY

Ravel, Maurice
BASILEUS QUARTET

Ray, Satyajit
HOME AND THE WORLD, THE
TWO DAUGHTERS

Reed, Les
GIRL ON A MOTORCYCLE, THE

Revaux, Jacques
JACKO AND LISE

Revutsky, Leonid
EARTH

Richards, Emil
EL NORTE

Rimski-Korsakov, Nikolay
APHRODITE

Rodgers, Richard
BASILEUS QUARTET

Romans, Alain
MR. HULOT'S HOLIDAY
MY UNCLE

Rosati, Giuseppe
OSSESSIONE

Rose, E.
RULES OF THE GAME, THE

Rosenberg, Hilding
TORMENT

Rossellini, Renzo
GERMANY, YEAR ZERO
GENERAL DELLA ROVERE
FEAR
STROMBOLI
OPEN CITY
PAISAN
FLOWERS OF ST. FRANCIS, THE

Rota, Nino
AMARCORD
LOVE AND ANARCHY
LA STRADA
LA DOLCE VITA
JULIET OF THE SPIRITS
FELLINI SATYRICON
8 1/2
I VITELLONI
NIGHTS OF CABIRIA, THE
WHITE SHEIK, THE

Rozsa, Miklos
PROVIDENCE

Rudich, Arik
DRIFTING

Rudin, Andrew
FELLINI SATYRICON

Rustichelli, Carlo
SEDUCED AND ABANDONED

Sahin, Ozan Garip
WALL, THE

St. Peters, Christian
KINGS OF THE ROAD

St. Pierre, Martin
DUST

Saint-Saens, Camille
AND THE SHIP SAILS ON
AU REVOIR LES ENFANTS
RULES OF THE GAME, THE

Saito, Ichiro
GOLDEN DEMON
UGETSU
LIFE OF OHARU
MOTHER

Saito, Takanobu
FLOATING WEEDS

Sakamoto, Ryuichi
LAST EMPEROR, THE
MERRY CHRISTMAS, MR. LAWRENCE

Salabert
RULES OF THE GAME, THE

Sarde, Philippe
BEAU PERE
CESAR AND ROSALIE
CHOICE OF ARMS
CLOCKMAKER, THE
CLEAN SLATE (COUP DE TORCHON)
I SENT A LETTER TO MY LOVE
SINCERELY CHARLOTTE
MY OTHER HUSBAND
TENANT, THE
LE CHAT
FRENCH DETECTIVE, THE
TESS
MADAME ROSA

Satie, Erik
MISS MARY

Sato, Masaru
HIDDEN FORTRESS, THE
RED BEARD
SANJURO
YOJIMBO
SWORD OF DOOM, THE
THRONE OF BLOOD
HIGH AND LOW
IREZUMI (SPIRIT OF TATTOO)
LOWER DEPTHS, THE
BAD SLEEP WELL, THE

Scarlatti, Alessandro
EXTERMINATING ANGEL, THE

Scarlatti, Domenico
DEVIL'S EYE, THE

Scherpenzeel, Ton
SPETTERS

Schierbeck, Poul
DAY OF WRATH
ORDET

Schirman, Peter
DESTINY

Schmidt, Ole
WOLF AT THE DOOR, THE

Schubert, Franz
AND THE SHIP SAILS ON
AU REVOIR LES ENFANTS
BASILEUS QUARTET
DIARY OF FORBIDDEN DREAMS
GET OUT YOUR HANDKERCHIEFS
PERIL
THREE MEN AND A CRADLE

Schultze, Norbert
KOLBERG

Schumann, George
COLONEL REDL

Schumann, Robert
SPRING SYMPHONY
LE CAVALEUR (PRACTICE MAKES PERFECT)

Schumson, Robert
FANNY AND ALEXANDER

Schwalz, Isaac
DERSU UZALA

Scotto, Vincent
BAKER'S WIFE, THE
CESAR
RULES OF THE GAME, THE
PEPE LE MOKO
FANNY

Senia, Jean-Marie
DIRTY DISHES
TENDRES COUSINES

Serra, Eric
SUBWAY
BIG BLUE, THE
LE DERNIER COMBAT

Serra, Luis Maria
CAMILA
MISS MARY

Seyrig, Francis
LAST YEAR AT MARIENBAD

Shankar, Ravi
APARAJITO
PATHER PANCHALI
WORLD OF APU, THE

Shostakovich, Dmitri
LAW OF DESIRE

Shuman, Mort
ASSOCIATE, THE
HOLIDAY HOTEL

Shuoo, Watazumido
SACRIFICE, THE

Skorik, M.
SHADOWS OF FORGOTTEN ANCESTORS

Slap Cat
SUGAR CANE ALLEY

Slickers, The
HARDER THEY COME, THE

Smetana, Bedrich
BASILEUS QUARTET

Solal, Martial
BREATHLESS
TESTAMENT OF ORPHEUS, THE

Stampone, Atilio
OFFICIAL STORY, THE

Stein, David
PLAYTIME

Sternwald, Jiri
TRANSPORT FROM PARADISE

Stora, Jean-Pierre
APHRODITE

Strauss, Johann
AND THE SHIP SAILS ON
BOUDU SAVED FROM DROWNING
COLONEL REDL
RULES OF THE GAME, THE

Strauss, Oscar
LA RONDE
EARRINGS OF MADAME DE . . ., THE

Stravinsky, Igor
LAW OF DESIRE

Su, Cong
LAST EMPEROR, THE

Sust, Jiri
CLOSELY WATCHED TRAINS

Takemitsu, Toru
KWAIDAN
HIMATSURI
DOUBLE SUICIDE
DODES 'KA-DEN
RAN
WOMAN IN THE DUNES

Tamassy, Zdenko
MEPHISTO

Tansman, Alexandre
POIL DE CAROTTE

Tchaikovsky, Pyotr Ilich
SUMMER INTERLUDE

Tchaikovsky, Pytor Ilich
AND THE SHIP SAILS ON

Telson, Bob
BAGDAD CAFE

Theodorakis, Mikis
IPHIGENIA
Z
STATE OF SIEGE

Third Ear Band, The
MACBETH

Tocnay, Brunoy
SUGAR CANE ALLEY

Troggs
WRONG MOVE

Trovaioli, Armando
LA NUIT DE VARENNES
FAMILY, THE
MACARONI
TWO WOMEN
WIFEMISTRESS
IN THE NAME OF THE POPE KING
DOWN AND DIRTY

Trovajoli, Armando
YESTERDAY, TODAY, AND TOMORROW

Umiliano, Piero
BIG DEAL ON MADONNA STREET, THE

Valero, Jean-Louis
SUMMER
PAULINE AT THE BEACH

Van Otterloo, Rogier
SOLDIER OF ORANGE

Van Parys, Georges
FRENCH CANCAN
EARRINGS OF MADAME DE . . ., THE
DIABOLIQUE
LE MILLION

Vanderson, V.
SUGAR CANE ALLEY

Vaynberg, Moisei
CRANES ARE FLYING, THE

Verdi, Giuseppe
EL NORTE
LA TRAVIATA
MANON OF THE SPRING
ARIA

Verdi, Guiseppe
AND THE SHIP SAILS ON

Vinicius, Marcus
HOUR OF THE STAR, THE

Virtzberg, Ilan
BEYOND THE WALLS

Visconti, Luchino
LA TERRA TREMA

Vivaldi, Antonio
GOLDEN COACH, THE
ELVIRA MADIGAN
LES ENFANTS TERRIBLES

von Koch, Erland
PORT OF CALL

Vuh, Popol
FITZCARRALDO

Wagner, Richard
BASILEUS QUARTET
WUTHERING HEIGHTS
WHERE THE GREEN ANTS DREAM
TESTAMENT OF ORPHEUS, THE
L'AGE D'OR
ARIA

Webern, Anton
GOSPEL ACCORDING TO ST. MATTHEW, THE

Weill, Kurt
THREEPENNY OPERA, THE

Weinberg, Herman G.
OPEN CITY

Wengler, Marcel
SWANN IN LOVE

Werle, Lars Johan
PERSONA
HOUR OF THE WOLF, THE

Wiener, Jean
CRIME OF MONSIEUR LANGE, THE
LOWER DEPTHS, THE

Wiese, Klaus-Jochen
WHERE THE GREEN ANTS DREAM

Wilhelm, Rolf
FROM THE LIFE OF THE MARIONETTES
TONIO KROGER
SERPENT'S EGG, THE

Wiren, Dag
LESSON IN LOVE, A

Wisniak, Alain
L'ANNEE DES MEDUSES

Wroclaw Rhythm Quintet
ASHES AND DIAMONDS

Xarhakos, Stavros
SWEET COUNTRY

Yardbirds, The
BLOW-UP

Yared, Gabriel
BETTY BLUE
DANGEROUS MOVES
HANNAH K.
MOON IN THE GUTTER, THE
INVITATION AU VOYAGE

Yatove, Jean
JOUR DE FETE

Yepes, Narcisco
FORBIDDEN GAMES

Yguerbouchen, Mohamed
PEPE LE MOKO

Yuasa, Joji
FUNERAL, THE

Yvain, Maurice
LE PLAISIR

Zeller, Wolfgang
VAMPYR

Zimmer, Hans
MOONLIGHTING

Ziv, Mikhael
BALLAD OF A SOLDIER

PRODUCERS

Adler, Stanislaw
KANAL

Adlon, Eleonore
BAGDAD CAFE

Adlon, Percy
BAGDAD CAFE

Alain Terzian
SCENE OF THE CRIME

Alatriste, Gustavo
EXTERMINATING ANGEL, THE

Alexakis, Costas
SWEET COUNTRY

Allen, Lewis
FAHRENHEIT 451

Alliata, Francesco
GOLDEN COACH, THE

Altolaguirre, Manuel
MEXICAN BUS RIDE

Amato, Giuseppe
LA DOLCE VITA
FLOWERS OF ST. FRANCIS, THE

Ammar, Tarak Ben
LA TRAVIATA

Amon, Robert
JUPITER'S THIGH

Angeletti, Pio
TILL MARRIAGE DO US PART

Ardy, Jean
SINCERELY CHARLOTTE

Ayala, Fernando
FUNNY, DIRTY LITTLE WAR, A
EL MUERTO

Bacquet, Edgar
FEMMES DE PARIS

Baldo, Angel
CAMILA

Balurov, Jordan
SHOP ON MAIN STREET, THE

Bannert, Walter
INHERITORS, THE

Barbault, Armand
CONFIDENTIALLY YOURS!
MAN IN LOVE, A

Barreto, Lucy
BYE BYE BRAZIL

Barreto, Luis Carlos
DONA FLOR AND HER TWO HUSBANDS

Baum, H.
EARRINGS OF MADAME DE . . ., THE

Baum, Ralph
EARRINGS OF MADAME DE . . ., THE
LOLA MONTES

Baylis, Robert
LOVE SONGS

Beineix, Jean-Jacques
BETTY BLUE

Belmont, Vera
DIRTY DISHES
TENDRES COUSINES

Bendico, Silvia D'Amico
DARK EYES

Benninger, Willim
LOST HONOR OF KATHARINA BLUM, THE

Berbert, Marcel
DAY FOR NIGHT
JULES AND JIM
STOLEN KISSES
STORY OF ADELE H., THE

Bergendahl, Waldemar
MY LIFE AS A DOG

Bergman, Ingmar
AUTUMN SONATA
CRIES AND WHISPERS
LESSON IN LOVE, A
FROM THE LIFE OF THE MARIONETTES
DREAMS
SCENES FROM A MARRIAGE
PERSONA
VIRGIN SPRING, THE
WINTER LIGHT, THE

Bernart, Maurice
THERESE

Berri, Claude
LE SEX SHOP
TESS

Bertolucci, Giovanni
INNOCENT, THE
STAY AS YOU ARE

Besson, Luc
SUBWAY
LE DERNIER COMBAT

Betzer, Just
BABETTE'S FEAST

Beytout, Christine
ONE DEADLY SUMMER

Bini, Alfredo
GOSPEL ACCORDING TO ST. MATTHEW, THE

Bittins, Michael
BOAT, THE

Bliokh, Jacob
BATTLESHIP POTEMKIN

Blondy, Raymond
GRAND ILLUSION

Bodard, Mag
DONKEY SKIN
UMBRELLAS OF CHERBOURG, THE

Bolary, Jean
MADAME ROSA

Bonin, Claude
BLIND TRUST

Borkon, Jules
HORROR CHAMBER OF DR. FAUSTUS, THE

Boustiani, Gabriel
DEATHWATCH

Boyd, Don
ARIA

Braun, Zev
PEDESTRIAN, THE

Braunberger, Pierre
SHOOT THE PIANO PLAYER
MY LIFE TO LIVE

Brauner, Arthur
LOVE IN GERMANY, A

Braunsberg, Andrew
TENANT, THE
MACBETH

Cacoyannis, Michael
SWEET COUNTRY

Cadeac, Paul
TWO OF US, THE

Cagarp, Carl-Henry
MAGICIAN, THE

Campos, Miguel A. Perez
LAW OF DESIRE

Cardarelli, Romano
LOVE AND ANARCHY
SEDUCTION OF MIMI, THE
SWEPT AWAY. . .BY AN UNUSUAL DESTINY IN THE BLUE SEA OF AUGUST

Carlsen, Henning
WOLF AT THE DOOR, THE

Carraro, Nicola
CHRIST STOPPED AT EBOLI

Carre, Leon
DIARY OF A COUNTRY PRIEST

Cervi, Antonio
RED DESERT

Chouraqui, Elie
LOVE SONGS

Christensen, Bo
BABETTE'S FEAST

Clair, Rene
A NOUS LA LIBERTE

Claudon, Paul
GOING PLACES
GET OUT YOUR HANDKERCHIEFS

Clementelli, Silvio
MALICIOUS

Clouzot, Henri-Georges
DIABOLIQUE
WAGES OF FEAR, THE

Cohen, Rudy
BEYOND THE WALLS

Cohn, Arthur
BLACK AND WHITE IN COLOR
DANGEROUS MOVES
GARDEN OF THE FINZI-CONTINIS, THE

Cohn-Seat, Gilbert
LADY CHATTERLEY'S LOVER

Colby, Ronald
HAMMETT

Colombo, Arrigo
SEVEN BEAUTIES

Committeri, Franco
FAMILY, THE
MACARONI
IN THE NAME OF THE POPE KING

Conti, Mario
PAISAN

Cottrell, Pierre
AMERICAN FRIEND, THE
CHLOE IN THE AFTERNOON
CLAIRE'S KNEE
MY NIGHT AT MAUD'S

Courau, Pierre
LAST YEAR AT MARIENBAD

Cristaldi, Franco
AMARCORD
AND THE SHIP SAILS ON
CHRIST STOPPED AT EBOLI
SEDUCED AND ABANDONED
WIFEMISTRESS
BIG DEAL ON MADONNA STREET, THE

Cucchi, Carlo
DARK EYES

D'Angelo, Salvo
LA TERRA TREMA
BELLISSIMA

Dancigers, Georges
LA BALANCE
JUPITER'S THIGH
LE CAVALEUR (PRACTICE MAKES PERFECT)
FRENCH DETECTIVE, THE
LE MAGNIFIQUE

Dancigers, Oscar
EL BRUTO
LOS OLVIDADOS
WUTHERING HEIGHTS
WOMAN WITHOUT LOVE, A

Danon, Marcello
LA CAGE AUX FOLLES 3: THE WEDDING
LA CAGE AUX FOLLES II
LA CAGE AUX FOLLES

Danon, Raymond
MR. KLEIN
LA PASSANTE
MADAME ROSA

Darbon, Emil
ORPHEUS

Dassin, Jules
NEVER ON SUNDAY

Dauman, Anatole
TIN DRUM, THE
WINGS OF DESIRE
MURIEL

de Beauregard, Georges
BREATHLESS
CLEO FROM 5 TO 7
CONTEMPT
LES CARABINIERS
LE DOULOS

de Broca, Michelle
CESAR AND ROSALIE

de Broca, Philippe
KING OF HEARTS

de Goldschmidt, Gilbert
GIFT, THE

de Gunzberg, Baron Nicolas
VAMPYR

De Laurentiis, Aurelio
MACARONI

De Laurentiis, Dino
LA STRADA
NIGHTS OF CABIRIA, THE
SERPENT'S EGG, THE

De Laurentiis, Luigi
MACARONI

de Micheli, Adriano
TILL MARRIAGE DO US PART

De Negri, Giuliani G.
GOOD MORNING BABYLON
NIGHT OF THE SHOOTING STARS, THE
PADRE PADRONE

de Noailles, Charles Vicomte
L'AGE D'OR

de Noailles, Vicomte
BLOOD OF A POET, THE

De Sica, Vittorio
BICYCLE THIEF, THE
UMBERTO D
MIRACLE IN MILAN

Del Duca, Cino
L'AVVENTURA

Delon, Alain
MR. KLEIN

des Fontaines, Andre Halley
CRIME OF MONSIEUR LANGE, THE

Donner, Jorn
AFTER THE REHEARSAL
FLIGHT OF THE EAGLE

Dorfman, Jacques
JACKO AND LISE

Dorfman, Robert
FORBIDDEN GAMES

Dorfmann, Annie
GERVAISE

Doynel, Ginette
PICNIC ON THE GRASS

Dreyer, Carl Theodor
DAY OF WRATH
ORDET
VAMPYR

Durniok, Manfred
COLONEL REDL
MEPHISTO

Dussart, Philippe
BAND OF OUTSIDERS
MON ONCLE D'AMERIQUE

Duval, Claire
LUMIERE

Eckelkamp, Hanns
COP AND THE GIRL, THE

Edwards, Robert Gordon
NIGHT PORTER, THE

Eisenstein, Sergei
ALEXANDER NEVSKY

Ekelund, Allan
DEVIL'S EYE, THE
PORT OF CALL
SECRETS OF WOMEN
SEVENTH SEAL, THE
SMILES OF A SUMMER NIGHT
SILENCE, THE
VIRGIN SPRING, THE
WILD STRAWBERRIES
THROUGH A GLASS DARKLY
SUMMER INTERLUDE

Ergas, Morris
GENERAL DELLA ROVERE

Farago, Katinka
SACRIFICE, THE

Fayolle, Lise
I SENT A LETTER TO MY LOVE
HEAT OF DESIRE
MOON IN THE GUTTER, THE

Fengler, Michael
MARRIAGE OF MARIA BRAUN, THE

Ferrari, Mario
DIVINE NYMPH, THE

Ferrario, Enea
EYES, THE MOUTH, THE

Francini, Paulo
PIXOTE

Frappier, Roger
DECLINE OF THE AMERICAN EMPIRE, THE
BLIND TRUST

Froelich, Carl
MAEDCHEN IN UNIFORM

Froment, Raymond
LAST YEAR AT MARIENBAD

Fujii, Hiroaki
ODD OBSESSION

Fujimoto, Sanezumi
SWORD OF DOOM, THE

Gallardo, Hector
CAMILA

Gance, Abel
NAPOLEON

Gasser, Yves
PROVIDENCE

Gault, Pierre
TONI

Gehret, Jean
BOUDU SAVED FROM DROWNING

Geiger, Rod E.
PAISAN

Genee, Peter
GOALIE'S ANXIETY AT THE PENALTY KICK, THE
WRONG MOVE

Genoves, Andre
BAD GIRLS

Giannini, Giancarlo
SEVEN BEAUTIES

Giovannini, Giuseppe
JOKE OF DESTINY, A

Girard, Roland
MADAME ROSA

Gomez, Alfonso Patino
CRIMINAL LIFE OF ARCHIBALDO DE LA CRUZ, THE

Gordine, Sacha
BLACK ORPHEUS
LA RONDE

Gori, Mario
SOTTO. . .SOTTO

Gori, Vittorio Cecchi
SOTTO. . .SOTTO

Gouse-Renal, Christine
VERY PRIVATE AFFAIR, A

Grade, Lew
FROM THE LIFE OF THE MARIONETTES

Graetz, Paul
DEVIL IN THE FLESH, THE

Grimaldi, Alberto
GINGER & FRED
FELLINI SATYRICON
1900
LAST TANGO IN PARIS

Grunhut, Moriz
ECSTASY

Grunstein, Pierre
JEAN DE FLORETTE
MANON OF THE SPRING

Guest, Don
PARIS, TEXAS
HAMMETT

Guissani, Roberto
MAN IN LOVE, A

Gutowski, Gene
REPULSION

Haenkel, Hans
LE MILLION
UNDER THE ROOFS OF PARIS

Haggiag, Ever
DAMNED, THE

Hakim, Raymond
LA BETE HUMAINE
ECLIPSE
PEPE LE MOKO

Hakim, Robert
LA BETE HUMAINE
ECLIPSE
PEPE LE MOKO

Halfon, Samy
HIROSHIMA, MON AMOUR

Hanus, Ladislav
SHOP ON MAIN STREET, THE

Hara, Masato
MACARTHUR'S CHILDREN
RAN

Hellwig, Klaus
PROVIDENCE

Henzell, Perry
HARDER THEY COME, THE

Herzog, Werner
AGUIRRE, THE WRATH OF GOD
EVERY MAN FOR HIMSELF AND GOD AGAINST ALL
FITZCARRALDO

Hommais, Pascal
LE GRAND CHEMIN

Horky, Frantisek
ECSTASY

Horsetzky, George C.
PANDORA'S BOX

Hosogoe, Seigo
TAMPOPO
TAXING WOMAN, A

Houwer, Rob
FOURTH MAN, THE
SOLDIER OF ORANGE

Hubschmid, Edi
YOL

Ichikawa, Kiichi
WOMAN IN THE DUNES

Imbert, Edecio
CAMILA

Israel, Marjorie
MAN IN LOVE, A

Javal, Bertrand
COUSIN, COUSINE

Jolivet, Pierre
LE DERNIER COMBAT

Jonsson, Bo
MONTENEGRO

Junkersdorf, Eberhard
COUP DE GRACE

LOST HONOR OF KATHARINA BLUM, THE

Kalatozov, Mikhail
CRANES ARE FLYING, THE

Kamenka, Alexander
ITALIAN STRAW HAT, AN

Kamenka, Alexandre
LOWER DEPTHS, THE

Kanamaru, Masumi
IREZUMI (SPIRIT OF TATTOO)

Karmitz, Marin
WALL, THE

Kikushima, Ryuzo
RED BEARD
SANJURO
HIGH AND LOW

Korytowski, Manfred
WANNSEE CONFERENCE, THE

Kuchinsky, V.
MOSCOW DOES NOT BELIEVE IN TEARS

Kupferberg, Robert
MR. KLEIN

Kurosawa, Akira
KAGEMUSHA
THRONE OF BLOOD
LOWER DEPTHS, THE
BAD SLEEP WELL, THE

Kuwata, Ryotaro
TWENTY-FOUR EYES

La Pegna, Arturo
BASILEUS QUARTET

Labrande, Jean-Pierre
MR. KLEIN

Lang, Fritz
TESTAMENT OF DR. MABUSE, THE
SPIES

Lanoux, Victor
MAKE ROOM FOR TOMORROW

Lassa, Henri
CLEAN SLATE (COUP DE TORCHON)

Le Clezio, Sylvie
COCA-COLA KID, THE

Ledoux, Patrice
BIZET'S CARMEN
BIG BLUE, THE

Lelouch, Claude
AND NOW MY LOVE
CAT AND MOUSE
EDITH AND MARCEL
MAN AND A WOMAN: 20 YEARS LATER, A
HAPPY NEW YEAR
MAN AND A WOMAN, A

Lepetit, Jean-Francois
THREE MEN AND A CRADLE
LE GRAND CHEMIN

Levine, Joseph E.
CONTEMPT

Levy, Alfredo
DAMNED, THE

Levy, Raoul J.
AND GOD CREATED WOMAN

Littin, Herman
ALSINO AND THE CONDOR

Lodi-Fe, Maurizio
CONFORMIST, THE

Lombardi, Francisco J.
LA CIUDAD Y LOS PERROS

Loulergue, Michel
SUGAR CANE ALLEY

Lucari, Gianni Hecht
INHERITANCE, THE
GARDEN OF THE FINZI-CONTINIS, THE

Luddy, Tom
MISHIMA

Lukas, Jaromir
SHOP ON MAIN STREET, THE

Macri, Antonio
THREE BROTHERS

Makovski, Claude
VERY CURIOUS GIRL, A

Malle, Louis
AU REVOIR LES ENFANTS

Malo, Rene
DECLINE OF THE AMERICAN EMPIRE, THE

Marthesheimer, Peter
DESPAIR
BERLIN ALEXANDERPLATZ

Marx, Joszef
COLONEL REDL

Mateos, Julian
HOLY INNOCENTS, THE

Matsue, Yoichi
DODES 'KA-DEN
DERSU UZALA

Melville, Jean-Pierre
LES ENFANTS TERRIBLES
BOB LE FLAMBEUR

Menegoz, Margaret
DANTON
LE BEAU MARIAGE
FULL MOON IN PARIS
SUMMER
PAULINE AT THE BEACH
SWANN IN LOVE

Mengershausen, Jaochim von
ALICE IN THE CITIES

Metzger, Radley H.
CAMILLE 2000
THERESE AND ISABELLE

Meyniel, Laurent
JACKO AND LISE

Michelin, Andre
ALPHAVILLE

Miller, Claude
TWO ENGLISH GIRLS

Milshtein, Oury
VAGABOND

Minervini, Gianni
WHERE'S PICONE?

Minoru, Jingo
RASHOMON

Mnouchkine, Alexandre
LA BALANCE
JUPITER'S THIGH
LE CAVALEUR (PRACTICE MAKES PERFECT)
LE MAGNIFIQUE

Molander, Harald
TORMENT

Motoki, Sojiro
DRUNKEN ANGEL
SEVEN SAMURAI, THE
STRAY DOG
THRONE OF BLOOD
LOWER DEPTHS, THE

Moussa, Ibrahim
GABRIELA
CRICKET, THE

Mukerjee, Amiyanath
WORLD OF APU, THE

Musu, Antonio
BATTLE OF ALGIERS, THE

Nagata, Masaichi
GOLDEN DEMON
FIRES ON THE PLAIN
RASHOMON
SANSHO THE BAILIFF
UGETSU
GATE OF HELL
SISTERS OF THE GION

Nakajima, Masayuki
DOUBLE SUICIDE

Nebenzahl, Seymour
M
THREEPENNY OPERA, THE
KAMERADSCHAFT

Nebenzal, Harold
GABRIELA

Nedjar, Claude
INVITATION AU VOYAGE

Nielsen, Jorgen
GERTRUD

Nocell, Georgio
THREE BROTHERS

Nounez, Jacques-Louis
L'ATALANTE

Ohono, Tadashi
WOMAN IN THE DUNES

Okada, Yutaka
FUNERAL, THE

Ophuls, Max
LE PLAISIR

Orain, Fred
MR. HULOT'S HOLIDAY
MY UNCLE
JOUR DE FETE

Ossard, Claudie
BETTY BLUE

Oves, Zdenek
CLOSELY WATCHED TRAINS

Pabst, G.W.
DIARY OF A LOST GIRL

Pagnol, Marcel
BAKER'S WIFE, THE
CESAR
FANNY
MARIUS

Paulve, Andre
BEAUTY AND THE BEAST
ETERNAL RETURN, THE
SYLVIA AND THE PHANTOM

Pegoraro, Lorenzo
I VITELLONI

Perrin, Jacques
BLACK AND WHITE IN COLOR
Z
STATE OF SIEGE

Peyrot, Yves
PROVIDENCE

Pflaum, Lujan
MAN FACING SOUTHEAST

Pialat, Maurice
A NOS AMOURS

Piedra, Emiliano
BLOOD WEDDING
CARMEN
EL AMOR BRUJO

Pines, Romain
SUNDAYS AND CYBELE

Pineyro, Marcelo
OFFICIAL STORY, THE

Poire, Alain
LA BOUM
MY OTHER HUSBAND
TALL BLOND MAN WITH ONE BLACK SHOE, THE
LA CHEVRE
PARDON MON AFFAIRE
RETURN OF THE TALL BLOND MAN WITH ONE BLACK SHOE, THE

Polanski, Roman
MACBETH

Pommer, Erich
SIEGFRIED
LAST LAUGH, THE
BLUE ANGEL, THE
VARIETY
CABINET OF DR. CALIGARI, THE
KRIEMHILD'S REVENGE

Ponti, Carlo
DIARY OF FORBIDDEN DREAMS
CONTEMPT
LA STRADA
PASSENGER, THE
TWO WOMEN
BLOW-UP
LES CARABINIERS
LE DOULOS
ZABRISKIE POINT
YESTERDAY, TODAY, AND TOMORROW

Porcelli, Enzo
HENRY IV
EYES, THE MOUTH, THE

Previs, Ludvig
DYBBUK, THE

Puldi, K.L.
YOL

Queffelean, Alain
ERENDIRA

Querejeta, Elias
GARDEN OF DELIGHTS, THE
SPIRIT OF THE BEEHIVE, THE

Rachedi, Hamed
Z

Rademakers, Fons
ASSAULT, THE

Ray, Satyajit
APARAJITO
PATHER PANCHALI
WORLD OF APU, THE
TWO DAUGHTERS

Ray-Gavras, Michele
HANNAH K.

Regis, Alix
SUGAR CANE ALLEY

Repetto, Luis Osvaldo
FUNNY, DIRTY LITTLE WAR, A

Rique, Newton
DONA FLOR AND HER TWO HUSBANDS

Rizzoli, Angelo
LA DOLCE VITA
JULIET OF THE SPIRITS
8 1/2

Robert, Yves
TALL BLOND MAN WITH ONE BLACK SHOE, THE
PARDON MON AFFAIRE
RETURN OF THE TALL BLOND MAN WITH ONE BLACK SHOE, THE

Roe, David
COCA-COLA KID, THE

Rohrbach, Gunter
BOAT, THE

Roos, Fred
HAMMETT

Rossellini, Renzo
LA NUIT DE VARENNES

Rossellini, Roberto
GERMANY, YEAR ZERO
FEAR
STROMBOLI
OPEN CITY
PAISAN

Rousset-Rouard, Yves
LA TRUITE (THE TROUT)
EMMANUELLE

Rouve, Pierre
BLOW-UP

Rovere, Luigi
WHITE SHEIK, THE

Rubeiz, Janine
DEATHWATCH

Ruggieri, Francois
SUBWAY

Saada, Norbert
L'ADDITION
JACKO AND LISE

Saadi, Yacef
BATTLE OF ALGIERS, THE

Safra, Michel
DIARY OF A CHAMBERMAID

Salkind, Alexander
BATTLE OF AUSTERLITZ, THE

Salkind, Michael
BATTLE OF AUSTERLITZ, THE

Sarde, Alain
BEAU PERE
CHOICE OF ARMS
SUNDAY IN THE COUNTRY, A
MY BEST FRIEND'S GIRL

Sassoon, William
GIRL ON A MOTORCYCLE, THE

Sato, Masahiro
GO-MASTERS, THE

Saura, Carlos
CRIA!

Scattini, Luigi
DIVINE NYMPH, THE

Schell, Maximilian
PEDESTRIAN, THE

Schidor, Dieter
QUERELLE

Schlumberger, Emmanuel
PERIL

Schroeder, Barbet
MY NIGHT AT MAUD'S

Seitz, Franz
TIN DRUM, THE

Senatore, Daniele
SEDUCTION OF MIMI, THE

Serrador, Cia
DONA FLOR AND HER TWO HUSBANDS

Setterberg, Goran
FLIGHT OF THE EAGLE

Shinoda, Masahiro
DOUBLE SUICIDE

Shivas, Mark
MOONLIGHTING

Sievernich, Chris
STATE OF THINGS, THE

Silberman, Irene
DIVA

Silberman, Serge
DISCREET CHARM OF THE BOURGEOISIE, THE
DIARY OF A CHAMBERMAID
RAN
PHANTOM OF LIBERTY, THE
THAT OBSCURE OBJECT OF DESIRE

SCREENWRITERS

Andre Techine
SCENE OF THE CRIME

Andrzejewski, Jerzy
ASHES AND DIAMONDS

Annaud, Jean-Jacques
BLACK AND WHITE IN COLOR

Antonioni, Michelangelo
L'AVVENTURA
ECLIPSE
RED DESERT
PASSENGER, THE
BLOW-UP
ZABRISKIE POINT

Arcalli, Franco
1900
LAST TANGO IN PARIS

Arcand, Denys
DECLINE OF THE AMERICAN EMPIRE, THE

Archard, Marcel
EARRINGS OF MADAME DE . . ., THE

Ardy, Jean
APHRODITE

Areero, Antonio
BLOOD WEDDING

Arenstein, Marek
DYBBUK, THE

Arthur, Donald
MONTENEGRO

Aseyev, Nikolai
BATTLESHIP POTEMKIN

Aubert, Pierre
MR. HULOT'S HOLIDAY

Audiard, Jacques
LA CAGE AUX FOLLES 3: THE WEDDING

Audiard, Michel
LA CAGE AUX FOLLES 3: THE WEDDING
JUPITER'S THIGH
LE CAVALEUR (PRACTICE MAKES PERFECT)

August, Bille
TWIST & SHOUT

Aurel, Jean
CONFIDENTIALLY YOURS!
LOVE ON THE RUN
WOMAN NEXT DOOR, THE

Aurenche, Jean
CLOCKMAKER, THE
CLEAN SLATE (COUP DE TORCHON)
GERVAISE
FOUR BAGS FULL
FORBIDDEN GAMES
DEVIL IN THE FLESH, THE
SYLVIA AND THE PHANTOM

Avanzo, Renzo
GOLDEN COACH, THE

Axel, Gabriel
BABETTE'S FEAST

Ayala, Fernando
EL MUERTO

Azcona, Rafael
GARDEN OF DELIGHTS, THE

Babenco, Hector
PIXOTE

Badalucco, Nicola
DEATH IN VENICE
DAMNED, THE

Bal, Walter
JACKO AND LISE

Balasz, Bela
THREEPENNY OPERA, THE

Bannert, Walter
INHERITORS, THE

Barbash, Benny
BEYOND THE WALLS

Barbash, Uri
BEYOND THE WALLS

Baron, Suzanne
DIRTY DISHES

Barreto, Bruno
GABRIELA
DONA FLOR AND HER TWO HUSBANDS

Bartolini, Elio
L'AVVENTURA
ECLIPSE

Bazzini, Sergio
INHERITANCE, THE

Becker, Jean
ONE DEADLY SUMMER

Becker, Jurek
DAVID

Beineix, Jean-Jacques
BETTY BLUE
DIVA
MOON IN THE GUTTER, THE

Bellocchio, Marco
HENRY IV
EYES, THE MOUTH, THE

Bemberg, Luisa
CAMILA

Bemberg, Maria Luisa
MISS MARY

Beraud, Luc
HEAT OF DESIRE
SINCERELY CHARLOTTE

Beresford, Bruce
ARIA

Berglund, Per
MY LIFE AS A DOG

Bergman, Ingmar
AFTER THE REHEARSAL
AUTUMN SONATA
CRIES AND WHISPERS
LESSON IN LOVE, A
FROM THE LIFE OF THE MARIONETTES
FANNY AND ALEXANDER
DREAMS
DEVIL'S EYE, THE
MAGICIAN, THE
PORT OF CALL
SCENES FROM A MARRIAGE
SECRETS OF WOMEN
SEVENTH SEAL, THE
SMILES OF A SUMMER NIGHT
SILENCE, THE
PERSONA
WILD STRAWBERRIES
WINTER LIGHT, THE
THROUGH A GLASS DARKLY
TORMENT
SUMMER INTERLUDE
SAWDUST AND TINSEL
HOUR OF THE WOLF, THE
SERPENT'S EGG, THE

Berri, Claude
TWO OF US, THE
TCHAO PANTIN
JEAN DE FLORETTE
LE SEX SHOP
MANON OF THE SPRING

Bertolucci, Bernardo
CONFORMIST, THE
1900
LAST TANGO IN PARIS
LAST EMPEROR, THE

Bertolucci, Giuseppe
1900

Besson, Luc
SUBWAY
BIG BLUE, THE
LE DERNIER COMBAT

Birinski, Leo
VARIETY

Blanche, Francis
FEMMES DE PARIS

Blier, Bertrand
BEAU PERE
GOING PLACES
GET OUT YOUR HANDKERCHIEFS
MY BEST FRIEND'S GIRL

Bogomolov, Vladimir Osipovich
MY NAME IS IVAN

Boileau, Pierre
HORROR CHAMBER OF DR. FAUSTUS, THE

Bond, Edward
BLOW-UP

Bonicelli, Vittorio
GARDEN OF THE FINZI-CONTINIS, THE

Bortnik, Aida
OFFICIAL STORY, THE

Bost, Pierre
CLOCKMAKER, THE
GERVAISE
FOUR BAGS FULL
FORBIDDEN GAMES
DEVIL IN THE FLESH, THE

Boulanger, Daniel
KING OF HEARTS

Bourguignon, Serge
SUNDAYS AND CYBELE

Boyd, Don
ARIA

Brach, Gerard
DIARY OF FORBIDDEN DREAMS
I SENT A LETTER TO MY LOVE
MY BEST FRIEND'S GIRL
TWO OF US, THE
TENANT, THE
JEAN DE FLORETTE
MANON OF THE SPRING
REPULSION
TESS

Brannstrom, Brasse
MY LIFE AS A DOG

Braun, Alfred
KOLBERG

Bresson, Robert
DIARY OF A COUNTRY PRIEST

Brook, Peter
SWANN IN LOVE

Brownjohn, John
TESS

Bruckner, Jutta
COUP DE GRACE

Brunelin, Andre G.
INVESTIGATION

Bryden, Bill
ARIA

Brynych, Zbynek
TRANSPORT FROM PARADISE

Buchwald, Art
PLAYTIME

Bunuel, Joyce
DIRTY DISHES

Bunuel, Luis
EL BRUTO
CRIMINAL LIFE OF ARCHIBALDO DE LA CRUZ, THE
LOS OLVIDADOS
EXTERMINATING ANGEL, THE
DISCREET CHARM OF THE BOURGEOISIE, THE
DIARY OF A CHAMBERMAID
WUTHERING HEIGHTS
PHANTOM OF LIBERTY, THE
WOMAN WITHOUT LOVE, A
VIRIDIANA
THAT OBSCURE OBJECT OF DESIRE
L'AGE D'OR
MILKY WAY, THE

Bussi, Solange
THREEPENNY OPERA, THE

Cacoyannis, Michael
IPHIGENIA
SWEET COUNTRY

Callegari, C.P.
STROMBOLI

Camus, Marcel
BLACK ORPHEUS

Camus, Mario
HOLY INNOCENTS, THE

Carere, Christine
LA CAGE AUX FOLLES 3: THE WEDDING

Carpi, Fabio
BASILEUS QUARTET

Carriere, Jean-Claude
ASSOCIATE, THE
DANTON
DISCREET CHARM OF THE BOURGEOISIE, THE
DIARY OF A CHAMBERMAID
RETURN OF MARTIN GUERRE, THE
PHANTOM OF LIBERTY, THE
SWANN IN LOVE
THAT OBSCURE OBJECT OF DESIRE
TIN DRUM, THE
MILKY WAY, THE

Castanier, Jean
CRIME OF MONSIEUR LANGE, THE

Cavalier, Alain
THERESE

Cavani, Liliana
NIGHT PORTER, THE

Cayrol, Jean
MURIEL

Cerami, Vincenzo
EYES, THE MOUTH, THE

Cesana, Renzo
STROMBOLI

Chabrol, Claude
LE BEAU SERGE
BAD GIRLS

Chendey, Ivan
SHADOWS OF FORGOTTEN ANCESTORS

Chiari, Mario
MIRACLE IN MILAN

Chukhrai, Grigori
BALLAD OF A SOLDIER

Clair, Rene
A NOUS LA LIBERTE
LE MILLION
UNDER THE ROOFS OF PARIS
ITALIAN STRAW HAT, AN

Clement, Rene
FORBIDDEN GAMES

Clouzot, Henri-Georges
DIABOLIQUE
WAGES OF FEAR, THE

Cocteau, Jean
BEAUTY AND THE BEAST
BLOOD OF A POET, THE
ETERNAL RETURN, THE
ORPHEUS
TESTAMENT OF ORPHEUS, THE
LES ENFANTS TERRIBLES

Cohn, Art
STROMBOLI

Colomo, Fernando
SKYLINE

Comencini, Luigi
TILL MARRIAGE DO US PART

Comolli, Jean-Louis
HEAT OF DESIRE

Companeez, Jacques
LOWER DEPTHS, THE

Conchon, George
BLACK AND WHITE IN COLOR

Constant, Jacques
PEPE LE MOKO

Corneau, Alain
CHOICE OF ARMS

Cossa, Roberto
FUNNY, DIRTY LITTLE WAR, A

Costa-Gavras, Constantin
HANNAH K.

Costa-Gavras, Constantine
Z
STATE OF SIEGE

Curtelin, Jean
L'ADDITION

Curzi, Pierre
BLIND TRUST

D'Amico, Suso Cecchi
DARK EYES
INNOCENT, THE
BIG DEAL ON MADONNA STREET, THE
MIRACLE IN MILAN
BELLISSIMA

D'Anna, Claude
TENDRES COUSINES

d'Ashelbe, Roger
PEPE LE MOKO

Dabadie, Jean-Loup
CESAR AND ROSALIE
MY OTHER HUSBAND
PARDON MON AFFAIRE

Dali, Salvador
L'AGE D'OR

Dancigers, Oscar
LOS OLVIDADOS

Danon, Marcello
LA CAGE AUX FOLLES 3: THE WEDDING
LA CAGE AUX FOLLES

Dassin, Jules
RIFIFI
NEVER ON SUNDAY

de Arminan, Jaime
NEST, THE

de Broca, Philippe
JUPITER'S THIGH
LE CAVALEUR (PRACTICE MAKES PERFECT)
LE MAGNIFIQUE

De Casabianca, Camille
THERESE

De Filippo, Eduardo
YESTERDAY, TODAY, AND TOMORROW

de Givray, Claude
STOLEN KISSES

de la Iglesia, Eloy
EL DIPUTADO

De Negri, Giuliani G.
NIGHT OF THE SHOOTING STARS, THE

De Santis, Giuseppe
OSSESSIONE

De Sica, Vittorio
SHOESHINE
TWO WOMEN
UMBERTO D
MIRACLE IN MILAN

DeForrest, Michael
CAMILLE 2000

Del Monte, Peter
JULIA AND JULIA
INVITATION AU VOYAGE

Dembo, Richard
DANGEROUS MOVES

Demy, Jacques
DONKEY SKIN
UMBRELLAS OF CHERBOURG, THE

Deville, Michel
PERIL

Dhery, Robert
FEMMES DE PARIS

Diegues, Carlos
BYE BYE BRAZIL

Djanelidze, Nana
REPENTANCE

Dobai, Peter
COLONEL REDL
MEPHISTO

Doherty, Christopher
BAGDAD CAFE

Dormann, Genevieve
COUP DE GRACE

Dorrie, Doris
MEN

Dovzhenko, Alexander
EARTH

Dowson, Jan
STORY OF ADELE H., THE

Doynel, Ginette
GOLDEN COACH, THE

Dreyer, Carl Theodor
VAMPYR

Dreyer, Carl Theodor
DAY OF WRATH
GERTRUD
ORDET
PASSION OF JOAN OF ARC, THE

Dreyfus, Mme. Jean-Paul
LA MARSEILLAISE

Dreyfus, N. Martel
LA MARSEILLAISE

Dumarcay, Philippe
GOING PLACES

Duncan, Ronald
GIRL ON A MOTORCYCLE, THE

Dupont, E.A.
VARIETY

Duran, Jorge
PIXOTE

Duras, Marguerite
HIROSHIMA, MON AMOUR

Durieux, Gilles
EDITH AND MARCEL

Duvivier, Julien
POIL DE CAROTTE
PEPE LE MOKO

Einstein, Carl
TONI

Eisenstein, Sergei
IVAN THE TERRIBLE PART I AND II
BATTLESHIP POTEMKIN
TEN DAYS THAT SHOOK THE WORLD
ALEXANDER NEVSKY

Ellis, Bob
WHERE THE GREEN ANTS DREAM

Erlanger, Philippe
RISE TO POWER OF LOUIS XIV, THE

Eschasseriaux, Bernard
SUNDAYS AND CYBELE

Estienne, Marie-Helene
SWANN IN LOVE

Fabbri, Diego
GENERAL DELLA ROVERE

Fabiani, M.
LA BALANCE

Fabre, Michel
VERY CURIOUS GIRL, A

Falkenberg, Paul
M

Fassbinder, Rainer Werner
QUERELLE
MARRIAGE OF MARIA BRAUN, THE
BERLIN ALEXANDERPLATZ

Feijoo, Beda Docampo
CAMILA

Fellini, Federico
AMARCORD
AND THE SHIP SAILS ON
LA STRADA
LA DOLCE VITA
JULIET OF THE SPIRITS
GINGER & FRED
FELLINI SATYRICON
8 1/2
OPEN CITY
PAISAN
I VITELLONI
FLOWERS OF ST. FRANCIS, THE
NIGHTS OF CABIRIA, THE
WHITE SHEIK, THE

Feret, Rene
MYSTERY OF ALEXINA, THE

Fermaud, Michel
MAN WHO LOVED WOMEN, THE

Ferrini, Franco
INVITATION AU VOYAGE
CRICKET, THE

Ferry, Jean
VERY PRIVATE AFFAIR, A

Feyder, Jacques
CARNIVAL IN FLANDERS

Fieschi, Jean-Andre
HEAT OF DESIRE

Flaiano, Ennio
LA STRADA
LA DOLCE VITA
JULIET OF THE SPIRITS
8 1/2
TONIO KROGER
I VITELLONI
NIGHTS OF CABIRIA, THE
WHITE SHEIK, THE

Forman, Milos
FIREMAN'S BALL, THE
LOVES OF A BLONDE

Franci, Adolfo
SHOESHINE
MIRACLE IN MILAN

Franju, Georges
HORROR CHAMBER OF DR. FAUSTUS, THE

Frank, Christopher
L'ANNEE DES MEDUSES

Freeman, Gillian
GIRL ON A MOTORCYCLE, THE

Frohlich, Pia
MARRIAGE OF MARIA BRAUN, THE

Frolich, Pia
COP AND THE GIRL, THE

Fuji, Yahiro
SANSHO THE BAILIFF

Furstenberg, Veith von
ALICE IN THE CITIES

Gades, Antonio
CARMEN
EL AMOR BRUJO

Gainville, Rene
ASSOCIATE, THE

Galeen, Henrik
GOLEM, THE
NOSFERATU

Gance, Abel
BATTLE OF AUSTERLITZ, THE
NAPOLEON

Gardner, Fred
ZABRISKIE POINT

Garland, Robert
BIG BLUE, THE

Gasiorowski, Jacek
DANTON

Gegauff, Paul
BAD GIRLS

Geiger, Franz
LOLA MONTES

Gelbert, Arnie
MONTENEGRO

Germi, Pietro
SEDUCED AND ABANDONED

Geronimi, Jerome
DIABOLIQUE
WAGES OF FEAR, THE

Godard, Jean-Luc
ALPHAVILLE
BAND OF OUTSIDERS
BREATHLESS
CONTEMPT
LES CARABINIERS
HAIL, MARY
MARRIED WOMAN, THE
MASCULINE FEMININE
MY LIFE TO LIVE
ARIA

Goicoachea, Gonzalo
EL DIPUTADO

Goldberg, Jakub
KNIFE IN THE WATER

Goldenberg, Jorge
MISS MARY

Goldin, Marilyn
BIG BLUE, THE

Goron, Joelle
SINCERELY CHARLOTTE

Gorris, Marleen
QUESTION OF SILENCE

Granier-Deferre, Pierre
LE CHAT

Grass, Gunter
TIN DRUM, THE

Gremm, Wolf
KAMIKAZE '89

Grendel, Frederic
DIABOLIQUE

Grevenius, Herbert
SUMMER INTERLUDE

Griffi, Giuseppe Patroni
DIVINE NYMPH, THE

Grisolia, Michel
CHOICE OF ARMS

Grossman, Ladislav
SHOP ON MAIN STREET, THE

Gruault, Jean
JULES AND JIM
GREEN ROOM, THE
STORY OF ADELE H., THE
MON ONCLE D'AMERIQUE
MYSTERY OF ALEXINA, THE
TWO ENGLISH GIRLS
LES CARABINIERS
RISE TO POWER OF LOUIS XIV, THE

Grumberg, Jean-Claude
LAST METRO, THE

Guerra, Tonino
AMARCORD
AND THE SHIP SAILS ON
BIZET'S CARMEN
L'AVVENTURA
HENRY IV
GOOD MORNING BABYLON
GINGER & FRED
ECLIPSE
CHRIST STOPPED AT EBOLI
RED DESERT
NIGHT OF THE SHOOTING STARS, THE
BLOW-UP
ZABRISKIE POINT

Guney, Yilmaz
WALL, THE
YOL

Guttman, Amos
DRIFTING

Gyongyossy, Imre
REVOLT OF JOB, THE

Hallstrom, Lasse
MY LIFE AS A DOG

Hampton, Christopher
WOLF AT THE DOOR, THE

Handke, Peter
GOALIE'S ANXIETY AT THE PENALTY KICK, THE
WINGS OF DESIRE

Hanke, Peter
WRONG MOVE

Hansel, Marion
DUST

Hara, Kenichiro
47 RONIN, THE (PARTS I & II)

Harlan, Veit
KOLBERG

Hasebe, Keiji
ODD OBSESSION

Hashimoto, Shinobu
IKIRU
HIDDEN FORTRESS, THE
DODES 'KA-DEN
RASHOMON
SEVEN SAMURAI, THE
SWORD OF DOOM, THE
THRONE OF BLOOD
LOWER DEPTHS, THE
BAD SLEEP WELL, THE

Henzell, Perry
HARDER THEY COME, THE

Hersko, Janos
FATHER

Herzog, Werner
AGUIRRE, THE WRATH OF GOD
EVERY MAN FOR HIMSELF AND GOD AGAINST ALL
WHERE THE GREEN ANTS DREAM
FITZCARRALDO

Hisaita, Eijiro
HIGH AND LOW
BAD SLEEP WELL, THE

Hojo, Hideji
SAMURAI TRILOGY, THE

Holierhoek, Kees
SOLDIER OF ORANGE

Holland, Agnieszka
DANTON
LOVE IN GERMANY, A

Hong-zhou, Li
GO-MASTERS, THE

Horky, Frantisek
ECSTASY

Horovitz, Israel
MAN IN LOVE, A

Hrabal, Bohumil
CLOSELY WATCHED TRAINS

Hubert, Jean-Loup
LE GRAND CHEMIN

Huppert, Caroline
SINCERELY CHARLOTTE

Ichikawa, Kon
ODD OBSESSION

Ide, Masato
KAGEMUSHA
RAN
RED BEARD

Inagaki, Hiroshi
SAMURAI TRILOGY, THE

Isaksson, Ulla
VIRGIN SPRING, THE

Itami, Juzo
TAMPOPO
FUNERAL, THE
TAXING WOMAN, A

Janowitz, Hans
CABINET OF DR. CALIGARI, THE

Jansen, Adolf
M

Japrisot, Sebastien
ONE DEADLY SUMMER

Jardin, Pascal
LE CHAT

Jarman, Derek
ARIA

Jeanson, Henri
PEPE LE MOKO

Jemma, Ottavio
MALICIOUS

Jolivet, Pierre
SUBWAY
LE DERNIER COMBAT

Jonsson, Bo
MONTENEGRO

Jonsson, Reidar
MY LIFE AS A DOG

Jul, Christen
VAMPYR

Kabay, Barna
REVOLT OF JOB, THE

Kacyzna, S.A.
DYBBUK, THE

Kadar, Jan
SHOP ON MAIN STREET, THE

Kaminka, Didier
MY NEW PARTNER

Kang-tong, Ge
GO-MASTERS, THE

Kaplan, Nelly
VERY CURIOUS GIRL, A

Kassovitz, Peter
MAKE ROOM FOR TOMORROW

Katsura, Chiho
IREZUMI (SPIRIT OF TATTOO)

Katz, Robert
KAMIKAZE '89

Kawaguchi, Matsutaro
UGETSU

Kessel, Joseph
MAYERLING

Kikushima, Ryuzo
HIDDEN FORTRESS, THE
RED BEARD
SANJURO
STRAY DOG
YOJIMBO
THRONE OF BLOOD
HIGH AND LOW
BAD SLEEP WELL, THE

Kinoshita, Keisuke
TWENTY-FOUR EYES

Kinugasa, Teinosuke
GATE OF HELL

Kirkland, Jack
GOLDEN COACH, THE

Kirsner, Jacques
LA PASSANTE

Klos, Elmar
SHOP ON MAIN STREET, THE

Knudsen, Poul
DAY OF WRATH

Koch, Carl
LA MARSEILLAISE

Koerpel, Jacques A.
ECSTASY

Kolpet, Max
GERMANY, YEAR ZERO

Konami, Fumio
GO-MASTERS, THE

Kramer, Robert
STATE OF THINGS, THE

Kurosawa, Akira
KAGEMUSHA
IKIRU
HIDDEN FORTRESS, THE
DRUNKEN ANGEL
DODES 'KA-DEN
DERSU UZALA
RAN
RASHOMON
RED BEARD
SANJURO
SEVEN SAMURAI, THE
STRAY DOG
YOJIMBO
THRONE OF BLOOD
HIGH AND LOW
LOWER DEPTHS, THE
BAD SLEEP WELL, THE

Kurys, Diane
ENTRE NOUS
MAN IN LOVE, A

Kveselava, Rezo
REPENTANCE

Kyser, Hans
FAUST

L'Hote, Jean
MY UNCLE

La Capria, Raffaele
CHRIST STOPPED AT EBOLI

Lagrange, Jacques
PLAYTIME
MR. HULOT'S HOLIDAY
MY UNCLE

Laine, Pascal
TENDRES COUSINES

Lamballe, Gerard
LA CAGE AUX FOLLES 3: THE WEDDING

Lampel, Peter Martin
KAMERADSCHAFT

Lang, Fritz
M
TESTAMENT OF DR. MABUSE, THE
SPIES
DR. MABUSE, THE GAMBLER (PARTS I & II)
DESTINY
METROPOLIS

Lang, Michel
GIFT, THE
HOLIDAY HOTEL

Lange, Monique
MAN AND A WOMAN: 20 YEARS LATER, A
LA TRUITE (THE TROUT)

Langmann, Arlette
A NOS AMOURS

Lania, Leo
THREEPENNY OPERA, THE

Larreta, Antonio
HOLY INNOCENTS, THE

Lattuada, Alberto
CRICKET, THE
STAY AS YOU ARE

Lautner, Georges
LA CAGE AUX FOLLES 3: THE WEDDING

Le Breton, Auguste
RIFIFI
BOB LE FLAMBEUR

Le Henry, Alain
ENTRE NOUS
SUBWAY

Lefranc, Guy
ELUSIVE CORPORAL, THE

Lelouch, Claude
AND NOW MY LOVE
CAT AND MOUSE
EDITH AND MARCEL
MAN AND A WOMAN: 20 YEARS LATER, A
HAPPY NEW YEAR
MAN AND A WOMAN, A

Leonhardt, Rudolf
DIARY OF A LOST GIRL

Leveque, Josiane
TENDRES COUSINES

Levy, Raoul J.
AND GOD CREATED WOMAN

Liebmann, Robert
BLUE ANGEL, THE

Lilienthal, Peter
DAVID

Limentani, Annalena
PAISAN

Lisandrini, Fr. Antonio
FLOWERS OF ST. FRANCIS, THE

Littin, Miguel
ALSINO AND THE CONDOR

Lizzani, Carlo
GERMANY, YEAR ZERO

Losey, Joseph
LA TRUITE (THE TROUT)

Loy, Nanni
WHERE'S PICONE?

Lustig, Arnost
DIAMONDS OF THE NIGHT
TRANSPORT FROM PARADISE

Maccari, Ruggero
LE BAL
FAMILY, THE
MACARONI
DOWN AND DIRTY

Macchi, Giulio
GOLDEN COACH, THE

Machaty, Gustav
ECSTASY

Magni, Luigi
IN THE NAME OF THE POPE KING

Maiuri, Dino
WUTHERING HEIGHTS

Makavejev, Dusan
MONTENEGRO
LOVE AFFAIR; OR THE CASE OF THE MISSING SWITCHBOARD OPERATOR

Makovski, Claude
VERY CURIOUS GIRL, A

Malle, Louis
AU REVOIR LES ENFANTS
FRANTIC
VERY PRIVATE AFFAIR, A

Manas, Alfredo
BLOOD WEDDING

Mann, Erika
TONIO KROGER

Marijan, Bojana
MONTENEGRO

Marquet, Henri
MR. HULOT'S HOLIDAY
JOUR DE FETE

Marquez, Gabriel Garcia
ERENDIRA

Marthesheimer, Peter
MARRIAGE OF MARIA BRAUN, THE
COP AND THE GIRL, THE

Masson, Rene
DIABOLIQUE

Matji, Manuel
HOLY INNOCENTS, THE

Mauprey, Andre
THREEPENNY OPERA, THE

Mayer, Carl
LAST LAUGH, THE

Mayersberg, Paul
MERRY CHRISTMAS, MR. LAWRENCE

Mayol, Jacques
BIG BLUE, THE

Mazia, Edna
DRIFTING

Medioli, Enrico
INNOCENT, THE
DAMNED, THE

Meerapfel, Jeanine
MALOU

Melson, Jean
APHRODITE

Melville, Jean-Pierre
LES ENFANTS TERRIBLES
LE DOULOS
BOB LE FLAMBEUR

Menzel, Jiri
CLOSELY WATCHED TRAINS

Mercer, David
PROVIDENCE

Mergault, Olivier
MOON IN THE GUTTER, THE

Meyer, Carl
CABINET OF DR. CALIGARI, THE

Michalek, Boleslaw
DANTON
LOVE IN GERMANY, A

Mikhalkov, Nikita
DARK EYES

Miller, Claude
HEAT OF DESIRE

Mizoguchi, Kenji
LIFE OF OHARU

Mizrahi, Moshe
I SENT A LETTER TO MY LOVE
MADAME ROSA

Mizuki, Yoko
KWAIDAN
MOTHER

Molinaro, Edouard
LA CAGE AUX FOLLES

Mommertz, Paul
WANNSEE CONFERENCE, THE

Monicelli, Mario
BIG DEAL ON MADONNA STREET, THE

Montanelli, Indro
GENERAL DELLA ROVERE

Moorhouse, Frank
COCA-COLA KID, THE

Moreau, Jeanne
LUMIERE

Morlion, Fr. Felix
FLOWERS OF ST. FRANCIS, THE

Moscati, Italo
NIGHT PORTER, THE

Moussy, Marcel
SHOOT THE PIANO PLAYER
FOUR HUNDRED BLOWS, THE

Nagibin, Yuri
DERSU UZALA

Nakagami, Kenji
HIMATSURI

Napolitano, Silvia
JULIA AND JULIA

Narcejac, Thomas
HORROR CHAMBER OF DR.
FAUSTUS, THE

Natanson, Jacques
LA RONDE
LE PLAISIR
LOLA MONTES

Nava, Gregory
EL NORTE

Nemec, Jan
DIAMONDS OF THE NIGHT

Nemier, Roger
FRANTIC

Neron, Claude
CESAR AND ROSALIE

Nezval, Vitezslav
ECSTASY

Nicaud, Philippe
LA CAGE AUX FOLLES 3: THE
WEDDING

Noda, Kogo
FLOATING WEEDS

O'Flaherty, Dennis
HAMMETT

O'Hagan, Colo Tavernier
PASSION OF BEATRICE, THE

Oddner, Georg
FLIGHT OF THE EAGLE

Oguni, Hideo
IKIRU
HIDDEN FORTRESS, THE
DODES 'KA-DEN
RAN
RED BEARD
SANJURO
SEVEN SAMURAI, THE
YOJIMBO
THRONE OF BLOOD
HIGH AND LOW
LOWER DEPTHS, THE
BAD SLEEP WELL, THE

Ohno, Yasuko
GO-MASTERS, THE

Oldoini, Enrico
SOTTO. . .SOTTO
STAY AS YOU ARE

Olivera, Hector
FUNNY, DIRTY LITTLE WAR, A
EL MUERTO

Olivier Assayas
SCENE OF THE CRIME

Onetti, Juan Carlos
EL MUERTO

Ophuls, Max
LA RONDE
LE PLAISIR
LOLA MONTES

Oroz, Alfredo
HOUR OF THE STAR, THE

Oshima, Nagisa
MERRY CHRISTMAS, MR. LAWRENCE

Otten, Karl
KAMERADSCHAFT

Ottieri, Ottiero
ECLIPSE

Ozu, Yasujiro
FLOATING WEEDS

Pages, Eduardo Ugarte
CRIMINAL LIFE OF ARCHIBALDO DE
LA CRUZ, THE

Pagnol, Marcel
BAKER'S WIFE, THE
CESAR
FANNY
MARIUS

Paige, Alain
TCHAO PANTIN

Palcy, Euzhan
SUGAR CANE ALLEY

Papava, Mikhail
MY NAME IS IVAN

Papousek, Jaroslav
FIREMAN'S BALL, THE
LOVES OF A BLONDE

Paradzhanov, Sergey
SHADOWS OF FORGOTTEN
ANCESTORS

Parenzo, Alessandro
MALICIOUS

Pascal Bonitzer
SCENE OF THE CRIME

Pasolini, Pier Paolo
GOSPEL ACCORDING TO ST.
MATTHEW, THE

NIGHTS OF CABIRIA, THE

Passer, Ivan
FIREMAN'S BALL, THE
LOVES OF A BLONDE

Pavlenko, Pytor
ALEXANDER NEVSKY

Penchenat, Jean-Claude
LE BAL

Peploe, Clare
ZABRISKIE POINT

Peploe, Mark
PASSENGER, THE
LAST EMPEROR, THE

Perier, Etienne
INVESTIGATION

Perilli, Ivo
TILL MARRIAGE DO US PART

Perrier, Marc
SUBWAY
BIG BLUE, THE

Petenyi, Katalin
REVOLT OF JOB, THE

Petersen, Wolfgang
BOAT, THE

Petraglia, Sandro
JULIA AND JULIA

Pialat, Maurice
A NOS AMOURS

Pietrangeli, Antonio
OSSESSIONE

Pinelli, Tullio
LA STRADA
LA DOLCE VITA
JULIET OF THE SPIRITS
GINGER & FRED
8 1/2
I VITELLONI
NIGHTS OF CABIRIA, THE
WHITE SHEIK, THE

Pinoteau, Claude
LA BOUM

Pirro, Ugo
INHERITANCE, THE
GARDEN OF THE FINZI-CONTINIS, THE

Pisier, Marie-France
LOVE ON THE RUN

Poiret, Jean
LA CAGE AUX FOLLES

Polanski, Roman
DIARY OF FORBIDDEN DREAMS
KNIFE IN THE WATER
TENANT, THE
MACBETH
REPULSION
TESS

Pontecorvo, Gillo
BATTLE OF ALGIERS, THE

Pope, Thomas
HAMMETT

Porta, Elvio
WHERE'S PICONE?

Pressmann, Elie
MAKE ROOM FOR TOMORROW

Prevert, Jacques
CRIME OF MONSIEUR LANGE, THE
LE JOUR SE LEVE

Pries, Eran
BEYOND THE WALLS

Puccini, Gianni
OSSESSIONE

Puenzo, Luis
OFFICIAL STORY, THE

Quarantotti;, Isabella
YESTERDAY, TODAY, AND TOMORROW

Querejeta, Francisco J.
SPIRIT OF THE BEEHIVE, THE

Rakoff, Ian
FLIGHT OF THE EAGLE

Rappeneau, Jean-Paul
VERY PRIVATE AFFAIR, A

Rather, Bjarne
TWIST & SHOUT

Ray, Satyajit
APARAJITO
HOME AND THE WORLD, THE
PATHER PANCHALI
WORLD OF APU, THE
TWO DAUGHTERS

Rayfiel, David
DEATHWATCH
ROUND MIDNIGHT

Redon, Jean
HORROR CHAMBER OF DR. FAUSTUS, THE

Remy, Chantal
MAKE ROOM FOR TOMORROW

Renoir, Jean
BOUDU SAVED FROM DROWNING
CRIME OF MONSIEUR LANGE, THE
LA MARSEILLAISE
LA BETE HUMAINE
GRAND ILLUSION
GOLDEN COACH, THE
FRENCH CANCAN
ELUSIVE CORPORAL, THE
RULES OF THE GAME, THE
ELENA AND HER MEN
PICNIC ON THE GRASS
TONI
LOWER DEPTHS, THE

Revon, Bernard
STOLEN KISSES

Rhone, Trevor D.
HARDER THEY COME, THE

Richard, Jean-Louis
DAY FOR NIGHT
SOFT SKIN, THE
FAHRENHEIT 451
EMMANUELLE

Richter, Erich A.
INHERITORS, THE

Riera, Albert
L'ATALANTE

Rifberg, Klaus
FLIGHT OF THE EAGLE

Rivelin, Michel
TWO OF US, THE

Robbe-Grillet, Alain
LAST YEAR AT MARIENBAD

Robert, Yves
TALL BLOND MAN WITH ONE BLACK SHOE, THE
RETURN OF THE TALL BLOND MAN WITH ONE BLACK SHOE, THE

Roddam, Franc
ARIA

Roeg, Nicolas
ARIA

Rohmer, Eric
CHLOE IN THE AFTERNOON
CLAIRE'S KNEE
LE BEAU MARIAGE
FULL MOON IN PARIS
SUMMER
MY NIGHT AT MAUD'S
PAULINE AT THE BEACH

Rondi, Brunello
LA DOLCE VITA
JULIET OF THE SPIRITS
FELLINI SATYRICON
8 1/2

Roodt, Darrell
PLACE OF WEEPING

Rosi, Francesco
BIZET'S CARMEN
CHRIST STOPPED AT EBOLI
THREE BROTHERS
BELLISSIMA

Rossellini, Roberto
GERMANY, YEAR ZERO
FEAR
STROMBOLI
OPEN CITY
PAISAN
LES CARABINIERS
FLOWERS OF ST. FRANCIS, THE

Rouffio, Jacques
LA PASSANTE

Rozov, Victor
CRANES ARE FLYING, THE

Rudkin, David
FAHRENHEIT 451

Russell, Ken
ARIA

Salvador, Jaime
WOMAN WITHOUT LOVE, A

Samperi, Salvatore
MALICIOUS

Sasek, Vaclav
LOVES OF A BLONDE

Saura, Carlos
CARMEN
EL AMOR BRUJO

GARDEN OF DELIGHTS, THE
CRIA!

Sautet, Claude
CESAR AND ROSALIE
HORROR CHAMBER OF DR. FAUSTUS, THE

Scarpelli
SEDUCED AND ABANDONED

Scarpelli, Argo
BIG DEAL ON MADONNA STREET, THE

Scarpelli, Furio
LE BAL
FAMILY, THE
MACARONI

Schamoni, Peter
SPRING SYMPHONY

Schatzky, Olivier
MAN IN LOVE, A

Schell, Maximilian
PEDESTRIAN, THE

Schiffman, Suzanne
CONFIDENTIALLY YOURS!
DAY FOR NIGHT
LOVE ON THE RUN
LAST METRO, THE
SMALL CHANGE
STORY OF ADELE H., THE
WOMAN NEXT DOOR, THE
MAN WHO LOVED WOMEN, THE

Schlondorff, Volker
LOST HONOR OF KATHARINA BLUM, THE
SWANN IN LOVE
TIN DRUM, THE

Schmit, Sophie
SUBWAY

Schrader, Leonard
KISS OF THE SPIDER WOMAN
MISHIMA

Schrader, Paul
MISHIMA

Scola, Ettore
LE BAL
LA NUIT DE VARENNES
FAMILY, THE
MACARONI
DOWN AND DIRTY

Scott, Helen
FAHRENHEIT 451

Seitz, Franz
TIN DRUM, THE

Semprun, Jorge
Z

Serge, Jean
ELENA AND HER MEN

Serguine, Jacques
VERY CURIOUS GIRL, A

Serran, Leopaldo
GABRIELA

Serreau, Coline
THREE MEN AND A CRADLE

Shepard, Sam
PARIS, TEXAS
ZABRISKIE POINT

Shima, Koji
GOLDEN DEMON

Shinoda, Masahiro
DOUBLE SUICIDE

Simoneau, Yves
BLIND TRUST

Skolimowski, Jerzy
KNIFE IN THE WATER
MOONLIGHTING

Skot-Hansen, Mogens
DAY OF WRATH

Smirnov, E.
MY NAME IS IVAN

Soeteman, Gerard
ASSAULT, THE
FOURTH MAN, THE
SOLDIER OF ORANGE
SPETTERS

Solinas, Franco
BATTLE OF ALGIERS, THE
HANNAH K.
MR. KLEIN
STATE OF SIEGE

Sonego, Rodolfo
WIFEMISTRESS

Spaak, Charles
CARNIVAL IN FLANDERS
GRAND ILLUSION
LOWER DEPTHS, THE

Stagnaro, Juan Bautista
CAMILA

Stawinski, Jerzy Stefan
KANAL

Steinhoff, Ninon
THREEPENNY OPERA, THE

Stok, Danuta Witold
MOONLIGHTING

Stone, David
REPULSION

Stoppard, Tom
DESPAIR

Sturridge, Charles
ARIA

Subiela, Eliseo
MAN FACING SOUTHEAST

Sulik, Boleslaw
MOONLIGHTING

Swaim, Bob
LA BALANCE

Szabo, Istvan
COLONEL REDL
MEPHISTO

Tacchella, Jean-Charles
BLUE COUNTRY, THE
COUSIN, COUSINE

Takemitsu, Toru
DOUBLE SUICIDE

Tambellini, Flavio R.
GABRIELA

Tamura, Takeshi
MACARTHUR'S CHILDREN

Tarkovsky, Andrei
SACRIFICE, THE

Tati, Jacques
PLAYTIME
MR. HULOT'S HOLIDAY
MY UNCLE
JOUR DE FETE

Tavernier, Bertrand
CLEAN SLATE (COUP DE TORCHON)
DEATHWATCH
SUNDAY IN THE COUNTRY, A
ROUND MIDNIGHT

Tavernier, Colo
SUNDAY IN THE COUNTRY, A

Taviani, Paolo
GOOD MORNING BABYLON
NIGHT OF THE SHOOTING STARS, THE
PADRE PADRONE

Taviani, Vittorio
GOOD MORNING BABYLON
NIGHT OF THE SHOOTING STARS, THE
PADRE PADRONE

Temple, Julien
ARIA

Thomas, Anna
EL NORTE

Thomas, Ross
HAMMETT

Thompson, Daniele
COUSIN, COUSINE
LA BOUM

Tomioka, Taeko
DOUBLE SUICIDE

Tonnerre, Jerome
MAN AND A WOMAN: 20 YEARS LATER, A

Treuberg, Franz
FEAR

Troell, Jan
FLIGHT OF THE EAGLE

Truffaut, Francois
CONFIDENTIALLY YOURS!
DAY FOR NIGHT
LOVE ON THE RUN
LAST METRO, THE
JULES AND JIM
GREEN ROOM, THE
SHOOT THE PIANO PLAYER
SMALL CHANGE
SOFT SKIN, THE
STOLEN KISSES
STORY OF ADELE H., THE
WOMAN NEXT DOOR, THE
TWO ENGLISH GIRLS
FAHRENHEIT 451
FOUR HUNDRED BLOWS, THE
MAN WHO LOVED WOMEN, THE

Tudal, Antoine
SUNDAYS AND CYBELE

Turrent, Tomas Perez
ALSINO AND THE CONDOR

Tynan, Kenneth
MACBETH

Uegusa, Keinosuke
DRUNKEN ANGEL

Ungari, Enzo
LAST EMPEROR, THE

Usigli, Rodolfo
WOMAN WITHOUT LOVE, A

Uytterhoeven, Pierre
AND NOW MY LOVE
EDITH AND MARCEL
MAN AND A WOMAN: 20 YEARS LATER, A
HAPPY NEW YEAR
MAN AND A WOMAN, A

Vadim, Roger
AND GOD CREATED WOMAN

Vajda, Ladislaus
PANDORA'S BOX
THREEPENNY OPERA, THE
KAMERADSCHAFT

Valdarnini, A.
DIVINE NYMPH, THE

Van Ackeren, Robert
WOMAN IN FLAMES, A

Van Hamme, Jean
DIVA

Varda, Agnes
CLEO FROM 5 TO 7
VAGABOND

Vash, Karl
M

Veber, Francis
LES COMPERES
LA CAGE AUX FOLLES II
LA CAGE AUX FOLLES
TALL BLOND MAN WITH ONE BLACK SHOE, THE
LA CHEVRE
FRENCH DETECTIVE, THE
LE MAGNIFIQUE
RETURN OF THE TALL BLOND MAN WITH ONE BLACK SHOE, THE

Verhoeven, Paul
SOLDIER OF ORANGE

Vigne, Daniel
RETURN OF MARTIN GUERRE, THE

Vigo, Jean
L'ATALANTE

Vince, Barry
MOONLIGHTING

Vincenzoni, Luciano
SEDUCED AND ABANDONED

Viola, Cesare Giulio
SHOESHINE

Viot, Jacques
BLACK ORPHEUS
LE JOUR SE LEVE

Visconti, Luchino
INNOCENT, THE
DEATH IN VENICE
OSSESSIONE
DAMNED, THE
LA TERRA TREMA

Vogel, Jesse
THERESE AND ISABELLE

Vollmoller, Karl
BLUE ANGEL, THE

Volpe, Les
PLACE OF WEEPING

Von Cube, Irma
MAYERLING

von Harbou, Thea
SIEGFRIED
M
TESTAMENT OF DR. MABUSE, THE
SPIES
DR. MABUSE, THE GAMBLER (PARTS I & II)
DESTINY
METROPOLIS
KRIEMHILD'S REVENGE

von Trotta, Margarethe
COUP DE GRACE
LOST HONOR OF KATHARINA BLUM, THE

Vucicevic, Branko
MONTENEGRO

Wada, Natto
FIRES ON THE PLAIN
ODD OBSESSION
BURMESE HARP, THE

Wademant, Annette
EARRINGS OF MADAME DE . . ., THE
LOLA MONTES

Wajda, Andrzej
DANTON
LOVE IN GERMANY, A
ASHES AND DIAMONDS

Wakao, Tokuhei
SAMURAI TRILOGY, THE

Watanabe, Jose
LA CIUDAD Y LOS PERROS

Wegener, Paul
GOLEM, THE

Wenders, Wim
ALICE IN THE CITIES
AMERICAN FRIEND, THE
KINGS OF THE ROAD
GOALIE'S ANXIETY AT THE PENALTY KICK, THE
STATE OF THINGS, THE
WINGS OF DESIRE

Wertmuller, Lina
LOVE AND ANARCHY
JOKE OF DESTINY, A
SEVEN BEAUTIES
SOTTO. . .SOTTO
SEDUCTION OF MIMI, THE
SWEPT AWAY. . .BY AN UNUSUAL DESTINY IN THE BLUE SEA OF AUGUST

Wheeler, Rene
RIFIFI
JOUR DE FETE

Widerberg, Bo
ELVIRA MADIGAN

Winsloe, Christa
MAEDCHEN IN UNIFORM

Wollen, Peter
PASSENGER, THE

Yoda, Yoshikata
SANSHO THE BAILIFF
UGETSU
LIFE OF OHARU
47 RONIN, THE (PARTS I & II)
SISTERS OF THE GION

Yornykh, Valentin
MOSCOW DOES NOT BELIEVE IN TEARS

Yoshow, Valentin
BALLAD OF A SOLDIER

Zamyatin, Eugene
LOWER DEPTHS, THE

Zanuso, Billa Billa
YESTERDAY, TODAY, AND TOMORROW

Zapponi, Bernardino
FELLINI SATYRICON

Zavattini, Cesare
BICYCLE THIEF, THE
GARDEN OF THE FINZI-CONTINIS, THE
SHOESHINE
TWO WOMEN
UMBERTO D
MIRACLE IN MILAN
YESTERDAY, TODAY, AND TOMORROW

Zeffirelli, Franco
LA TRAVIATA

Zidi, Claude
MY NEW PARTNER

Zieman, Ulla
DAVID

Zimmer, Bernard
CARNIVAL IN FLANDERS

Zuckmayer, Carl
BLUE ANGEL, THE

Zwerenz, Catharina
WOMAN IN FLAMES, A

SOURCE AUTHORS

Abe, Kobo
WOMAN IN THE DUNES

Adam, Alfred
SYLVIA AND THE PHANTOM

Adlon, Percy
BAGDAD CAFE

Akae, Baku
IREZUMI (SPIRIT OF TATTOO)

Aku, Yu
MACARTHUR'S CHILDREN

Akutagawa, Ryunosuke
RASHOMON

Alberti, Barbara
NIGHT PORTER, THE

Amado, Jorge
GABRIELA
DONA FLOR AND HER TWO HUSBANDS

Amar, Denis
L'ADDITION

Amidei, Sergio
OPEN CITY
PAISAN

Andrzejewski, Jerzy
ASHES AND DIAMONDS

Anet, Claude
MAYERLING

Ansky, S.
DYBBUK, THE

Antoine, Andre-Paul
FRENCH CANCAN

Antonioni, Michelangelo
L'AVVENTURA
WHITE SHEIK, THE
ZABRISKIE POINT

Arbiter, Petronius
FELLINI SATYRICON

Arnaud, Georges
WAGES OF FEAR, THE

Arsan, Emmanuelle
EMMANUELLE

Arseniev, Vladimir
DESPAIR
DERSU UZALA

Ayme, Marcel
FOUR BAGS FULL

Bandapaddhay, Bibhutibhusan
APARAJITO

Bandopadhaya, Bibhutibhusan
PATHER PANCHALI
WORLD OF APU, THE

Bang, Oluf
DEVIL'S EYE, THE

Bany, Jean
INVITATION AU VOYAGE

Bartolini, Luigi
BICYCLE THIEF, THE

Bassani, Giorgio
GARDEN OF THE FINZI-CONTINIS, THE

Bastid, Jean-Pierre
L'ADDITION

Belletto, Rene
PERIL

Bemberg, Maria Luisa
MISS MARY

Bendico, Silvia D'Amico
JOKE OF DESTINY, A

Bergamin, Jose
EXTERMINATING ANGEL, THE

Bergman, Ingmar
SEVENTH SEAL, THE
SUMMER INTERLUDE

Bernanos, George
DIARY OF A COUNTRY PRIEST

Berr, Georges
LE MILLION

Bertolucci, Bernardo
LAST TANGO IN PARIS

Besson, Luc
BIG BLUE, THE

Bessy, Maurice
KING OF HEARTS

Bizet, Georges
BIZET'S CARMEN

Blier, Bertrand
BEAU PERE
GOING PLACES

Boehme, Margarethe
DIARY OF A LOST GIRL

Bogomolov, Vladimir Osipovich
MY NAME IS IVAN

Boileau, Pierre
DIABOLIQUE

Boll, Heinrich
LOST HONOR OF KATHARINA BLUM, THE

Bonheur, Gaston
LADY CHATTERLEY'S LOVER

Borges, Jorge Luis
EL MUERTO

Bost, Pierre
SUNDAY IN THE COUNTRY, A

Boyer, Francois
FORBIDDEN GAMES

Bradbury, Ray
FAHRENHEIT 451

Brecht, Bertolt
THREEPENNY OPERA, THE

Bronte, Emily
WUTHERING HEIGHTS

Buchheim, Lothar-Guenther
BOAT, THE

Bunuel, Luis
VIRIDIANA

Cain, James M.
OSSESSIONE

Calef, Noel
FRANTIC

Carlsen, Henning
WOLF AT THE DOOR, THE

Carriere, Jean-Claude
WOLF AT THE DOOR, THE

Carson, L.M. Kit
PARIS, TEXAS

Castanier, Jean
CRIME OF MONSIEUR LANGE, THE

Cavani, Liliana
NIGHT PORTER, THE

Cayrol, Jean
MURIEL

Chekhov, Anton
DARK EYES

Chelli, Gaetanp Carol
INHERITANCE, THE

Chikamatsu, Monzaemon
DOUBLE SUICIDE

Cocteau, Jean
ORPHEUS
LES ENFANTS TERRIBLES

Coetzee, Jean-Marie
DUST

Cohen, Olivier
ENTRE NOUS

Compton, David
DEATHWATCH

Consiglio, Alberto
OPEN CITY

Cortazar, Julio
BLOW-UP

Curtelin, Jean
L'ADDITION

D'Annunzio, Gabriele
INNOCENT, THE

d'Ashelbe, Roger
PEPE LE MOKO

D'Aunia, Marina
CRICKET, THE

Dabadie, Jean-Loup
PARDON MON AFFAIRE

Danon, Marcello
LA CAGE AUX FOLLES II

de Beaumont, Mme. Marie Leprince
BEAUTY AND THE BEAST

de Falla, Manuel
EL AMOR BRUJO

De Filippo, Eduardo
YESTERDAY, TODAY, AND TOMORROW

de Guichen, R.
L'ATALANTE

de Mandiargues, Andre Pieyre
GIRL ON A MOTORCYCLE, THE

De Maupassant, Guy
WOMAN WITHOUT LOVE, A

de Maupassant, Guy
LE PLAISIR
MASCULINE FEMININE

de Moraes, Vinicius
BLACK ORPHEUS

de Rothschild, Philippe
LADY CHATTERLEY'S LOVER

Del Monte, Peter
JULIA AND JULIA